ISBN 978-1-330-01669-5
PIBN 10004810

THE

COMBAT OF THE PEOPLE:

OR

HILLEL AND HEROD.

A HISTORICAL ROMANCE

OF

THE TIME OF HEROD I.

BY ISAAC M. WISE.

CINCINNATI, OHIO.
Printed and Published by BLOCH & CO., at the Office of The Israelite and Deborah.
1859.

Simon. "Every man, coming from the vicinity of Jericho, is suspected to be an enemy of Herod, and must submit to the turmoil and drudgery of a thousand spies. The blood of Aristobulus, the youthful Highpriest of the heroic race of the Asmoneans, yes, the blood of the assassinated servant of the Lord, cries and threatens from the pool of Jericho, where the despot's hirelings extinguished his pure lamp of life. Ah, the blood! the blood of Aristobulus haunts the "Half Jew," the proselyte ruler. He sees drops of this blood on every man's garment coming from Jericho, or its environs. Therefore, his spies are after every one coming from thence.

"Ah, my good natured fellow," Jonathan said, "you suppose, every man has a conscience, that revolts against crime and incessantly haunts its perpetrator. If Herod had a conscience, he could have no rest, no hour of happiness; remorse and self-contempt must overawe him day and night.—From Antioch the blood of the heroic Antigonus cries for vengeance; from Galilee sound, like specter's music in midnight hour, the voices of the hundreds murdered by Herod and his hirelings. Jerusalem, the city of peace, the habitation of our God, is red with the blood of the pillars of Israel, our Sanhedrin, our great luminaries.—Blood, assassination and violence cry from every corner of this blessed land; still you believe Herod has a conscience? Herod is haunted by his conscience, because one person was slain? I rather believe, he has information of our friends' doings in Jericho. He most likely knows, that the heads of the Pharisees congregate in that city and devise means to throw off the intolerable yoke, to restore law and justice to Israel. Therefore, he suspects every man coming from Jericho, or its environs."

"You may be right, Jonathan," said Simon; "Uziel's sagacious son never errs greatly. If Herod is aware of the brethren's council in Jericho, he will, if he descries us, have us watched closely. We must deliver our message to the council of Jerusalem, in spite of vigilance itself; but we must be careful, that we, by our going to the council, betray it not to the spies."

"Our disguise will protect us," said Jonathan. "I walked yesterday through all parts of the city, and everywhere I was taken for an *Amhaarez.** Let us only be careful to sustain our assumed character well."

"How little knowledge of man must the people of Jerusalem have," said Simon, "if they could take you for a simple and illiterate peasant. But I fear the spies of Herod are better judges of human countenances than the unsuspecting community. We must, before we go to the council, ascertain that we are not suspected at all; for, if we are, we betray the place of meeting to the vigilant spies, and this would bring misery on our friends, and frustrate our schemes."

"But how will you ascertain it?" Jonathan asked.

"I do not know yet," said Simon; "but I will see Abba Shaul and confer with him on the subject."

The messenger of the Highpriest arrived among the peasants, and informed them that they could not be received to-day with due honors, as a party from the district of Bethlehem had arrived before them with the first fruits, who would to-day be received, it being contrary to the established usages to receive two parties the same day.—The day next following, however, was set apart for their solemn reception.

Jonathan cast a significant look on Simon, and when the messenger was gone and the peasants each went his way to amuse himself, Simon whispered to Jonathan: "I understand the import of this measure. It would not do to arrest or molest one of those who come to Jerusalem to bring the first fruits; hence, before receiving us in solemn procession, they want to ascertain, whether no dangerous character is among the crowd. I understand them well."

"But this gives us also ample time to examine our path carefully," said Jonathan. "Let us, each for himself, wander through the city and learn as much as we can."

While this occurred on one side of the city, another meeting of interesting char-

* An ignorant peasant.

acters took place at the opposite side, at a moderate distance from the city. There was the place of repose to the dead, and sepulchres and stones, of all descriptions, marked the last abode of thousands of human beings. An humble cottage, the home of the grave digger, was the only habitation of the living among the dead, found in this vicinity. Before the cottage door stood a man, tall, muscular and robust, as few inhabitants of cities, especially in the torrid climate, are. His dark colored face was covered with a bushy, black beard. His small grey eyes were overshadowed with heavy brows. The furrows of his forehead betokened the storms of life that had passed over his head. The features of calm indifference, which marked his countenance, contrasted peculiarly with the melancholy smile that appeared to play around his lips, and the stern resoluteness marking his temples and looks. The scars in his muscular face told a story of many a hot battle fought, and his gigantic form testified to his being a terrible antagonist in the combat. It was Abba Shaul ben Botnith, the gigantic grave digger, the tallest man of his age, the terror of his enemies, and a trustworthy rock to his friends. Abba Shaul prayed as the sun rose, with countenance turned toward the *sanctum sanctorum* on Mount Moriah.

Two females, richly dressed and thickly veiled, followed by a man servant, riding on white asses, came up the road from the city, and alighted before the cottage of the grave digger. The salutation of peace, uttered with a musical voice, by one of the females was returned by Abba Shaul in an unintelligible murmur.

"Lead me to the sepulchre of my beloved mother," the same female said, "and I will pay you well for your trouble."

"Many beloved mothers lie beneath the frigid sod," Abba Shaul remarked, monotonously; "also those who died in the agony of despair and bereft of their children."

"Do you not know me, Abba Shaul?" she asked, surprised.

"I only know what I dare know, and this is very little in our days," he replied. "How dare a vulgar grave digger know an aristocratic lady, in Rome's richest attire?"

"Have you indeed forgotten my name?" she continued asking.

"I have tried to forget all that is past," he said, "as the memory of the past is the most obnoxious crime of the present. No man, in our days, dare remember of the past more than the last six years. But these, (pointing to the graves,) these are the silent witnesses of a terrible past. To forget them is a magnanimous virtue at present."

"You speak in riddles, I do not understand you, Abba Shaul," the female said.

"Yes, yes, I speak in riddles," said he; "if words plain and intelligible are no longer tolerated, men must speak in riddles."

"Do you speak of our king and his last mandates?" she asked naively.

"Like others, I most always speak of myself," Abba Shaul said, drily. "A grave digger never must speak of a king, such is the law of decency in our days."

"Tell your young man to lead my attendants to the family vaults of Sabion, king Herod's illustrious friend," the female said, "and while they fumigate the vault, I will speak a few words more to you."

"It is true, the vaults of the mighty and wealthy also need fumigation, about as much as those of the poor," said Abba Shaul, while going away to call his young man. When returned, the young man with the attendants went away; Abba Shaul was alone with the female. She lifted her veil, and a countenance of exquisite charm, one of those indescribably luxuriant beauties of the Orient, especially of the daughters of Zion, became visible to Abba Shaul. She fixed her fiery looks on the man before her when asking: "Do you now know me, Abba Shaul?"

"Do I know Sabion's fairest daughter? Do I recognize sweet Helen, I so often rocked on my lap?" said Abba Shaul. "What a question! Once your father also knew me, and I knew him, you, and your deceased mother. But now the mighty Sabion knows not the vulgar grave digger. It would be a disgrace on you, if it should transpire that I know you, or you recognize me. Therefore, I did not know you in the presence of your attendants."

"Tell me, Abba Shaul," she said hastily, "have you heard from Jericho? have you no tidings of Hillel's son? I have heard the peasants near Jericho have come to present their first fruits in the Temple. Did he not improve this opportunity, to come in peasant's disguise with them, to see me again, after many moons of painful separation? Speak! Abba Shaul, is he dead? has he forgotten poor Helen? or is he here to renew the covenant of love? O, I pray you, speak, tell me all you know."

"Simon, Hillel's son lives," Abba Shaul said; "he has not forgotten Helen, for his love for her is imperishable as the powerful mind is that conceived it. I know of the peasants' arrival, but whether Simon is among them I can not tell. To morrow I will know it. But, behold! there a peasant comes from the city; so early, a peasant from the city, he is clad in his festive garb, he wears a verdant wreath on his turban, it is undoubtedly one of the men of Jericho. Go to the vault and pray. I will ask him and you shall have the answer. Say you are tired, wish to rest in my cottage, leave your attendants outside, and I will tell you all I learned."

She hastily threw the veil over her face, and went to the vault. She was but a few minutes gone when Simon ben Hillel alighted from his ass, and was received, by Abba Shaul, with a kiss impressed on the young man's forehead.

"Jonathan ben Uziel and I," said Simon, but little louder than a whisper, "have come among the peasants of Jericho with a message of the scribes to the people's council of Jerusalem. Can we deliver it without apprehension?"

"They watch closely every person coming from Jericho," Abba Shaul replied. "It would be marvelous, should they not regard you among the multitude, and none must wait for miracles. Go back, and tell Jonathan to be cautious. Go not about the city till after the solemn reception. Keep yourselves close to the other peasants till dusk. When the Temple closes, to-morrow, go down to Bezetha to the house of Baba ben Buta; there you will be received by our secret friends, who will ask you, 'Is the house of the Lord closed?' then you answer, 'When night sets in, the house of the Lord closes.' They will then lead you to the right place."

After a pause, Abba Shaul invited Simon to his house, and told him, he would call in some body who was able to give him a full account of the intentions of Herod and his spies.

Simon entered the house, and, after he had partaken of a repast, Abba Shaul left the room and after a few minutes Helen came in. Simon, surprised by the approach of a veiled lady so costly dressed, rose, but could say nothing. Helen also was unprepared to say any thing, and so they stood for some time silently opposite each other. Helen composed herself first and asked with a tremulous voice, "Are you not Simon ben Hillel?"

"Helen, only beloved, dearest, sweetest Helen," Simon cried, passionately, "it is your voice. If it is you, speak, speak, my only hope, remove this heartless veil, and let me gaze once more in your angelic countenance. Once more, O, dearest beloved, let me have the paradisian rapture of reading love and fidelity in your starry eyes. If you are Helen, still mine, still the kind, affectionate, beloved dove, torture me no longer."

She removed the veil and sank, speechless, in the embrace of the passionate youth, who pressed her with unutterable delight to his enraptured breast. The excitement of the unexpected meeting, however, soon gave way to melancholy presentiments. Simon's arms, almost paralyzed, sunk down as though he had no strength to press the beloved longer to his heart. His head dropped to his bosom, his countenance pale and his voice hollow, he said, "It is over, it is all over.—It is the will of God, that it should be so. Helen, we must part, now and forever." The pale countenance of Simon gave his words an unusual force. It was only after long hesitation, that Helen could ask as to the cause of this sudden change of mind. "Have you forgotten, good Helen," said Simon, "that you are the daughter of the proud and wealthy Sabion, Herod's mighty friend and counsellor, and I am the poor son of a poor Babylonian emigrant? Are you not aware, that my father split wood in this city for a scanty pay, to support his family and pay his admission to the academy, while Sabion was the favorite of kings and queens? You must know, that your father, like Jephtah of old, rather would sacrifice you with his own hands than allow you to be mine.—There is no hope for us, none for our love. I can not, I dare not tie your fate to mine; for your prospect is bright, the sons of the noblest of our people look on you with anxious hopes, you are the favorite of a noble queen, the pride of the court, the object of contention to the richest and noblest, and I am the poor son of a Poor and insignificant Babylonian emigrant, the meek, humble, unpretending Hillel. We must part now and forever. Had I known when first I met you under yonder Palm trees, when first love, irresistible love to you, chained me to your footsteps, that you were Sabion's daughter, never would I have given utterance to my glowing passions. But, it is not too late yet; let us part now and forever."

"Simon, be like yourself," she said in a calm, composed manner; "be honest, upright and sincere as your heart is. You know, that this is a poor excuse for your alleged determination. Play not cruelly with my heart, when you know that I can not live without your love; the love I bear to you, is the essence and cause of my very existence. Tell me, what ails you? I am the favorite of a noble queen, it is true, and she loves me better than any of her ladies. One word from her lips and Simon ben Hillel occupies that envied position, in which Sabion must consider him worthy to be his son-in-law."

"I accept no favors of a monarch's hands," said Simon, hastily and determinedly.

"I know it well," said Helen, "therefore, I never asked for any in your behalf. But if I offer you my hand with the consent of my father, would you not accept it? And, if the queen wills it so, can my father refuse it? Simon, if I tell the queen of my love, I am sure she will favor me with her successful interference. You know this; I have told you so, frequently; hence it can not be this. Let me know, I prithee, let me know what ails you?"

"You know, dearest Helen," said Simon, with much embarrassment, "you know, I can not deceive you. It is indeed not this alone, there is yet something. I scarcely know how to say it without giving you offence."

"Speak, my friend, I must know your heart," Helen said.

"My father stands high in the estimation of those who know him," said Simon; "he is the most respected among the Pharisees and is a firm Pharisee himself. You know the hatred and bitterness existing between the Pharisees and Sadducees, especially since the latter have sworn allegiance to Herod. Your father, Sabion, noble Helen, is an influential leader of the Sadducees who hates and despises the Plebian multitude of Pharisees. It is next to an impossibility for him thus far to condescend, as to give his daughter in marriage, to an insignificant Plebian, the son of an emigrant, an obscure Pharisee. Do not deceive yourself, noble Helen, do not believe that your father, the queen or any body else thinks, feels and would act by your generous impulse. I would only set you at war with your father, with the queen, with all your friends, without the least hope of a favorable result. Helen, magnanimous virgin, stainless soul, the ravine between you and me is too deep; the daughter of the Patrician Sadducee and the son of the Plebian Pharisee stand too far apart from each other. I feel my heart will break, joy will never smile on me again, love and happiness are forlorn to me; but it must be. Better now, when we alone know it, than after I have caused you the painful misery of severing your heart from your father and your friends. Take this parting tear, as the expression of my breaking heart, hundreds more will flow; but forget not, we have no dominion over the unfortunate causes which tear asunder the families, the most sacred ties of our country. Farewell, farewell, Helen, forget me."

The tears glittering in Simon's black eyes

were not calculated to calm Helen's passions. "Leave me not, desert me not, Simon!" she cried, vehemently, "plunge this dagger in my aching heart, before thou abandonest me. God knows, I can not live without thee."—"And if all this is true," she said after a pause, "if the queen and my father can not be moved in my favor, then, I swear it by the spirit of my departed mother, then I go with thee to Arabia, beyond the Euphrates, beyond the Tigris, to distant India, to any part of the world, wherever thou goest. An oasis in a howling desert, an humble tent in the wilderness, anything will satisfy me that pleases thee. Simon, stay and let us scheme our flight, if I fail in my attempt with the queen."

"I dare not leave my country," said Simon. "Whoever deserts his people in days of affliction, shall not behold Israel's salvation. I can not, I dare not leave this unhappy land, even to save my life, not even for the prize of the unutterable happiness smiling in your embrace. Helen! it is easy to descend from the proud palace to the shepherd's tent, when love urges; but, forget not, my good Helen: Life is long, poverty is a cruel master, the affections of youth soon give way to sober sentiments, and repentance is a gnawing monster in the heart. One look of dissatisfaction from you would make me miserable beyond description. Helen, my only love, we must part forever, the happiness of all your lifetime demands it."

"No, no, no, I can not be happy, I can not live without you," she exclaimed, with tears in her eyes. "It can not be, it must not be. But, Simon ben Hillel," she said resolutely after awhile, "if you are tired of my love, if your heart is no longer mine, and such appears to be the case, then say it without faltering, say it and"—here a flow of tears interrupted her speech.

Simon clasped both her hands and, overpowered with love and tenderness, he exclaimed, in frantic accents, "Helen, idol of my heart, queen of my soul, thou fairest and most amiable of Zion's daughters, I prithee, accuse me not of what I am incapable of doing. I can not forget you, I can not love another woman, my love to you is boundless, omnipotent, eternal. But, tell me Helen, could you love the murderer of your own father? Why do you thus stare in my countenance? Not yet; I am not yet the assassin of Sabion, but I swore by the Almighty God to perform this horrid duty at the first opportunity that offers, at the risk of my own life. Tremble not, Helen, condemn me not till I have spoken. When I first learned your father's name, he was a Pharisee, and a sworn friend of the unhappy Asmoneans, the favorite of Mariamne, Alexandra, and of the generous and harmless Hyrcanus. But he turned a traitor, a foul and heartless traitor to his country; he betrayed the flight of Hyrcanus; he lent his bloody hand to Herod, to assassinate the youthful highpriest Aristobulus; he stands now at the head of a thousand spies who daily deliver some of the best men to the jailor's ruthless hands, or to the scaffold. He is the right hand of Herod, the foul murderer of his own people, the teacherous hireling of Rome. The council of the people condemned him to ignominous death, thousands of young men swore to excute the decree, and one of these thousands is Simon ben Hillel. With this dagger, it is a sanctified instrument; with this steel, I will, wherever I see him, pierce his heart, mine, if necessary, in the name and in behalf of my downtrodden, outraged people. Helen, do not look so angry, so desperate; bethink thyself, an outraged people speak from my lips, and every other sentiment in my heart must be dumb as the grave."

"It is enough, gracious God in Heaven, it is more than enough, it is more than woman can bear," Helen exclaimed with a hollow voice. "Simon, hear me pray; see, O behold the agony of this tortured heart. If blood must flow, murder me, for I feel that I can not live much longer. Simon, break asunder the terrible bonds which chain you to treason, conspiracy and assassination, and flee with me to a desert land. But if thou canst not break them, have mercy with me, first murder me, before thou thinkest of assassinating my father."

"Farewell, Helen!" Simon cried, in accents of madness, and ran toward the door. "Not one step further!" Helen exclaimed powerfully, with wild looks flashing from her large, black eyes. "You are mad, and it is my duty to protect you, my father, myself and other people against the rash acts of a madman. You are a member of the secret conspiracy of Jericho, I know it, and you are arrested in the name of the king."

Simon crossed his arms over his breast, fixed his looks on Helen and responded, calmly: "I am not mad. I know no king in Israel. Herod is an usurper, the vilest assassin in this country. I am no one's prisoner, as long as a sword hangs from my girdle. Your attendants, madam, can not arrest me. You must go home, tell your father the secret I have broached to you, and you and he might be avenged."

Helen fell down upon her knees, lifted up her hands to Simon, and prayed him vehemently not to consider her a traitor. Again and anon she prayed him, to change his determination; but, when she found out, that words were wasted in vain, she rose, and with a manly resoluteness she stated: "I can not, God witness, I can not leave you; still I must hate him who schemes the death of my father. I am determined to die or to prevent you from committing the horrid murder. Simon, here in the presence of these graves I swear that I will always love you, never for a moment shall a faithless thought defile my heart; but I will have resort to extreme measures, if necessary, to prevent you from the performance of an act, which would forever sever us. I swear it, by the spirit of my departed mother."

She was gone before Simon could reply, leaving him in the most wretched condition, tormented, tortured between love and duty, an indomitable affection and a glowing patriotism. He had not much time to reflect on his condition, for Abba Shaul came in and advised him, not to return to the city, but to choose by-ways to reach his companions encamped outside the Fishgate. Simon obeyed, silently. Thoughtfully he mounted his ass and pursued the by-ways around the city as Abba Shaul had told him.

On returning to the camp of the peasants, and he had to travel many furlongs before he reached it—Simon found Jonathan anxiously waiting for him.

"We are lost, if we do not act speedily," Jonathan whispered. "When walking the Upper Market a peevish boy stept up to me and most impertinently told me: 'Jonathan ben Uziel and Simon ben Hillel are detected, notwithstanding their disguise. Toward evening they will be arrested.' I looked, amazed, at my voluntary companion, and closely scrutinized the peevish countenance, but made no reply. He then continued with a pertinent smile, 'I am no spy,' and left me. For some time I was undecided what course to pursue, when a Roman soldier asked me, 'How many peasants in your place are called Jonathan ben Uziel?' I marveled long after the soldier had gone, and can not tell yet what all this means; but I know we are betrayed and in imminent danger."

"This is marvelous, indeed," said Simon. "We must take proper care to evade detection, and I have a good plan to do so. I have a wealthy uncle, a brother of my father, whose country residence is a few furlongs from here. He has plenty of Babylonian costumes, and we have false beards, which baffle detection. We speak well all dialects of the Aramees and Chaldees. Not far from here, a Babylonian caravan is encamped. Let us dress at my uncle's, join the caravan, and be Babylonians for some time. You know Herod favors all foreigners, especially the Babylonians."

The plan was agreed upon. Both men went away, unobserved, to carry out their scheme. When scarcely gone, several officers arrived among the peasants, and informed them of two young men having come up with them from Jericho, who must be presented to the governor of the city. The peasants were all assembled, every one's name was asked, but none called himself either Simon or Jonathan. On inquiry whether any was missing the officers were told, that all were present; none of the peasants would have betrayed the two young men, whose secret mission they appeared to have guessed. The officers took two young men along, answering best to the description of the persons wanted, notwithstanding the loud protests of the arrested and the other peasants. The assurance that no harm should be done to them, pacified the agitated multitude, and they patiently awaited the result. When, however, the next morning the messengers of the Highpriest came to array them in a solemn procession to enter the city, and the two peasants had not returned; it took the whole influence of the priests to pacify the agitated minds, who considered it an unpardonable sin, that their two neighbors were prevented from paying obedience to the law.

The procession was headed by the musicians who, with their flutes, trumpets, cornets, harps, cymbals and other instruments, discussed Davidian music. Then were led the sacrifices, the bullock first, his horns gilded, on his head the olive crown, and the whole animal was covered with fruits and flowers. And then came the smaller animals, as every comer thought proper to offer. One brought a calf, another a lamb, the third a young goat, as a peace-offering, a thank-offering, or to pay a vow, while others brought their first horn animals along to the priest. All the animals were more or less ornamented with fruits and flowers, each led by a boy, who came up to see the city. Then came the peasants, with their baskets of gold, silver or palm branches filled with the finest tropical fruits and ornamented with flowers, each carrying a pair of pigeons as the requisite sacrifice. In the midst of the procession was carried a large banner with the shield of David and Judah's lion on it, surrounded by palm trees, as Jericho was commonly called the city of palms.

As they slowly moved toward the gate of the city they sung, to the sound of music, the one hundred and twenty second Psalm:

"I am glad, I am glad
In my soul, in my heart,
When they say: For the house
Of the Lord we'll depart.
Jerusalem! Jerusalem!
Within thy gates our feet shall stand.
Compact and strong thou art, our gem,
Our joy, the queen of Judah's land.
And to thee flock the tribes,
Come the tribes of the Lord—
Come with dance and with song,
And with thanks to the Lord.
For there the thrones of judgment stand,
The Lord rules from this loved place;
And there the throne of Israel's land
Once filled by David's royal race.
Do bid hail, greet with peace
Jerusalem's towers.
They prosper who do wreathe
With sweet love thy bowers.
May peace within thy walls abide,
And plenty in thy mansions be.
In thy Temple our God reside—
Jerusalem! be peace with thee."

Arrived at the city gate, the procession was received by the officiating priests, Levites, treasurers of the Temple, and the representatives of the Israelites at the sanctuary, all clad in their sacerdotal vestments, bearing the banners and ensigns of the city and the sanctuary. Before them went the Levites, with their cornets and trumpets, and after them came the curious multitude. Also, a deputation of the city bearing the standard with the *Ariel*, a deputation of the Sanhedrin carrying a representation of the scroll of the Law, and the messengers of the King, before whom a Roman standard, united with Judah's lion, was carried, came among the rest, to receive the strangers.

After the deputy of the Highpriest had spoken the blessing over them, the King's messenger had Promised them his protection, and the city authorities had offered them the hospitality of the capitol, the representatives of the Sanhedrin admonished them always to obey the will of God with a willing heart. Then the procession organised again, and, with music and song, with floating banners and standards, with numerous ensigns and golden emblems, the gay and delighted procession moved through the city, through the dense crowds of Jerusalemites, country people, Egyptians, Ethiopians, Arabs, Syrians, Babylonians, Persians, Greeks and Romans, each in the peculiar costume of his country. All the mechanics rose from their seats, and each greeted the passing: "Our brethren, men of Jericho welcome in peace."

Arrived in the crowded court of the Temple, the music ceased and all, taking their baskets on their shoulders, listened with sacred delight to the currents of music resounding from the outer apartment of the Temple. The Chorus of the Levites sung the thirtieth Psalm to the powerful orchestre of their brethren. On each side of the fourteen steps leading to the second court stood the officiating priests to assist the comers in making their sacrifices. And as they ascended the steps they were saluted by the full orchestre and chorus, and every heart was filled with heavenly harmonies, and every eye was directed to heaven. Every soul soared aloft on the pinions of sacred psalmody, every mind felt the presence of Israel's God. From the golden gates, the onix and sapphire, from the thousand gems set in the wall, the light of the Lord was a thousandfold and brilliantly reflected, and fell enlightening and warming in every heart. The gorgeous columns with the glittering capitulars which run in double rows around the cloisters and supported the arched roof, were ornamented to-day with fruit and flowers of all sorts which the land produces, and proclaimed, in a powerful language, the bountiful goodness of our God.

When, however, the procession ascended the twelve steps leading from the court to the holy house itself, silence ruled supreme; not a sound, scarcely the palpitation of the hearts was audible. All, priests, Levites, musicians, singers and worshippers appeared overawed by the sacredness of the place, where the Most Holy of Israel throned among Cherubim. Arrived at the altar, each took the basket on his hand, the priest waved it before God and the multitude read the word of Scripture: "I wish to say before God thy Lord, that I came in the land which God has sworn to our fathers, to give it to us." The priests then took the baskets and set them down before the altar, and the multitude continued to read the scriptural passage, thanking God for his goodness, and praying as every heart dictated. When this was done the sacrifices were brought under the solemn performances appertaining to it, accompanied by the song and music of the Levites, the prayers of the people's representatives, and the devotion of the worshipping multitude.

When the solemn service was over, the peasants repaired to the cloisters, to eat the sanctified meat, and then prepared for the banquets following the sacred ceremonies. A man dressed in white, with a girdle and apron of white leather and an axe on his shoulder, an Essenee of the first degree, addressed the peasants as they passed the outermost court of the Temple. "Not all sacrifices are acceptable to God," said he, "the sacrifice of the wicked is an abomination. God has given us ears, that we hear his commands, and do them; he asks neither fire offering nor sin-offering of us. Whoever kills an animal, without repentance of sins, commits murder on that animal; but the Lord never despises an humble and contrite heart. His are the first fruits and the last, the first born animals and the last; His are the beasts of the forests and the animals of the meadows, the gold and silver are his. Hunger troubles him not and he suffers not by thirst; for God is no man, and the infirmities of the mortal ones befall him not. Repent, repent of your sins; let your garments always be white, and let the oil not be wanting on your head; wash away your guilt and clothe in innocence; this is the sacrifice which pleases God."

A dense crowd surrounded the fantastic man as he spoke, and listened to him with profound attention and silence. "A sacred angel stands in the midst of heaven," the Essenee continued, "Israel is his name. The heavenly host look on him, to know when night sets in and when the day breaks, in order to render praise to God on high when Israel chants His praise; when the day breaks, the sacred angel has the word, "Truth," on his forehead, and when night sets in he bears the word, "Faith," upon his brows. The angel teaches you a sacred lesson: As long as the bright sun of life and happiness shines on you, let truth be the highest aim of your endeavors; listen to truth, and walk in its path; for truth is the signet of our God—in order that faith and confidence in God's justice and goodness be your guiding star through the night of misery, pain and death. Wherever God's glorious sun of revelation illuminates our mind, let us search after truth as after hidden treasures, and love it as our life; for it is costlier than fine gold, more precious than the treasures of Ophir; it elevates to honors those who honor it, and watches over those who trust in it—in order that faith, that faith which is the offspring of truth, guide us safely through the night of ignorance, and protect us against the dangers of darkness. Trust in the truth and faith which are inscribed on Israel's forehead, and follow not after strange gods. Be not led astray either by the philosophy of the Greeks or the learning of the Romans; mind neither the wisdom of the Orient nor the erudition of the Alexandrians. Israel's truth and faith alone be your guide."

By this time the attention of all was attracted by the Essence, the multitude listened in silent suspense. A lad of superior beauty, whose delicate limbs were covered with a black cloak of coarse material, slowly and cautiously made his way through the crowd, and on reaching a bearded Babylonian, he whispered: "The Philistines are on thee, Samson. Follow me to Baba ben Buta." Jonathan ben Uziel, for he was the Babylonian in disguise, found no time to ask an explanation; for when the Essence spoke again, the lad pressed its way through the crowd, followed by the two Babylonians in disguise—Jonathan and Simon. The lad went so fast, that they, without attracting particular attention by fast running, could not overtake him. Before a low building in Bezetha, the lad stopped, and when the two men had reached him, he said: "Here is the house"—"And who are you?" Jonathan asked, hastily. "Now, I am your angel, after awhile, you will be mine," he said with a peevish smile, and turned quickly around a corner.

"I do not know what to make of the officious boy," said Jonathan, "it is the same who met me yesterday at the Upper Market."

"I suspect the boy to be a girl," Simon replied, with a smile. "Have you ever seen a boy with such a beauteous countenance, so peevish, still so chaste a look? I must be much mistaken if the boy is not a girl."

Jonathan made no reply. Both entered the house, and were welcomed by a man, with the question: "Is the Temple of the Lord closed?" Simon answered according to instructions, "When night sets in, the Temple of the Lord closes?" The man then asked them, "Which side of the Temple is dark?"—"The north, the north, the north," was the monotonous reply. This appeared to satisfy the man, and he bid them follow him. Long after sunset the party arrived in the valley of Hinom and, walking through it they reached, at its extreme, a low hut. On entering this a man received them and the above questions were repeated and answered as before, when their eyes were bandaged and they were led down many, many steps, then again onward and down again, then again forward on a level. After a long and winding walk, they were stopped, the bandage was removed from their eyes and they stood in a large and high hall, in which a flood of light fell upon gigantic stone columns, on which the stony roof rested, and upon several hundred manly figures, wrapped in black cloaks and blank swords in their hands. The bandages being removed ten swords were swung above each head, when a rough and powerful voice asked them: "What can save your life?" — "The liberty of Israel," was the immediate reply.. The swords were returned to their sheaths, and the strangers welcomed and invited to a seat in the hall.

A man yet young, still bent as with old age, his hair half grey, his countenance furrowed and painstricken, a blind man sitting on an elevated chair rose, after a moment of silence, and every eye in the hall looked on him who could see none of them. It was Baba ben Buta, formerly a senator in Israel and a wise judge, now a hapless blind man, who was deprived of his sight by order of Herod, when after he, supported by Sosias, a general of Antony, and a Roman army, had taken Jerusalem, he massacred the senators who were opposed to his claims upon the throne. Baba ben Buta being an admirer of Herod (Josephus calls him Pollion,) but a strong opponent to his violent usurpation, was not massacred; he was deprived of his eye sight, to render him harmless and unfit to sit in the Sanhedrin.

Baba ben Buta rose and addressed the strangers with a clear and powerful voice: "Peace be with you, brethren. In the name of Israel's God and in behalf of my mortified and tyranized people, I bid you welcome in the people's council. You stand here in the hall of King Solomon, here are kept the implements and tools with which the first Temple of the Lord was built. This is a sacred place. It is located beneath the Temple on Mount Moriah, known traditionally to a few. Here, the prophets of the Lord assembled when idolatry and corruption held their sway over the throne and the people. This is the place where the royal child Joash was hidden for six years and escaped the bloody hands of Athaliah. Here we meet again to devise means for the salvation of Israel.—Tell us from whence you come, who you are, and what tidings you bring us."

When Baba ben Buta had resumed his seat, Simon rose and replied: "Israelites, men and brethren, your servants, Jonathan ben Uziel and Simon ben Hillel, the pupils of my illustrious father, come messengers from the council of the Scribes, of Israel's wise men, in the vicinity of Jericho, the place where once the prophet Eliah held his councils. They desire us to tell you, your cause is also theirs, your grievances are theirs also; therefore, they desire to act in unison with you, to redress our grievances, break asunder the shameful yoke, the bonds of slavery and subjection weighing down to the dust the virgin daughter of Israel. Your servants come to receive instruction from you, as to the best and safest mode of speedy operation, and convey word to those who sent us."

"And how did the wise men of Jericho know of the existence of the people's council," Baba ben Buta asked.

"Abba Shaul ben Botnith knows, that both your servants are members of the people's council in Bethlehem. We have sworn the same oath as you have. We are ready to act whenever you command. We advised the Scribes and the wise men of Israel to unite with you. They sent us, because it was easy for us to gain admission to your wise council."

"I witness," said Abba Shaul, with his powerful and monotonous voice.

Baba ben Buta examined the strangers thus: "What is your first duty?"

"To restore justice, liberty, independence and peace to Israel?" was the reply.

"What is your next duty?" Baba ben Buta continued.

Simon faltered. "Speak, speak, strangers," the blind man urged, "you put your lives in jeopardy." Simon hesitated. A hundred swords rushed from their sheaths and the metallic sounds reverberated like the herald of death through the subterranean hall. "Speak or die," it roared like thunder from hundred throats. A deep sigh escaped the tormented bosom of Simon, on uttering the fearful words, in a tone frantically wild; "My second duty is to slay proud Sabion."

A shriek, shrill and painful, resounded from another part of the hall; every look turned in that direction. "Treachery!—Treachery!" several exclaimed, simultaneously, "it is not Baruch ben Menahem, it is a"—

"A woman!" said Helen, throwing off her mask and cloak, "a woman in the disguise of Baruch ben Menahem, who has instructed her in the secrets of this place."

"Death to the intruder!" several men cried, and rushed toward her. Simon and Abba Shaul protected her. "None shall kill her as long as Abba Shaul lives," the powerful man thundered, swinging his sword. "Shed no innocent blood," Simon cried, vehemently. "None shall die in Israel without a trial, before the tribunal of law and justice: none shall die in Israel, unless the law commands his death," Baba ben Buta calmly said. The swords were returned to their cases, and Helen was led up to the chair of the blind man, to stand a lawful trial for her intrusion.

Trembling and amazed, Simon looked on the beloved maiden, as she stood at the brink of death, on account of a rash act, to which love and filial affection prompted her. He could scarcely breathe, nor could he turn his gaze from her. Now, she descried him among the multitude, her eyes darted forth looks of love and affection, no fear was visible in her countenance; she stood firm before her judge. Simon, overpowered with feelings he could repress no longer, fell upon his face before the chair of the blind man, and prayed vehemently: "Baba ben Buta, spare, spare her. In behalf of Hillel, I pray spare her, my life as a pledge for her generous intentions."

CHAPTER II

A SCENE IN THE ROYAL PALACE.

Passing through the rows of palaces north west of the theater, which stood nearly in the center of Acra, or the Lower City, as one part of Jerusalem was called—we stop before a large park, in which nothing is omitted which nature and art combined produce to charm and captivate even the over-irritated sensualist of tropical lands. The verdant carpet variegated with Flora's blooming children was intersected with shady walks, while the palm tree, the cedar and the fig tree stood peaceably together. There the rich foliage of the vine protected an artesian well from the heat of the sun; here the olive and Jericho's balm shrubs were intimately crowded together, upon which the pomegranate and the golden orange appeared to look down with elated pride. Aloes and myrtles by the side of lemon trees impregnated the air with their sweet scent, in rivalry with their precious neighbors, the narcissus and the clove.

We pass these shadowy ways, up the slight declivity, and arrive before a magnificent palace of Tuscan structure. Passing through the marble portal, we step into a square court surrounded by colossal columns, upon which the front of the upper story rests.—Under it, upon the mosaic floor, low chairs, rich sofas, and little round tables are placed. Sentinels and servants haste to and fro, courtiers and high dignitaries in their state costume come and go continually. Every where, Grecian art and taste appear combined with oriental luxury and royal opulence. We ascend the marble stairs, and passing by the sentinels and servants, leaving unnoticed their tokens of respect, we open the doors and enter one of those spacious saloons, the walls glittering with the richest mosaic, and the floor covered with the heavy silk carpets of Damascus. The windows are replaced by Egypt's finest linen, and metallic mirrors reflect the brilliant gems set in the walls.

In the center of the saloon, on a platform several steps high, covered with red velvet interwoven with flowers of gold and silver, there rested the rich sofa, on which the most beautiful, most virtuous and at the same time most unfortunate of Queens, Mariamne the last daughter of the heroic family of the Asmoneans sat. Her head reclined upon her white, round arm, on which fell a profusion of black tresses, contrasting beautifully with the three strings of Persian pearls around the head, to keep uncovered a prominent and lilly white forehead. Her eyes which, like two solitary stars glittered under the dark brows, were fixed on her mother, Alexandra, who sat on the same sofa, and spoke to her on matters of momentous importance. None, beside the two ladies, was in the saloon. They spoke little louder than a whisper, still we must know part of the conversation.

"He is the father of my children," said Mariamne, with much feeling, "I can not consent to his destruction."

"And the murderer of your race," said Alexandra, in a tone of bitterness, "the wilful and malignant assassin of your brother, Queen. Do you know, daughter, the heart, the love, the inexpressible affections of a mother, for her children? Why, then, would you not comprehend the pain, the unutterable affliction of a mother bereft of her only son by the assassin's vile schemes, by foul and cowardish intrigues, by a despotic and self-deifying King? Why, then, would you not understand the mother's intense desire, to avenge her murdered child?"

"Because it is ignoble and impious," said Mariamne, briefly. "God who knows man's motives, God alone can judge man's actions, and He, only He, has a right to punish a

King. I believe, mother, Herod is my brother's assassin, but I do not know it. I can not condemn him because I believe him condemnable: for he is the father of my children."

"Pshaw, a King!" Alexandra ejaculated, with a contemptuous sneer. "Who, besides the Romans, ever said, Antipater's son was a King? A King must be the favorite of his people, else he is a monster. Herod's intention to exterminate a race of heroic Kings which he has partly realised already, is all the claim he has, upon the royal title. What else has he done, becoming a King? You believe, and I know, Herod is your brother's assassin. I know he designs the death of all whose veins contain the royal blood.—Now, ask yourself, what is your duty?—Must you, your mother, your grandfather, your own children, the last hopes of our family, and of Israel—I say, must you patiently and inactively, wait for the fatal blow; it may fall any day—or must you save yourself, us, your children, the hope of our family and of Israel? Tell me, Queen, which is nobler, to die cowardly and foolishly, or to live and act bravely and usefully? Or do you believe Herod can enjoy an undisturbed night's rest, as long as an Asmonean lives? Or did the assassination of your brother, God's Highpriest, not convince you, that he is capable of any crime, any outrage, before which hell and Satan themselves would blush?"—

"Mother, mother, I prithee," Mariamne supplicated, "bereave me not of the last spark of affection I bear to the father of my children. No, he can not be so monstrous, so diabolic as to slay his own children. You know how passionately he loves me."

Alexandra laughed angrily, on saying: "Yes, yes, my magnanimous daughter; I recollect how passionately he loves you, so passionately, indeed, that on being summoned to appear before Marc Antony to clear himself of the charge of having murdered my son, the Highpriest, he commanded Joseph, his brother-in-law to slay all of us, even you and your children, in case he should be punished for his crime. O yes, I recollect now, that he killed Joseph, his brother-in-law, because he broached the secret command to you. I recollect now, his furious conduct when he assailed you with the infamous charge, to have enjoyed a prohibited intercourse with his brother-in-law. I recollect the passionate love he bears to you. This very passionate love, I apprehend, will one day be the pretext to effect your and our destruction; for Herod does nothing without a wise and judicial pretext."

"Then, let it be so, in the name of God, who elevates and dethrones Kings," Mariamne exclaimed, with a solemn emphasis. "Let any misfortune come on me, the consciousness of spotless innocence, of a stainless character, of an unexceptionable adherence to duty and justice will sustain me on the scaffold, in the dark prison, in any and every scene of misery. God guard me, that I perpetrate no wrong. I shall not be auxiliary in any crime. I would blush before my own sons, before my people, nay, before the light of God's sun, should I have wronged my children's father, my people's King."

"Who wants you to perpetrate or be auxiliary in committing any crime?" Alexandra asked. "None wants your support in committing regicide. Still the man who murdered hundreds, who killed his own brother-in-law and two of his brothers, the man who assassinated the Lord's Highpriest, the exterminator of your race, you must affirm, deserves an ignominious death. But it is not this which your mother, in behalf of your royal family, of your own children, in behalf of your life and your people's wish and hope, asks of you. I wish you to embrace this favorable opportunity, and flee with your children to the King of Arabia, flee with your mother and your aged grandfather and ask the protection of the King against the violence, bloody and treacherous intentions of a slave, whom you have made a King. Cleopatra promised me her intercession with Marc Antony, in our behalf. Our people will rise in your favor. You must return as Queen of Judea, to secure the throne of the Asmoneans to your children, the lawful heirs thereof, and Herod must return to that obscurity from which he emerged by violence and bloodshed. Queen! this is your sacred duty, and this is the proper time to effect your escape. While Herod, with his army is engaged near Cana, opposed by the Arabian army and watched closely by the Egyptians, we can make good our escape. Dositheus, the governor of the palace, has not forgotten the death of his three brothers. He is our friend, because he hates Herod, and he favors our schemes."

"Mother, I caution you against the servile Dositheus," said Mariamne. "he is too servile to be honest, and too proud upon being a relative of Herod to be of any service to you. Dositheus may be the conscious or even unconscious tool of Herod, instructed to favor your escape, in order to gain a pretext to your destruction."

"I have positive proofs of his fidelity," said Alexandra.

"So you had of Sabion, still be betrayed you," Mariamne remarked.—"But it is not this alone, I wished to say. You advise me to seek protection with the enemy of my country against my own husband. Arabia's King in war with Judea on account of Cleopatra, to whom he refuses the payment of tribute, to become my protector, and there with one in rebellion against Cleopatra and Rome, I should wait for the favor of both? It is both wrong and foolish. You can not, after mature reflection, advise me to such a hazardous step."

"Ah, the Queen of Judea appears not disposed to understand this scheme," said Alexandra, smilingly. "Now, suppose for a moment, Cleopatra occasioned Marc Antony to appoint Herod to collect her tribute in Arabia; suppose she advised the King of Arabia to refuse payment, in order to involve Herod in this war, and offer us an opportunity to escape, and a place of safety; suppose, furthermore, she sent her troops to Cana for the purpose of engaging Herod so long, if the Arabs fail, until we have effected our escape, could you then call this scheme foolish? Evidently not. As regards the wrong, only the alternative is left you, either expose yourself, your children and your royal family to certain death, which will eventually come, or escape and secure the throne of your fathers to your children."

"Be merciful, my God, be merciful and punish us not in thy just wrath, for the innocent blood, shed in this unholy war," Mariamne cried. "Mother, this is a foul scheme, a vile treachery, which costs more human lives than I would wish to be made responsible for, before the throne of everlasting justice. Mother, my hands have not spilt that innocent blood, and I, even if death was certain to my children, my family and myself, as you suppose, I would take no advantage of this criminal scheme. Mother, I stay, let the consequences be as God pleases. If I must die, I shall die worthy of the last daughter of the Asmoneans, consoled and sustained by a stainless conscience."

The Queen observing the painful effect of her rebuke on her mother, and unwilling to continue the unpleasant conversation, called for her ladies. Helen, Sabion's beauteous daughter, whose acquaintance we made at the cottage of Abba Shaul, stepped into the saloon. "Bid my servant, fair Helen, to bring my sons," the Queen said; "I have not seen them to day." Helen obeyed, and returning to the saloon she told the Queen secretly, that Menahem's son urgently wished to see her. Alexandra, observing the secret conversation withdrew from the saloon. The Queen requested Helen to admit the man, and withdraw herself, as she wished to be alone with him. After Helen was gone, Baruch ben Menahem was ushered into the presence of the Queen. Without giving him time to go through the usual formalities and ceremonies the Queen urged: "Be short, my friend, tell me as quick as possible what you have to say. These walls have ears and treacherous lips."

"My gracious Queen, I bring you sad news," Baruch said. "Salome, the King's malignant sister, sends me to Cana, to deliver this letter to Herod. This letter says,"—Here he paused, as though he could find no words to express the criminal contents of the letter.

"Speak, speak, my friend," Mariamne urged, with a smile, "I am prepared to hear the worst."

"This letter contains an ignominious and

false, utterly false charge against you," Baruch resumed. "It says, you, my gracious Queen, you had yielded to the impure requests of Dositheus."

The Queen laughed. "Do not trouble yourself about that," she said, kindly, "Salome has done so once before. Having then charged me with the same crime with her own husband, of whom she appeared to be tired, the consequence was the death of her husband by the hands of the King. This is not a plot against me, it is one against poor Dositheus. It is better you deliver the letter in the hands of the King, than any body else, for I know your faithful heart."

"I will deliver it, and I will say all I know about the letter," said Baruch.

"And what do you know about it?" the Queen asked.

"I offered my services to Herod's sister, because you, my noble Queen, desired me to do so," said Baruch. "My surprise about my easy success with her was soon explained to me. From that very hour she spared no trouble, all her beguiling and lubric arts were employed, to win me for her sensual propensities. It did not require the virtue of Joseph to resist her, as she is far from being Potiphar's beautiful wife. She waxed daily more arrogant and shameless, and I more disgusted with her. She begged, promised, menaced; I was deaf to her words. Still, I flattered her, because you wanted it so. I gave her some hopes and when she pressed me to the utmost, I told her that I never would accede to her wishes, unless united with her in lawful marriage. Wishing, as I did, for your sake, to have her entirely under my control, I threatened to reveal her conduct to the people and scandalise her name, publicly, if she refuses to be mine. She reflected several days and the result was, that she promised to be mine, if I would stand this trial, to deliver this letter to the King and tell him this was no secret at court. I consented. She wrote the letter, I read it, she sealed it carefully in my presence, and bid me haste."

"I think I understand these intrigues," said the Queen, deliberately. "Dositheus is the only remaining brother of her deceased husband. None can contest his rights upon her, for she is childless. He must die before she can marry you. This is the whole secret. But how will you prove the innocence of poor Dositheus before the enraged King?"

"Very easily, indeed," said Baruch. "Before delivering the letter to him, I shall reveal to him the shameless conduct of his sister. I will also tell him, that she, in my presence, wanted Dositheus to write a similar letter to the King against you and the Nassi, the son of Bethera. When Dositheus refused, she became so enraged, that she slapped him in his face. Had I not stepped between them, the offended man would have massacred her, on the spot. I will tell him all this, and then deliver this letter."

"Has that ignoble woman also a grudge on the Nassi, that blind and obedient tool of Herod?" the Queen said, astonished. "This is a novel discovery. I did not know that. He was, indeed, several times with me, asking my advice in important matters. But he is an old man, the King would scarcely have believed the scandalous report."

A noise in the reception room interrupted the conversation. The doors were thrown open and, without any ceremony, Herod, followed by Dositheus, armed to the teeth, rushed into the saloon. Without paying any respect to his Queen he harshly asked the young man, "Who are you?" With a tremulous voice be replied, "My royal master's servant, Baruch ben Menahem."

The King laughed so savagely, that it frightened his own attendants. "What means this letter?" he said, snatching it out of Baruch's hands.

"Mercy, mercy, my royal lord!" Baruch cried, falling upon his face, "read not this damnable letter, before you have heard me."

Herod kicked him away with his foot, opened the letter and cast a hasty glance on it. Then he turned to Dositheus. "Secure this traitor?" he thundered. Baruch was immediately led away, and Herod was alone, with Mariamne. At this painful moment Helen with the two little sons of Herod entered the saloon. The children hastened to embrace their father, but he pushed them away, with a curse on his lips. They sought refuge with their mother, who pressed them affectionately to her heaving bosom, and with a tear in her eyes, she said, "Be content, my darlings, father is cross." Helen fell down before the King and prayed, "Do no harm, my royal lord, to Baruch ben Menahem. He is the son of the Essenee Menahem. He is harmless as a dove."

"Is he also your lover, young lady?" the King asked, ironically. "Begone, I must be alone with the Queen."

"Mercy, mercy for the young man," Helen, cried, and refused to leave the saloon.

"Call Sabion," the King commanded. Helen, refusing to rise, she continued suing for mercy, until her father came.

"It appears that also your daughter conspires against me," Herod said. "Get her out of my way."

Helen obeyed, silently, the command of her father, and went away with him. The King followed them to the anti-room, where he asked Sabion, "What news do you have?"—"Nothing important," said Sabion. "The peasants of the district of Jericho have come to offer their first fruits. They are encamped outside the Fishgate. I have made the proper arrangements."

Helen blushed, on hearing the peasants of Jericho mentioned, but none observed her.

"Be careful," the King said, and returned to the saloon, where he found his children were yet in the embrace of their mother.

"I must be alone with you, Queen," Herod said, in a harsh and agitated tone.

"My children are the most preper witnesses to every thing King Herod has to say to his consort," the Queen responded, in a calm tone.

"Will it benefit them to hear of the faithlessness of their mother?" the King asked, trembling with excitement.

"They are innocent children and understand little of the crimes and follies of the world," Mariamne said; "but they are sensitive enough to feel the frigid conduct of their father; they can not do the whole day without the love of their mother. They need it doubly. Speak, my lord, without restraint. Your children understand only your anger, but not your words."

This appeared to pacify the excited King, for he spoke calmly. "Mariamne, Queen of my heart"—

"Asmonean princess and Queen of Judea, you mean to say," Mariamne proudly interrupted.

"Any title you please to claim," Herod said, "but tell me, what this young man had to do in your private apartment, alone, all alone with you."

"Important business, concerning none but myself," the Queen replied. "Did not your sister's letter inform you—you read it—of the nature of Barueh's business?"

"The letter? which letter?" Herod asked, feigning calmness.

"Well, the letter you hold in your hands," Mariamne said, "accusing me of a criminal connection with the aged Dositheus, your obedient tool."

"How do you know the contents of this letter," the King asked, with increasing excitement.

"Your treacherous sister gave it to Baruch ben Menahem," the Queen replied, "and he being her favorite was acquainted with its contents. He came and told me of the treacherous and infamous plots of your sister against me."

"He told you," Herod thundered; "then your intimacy with him is evident. Confess your crime, Queen, and bear witness, that my wrath is deserved."

"I do not understand you, King," she said, contemptuously. "Tell me what you mean, and I will give you an explanation, if honor permit it."

"Hear then, and be convinced, that nothing remains a secret to Herod," he said hastily.

"In Cana, I met the Arabian army. I attacked them and they fled. They could not stand the charge of my well-drilled army. Athenio, the general of Cleopatra, commanding a corps of observation, said he came to support me, if I should not be able to repulse the Arabs. I mistrusted his words. No sooner were the Arabs defeated than he supported them. The united armies of Cleopatra and Arabia fell on my men. They stood their ground like giants; but they were overwhelmed by superior numbers, and were defeated, defeated by treason, by the treachery of Cleopatra, roused against me by the members of your family. Cursing and trembling with rage, I returned to my quarters. Here I found a letter of my sister. Read it, read it, yourself."

Mariamne read: "Baruch ben Menahem is the suitor of your Queen. This is no secret to any one at court. Their relations are most intimate, thus much is known to every body. I, wishing to prevent the scandal and deliver the young sinner into your hands, attracted him to myself, promised to marry him, if he convey a letter to you, saying that Dositheus courts the Queen; because I knew he would open the letter, and you would scarcely believe such a crime of Dositheus. When delivering the letter to you, he is in your power. Your sister,

SALOME."

"Foul, diabolical lies!" Mariamne exclaimed, violently. "All is an invention, a malignant, despicable invention."

"Do not rage in vain, fair Queen," Herod said, with a sneer. "I at once ascribed the treason of Cleopatra's General to your arts, and thought there must be some truth in my sister's letter. I hastened home to my capital, to my palace, to my wife's private apartment, and here I find the identical Baruch ben Menahem, alone with you, having in a moment of repentance told you the contents of this letter. Queen, you are guilty, according to the best of my judgment. Confess your crime, and yield to the arm of justice."

"Father is very cross to day," the oldest of the children said, pressing himself timidly to his mother.

"Yes, my child," Mariamne said, proudly, "your father is very cross to day, and misinformed. Let us go, and return when his anger is over." She went toward the door, but Herod stopped her, and cried furiously, "You shall not go from here before I know the truth in these matters."

"I shall not stay, quarreling with a mad man," she replied, calmly. "Your morbid conscience is your interpreter of events. You see all things in a delusive light." She again attempted to leave the room, but Herod seized her and dragged her back. The children cried violently. Mariamne silenced them. "Do not cry," said she, "it is nothing; your father was beaten by the Arabs and wants now to make good his courage with his defenceless wife and children."

Herod gnashed his teeth, and roared lionlike. Helen and the other ladies of the Queen rushed into the room and surrounded the Queen, who sunk half-fainting in Helen's embrace. "What is it, my gracious Queen?" the ladies asked. "Nothing, nothing; the King told me our army was defeated," she said with a faint voice. "Conduct me to my private chamber. Take care of my sons."

The Queen, the children and the ladies went away, leaving Herod alone in a state of fury. He plucked the hair from his beard, in his violent rage, pushed his head against the wall, and struck his breast with his own fists; then, he cried furiously, "She is faithless, she betrayed me." Opening the door he called out the name of Sabion. The man appeared. Herod seized him, and, infuriated with rage, he cried in a hoarse and depressed voice, "Take that young man, that Baruch ben Menahem, torture him with all possible instruments. Tear his limbs slowly from his body, burn his eyes out with hot iron, tear the flesh from his breast, with sharp tongs, until he confesses his crime, then let him die, and tell me his confession."

"My lord," said Sabion with a faltering voice, "he is the son of your best friend, Menahem the Essenee."

"Traitor, do you also conspire against me?" the King roared. "Do what I told you."

When Sabion was nearly out of the room, the King called him back. "The Queen and her children, her mother and grand father must be closely watched."

The trembling courtier bowed, submissively, and turned to withdraw. "Stay!"

the King thundered. "Who are the peasants from Jericho?"

"Peasants who come to offer their first fruits, I believe," said Sabion.

"Be careful," the King said, in a milder tone. "You know, Sabion, Jericho is the property of Cleopatra and the refuge of conspirators and rebels. Take care that no spies are among the comers."

Sabion again bowed submissively, and withdrew. When Herod was alone he cursed, wept, raged, and wept again, for many hours.

Sabion returned late at evening to his father's house, humiliated and disgusted with the ruthless despotism of his royal master. Helen waited impatiently for her father's return, and when he came he first of all things went to her apartment and kissed her affectionately.

"Helen, my daughter, my only child," said he, "you are my only joy in this world. Since your mother has returned to mother earth, I have none beside you to console me."

"Mother returned to our Father in heaven," Helen said; "after awhile we shall meet her again."

"Nonsense, nothing but supreme nonsense," Sabion ejaculated, "the dead are dead and rest in the bosom of eternal peace. This is the belief of all Saducees, and is also mine. But let this be as it is. How is the Queen?"

"The Queen is sick," said Helen, quickly, "and the dead live, my mother lives. I feel it in spite of all the Saducees in the world. Whatever the yearning hearts of all good men proclaim, can be no delusion. My mother lives and hears me, when I remember her in my prayer."

"You are a good, pious soul, my darling," the father said, smilingly, "and I dislike to dispute your pious opinions But do tell me what the Queen said after the meeting with the King."

"Nothing in the world," said Helen, "she is too unwell to say anything. But allow me, dearest father, allow me also a question, what did Baruch ben Menahem say, when you saw him last?"

"Do not care, my child, for the peculiar youth," Sabion said, "he must die."

"Die! Baruch, the innocent, harmless, pious youth must die?" Helen exclaimed, bewildered. "Father, you must be mistaken, he is gentle as a dove, kind as a lambkin, he can have done no wrong, why should he die?"

"You are foolish, Helen," Sabion gainsaid, with a smile. "In our days, the most unpardonable crime is to displease the King, and this is the very crime of which Baruch is guilty; therefore he must die, breathe his last under the tortures of modern invention. They have imported quite new tortures from Rome, as Anteny, Augustus 'and Lapidus invented them to establish their power and secure their dominion over Rome."

"God, merciful God, must Baruch die?" Helen lamented. "It can not be, it must not be. How the poor youth will struggle with the torments of death!"

"Who cares in our days about death!" Sabion vociferated. "It is something so common, so much of every-day occurrence, that none cares for it, except nervous women and cripples. Men have become indifferent to life and death."

"Father this is a sinful time," Helen said. "I will go, early in the morning, and pray at the tomb of my mother."

"What good will it do you, foolish child?" Sabion asked.

"It will relieve my heart," said Helen, feelingly. "It will sustain me, that I be not infected by the raging vices of the day. It will invigorate me, that I despair not of man's humanity, and of God's godliness."

"The King, sir, wishes to see you immediately," a servant entering said hastily, and retired.

"So late at evening, it must be important," Sabion murmured between his teeth.

"Father! one request I have to make, do not refuse it to your child," Helen prayed. "Let no harm be done to Baruch, till I have seen him in his prison. Early in the morning, I will go and pray at the tomb of my mother; then I will go to see him."

"I will, my child," Sabion replied, and left her room.

Early in the morning Helen, in company with her friend Elvira, whom she regarded as a sister, and an old servant, went out to the tomb of her mother. She intended to consult Abba Shaul, in whom she placed much confidence, in regard to the fate of Baruch ben Menahem. But finding there Simon ben Hillel, and having with him the exciting conversation, which we noted before, she forgot all about Baruch, and returned to the city in a state of intense excitement. On her way home she spoke very little to Elvira. After a long silence, she asked her, "Who is the steady companion of Simon ben Hillel?"

Elvira replied, "Jonathan ben Uziel." Notwithstanding the hundred questions of the lively and active Elvira, Helen could not be induced to speak again. Having arrived at her residence, her servant was immediately dispatched to call two of her father's secret men. They came. Helen mastered her temper and, in the calmest manner, she told them of the peasants, encamped outside the Fishgate, gave them a description of the two young men she wished to have arrested forthwith and locked up in a room which she pointed out. The two men grumbled, but a handful of glittering gold going to their pockets, and the promise of more, if her orders were well attended to, silenced the bearded and sun burned spies. They promised to do their best, and went out on their errand.

Elvira was more curious and inquisitive to day than ever before. After she had proposed a hundred questions, in a joking and laughing manner, peculiar to herself, she asked, "Tell me, fair Helen, why do you have arrested TWO young men, when I scarcely can arrest the attention of ONE?"

"That none else arrest them," Helen replied drily, apparently not having understood the wit of her companion. "They play a hazardous game which I must prevent."

"Would not you allow me to arrest one of them?" Elvira asked, peevishly. "The description you gave of them is so charming, indeed, that I would like to arrest one of them."

Helen was not well disposed to day. "This is no time for jokes," she said, earnestly, "nor is it right of you to suspect my motives. I tell you, I have those two men arrested, because they are in imminent danger."

"Danger?" Elvira repeated, thoughtfully. "And you entrust those you wish to save in the hands of your father's suspicions servants?"

"Are my father's servants suspicious?" Helen asked, with no little surprise.

"They are suspicious to the people," Elvira said, "but to those who know them well, they are acquainted as a ruthless and reckless band of spies and assassins, who lurk in dark places and listen after every secret word, to provide the scaffold with new victims and the prisons with afflicted hearts, to bring misery into peaceable families and tear asunder, the most sacred and dearest ties of endeared companions."

"Gracious God! Elvira what do you say?" Helen asked, "Do we live in a den of murderers?"

"Worse, much worse than this," Elvira said. "And you entrusted two innocent young men into such reckless hands."

"Fear naught, dearest," Helen said, "they promised to bring them to me, and there is an honor also among thieves."

"There may be an honor among thieves," Elvira said, "but not among hirelings and spies; certainly none among Herod's cruel tools, who are feared, hated, despised by every body and tyrannized over with an unbending, iron rod, by Herod and Sabion. They will certainly inform your father of your command before they obey it. In a few hours you and the two young men are in the hands of your father."

"There is yet no cause of alarm," Helen said. "I am my father's only child, and he loves me affectionately. I can do a great deal with him."

"You are decidedly mistaken," Elvira contended. "No affection is too holy, no ties are too sacred to Herod. If he bids, your father must obey, whatever his objections might be. If the two young men displease Herod, they or you must die, and your own father must be your executioner."

"You are terrible to day," Helen said.

"Your imagination is fraught with evil demons. There is no such a thing.—I must now go to Baruch ben Menahem, and you stay and take proper care of the two young men, when they are brought, that no harm befal them." She kissed Elvira, and left.

"Not so hasty, young lady," Elvira said to herself; "you shall not arrest Jonathan ben Uziel. I shall not entrust his fate to such hands." She went away, and in a few moments she returned dress d in boy's clothes, and her servant in the disguise of a Roman soldier.

"How do I look?" she asked her servant.

"Amiable, upon my honor, amiable," the servant ejaculated.

"Fool; why do you say this?" Elvira scolded; "Is there a young lady in Jerusalem who does not know that she is amiable? And if she should happen not to know it, aré there not plenty of men here to tell her? I wish to know, whether I look precisely like a naughty, peevish, saucy boy; for that is the part I am going to play."

"You look so, exactly so," said the obliging servant.

"Ah, you fool, dare you say to a lady, that she looks like a naughty, peevish, saucy boy?" Elvira rebuked. "If I look so, indeed, you are the first man in Jerusalem who has the impudence to tell truth to a young lady. If you say so to another, she will slap you in your face. How do I look, Marc?"

"To be sure, young lady—young gentleman, I was going to say," the servant stammered, "you look exactly as you please,"—

"You are a stupid ass," she scolded, "I do not wish to look as I please; I wish to look as others please to imagine a naughty boy. No young lady pleases to please herself, but to please others. I see you are a foolish Babylonian, a ridiculous Greek, a stupid Samaritan, you do not know much. Marc, how do I look?"

"By the beard of the highpriest," the poor fellow ejaculated, "I do not know how you look."

"Who are you, Marc?" Elvira said. "Stand straight and answer."

"I am Portubius Samouius Hervasto, a soldier of the fifth legion," the fellow said, stretching his figure.

"And I am Saltulis Antonio Pompius, a wealthy patrician," she said, haughtily, "who lives at present in Jerusalem. You know it now?"

"To be sure I do," the man said, and both went out on an errand already known to us.

"Baruch ben Menahen, beloved companion of my childhood," Helen said, with two large tears in her eyes, "are you of a good spirit?"

"I am," said he, smilingly. "I know my doom is sealed, I must die. Herod the King, by the will of Rome, wills it so. But I have no crime on my soul. My conscience is free of every guilt. Helen, I am happy now, that I lived with God and according to His will. I can now look fearlessly into the very jaws of death. Helen, I thank you that you descended to this prison, to see me once more. Go back to my companions, and tell them Baruch ben Menahem has lived long enough to die happily, if God has so decreed. Farewell, Helen, forever, farewell."

She could make no reply; she could not even clasp the outstretched hand of her friend. "Can I not save you?" she asked, after a long pause. "Speak, my friend, can I do nothing for you?"

"Nothing for me, I believe," Baruch said, after some reflection; "but you may be of much service to somebody whom I love better than my life."

"Tell me, Baruch," she said, hastily, "O tell me, what can I do to please you. Let it cost my life, I will gladly do it."

"Noble Helen," the young man exclaimed, much moved. "Look out doors and see that none overhears our conversation."

"My old and faithful servant watches," she said, "we are undisturbed. Speak my friend, that I may act speedily."

"Do you love our Queen?" he asked.

"With all my heart," she responded.

"Swear by your God, by your hopes of eternal salvation, swear by your life and love," he said, "that you will never desert, never betray her, and I will speak."

"I do solemnly swear," Helen said, having laid her right hand upon the heart and having lifted up her left hand to heaven.

"Hear me, Helen, and then tell me what you will do," he said, with increasing emphasis. "No mortal being ever has loved a woman so affectionately, so passionately, so sincerely, as I have our Queen. No mortal ear has ever heard this confession; this broken heart alone knew it; and I alone felt the nameless torments of a hopeless raving passion. I embraced every opportunity to serve her, and so I ingratiated myself into the confidence of her deadly enemy, the Queen's malignant sister. You know diabolic Salome. Hell itself dare not boast upon a more degraded, more satanic woman than she is. She plots incessantly the destruction of the Queen and of every member of the Asmonean family. She knows that I learned her satanic schemes and revealed them to the Queen; so I must die, and the next victim of her malignity is either the Queen or her aged grandfather. She knows the passionate love of Herod for his royal consort, and, behold jealousy is her ally; Satan can make no better plots—She says, that Dositheus and myself, as I just now learned, prostituted the Queen.

"Speedy assistance only can save her, or else she is lost, lost probably in a few hours," Baruch continued; "speedy assistance is necessary, energetic action alone can save her."

"Tell me, what shall I do for her," Helen urged, "tell it quickly, I am prepared to die for her, if I can not save her otherwise."

"Go down to Bezetha," Baruch said, "in my father's house you will find my clothes and a false face, looking exactly like myself. Go to the valley of Hinom, and with the instruction I hereby will give you, you will find admission into the people's council. There you tell all you know about the Queen and myself, and tell them, I hope they will act speedily, and energetically in behalf of the Queen"

Baruch having instructed her in all she should know, she left him resigned to his unhappy fate and prepared to die. The tears of Helen were dried by the calm resignation of Baruch, and her desire to save the Queen. In a few moments she was again in her private apartments, where one of her father's servants informed her of the arrest of the two strangers who were secured in an adjoining apartment. Helen blushed. Having paid the man for his services, she dismissed him, and thought of the best way to pursue, to bring Simon out of the city and prevent him from coming in conflict with her father. After some deliberation she went to the apartment described to her by the servant. Her heart beat more violently with every step she progressed toward the room. Modestly and blushingly she opened the door, but two peasants, entire strangers, stood before her. She stood paralyzed at the door, and was for a good while, unable to speak.

"Who are you, and what do you want here?" she asked, feigning calmness.

"We have been arrested," one of the peasants said, "we know not why or wherefore. We are kept here in close confinement, we can not tell to what end."

"It is a mistake," Helen said. Giving each of them a hand full of gold coins, she requested them to be silent on the matter, leave the palace and join their friends.

The peasants, glad of the easy escape, cordially thanked her and attempted to go, when a secret door in the wall opened, and Sabion, with several servants, entered. Helen looked with consternation on her father, when he calmly and imperatively said, "Simon ben Hillel and Jonathan ben Uziel, you are my prisoners." Waving with his hand, the officers were called to their duty and, notwithstanding the protests and petitions of the peasants they were led away. Sabion eyed his daughter closely when saying slowly and emphatically, "My daughter is well instructed in the functions of her father, she can effect arrests in the best way. She has also studied the art of courts, and feigned not to know the strangers, when she perceived the presence of her father. You are quite a promising child. I ought to be proud of you." Helen attempted to speak, but Sabion would not let her. "Not necessary," he said, in a bitter tone, "I know enough of your affairs. It is a pity that the affectionate meeting was frustrated, quite an officious and imposing father you have, but it so happens, that official duties required my presence hereabout. But, young lady, I must know two things before hand. Do you know the character of these two men, and what connection have you with them?"

"I do not know these two men, nor do I know their characters; I have no connections with them," Helen said, calmly and composedly; "they are innocent peasants whom I know not."

"Perfectly well," said Sabion, sneeringly; "masterly perfect. My daughter perfectly sustains the character of a lady at court.—She looks innocent, harmless and sweet as though nothing wrong, nothing strange had happened. She pleads a total denial of all facts, and it is for me to prove them. Sagacious, very sagacious, indeed. But the evidence is in my hands and it shall not escape."

"I do say here, in the presence of my God and my father," Helen said, solemnly, "that the two men you have arrested are strangers to me, I know them not. Their very countenances prove them to be innocent and harmless peasants."

Sabion smiled cunningly, when saying, "Very good. A Queen could not do any better. They are all innocent, my daughter, her secret friends and all mankind besides. It is a capital joke. But my innocent daughter should know, I believe, that Hillel's son and his pupil are sworn and avowed enemies of Herod and her father. If she does not know it, I do hereby inform her. I also inform her that she having secret communications with the enemies of the King and her father, is a traitor"——

"Father, for God's sake continue not!" Helen cried vehemently, "do not accuse your only child of crimes she is incapable of committing. I do declare, that the two peasants you just now have arrested are perfect strangers to me. I know them not, nor do they know me. I only then will give you an explanation, when the peasants are restored to liberty."

"You shall not fool a man, I say," Sabion remarked. "The two prisoners remain in my power, till I know the truth about this affair. Woman's tears and her persuading voice are insufficient to make me forget the duties I owe to my King."

"And your only child's petition?" Helen asked.

"Is of no avail," Sabion replied. "I am the King's servant"——

"And the people's opponent," Helen remarked, imprudently. But, frightened by her own words, she added, "Baruch ben Menahem, the innocent Essence, the son of your King's friend, is my testimony."

Sabion scrutinized her sharply, with his piercing look, which darted arrowlike from his small black eyes. "Do you know this?" he asked, slowly and shrewdly. "Ah, I believe Simon ben Hillel told you. Therefore he must die."

Helen trembled, when her father articulated the last words, so firmly and resolutely, that no doubt could be entertained as to their meaning. She quickly recovered her self-possession, and asked, smilingly, her father, "Would you have Simon ben Hillel die, if he is my lover, if I must die on his grave?"

"Your lover, unhappy child?" Sabion asked, in a tone of consternation, "You do not mean this, in earnest, my child, do you?"

"Whenever your anger will be over, I will tell you truly, what I know," Helen said. "I speak not to Herod's stern officer, I shall gladly and sincerely speak to my father."

"Speak, my child," Sabion said, half smiling, "but speak the truth and nothing but the truth."

"I do my father," said Helen. "I love but one man, I will ever love him only, and he is indeed, Simon ben Hillel. But neither of the two men arrested is Simon ben Hillel."

"Treacherous child, unnatural daughter," Sabion exclaimed, angrily, "you love the son of our archenemy; for Hillel is the head of the Pharisees. Never shall you be his wife. Never shall you be the partner of a despised Pharisee, a poor Babylonian, a foe of King Herod. Never will I give my consent to this unnatural union." After a while, he composed himself and, in a milder tone, he asked, "Who are the two men, I found with you?"

"Two innocent peasants," Helen said, "you can see it in their countenances."

"And how did they come to you," Sabion inquired, "when you ordered my servants, to arrest Simon ben Hillel and Jonathan ben Uziel?"

"Your servants missed the right men," said Helen. "On entering this room, I perceived the mistake."

Sabion opened the door, some of his servants were called and came in. "Take the two prisoners," said he, "and go with them about in search of Simon ben Hillel and Jonathan ben Uziel. They can point them out to you. Whenever those persons are in my power, these prisoners are dismissed."

The servants withdrew. Helen fell down, embraced the knees of her father, praying him to do no harm to Hillel's son; but the hard man turned away his face. He left the room, leaving Helen in tears and resting upon her knees. When he was gone she rose slowly and cried vehemently, "Am I not the unhappiest woman, placed as I am between two bitter enemies, both of whom I love? God assist me, that I prevent both from the commission of an act which surely would forever render me most miserable."

After some reflection, she called Elvira.—The girl came. "You are right, my good Elvira," Helen said. "My father's servants informed him of my orders, and I despair."

"No cause for it," said Elvira, "I do not know what interest you take in the two young men; but I know them out of Sabion's reach!"

"Where, my beloved sisterly friend, where are they," Helen inquired anxiously, "I will, I must know it."

"I can not tell you, beloved Helen," Elvira said, "I can not tell you."

"O behold the anxiety of my trembling heart," Helen said, "behold me pray, beseech you, dearest Elvira. Know the secret, that Simon ben Hillel is the friend of my heart. I must know where he is, the whole happiness of all my life depends on it. My life and his, my happiness and his, Elvira, my paradise and his depend on it, that I see him, speak to him ere the next morning dawns. Tell me, hesitate not, I beseech you, I conjure you in the name of thy God and mine."

"If I tell you, good Helen," said Elvira, "you do not know the place, you can not find him."

"Speak, only tell me the place," said Helen. "If it is in the highest heaven, my love will furnish me with wings and I will reach him. If it is in the lowest regions of the nether-world, my affections will safely guide me through the terrible gates of hell. O tell me, where is he?"

"If I tell you, beloved, you will not understand me," said Elvira. "Still I will tell you, just to satisfy you. Simon ben Hillel will be this evening in the people's council."

Helen seized her violently and cried passionately, "This is the voice of God speaking through you, Elvira. You are the oracle of the Almighty. Tell my father, I want to pray all night on the grave of my mother. Tell him I am mad, I am sick, I am enraptured, no, I am deadly sick in my brains. Farewell, farewell."

Before Elvira could speak Helen was gone.

CHAPTER III

THE TRIAL AND THE SCHEME.

"Save the Queen, ye men, with the muscular, sunburned countenances," Helen cried in the subterranean hall of the people's council, after she was detected; "save the Queen, she is in imminent danger. Herod returned enraged from Cana. He considers his wife and her family the efficient cause of his defeat. His treacherous and malignant sister Salome conspired and plotted against my gracious Queen. She made the King believe Baruch ben Menahem was the lubric favorite of the Queen. Both Baruch and the Queen are in close confinement, both expect torture and death with every moment."

Profound silence reigned supreme, in the wide, subterranean hall. Simon ben Hillel breathed again; his heart was somewhat relieved. The men, with the bearded, rough countenances, looked amazed on the courageons culprit. Her vehement voice and heart-piercing clamor appeared to inspire the stoutest hearts with sympathy for her.

"Who sends you here, the Queen or Baruch ben Menahem?" Baba ben Buta asked, in his usually solemn tone.

"Baruch ben Menahem in behalf of the Queen," said Helen. "He knows as I do through my father, that both are in the most imminent danger."

"And who is your father, that he knows the secrets of Herod?" Baba ben Buta asked.

"My father is Sabion, King Herod's confidential friend," Helen responded, boldly. "You wrong him, he is not the man who leads Herod, he is the mere servant, a tool of the King, his death would not benefit you."

"Enough heard," one of the multitude vociferated. "She is Sabion's daughter. This is foul treachery, to which Baruch ben Menahem has given his aid."

"It is not for you alone to decide," Baba ben Buta admonished. "There are many of us, and all of us claim equal rights on every question. First, I will hear, then we will judge." Turning to Helen he continued, "Is not Baruch ben Menahem your husband, your groom, or your lover?"

Helen blushed, she was not prepared to answer this question. At this instance Simon rose and, lifting up his right hand, he exclaimed, solemnly, "I witness, that he is not."—"I witness that he is not," Abba Shaul repeated, in a monotonous voice, sounding like distant thunder. Helen rewarded them with a look more eloquent and affectionate than Homer and Virgil ever were. All eyes were directed to the two emphatic witnesses, so Helen was unobserved and won time to regain her self-possession. — "No, emphatically no!" Helen exclaimed. "Baruch ben Menahem is no more to me than the playmate of my childhood. I know his generous heart is incapable of any crime. I know that Herod accuses him of a criminal connection with the Queen, on account of which both their lives are in jeopardy. Before the morning dawns he most likely will be among the dead; for in the silence of night Herod executes his opponents, and none knows how they came to their death, when in the morning they are found slain in the lanes of Jerusalem. To morrow probably, the Queen is no more, for the wrath of Herod is indomitable. I beseech, I entreat you to save the Queen and young Baruch, if it is in your power," Helen prayed vehemently, and a current of tears gushed from her eyes.

"How do you know the method of Herod to assassinate his victims?" Baba asked.

"By my father," the damsel said.

"Who is the chief executioner," one of the multitude interrupted her.

"My father is the King's confidential friend," Helen said, "but not his executioner."

"And his spy," one added, "his cunning, heartless adviser, and the people's villanous assassin."

"Gracious God, Thou knowest it can not be, it dare not be so," Helen exclaimed, with painful emotions. "He is my father, I love him, affectionately, he can not be as bad as you imagine him. It is a malignant invention of slanderous souls, my father is not guilty of such hideous crimes."

"Spare your words, woman," Baba ben Buta rebuked her, earnestly, "your plea for your guilty parent, however much honor it may do to your generous heart, only renders you suspicious in our eyes, as we know Sabion too well. Speak no more in his favor. Answer me one more question. Are you prepared to take a solemn oath in substantiation of what you have said, in regard to the Queen and Baruch ben Menahem?"

"I am, I am," she responded, solemnly.

"And are you ready to die without a murmur," the blind man continued, in a guttural tone, "if your statements regarding the Queen and Baruch ben Menahem are not true?"

"I am, I am," said Helen firmly.

"Then lead her into one of the secret chambers," said Baba, "and secure her, that we, in due time, might call her back."

Helen was led away. One more affectionate look she cast on Simon, and disappeared.

"I witness," said Baba ben Buta, "that the woman who stood before you, spoke the truth. I was informed of his defeat near Cana by the joint attack of the Arabs and Egyptians; of his hasty return to Jerusalem, and his suspicions on the Queen and her family. I am informed, that on returning, unexpectedly, he found Baruch ben Menahem alone with the Queen in her private saloon; the unfortunate youth was instantly arrested, and is most likely doomed to death, while the Queen was so ill treated, that she lays sick on her bed and is closely watched by Herod's servants. Also, her mother and grandfather are closely watched."

"I witness," said Abba Shaul, "I have learned all these things, and say we must act speedily."

"And what kind of action do you propose?" one asked Abba Shaul.

"Herod's army stands discomfited and discouraged near Cana," said Abba Shaul.—"The queen of Egypt is his bitter adversary, hence our friend and ally, if we need her assistance. Marc Antony expects daily the approach of the Roman army under the command of his powerful adversary. He can not assist Herod. This is an opportune time to shake off the intolerable yoke. Let us, before the morning dawns, take possession of the Temple. Let us, early in the morning, give the signal to a general insurrection in the city. Ten thousand brave hearts are ready instantly to join us and die with us, if God so decrees. I call this speedy action."

After the powerful voice of the gigantic man had subsided, silence reigned supreme. None appeared sufficiently prepared to appreciate the merits of the bold and dangerous scheme. Abba Shaul looked about himself as though he was to press his looks into every heart, and when none spoke, he resumed, "Why are you silent, ye men with the iron muscles, are your hearts not bold enough to strike the fatal blow? The last of the Asmoneans, the offspring of those who saved you from the hands of Antioches Epiphanes, are in imminent danger; you must repay part of the debt, you must save them. Or have you not long enough been trodden under the feet of a bloodthirsty tyrant? are you not tired yet of the insufferable yoke which Antipater's son imposes upon your neck? Ah, the lashes upon our back do not pain us, the blows do not harm us. We can wait yet. If we are trampled upon, have we not manly patience? If our brethren are murdered in the darkness of the night in the royal palace, and like dogs thrown into the street; dare we not bury them and weep a tear upon their graves? If the King sends away our treasures to foreign, heathen temples, are we not still an opulent people? If he by his spies prohibits us to speak, can we not think? If he drinks our warm hearts blood, have we not still sufficient thereof? Ha, ha, ha, we are a rich, patient and virtuous people!—Why do you thus gaze at me? You think I am mad? Yes, I feel my brains glow, my blood boils, a blast of fire is in my heart. My patience is consumed, I can stand it no longer."

"Long live Abba Shaul!" it thundered from a hundred lips and the swords rushed from the sheath. "Let him lead us, we will follow," they cried.

It took the whole influence of Baba ben Buta to pacify the agitated multitude.—When he succeeded in obtaining a hearing, he said, "Men and brethren, your heroic determination is laudable, but your impatience might cost all your lives and administer the fatal blow to the very cause which we intend to carry victoriously through this beautiful land. We have just commenced to deliberate. We are not prepared yet for the outbreak. We stand in opposition to a powerful and cunning tyrant. Both power and prudence must be united to defeat and dethrone him. It is noble to act by the generous impulse of a heroic heart. It is brave and valorous to fight where danger is most imminent, and death most certain. But it is wisest and most advisable to have a plan of action, by which success is likely to be attained, before we advance one step. Can any one of you give us such a plan? And if we are defeated our cause is lost."

"I have but one plan," Abba Shaul said,

"and this is to start the insurrection, and it will roll like a ball of wild fire all over the city, all over the land and re-kindle the fire of liberty and bravery in the hearts of Judah's heroic sons. Never a just cause appealed in vain to the sons of my people.—Those who defeated the armies of Syria and of Rome are men of iron hearts. Those who obey the Law of the Lord love liberty and independence. It is their very element, in which only they can live. It is the air which they breathe, the sustenance which keeps them alive. Antipater's son has deprived us of our element, our air, our sustenance, we can stand it no longer. We appeal to our suffering brethren from the hight of the Temple; will they not hear us, not hasten to our support? O do not thus slander the sons of Israel, say not they will not come and go with us."

"Allow a young man and a stranger among you to say a word or two," said Jonathan ben Uziel. "We must not forget, that at the first voice of open rebellion, that reaches the ear of Herod, the heads of all the Asmoneaus must fall victims to his rage; for any and every rebellion, as every misfortune that befalls him, he would ascribe to the intrigues of the Queen and her relatives. If the Queen is not dead yet, if Baruch ben Menahem lives yet, we kill them by our insurrection. The kingdom shall fall forever, but the Asmoneans shall live happy among us. We owe them a debt for their father's sake; we must pay it. Let us adopt a wise plan to save the Queen and her relatives, then let us appoint a day for a general insurrection to proclaim the republic, under the government of the Sanhedrin and the High-priests, as we had it heretofore."

"Listen to the advice of Uziel's sagacious son," said Simon ben Hillel, "for it is the counsel of the wise men and scribes of Jericho. Tell our brethren in Jerusalem, they did say, to appoint the feast of passover as the proper time for the great work of Israel's redemption. Once redeemed that day from the bondage of Egypt, let it be the day of our redemption from the yoke of Herod, Rome and the royal power. Till then, let us prepare the people for the great day of redemption. When the ten thousands of Israel come to Jerusalem, to offer the Paschal sacrifice, let us be ready for energetic action, and strike the blow with united strength. If you think proper to do as our wise men said, I promise, and my life be pledged to you for its faithful execution, that I shall protect the Queen against every violence; I shall save Baruch, if he lives by to morrow. All this I will do, if Abba Shaul supports me and you are satisfied."

"Believe him, for he is wiser than Herod," said Abba Shaul. "If the wise men and the scribes of Jericho do think as their messengers state, I submit."

Long and lively was the debate of the secret council. Still finally the plan of the men of Jericho was adopted. The feast of Passover was appointed the time of the insurrection. Simon ben Hillel and Abba Shaul were commissioned to protect the Queen and rescue Baruch ben Menahem.—They swore a solemn oath to this effect, and were given on hand all the means they required. Simon was absolved till the day of passover from his duty to slay Sabion. Jonathan ben Uziel was sent back to Jericho to announce to the wise men of Jericho the resolutions of the people's council.

"I can not perform my duties," Simon said, "which you entrust to my care, without the assistance of the damsel you have in your power. She must assist me and she will do it."

"Will you entrust so important a secret to Sabion's daughter?" one of the men asked.

"My life and my honor as a pledge," Simon said, "for her fidelity and honesty of purpose. Behold, she came here, risked her life, exposed herself to the gaze of strangers, only to save the Queen. Why should we doubt her fidelity? Let her be sworn to perform her duty and keep secret what she knows, and if she violates her oath can not your daggers reach her in time?"

"Women are cunning," another said, "and she might out-manoeuver us before we would be aware of it."

"Are you afraid of a woman?" Abba Shaul asked, contemptuously. "I guarantee for her."

The conclusion to which the council came was immediately carried out. Helen, being again brought before that body, and after having been instructed in the dangers threatening her if she violate her oath and betray their secret assemblies, a terrible oath was administered to her, which she affirmed with a loud and strong, Amen. Next she was made acquainted with her duty to support Simon ben Hillel and Abba Shaul in all things they would do to save the Queen. She turned toward Simon, and requested him not to engage in this dangerous enterprise. Simon telling her he must do so, she told him, that he risks his liberty and probably also his life, if he was detected. Simon insisted upon his determination and Helen incessantly remonstrated, but in vain—Simon had taken an oath, that he would perform this task, and his resolution was unalterable.

"Know it then," Helen said, "two peasants were arrested instead of you and Jonathan ben Uziel. When the mistake was discovered the spies were charged to go about in search of you, the two peasants being able to identify you must go with them and remain so long in the hands of the spies until you are found. They will most certainly identify you, then your liberty and life are in jeopardy."

Simon laughed when saying, "that is Sabion's abominable scheme," but then he remembered the presence of Helen, and continued in a mild tone, "Care not for me, fair damsel, I am Herod's master in cunningness. I will successfully deceive him, I will save the Queen. You must co-operate with us and we promise you, no harm shall befall either you or the Queen."

"And my father," Helen asked, anxiously.

"Your father's head is forfeited to the people's council," Baba ben Buta answered, solemnly and seriously.

"Mercy, mercy for my father," Helen cried, "he is but the tool of the King, be not too severe against him."

"Your father's head is forfeited to the people's council," Baba ben Buta repeated.

Then let not Simon ben Hillel return to the city," Helen prayed, "let not him be the executioner."

"He is dispensed from that duty for a certain period of time," Baba ben Buta said.

"Then I am ready to support and assist, in the glorious work of rescuing the Queen from the iron grasp of danger," Helen exclaimed joyfully. "Your life, Simon ben Hillel is at stake, but I shall die with you, if I can not rescue you."

CHAPTER IV.

A DAY IN JERICHO.

In the outskirts of Jericho there stood a solitary, humble cottage, debarred of every ornament, stripped of all luxury, and poor in its appearance. The garden in which it stood, was not diversified with the variegated colors of Flora's blooming children; it was a plain kitchen garden, in which the common vegetables grew, supplying the poor man's table. Two she-goats, feeding upon the shrubs in the rear of the cottage, completed the whole wealth about the poor man's home. Every thing about the cottage, as the small building itself, was neat and clean, like the homestead of poor and industrious people.

Stepping into the low cottage our look first meets a small room filled with scrolls of parchment and Egyptian papyrus, in the midst of which, at a small table, sits an old man. His long beard and the locks of his head are grey, still luxuriant and long. Under a prominent forehead two brown eyes set in a bushy frame of grey hair, animated with almost a youthful fire, rest on the parchment. A smile plays softly around his lips which contrasts peculiarly with the solemn seriousness of the whole countenance, which, pale as it is, bears no furrows of old age, and its muscular strength presents no marks of the gnawing teeth of decay. That peculiar luster, that nameless and unfading beauty of the human face which is the efflux of a strong intellect, illuminates the whole countenance of the old man before us and commands veneration. He sits as motionless as a marble statue and it appears as though none had the impudence to disturb him in his silent meditation which occupies his whole soul. Still a tall man dressed in Greek costume most unceremoniously opens the door hastily, and, without saluting the old sage, he ejaculates: "Are you Hillel?"

"I am Hillel, so may God bless thee."

The stranger interrupts him, "I am a Greek who has heard much of the religion of the barbarians who dwell between the sea and the Jordan river. They say, you know the laws of the gods and the path of happiness to man. I have no time to spend with you. I am a Greek who learns very fast. I came to your brother Shamai and requested him to teach me his religion in as short a time as I can stand on one foot.—But he pushed me aside with the measuring rod in his hand, and in his indignation bid me leave directly. I left and through the aid of others, I come to you, Hillel and ask you, can you teach me your religion while I stand on one foot?"

"Why art thou so in haste my son?" Hillel asked.

"Because I dislike to be much longer among barbarians," the Greek answered, saucily.

Hillel was silent for a moment, he apparently reflected on a preper answer to the insult offered him. Then he said in a mild tone, "Thou mayest be right. I hear the Greeks are very wise, and it behooves thee to live in a land of learned men."

"Is this all you have to tell me?" the Greek asked, somewhat embarrassed.

"If this is all thou wishest to know, yes," Hillel responded, quietly.

"But, I wish to know your religion," the Greek said.

"The Greeks are very wise, why should they learn anything of barbarians?" said Hillel.

"Yes, indeed, they are very wise," said the Greek, "but in Religion, it appears to me they are quite foolish. Therefore I come to learn of the barbarians."

"In what are the Greeks wise?" Hillel asked.

"In everything, except Religion," the Greek replied.

"Can the Greeks tell us, why and how we and the things around us exist?" Hillel asked. "Can they tell us, how the sun shines, the thunder rolls, the hurricane roars, the ocean heaves its mighty treasures, and the earth reels on command of the Great Unknown? Can they tell us how man thinks, feels or lives, and why he is conscious of his consciousness? The Greeks are very wise, still can they tell us the ends of the world, the size of the heavens, the depth of the ocean or the compass of the air? And if they can not tell this in any time, why wouldst thou assume to know the will of the Creator and Great Cause of all these things in so short a time as thou canst stand on one leg?"

"I am foolish, pardon me my venerable master," the Greek said, overcome by the kindness of Hillel. "But I vowed a sacred vow to Minerva, that if I could not learn the religion of the eastern Barbarians in as short a time as I can stand on one leg, I would return and bring incense to her shrine. I must keep my vow."

"Speak, I prithee," said Hillel; "If I had vowed to my table to return to it and do homage to it, must I do it? Still this table exists and Minerva exists nowhere."

"Minerva exist nowhere?" the Greek asked, astonished, "also not in Olymp? Speak! old sage. But no, speak not, I dare not learn anything of you unless you can teach me everything concerning your religion, while I can stand on one leg. I shall not violate my vow."

"Before I do so," said Hillel, "let us understand each other what religion is. Is it not to worship God or the gods, as He or they wish it? and is not to do the will of God or the gods, to worship Him or them? Speak, my son, is it not so?"

"So it is," said the Greek, "I agree."

"Then, stand on one leg and hear my religion," said Hillel, solemnly, while rising. The Greek looked with surprise at the straight, colossal figure of the ancient sage, on assuming his position.

"Whatever hurts thee, thou shalt not do thy neighbor," Hillel said, slowly. "This is the principle part of my religion, the rest is a mere explanation. Go and finish thy studies."

The Greek stood awhile as though rooted to the ground, gazing aghast into the open and manly countenance of Hillel. Then he drew forth a dagger from under his cloak, and, laying it on the table, he said: "You are my lord and master, yours is that dagger and this arm. Command and I obey."

"Neither thy dagger, nor thy arm is any way available to me," Hillel said. "Remember, my shield is the arm of God, and my weapon is my confidence in Him."

"And your God is truly a marvelous God, who watches over his saints," the Greek said, "for I was sent here to assassinate you, but I can not. 'Whatever hurts thee, thou shalt not do thy neighbor,'" the Greek repeated, slowly.

"Dost thou repent now thy sinful conduct and wicked thoughts?" the old saint asked, mildly.

"I do sincerely and truly," the Greek replied, much humiliated.

"Then God will forgive thee," Hillel said, "if all men thou hast offended will do the same."

"You first, noble, generous demi-god," the Greek supplicated, kneeling before Hillel, "you must first forgive the villain who has been hired to execute a foul villany, a horrid outrage."

"Rise, my son," Hillel said, "and remember my religion 'Whatever hurts thee thou shalt not do thy neighbor.' Would it not hurt me to pray thee for pardon and not obtain it? I have no grudge against thee, there is nothing to be pardoned, rise and be henceforth a good man. So may all men thou hast hurt forgive thee, as I do with all my heart."

The Greek rose, clasped his dagger and lifted it up exclaiming enthusiastically, "none shall outdo me in magnanimity! Great Hillel, I will avenge thee and let it it cost my life. I will assassinate him who sent me to assassinate you. Know it, venerable man, the man who sent me is"——

"Not one word more shalt thou speak; my son," Hillel interrupted. "Would it not hurt thee to hear the name of thy enemy mentioned? It might hurt me, therefore thou shalt not tell me. Would it not hurt thee to be murdered? Therefore thou shalt not murder him who hired thee to do the sinful deed. Vengeance and punishment belong to God alone, thou must commit no crime."

Surprised to the utmost, the Greek embraced the old saint. "Thou art the god of virtue," he exclaimed, "I am thy child, thy servant, do with me, as thou pleasest.—But forget not, magnanimous man, that it is indipensably necessary that you should know the name of the man who, for no cause known to me, desires after your life and also hunts after your son to do him, as I was hired to do you."

"That is Sabion," said Hillel, "none else. But tell me where is my son?"

"In Jerusalem, most likely by this time, in the hands of Sabion," said the Greek, "and there he is in the very worst hands."

"God will protect him," Hillel said, calmly. "I know not why he went to Jerusalem, where danger now lurks in every corner; but God will protect him."

"Are you so sure of God's protection?" the Greek asked.

"Sure, quite sure, my son," the sage replied. "I hurt none, why should God hurt me? God is the All-just. If He inflicts punishment, it must be deserved. There, in yonder rivulet, I once saw a skull floating, and I said 'As thou hast thrown others in the water, thou wast thrown in thyself, and finally, also he will float who caused thee to perish in the water,' and the wise men approved of my doctrine. God will do me no harm, no wrong."

"But tell me, my master," said the Greek, "is it enough in the sight of your God, if man does no wrong? If all of us do no wrong, none will do any good, and virtue will have no patron."

"Do harm to none, and thou wilt certainly do good to all with whom thou comest in contact," said Hillel; "for man must be active God gifted him with an active soul. The great lesson he is commanded to study is to hurt none, harm none. He must do something, so he can do but what is good."

"Did you not say God protects you?" the Greek asked; "If so, how does he protect you?"

"I know not how," said Hillel, "but I

know he protects me. God has many messengers."

"And I will be one of them," said the Greek, "I will practice the first lesson I have received. I will go to Jerusalem, harm none, hurt none, and protect your son. Then I will return with him, and learn of you my second lesson."

"Go with God, my son," said Hillel, "but never forget my first lesson." He took a spade from a corner of the room and went to the door with the Greek, who asked him, "What will you do with this spade?"

"I will work in the garden" said the sage.

"You will work? no, you shall not," said the Greek. "Here is the money I was paid for your life It is enough to support you and your family one year."

"Whoever despises gifts will live," said the sage, "so the wise King said; because the poor only takes gifts, and the poor is esteemed like the dead. I am not poor, I can work."

The Greek finding his repeated attempts to give Hillel the money a vain and fruitless task, asked again: "Why should not your wife and children work for you?"

"Because it is my duty to support them," said Hillel. "My wife and my children are my best friends, the partners of my joy as of my affliction; why should I not work with them?"

"You should not work at all," said the Greek, "you are so wise and learned in your Law, that others should work for you while you study for them."

"None can study for his neighbor," said Hillel. "If thou knowest much, do not think more of thyself on that account; for thou art created to this very purpose. Degrade wisdom not to a stepping stone to wealth and honors, or to a spade to dig for a sustenance. Whoever wears the *Toga* changes for the worse; for honors and wealth are dangerous companions."

By that time they had come to the end of the garden. A clamor of wo was heard in the neighborhood. The stranger turned quickly round, looking toward the cottage. Hillel smiled. "Fear not, stranger, the noise is not in my house," said he, "for God protects it, and my wife and children cry not if a misfortune befall them. They know that no actual evil can befall them."

Astonished and heartily admiring the man of a thousand virtues, the Greek leaving Hillel wished to return to Jerusalem.

"Let us go and see what this noise means," said Hillel.

"I will go and inquire," said the Greek, "you must not leave your study; for you are a wise man, every moment you spend outside of your study is a loss to you and to your people's literature."

"Would I like to cry for help, or lament over my misfortune, and none come either to assist or console me?" Hillel asked. "If you are wiser than the rest, you are expected to do more than they do; for if wisdom is not a prompter to noble actions, it is a dead treasure in the hands of an avaricious man. He, whose wisdom is greater than his virtuous actions, compares to a tree with wide-stretched branches, a rich foliage and small roots, the slightest storm will upset it. He, whose virtuous actions predominate over his wisdom compares to a tree with small branches, a thin foliage and powerful roots, all the hurricanes may rage against it, still they will not move it from its place. Let trunk and branches be strong and large, the foliage rich, and the roots powerful, and stand fearless in the storm.—Come, my son, let us see whence the calamity comes. Let us help them if we can, or console them, if help is impossible."

The Greek kissed the garment, of the old sage, and followed him silently. In the central market space of Jericho, under the palm trees, a large concourse of people met, clamors of grief and woe were heard among them, and the name of Baruch ben Menahem was connected with the accents of lamentation.

"The dead body of Baruch ben Menahem was found in a street of Jerusalem," said one, in reply to Hillel's inquiry; "they brought it home to the woe-stricken parents. He was Menahem's only son."

"The lanes of Jerusalem are soiled with blood," one exclaimed, "the holy city is defiled by the hands of assassins. The best and most godly are daily killed and thrown in the street as the mud, the nuisance of the houses."

Meanwhile the multitude had rapidly increased, the murmurs and the lamentations had become louder and more painful, and the indignation of the populace had grown into fierce wrath. The stump of an old palm tree was mounted by a young man who, waving with his hands, bid silence.

"Be silent here and listen," one admonished the other, "Jonathan, Uziel's sagacious son wishes to speak to you." The multitude listened, when he said: "Men and brethren, Menahem's only son, Baruch, among the good and noble the best and most generous youth, Jericho's pride, a wretched mother's only love, has been found slain in the streets of Jerusalem. How could she become a harlot, the faithful fortress, justice once dwelt in her, and now murderers."

Accents of weeping and lamentation, proceeding from the agitated multitude, interrupted the speaker, who continued after awhile: "Tell it not in Gath, bring not the terrific tidings to the market spaces of Escalon, unless our enemies would rejoice over our downfall, our adversaries laugh at our degradation. Let the daughters of Zion dress in mourning and weep over their loss; for Menahem's son, the fairest of men, has been found slain in the streets of Jerusalem."

Again, the voices of lamentation and weeping interrupted the speaker; but he resumed after awhile: "Know ye, men and brethren, no heifer's neck will be broken, no judges will wash their hands over the spot where the corpse was found and say: 'Our hands have not spilt this blood, and our eyes have not seen it;' none will ever search after the assassin, for none dare do so. Justice has deserted us, honor is exiled from Israel, God is no longer enthroned in Jerusalem; for the city is filled with murderers. Her princes are slaves, her judges are blind tools, and her rulers are men of violence and injustice who thirst after their people's blood, and fatten themselves with the substance of their hungry brethren Know it, ye men of Israel, Herod and Sabion are the murderers of Baruch ben Menahem."

Like distant thunder in silent night a murmur arose among the multitude, which gradually increased into a roar of wrath and fierce anger. Curses and menaces were heard among the voices of lamentation, and, as Jonathan proceeded to tell the story of Baruch's fate, as he had learned it in the People's Council, the cry of vengeance waxed louder with each moment. The lamentations gave way to the outbursting fire of inflamed passions, and the metallic sound of swords, and the cry of "Down with the tyrants!—To the scaffold with the murderers!" were the only articulate sounds, that could be distinguished, and they appeared to find a re-echo in every manly breast.

Menahem, bent with grief, had made his appearance among his sympathising friends. His appearance calmed the excited passions of the populace. Every eye was directed toward the mourning father, his grief was honored by an awful silence. He looked upon the multitude first, then he lifted up his look to the skies, and, in a voice of painful resignation, he said: "God hath given and God hath taken away, the name of the Lord be praised." Then he looked again on his friends, while saying, "As we accept gladly the good from the Lord, should we not even so receive the evil? Men and Brethren, I thank you, for your kind sympathy with a bereft father, a childless mother. 'Thou shalt honor thy father and thy mother, that thy days be prolonged upon the land which the Lord thy God hath given thee,' is the commandment of the Lord. My son, having been sent to the Essences to be initiated in their mysteries, violated the express command of his parents, and went to the city of Jerusalem. Behold! God is strict with his righteous ones even upon a hair's breadth. My son immediately found the punishment, because he was righteous before God and man. I acquiesce in the justice of God.—Believe not, men and brethren, the words of Uziel's son; his affections for my unfortunate son and his hatred against Herod lead him astray. Love disturbs the balance of the mind, and hatred disturbs it. Be not led astray, not incensed to rash and imprudent deeds by the offended affections of a sensitive youth. You know Herod and Sabion to be my friends; they cannot have slain my only son; I exonerate them."

"Herod's officers arrested two peasants," one of the crowd interrupted, "who came to Jerusalem to fulfil the Law concerning the first fruits. He prevented them from worshiping God in His sacred Temple, and nothing has been heard of them as yet. Herod is a wicked man, and the wicked is apt to commit wickedness."

"So it is," said Jonathan. "But the venerable Menahem should know, that the man who massacred his sister's husband, the monster who slew the Highpriest, his own wife's only brother — is capable of any and every crime. He has no friend, because he loves none; he deserves the friendship of none, because he can not reciprocate it. Menahem's son, I do say, because I know it, was slain by the command of Herod, and by the hands of Sabion. The crime is double, tenfold: he slew an innocent youth, beloved by all who knew him, the son of his friend and advocate; slew him in the darkness of night, and, too cowardish to defend his own terrific crime, has the corpse thrown into the street to make the unsuspicious believe, Baruch fell by the robber's hand, that he might double the number of his spies and heartless slaves, to enslave the free-born sons of Judah. The law and justice are God's, and we are God's people, His servants and messengers. Herod and Sabion violate the law, trample it under their feet, enslave the people, rob us of our rights, and it behooves us to execute judgment in the name and in behalf of our God."

"Who appointed you the avenger of my son's blood?" Menahem asked. "Has he no relative to persecute the assassin? None has called upon you to judge a King—"

"He is Rome's King, Rome's creature," the multitude cried, "we may judge a hireling, a spy, an assassin."

"Hillel speaks, be silent, Hillel speaks," they admonished each other, and all were silent.

"The King is no less subject to the Laws of God, than the humblest of his subjects," said Hillel. "If the King is a criminal, the laws prescribe his punishment. The murderer should be taken even from God's sacred altar, if he be the Highpriest and worship God in behalf of Israel — and receive the punishment due to him. Whoever spills the blood of man, his blood will be shed by man, such is the wise decree of Providence. If you know Herod and Sabion to be guilty of this crime, you may condemn them, but you can not execute your judgment on the culprits. You are weak and they are powerful, you are a few and they are many, you are in Jericho and they are in Jerusalem. Therefore let us not waste words. Mourn over the dead, console the bereft parents, and return each to his house, God will judge and punish the guilty. Wait, my people, wait patiently until the day of divine vengeance comes, then the wicked will be punished, and the righteous will be triumphant."

A body of Egyptian soldiers arrived at the spot to disperse the crowd, the eloquence of Hillel and his influence over Jonathan ben Uziel prevented the outbreak of serious disturbances.

"Woe unto thee, Judah," Jonathan ben Uziel cried, on entering the hall of Gurion, where the sages held their meetings, "woe unto Israel, that Egyptians rule over thee and disturb thy councils. Let every patriot clothe in sack and ashes and cry woe, that the birds stop their merry melodies, Tabor and Hermon pour down currents of tears to drown the beauty of the valleys. Let Jordan's waters be congealed with shame, and the hot springs of Tiberias be frozen with consternation, on account of the strangers who set their feet on the neck of Israel, and trample the daughter of Zion in the dust."

The sages and scribes assembled in the hall listened with much sympathy to the outpouring of offended and wounded sentiments, and none interrupted the young man. Apparently overcome by his painful emotions, he stopped awhile, then he resumed:

"If this is the will of Cleopatra, if she has taken possession of Jericho, that we be not allowed to speak out what we think, what profit have we by not being under the immediate dominion of Herod? Let us, my lords and masters, let us forthwith send deputies to Egypt's Queen and complain of the injustice committed in her name on a loyal people, who hate their enemies only. I most respectfully submit to your wise consideration, my humble opinion, not to stand this outrage."

Shamai, the mighty antagonist of Hillel and his school, rose gravely and, locking about in the hall as though his looks intended to subjugate every heart, he said slowly and sonorously: "Are you not glad to be protected by Cleopatra against the will of Herod, who massacred as many of your colleagues as fell in his hands, why would you trouble her with complaints? Or do you wish to occasion her to withdraw her protection from this city; where will you meet, where live, where maintain and promulgate the sacred traditions of our nation? Uziel's sagacious son is beyond the venomous eye of suspicion, his motives are undoubtedly pure and patriotic, his purposes pious and godly; none dare question the wisdom of Hillel's most renowned pupil, and none should oppose his opinions. But, my hair begins to be grey, stored away in my memory lies the history of half a century, as bloody, unfortunate and disastrous to Israel, as the days of Syrian oppression. I have seen a King who committed fratricide, and a prince who appealed to a foreign power, to slaughter his own people and secure him the throne of his fathers. I have seen the brother in arms against his own brother, and cruelties and inhuman outrages, innumerable almost, committed by the combatting parties, who soiled the earth with blood, and filled the land with misery and sore affliction. Still, every party appealed to the people, and each found its zealous supporters. The people are withering leaves, every wind can carry them off to any direction. The people are slumbering sparks, harmless and unconscious of their monstrous strength. My people bleed from a thousand wounds and Jonathan ben Uziel pours vinegar into the aching bruises. Woe unto him, I say, who disturbs my people while dressing its numerous wounds. 'Woe unto him who stirs up the enraged lion from his refreshing slumber, to tear and devour and run roaring and raving through the depopulated forests. Let the people rest a few years, when rest is granted them; let them recover from the mournful misery they have suffered for years passed. Have mercy with the wretchedness of my brethren, and be silent yourselves. But no, so all do not think; patriots, wise and excellent, like Jonathan ben Uziel, waken the people from their benevolent repose, to behold their own misery and run deeper yet into the mire of wretchedness. Men, zealous and patriotic, excite the dormant passions of the populace against those who brought us a few years of release. They agitate against Herod in Jericho and in Jerusalem against Cleopatra to shake off the dominion of strangers and tyrants, as they say, when we know that the Kings of our own race could not bring us either rest or peace. Therefore I say, let the people alone, undisturbed, calm the agitated passions, and pour no oil in the blasting flame; let my people rest a few years and recover its heartpiercing losses. We have a spot in Jericho where to preserve, discuss and promulgate the laws and traditions of Israel, and none disturbs us. We have a place in Jerusalem where the priests worship the Most High, and none interferes with them. We have a King who is capable of maintaining the peace and tranquility of this country, and none can hinder him. Prosperity and happiness gradually return to Israel, and none should prevent it. Whoever wishes to study the Law, let him come to Jericho. Whoever desires to worship in Israel's glorious house, let him go to Jerusalem. Whoever values his life, let him not go near the royal palace. Let every political ambition slumber a few years, and let us wait patiently for the help of our God. He redeemed us from the Egyptian bondage, smote Sissera and his host, slew Sanherub and his powerful army; with a mighty hand He smote powerful Babylon and restored Israel's faithful children; behold he vanquished Syria and its presumptuous rulers before our fathers, and chastised yonder Greece on account of her sins: Wait for a moment until the wrath is passed, and our sun will rise again, God will be again with Israel and be gracious of His faithful children."

When Shamai resumed his seat, every eye looked on Jonathan ben Uziel, who was presumed to refute the arguments of the sagacious master. But none observed the presence of Hillel in a retired corner of the hall, as Jonathan did, in whose presence the young man would not speak without his permission; hence none could account for the painful silence reigning for some time in the hall. Akabiah ben Mahalalel broke the silence thus: "When yesterday I walked through the lanes of Jericho, I heard the people say, 'There is one in this city who like Moses is worthy to communicate with the Holy Spirit, were his generation worthy of it.' Every wise man in this city whom I told this voice of the people, casts his look on Hillel the great Babylonian, the meekest of mortals and the most learned of Shemaiah and Abtalion's academy. Let us consult him who is the friend and favorite of the people; for know it, ye sages of Israel, Whoever is beloved in the sight of the people is also beloved in the sight of God, and whoever displeases God is also disliked by the people. The people's voice is God's voice, the will of God expressed by this medium. Let us send for Hillel and hear his opinion."

"Who is Hillel, the unknown stranger, that Israel's sages should ask his advice!" one of the friends of Shamai stated, haughtily.

"The inoffensive, unpretending and meek Babylonian," said Akabiah, "who left his home and, with his wife and children came to Jerusalem to hear the Law of God expounded by Shemaiah and Abtalion. The poor Hillel, who split wood for a scanty pay in the streets of Jerusalem, to support his family and pay the admission to the academy when the King ordained it so. When one winter day he could obtain no work and could not pay his admission to the academy, he sat all night before the window, to listen to the words of sagacious masters. The snow fell fast from the clouds and covered the benumbed form of the inquisitive stranger. When the morning dawned, and light penetrated through all windows except one, the disciples being sent out to discover the cause brought the benumbed man into the hall of the academy. By the application of the proper remedy the frozen limbs of the poor man were restored, and I heard Shemaiah say, 'This man is worthy to be *Nassi* in Israel, he is worthy that all Israel should violate the Sabbath to spare his life.' That very man you appear not to know, never to have heard of him, that very man is Hillel, whose advice we want."

When Akabiah mentioned the word *Nassi*, (prince, president of the Sanhedrin,) the friends of Shamai murmured audibly, as they considered only Shamai and Menahem capable and worthy to the high positions in the nation's supreme council. Therefore the Shammaites appeared much displeased. When Akabiah was done, one of them rose to give utterance to the opinion of all of them. He said: "Akabiah ben Mehalalel is entirely too partial in the appreciation of Hillel's virtues. Meekness and poverty combined with fortitude and self-denial inspire respect and sympathy. We appreciate the humane and charitable sentiments of Akabiah ben Mehalalel. But the goodness of his heart is no valid reason, why the sages of Israel should consult an obscure stranger."

"An obscure stranger!" Akabiah exclaimed, amazed and offended. "Is the master and teacher of Jonathan ben Uziel, Simon ben Hillel, and seventy eight more renowned disciples, of whom Israel is justly proud, an obscure stranger? Verily, the disciple's wisdom is the master's crown of glory.—Take back your offensive words."

"Will Akabiah understand me right," the answer of the Shamaite was, "I meant no harm in what I said. I think, in comparison to Shamai and Menahem, Hillel can be regarded merely an obscure stranger."

The Hillelites evinced much dissatisfaction at this explanation, and harsh words would have followed, had not Shamai in proper time given the debate a favorable turn. He rose and said, "Whoever seeks to acquire honor by the shame of his neighbor, is no man, and can find no favor in the sight of God. As my friends have gone so far in depreciation of Hillel, it becomes my duty to say, that none can raise a valid objection to the proposition of hearing the advice of a man, whose heart and soul is with his people, whose eminent wisdom must be acknowledged by every impartial man, and who is too meek and unpretending to raise his voice in the council of Israel's sages. Why should we not hear his opinion? I say, let him come and be requested to speak."

A storm of applause, in approbation of Shamai's words, stopped the debate. Messengers were dispatched to bring Hillel in, who after a painful search was found in a deserted corner of the large hall, and, notwithstanding his objections, was introduced to the council and received with much enthusiasm. He was given a seat at the right hand side of Shamai, who received him with marked tokens of profound respect.

Silence and quietude being restored, Jonathan ben Uziel rose and, after having paid his respects to Hillel and Shamai and others superior to himself in age or authority, he said, "I come to you, men and brethren, greeting from the people's council of Jerusalem. But before I speak, I desire to know, whether none is among us who is capable of betraying us."

After a few minutes of recognition it was admitted on all hands, that none was among them capable of being a traitor. Jonathan resumed, and in a most eloquent strain he communicated what he was charged with, by the People's Council. He depicted, in words glowing with eloquence, the indignation of the people, the agony of every manly heart on hearing of the Queen's life being in jeopardy. He then communicated the fact, that the people's council charged competent men with the duty of protecting the Queen, and that the Passover week was appointed for the final action of the people, as they would suffer no longer the intolerable despotism of Herod and his hirelings.

"Not we, indeed, agitated the revolution among the people of Jerusalem, as our learned master Shamai thinks," Jonathan said, "the people, feeling the burden of despotism imposed on them, the people beholding the crimes perpetrated daily by the King and his co-adjutors, the people revolt, because they would stand it no longer. We did not agitate this state of things, nor is it in our power to change it. The only question here is, shall we choose sides with the revolution, or submit to Herod's tyranny. Must we desert the people and coincide tacitly and inactively with its tyrant, or must we lend a helping hand to our brethren, to justice and liberty, and we insist on the restoration of the Sanhedrin, our courts of justice, our laws and our rights. Herod will not and dare not grant those things to us, the people will and must. The question, therefore, is easily decided. But it is not for me, it is for you to decide upon the course to be adopted. Let us first hear the advice of our venerable master, let Hillel speak, and then let us decide."

It was only after the request to give utterance to his opinion was repeatedly addressed to Hillel, that he rose, and after having humbly asked the permission of all that were wiser or older than himself, he said: "Who am I, that I should lift up my voice among the wisest of Israel? I am the least of my family who is the least regarded in Israel. But you ask and I must answer; you command and I will speak. I saw the bloody contest of two royal brothers for the dominion over my people. I saw them deliver my people into the hands of Pompey, the haughty Roman who murdered and plundered thousands, and the blood of the bravest soiled the ruins of the defended walls. I wept over the house of the Lord thus desecrated, and over the people of Israel slain and hunted like wild beasts."

After a pause Hillel continued: "I saw Antipater reiterate the brother's unhappy quarrel, to satisfy his own ambition. I saw the bloody catastrophe of the Asmonean house, the return of Herod from Rome, the barbarity of the Roman hirelings, the fall of Jerusalem, the massacred multitude of my brethren, the slain Senators, the murdered teachers of Israel; I saw the man, who defied Israel's Sanhedrin, mount the throne of Judea over the corpses of the thousand patriots slain without mercy; I heard the savage triumph of our enemies and wept ever our misfortune; but no thought of resistance entered my mind, as the people were divided in their sentiments, and I thought it was the will of Providence. I hoped Herod would restore peace and justice to this country. The hyena itself drinks no more blood than to satiate his appetite, why should Herod not cease feeding on human blood? The barbarians, our fiercest enemies, themselves respect the laws of Israel, why should not Herod do it, after his fierce anger be gone? So I thought, but, behold! we are deceived. There is neither peace nor justice in our land. The Sanhedrin and the judges are the King's creatures. The wise men are prohibited from entering the city of our pride. The schools of the learned, our pillars and our hope, are closed. The blood of the slain, both Highpriest and people, cries for vengeance from every corner of this land, and there is none to listen. The tyrant rages against his own wife, spares not the beloved of his bosom; who can expect mercy or justice from his hands? He is Rome's hireling, to exterminate Israel's laws and religion, and the hire he receives, are crown and scepter. On the one side then a King pleads for his rights, with which Rome invested him, and on the other hand an outraged, down-trodden and strangled people, bleeding from a thousand wounds, cries before the throne of justice—the decision is easily given; if I am not for myself, who should be for me? If I am only for myself, who am I? If I am not now for myself, when should I be it?"

The loud murmurs of the Shamaites and the cheering hurrahs of the Hillelites interrupted the speaker for a moment. But an ardent enthusiasm appeared to have seized on him, and with a voice which sounded powerfully through the hall he continued: "Two dreadful scenes open to our vision. Here, behold! here stand the indignant men with the arms of destruction in their hands to attack the tyrant and compel him to yield to the people's will, to the law of God. Behold! the dead heroes, the revolution has slain them; behold! the mourning parents, the weeping children, the lamenting wives and brides, the revolution! ha, the revolution killed our beloved, the crown, the hope, the joy of our life—who must not shudder at the very thought of a bloody revolution? But there, there the graves open, and behold! Israel's thousand sons, the noblest and wisest of my people, rise and show the wounds inflicted by Herod. A King and a Highpriest, Matathia's noble sons lead the dreadful procession, who in the silence of night move through the cities and cry, vengeance! vengeance! vengeance! Behold the thousands of afflicted parents, weeping children, despairing wives and brides, behold! they like the howling wilderness re-echo in accents of madness, vengeance! vengeance! vengeance! There lie the prostrated people of Israel, deprived of every right and might, its crown trampled in the dust, its laws, justice, religion, its valiant men and its heroic defenders—ha, wretched Israel, thy voice is impotent, thou art helpless. Who conjured me up here, that I see death, blood, destruction here and there? Who called me up to delight in my hot tears, and scoff at my bloody grief? Away, away, ye specters, away ye bloody shades of my assassinated nation! I feel, that I stumble, I fall; revolution, revolution alone can save thee, Israel, and revolution is bloodshed, misery and wretchedness. Still God commands the revolution through the voice of his people."

The thunder of enthusiastic applause which resounded through the hall was interrupted by the voices of the extreme Shamaites who exclaimed: "Hillel is no longer like himself, he is no longer the pious, meek and submissive Hillel. His words are fire, his sentiments are bloody. He is another man."

"Verily, I am not I, I know myself no more," said Hillel, "my soul is sore, my heart is wounded, my breast is tortured, tormented most cruelly. The affliction of my people, the tears and blood of my nation, the enemy's scoffing at our sacred religion, our laws, our hopes, at justice itself, turns me into an agitated lion. I feel that it is our duty to countenance the revolution."

"Then let us complain to Cleopatra about the conduct of her servants," Jonathan proposed.

"The revolution, the revolution!" it sounded through the hall, "send to Cleopatra and let her know that we would not stand such a treatment."

The revolutionists being in the majority prevailed; Shamai with his friends being overruled left the hall, angrily; but the Hillelites completed their plan and acted accordingly.

CHAPTER V.

THE KING AND THE ESSENEE.

The consistent assurances of Baruch ben Menahem in torture and death, that the Queen was innocent and spotless, diminished not the jealousy of Herod, nor did the sickness in which the Queen suddenly fell after the King had treated her, as we have already seen, disarm his suspicion, that his wife with her family conspired against him with Cleopatra. He passed a night of intense excitement. The servants were scarcely allowed to sit down and breathe. "Is the Queen indeed sick?"—"Is the Queen very sick?"—"Does the Queen's health improve?"—"Has Baruch ben Menahem confessed his crime?"—"What degree of torture have they applied?" and similar questions he proposed every minute of the night, and kept his servants always busy. He cursed, raged against every body, then again wept and lamented his and the Queen's fate, so that it sometimes appeared, he had lost his senses. Toward morning the Queen's disease became alarming. In a delirious state she repeated the best part of the conversation she had with her mother, every word of which was brought to the ears of Herod. The physicians said the disease of the Queen was alarming, as the rushing of the blood to the head could not be stopped, notwithstanding all the means applied.

Sabion stepped into the cabinet of the King and announced the death of Baruch ben Menahem under the torturers' hands. He said the last words of the expiring youth were, "The Queen is innocent." This set Herod completely crazy. He ran about in the palace like a madman, and when the physician again told him on his own inquiry, that the sickness of the Queen was dangerous, he struck the physician and gave orders to set all those "Greek dogs" outdoors and call Essence physicians. This was done immediately. Among the five Essence physicians at the bed side of the Queen was also Simon ben Hillel, dressed in white garments with a leather apron. After some consultation they determined upon the treatment they thought best to apply. Toward the dawn of morning the fever subsided, and the Queen slept. Herod desired to see one of the Essenee physicians and Simon ben Hillel was ushered into his presence. The exquisite beauty of the young man, his open, manly and intelligent countenance, his fiery and penetrating looks, and his proud and firm bearing made a surprising and favorable impression on the King. He regarded the young physician for several moments with apparent delight. "Are you one of the Essence physicians?" the King asked, somewhat surprised by the youth of the man before him.

"I am, my lord," was the short answer.

"What do your colleagues think of the disease of the Queen?" Herod inquired.

"The disease was dangerous," Simon replied, "but is so no longer. Silence, repose, a careful diet and the right degree of warmth will cure it in a few days."

"What medicine do you give?" the King asked.

"None, my lord," was the reply of Simon.

"Do you mean to cure the Queen with amulets and prayers?" the King asked, smilingly. "I must inform you, that neither the Queen, nor myself believe much in those things."

"Prayer cures wounded hearts, and amulets heal the morbid imagination," Simon replied. "My colleagues can not think for a moment, that Herod's royal concort suffers of either of those maladies."

Herod was visibly embarrassed, and walked the room, in rapid strides, his arms crossed over his breast, to hide his emotions. "But how do your colleagues know, where and when to apply those peculiar remedies?" he asked, without looking on Simon.

"Besides the numerous symptoms of the patient," said Simon, "and the information we gain by the attendants, we look into the eye, the mirror of the soul, to read the sufferings of the heart, or the aberration of the mind. The eye of the patient, who discards every etiquette and forced appearance, and allows human nature to operate on its own laws, seldom if ever deceives the physician."

This reply was not calculated to relieve Herod from his embarrassment. He tried to give the conversation another turn, and asked, "Who are you, that you speak such an elegant Grecian dialect, and that your old and renowned colleagues introduce you to the Queen?"

"I am a Babylonian, my lord," said Simon, "the son of a family little known beyond the limits of our village on the Habor river. In my early youth I studied the wisdom of Palestine's wise men, then went to Alexandria, to the Egyptian Therapeuts, to Athens and Rome, and learned as much of science as I could retain. Now I return to Babylon, to make use of my knowledge. Being known to my colleagues here, they conferred on me the distinguishing honor, to introduce me to the Queen of Judea."

Meanwhile Herod composed himself, and turning again to Simon, he said, "Your learning might be useful to us in Judea. Why should you return to Babylon? But tell me first, do you not believe an evil demon has seized the Queen, which, by the power of pious men, could be driven out?"

"I know of but four evil demons," said Simon, slowly and significantly, "none of which should ever trouble a Queen."

"Yes, yes, they say the Essenees know the names of the angels and the evil demons," Herod said, hastily, "let me know the names of those four."

"Ambition, passion, avarice and superstition are the four cruel demons which seize upon the unguarded man," Simon responded, earnestly, "none of which should ever trouble a Queen."

"Either of which is enough to derange a man's sound brains," Herod said, wildly laughing. "The Queen is troubled with an evil demon. Go and tell it to your colleagues, that their treatment be shaped accordingly."

Simon bowed and was about retiring, when Herod stopped him. "Not so hasty, young man, I desire to speak one word more to you." Simon bowed, and Herod continued: "You have told me the symptoms of a wounded heart or a morbid imagination, together with the remedies for those maladies. I wish now to learn of you the same in regard to evil demons."

"A man's words and actions, besides his looks and the features of his countenance," Simon responded, "are the symptoms of his being possessed by either or all of those demons. The name of God, the word of God, and the counsel of true wisdom are the only remedies."

Herod looked penetratingly into the eyes of Simon, and after an emphatic pause, he said, "Speak, young man, am I possessed by either or all of those demons? Speak truth, and nothing but truth."

"The anger of a King is the angel of death," said Simon.

"But a wise man can appease it, says the same wise King," Herod added.

"Life and death are in the power of the tongue," Simon continued.

"Righteousness saves from death, says the same ruler of Israel," the King remarked.

"If God gives freedom to the destroyer, he distinguishes not between the good or the evil one, Israel's sages said," Simon observed.

"I am Israel's King, and no destroyer," said Herod.

"And Kings hate to hear the truth," Simon responded.

"But I insist to hear it now, just now and of you," Herod said, impatiently.

"Listen, Herod to the words of truth," Simon said, in a sonorous tone. From his eyes, looks of fire darted forth, his countenance colored to a scarlet hue, his right hand was lifted up and his whole frame appeared to grow under the eyes of Herod. "Hark! son of Antipater, and I will tell you solemn, sacred truth. I had a nocturnal vision before I was called hither, that made the blood congeal in my veins. I saw Israel's patriots prostrated in the dust and lamenting over the desecration of Zion's virgin daughter. Blood, human blood, corpses and specters, awful to look upon, bewildered my sight. The cry of violence and injustice sounding ghost-like from deserted graves struck my ear and pierced my heart. Meteors of fire flashed through the atmosphere and combined into the words, reaching from heaven to the earth, RETRIBUTION! JUSTICE! Then they changed into a seraph of fire who lifted up his flaming sword over Jerusalem, and cried LET JUSTICE BE DONE! that the hills trembled; and the mountains fearfully re-echoed LET JUSTICE BE DONE! I trembled, I wept. There appeared an angel of the Lord in the form of a young Essenee. His limbs were disjointed by inhuman torture, pale was his countenance, distracted his features, dim and breaking his eyes. But, on a sudden, the body of clay disappeared and an angel of light, surrounded with rays of celestial suns, stood before me and bid me, Go and cure Herod, he is possessed by evil demons. Ambition, passion, prejudice, mistrust and a morbid conscience make him sick, very sick in soul and body. Go and tell him, the Queen and Baruch ben Menahem are innocent, and he is guilty of horrid crimes."

"Be dumb, everlastingly dumb, thou infernal liar," Herod raged, and, drawing his sword, he advanced furiously upon Simon. "Traitor, liar, dog, follow that accursed Baruch," he cried, raving with madness.

Simon laughed loudly, and, looking firmly into the eyes of Herod, he said, "No, you can not, you dare not lay hand on me. I have the power to banish evil demons and subject them to the will of God."

"I will not do it," said Herod, monotonously, and the sword fell from his hand.—He crossed his arms over his breast and stared into the countenance of Simon, who looked calm as ever. "Who told you the secrets of my court, of my private cabinet, who told you what happened this night?"

"There is an eye of God that penetrates into the secret recesses of royal palaces and royal hearts," said Simon, "and He chooses His servants, the messengers of His will."

"There must be traitors in this palace," Herod murmured to himself.

"The slave who trembles before his master is easily turned into a vile traitor," said Simon. "You, King, should know best, whether your servants can be traitors."

"All of them are slaves and cowards who tremble when I look cross," said Herod, "weep, laugh, dance, sit, lie, cheat, do anything, if I want it, why should they not be traitors? There are no angels to tell you what I do. A traitor did. Confess, that I punish the guilty head."

"I have said every word you wished to know," said Simon, "more, I dare not tell. If there are evil demons, why not also angels? If the former prompt man to wickedness, why should not the latter attempt to oppose it? There are angels, but they appear only to the righteous and good. Herod is surrounded by men who tremble when he looks cross: weep, laugh, dance, sit, lie, cheat do anything, if he wants it, because he drives the angels from his presence, invites evil demons to rule over him, and attracts others around him. My lord, there are angels, but you do not wish to communicate with them."

Herod's agitation was over. True to his peculiar nature, moments of almost a feminine sensibility followed the hurricane of wild passions. His voice became soft and sonorous, his looks mild and kind, his countenance assumed an expression of intense suffering of the mind, which inspired compassion and sympathy. Thus he now stood before Simon, and stared for several minutes into his calm countenance, mild and firm looks. "It does my heart good once to see a man of truth and integrity before me, who trembles not when I am angry," said Herod, "and gives utterance to his conviction, notwithstanding my hot displeasure. Kings seldom have the good fortune to meet with such men. I am only sorry, that you have not had experience enough to agree with me that there are few angels on earth. If such there are at all, they are few and far apart. There in rural districts, in retired valleys, on solitary mountains, there innocence dwells and kindness has made its home. In the cities corruption reigns, and vice has pitched its tents. The angels fled the dust of the cities, to rusticate on the mountains."

"Because those who are greedy of power and dominion, of wealth and honor," Simon said, "who consider man a mere auxiliary to their selfish purposes, dwell in the cities, and by oppression and injustice, by their violation of sacred laws and setting bad examples, they demoralize the community.—Sir, this very people was for many centuries the pattern of virtue and justice. It was the only people on earth, that respected justice and virtue as the will of the Most High.—This very respect was its pride, its pillar of fire and of smoke to lead it in the right path; its strength, its buoyancy, its indestructible vigor, the foundation on which its hopes and its future rested. Look back but one century and behold the energy, national buoyancy and patriotic spirit of the armies who routed the proud and mighty Syrian, and tell us whether a demoralized people can perform such miracles of bravery? But evil demons took possession of our lords and rulers, our mighty and wealthy men, and they spent all their influence, to corrupt our people.—Still demoralization has yet not attained such an alarming altitude, that the cities are as corrupt as they appear to the morbid ambition of arbitrary lords who, having no better excuse to make, attempt to justify their conduct by the supposed demoralization of the community. Also in the days of King Solomon, wealth and luxury corrupted the people, and the wise man's son, calculating upon a total relaxation of the moral vigor, attempted to play the tyrant; but he was mistaken, it cost him ten parts of his kingdom. Be careful, King of Judea; the weakness of your courtiers, the demoralization of your wealthy favorites are no fair test of the people's real character. I who caution you, and not he who flatters you, I am your real friend. I repeat it, be careful, King of Judea! The people are a reposing volcano, a smooth sea, a depressed earthquake."

"You are not well enough versed in the state of things," said Herod, much humiliated. "Still I wish to speak more to you. But first promise me to be my friend and stay with me."

"A King who rules over all can have no friend in the strictest sense of the term," Simon replied coolly, "I can not flatter."

"Are you an insane man, to refuse the friendship of your King?" Herod asked.

"If I was insane," said Simon, "the wise Herod would not attempt to deprive me of my manhood and make of me a tool of his. Kings, especially those who stand in a relation to their people as you do, can not expect, do not wish to have a friend. But they need many tools. Money, honors and fear work wonders with many, but where those means would not work, a king's friendship you think, would operate very well.—Sir, I can be no tool."

"Stay with me and I will teach you to be my friend," said Herod, much mortified; "stay, I have none like you among all my officers and servants. I want a man who utters freely what his heart feels."

"I consent to remain with you," said Simon, "if you agree, whenever we are alone not to play my superior, for I am not your subject, I am a Babylonian, and not to violate the rights of truth in my presence."

"I agree and give you my royal word so to do," said Herod. "But now, sit down here, and I will first convince you of your erroneous conceptions of the people."

A chamberlain stepped in. "Sabion says, he must see my royal master immediately," said the man. "The business must be urgent," said the King; "for this is an unusual hour for him to appear before me. Admit him." The chamberlain retired and Sabion entered. He looked bewildered and sorrowful. "I wish to see you alone, my royal master," said Sabion.

"I have no secret before this stranger," said Herod. "I wish you to notice, that this man whose name will be told you hereafter, is my friend."

Sabion bowed, submissively, and began his report: "For several weeks past I have noticed a secret movement among some suspicious characters. I was on my guard and succeeded in detecting their place of nocturnal meeting. It is in the valley of Hinom. My only daughter Helen, whom I fondly loved and cherished, sent out two of my servants, to bring to her two young men of Jericho; Jonathan ben Uziel is the name of one and Simon ben Hillel the other. The servants by mistake arrested two other men. I was informed of all this. I gave the two men in charge of my servants and bid them not to dismiss them, until they have arrested the two young men who belong to the conspirators of Jericho. They followed their trace to the valley of Hinom, where they watched for them. After midnight both young men came out from a low hut, my servants attempted to arrest them, but a body of armed men interfered, killed two of my servants, wounded several and the rest were obliged to flee. The two peasants also took advantage of the attack and made good their escape. This morning I received the report, that among those who attacked them was Abba Shaul, the notorious grave digger, and my own and only daughter Helen."

Here Sabion stopped, apparently incapable to continue. The King looked scrutinizingly on Simon, but no feature of his countenance was changed.

Sabicu continued, after a pause: "Helen was missing all evening, and her old servant could be found nowhere. I inquired after her, but none could tell her whereabouts — She confessed her foolish love for one Simon ben Hillel, and, having heard me giving orders to my servants to arrest that rebel, I expected, she went out in search of him, to caution him. When she returned I examined her sharply, but nothing could be learned from her. I examined the servant, but it also was, in vain. When I received this morning the above report, I examined the grey sinner upon the torture, and he confessed to have been with his mistress in the valley of Hinom, where she disappeared, then returned in company of many armed men, who attacked others, he could not distinguish in the darkness.—Now, my royal lord, I pray you, not to charge me with the crimes of my daughter. I am innocent. She is arrested, closely and safely confined, and here I am to lay the matter at your feet. I can not implore your pardon for her, justice only must be done.—I have dispatched ten men to arrest Abba Shaul and others whom I suspect. Command, my royal master, what shall be done with my daughter!"

"You think conspirators meet in the valley of Hinom, at a nightly hour?" the King asked. This being affirmed he continued, "Where was Helen before she went away?"

"That morning she was at the grave of her mother," said Sabion, "where Abba Shaul must have met her. Then she visited Baruch ben Menahem in his prison. The rest of the time she spent at the bedside of the gracious Queen, and in the house."

Herod laughed savagely, and run up and down the room. "I understand the diabolic scheme," he said. "The Queen and Baruch knew of the secret conspiracy. They sent your daughter to inform the rebels of their perilous position, and conjured them up to help them if possible. Ah, ye hissing, venomous serpents, you are in my power, the host of hell itself can not save you. Sabion, be vigilant, something great will be undertaken against us. Tell my captains to meet me within one hour in the private chamber. Keep your daughter in close confinement, my honest Sabion. Your King's favor and best will are well deserved. Begone, and perform your duty."

Sabion bowed again and anon, and then disappeared. "Speak, visionary Essenee," said Herod, "is there an angel in this city, if the wife conspires against her husband, the daughter against her own father, the people against their King? O you good-natured, deceived philosopher, you do not know the wickedness and baseness of man as I do, or you must admit, that this treacherous and maligeant race must be ruled with an iron hand. Blood and terror only can bend their proud neck and make them submit to law and order. Speak, if you can, can this nation of rebellious men, women and children be governed without an iron rod? Ha, ha, ha, you are dumb, convinced, defeated, you see your own folly."

"Whenever Herod will have regained self-dominion," said Simon, "I will speak, but not till then. How should a man rule over a nation, if he can not master himself?"

Herod pressed his under lip between his teeth and struggled visibly to gain dominion over himself. He appeared to be ashamed of the calm, impassionate Essence. "Speak, Essence, and I will hear you without interruption."

"All of them are slaves and cowards, who tremble when I look cross, Herod said of his courtiers," Simon said; "Still you place implicit confidence in the words of the courtier who just now retired. Herod, is it patriotism, high-souled friendship or cowardice, that causes a man to betray his own daughter, and as he said his only daughter? If it is the latter, how can you place implicit confidence in the words of a coward, will he not just as soon betray his King as he will betray his child? How do you know that this man Sabion has any other object in view than to gain your full confidence, in order to ruin you, and to carry this he sacrifices his own child, if she plays not a part of the drama which her father arranged?—A body of armed men rescued some prisoners from the grasp of their captors, and Herod sees in this a conspiracy of his royal consort with his enemies Perhaps a gang of robbers held a nocturnal rendezvous in that abominable valley and thought to find a rich booty? or probably the very servants of Sabion's daughter attacked those who arrested her lover? There is more probability for the truth of my hypothesis, than for yours, my lord."

Simon paused here, for he saw the King wished to say something. Herod again asked, "Can you be my friend, young Essence?"

"As long as you suspect your own wife, the partner of your bosom, no!" Simon responded, promptly. "It is impossible for you to have confidence in a friend, who disagrees with you on many essential questions. You only listen to your slaves. Equality and confidence are the very first conditions of friendship."

Herod again paced his saloon, in rapid strides. A legion of combatting thoughts appeared to trouble his mind. After awhile he stopped again before Simon, and addressed him thus: "I do not know you, still I feel my heart attracted by you. I wish to have a friend. It is so great and pleasant an idea to have one in this world who rejoices in our prosperity, weeps over our affliction, sympathizes with our distress, has an honest smile and tear for us. It is the pride and prime of humanity. But I will hear some other time the causes, why you can not be my friend. Now, I will teach you, that I have confidence in those who deserve it.—I wish to teach you, that Herod deserves an honest and upright friend. What is your name?"

"Call me Aurion, my lord," said Simon, "it is my gentilized name."

"Then you hear well," said Herod smilingly, "so hear me, Aurlon; I commission you, and give you all the power you need, to investigate into the cause of Sabion's daughter, the fight of last night and the supposed conspiracy. I will issue orders to this effect. Now, I must see my captains. Farewell."

"My lord, I am a stranger at your court," Simon stammered, taken with surprise.

"A wise man is nowhere a stranger," said the King, bowing Simon out of the saloon.

"But what means do you place at my disposition," Simon asked.

"Any you want," said the King, and disappeared through another door.

Simon, when alone involuntarily fell upon his knees and exclaimed, "Lord, my God, relieve me from this intolerable torture, this damnable mask, I can bear it no longer."—Then he rose suddenly, and looked about himself, as though he was afraid the walls would betray him. "Helen! Queen! I come, I save you or die with you," he exclaimed, loudly, overwhelmed with enthusiasm, and went away to think of a proper plan of action.

Having told his colleagues that the King desired him to stay with him, for some time, he managed it to approach the Queen close enough, that he, without attracting particular notice, could whisper in her ear: "Fear not, your people watch at your bedside," and without waiting for an answer, he left the apartment, went down stairs, to breathe the fresh air in the court. Walking about the park he observed a Greek who followed his every step. He considered him one of Sabion's spies and went out of his way, but every where the Greek was after him. Finally, in the dark shade of a cypress walk he murmured half audibly, "What thou wishest not to be done thee, do not to thy neighbor." Simon still fearful that the man might be one of Sabion's spies, took no notice of what he said; but he knew, that he was either detected or at least suspected. This had its good effect. The Greek believing he was mistaken in his man, bent his steps to another side of the park, and sat down at a retired corner to think of a plan of operation.

"I have done my duty, let the consequences be as God pleases," Helen said to herself, after her father had secured her behind gates and bars, and she had felt the whole crushing weight of his wrath. "God save the Queen and Simon, and let there be done with me as the Lord pleases," she murmured then, and resigned her fate into the hands of Providence. Her father had treated her so unkindly, that she could not pray for him. She felt mortified and disgusted, and even against her own inclination, she commenced to believe her father's enemies knew him much better than she did. Not long, however, did she yield to these angry emotions of her heart. Filial affection, the noblest gem in the diadem of humanity, moved her heart again, and she stretched out her arms after her father, determined upon a full confession of her adventure and to pray his forgiveness. "I will move his heart," she soliloquized. "I am his only child, he can not abandon me. For my beloved mother's sake he must forgive me"—here she paused for a moment. "My mother? My mother?" she then continued; "did she not die with a broken heart, because my father betrayed the old King, deserted the Pharisees, and turned a friend of Herod? O, he did not love her, he does not love me; he has no heart for his child." Then she thought of all the kindness he had shown her ever since she could remember, and again she lifted up her hands, and begged her father's pardon, that she could for one moment wrong him. "My love, my passionate love for Simon," she soliloquized, "makes me blind to the love of my father, and I harbor the criminal desire to see him guilty, that my lover, his deadly enemy, be right, and I have an excuse before God and man, to love the violent enemy of my father, who is sworn to take his life. I am revoltingly wicked, I disobeyed and mortified my affectionate parent, and now I am angry because he administers to me the well deserved punishment. I will not murmur. I will confess my guilt and sue for pardon. He will, he must forgive me."

Helen had not slept much for two nights. She was exhausted by the occurrences just passed. Her agitation gave way to relaxation. Her eyes were half closed, when the door opened, and Elvira in company of another servant stepped in and brought Helen the news, that she would be removed from here to a prison, and they had come to see her once more, as none is allowed to see her hereafter.

Helen embraced Elvira, and asked who had given them permission to see her once more. "Your father," said Elvira, "your father heard my ardent prayers, and allowed me to see you before you be removed to a solitary prison."

"O, my father is so kind!" Helen exclaimed.—"But why must I be removed to a prison? A prison?—Heaven! Baruch also was in a prison! Elvira, my beloved soul, why must I be removed to a prison?"

"Your father is so very kind," said Elvira, sarcastically, "he is afraid you might meet with any harm, therefore, I suppose he will keep you safe. O, the kind, kindest father!"

"Suspect not the motives of my father," Helen replied, imperatively, "the father must know best, what he must do with his child. My father loves me, fondly, he will do me no wrong. I have disobeyed his behests, and am ready and willing to receive my punishment without a murmur."

"And you will receive a full measure of it," said Elvira, "for he is enraged at you.—Poor Helen, the sword of death is suspended on a hair over your head, every moment the fatal blow may fall, and you are yet confident in your father's love? He has informed the King of your adventure. With your life he will demonstrate his patriotism and his fidelity to the King, and you are still confident in your father's love? O, my good Helen, beloved friend of my heart, prepare for misery, for nameless affliction, for death prepare. I am done, I told you the whole secret."

"And why, beloved Elvira, why do you tell me my miserable fate," Helen asked, "could I not learn it in due time yet?"

Elvira approached her closer and a little louder than a whisper she said, "Because I will, I must rescue you from certain death. Ten armed men were sent out this morning to arrest Abba Shaul, but the bold man offered an unexpected resistance. He killed three and forced the rest to flight. Your father enraged at this took forty of the royal guard and went out to arrest the heroic man. The King holds a secret meeting with his captains. I, taking advantage of the favorable moment, bribed the guards at your door, stole the key from your father's secret apartment, and here I am. Every thing is prepared; Helen, flee this moment, the mules are ready, I have clothes for you, that none know you. Flee this moment, and in a few hours you are in Jericho and out of Herod's reach."

"No, my good Elvira, I shall not flee," said Helen, composed. "I dare not flee, not only because my confidence in the love of my father is unlimited, but also because an oath, sacred and inviolable, forbids me to leave this place. I thank you my beloved Elvira, you are a true and warm friend: but I must stay, let the consequences be as God pleases."

Elvira prayed with tears in her eyes, but in vain; Helen's determination to stay was firm and unalterable. "Know it then," Elvira said, "if so it must be, I heard the oath you have sworn last night in the People's Council, and I informed Baba ben Buta instantly of your perilous situation. He and his friends being afraid you might be occasioned to betray them, for woman is weak—and knowing that torture and death threaten you, they absolved you of your obligation to stay here any longer, and charged me with the duty to effect your escape. Hesitate no longer, my beloved Helen, flee or you are lost, lost anyhow; if you confess, the people's daggers will reach you, and if you be firm, the King's anger is certain death to you."

Helen, after a long pause said, calmly and resolutely, "Elvira my love, tell Baba ben Buta, I flee not, and, although I am a feeble woman, I violate not my oath, let it cost my life. Here I remain, here where Simon spurns peril and danger, here, I trust, I will assist in saving the Queen, and none shall take me from this place.

All being in vain Elvira wept a parting tear, and after affectionate embraces she left Helen. The door was locked, Helen was alone with her love, grief and apprehension. She was satisfied that she acted right in staying where she was. She could not doubt the love of her father, still the words of Elvira, who was so dear to her heart, re-echoed painfully in every recess of her soul. She struggled powerfully against every accusation, that rose in her heaving bosom, against her father. She subdued them all except one—his order to arrest Simon. This was in her eyes a crime for which the mercy of heaven itself could find no forgiveness. Simon appeared to her pure and innocent as the angels who sing the praise of the Almighty. Remembering now the imminent danger in which Simon was placed, and being disabled herself to assist and caution or die with him, she altogether forgot her own perils, and her sighs followed the beloved friend whom she imagined in the hands of his enemies.

Again she heard a noise before her door. The heavy steps of warriors re-echoed through the hall, an attempt was made to open the door. "They come to remove me to a prison," she thought, and shrank at the recollections of the dim cell in which she had seen Baruch ben Menahem. The door opened, her father, attended by five men of the King's guard entered. "This woman must be conveyed to yonder prison, and well taken care of, that none have access to her," said Sabion to the guards, without looking on Helen.

"My father wounded," Helen cried in painful accents. "O tell me who dared lay hand on my beloved father?"

"Your friend and co-adjutor Abba Shaul," said Sabion gnashing his teeth. "These men saved my life. Abba Shaul escaped; but you are in my power, you and your accursed lover, and you shall pay for the rebel's daring conduct."

Helen hastened toward the guards and kissing every one's sword, she thanked them with tears in her eyes for having saved the life of her father. Then in a state of affectionate ecstacy she stretched out her arms and went to embrace her father. "Away, shameful actress," Sabion roared, "treacherous, infamous woman! I know the serpent's venomous hissing. You go to prison and await your trial before the King's authorities." He pushed her violently to one side of the room, and bid the guards to conduct her to the prison he had told them. The guards, however, struck with the beauty and filial affections of Helen, hesitated. Sabiou bid again, and none appeared to be disposed to obey. Helen recovered her presence of mind. Dismayed, mortified and tortured she looked frigidly on her father. "You need not be angry," she said, calmly, "if Sabion considers it necessary to accuse his own and only child of any crime before the King's judges, Helen knows how to obey her father's command, without the assistance of those strangers. Let them go out of this room, that I may speak one word more alone to my father, and without a murmur I follow you to the prison, to the gates of hell, if so you desire."

Sabion laughed furiously, and said, "Be alone with you, that it be said I was aware of your treacherous designs, that your sins fall on my head? No, woman, I am no longer your father, and unless the King exonerates you, I never shall be. You are Satan's child, Sabion nourished a poisonous scorpion. Begone to yonder prison."

"I must speak a few words alone to my father," Helen said, resolutely, "otherwise the King's armies can not convey me alive to yonder prison."

"No defiance, degraded woman," Sabion said, "Soldiers, do your duty."

Reluctantly the soldiers attempted to lay hands on her, but, with the strength of an enraged lioness, she pushed one after the other from her. "Not alive, I say," Helen cried, "not alive shall you move me from here, unless my request be granted."

"No violence," Sabion said, with a diabolic smile on his lips. He advanced toward her, grasped both her hands, and tied them together with a cord. Helen, dumb and motionless like a marble statue, offered no resistance. When her hands were tied, she said, slowly and monotonously, "The father ties the hands of his own and only child, to deliver her without a hearing, into the hands of the executioner.—Mother, beloved, dead mother, thou hast seen it, I offered no resistance." Two large tears glittered in her eyes. "Remove her," Sabion commanded, and the soldiers went to do their duty.—Again the door opened, and in the midst of a royal guard, Simon ben Hillel entered the room. A scream, shrill and piercing, escaped Helen. Simon fearing the consequences of unguarded words, said, "Fear not woman, although my clothes are white, yet I am no dead man. I live. I am the King's physician and friend, an humble Essenee. My lord," he said to Sabion, "you are requested to withdraw. This signet and this chain, sir, are the evidence of my authority. No harm shall be done to your daughter, unless justice so demand it."

"The King is very gracious," said Sabion meekly and bowing profoundly before Simon, "I gladly obey. I am relieved of a painful duty." He left the room with his guards.

"Stand outside, guard the door, admit none, and wait for my orders," said Simon to his guards, which was immediately done. He untied Helen's hands, and quivering with excitement she sunk into the embrace of Simon, who pressed her close to his bosom.—A long kiss was the whole conversation which passed between them the first few moments. It was a profusion of presentiments, that laid in that silent eloquence which baffles description. The heart of the offended and mortified daughter, the tormented bosom of the affectionate child heaved again with love and unutterable bliss, on the high beating breast of the loving friend. The frigid despair poured into her affectionately glowing soul, by a heartless and cruel father, took wings and gave way to the shouting joy of boundless happiness, engendered by the love and fidelity of him whom she loved best on earth. Closer and still closer Helen clung to Simon who, liberated of the hated mask he bore so long, joyful to be free of the oppressive and cold etiquette and eternal vigilance, and elated with the idea, that he could save the beloved of his heart from the cruel and merciless hands of her unnatural father, pressed her in silent rapture to the stormy heart, and for a long time he had no word to say.

A man whose heart was never moved by an intense and powerful passion, can hardly imagine the bliss of the two lovers before us. Imagine the first blossoms of spring after a dreary winter, the rising sun after a dreadful and stormy night, the first words of a beloved patient who laid dumb in the cold embrace of death, imagine you hear the harmony of the spheres after the roars of a hurricane over a storm-tossed ocean subsided, the swelling accords of the seraphic lyre resounding through a night of darkness and pain, imagine tenfold all these various emotions, and you approach the paradisian rapture of Simon and Helen.

"Fear not beloved Helen," said Simon first recovering his full presence of mind, "Herod and your father are more in my power than you or I am in theirs. I have tried the experiment of confronting wickedness and corruption with the bold countenance of justice and innocence, supported by cunning wisdom in the service of a good cause, and I have found verified what I always supposed must be the case, wickedness is a sneaking coward. Herod and Sabion are my slaves."

Helen stared, delighted and amazed, into the glowing countenance and radiating eyes of Simon, who continued in an emphatic tone: "If you, dearest Helen, will hear what I say, speak and act exactly and literally as I tell you, and you have sworn a solemn oath so to do—you are free and exonerated before the sun rises again over Zion's towers; Abba Shaul will be declared a patriot and hero, worthy of the King's best confidence, and the Queen is saved. Herod's anger, however, falls with crushing weight upon the guilty head of him whom our whole nation curses, and it shall annihilate him."

"Simon! Simon! dearest friend of my heart," Helen interrupted, in painful accents, "Do tell me, I pray, I beseech you, who is the wretched object of your fierce displeasure?"

"Sabion, your murderer and the foul assassin of your nation," Simon responded, firmly.

"Away from me, beguiler," Helen cried, passionately, "he is my father. Away with thy smooth, murderous tongue, I say. I stay here and die, if so it must be, but I shall never, never be auxiliary or even suffer, that my father be wronged."

"O, the dear father, whose hands are soiled with innocent blood," said Simon, "who sacrifices his own daughter for the momentary favor of a despotic King. O, the kind father, whose hands, yet red with Baruch's blood, murder his affectionate child. I was present when he accused you before the King, of treason and conspiracy. I made an unnatural exertion to restrain myself, not to trample his black heart out of his bosom.— This dear father must be spared, the Queen must fall and Israel wrince itself in its own reeking blood. Helen, Helen, your affections make you blind. Not you—I will do the work of justice and it is for you, your oath dictates it—to support me in saving the Queen."

"Simon, O hear me pray," Helen said, 'behold me weep and tremble before you, like a wretched sinner. O, that you could feel the nameless torment which seizes upon my heart. Simon, my father is not as wicked as you, in your boundless hatred, imagine him. Spare, O spare his life. Bid me go through the shadow of death, through the fire streams of the nether world, and I will cheerfully obey, because I love you with every fiber of my heart, and I have sworn to assist you. But spare my poor, wretched father. I am his only, only child, probably his only friend on earth. Let God judge and none else."

Simon.—And your oath?

Helen.—And my father!

Simon.—And your love?

Helen.—And my filial duties!

CHAPTER VI.

COURT INTRIGUES.

"Who is the strange wizard, that he so quickly captivated the heart of the King?" Salome, the King's intriguing sister, said to the servile Sabiou, who stood before her in a most humble attitude.

"I know not, my lady," said Sabion, bowing deeply. "He came into the palace I know not how. He was ushered into the King's presence I know not why or by whom. He captivated the royal heart in one hour. He rules over all in the palace. His commanding and penetrating looks are everywhere."

"He spoils the King," said Salome. "The King begins to be pious, virtuous and humble like a Pharasean scribe. He appears to forget altogether, that the Asmoneans and their friends plot against him, and leave no means untried to ruin him, This Essenee is an agent of the conspiracy. He came to rock the King into a careless sleep. So it is, and we must render that man powerless."

Sabion smiled, and bowed as deep as he could. "So it is my lady," said he, "that is also my opinion. But who dare tell this to the King? He is in love with the young Essence. Still it is our duty to caution the King against the man who assumes the countenance of a saint, personified justice and virtue. He plays the Essence in simplicity of manners and blunt frankness of language. But there is not a spark of Essenean submissiveness about him. He commands where he should obey, and begs politely where he should command. He examines every person and thing in his way, with scrutinizing and penetrating looks, still maintains the appearance of calm indifference. He speaks when he must, but every word of his is sagacious and to the point, and appears to be the product of the moment, the result of a natural impulse without forethought or secondary purpose. None is his companion, still he knows every body's name and function. This is a studied and assumed character, my lady. But the man who succeeds so well in an assumed character, that he deceives Herod, is not easily unmasked."

"And still we must unmask him," Salome ejaculated, passionately. "Who has called him hither to govern and master all? He is an agent of the King's antagonists, but the King is smitten with blindness. We do see, and we feel it our duty to expose the actor to the impartial gaze of our lord. I am the King's sister, it behooves me to watch over him. Sabion, sagacious man, think of proper means."

Sabiou's bow and smile were significant, they appeared to tell, that he had done so already. "You are very kind, my lady," said he. "If I should propose means to expose the real character of the young stranger, it would be to rouse his dormant passions. A young man with so much fire in the eye must have powerful passions. They are subdued by a controling intellect, but will ultimately break forth with increased violence, if they meet with an adequate irritation. Let once the passions have the sway over his intellect, and he stands exposed to our gaze. The studied and assumed character explodes, and the man, as he is, appears in words and actions."

"Your sagacity is admirable," said Salome, smiling complacently. "But you have no opportunity, he studiously avoids it — to ascertain his infirmities. Which of his passions predominates, which, if properly roused will most likely govern him? This is the question you must answer first."

"This is another cause of my suspicion," said Sabion, "he avoids every opportunity where his passions might be learned. There is no man without them, and he who hides them most is sorest afraid of their operation. In examining the catalogue of human passions, I first thought of ambition — but the young Essenee appears to have none, for he never shew his face at court, and at his appearance he at once rose to the highest position. Then I thought of avarice — but this is seldom the dominating passion of the young; the practical man only knows the value of wealth. Love, I thought, love must be the most powerful passion of the young man. Where is the youth who will effectually resist female charms? Let him be a Solomon, Samson or Socrates, woman's bewitching power will, if she desires, make a fool of the one, a feeble child of the other, and an Epicurean of the last. We must think of a Delilah to manage our Samson.— A shame it would be, if Herod's court could not boast of a Delilah."

Salome listened with peculiar delight to the words of Sabion. "I see," said she, "Sabion needs no counsellor. Still I must observe, that he is not sufficiently versed in human feelings. Great, almost omnipotent is love; but the most powerful passion, that ever swayed its iron scepter over man, is jealousy. Jealousy is the name of the serpent, that eats his own excrement, and devours both the blood and intellect of man.— Love is gentle and generous, jealousy is savage and cruel. Love tames the lion, jealousy changes the lamb into a raving tiger.— Love makes precautious and shrewd, jealousy breaks through the limits of wisdom and crushes every opposition; for jealousy has the power of both love and hatred."

Salome invited Sabion to be seated at her right hand side, then she told him in an intimate tone: "I will tell you my plan, my good friend, and I expect you will approve of it. The young Essence is gifted with every charm to win a woman's heart. It is an easy task for you to engender a passionate love for him in the heart of your daughter, especially as she now frequently comes in contact with him, and he will extricate her from the trouble of her last adventure. Love begets love. Helen is too beautiful not to be loved. She is Sabion's only daughter, he is the King's favorite, the match is fine. The part you have to perform must be perfectly clear to you. Your daughter, you told me, has a love affair with one Simon ben Hillel. This must before hand remain a secret to the Essenee. He has free access to the Queen, and that gives me a good opportunity to play my part in the drama. After a while your daughter must be informed of the Queen's intimacy with the Essence, and he must learn the affections of Helen for his rival. This is my part of the play. You understand me now?"

"Perfectly, my lady, and I am astonished at your sagacity," said Sabion; "but my daughter is a whimsical woman. I fear her love to that Simon ben Hillel will be in our way. She says she can love none besides him."

The lady laughed, excessively, at the courtier's folly. "Do you, indeed, believe," said she, "a young woman's love is so consistent? O, then you are deceived. A man, so beautiful as that Essence, and so high in the King's favor, is a bait savory enough to catch every woman's heart in the Roman empire. That is a mistake of yours, my good friend. Go and convince yourself."— Sabion rose and went to the door. "One moment longer," said the lady, "I claim your kind attention. Tell me who is Simon ben Hillel?"

"He is the son of that woodsawyer," the courtier stammered, "who, together with Abba Shaul, the grave digger, are the only living witnesses of our"—

Here he stopped abruptly, and the lady appeared to understand him; for she asked, astonished, "And they live yet?"

"Hillel was out of my reach in Jericho," said the courtier, "but a Greek, was in Jericho when the body of Baruch ben Menahem was brought there, and the stupid multitude congregated around it, inflamatory speeches being made, Hillel attempted to pacify them, the anger of the crowd was excited, and the Greek singled Hillel out among the multitude and killed him. The wicked Greek! Abba Shaul was among the rebels who attacked my servants the other night in the valley of Hinom: his head is forfeited to the arm of justice."

"The excited rebels killed Hillel," the lady said, laughingly, "because he exhorted them to peace and justice, and Abba Shaul's head is forfeited. Is it not so? O, you are a wise man, and the rebels are very stupid; they kill their own friends. They must be watched much closer, and punished rigorously. Is it not so? Now, go, my wise friend, and play your part with due caution and very gentle, that your daughter detect nothing of our plan." The lady left the room, Sabion looked a good while at the door through which she left. Then he murmured, "Yes Lilah, primitive serpent, I can do all this to get rid of my enemies; but then and next your turn comes. You have long enough been the curse of mankind, your death shall be my sin offering before eternal justice, if such a being exists."

Sabion went directly to the room, where his daughter was still kept confined, with a sentinel at her door and one servant to wait upon her. Elvira was the only person besides Simon, who had free access to Helen's room. Sabion, on arriving at the door, was not a little astonished to be refused admittance. A bitter, malicious smile played around his lips, on murmuring, "They prohibit me from seeing my daughter,"—But quickly collected, he asked the sentinel whose orders he obeyed. "The orders of the King's physician," was the short reply Sabion gnashed his teeth, when he had turned his back on the sentinel. Simon stood on the upper portico absorbed in thought, so that he did not observe Sabion when he stepped up to him.

"My lord," said Sabion, several times, before Simon heard him.

"I am not your lord," said the young man, awaking, as it were, from a dream, "I am the King's body physician."

"And Herod's privy counsellor," the cunning man added, with a smile, "and the favorite of Antipater's son. But it is only the well deserved reward of your wisdom. The King understands how to choose his friends."

"Great men have great passions, and are apt to commit great errors," said the Essence, in his usual, calm manner. "I am young, and my good will is much greater than my wisdom. I never had the fortune to be among the great men of the country, and need the forbearance of the wise."

Sabion bowed profoundly. "You are already the favorite of every person at this court, especially the ladies are very eager to cultivate your friendship. I heard but this morning the King's sister say, that she was very desirous to see you in her saloon."

"I am sensible of the honor," said the physician, "but I scarcely dare venture in such noble company, as my manners are too impolite, too much like the rustic for the first time in the city. —But I have been charged by the King with a difficult task, in which you could best assist me. I must bring him a full report of the conspiracy which you detected, and of your daughter's part in that matter. Will you be kind enough to give me all the information you have on these matters."

"If you know the heart of a father whose only child rebels against him," said Sabion, in a lamentable tone, "call me not as a witness in this case, I know too much. Permit me, my lord, to see my daughter occasionally, remember my affliction, and let me altogether out of the affair. I am a fond father and an obedient servant of the King. Love and duty came in a clashing conflict, and I sacrificed myself to stern duty. But you can save my child, you can restore the daughter, the only darling child to her father; for you know not what I do. Do not call me, and I will be dumb as the grave."

Simon regarded every feature of the speaker's countenance with particular care, as long as he spoke. When he was done he thrust such a penetrating look on the sapient courtier, that he looked aside. "I must know all the particulars of this affair," he said firmly and resolutely; "the King charged me with this painful duty, and I shall prove myself a strict commissioner. In yonder room is your daughter, you may see her, whenever you please; but I must have all the information you can give."

The sentinel was ordered to admit Sabion, and Simon went away. "Confounded scoundrel," Sabion muttered, "he would not expose a weak point of character. Still I will ruin him."

The door was opened, Helen hastened to embrace her father, who returned her tenderness, most affectionately. "And so you have forgiven me, my dear child?" said Sabion, in a soft and flattering tone. "I was bound in duty to act as I did, but the King, perceiving the painful position in which I was placed, released me, by the appointment of his body physician to investigate into the matter. He appears to be so kind and well intended, that you have nothing to fear of him. He will certainly release you and also defend my character before the King."

Helen's surprise of her father's unexpected change of mind was equalled only by the joy she felt about the good opinion her father had of her lover. Again and anon she embraced her father, and assured him that she never felt the least anger in her heart, that her filial affections were not the least impaired. Her surprise and delight reached the highest altitude on hearing her father, say, "My child, we have great cause to be grateful to the Essenean physician. He is very much inclined in our favor and his influence with Herod is very great. I have closely watched the young man and convinced myself, the manly beauty of his exterior is by far inferior to his excellent qualities of heart and mind."

Helen was all enthusiasm, her whole heart laid open before her sagacious father who, making the best use of the happy moment, continued, after a smile, "If you could forget Simon ben Hillel and lavish your affections on the great Essence, you would at once atone for all the past follies. The King and your father would be decidedly pleased with your determination."

"Forget Simon ben Hillel?—No!—Love the young Essence?—Yes!" said Helen, somewhat perplexed. "But, my father, do you know that the calm, cool and sagacious physician is capable of love, that he would love me?"

"My daughter is so beautiful," he said, smiling complacently, "and her father is so wealthy and influential, that no man can resist her charms. I am glad to find you thus disposed. Shape your conduct toward the physician accordingly, without overstepping the limits of etiquette and propriety, and I will take proper care of the rest."

"If this is your will, my father," said Helen, "then give me a token, that such is your paternal wish, a token which I can show the young physician. He is meek and bashful beyond description. He never would have the courage to ask my hand from you, if I could not encourage him with some token."

"Here is the ring which I received of Cleopatra, as a token of her esteem," said the father. "This ring is valuable and of particular interest to me. I entrust it into your hands as a token of my wish, that you be the wife of Aurion, the King's body physician."

She grasped the ring so eagerly, and covered the hand of her father with so many kisses, that he was baffled with the unexpected change in Helen's mind. He left her fully satisfied, that he had carried out well, his part of the plot. He was scarcely gone when Simon paid Helen a visit. "Aurion, body physician of the King," said Helen, "what signifies this precious ring? Essenee, sagacious and sapient, tell me the import of this costly jewel."

Simon scarcely knew how to account for the happy humor of his beloved. He inspected the ring closely, then he said, "It is your father's ring, I saw it on his finger; hence it signifies a new trick or trap."

"How unkind you are!" Helen said. "The ring signifies the wish and will of my father, that I be your bride, your wife, yours in life and death, in time and eternity. This is the import of the costly jewel."

"Is it a dream, a fantasy, that makes you speak thus?" Simon asked, surprised. "Do tell me, beloved Helen, what do you mean by all this?"

"I mean, that my father advised me, earnestly, to love the young physician, whose praise he sounds exaltingly," said she, "and as a token, of his will and wish he gave me Cleopatra's ring, to encourage you with it."

"Do you deceive me with false hopes?"

"No, I only tell you what is literally true."

"Helen, my love, this is a new plot; by

the God of Israel, it is a plot. Either this is intended to restore his influence over the King, by my agency, or to ruin me. Dearest beloved Helen, caution, very sagacious caution is necessary in this affair. I remember now, that he told me of the King's sister who wished my company. She is the worst trickster at the court. I must see her, to ascertain what this means; for your father had a long conversation with her this morning. Let them plot as much as they please, if you will be wise, we will make the best of it. But at present I advise you, to tell your father, that I was so cool and distant, that it is very hard to gain access to my heart. Still, take care of the ring, we might need it."

"It is strange, that you suspect every thing proceeding from my father," said Helen, in an offended tone. "If he is ever so wicked, has he not a paternal heart?"—

"No, he has not," Simon interrupted, "I know he has not. He informed Herod of the supposed crimes of his own child, just to ingratiate himself in his lord's favor. He just as easy will dispose of you in any way to suit his selfish designs. But, we must be wiser than those corrupted courtiers. Ours is the sagacity of love, the boldness of justice, and the firmness of virtue. Helen, they shall not deceive us. I must now see Herod, he called me; then I will see his plotting sister, and teach her a lesson on plots and counterplots."

Herod was alone when Simon entered the saloon. Without giving him time to utter one word Herod asked hastily, "Well, my faithful Aurion, have you ascertained any thing in regard to the conspiracy?"

"I have ascertained more than sufficient to convince you, my lord, of the hazardous game you play with your people, by the wicked advice of your courtiers," said he. "But, before I speak, permit me to ask you, do you hire an assassin to kill an old and inoffensive man on a mere suspicion, or do your servants do so with your permission?"

Herod looked somewhat displeased about this direct and perplexing question. Simon continued not, and Herod was obliged to say something. "Why do you ask me this question?" he said.

"Because, if this is the case," was the reply, "I must beg your permission to leave this court, this city, this country."

"To what particular case do you have reference?" the King asked.

"In Jericho, I am informed," said Simon, "lives a Babylonian sage, Hillel is his name, a man as inoffensive as a child, and highly respected by the Pharasean sages. Sabion hired an assassin to slay the old man, I know not why. But the ruffian could not do it. He came back, deceived Sabion, who thinks that man killed, and on inquiry I learned the whole story. My Lord, if this was your will I submit, but I must leave you instantly; but if it is your friend's private enterprise, I must caution you against him. Had that man, Hillel, been assassinated, and had it transpired, that Sabion has ordained it so, your enemies would have increased by thousands."

"I am ignorant of this affair," said Herod.

"That self-same Sabion," he continued, "sent out your officers, my lord, to arrest a grave digger, called Abba Shaul. He offered resistance, and Sabion himself went there with men of your guard to arrest the bold warrior, who fought more than one battle, but succeeded not in his attempt. Abba Shaul fought them all and escaped. The man stands accused of knowing about, and being himself concerned in the conspiracy. The truth, however, is that Hillel and the grave digger are the only witnesses of the shameful and criminal connections of Sabion with a lady high at the court of Herod, a connection upon which the law sets the penalty of death. The private affairs of your chief spy are the main cause of this last onslaught of his. His daughter having fallen in love with the son of Hillel, feeling as Sabion does the power over him held by those two men, and unwilling to give his daughter to an obscure Babylonian, he found it necessary to have those two men out of his way, one by your royal authority, and the other by an assassin."

"Why do you tell me all this?" Herod asked.

"Not to rouse your indignation against your chief spy; for you have too much knowledge of the human mind not to know him already. I only intend to give you the whole story of the supposed conspiracy," the physician continued. "Two young men from the vicinity of Jericho, both innocent peasants, were arrested. Their companions roused an indignation in the city which bounded on madness. The men came to worship the Lord, have done no wrong, still they are captives. No sooner were those men seen in the hands of the officers, than an excited multitude with the grave digger followed them, and at an opportune time rescued them. The Queen knew as little about all this, as you did. The son of Hillel and the son of Uziel naturally were among those who went to rescue the two young men arrested in their place. Helen, wishing to caution her lover against the intentions of her father, followed his trace to the very spot where the fight occurred. Sabion, terrified at this demonstration of his daughter's indomitable affections for the son of one who is a witness of his shame, thought best to secure his daughter behind gate and bars, and make the best use of the occasion, to ingratiate himself in your confidence. But, in order to prevent any further communication of his daughter with the son of Hillel, he instructed her this day to love me, and attempted to put his two enemies out of his way. This is the whole story. I have good testimony for every part of it."

"Then you say there is no conspiracy in existence?" Herod asked.

"No evidence of one is in existence," said Simon; "still I should not be surprised at all, if conspiracies against you exist."

Herod looked surprised on his physician. "What makes you think so?" he asked, with a strong emphasis.

"The conspiracies at your own court, and the outrages committed on the people in your name," was the short and significant response.

"It is enough, more than enough," Herod cried, intensely excited. "You bring into my presence Hillel, Abba Shaul, the hired assassin, and Helen, as soon as I return rom Cana. I must go there to give battle to the King of Arabia. When I return, I will investigate closely into these affairs.—You say, the Queen is innocent?"

"Like a child, my lord," he said.

"How do you know it?" the King asked.

"By the forcible evidence of the combined circumstances," was the reply, "and whenever you please, my lord, I will convince you of it.—Can I give those men your royal word, that no harm should be done them?"

"You may," he said. "During my absence continue to investigate those matters. Dismiss Helen from her prison, have a careful eye on the Queen"—

"No, my lord," Simon interrupted, "I hate to share the fate of Baruch ben Menahem. The Queen is too virtuous to need my watching eye, and too wise to stand in need of my advice."

"You fear the effect of her beauty, Essenee," said Herod, smilingly.

"I admire her beauty and love her magnanimity," he replied; "but I fear your jealousy and the intrigues of your courtiers. Helen, your favorite's daughter, will on your return tell you the fearful story, how you were deceived in regard to Baruch ben Menahem, and, sir, you will be surprised at the impositions practiced on you."

"Young man, I bid you farewell," said the King, when rising, "and require you to collect all the evidence at your command, necessary to convince me of all your statements. Dositheus, the governor of the palace, Joseph my treasurer, and Sabion know my will to support you in all things, and they will do so. I will hold a terrific investigation on my return, and woe unto him who has deceived me or made bad use of my confidence."

Helen laid in the embrace of Elvira and rejoiced over her rescue from a perilous state in which, as she said, her adventurous and thoughtless enterprise had brought her. She believed she had played her part well in the great drama which she considered to be at its close, as the Queen was safe. "Now I must go to see the Queen," said she, "and tell her the story of my adventures."

"The Queen should not know too much of it," said Elvira. "The less she knows, the better it is for herself and for us. I fear the peculiar and sagacious performance of Simon will, some time or other, be understood by Herod; then his anger will know no limits. Simon and any one of us can escape his wrath, or can stand the consequences if necessary; but the Queen would be wretched, miserable, if she was recognized as one of our co-adjutors. She must know nothing of our designs."

"So it is, my beloved Elvira," said Helen, "and I will tell her no more than is absolutely necessary to explain my absence from her. Will you, my sweet sister, answer me one question, fairly, openly and truly?"

"I will, my lady, if I can."

"What brings you in the company of those bearded and rebellious men, my sweet Elvira," Helen asked, "what brings you in that subterranean abode in a nightly, unfriendly hour?"

The countenance of Elvira resembled a fresh rose in color and a violet in modesty. Perplexed, visibly embarrassed, she cast her looks on the floor. Helen waited for an answer which came not for a good while. Still, Elvira felt that she owed some answer to her friend and mistress. She fixed her black eyes on Helen, when saying, "A mysterious fate guides my steps, and I dare not tell whither. I will answer this question in a few short months, when the seal will be broken from my mystery. Now I can not, I dare not. Mistrust me not. I love you better than a sister, but I can not yet tell you this secret."

"And Jonathan ben Uziel?" Helen asked, smilingly.

"Knows me not, although I love him," said Elvira. "Still, he is not the cause of my acquaintance with those men." Elvira, apparently afraid to betray herself, quickly disappeared through the door, leaving Helen alone.

Helen went to the Queen, who yet sat pale and sickly on a sofa of white silk, with silver embroidery, her head leaning on the bosom of one of her ladies. The two young princes sat at her feet and from time to time looked compassionately in her countenance. When Helen opened the door, one of the princes ran toward her, and clapping his hands, he exclaimed joyously, "Mother is well again, she will not die!" Helen kissed the child, and approaching the Queen, she kissed the end of her garment, and congratulated her on her recovery.

"And I congratulate you, fair Helen, upon your happy escape," said the Queen, with a painful smile.

Helen blushed. She did not suspect she knew anything about her imprisonment, and thanked her for her kindness. The Queen moved with her hand, kissed her children, and in a few moments she was alone with Helen. "Tell me, good Helen," the Queen asked, "why you were kept so closely behind gate and bars?" Helen stammered unintelligible words, but the Queen would not let her off without confession, and encouraged her most kindly to speak. Helen, having regained her presence of mind, fell down before the Queen and prayed ardently; "Pardon, my gracious lady, pardon the weakness of an unguarded heart! If you will not be angry at my frivolous doings, I will confess every word."

"My good and fascinating Helen," said the Queen, playing with the girl's curls; "is incapable of committing a wrong. Speak, my pardon is granted you in advance."

"You know, my gracious Queen," said Helen, "you know the power of love. Providence decreed that I should feel its unlimited force. A young man, in beauty equal to Joseph, captivated my heart and its best affections. Waking, I think but of him, and sleeping he is the object of my dreams. My fantasy adorns him with a thousand graces, and each endears him a thousandfold to my loving heart. When he first, in yonder vineyards, singled me out among the maidens who celebrated there the fifteenth day of Ab, first clasped my hand between his and whispered, 'I love thee,' I imagined I heard all the melodies of heaven, and saw the charming scenes of paradise. This young man, a Babylonian by birth, came with the pilgrims of Jericho to this city to offer the first fruits in God's temple. With a yearning, longing, panting heart, I hastened to meet him, and when I saw him again, heaven and earth appeared to change into the gardens of Sharon, the air turned into Gilead's balm, my heart and soul turned a harp, resounding the praise of love. On returning to my home, I learned of my father that my lover was suspected of being a member of a secret conspiracy. I heard orders given for his arrest. My heart trembled in my bosom, and had he been in the heavens above, or in the nether world below, beyond pathless deserts or fathomless oceans, I would have hastened to caution him, and my love would have directed me in the right path. So I did, my gracious Queen; I could not do otherwise. In the valley of Hinom, surrounded by friends, I met him and saw him persecuted by my father's servants—They attacked him, he and his friends resisted and defeated my father's men, three of whom fell, the rest fled. He being safe, I returned home, but the servants knew me, informed my father, and I was arrested.—The King, however, through his Essenee physician, heard my story, restored me to liberty, and my father has forgiven me. Now, my gracious Queen, let me not feel your just displeasure, pardon a meek, unhappy maiden."

"Unhappy?" the Queen repeated several times, "No, my good Helen, those who love as ardently as you do, are not unhappy." After a deep sigh, the Queen offered her right hand to Helen which she covered with kisses, and bid her rise and be seated by her side. "What is the name of your friend?" the Queen asked

"Simon ben Hillel, a man little known beyond the limits of his humble home," said Helen, "still his wisdom, integrity and zeal deserve a better place in this community than he has always occupied."

"Hillel's name is not altogether unknown to me," said the Queen, "he is a distinguished teacher among the Pharasees. But I never heard of his son.—Is your father opposed to your love?"

"He is, my benign lady," said Helen, "he is unappeasably opposed to Simon. He hates him violently."

"As he hates all the Pharasees, I suppose," said the Queen.

"No, my noble dame, much more, infinitely more," Helen complained; "he hates him deadly, and would certainly have him killed, could he lay hold on him."

"That is strange," said the Queen, considerately. "But Helen shall not weep, if I can dry up her tears. Helen, I must see Simon ben Hillel, and if he is the son of his father, I shall be your patron, the advocate of your love."

"Thank you, gracious Queen, thank you a thousand times," Helen stammered, and two tears glittered in her black eyes. "The God of love will reward you with a thousandfold love."

"Not too many words, my good maiden," the Queen said, feelingly. "Send him word; let him know that I wish to see him."

"And my father's deadly hatred?" Helen stammered.

"I will protect him against it," the Queen said, earnestly. "None shall dare to harm him."

"My gracious lady, if you pardon me, that I did not tell you the whole secret," said Helen, "I will—I do—I inform you, that you know him already."

"The Essenean Physician!" the Queen exclaimed, suddenly. "Is it not so, Helen?"

Helen bowed, blushingly, to express affirmation, when the Queen continued, "Be careful, Helen, that man is too shrewd, altogether too deliberate and sagacious for his age, to be an affectionate friend, or ardent spouse. Helen, be careful, I mistrust that man. He has too suddenly gained the King's favor and confidence. I apprehend a treachery behind that mysterious man."

"You had no opportunity, my gracious Queen, to read his heart," said Helen, "or to study his character. He is as wise as he is kind, as shrewd as he is upright, and as determined and bold as he is true and faithful. He is a rock of truth in his words, and a fiery seraph in his love."

"The advocate is eloquent but suspected of partiality," the Queen said, smilingly. "Helen, you have never been deceived, you know not, how smooth the tongue, and how black the heart of some men is. Those who must hide the most baseness avail themselves not unfrequently of the sweetest words. Integrity is most always plump and simple, while deceit, like the venomous serpent, chooses the variegated garb, and hides itself in the shade of roses. Helen, good, innocent maiden, your friend is too wise, too shrewd altogether, I suspect him."

"Do not, my gracious Queen," Helen prayed. "Look first into his great and magnanimous soul, then judge, and you will think of him as I do."

A lady came in and whispered a few words to the Queen. After she had left the apartment the Queen again turned to Helen, "I am informed," said she, "that he, whom you love so much, is engaged deeply and for several hours too, in a private conversation with Salome, the chief and most unscrupulous authoress of court cabals What means this, if Aurion's intentions are honest and manly?"

"I can explain it," said Helen hastily. "My father contracted a particular affection for him, and desired me to marry him. He gave me this ring as a token"—

"This ring!" the Queen interrupted, much agitated. "Whose is this ring?"

Helen, somewhat terrified by the agitated voice of the Queen, stammered. This occasioned the Queen to pacify Helen with a painful smile on her lips. "Speak,my good Helen," said she, "do not care about my agitation. I had felt again a pain in my head, but it is all over now."

"My father gave me this ring, to show it to Aurion as a token of his wish concerning Aurion and myself," Helen continued. "I told him of my father's words, and on showing him the ring he remembered that my father, whose friendship he suspects, had told him of Salome's wish to see him, and had himself a long conversation with Salome. He apprehends a plot against himself and went to Salome, to learn my father's real intentions."

The Queen was visibly confused. She said little and what she did say had no meaning. Helen requested her to rest a little, as she was yet weak. But instantly she recovered. "I pity you, Helen," she said, "your father's sudden friendship for Aurion and his excuse to visit Salome, do not the least improve his case; I rather still more suspect his integrity. He wants to learn Sabion's intentions of Salome. Either he must be on confidential terms with Salome, more so than Sabion, then he certainly is dishonest, or he must be ahead of her in intrigues and cunning; then I certainly suspect him. Still for your sake, I will observe him closer. If I learn, that virtue also can assume a mask, if a noble end can be obtained, then I have profited an entire new lesson." She gave the conversation another turn, joked, laughed, teased Helen with her lover. But after awhile she asked naively, "Who gave this ring to your father?"

"Cleopatra, the Queen of Egypt," Helen answered, but was afraid of her own words, on observing the scarlet hue which flushed over the pale countenance of the Queen.

"My head-ache troubles me now, more than ever," the Queen said. "This is a costly ring for you," she continued, with a smile on her lips. "Give it to me, I will keep it for you, to be your witness, if your father should not be willing to keep his word."

Helen bowed, and gave the ring in the custody of the Queen. She examined it closely, then she requested Helen to call the Queen her mother, which Helen did.

The agitation of the Queen now could burst forth unobservedly. "My ring to Cleopatra!" she exclaimed, passionately. "Did I not give him this ring when he knelt before me, the King's daughter, and swore to love me forever? Ha, treacherous monster, where are thy oaths, thy thousand assurances of love; they are all forgotten in the presence of that passionate, beguiling, lubric wench, that prostitute of Antony. Now, I know, Herod, why not a spark of love glows for you in this hapless and cheerless heart. Now I know, why no sentiment of my soul pleads for the cold-blooded assassin of my brother. Herod, slave-born son of Antipater, werest thou not the father of my children—O how unhappy Mariamne is! she must hate the father of her children, or love a traitor, an assassin, a wretch."

Mariamne's mother, Queen Alexandra came. "I am happy to see you as well as you are, Queen," said Alexandra, "and hope you will go down in the park, to breathe fresh air."

"Mother, do you know this ring?" Mariamne asked, in a slow and emphatic tone.

"I believe I have seen it on the finger of Herod. It is, yes, it is the ring you gave him, when first"—

"Yes, yes," Mariamne said, "when first I listened to the courtier's thousand representations, first I silenced my heart, as a princess invariably must to suit the politics of the court, when first I concluded upon sacrificing myself for my family, when first Herod knelt in the dust before me and begged, implored, entreated, wept, as only the son of a slave can; then I gave him this ring and my consent to be his. This very ring, mark, this pledge of my love, was given to your friend, to lubric Cleopatra; but she, most likely afraid her Roman liege lord might descry the valuable ring and inquire after the price, yes the price—she made Sabion a present with it. So the story runs, and I tell you this only to convince you, that your confidence set in Cleopatra, to say the least, is very foolish."

"Not quite as you believe," said Alexandra, somewhat offended. "She kept her word, but I could not keep mine."

"Thank Providence, that it did not cost your life," said Mariamne. "Herod returned from Cana with the firm conviction, that I betrayed him to Cleopatra. I bore it patiently, and would have stood the consequences without a murmur, had not some one convinced Herod of my innocence in this matter, some one I know not who."

"Dositheus, I believe, has done so," said Alexandra. "We ought to be grateful to him for his interference. The influence of Dositheus on Herod is considerable, and he uses it much in our favor."

"I have no confidence in the cold and heartless courtier," said the Queen. "He studies his smiles, weighs his words and circles his tears. He is too polite for an honest man, and too submissive for a friend. He could not be my confidential friend. Mother, I caution you against Dositheus."

"You are not versed well enough in human nature," said Alexandra. "Dositheus is an ambitious, revengeful and treacherous knave as well as a thousand others. But he hates Herod on account of his murdered brother, and his hatred renders him a tool in my hands without a will, as soon as I need his services. The honest man can not be made subservient to other people's plans; rogues and knaves properly managed will do the best service."

"Such is not my doctrine, mother," said Mariamne. "I would have no dealings with the debased, even not to save my life."

"Yes, it is true, you are admirably honest, and your patience and forbearance are the demonstration of high virtue," said Alexandra. "The ring which Herod gave to Cleopatra testifies to the contrary of what you pretend.—This ring, my daughter, tells that our position is most dangerous, nay, even that our doom is sealed. As long as Herod loved you, we had one angel to plead our cause. But now he having betrayed your love to another woman, now we stand exposed to his hatred, ambition and jealousy. The last time, Queen, I propose to you to do your duty to your children and to yourself. Leave this country, go directly to Alexandria, entrust yourself to Cleopatra, and I give you my word the throne will be secured to your children, you and all of us will be safe."

"If Herod loves me no more," said Mariamne, "he is no worse than I am. If he has no affections for his children and their mother, I have and I will, as much as is in my power, see their father respected. Herod furnishes Antony with men and money in the great struggle which will take place between him and Octavius, and Antony, my mother believes would protect me against the wish of Herod! Cleopatra succeeded in obtaining from Herod my ring, and she should take my part before Antony! Is the world thus out of shape and form? Have reason and understanding thus turned into falsehood, that my wise mother speaks utterly contrary to them? I should think, put Mariamne out of the way, must

Cleopatra think, and Egypt and Judea might be united by marriage or treachery. This is more likely than your supposition."

"Will you not understand me, my daughter?" Alexandra asked, impatiently. "I see I must be plump. Cleopatra's greatness is her influence over Antony, which she has by her beauty, a beauty that just begins to fade away. Make your appearance at the court of Egypt, and every eye will look upon you; you outshine her a thousand times. You are an enemy too formidable for her in the eyes of Antony, that she should not do any and every thing to get you away, far away from her lord. He will anyhow be induced to comply with your wishes."

Mariamne made no reply. Displeasure and mortification were visibly depicted on her pale countenance. Alexandra, however, continued speaking on that topic and praised Mariamne's charms so much, that she exclaimed in a tone of disgust, "The daughter of the Asmoneans, Israel's Queen, the mother of Judah's princes should vie with a harlot for the favor of voluptuous Antony? No, I shall not. I prefer the scaffold to shame, and the greatest shame is that which we procure with the charms God has bestowed on us, at the expense of innocence and purity. Mother, I caution you, not to bring misery upon yourself and my grandfather, and shame upon your family. A princess should know how to die honorably and bravely for the glory of her house, in preference to living covered with shame, a stain upon the name of her house. Let Cleopatra's name be handed over to infamy, the Asmonean sun shall have no spots on account of suffering Mariamne. Mother, it appears as though we have changed parts in this tragedy. Let us stop here."

The earnest, high toned language of Mariamne failed not to impress her mother with the conviction, that she could not be persuaded to leave Jerusalem, or turn a traitor to her husband. She gave the conversation another turn by speaking of the unexpected progress which the Essenean physician made so rapidly in Herod's favor. "We could derive many a benefit from the young man," said Alexandra, after awhile. "It appears to me, that he stands as high in the estimation of the people as in the favor of Herod. The people are our guardians, if they have the power."

"I remember now," said the Queen, suddenly, "when sick, lying in a state of delirium, he whispered in my ear, 'the people watch at your bedside.' It is true, there may be something better in that man than I expected of his shrewdness: but, mother, I fear he turned a traitor to us and the people, for he gained too fast the favor of Herod, Salome and Sabion. If he gained their favor by honest means and for upright purposes, he plays a dangerous game, that may cost him his head. But still, I must know him. This is the advice I take of you, mother; if Herod has evil intentions against the remains of my family, I will appeal to my people. They will hear the daughter of Matatthia. They have hearts, souls and arms. This last resort, this final appeal suits me. I must see that young Essenee.—Mother, do you know the Pharasee Hillel?

"Pst, mention not the name of a man," said Alexandra, "who is a horror to Sabion and Salome. Besides this," she continued, whispering, "he is known as an opponent of Herod and a friend of the Asmoneans. His influence, notwithstanding his poverty, is great, very great. But what makes you ask this question?"

"The Essence Physician is the son of Hillel," the Queen answered.

"Then we should, we must see and study him," said Alexandra. "The son can not be altogether averse to his father."

"But we must be very careful with him, for he is very shrewd," the Queen remarked. "Attempt to form his acquaintance, inquire into his purposes and intentions, and let us see what we can do with him."

Simon was received with distinguishing kindness by the King's intriguing sister Salome. Having inspected the youthful Adonis for some moments, with visible delight, she invited him to a seat, reclining herself opposite him on a low sofa under a canopy of the finest weaving of Damascus. She had thrown back her veil and Simon could gaze at the profusion of tresses, the pearl teeth, the coral lips and the unfaded beauty of a young widow. Simon, who did not even suspect that hair and teeth were borrowed from art, the red and white of the cheeks were the painter's work, and the luster of the countenance was the product of artificial drugs—wondered that such a beautiful form should be the abode of so deep-dyed a soul. He almost changed his opinion about her, thinking that the faults of the great and mighty are always magnified, when, on looking deeper into her eye, a ray of malice darted forth, which went chilling through his soul.

Salome, on her part, and Castobarus a man of about forty who sat at her side, inspected Simon no less closely, while they went through the usual routine of compliments and established figures of speech, so that he felt more than ever the difficulty of playing successfully before them, another man than he really was.

The usual phraseology of court chats was interrupted by Simon with the question, "You expressed the wish, my lady, to see me, and I gave myself the pleasure to make my appearance in your saloon. If you desire me to render you any service, I am at your command."

"Very polite, sir, and very obliging," said the lady. "When I wished to see you, it was not to trouble you with any of my business; I only wished to become better acquainted with the man of whom my royal brother speaks with so much kindness and regard, and who has, in so short a time, bewitched every heart at this court. My friend Castobarus just now told me, how the King honors you particularly with his confidence."

Simon expressed thanks for the numerous compliments the lady had made him, in few words, and attempted to start a conversation of which he was not both subject and object; but in vain, both the lady and Castobaros continued to laud his wisdom, his manly beauty, his sublime virtues, his beneficial influence on the King, oppressed with care and trouble, and the hopes stored in his future. Disgusted, Simon yielded and listened with aversion to the flatteries with which he was overpowered. He looked especially with contempt upon Castobarus, who appeared to be the re-echo of the royal dame. The man with his small gray eyes and ever smiling countenance appeared to him like an automaton, whose locomotive power was the will of the lady. He remembered the description which Herod, in a moment of excitement, gave of his courtiers and servants; an exact specimen was now before him.

"I doubt, my lady," said Simon, "that I will meet, for a long time, with the favor of our sovereign. The novelty of my plain and simple deportment will not please him long, I apprehend, and I doubt that I ever will be capable of acquiring that politeness, that courtesy and accomplishment, which distinguishes so eminently the hightoned ladies and gentlemen of this court."

"Wisdom and virtue stand aloof of all forms," said Salome, "because they need not that embellishment, in which empty heads and vicious hearts hide themselves. The King values the diamond but cares little for its encasement. He will always respect and love you, and you can render invaluable services to him and our people."—

"The King will appreciate and reward your services," said Castobarus, with a bow, "and the people's gratitude will be great and everlasting; for a people forget not their benefactors."

Simon deciphered at once the object of this conversation, and with the adroitness of a practiced courtier he responded, quickly, "I am fully satisfied with our monarch's grace and your kindness, for all the services I am capable to render. A service rendered to a monarch must also be one to the people, for he is the people's head. The King's appreciation is the people's praise, for he speaks for all of them. Allow me, noble lady, to correct a mistake of your sagacious friend. Short, very short indeed is the memory of the multitude. The people but seldom know their true benefactors. They idolize the impostor and persecute their best friends. History speaks with a thousand tongues of the victims which popular fury demanded of those very men, the popular enthusiasm idolized. Permit me to say, my lady, happy, thrice happy, must every man feel who can tell himself I have contributed to the weal of my people, have alleviated the sufferings of humanity; but, disappointment is sure to him who expects thanks or appreciation."

It did not escape the attention of Simon that the two persons before him eyed each other occasionally, apparently disappointed with the Essenee's eloquence. He, therefore, continued with rising emphasis, "The great lesson which I studied, and it is the key to the secret of success—is to work and toil in the vineyard of humanity, without the least expectation of reward or praise. Praise, like slander, passes away, tracelessly as yonder shadow, as the moment rushes into the bosom of eternity. Victory is the warrior's prize, wisdom the student's remuneration, the voice of satisfied conscience is the only reward, of which we can not be deprived, and must invariably gain by manly and virtuous exertions. If our monarch offers me an opportunity to do more for humanity than I can do in another station, I will be grateful to him, and sure I am of the entire reward which I claim."

Salome commenced to feel, that she was in the presence of one who was her superior in mental powers. The sound principles of the Essenee, uttered in such a simple-sublime eloquence, and in so solemn a tone, having become entirely strange to her, fell heavily upon her heart, and failed not in drawing a silent comparison between the Essence's sublime principles and her own depraved ambition. She could not continue the conversation when her guest was silent, and Castobarus relieved the company from the painful silence with the remark, "It is to be wished to yourself, my lord, and your fellow men, that you lose not these sublime principles in the tumult of practical life. You are yet young, gifted with warm and generous impulses; but practical life, like the winds blowing from Lebanon's snow-crowned summits, temper the warmth of the heart."

Simon cast a contemptuous look upon the man. "May God, in His infinite mercy, protect me against experiences like those of which you speak, my lord," said Simon. "I would despise myself and attempt to be out of my own way, if possible, should I feel a change of principles in myself."

"That is right, sir," said Salome, with a feigned smile on her lips. "It is time enough to think of the unpleasant occurrenees of life, when they force themselves upon us; till then, it is best that man should please himself in the best way he can, without interfering with the happiness of his neighbor.—But sir, your conversation is altogether too serious and profound for a woman. Let us come to another theme. I was astonished, that you ingratiated yourself so quickly in the hearts of our ladies. But, since I have the pleasure to see and hear you, I am no longer surprised, that several ladies, especially one, who have a happy opportunity to see and hear you frequently, are so much enamored with you. You know, my good sir, love is a female theme, and so it is most natural, that I should come to it at last."

That was also the topic to suit Simon, and, having thanked the lady for the good opinion she had of him, he continued: "Love is such a pleasant, inspiring theme, a topic so amiable and fascinating, that you most naturally must come to it at last. A kiss, a smile, a whisper of affection is so natural to woman, that her lips appear consecrated to this very purpose. I always envy the happy man who feels the power of love. It must be the golden era of the heart, the paradisian days of the soul. But, I can not feel it, my heart is too coarse for such eminent presentiments. Now, more than ever, I ean only admire beauty and magnanimity, but it leaves my heart cold. I believe I am a fantastical being."

"You only believe so," said Salome, "but you will soon find out the contrary. I know you have bestowed too much attention on books, your heart must be refreshed before it can appreciate the happiness of love. Two fiery black eyes often perform miracles in a short time. I will prove to you that I am right. You have lately come much in contact with Sabiou's beauteous daughter; she loves you, I am told by reliable authority, and in two weeks from now, you shall tell me, whether two fiery black eyes can not work wonders. But, if you then must confess, that the daughter of my friend taught you the great lesson to love, in so short a time, I shall be satisfied with your repentance."

It was clear now to Simon, that Sabion and Salome had plotted together, the scheme to unite him with Helen by the sacred ties of love, in order to ruin either or both of them, but he could not yet look through the scheme. A shock of wrath and indignation chilled his blood and almost stopped its course for a moment, on thinking of the baseness of the father, who thus sacrifices his own child, to ruin his rival in the King's favor. He almost forgot the part he acted, and the sudden paleness of his countenance betrayed the painful emotions which tormented his bosom.

"My God, you are deadly pale!" Salome exclaimed. "What ails you? Speak, can I do anything for you?"

Simon composed himself. A feigned smile was the only reply Simon could make. After a short pause he said, "There is an incidence connected with the investigation into the cause of your friend's daughter, with which the King charged me, unfit for woman's delicate ear, which makes my blood congeal, as often as I think of it. Permit me, my lady, to speak of quite another subject."

This had an electrifying effect on the lady, and she desired him to communicate his secret. The more Simon hesitated, the more curiosity the lady evinced, until he finally said, "You are too enlightened, my lady, to believe in the appearance of spirits and demons; but I am an Essence, I do believe many things which you would discredit. You most likely would laugh at the very thing which fills my heart with horror."

This only increased the curiosity of the lady. "I promise not to laugh," she said, naively, "whatever strange things you may have to say."

"When our monarch charged me with the painful duty to investigate into the cause of great Sabion's daughter," said Simon, "orders had previously been given to remove her to a subterranean apartment of the palace. I accordingly went there with the intention to examine. Leaving the guards outside, I entered the apartment, where to my greatest surprise I found, in the place of a woman, a young and intelligent Essence. White as alabaster was his garment, his apron was the skin of the innocent lamb. A profusion of black curls encased his pale countenance, in which two black eyes, full of fire, betokened life and emotion. I looked on him, but he spoke not. I addressed him, but he answered not. I stepped up closer to him, and, by the light of the lamp, I saw the curls soiled, the white cloth bespotted with blood. 'What ails thee, brother?' I cried, but received no answer. 'In the name of God, and his angels, what ails thee, brother?' I continued, and suddenly the Essence was transfigured into a skeleton, awful to look upon. He stretched out his fleshless arm and hollow as the grave he told me, 'leave this place, death lurks here, in every corner.' I felt that I trembled. Still I attempted to speak again. But, behold, a light, such as I have never seen, filled the subterranean abode, and suddenly the vision vanished, my lamp was blown out, and I stood in the dark. I called the guard, light was brought, but I found nothing strange in the room. I left the apartment to do my duty.—Since then, I can not think of the strange vision, without being subjected to a feeling for which I have no name.—You have kept your word admirably, my lady, you did not laugh. Ah, you are frightened yourself. Are you afraid of specters?"

"Not exactly," said Salome, hiding her emotions, poorly; "your story, however, is so appalling, so shocking, indeed, that it makes one tremble." After she attempted in vain to give the conversation another turn, her whole mind appeared absorbed in that specter story—she asked Simon, "Who do you believe that demon was?"

"About that time, a young Essence was assassinated somewhere near the royal palace," Simon said, "I believe it was he that cautioned me. Sabion tells me the name of the slain was Baruch ben Menahem." He saw it well enough, that her face was deadly pale, trembling, he the physician looked beyond the paint, although it escaped the attention of Castobarus; but Simon let it pass unnoticed.

"I have heard the story told," she said, after awhile. "It is unpardonable, that such an outrageous murder should be committed in the immediate vicinity of the palace. The governor of the city should be called to account for it. Was the murderer not reached by the arm of justice?"

"Not yet, my lady," said Simon. "The governor of the city having not succeeded in detecting the perpetrator, I sent messengers to the most pious of the Essences with the request to ascertain by their secret arts the names of the murderers.";

"I do not believe in their secret arts," said Salome.

"Also my faith is somewhat lessened," said Simon; "for one says the murderer is a man while the other says it was a woman. One says love while the other maintains deep-rooted hatred was the cause of his death. One says an old widow seeing herself refused by the young man hired an assassin to take vengeance on the man. So each tells another story." Simon laughed loudly about the contradictory stories, on beholding Salome nearly fainting; and she feigned to laugh with him.

"It is amusing, indeed," said Castobarus, "to know how much superstition there is among the people. But I did not believe you, my lord, could believe in such things."

"Can I help believing what my eyes see and my ears hear?" said Simon. "There are many things hidden to one and known to the other. I could tell you stories, sir, which might cost your wits; but I am obliged now to leave your pleasant and honorable company. My duties call me hence"

Simon bowed and left the room. "A hell of shrewdness is in this man's words and looks. Castobarus, if it is true what you so often told me, that you love me," Salome cried, "get that hated man out of my way. This be the proof of your love, get that man out of my way. I hate, I abhor him. Prudence shipwrecks on his satanic self-possession, and I am certain he harbors evil intentions against all of us. Get him out of my way."

Castobarus said, this was no easy task, but he would try his best. He only begged for some time, to reflect on the subject. He went away and Solome immediately dispatched a messenger to invite Simon to another visit, appointing the hour most convenient to her.

"Thank heaven, that I see you again," said Helen, when Simon stepped into her room. "I have heard Castobarus speak to my father, and your name was frequently mentioned. And I hate that man, I know not why; so I apprehend a misfortune."

"Fear not, my sweet, beloved Helen, Providence watches over my unworthy head," said Simon. "I am Hillel's son, and the father's piety is not unfrequently the son's protection. This hated mask which I must bear, these tricks which I must play, this abuse of God's best gifts, language and intellect, which I must practice—crush me, cause me to blush at my own shadow, when I am alone. But surrounded by devils, watched by the messengers of hell, sworn to save the Queen, I must play the man whom I would have despised but a few weeks ago. Often when repentance comes over my heart and represents me to myself a roguish wretch, I think of Matatthia's daughter and my oath, and I think God must forgive me. Then I think of the prize now certain to me, the prize for which the angels would leave their heaven and combat with the demons of darkness; a prize to which nothing on earth is equal and nothing in paradise is better; Helen, my beloved, dearest, only Helen, for this prize I wrestle with Satan's guard, and now this prize is certain to me. It is certain, that your father and the King's sister, in order to complete a cabal not known yet to me, desire to see us either in love or wedded. It will not cost them much trouble to carry this point of the scheme."

Helen extended her hand to Simon. "I thank you for these words," said she, feelingly, "you spoke as though you had looked into my heart. Just now, I was with the

Queen. She, not knowing you, suspects your sincerity. I advocated your cause. She, however, thought love and sincerity can not bear such a wise and shrewd mask as you do. She is afraid you gained too fast in the favor of Herod and his particular friends, to be considered honest"—

"It is well, that she suspects me," said Simon, "it will save her much trouble."

"But, I love you too much and respect the Queen too highly," said Helen, "that her words should not have some effect on my heart. Your words, Simon are a Balm of Gilead to my heart. In this hazardous game which you play, Simon, forget not Helen's love. O, do not forget, that death in your embrace is paradisian joy, in comparison to life without you."

"No, no, no, you can not, you must not doubt my sincerity, not doubt my glowing passions," said Simon. "Doubt the purity of the angels, suspect the benevolence of light, but doubt not my love, the paradisian affections which are my source of life and happiness. I prithee, my angelic Helen, be firm in your love, firm in your confidence; for we have to go through many an ordeal before this drama will close. I must save the Queen, and I will attempt to save the King from his friends, if possible, and the people from their tyrants. If Herod listen to the voice of truth and justice, purify his court, change his Sanhedrin and alter his system of government, the revolution is made and the victory is ours. This is the object of my ambition. For this I risk my life, nay, I do still more, I bear this hated mask. But, Helen, I beseech, I implore you, let me not be tortured with the thought that you suspect my integrity. It would cripple my energies, slothfully would the blood flow through the veins, I would be no longer myself. Speak, beloved, shall your confidence be mine into whatever situations this drama forces me? Will you always remember, that my heart, my soul, my life are yours, wedded to you by the most sacred affections, a most solemn oath? O, speak, Helen."

She sunk enraptured in the embrace of Simon, and solemnly promised never to listen to the voice of suspicion, even if the Queen should speak it.

"Then, my beloved, tell your father, that I paid you a visit by your request," said Simon, "but I am cold, distant, proud, inaccessible, heartless. Tell him you doubt ever to succeed with me. But, give him a glimpse of hope, tell him you would not give up so easy. Tell him that you love me passionately, and implore his assistance to win my love."

"And what shall I tell the Queen," Helen asked.

"If, after our first interview, she suspects my motives," Simon said, "and I will attempt to deceive her—you need not contradict her. It is best for her not to be concerned in our schemes, nor to be too intimate with me. As soon, however, as she knows my intentions fully, I have cause to be less confident of success."

Several times rapping was heard at the door, but Helen would not open; but now Simon requested her to do so. Elvira came in and said a Greek wishes to see the King's physician immediately. The Greek proselyte was ushered in the presence of Simon.

"Here is the dagger and here the purse," he said. "I am hired to kill you."

Helen shuddered back, Simon laughed. "Who hired you, honest Greek?" Simon asked.

"A gentleman, a friend of yours, a suitor of a highborn lady, Castobarus," said the Greek.

"Flee to Jericho and stay there till I call you," said Simon. "The dagger and the money must be left with me. I thank you. Begone."

"Salome sent for me when I was but a few minutes gone,'" Simon said, after the Greek departed. "Was this done that I should not suspect her, if this foul assassination fails, or was Castobarus driven to this by jealousy? Hypocrisy! be thou my shield, I go to chastise the enemies of God and man. This foul, cowardish design delivers them into my hands, and, with the help of Providence, I will crush them. Helen, do you know now the object of your father's conversation with Castobarus?

This Greek is your father's bandit. Be careful, my love, you see with what a class of men we have to deal. Farewell, and be very cautious"

"Do not go from me and leave me thus alone with my agony, my fear," Helen cried; "Simon, I fear, we are lost."

"Who fears is lost," said Simon, "Fear nothing, suspect every thing, and forget not, that God watches."

Simon went to see Salome at the appointed hour. He found her in another room more elegantly furnished than the Queen's apartments. The sweetest perfumes impregnated the air. Flowers from the distant East, and birds distinguished by a gray plumage or a melodious voice, ornamented the apartment. Salome herself was so skilfully painted, and dressed so luxuriously and tastefully, that it dazzled Simon. On opening the door, when this rich and elegant scene at once burst upon his soul, he imagined he was stepping into the temple of some goddess, and Salome appeared to him like a being from a fairy world. With a smile fascinating, pleasing and beguiling on her lips, with looks half bashful and half joyful, apparently mute with joy, she extended her hand to welcome Simon. He clasped it and attempted already to persuade himself, she must be better than I first believed, when looks, malicious as a basilisk, inadvertently darted from her eyes. He pressed her hand passionately when thinking, "You shall be my slave, all your trumpery and artfulness shall not save you."

"You have invited me, noble lady," said Simon, somewhat perplexed, "and I am happy to report myself to you. I reflected all the time on another opportunity to see you, when your servant brought me your message."

"You need not wait for an opportunity; you are always welcome to me," said Salome, pointing Simon to a seat opposite her own.

"You are so kind, my lady," said he, "that I must at once tell you all I have to say, before I can have the pleasure to listen to your kind words."

"Speak, sir; I love to hear you," the lady said, smilingly.

He took the dagger from under his cloak and exhibiting it to the lady, he said, "This dagger was placed in the hands of an assassin, to render me powerless," eyeing Salome so closely, that she was alarmed, "and your friend, my lady, I mean Castobarus, paid the wages."

Here she rose suddenly, and exclaimed, "Is it possible, that he did! Are you certain, sir, that he did?"

"As certain as I am, that your intrigues, madam, killed Baruch ben Menahem," he said, "as certain as I am, that Hillel and Abba Shaul know of your criminal connection with Sabion, and can tell where your children are; yes, madam, so morally certain I am, that Castobarus hired a ruffian to render me harmless, and Castobarus is your friend."

The woman stood before the dreadful man, as the trembling culprit stands before his stern judge. Simon laid the dagger down at her feet, and, calm and cold as a hoary-headed priest, he said, "If I am in your way, kill me. You need not the agency of Castobarus and a hired assassin. Kill me, and I will die without a groan."

"By the mercy of heaven, you are mistaken," Salome cried, "I did not tell him to commit this outrageous crime."

"I am happy to hear you say this," said he, "but he interpreted your words to this effect. Is it not so? O, speak, my lady, I wish to know my deadly enemies; speak, is it not so?"

"Jealousy was his interpreter," said the lady, "I swear that he read in my heart, he detected the affection I contracted for you, and misinterpreted my words."

"What do I hear?" Salome, mighty Herod's sister, considers an obscure stranger worthy of her love?" he asked, surprised. "Nay, my ears must be sick, I dream, my brains are deranged; Salome love a nameless and friendless stranger? It can not be true. Herod's wise and shrewd sister would have me believe, that she who caused the death of her husband, lived for years in a criminal connection with Sabion, disposed of Baruch ben Menahem much in the same way as of her husband, and is guilty of this and that crime, could love, truly love a young and spotless Essence, whose every trait of character is a condemation of her numerous offences. Ah, let us not deceive each other, madam you are in a dilemma, for I know your crimes, and you are aware that I know them, therefore you desired your friend to render me harmless. But he, like all the slaves of your passions and whims, is a coward, and a hired assassin must perpetrate the deep-dyed crime. Thus the evil has become worse, and you attempt to extricate yourself by feigning love, and accusing your suitor of jealousy. Is it not so, madam? Let us be open and sincere, as falsities would do us no good. Is it not so, madam?"

"No, it is not so," she cried, violently. Grasping passionately the hand of Simon, she said, "I feel that I tremble as though I stood before the omniscient judge. I can not deny my faults; I am guilty of this and that crime, although I can not imagine how you know so much of me. Still I am not guilty of this last crime, which you lay to my charge; for I love you passionately, desparately. Like madness it burns in my brains, fury-like it storms in my breast. I could not resist. I must call and tell you, let it cost my life. I have hired no assassin, I rather would expose my breast to the assassin's dagger than yours. Load not that guilt upon my head; I am oppressed enough already."

"Is it possible, that hypocrisy, intrigue, and delusion should speak in such charming sounds!" Simon said. "Is nature thus a falsehood, that deception can assume the language of the heart?"

"O, doubt not my words, I prithee," she said, imploringly. "My heart is on my lips. I feel what I never felt before, I love for the first time in my life."

"No, it can not, it dare not be," Simon responded, in a solemn tone, "woman, thus deeply fallen, can be woman no longer, and only a woman can love. Defile not this sacred word, it signifies more, infinitely more, than the adulterous woman with murder on her soul can feel, or even imagine to feel. Passion, wild and violent, like the benumbed serpent warmed again, rages in your bosom, and you, not knowing what this means, call it love. Love is not for the wicked, not for the fallen. So God punishes sin and crime. The heart that abandoned virtue, abandons its paradise. The bosom opened to hatred and love deserts. O, do not profane the sacred word love."

Salome sank upon the sofa and covered her face with both her hands. "True, just as God is," she exclaimed, in a heart piercing tone. "I feel the crushing weight of your words. It prostrates me in the dust. But Aurion, man of iron virtue, be not more righteous than your God. Condemn not ere you have heard me. I never felt so deeply the burning shame of my life as I do now, and now and on your hands, I will return to virtue and purity. Aurion, hear me; God hears the voice of the repenting sinner, refuses not his grace to the contrite heart, eradicates the guilt from the book of everlasting memory. Aurion, here I stand and confess and repent my guilt. I am ashamed of myself; I feel bitter remorse at my own conduct. Aurion, should there be no mercy for Salome? I was thrown in a den of vice and crime. I was young, frivolous, unguarded, and being forced into the embrace of a man I hated, I fell deep, very deep, indeed. But, Aurion, help me rise again; offer me your hand, I will rise, support me and I will stand as firm and straight in the path of virtue as you do."

Simon was undecided what to say. The idea of reclaiming Herod and his vicious sister to the path of righteousness and thus to free his people from the scourge of despotism, and celebrate a decided triumph over the people's enemies, without bloodshed, was so very pleasing to him, that he wished its realization, even at the expense of his own life. The confession of Salome and her repentance sounded so sincerely and truthfully in his ear, and corresponded so entirely to his wishes, that he was inclined to believe her. Still it appeared so improbable, that a woman as vicious and corrupt as the one before him, should on a sudden leap into the embrace of virtue, that he suspected her sincerity. Then again he thought of the heavy responsibility placed on his shoulder; how he could save her or thrust her down in the lowest mire of vice; how she would be auxiliary in converting Herod, restoring the peace of the royal family, and the happiness of the country; how she could be instrumental in saving the lives of hundreds whose blood would flow; if the revolution must decide between King and people. All these thoughts with all the doubts connected therewith heaved the bosom of the Essenee and made him undecided. During this painful silence Salome sat, her face covered with a neckerchief. She sobbed audibly, and Simon could not resist. In a voice soft and fascinating as the notes of the nightingale, he asked, "You weep, cheerless daughter of Antipater?" A heaven of sympathy and kindness sounded thro' this question. She let the neckerchief fall, and exclaimed, "Ah, this is the voice of mercy, it is a tone warm from the heart. O, speak it again, my God proclaims forgiveness of sin through your lips. Once more, I beseech, I implore you, once more let me hear these glad tidings from the seat of mercy, once more and I will shout with the redeemed ones of the Lord."

"If all this is deception, then hell with all its demons are enviably innocent in comparison to yourself, madam," said Simon. "I will not slander human nature, I will not defile woman's name so outrageously, as to imagine for a moment, you play one of the studied parts of common court intrigues. I believe you are sincere this very moment, you are conscious and ashamed of your past conduct. If this is so the mercy and forgiveness of heaven may pour the Balm of Gilead in your wounded heart. If so it is, may God bless you with new strength to become a blessing to yourself, to your royal family and your people. Behold, heaven weeps over the fallen angels and rejoices at their rise. Woman is an angel on earth. However deep she sinks, she is an angel still—a fallen angel. Hold yourself not to my feeble hand but to that of God; rise and walk in the light of God and virtue. But I must tell you also this. Great sins are chronic diseases, the cure of which must be radical and requires a long time. Deceive yourself not. If you repent now, you may relapse to-morrow. Stand first again at the brink of beguiling sin and turn victoriously from it. Stand once more at the gate of shame and lock it with your own hands. Triumph gloriously over vice and crime when beguiling and flattering they knock at your door. Then know that you have truly repented your sins and are again heaven's child, God's angel. Then feel the zephyr of peace from a better world, gently cooling the glowing bosom. Then approach the heaven of love, and be enraptured with the golden rays of its thousand suns. Till then, farewell."

"Ah man, leave me not, abandon me not again into the dark hell of vice, let me not alone with my remorse, my repentance, my mortification, my love, my despair," she cried, in accents of madness. "I am too weak to walk alone the unknown path of virtue. Lead me, for heaven's sake lead me with your love, your wisdom, your virtue."

She fell down and embraced the knees of Simon and cried, "Behold, Herod's sister at your feet like a low slave, behold her pray and weep for mercy. Aurion, have mercy on the fallen woman, who wishes to rise on your hand. O, have mercy with a wretched, cheerless heart which yearns after love and happiness, after the bliss of innocence and purity."

Simon lifted her up, and, in the most flattering and soothing terms, he begged her to be quiet. He told her, that he would regard and lead her with a truly brotherly love, that he would be at her side as often and as long as he could; but he could not promise what his heart did not feel, he could not deceive her. She was satisfied and dismissed him with much kindness.

"Ha, ha, ha, young Essenee, you are not practiced enough yet in high life," Salome laughed, when he was out of the room. "He is too beautiful not to be a most enviable prize to any woman. My good man, you must be my husband or I am determined to ruin you. Why, with such a husband, I believe I could be as virtuous as Susanna and as kind as mother Rebecca. Wisdom, wealth, rank, beauty, nothing it appears would catch him. Virtue, repentance, a fallen angel attempting to rise, ha, ha, ha,—that is his passion. He shall have it as often as he pleases, and I will climb up the whole ladder of Jacob, if I can reach him. He is too excellent a man, that he should not be a high recompense for my trouble to become virtuous."

Simon never was so undecided, as he was when leaving Salome. He could not imagine that her repentance and love were not sincere; still he could not persuade himself to believe that his appearance and short conversation should have so wonderfully, affected her, as to change at once her whole course of life. He considered it impossible to return her affections; his love to Helen and his aversion to the King's sister were too powerful, to allow him to think otherwise. Helen's wretchedness, if he should violate his pledge of love, he thought would fury-like persecute him through the rest of his life. Still he was convinced of his capability to save Salome from the abyss of vice, reclaim her to virtue and goodness, and thus also turn Herod for the better, and spare to his people the horrid scenes of a bloody revolution.

In such a dilemma Simon walked about in the park, blind for the beauties of nature and the luxury of oriental vegetation. He saw not how profoundly those bowed whom he Passed, for he was engulfed in a train of thoughts which appeared to have the mastery over him. Suddenly he stood still, gazed on the artesian well as though he was to ascertain the laws on which it operates. "I must see her first and then to Jericho. My father's wisdom will guide me," he murmured. Quick as lightning he returned to the palace, bid farewell to Helen, and told her that he immediately must return to Jericho, to be back in a few days. Helen appeared very much displeased with her friend's determination. She could not resist giving expression to her apprehensions; but Simon pacified the apprehensive heart. Kissing her hand he turned to part, but she again requested him not to leave her so suddenly and unexpectedly, as she had evil omens.

"Be not foolish, my beloved Helen," said Simon, "I am the messenger of a good cause, and can not stumble. I must go to Jericho, to hear the advice of my father, and ascertain where the people's council now meets. None at this court must know whither I went, or that I am absent. Tell the Queen I will see her again in a few days, at present my duties call me hence. Tell your father"—Here he suddenly stopped and, after reflection, he continued, "tell your father, you suspect Salome to be passionately enamored with me, and I, therefore am cold and distant."

"But this is not true," Helen remarked, quickly.

"I tell you it is true and a good piece of news for your father," said Simon. "It will set him mad."

"You are mistaken; my father hates her," Helen interrupted. Then she looked upon Simon so inquiringly and sadly, that he instantly understood her. "Fear nothing, my only love," he said, "Helen is the name of the angel who shall lead me over the rugged path of life. My love is part of my life, one terminates with the other. But your father, good Helen, is lost, as he deserves it. Embitter not this parting moment with unkind words, my sweet love, I must act as I do."

He left the room. Once more she stretched her arms out after him, then he was gone. Simon met Castobarus in the hall. "My lord, your purse and dagger reached me," said Simon, "I shall return the compliment at the earliest occasion."

"I do not understand you, my lord," said Castobarus.

"Never mind, I understood you," said Simon, "the Greek, ha, ha, ha, the Greek is a very good interpreter of secret thoughts."

He went away leaving, Castobarus alone with his surprise. He went instantly to see Sabion.

Sabion came into the apartment of Helen and found her in tears. "What ails you, my child? Why do you weep," he asked, in a sympathising tone.

Helen looked on him for some moments, without knowing what to say. "If the father deceives his own child," she said, after awhile, honesty and integrity must no longer be sought among men."

"What means this, Helen?" Sabion asked, "I do not understand you."

"It ill becomes the daughter to admonish her father," she continued; "but the wrong is so great, indeed, that I must speak what I feel, what mortifies, torments me."

"I am curious, indeed," said Sabion, resuming a seat. "Let me hear, Helen, what ails you."

"Was it not you who directed my attention to the King's physician, and taught me to love him?" Helen asked. "Did you not do so by the advice of Salome, whom you know to be every body's enemy? And did you not hire an assassin, you and Castobarus to kill that very man, you have taught me to love? You can not deny it; for here, in this very room and in my presence, the Greek ruffian confessed his guilt, confessed still more, that you hired him to slay an old man in Jericho, which he could not do. Do you know now, why I weep? I weep because I have no father."

Sabion was perplexed. He walked the room in rapid strides. His small eyes rolled unusually quick in their sockets. He bit part of his underlip between his teeth, so that agitation spoke from every one of his features. When Helen was done he frequently exclaimed, "What a lucid imagination this girl has! She imagines things which are not even possible."

"No imagination, truth as clear as heaven," Helen said; "reality is every word I say. You denounced your own child to the King, and put my life in jeopardy, not a word of rebuke passed my lips. But I can not stand this outrage. You yourself, I have yet your ring, you wanted me to marry Aurion, and you yourself hired an assassin to slay him, slay him after he has rescued me from the executioner's hands, after he has become so dear to my heart. A father hires an assassin to kill the lover of his daughter.—All ties of nature are broken; honor, humanity, charity, affection, all that is dear to man fled to the wild beasts; monsters, devils in the shape of man, have remained, and you can ask me yet, why I weep? I weep that my mother is no more, and I have no father."

"Go, Helen, and tell what you know to the Queen, that your father may receive the punishment due to him," Sabion said, with a malicious smile on his lips, "so that it be not said, the daughter being aware of the father's guilt was his co-adjutor."

"Thus you did, but I shall not do it," said Helen, "you tied my hands to deliver me to the executioner, to ingratiate yourself in the King's favor; because you are no father. I am a child, and a child betrays not its father."

"Then go and tell your lover to do it," said Sabion, "that you be free of the guilt."

"I exercise no influence on him, he is cold and distant," said Helen, "and after this occurrence, I will most likely see him no more. I can not tell what he will do."

"Have you said all you know?" Sabion asked. "Now I will tell you the contents of the story. The cunning Essenee finding himself ingratiated in your favor invented this story for two purposes, I suppose; to have an excuse not to pay you his address any longer, and to carry out his evil intentions against me; he proves to be an enemy of mine:"

"Aurion invents no stories," Helen said, "he is a man of integrity such as this court has none."

Here Castobarus entered hastily. "I must be alone with you, my lord," he said. Both looked most embarrassed on each other. Helen observed it and rising from her sofa she said, "You may speak out, my lord, the secret is broached, the Greek assassin confessed every word, your dagger and purse are in the hands of Aurion. Just speak out, what you have to say, I know the secret."

"I understand now, you, desirous to ruin me, hired a man of whom you knew, that he would betray me," Castobarus said, rashly. "I understand Sabion's tricks and I will make up for it. Now, just now, I go to Salome and tell her how faithful her friend Sabion is."

"Be dumb, infernal liar," Sabion cried.

"I shall not be dumb, I shall speak," Castobarus replied. "I will have you rewarded for your kind services."

"You both deserve the golden medal,"

said Salome, on entering the room, "and you shall have it."

"You shoull long ago have been exposed to the contempt of a world," said Sabion, "and you shall have it."

CHAPTER VII

THE SCHEME DISCOVERED.

"Remember, Menahem, I know to a certainty," said Abba Shaul ben Botnith, "that Sabiou, in executing the orders of Herod, killed your son Baruch. He was represented to Herod by his sister, as the particular suitor of the Queen. Jealousy was the cause of his violent death."

Neither Menahem nor Shamai was prepared to answer. It was impossible for them to doubt the words of Abba Shaul. "This one act, if no other crime could be proved on Herod," Abba Shaul continued, "is all-sufficient to justify the revolution The King has no right to condemn a man without a hearing before the Sanhedrin. This is our security of person opposite our rulers. Herod violated this dearest of our rights. The compact between King and people is broken. Our lives are in danger, we must protect ourselves. Baruch was the son of Menahem, the particular friend of Herod, yet the young man was slain. Hence, neither our rights nor personal friendship are a sufficient guarrantee against the violence and wicked passions of Herod. Our arms are the only security of person left us, and if we do not make proper use of them, it is our own fault; we commit suicide."

"Abba Shaul, jealousy is a dreadful monster," said Menahem. "A man is scarcely responsible for what he does under its influence. As little as the intoxicated man can be judged by his doings in that condition, so little, indeed, can you judge a man by what he does under the influence of jealousy. Great men have great passions; hence Herod's passions are greater and more violent than ours. Will you condemn him for his greatness?"

"The greater the passions, the more powerful is the intellect in man to control them," said Abba Shaul. "So harmoniously, indeed, and so wisely proportioned the soul goes forth from the hands of its Creator. Wickedness is the nutriment of the passions, and gives them the superiority over man. Righteousness elevates the mental powers of man to dominion and superiority. Herod's unbridled passions demonstrate his immense wickedness. Not his Creator, but Herod is accountable for his unlimited wickedness. The wicked should not govern a nation whose mission it is to preserve and promulgate justice and virtue. Therefore Herod has forfeited his claims upon the crown of Israel, and the revolution is a sacred right, a divine judgment upon the guilty head of an arbitrary ruler, whom every patriot curses."

"'Thou shalt not curse the prince of thy people,' sacred scripture says," Menahem interrupted.

"'If he acts becoming thy people,' Israel's sages added," Abba Shaul said, hastily. "Herod acts unbecoming even the notorious violence of Roman lords. Trained in the bloody school of the triumvirate of Antony, Octavius and Lepidus, whom he saw wading through the blood of their countrymen, and passing recklessly over the mutilated bodies of their fellow citizens to power and dominion—backed by those very legions who committed all those outrages in Rome, hired by Rome and hated by all Israel; he attempts to fortify his tottering throne with our corpses. If we can stand this, we deserve no longer to be God's chosen people. Therefore the iron dice of the revolution shall be cast to decide, whether this land belongs to Israel or to Rome and her royal slave."

"Two wrongs never made one right," said Shamai. "Revolution is synonymous with murder and massacre; but God commands, 'Thou shalt not kill.'"

"Tell it to your King," said Abba Shaul. "Tell him, morever, that God commands him to write a copy of the Law, to be perpetually before him, that he depart not from its commandments, either to the right or to the left. O, do tell it to your Herod, that the Highpriest Joiada also knew the Law, when he commanded the death of the wicked Queen Athaliah. Also the prophets Elija and Elisha were godly men, still they preached rebellion against the house of wicked Ahab, and the prophet Amos was a righteous man who advised the people to insurrection against the second Jeroboam. Tell your King, Israel is the people of justice, and the highest tribunal thereof. If the King is a murderer, the people will try, condemn and execute him, as God has commanded. Those who offer resistance to the arm of justice, who shelter or defend the murderer, are guilty of the same crime, and their heads are forfeited to justice, to the People. The revolution is the tribunal designed to do justice to the murderous King. Tell him we come to punish a vulgar assassin as the Law commands."

'To increase the hatred of Rome against Israel," Shamai said. "You kill the King whom Rome has given us, and Rome's legions will punish every man who was concerned in it, and give you a King worse than Herod."

"Worse? I deny it," said Abba Shaul. "The Roman legions are of bone and flesh, so are we. If they come to fight us, we will go to fight them. The death of the brave is preferable to an inglorious life. If the King which Rome might again impose on us, will know that we executed his predecessor, because he was a murderer, he will respect our laws, and if he does not, we will, and his death is certain. This is my doctrine. But, it is not quite as certain, that Rome can take care of Herod. The two greatest armies the world ever saw prepare for a deadly combat, in which only one, either Antony or Octavius can be victorious. If Antony is defeated Herod is lost in Rome, and among us he is lost long ago. We must strike the blow, and trust in God and the justice of our cause."

"Say but little, do much, and let all thy doings be in the name of heaven, is my adage," said Shamai. "Why do you speak of revolution, if you know, that you can not make it? Herod stands with a faithful army near Cana, and the people have no power to oppose it. Why do you speak of revolution, if you know, that God hates violence and bloodshed?"

"The armies of Herod are of our blood and of our flesh and will hear our cries of woe," said Abba Shaul, "and if they hear not, they will feel the unimpaired strength of Israel, the power of an outraged people. I know that God hates violence and bloodshed, therefore I speak of revolution, to break the arm of violence, and make an end of bloodshed which marks nearly every day of Herod's reign."

"Your anger and hatred exaggerate the crimes of Herod," said Shamai. "Look upon them from the point of view which others choose, and they will be much diminished."

"Diminish them as much as you please, reduce them to a thousandth part of their real magnitude," said Abba Shaul, "and they are still monstrous enough to be condemned to ignominous death by any impartial Sanhedrin, if the perpetrator was no King. Was there ever a time when Israel's King stood above the law? Herod is the first to whom this exception is granted. This exception is fatal to Israel's rights and liberties, is the sword of destruction suspended on a hair above our heads. This exception, sires, demands a bloody revolution."

"Do not pronounce these words with such terrific pathos," said Shamai; "they offend every sentiment of my heart. But one thing is fatal to Israel, to desert the laws of God. God's laws are not of a political character. Let him govern who is best fitted for it, and let us worship the Lord and be pure. None dies except Providence decrees his death, and none rules unless God tells him to do so. Ye Pharasees connect the laws of God with the rules of government, to the detriment of the former. Abba Shaul, worship God, and know, who ever submits faithfully to the kingdom of heaven, feels no longer the yoke of earthly rulers; but whoever shakes off the laws of God, presses on his neck the kingdom of man. Let those rule who do so, and worship God. Better that Herod kills than you do. It is better to suffer injustice than do it. Correct not your neighbor's faults by your own. Assume not the executive staff of Providence; for the hands of man are frail. Man's destiny on earth is to worship God and be pure. Who governs worships not, and whoever soils his hands with the blood of man is impure."

"Such are the sentiments of the Essenees," said Abba Shaul, "but they are not mine. Although I am not capable of refuting your arguments, still they do not convince me, and so they would none who is not an Essence. Israel's happiness rests on three divine pillars; truth, justice and union are their names. Remove either and the old superstructure crumbles to fragments. Herod attempts to remove the central pillar of the colossal palace, and it must fall. It is not the will of God that man should suffer injustice, I feel it. It can not be the sole object of man to die always in order to live an eternal life; for God taught us, what man must do to live happy. O sires, you move in your own sphere of learning and piety, so that the humble cottage of the plain, common man is unknown to you."

Menahem who had been a silent spectator all this time asked Abba Shaul, "How do you know, that my son was killed by order of Herod?"

"A sacred oath seals my lips," said Abba Shaul, "I can not tell you the particulars; but rest satisfied, that I know it for a certainty."

"Also, Jonathan ben Uziel said so, and many other men, whose veracity is beyond doubt," said Menahem. "Let us now go to the academy and hear what news Jonathan ben Uziel brings from Egypt. Then I will go to Jerusalem. I must ascertain the fate of my son."

"Help, help me!" the Greek proselyte cried, running into the house of Menahem, pursued by several armed men. The three men rose from their seats to protect the man. Abba Shaul stepped in between the persecutors and the persecuted with the question, "What do you want here?"

"In behalf of justice," said one of them, "this man is a murderer, he killed a young man in Jerusalem."

"It is not true, my lords," the Greek cried.

"Who in Jerusalem authorized you to arrest a man in Jericho?" Abba Shaul asked.

"The Sanhedrin," was the short reply.

"There is none in Jerusalem, except you call Herod's creatures by that honorable designation," said Abba Shaul. "The members of the lawful Sanhedrin are in Jericho. If the man is a murderer he is now here in the city of refuge, and here he will be tried."

"We must convey him to Jerusalem," said the men, "if you refuse we must apply force."

"Beware, or you are lost," Abba Shaul thundered. Drawing his sword, he continued, "he is a dead man who touches this Greek."

"He is a murderer."

"Prove it before the Sanhedrin."

"We will do it in Jerusalem."

"No, you must do it in Jericho."

"He killed Baruch ben Menahem."

"It is an infernal lie," Abba Shaul vociferated. "You are the blind or the willing tools of a vile and satanic plot. You stay in Jericho to prove your own innocence." He gave a signal with a small whistle, and in a few moments the shrill notes resounded through all the lanes of Jericho. A large number of men immediately surrounded the house. Abba Shaul called several in and told them to take care of these men and this Greek, whom they accuse of murder, as all of them must be tried by the lower Sanhedrin. The men were disarmed and, together with the Greek, led away.

"These are the servants of Sabion," Abba Shaul said, "the very same men who attempted to arrest me. Desirous to remove the suspicion from Herod and his co-adjutors, he accuses a stranger, who he thinks has no friends, of the foul murder they themselves committed. Is there none in Israel whose gall overflows at such schemes? Are we all heartless slaves? It must be tried, we must appeal to our people, let them respond to my questions."

Abba Shaul hastened after the prisoners, while Menahem and Shamai bent their steps to the academy.

The whole city was in a state of intense excitement when this news spread. "We are not safe even in Jericho," some vociferated. "If he is the murderer of Baruch ben Menahem, he must die," others exclaimed. "It is one of Sabion's foul plots," a third party maintained; but none advocated the return of the Greek to Jerusalem, until he was tried by the Sanhedrin of Jericho. When, therefore, the Sanhedrin opened its session the next day, all the doors and windows of the building were thrown open, to satisfy the curiosity of the excited multitude who filled and surrounded the house.

On an elevated platform sat Akabiah ben Mahalalel, the chief judge of the Sanhedrin of Jericho, with two secretaries on both sides of the platform, before which in a semicircle sat twenty two judges, behind them sixty nine graduated pupils in three rows, and around them the curious multitude. Menahem stepped before the judges and, bowing reverently, he said, "I in the name of the God of Israel and in behalf of his holy law, demand justice of you, venerable Sanhedrin."

"So may God do unto us now and for evermore, Amen," the judges responded.

Menahem then narrated the story, how his son was found slain in the city of Jerusalem, and how several officers came to this city to arrest a Greek, as being the murderer of his son, but the people insisted upon trying the case before the Sanhedrin of Jericho. He concluded with the consideration, that the Sanhedrin of Jericho had no right to try a man for a crime which he committed in Jerusalem. He thought the duty of the Sanhedrin was to ordain that the Greek be placed before the Sanhedrin of Jerusalem.

When Menahem had resumed his seat, Jonathan ben Uziel rose on the opposite side, and said, "It would not be right for me to rise and speak in the presence of so many sages of Israel, so much older and more learned than myself, if it was not as the sages of old said, 'Where the name of the Lord could be desecrated, one may violate the respect due to his superiors.' The name of the Lord is desecrated, if it should be said among the Gentiles, there is no justice in Israel. Our fundamental doctrine is, 'There shall be one law and one statute for you, the native and the stranger.' Violate this law in the least point, and the name of the Lord is desecrated among the Gentiles. Therefore I rise in the presence of these venerable masters, to defend the Greek accused of the murder of Baruch, my deceased and lamented friend."

Every eye was fixed upon the young sage, when the chief judge said, "The Sanhedrin grants you permission to defend the culprit."

"Jericho is now the city of refuge," said Jonathan, after bowing to designate his gratitude. "The law states, plain enough, the procedure in this cause. The Greek is among us and claims our protection, and the law imposes the duty on you to decide, whether the Greek is a murderer. I claim, that he is innocent. But should you ascertain the contrary to be true, you must refuse to protect him any longer, and deliver him to the officers who claim to be the avengers of the blood of my deceased friend. This is the meaning of the law, take its letter or its spirit."

The secretary read the argument of Menahem, and his colleague read the reply of Jonathan to the listening judges and the silent spectators. This done, Menahem rose and replied: "Moses pointed out three cities of refuge, Bezer, Ramah in Gilead and Golan. Joshua, in obedience to the law, appropriated three more cities to the very purpose, Kedesh, Shechem and Hebron, this side of the Jordan. Jericho is not among these cities; it is no city of refuge. If Moses and Joshua named the cities, how can we add a seventh city of refuge to the six prescribed by the law? If this is no city of refuge the murderer must be sent to the place where the crime was committed, where the witnesses are found and the circumstances can best be ascertained. If Jericho is the altar of learning and piety, our law commands the murderer must be taken from the altar, to die. If justice dwells in Jericho she must eject the murderer."

"If he is a murderer," said Jonathan, when Menahem had resumed his seat. "But to ascertain this is the duty of this Sanhedrin. Jericho, I maintain, is a city of refuge by the force of circumstances, and by appointment of the sages. Look into the law and behold, first it ordains, that cities of refuge should exist in Israel. Then it says six such cities should exist. And finally Moses named three cities and Joshua three more, in obedience to the law. The law exists independent of the number and names of the cities. If these cities be destroyed, the law is not abolished, and other cities must be appropriated to this purpose. Herod has decided that the cities above named should no longer be cities of refuge; for whoever of his opponents escaped to any one of those cities, was nevertheless arrested, carried away and executed. The cities of refuge are no more, but the law still exists. It is the duty of the Sanhedrin to enforce the law, hence they must appoint other cities of refuge. The members of the lawful Sanhedrin escaped to this city, and only in this city they have jurisdiction, beyond its limits, Herod and violence rule supreme; hence Jericho must be appointed the city of refuge. If our sages had not decreed so, they have proved by their actions, that such is their will. They sought refuge in Jericho and refused obedience to the summons of the King and his Sanhedrin, where they stand accused of high treason. How dare they refuse obedience, if they considered not this a city of refuge?"

Menahem attempted to refute the arguments of Jonathan. When he said the sages refused obedience to Herod and his Sanbedrin, because they consider them illegally constituted, Jonathan told him therefore no obedience must be paid them in this case. When both were done and the secretaries had read again both sides of the argument, the Sanhedrin after a short debate decided, Jericho was a city of refuge, under the prevailing circumstances, and the cause of the Greek must be tried by them. The Greek and the officers from Jerusalem were arraigned before the judges. Having read to them the usual formula of the oath, to which they responded Amen, and the law concerning false witnesses which ordains the same punishment for the false witness which his testimony, if true, would bring on the culprit, and having admonished them solemnly to speak the truth before God, at the sacred seat of justice, all except one were led into an adjoining chamber, and one after the other was examined and cross examined. Aware of the severity of the law, and knowing the unexceptionable justice of the Pharasees, the officers only stated, that they were sent to Jericho by Sabion, in the name of the lower Sanhedrin of Jerusalem, who considered the Greek guilty of the murder of Baruch ben Menahem. Nothing more could be learned of them. When Jonathan asked the multitude whether there were witnesses in favor of the Greek, two peasants came forward and told the story, how they when taking the first fruits to Jerusalem were arrested by the men now before the judges, taking them for two other men, and how they were treated until a party of strangers rescued them from their hands in the Valley of Hinom.

It was evident to the initiated, that the officers were the servants and spies of Sabion. The first idea of many was, those spies came for a double purpose, to arrest the Greek in order to remove the suspicion of murder from Herod and his servants, and to ascertain the doings of the Pharasees at Jericho. Abba Shaul's testimony only confirmed that of the peasants, but threw no light on the principal point of the case. When Jonathan asked again, "Are there any more witnesses among you?" a boy whom Jonathan instantly recognized as the one who was his guardian angel in Jerusalem, came up and stated, "I am a servant of Sabiou's daughter. I saw Baruch ben Menahem in the subterranean room of Herod's palace. The men before you tortured him till he died. They executed the command of Sabion, which he received of Herod. I administered the last drops of water to the parched lips of the expiring victim of wickedness. When I wept, yonder wretched man dragged me out of the room, and there I heard the last groan of Baruch. So help me God, now and forever."

Two men supported Menahem who sunk, fainting, from his seat. "I can tell you still more," said the boy. "This Greek was hired to kill Hillel and his son Simon, hired by Sabion. But the Greek informed Hillel and his son of the murderous intentions of the vile and wicked man. Therefore, he is desirous to have this Greek in his power. I can tell you still more, but this is enough at present."

A shriek of terror and indignation was heard like distant thunder, from the multitude. Akabiah restored order, when Menahem rose, deadly pale was his countenance, blue and quivering his lips, dim and nearly breaking were his eyes. "I retract. I take back my accusation. The Greek is innocent," was all he could stammer forth, then his friends led him out of the hall, a picture of calamity.

The Sanhedrin dismissed the Greek and retained the four officers for a further hearing.

Then the Sanhedrin adjourned, the indignation of the people became so loud and violent, that it was difficult even for Abba Shaul to conduct the four officers to their prison. Jonathan searched in vain among the crowd after the mysterious boy; he had disappeared.

"I know everything thou canst tell me," said Hillel to his son Simon, "The Greek proselyte has told me, how thou art the physician and friend of Herod, and of several of his courtiers. Thou shouldst never have forgotten the admonition of thy father. Behold! my mother was a daughter of the royal house of David, and my father was a nobleman of Benjamin, of King Saul, some maintain. When she died, and she was a great and good woman, she called me to her couch, and bid me to bring honor upon our family. Her voice always re-echoed in my heart. As Joseph saw the portrait of his father when sin threatened to beguile him, so did I see on all occasions the picture of my dying mother, and heard her last words, 'Bring honor upon our family.' I began to inquire after the meaning of those words, but was much puzzled with their ambiguity. To amass wealth, I thought, must be the way to honor; for I saw nearly every man did bow at the shrine of Mammon and its lucrative priests. But then I thought, is it really an honor to see my money respected by others? What is it to me or to the house of my father, if a number of selfish men worship the chests filled with gold which happen to be mine? I am not the chest, nor am I the gold, both have not the least affinity to myself. Then I saw my opinion corroborated; for as long as my neighbor Adoniram was wealthy he had many friends and admirers; but as soon as he was poor, he was an object of ridicule to those who formerly honored him, and his faults were heralded to the world.

"Then I thought to study the wants and wishes of the people and attempt to satisfy them, in order to be elevated to offices and high dignity—must be the way to honor. But then I saw Kings who were murderers, a curse upon their people, and the lowest slaves of their passions and their accomplices. I saw men high in rank and low in the scale of virtue, eminent in position and despicably low in the estimation of their fellow men, honorable in dignity and disreputable in their doings. Then I saw the honorable and dishonorable condemned at once by a thoughtless multitude, and thought, also this is vanity and windy thought.

"Be poor, and no false friends will deceive thee, I thought. Govern none and none can condemn thee. Let all thy worth and thy value be in thy heart, so that but thou and thy God know them, and none will envy thee. Be humble and live retired, and none will defame thee. Respect thy neighbor, and he will respect thee. Honor thyself with virtuous doings and wise pursuits; and rest secured, honor will ultimately come; but if it come not it is not thy fault, and thy God knows it. So I thought I would obey the behests of my dying mother, and I have honestly attempted so to live.

"Are not these the doctrines I have implanted in thy youthful heart, and was it not my best joy, my only pride, thy mother's delight and thy sister's and brother's hope, to see thee walk on the path of righteousness? My son, if thou departest from it, thou art guilty of patricide and matricide, for both of us must be dead to thee. My son, my son, I fear the favorite of Herod must be a wicked man or become one. Who walks in the council of the wicked, stands on the path of sinners, sits in the company of scorners, must he not be or become one of them? My son, my son, my apprehensions are dreadful."

"O do not suspect my motives, my father," Simon cried, in accents of acute pain, "do not thus doubt the sincerity of your first born son. The praise or condemnation of a world besides you is indifferent to me; but I can not bear the thought of being misunderstood by my own father and great teacher. I thank God every morning, and praise him every evening, that you are my father and my teacher, and your lessons are deeply rooted in my heart. O do not suspect me, I beseech, I implore you. Hear me, I will explain my conduct, then judge. Correct me, if I am wrong, and your word shall be my law, encourage me if I am right, and your words shall be my pillar of fire in the obscure path of life."

Hillel appeared to be appeased, and, in a mild tone, he said, "Speak, my son and I will hear."

"Herod returned from Cana," said Simon, "with the firm conviction, that the Queen and her family, together with Cleopatra, conspired against him. Since then I have ascertained, that not the Queen but one of her relatives is guilty of this crime. I was selected by the representatives of the people, to go and save the Queen and Baruch ben Menahem from the iron grasp of Herod. I was introduced to him as an Essenean physician. I met him as virtue confronts wickedness, and he submitted, after a short struggle. The Queen is saved, but Baruch ben Menahem was executed before I reached the palace.

"While in the palace I came in contact with the courtiers, counsellors and creatures of Herod, as also with his sister, Salome, and I found Herod's wickedness to be angelic virtue in comparison to his friends and officers. People say the Essences can cast out devils and banish malicious demons. I thought the learning of the Essences and their practical arts might be well applied in this case. Cast out the devils and banish the malicious spirits from the court of Herod, and he might be saved yet. Our people might be spared the calamity and bloodshed of a revolution. Justice and internal peace being thus restored, Israel might gain new strength, revive, rejuvinate, heal its wounds and regain its native buoyancy, to win its independence of Rome, to be Israel, free and united once more as in days of yore. Is not this sacred aim worthy of an attempt? Father, it may cost my life, but not my virtue."

"Praise and glory be rendered to God on high," said Hillel, "that I hear my son speak thus. Death is not the loss of life, for endless is the life of the righteous; the loss of virtue is death, irreparable death. Thank God, my son is determined to live.—What are the means thou wilt apply to effect this reform? It is a difficult task and requires a colossal exertion."

"In the presence of Herod but one sort of means is effective, and I have applied it with success," said Simon. "Honesty, integrity and uprightness connected with the natural boldness of virtue and innocence, are the means to make a man his superior, and this proves, that there is still a spark of goodness and humanity in him which, if properly nourished, might yet become a sacred flame, to burn out of him all that is vicious and corrupt. But his courtiers, friends, officers and servants, all who surround him, are irrevocably lost, not a touch of humanity, not a trace of goodness is discernible in them. Shrewdness, cunningness, avarice and ambition lead them, and no means are too low or base to them, if they are subservient to their purposes. Shrewdness, cunningness, adroitness, superior to their outworn wits, are the only means to be applied in managing them. It is difficult to poison a serpent, to entangle a fox in his own schemes; but I can not master them otherwise."

"This is a dangerous game, my son," said the old man. "The upright man never should assume a mask. The mask for wickedness, and honesty to the righteous is the straight way."

"Truly, my father, so it should be," said

Simon. "But when it has come so far, that virtue must hide her face, piety must be ashamed of herself, and innocence is the object of ridicule; then a mask is necessary to dethrone the despots, cast out the devils and banish the malicious demons. A mask woven of shrewdness and cunning, a mask to baffle their feeble heads and dazzle their dim eyes—will do the work which virtue fails to accomplish by her usual frankness and uprightness."

"So it must be, my son, so it is the will of God," said Hillel. "Disguise and cunning are the crutches of baseness, on which the vile man, for awhile, passes through the world, until they break, and he lies prostrated in the dust. But virtue makes no use of those crutches, nor can the man with sound limbs handle advantageously the support of the lame. My son, thou wilt not succeed with them on this score, for they, by the very nature of things, are thy masters. David could not smite the Philistine with the best arms of the warrior, for he was not practiced in using them. The simple implements of the shepherd sufficed to secure him the victory; for his hand was trained to handle them, he smote the lion and the bear, why should the Philistine have escaped his well practiced eyes and hand! Cast away the disguise and the mask, they are the crutches of the base and depraved, the arms with which thou canst not smite the Philistines, thou art not practiced in the use thereof. Confront Golia with the shepherd's cane and flat stones, with thy own arms, and if thou canst not smite him, he will not slay thee."

"What a contrast, Hillel and Herod, Hillel and Sabion!" Simon exclaimed, enthusiastically. "My heart revives in your presence, my glorious father, my great teacher. After having heard for weeks the voice of crime, corruption and depravity, after I nearly turned away with disgust from mankind, it is Balm of Gilead, the light of heaven, the voice of Seraphs to my heart, to hear you speak again, so noble, so true, so generous, so wise.—How happy a son I am, Hillel is my father." He embraced and kissed his father. In a state of fervent enthusiasm he continued, "How good would Herod be and how happy Israel, if Hillel occupied the position of Sabion. How great is Israel, it gave birth to Hillel!"

"Thy filial love and enthusiasm mislead thee," said Hillel. "I am neither better nor wiser than a thousand others in Israel. A thousand other men would tell thee the same, under similar circumstances.—But we are not at the end of our conversation. Tell me all thou hast to say."

"Sabiou's only daughter Helen, the fairest and loveliest of the daughters of Israel," Simon continued, "is the object of my fervent love"—

"Beware, young man," Hillel said, rising from his seat, "beware, Samson against that Delilah!"

"Do not say so, my father, I prithee," Simon continued. "Helen is worthy to be Hillel's daughter. She is pure and spotless as the blue vault of heaven. The maiden's heart is innocent and modest as the rose of Sharon, smiling blushingly under the verdant foliage. Her soul is the breath of heaven, capable of all that is good, noble and generous. She is the fairest form, inhabited by the noblest soul, which peeps in heavenly glances through her eyes. I loved her and she knew it and swore to be mine, before I was aware whose daughter she is. To desert her now would be vile treachery and a hell of torture to my soul."

"Well do I know what the Law ordains, the child should not suffer for the sins of the parent," said Hillel. "God himself visits the iniquity of the fathers only on those children who continue to hate Him, abide in the wickedness of their fathers. No man is better than the Law of God. But I fear, my son, love bedims thy vision, thou seest the beloved in the soft beams of the moon, where the beautiful and perfect only are visible, while the imperfections are in the dark shade hidden to the delighted spectator."

"You, my father, by your wise and generous teaching formed my heart, to be a safe touchstone for virtue and wickedness," said Simon. "There is an impulse in me, that never deceived me, by which I discriminate at once the virtuous from the vicious. There are certain criteria, undeniable symptoms, in the sound of a man's voice, the looks of his eyes, the totality of his features, the posture of his body, the formation of his mouth, which are the correct expressions of the soul. The soul is the cause, the outward appearance of man its effect. Do not similar effects entitle us to think of similar causes? Yes, so benign is our God, that he gives us eyes to look into the heart of man. He gives to virtue another visage than to vice. If not all my knowledge of man deceive me, if my heart belies me not, for the first time, Helen is as kind and pure as Heaven's angels. She looks so much like the deceased Baruch ben Menahem, that she must be as good as he was."

"Also, this philosophy is not without exception," said Hillel, "but I am inclined to trust in the impulses of thy heart. The similarity of Baruch and Sabiou's daughter is quite natural, for their mothers were near relatives."

"Still Sabion was his murderer!" Simon exclaimed, despondently.

"He would execute his own child, if it serves his base purposes," said Hillel.

"True, my father, very true, and Helen knows it by sad experience," said Simon. "But, let us not forget the trial, my father; the Greek proselyte will be tried to-day."

"Do not care for that," said Hillel, "no injustice is done in Jericho, where the Law reigns supreme, and no point of law can be disregarded or falsely construed, where Jonathan ben Uziel pleads, and Akabiah ben Mehalalel presides. Both are there. Let this not disturb thee, go on, tell all thou hast to communicate."

"My love for Helen is my safeguard," said Simon, "that no woman will ever capture my heart. One, however, attempts mightily to conquer it, and this one is Salome, Herod's vile and debased sister."

"She is an adulterous woman," said Hillel.

"With a double murder on her soul," Simon added. "I know all this and still more, she is the worst devil at the court of Herod. The most bloody cabals and treacherous designs are her work. Sabion, Castobarus and Dositheus themselves are her slaves, she is the primitive serpent which poisons the heart of Herod. This very woman, my father, knelt in the dust before me, gave free utterance to her repentance and remorse, swore that on my hand she would rise from the mire of vice, walk the path of virtue, and become an ornament to mankind. First, I thought I must crush the serpent's head at my feet; but then I hesitated. If she could be reclaimed to God and virtue, Herod's change for the better, the fall of his slaves, is a certain fact. The responsibility thus laid on my shoulder is so great, that I could not decide without your paternal advice. Shall I thrust her back into the embrace of triumphing Satan, and let the revolution decide between Herod and Israel; or must I offer her my hand to reclaim her, reclaim Herod, heal the breach between him and his people and give to Israel years of peace and happiness? The struggle in my soul is violent, tormenting, burning, I can not decide. Every tho't is a tear, every idea is a painful sigh, I can not decide. Here is Helen, love, happiness, paradise, a sacred oath and—a bloody, desperate revolution; there is Salome, a life full of hell, torment, despair, a cheerless and joyless existence, and—peace and happiness to Israel. My father, I am not virtuous enough to decide. Your word shall be my law, my pillar of fire."

"There is the error under which thou laborest, my son," said Hillel, "thou believest to outdo the wicked by disguise and dissimulation, and this is the handicraft of the wicked only. I tell thee, Salome deceives thee. A woman fallen so deep, so low into adultery, murder and heartlessness, can rise no more, except God's punishment, pain, disease, poverty or misery awaken her from the horrid slumber. She lives in wealth and superabundance, surrounded by the luxuries and pleasure of a court, her conscience is deafened daily by a roar of interchanging hilarities. It would be a wonder, indeed, as marvelous as the death of the Egyptians in the Red Sea, should she repent her sins and feel shame and remorse about her past conduct; and wonders are not wrought every day. Didst thou do anything there, which should have prompted her to so sudden and unnatural a change of mind?"

Simon answered this question in the negative, and Hillel continued, "Then believe me, either that lubric and voluptuous woman lusts after thy youth and manly beauty, or she intends to destroy thee, and therefore she feigns repentance.—Thou just hast told me of Salome's crimes, tell me also, does she know of thy knowledge of them?"

When Simon affirmed also this Hillel continued, "And still thou believest her sincere? still thou supposest she does not intend to ruin thee? Be wise, my son, and beware of the fallen woman, who must hate thee violently on account of thy knowledge of her crimes."

"Does Hillel live here?" was heard outside, and in a few moments the door opened and Elvira, dressed as a boy, as we have seen her before the Sanhedrin, came in, and having bowed respectfully before the old man, she said to Simon, "I must see you alone."

"I have no secret before my father," was the answer.

"Well then, I will speak," said Elvira. "When you scarcely was out of the gate, Helen came to me, she was irritated, shocked, as I never saw her before. I inquired after the cause, and she told me, how she accosted her father in an unguarded moment, and called him to account for all the wrongs he had committed, especially being concerned in the assassinating scheme. The three good creatures, Sabion, Castobarus and Salome met and accused each other of the most shocking crimes and treacheries, in presence of Helen, who gave free utterance to the disgust she felt, until her father violently pushed her out of the room, when she came to me. I trembled for her safety and advised her to flee instantly to Jericho, but she refused. I never left her, for I feared the worst. Toward evening she was called to the Queen, and since then I have seen her no more."

"Where is she?" Simon asked almost paralyzed with surprise and apprehension.

"Besides God, only the three monsters and their accomplices know it," Elvira responded. "Sabion laments, so loudly and genuine paternally, the disappearance of HIS ONLY child, that any intuitive mind must decypher his guilt at the first glance. I went to the Queen and told her all I knew, and her indignation is unlimited. She has immediately issued orders to all officers in the city and country; but I am afraid it is in vain, Helen is somewhere, where the Queen's power has an end."

Simon regained his presence of mind. He looked about himself as the lion before he rushes to the deadly combat. "And if they have sent her to the end of the world," he roared, "I will find her. And if the shield of Judah Maccabee protects the perpetrators, I shall dash it in pieces and punish them for their outrages, their satanic crimes. We shall measure our strength in a few short days, either I crush them, or the arm of the people, the hand of justice shall overreach them and"—

"Not so hasty, young man, not so desperate," Hillel said, slowly. "Do not speak what thou knowest not yet to be in thy power to do."

"I only see my power in all this," said Simon, "they are afraid the assassinating scheme will enrage Herod against them, and they remove the two witnesses Helen and the Greek out of their way. The onslaught to arrest the Greek failed, and I am Helen's patron, I will bring her back to annihilate her monstrous father.—She would not believe me, how wicked and monstrous he is, she defended him, advocated his cause. Ah, Helen, poor maiden, now she must suffer for it, for her filial love and confidence." —Here, he suddenly stopped, turned slowly to Elvira, grasped her hand and asked in a hollow tone, "Elvira, is she not dead?"

"I know not," she said, despondently. "I believe not, that the father would murder his own child."

"I know that he is capable of the worst," Simon said, slowly, and looked upon his father, in whose countenance he supposed to read an affirmation of the latter sentiment. "Bless me, my father, that my strength fail not," Simon cried. Hillel laid his hands upon his head and said, solemnly, "God giveth and God taketh away, the name of the Lord be praised."

CHAPTER VIII.

THE DECISION OF THE PEOPLE.

East of the Jordan river, opposite Jericho, Mount Nebo looks down upon the plain of Moab, and tells the glorious story of Israel's victories under the lead of Moses, the last days of that giant of antiquity, his death and mysterious burial. There is a cave in Mount Nebo, in which the prophets held their secret councils, when the Kings of Israel or Judah went astray; in that cave the prophet Elija was hid, and the people surrounded it with a thousand marvelous stories. The cave after many windings, ascends and descends, leads to a valley thro' which the Zered passes, a valley almost inaccessible from any other point, as the Zered winds its way to it through perpendicular rocks and narrow arches, and leaves it in the same manner. The palm trees which crowd the fertile valley of a perpetual spring gave shelter and food to many fugitives. It was the principal place of meet ing for secret bodies. It was, therefore, called the valley of Zanaim, or the humble.

Many a solitary wanderer at that day bent his steps toward Nebo, some riding on asses, while others walked slowly over the plain with rude staffs in their hands. At the mysterious cave a fire burnt, around which some fantastical shepherds danced whenever a stranger appeared. Then they would ask him, "Whence comest thou and whither doest thou go?" If the stranger answered, "I come from the mountains and go to the valley," they would continue asking, "And what seekest thou in the valley?" If the stranger answered, "Light," and added to it "Nena," which are the initials of the Hebrew verse, "The light of the Lord is the soul of man," the shepherds would tell him to stay, and whenever a party was together, one would take a torch and lead them through the cave to the valley. Near the end of the cave a band of armed men stopped the strangers, and asked them the same questions which Simon and Jonathan were asked on entering the secret hall under the Temple of Jerusalem. The answers being correct they were given another leader to the valley of Zanaim. But if the answers could not be given they were led into a branch of the cave, where they were instructed in the secrets and sworn to support the revolution.

The valley was soon filled with a large number of bearded men, upon whose countenances a solemn earnestness was enthroned. They stood or laid together in groups, and conversed on serious topics.

"Hark! Jonathan ben Uziel speaks," said some. "He was in Alexandra and knows a great many new things." The crowd congregated around the speaker, who gave a full description of the grand preparations making by Antony to meet the armies of Octavius. He said that Cleopatra promised, none should interfere with the people of Jericho as long as it was under her protection. She issued orders to give effect to her words. "She also promised her aid and cooperation in case of revolution against Herod whom she hates violently. But all this is of no particular consequence to us," Jonathan continued, "for if Cleopatra aids us she will long after the land of Judah, and Antony will give it to her, if he is the only lord of the Roman empire. What profit is it to us to serve Cleopatra instead of Herod?"

"First let us dethrone Herod," some of the crowd vociferated, "then let us talk of the intentions of Cleopatra."

"So it is," said Jonathan, "we are strong enough to dethrone our tyrant. If Antony is victorious, Cleopatra will prevent him at least from supporting Herod. If Octavius is the hero of the day, we have nothing to fear of him; for Herod supports Antony. Cleopatra is a woman and resides in Egypt, she can not be as dangerous to us as Herod is. Besides this she promises not to interfere with our laws and religion. Cleopatra can easily be dethroned in Judah at an opportune time Her beauty is her power and this will soon fade, then we are again independent."

"We need not wait so long," one ejaculated. "First dethrone Herod, Cleopatra is not fit to govern Judah, she will soon learn this and let us alone."

"Let us have a plan of action," said Akabiah ben Mehalalel, "understood by every leader, and let us agree here to act accordingly. The sages and scribes of Jericho have agreed upon a plan; let us examine it first. Simon ben Hillel is commissioned by them to inform you of their scheme of action."

Simon ben Hillel appeared before the people, and after having communicated his experiences at the court of Herod, and having given expression to the hopes, to reform Herod and banish his present courtiers and officers, he continued, "The wise men of Jericho abiding by the decision of the people's council at Jerusalem propose to extend the time of operation to the Passah week. They desire Herod to agree and swear to the following points:

"1. He must banish from this country all his courtiers, officers, servants and spies, and fill the vacant offices with faithful Pharasees, such as are known to the Sandedrin as capable men and friends of the people.

"2. The present Sanhedrin of Jerusalem to be dissolved and a new one formed under the presidency of Hillel and Menahem. The members of the new Sanhedrin are written down on this scroll, which I hand you for examination.

"3. The Sanhedrin must be fully reinstated in its functions and powers as the laws of Israel ordain

"4. None shall be entitled to fill the office of a judge in Israel, unless he has obtained this right from the superior officers of the Sanhedrin. The people shall elect their judges from the candidates so qualified, and none shall interfere with them. The lower Sanhedrin shall fill its vacancies from among the judges so elected by the people. The highest Sanhedrin shall fill its vacancies from among the most prominent members of the lower Sanhedrin, without interference of the King.

"5. The decisions and laws of the Sanhedrin shall be supreme without any other sanction.

"6 The King shall have no right to interfere with the dispensation of justice; nor shall he be accountable to the Sanhedrin. But all his officers shall be subject to the law.

"7. None in Israel shall be prohibited to speak, write or teach what he thinks proper. None of them shall be accountable to any other than the legal authorities. None shall be punished for any crime except a Sanhedrin so ordains. None shall be obliged to go to any foreign land except the Sanhedrin commands it.

"If Herod agrees to these stipulations, we swear him the oath of allegiance to be sacred and inviolable, as long as he faithfully adheres to these points. If he refuses, the revolution is an act of necessity and must be carried into effect, notwithstanding the precious blood that will flow.

"Let all be prepared for the Passah week, let the thousands of Israel come to Jerusalem with their paschal lambs and be ready for action at any moment's notice. Abba Shaul with his chosen men will be in the hall under the Temple. At a given signal they will break forth through the secret entrance, take possession of the Temple and appeal to the people. Then let every man be ready for action, and take Jerusalem. Abba Shaul will make the proper preparations to this purpose and appoint the chieftains of the different divisions. If at that time Antony is lord of Rome, we can only force Herod to accept our terms and cause Antony to withdraw forever all Roman troops from our territory. But if Octavius is lord of Rome Herod and his officers shall be tried before the new Sanhedrin and punished according to the mandates of our laws. In this case the Sanhedrin shall be permanent and supreme, until the people have agreed upon a government and carried it into existence."

A shout of joy, resembling the roar of a cataract, resounded after Simon was done. Powerful was the re-echo from the ancient mountains, clefts and caverns. The plan was accepted with enthusiastic applause. Some, however, objected to some points.

"Why should Menahem sit at the side of

Hillel," one asked, "when we know him to be no friend of the people, but an admirer of Herod?"

"He was but is no more an admirer of Herod," Jonathan said. "Ever since he is convinced of the atrocious murder of his own son, he knows the true character of Herod. Besides, it is well known, that Menahem and Shamai are the heads of the Essenees and of a powerful faction among our students. One of them must be elevated to honor and high dignity to satisfy the rest. Menahem is preferable to Shamai, being of a milder disposition and sweeter temper than the former. Also among the Sanhedrin there are, besides Shamai, many prominent Essenees, especially as they are well acquainted with therapeutics, demonology and the kindred sciences, which a Sanhedrin must know, as you are all aware."

"Why should we grant Pardon to Herod," another asked, "if the revolution be victorious, in case Antony remain the lord of Rome?"

"Because we are not prepared to fight the Roman legions," said Abba Shaul, "but we can force Herod to subscribe to our terms, and send the Roman legion from the country. As long as the dispensation of justice is in our power our rights and liberties are secured, and Herod can not wrong us. This is the main point in the contest."

"We want no King, we need no King at all," several of them vociferated. "As long as Israel had a King, there was no end of the national misfortunes. If we are victorious let us have the republic again. We are capable of self-government, we need no guardian. Down forever with the King; the Sanhedrin and the judge, as in days of yore, shall govern the nation."

"None of us wants a King," Simon responded; "but every one of us is convinced that we must have one if Antony is the lord of Rome; it must be either Herod or Cleopatra. If Herod swears to our terms he is preferable to Cleopatra, because he is a man and a heroic warrior. With Cleopatra at our head we are a dependency of Egypt, and with her we are the tail of Rome. If Octavius is victorious we are free of our tyrant, and may carry out all our wishes."

"Why should you have Hillel as your Nassi of the Sanhedrin," urged one of the Shamaites, "when you know the man's humility and softness of character? If we have a republic, that man with his excellent virtues would exactly suit to watch over the dispensation of justice, especially as he has no ambition, not the least desire after wealth, not the remotest aspiration to appear to his neighbor any better than he is. Yes, if we have the republic again, Hillel is our best man to preside over the Sanhedrin. But if Israel remain a monarchy under Herod with his iron will and intriguing ways, will Hillel be firm enough to protect the interests of Israel? Would not Shamai be the best man to oppose Herod, to hold him within the limits of the law? Shamai's energy and firmness of will, connected with his eminent piety and excellent virtues, would be a barrier to our rights insurmountable to Herod or any other ambitious tyrant. Reflect well on this point, it is the most important of the programme exposed to your consideration."

Akabiah ben Mehalalel responded promptly. "I appreciate the philosophy of my neighbor. The highest virtues make the best man of a republic, and the best man must preside over the Sanhedrin. But in a monarchy where the interests of the people must be guarded against the encroachments of a grasping ruler, determination, boldness, firmness of will and purpose must be added to the other virtues, to befit a man to the highest civil office in the country. Let any man come and say, he has discovered a weak trait in Hillel's character, unless he calls goodness or deliberation a weakness. My neighbor agrees with me, that Hillel is the best Nassi of a republic we could find. I will prove, that he is also the best man for that office in a monarchy. First, I must tell him a story. A pagan had seen the Highpriest in his official attire. He went instantly to Shamai and desired him to be received in the covenant of Abraham, provided that he might become Highpriest. Shamai indignant at the ambitious motives of the pagan, drove him out of his room. The pagan went to Hillel and stated his request. 'Sit down my son, study the Law, I will assist thee, and decide thyself, whether thy request can be granted,' said Hillel. The pagan studied the Law diligently and became daily more delighted with its wisdom and purity. When he arrived at the passage, 'And the stranger who comes nigh (the altar) shall be put to death,' he asked Hillel, 'does this law also refer to the Israelite?'—'To every man who is not a son of Aaron,' Hillel replied.—'I do not wish to be better than Hillel,' said the pagan, and he became a pious Israelite. Hillel's humility and kindness opened to the inconsiderate man the gates to the kingdom of heaven, which Shamai's rashness barred before him. Place Shamai in a juxtaposition to Herod, and they will quarrel perpetually. Let Hillel occupy the same position, and he will master any despot by wisdom, goodness and mild words. He is the man to meet Herod."

"With due deference to the excellencies of the learned Shamai," said Jonathan ben Uziel, "it must nevertheless be admitted, that Hillel is the favorite of the whole people, and every man is convinced he will defend our rights at any risk and hazard, as there is nothing in this world which could bribe or delude him, for he wants nothing. The bread he eats and the garment he puts on are barely enough to sustain a beggar. Wisdom and knowledge form the aim of his existence. Virtue and kindness are parts of his nature with which he can as little part as with his hands or his legs. The Nassi of Israel is our representative, the depositary and bearer of Israel's laws and traditions. This is Hillel, and Hillel only. Deny it who can. But if none can deny it, the question is decided, the greatest man must be our Nassi."

"'There is a time to do for the Lord, they set aside Thy Law,' said the Psalmist," one called from the crowd.

"Read it right," said Akabiah, "'This is the time to do for the Lord, they have set aside Thy Law.'"

"Are you sure, that Hillel will accept this high dignity?" another asked.

"None asked him," said Jonathan, "but we all know his doctrine. Since there are no prophets and no *Urim* and *Thumim* anymore in Israel, God reveals His will through the voice of the people, is his doctrine. He pays obedience to the will of the people, if they require no wickedness of him, for in this latter case God has spoken, 'Thou shalt not follow the multitude to wickedness;' God has forewarned us, not to listen to the voice of prophets, who preach against the Law of God, 'For the Lord your God trieth you to wit whether you love the Lord your God with all your heart and all your soul.'"

The decision of the council was unanimous in favor of Hillel and Menahem. Also the rest of the programme was adopted with the exception of one clause. Jonathan ben Uziel, and with him a great many others, defended their opinion, in case Antony become the sole master of Rome, Cleopatra was preferable to Herod. The arguments on both sides were so wise, that the council could arrive at no decision. Here a messenger from Jerusalem was announced. The man stepped in the midst of the council, and announcing himself as a messenger of Babah ben Butah, he informed them, that Herod in battle utterly discomfitted the King of Arabia, and now pursues him to his very capital. This gave another turn to the deliberations. A shout of enthusiastic and patriotic applause inadvertently burst forth from the multitude. The victorious arms of Israel, the proud lion of Judah, the triumphant warriors of Jacob were so loudly and enthusiastically applauded, that even Abba Shaul thundered forth his admiration and joy.

When the noise subsided, Abba Shaul said, "If we must have a King, let us have a man who is capable to lead our armies, protect our country, and maintain the honor of our warriors. If Providence decrees that we must have a King, let it be Herod, if he swears to our terms."

A thunder of enthusiastic applause was the response of the multitude, and this point was so decided. Abba Shaul having appointed his captains and subaltern officers, the men from the different parts of the country were instructed to prepare their neighbors for the outbreak of the revolution, let them come to Jerusalem the week before Passah feast, where plenty of arms would be in store for them, and at the first appeal from the Temple let every man do his duty. Then the council adjourned to meet again in the subterranean hall of the Temple, Sunday night before the Passover.

"Abba Shaul, where is Helen?" Simon asked, when they went back to Jericho. A sigh, deep and painful wrung from his bosom, when he asked this question.

"I can not tell yet," said Abba Shaul. "Sabion has a private house, now almost a castle in the valley of Sharon, separated from the next town by a thicket of Sycamores. There he lived for months with Salome alone and undisturbed. If she lives, she might be there. I will go there and see. You shall hear of me in Jerusalem."

"And if she is not there?" Simon asked in a melancholy tone.

"Then may God help her and console you," said Abba Shaul, "then I fear for her life."

Simon did not speak one word more that day. He returned to Jericho panting after the consoling word of his pious father. There, indeed, there he found the balm of consolation, as such a father can distil into the wounded heart of a wise and beloved son.

CHAPTER IX.

DAY OF ATONEMENT.

The streets and lanes of Jerusalem were thronged with people at an early hour of the morning. A checkered line of human beings floated through the avenues, and rose like gigantic and variegated columns to Mount Moriah, where the morning dawn was greeted with the powerful and harmonious accords of the levitical chorus and orchestra. The Hallelujah of the mighty chorus was borne aloft to the blue vault of heaven, on the wings of harmonious music, in which the powerful notes of the trumpet, cornet, and drum were blended with sweet sounds of the flute, the cymbal, harp and *cystrum*. Solemnly these currents of music re-echoed in the colossal dome, greeted and invited the thousands of pilgrims who hastened toward the sacred spot.

The Temple, its numerous cloisters and spacious courts, filled rapidly with myriads of worshippers from all parts of the eastern lands. The Roman and Grecian costumes, the wide and white cloak of the Egyptian, the Persian parti-colored tunic and gold embroidered girdle, the turban, brass helmet and scarlet cap with gold tassels, variegated the waving ocean of human beings. The luxury and gaiety of the orient, contrasted with the simplicity of the Essences and Galilean peasant, the solemnity reflected on every countenance, the silence reigning supreme among the innumerable multitude interrupted only by the occasional strains of sacred music resounding from an invisible chorus, rendered the scene grand and sublime.

Herod, Mariamne, the royal family in the state vestments, preceded by a guard of honor, surrounded by the courtiers, in their rich costumes, and followed by the Sanhedrin, the highest dignitaries of the state and the city, the delegations from Rome, Athens, Alexandria and Babylon, and another guard of honor closing the grand procession —entered the court of the Temple. The people gave room to the approaching dignitaries; but none saluted them with a word or mien, for here a higher than a mortal King resided, He before whom all men are equal, because all are His children. Every look followed the stately procession, but none spoke or bowed.

But when the Highpriest appeared in the white, sacerdotal vestments of the day, and approached the sacrifice between the *Ulam* and the altar, a sacred awe appeared to electrify the multitude. The chorus and orchestra were silent, the myriads of worshippers presented a smooth sea untouched by the wings of the wind, the Highpriest laid his hand on the head of the sacrifice and confessing his sins he implored God's pardon with a loud and sonorous voice, concluding with the scriptural passage, "For this day I will be appeased unto you to purify you from all your sins before God," here he stopped abruptly; for as he pronounced the ineffable name of the Lord of the universe, all the people from the King to the humble peasant, priest and layman, men and women, fell down upon their knees, prostrated themselves in the dust before the Lord of Hosts, each repented his sins and transgressions, and worshipped the God of grace and unlimited mercy. The thousand fold Hallelujahs which now resounded from the levitical chorus, accompanied by the thunder of trumpets and warbling flutes, melting gradually into the soft piano of the harps—appeared to announce the pardon of God to Israel, seemed to be a greeting voice from heaven to his children. When the people slowly rose the Highpriest with his hand stretched forth to bless the people finished the biblical sentiment, "Ye shall be purified," and the multitude in an awful chorus exclaimed, "Praised for ever and ever be the glorious name of Israel's Majesty on high." Then the Highpriest concluded, "And Thou extend thy mercy to the congregation of Jeshurun."

Thrice was this solemn scene repeated. The Highpriest confessed his sins, the sins of his tribe, and the sins of Israel. During the intervals priests and people sung solemn psalms. But when, after the last confession, the Highpriest with the censer of burning incense entered the *sanctum sanctorum*, a silent awe rested upon the multitude, and every one yielded to the devotions of his heart. Every knee was bent, all hands folded and every head dropped in prayer and silent meditation. Then the Highpriest appeared again on the steps of the Temple. His solemn words, "Rise Israel, from the dust, God thy Redeemer liveth, He forgives sin, iniquity and transgression," rushed like an electric stream through the thousand hearts. All rose suddenly and the most unbounded enthusiasm broke forth in joyous hymns, in harmonious shouts of happiness and sacred delight. The trumpets, cornets and drums thundered forth the enthusiasm of the thousand happy hearts and vied in delightful excellency with the power of the people's voice, the sweetness of the flutes and harps, and the notes of the thousand singers in the levitical chorus. When the Highpriest had blessed the people and changed the white for the usual vestments of his office, the people thronged around him to congratulate him, shake his hand or kiss the borders of his cloak.

All rejoiced, every heart appeared filled with delight and gladness, except one, and this one was Mariamne, the Queen. She could not help remembering when her grand-father, her uncle, and last her youthful and admired brother filled that place of high honor, which now an obscure stranger occupied. And these reflections on the side of Herod, of whom she was sure he was the murderer of his brother, were the more dreadful and tormenting. All others rejoiced, but her eyes were filled with tears, tears of sadness.

Meanwhile the grand procession formed, to escort the Highpriest home to his palace. The man with the ram having left for the mountain of Azazel, under the salutations and congratulations of the priests, the procession commenced to move out of the courts of the Temple. A herald proclaimed, "Thy sins, Israel, are forgiven, the Highpriest returns to his house. Come, come, do honor to the man of God." The descendants of the different royal houses of Israel, followed by the descendants of David, headed the procession. The Davidians also had a herald who exclaimed, "Do honor to the house of David." Then came the Levites and Priests. The Chiefs of the former were dressed in blue silk, and the chiefs of the latter were dressed in white silk. Next came all the singers and musicians in three divisions, first the vocalists, next the band with stringed instruments and last the orchestra with the trumpets, cornets and drums. Behind them the sentinels of the Temple-gates, the artists and garrison followed. Next came the treasurers and the key-bearers. The first division of the procession was followed by the King, his court and body guards. After them came the Sanhedrin followed by one hundred constables, bearing silver axes, as an emblem of their office. They preceded the Highpriest who was surrounded by the oldest priests, who were followed by the authorities and guards of the city, and the multitude of the people who chose to follow. The rich men of Jerusalem were dressed in white silk, rode on white asses and bore white wax tapers in their hands.

As the procession moved through the city the windows were brilliantly illuminated and decorated with versicolored banners. The strains of music and song were drowned by the powerful voice of the people's enthusiasm, greeting and saluting the returning Highpriest, and giving free vent to its feelings as the different divisions passed. Also groans and hisses were heard sometimes amid the cheers. "Where is the old King?" several shouted at different spots when the King and his court passed; for the old King, the grand-father of Mariamne was not among the courtiers. Angry looks and angry words followed. The officers attempted to arrest some, but it was impossible to do it in the dense crowd. "This is not OUR Sanhedrin," was the cry at some other places, heard in the midst of the cheers. "This is not OUR Highpriest," some few had the courage to remark, but were silenced by their neighbors. The efforts of the officers to silence the people were in vain, the crowd was too dense and unmanageable. The sacredness of the day was a sufficient guarantee to all, that no disturbances would take place. The procession, indeed, moved on without any disturbance, to the palace of the Highpriest, where the *Nassi* gave him a golden tablet bearing the inscription, "I, Onias, the Highpriest, conducted the sacred ceremonies in the Temple of the Lord, the Day of Atonement, 3659 years after the creation.' Then the great banquet in the palace of the Highpriest concluded the festivities of the day.

Otherwise the Day of Atonement was celebrated in the Synagogues of the Essences and also otherwise in the Synagogues of the Pharasees. But altogether different the day was spent on the hills and mountains, in the vineyards and olive gardens. The daughters of Israel borrowed white garments of each other, so as not to put to shame those who had none. All of them, the princess no less than the daughter of the humblest citizen, were dressed in borrowed white garbs. No Jewels were worn this day, also on account of those who had none. Head, neck and arms were ornamented with wreaths of flowers, blossoms, myrtle and vine leaves, which to wind tastefully was a particular skill of the oriental women

Early in the morning the young women left the city in different groups with their harps, tambarines, *cystrums* and flutes and went to a vine-crowned hill, followed by the young men. Arrived on the hills, they sang, played and danced in their peculiar style. Forming a group opposite the young men they sung somewhat like this:

"Rejoice in the grace of God who pours the Balm of Gilead into the wounded heart. This is the Day of Atonement. God pardons sins and iniquity; he eradicates Israel's transgressions from the book of everlasting memory. The Highpriest enters the most sacred apartment, approaches the seat of mercy, and behold God is nigh. Thy sins, O Israel! are forgiven, thy God looks graciously down upon thee. So strike the timbrel, let resound the sweet accords of Judah's harp, proclaim the grace and loving kindness of our God."

Then again they played and danced. When again they formed into a group the young men answered in about the following words: "The daughter of Israel in her white garb, the finest symbol of innocence, praises the grace of our God, heralds the forgiveness of sin to Judah's happy sons. The heart revives, silent are the sighs, joy divinely fills the soul. Shout glory and joy to the majesty on high, thy sins are forgiven, thy guilt is forgotten. How pure and fair, how beauteous and dear are God's heralds of pardon to Israel's sons."

Then the young men danced and when they halted again the maidens responded somewhat to this effect: "Look not upon beauty, turn thy eye from female charms. Beauty like roses fades, the luster of the eye like star-light vanishes. A generous heart with noble virtues adorned like the precious stones on the Highpriest's shield, emanates a light soft and pleasing, a light that never dims. A soul free from guilt is a sun that never sets. The heart of woman is a temple of God. Love is the highpriest, forbearance prepares the sacrifice, innocence is the light that burns on the golden candlestick, affection is the incense rising from the golden altar to the Lord of Hosts. Look not upon beauty, turn thy eye from female charms, look upon the heart, the soul, the family."

So the day was spent until the signal was given from the Temple roof, that the High-priest left the Temple, when the different groups and companies returned with song and music to the city.

Simon and Jonathan went the whole day from one public place to another, to ascertain something of Helen's whereabouts. But in vain, they had discovered no trace, not even the remotest idea of her place of existence could be formed. But Jonathan had seen Elvira in woman's dress. She appeared so beautiful to him, that he could not help thinking of her all day. They had returned to the city. Jonathan went to the place which Simon had told him to choose, and Simon went to the palace to see Herod.

Arrived at the palace, Simon was requested to appear instantly before the Queen. This was a welcome opportunity to him, as he expected to learn something about Helen. He repaired to the Queen's apartment without delay. He was admitted without cere mony. When he stepped into the brightly illuminated saloon and cast a shy look on the great and beautiful woman in the flowing white robe, who received him standing, a model statue of a model artist—when his look met the large black eyes of the Queen staring obliquely on him, he inadvertently knelt down before the majestic daughter of the Asmoneans.

"Rise and stand erect," said Mariamne, "none must bend his knee before a mortal being. This homage is due to God only."

Simon rose and looked firmly into the countenance of the Queen. There was a pride and a self-conscious majesty in that countenance, softened by features of the most tender goodness, which he had never observed before. "You are the image of God, my gracious Queen," said Simon, in a fascinating tone, "I adore the Creator in His most perfect likeness."

The Queen smiled on remarking, "Is this the language of the stern Essence or of the courtier ?"

"It is neither," Simon replied, quickly; "for truth is not in the extremes."

"Then let Hillel's son speak to me in his honest, free manner," said the Queen, while resuming a seat. "I know that you have been my savior, when Herod suspected me of treachery. Elvira, in the anguish of her soul when Helen was lost, told me more than I expected. I know of your laudable affection for Helen, her unlimited love for you, and the part you played with Sabiou. I am in possession of his ring. Hence an open and frank conversation will do good to both of us. I must first apprise you of two facts. I can not find Helen, notwithstand the most diligent search all over my domains. Yet I do not despair of escrying her prison. The second fact is, that my good, unpretending and harmless grand father, the venerable old King and highpriest, the man of a thousand misfortunes—is accosed of treachery, of a secret correspondence with the King of Arabia. Herod, on returning from the seat of war, begged pardon of me in a most fervent eloquence, begged me to forgive him the error of accusing me of treachery. But he told me, that he is certain, he holds the evidence in his hands, that my good, old grand-father, who suffered so much, in this world, the hoary King and highpriest, held a treacherous correspondence with the King of Arabia. I beseeched, I implored him, not to believe it; but be insisted upon it, and swore that the matter should be laid before the Sanhedrin"—

"Then he is lost," Simon interrupted, "for the whole Sanhedrin are the creatures of the King, and the presiding officers are weak and pliable men."

"O, do not say so, young man," the Queen lamented, "I can not bear the idea. If he is lost, I can not live. I can not outlive this sad and cruel injustice sanctioned by the Sanhedrin of Israel. Devise means to save him, and let me find the means to rescue Helen. Young man! Helen for my old grand-father. If she is beyond the deserts, in the distant Germania I will find her, and return her to you. Devise means to save my grand-father, I will love you as my brother, the savior of my family. My wealth is yours, your wishes shall be mine. You have risked your life to save mine, do not stop at a work half done, devise means to save my grand-father."

"I know not, my gracious Queen, that I have the power to devise such means," said Simon; "but, if I have, no promises are necessary to prompt me. 'Who saves one human life has observed the whole Laws of God,' say our sages. This is enough of promise, a sufficient reward to me. To prevent so hideous a crime, so burning a shame to rest upon our country, is a stimulus which must prompt every patriot to risk his life. Whatever my humble abilities allow I shall cheerfully do. But, my gracious Queen, Helen, where is Helen? I can not think, am incapable to concentrate my thoughts on any subject."

"Therefore I tell you, let me have the care and pleasing duty, to find Helen," said the Queen. "Let my grand-father be your only thought, and entrust your love to my care." The Queen extended her hand to Simon, "Give me your hand and your word," said she, imploringly, "that you will do so."

"I can not," said Simon, "I can not promise, my gracious lady, that which I am not certain of performing. I can not master my affections, they have dominion over my thoughts. I think of Helen, when I wake, I dream of her when I sleep. My soul is engulphed in the wounds of my heart. I can not yet think. But I promise you, my noble Queen, that I will attempt, manfully will I attempt to do my duty, to regain dominion over myself. I will honestly attempt to devise means; but I can promise nothing."

"I am satisfied," said the Queen. "Whenever you desire to communicate with me, you are the King's body physician, you may at any time call on me."

"I thank you, my gracious lady," said Simon; "but at the same time I must beg you to remember, that Herod dislikes"—

"He was delighted to hear of me, that you did not speak to me of his suspicion," said the Queen. "He called you the most upright man of his acquaintance. He said you, more than all, were capable to be a friend, and recommended you highly to my particular attention."

"Still I must request you, noble lady," said Simon, "not to speak favorably of me to your royal consort. I have good reasons to prefer this humble request to you."

Mariamne blushed. "Do you speak of Baruch ben Menahem?" she asked somewhat perplexed.

"I know that Salome's intrigues killed him," said Simon, "I fear no intrigues. There are certain things of which ignorance is bliss. My gracious Queen, I beg this favor of you, do not speak favorably of me in presence of your royal consort."

"I do not understand you," said Mariamne, "you hide a terrible secret in your bosom, it appears.—But I do not wish to know it. I have full confidence in your honesty of purpose, and promise you to be careful with my words, when speaking of you in the presence of Herod."

Simon bowed, designating his intention to leave; but the Queen asked him, "Have you seen Salome since you returned from your journey?"

"Not yet, my noble lady," he answered, "I suspect her of co operation in the abduction of Helen, and determined upon not seeing her before I am certain of it."

This gave no satisfaction to Mariamne, she could not discover Simon's secret; still a knowledge thereof appeared important to her. She attempted several times to learn something of Simon, but in vain, he was mute on this point, and answered every question with so much frankness, that the Queen came to the conclusion, that nothing could be learned of him, and dismissed him with tokens of kindness and particular grace.

Simon thought this was a proper time to see Herod. He was at the highpriest's banquet, wine and hilarity may have rendered him more communicative than usual. He went to the King's reception room where he met Sabion. Without returning his compliments, Simon said, in a tone of bitter sarcasm, "The great Sabion watches at the King's door that he be not abducted, like his only daughter."

"What means this, my lord?" Sabion asked, somewhat perplexed.

"It means the ring, you understand, Cleopatra's ring, which you sent me through your daughter. It means the assassin's dagger which you and Castobarus sent me afterwards. It means that Helen and the ruffian, my witnesses, must be disposed of in the best possible way," said Simon. "It means nothing of importance, only plain things. You know how easy it is to abduct, to assassinate an individual, and you, faithful man, watch at the King's door, that no harm befall him. O you are an honest servant."

Observing the embarrassment of Sabion, Simon continued. "It was very wise and truly paternal of you, that you sent Helen away from this court to a quiet country place, so that her young heart be not infected with the reigning vices of the court. You are not only a faithful servant, but also a kind father."

"I do not understand a word of what you say," Sabion ejaculated. "You are terrible in your accusation."

Here the door of the King's saloon was opened and Herod called out, "Is not this the voice of Aurion?" Simon bowed respectfully, and Herod invited him to step in the saloon.

"I am very happy to congratulate you, my lord," said Simon, "on your glorious victory over your enemies."

"And why is Aurion so late with his congratulation?" Herod asked.

"I returned to the city but yesterday," said Simon. "To day, being Day of Atonement, I could not have the pleasure to do my duty."

"And where were you so long?" Herod inquired.

"I went after the witnesses to prove my report," said Simon.

"Is proved already," Herod said, hastily. "The Queen is innocent. The conspiracy in the valley of Hinom was a product of Sabion's imagination, and his daughter, who then attempted and failed to run away with her lover, succeeded after all; for gone she is, and the old father knows not whither."

"My lord, you are again misinformed," said Simon; "in regard to Helen, you are decidedly misinformed."

"Again misinformed!" Herod ejaculated. "Who misinformed me?"

"He who told you Helen run away with her lover," said Simon. "I know this affair much better."

"Her own father, sir, her own father says so," said Herod. "Must not I believe what the father says of his daughter?"

"If the father is not Sabion," Simon responded, dryly.

"You are no friend of Sabion," said Herod, "the much more cautious should you be with your words."

Simon bowed reverently; then he said, "My lord, what is my sin or transgression, that I am attacked by an assassin in your very palace?"

Herod looked surprised on Simon, who continued, "I was attacked by a paid assassin, and Helen is my witness; therefore Helen disappeared."

"Have you an idea of him who hired the assassin?" Herod asked.

"I have no mere idea, but the positive knowledge, that Sabion and Castobarus hired the assassin," said Simon. "Their foul play being discovered, Helen was removed to some unknown place, and the assassin was arrested in Jericho by order of the Sanhedrin, through the servants of Sabion, accused of the murder of Baruch ben Menahem. That was done to get the second witness out of the way. But there is yet a third witness in existence, whom they forgot to silence, and this is Salome, my lord's own sister, she has knowledge of the whole scheme."

"Is it possible! Nay, it is certain, slaves, yes slaves are cowards, and cowards hire assassins," Herod cried. "Scandalous, the father brings his own daughter into ill repute, to cover his shame; and I, how unhappy a man is a King, and I must entrust my honor, my life into the hands of such slaves. Curse on royalty, it needs slaves. Vile instruments, despicable and disgusting, are necessary to protect thrones. Curse on royalty, for the crown must perpetually be watched by unmanly spies. The sword, ha, ha, ha, the sword! Ah, enemies can be chastised with the sword; but nations must be governed with prudence, that is with spies, soulless tools, saleable hirelings, passionate cowards, who report every secret thought, every word to the King, that the royal master sleep not too well, dream not too sweet and know his dependence on his own slaves. Curse on royalty, for Kings must be the servants of their own slaves."—Herod run fast up and down the room, gnashed with his teeth, cramped his fists, and his eyes rolled wildly in their sockets. "But it is a great satisfaction to be a King," he continued, after awhile, "and I can not be King without those slaves, those despicable creatures. I can not lose Sabion nor Castobarus, they are my chief spies. But they shall give you satisfaction."

"Not I, but the offended majesty of justice demands satisfaction," Simon replied. "But here is the mistake, my lord. You curse royalty, because you misapprehend its mission and duties. Cast away the curse attending royalty, cast out the devils of your court, let justice govern, and be governed by it yourself, and you need neither slaves nor spies."

Herod laughed violently, when Simon was done. "Do you know this nation of republicans, young man?" Herod asked with much emphasis. "Do you think a people with the strongest passions and a cutting and dissecting intellect can be governed by good words and sweet sentiments? Are you informed of the inflexible character of the Pharasees, with whom religion and liberty are synonymous terms? Are you acquainted with the fanatic zeal of that party, their reckless and self-denying bravery, when they see only a glimpse of hope to establish their delusive form of popular government? Ah, you do not know the people. None can rule them otherwise than with an iron rod; they submit to superior force only. If they detect the least weakness in the government, they are sure to overthrow it by laying hold on that weak point with a remarkable shrewdness and power. Crushing force and an all-seeing eye alone can govern them. My army is my force, and my spies are my all-seeing eye. You can not expect a spy to be an upright man, how can you marvel at Sabion, that he is a rogue, if he is the chief of the spies? But they shall not molest you. You have my royal word, none shall molest you."

"Do not speak of me, my lord, speak first of yourself," said Simon. "Your armies and your spies are insufficient to protect you, as long as you change not your system of government. It is a grand mistake of rulers to imagine themselves wiser than the people. All men know all things, but spies know very little, and to suit their masters they must fabricate dangerous plots which they discovered, schemes and conspiracies which only they can defeat, an obstinacy and rebellions spirit which can be governed by their shrewdness only. In fact, however, they only render themselves and their masters odious in the sight of the people, and the people is made suspicious in the estimation of its ruler. They destroy that mutual confidence and regard which makes nations happy and Kings enviable. My lord, this is the true picture of things. A nation of republicans, as you call yours, gifted with strong passions, a fanatic zeal, an acute intellect, a reckless bravery, with whom religion and liberty are synonymous terms, bids defiance to your armies and laughs at the sagacity of your spies. Whenever your system of government will bear too heavy on your people, they will break the yoke, be sure they will break the chains, and then it will be too late for you to listen to the advice of better men than your courtiers."

The emphasis which Simon laid upon his words and the uncommon animation of his voice roused the suspicion of Herod. He scrutinized him with his shrewd and piereing looks, on asking him, "How do you know all this?"

"By the little wisdom God has been pleased to grant me," said Simon, "and by daily experience. Or should sagacious Herod not have heard to-day the groans of a dissatisfied people? Should his spies not have informed him that, notwithstanding the sacredness of the day, some of the people exclaimed,

This is not our Highpriest'—'This is not our Sanhedrin'—'Where is the old King'—and similar exclamations of their dissatisfaction? But if they should not have told you, I do"

"Carpenters, tanners, sandal makers, wood sawers, and other such rebels," said Herod. "Who cares for such brainless fellows."

"They have the fists and the bold hearts, Sire, to strike the blow, after the scheme is ripe for execution," said Simon. "A nation of such an intellectual superiority, as you say yours is, has plenty of men, to make good schemes. They must have the very rebels of whom you speak, and these very rebels have hearts to feel when they are wronged; but they seldom speak, they most always act. The words of those carpenters, tanners, &c., are the echo of a pride so wounded, an ambition so depreciated, and a consciousness so disregarded, that even they feel and utter it."

"Induction, nothing but induction," said Herod. "Ten of my soldiers are sufficient to fight one hundred of them."

"You are not sure, however, that your soldiers will kill their own fathers, brothers and friends," said Simon. "You are not sure that you can send ten soldiers to fight every hundred rebels, that might rise against you. You are not positive, that ten soldiers will fight one hundred agitated and desperate men. A man in a moment of passion, when he fights for his rights, his family, his country, is no coward. His blows are heavy, his sword is sharp. You are mistaken in the nature of man. He who is submissive to servility when his passions slumber, becomes a lion, a bloodthirsty tiger, when his passions are aroused. He who suffers wrong, because he can not help himself, becomes cowardish, malicious and servile. Give him a spark of hope, and vengeance, the venomous passion of vengeance, renders him at once a giant, a reckless and fearless hero. Such is the fact of human nature, no inductions. Those groans of to-day which fell on my ears, not only are the expression of suffering wrong but of a determination to avenge it. I caution you, Herod, against your spies and your system of slavery. Remember it, this evening concluding the Day of Atonement, I caution you against yourself and your vile friends."

"Are you my friend?" Herod asked.

"No!" Simon responded, promptly, "tyrants have no friends, want none, and deserve none. They may be feared but not loved; they may strike terror into the hearts, but can not inspire them with noble affections; self-interest, fear, vain ambition may procure slaves for them, but no friends. There again is your error, you flatter yourself one on earth might love you, when you know well enough, that you can love none. Poor Herod, who loves none is loved by none."

"Therefore I must rule, therefore I must be a King," said Herod. "You speak against yourself. If I can not govern by terror, by love I can certainly not; for none loves me. If I show them less rigor, the very cowards will turn lions, you say yourself, and tear first myself. Their groans do not disturb me. Let them bow down to their lord and King and be happy. Their exclamations do not frighten me, I am prepared for all eventualities. Let them hate me, but they must obey me. Obedience is a virtue which is a stranger to a large number of my people; terror teaches them this duty of a loyal subject. You are a physician and a wise man, but you would be a poor King. But let us speak of another topic. Where have you been all this time?"

"Among your enemies, Sire," said Simon, dryly, "a place where you never go, still are always there. I heard them speak as they feel, and you never do. Still it is true, that we must learn our deficiencies and demerits of our enemies."

"Aurion, Aurion, your words are too bold," said Herod, rebukingly. "Cunningness and deception also sometimes assume the mask of plump honesty. If you go among my enemies, are you not one of them?"

"Can I go among your friends, where are they?" Simon asked. "I act the friend to you, that is more than your courtiers do, and, therefore, I went to your enemies, I mean to those who speak, in order to serve you with plain truth, such as you rarely hear. No wonder that Herod, surrounded by vile servants, sees a rogue in every man, hence not always in the right place. But you sent me to Jericho, to bring Hillel and Abba Shaul before you, and there your enemies speak. But I shall not deprive you of your sleep to night by telling you what they say."

"Nor do I wish to know it," Herod said. "Did you also hear of a conspiracy there, a meeting somewhere near Mount Nebo?"

"I did, Sire," said Simon, slowly. "But you do not call the thing by the right name. The dissatisfied portion of your people met somewhere in the desert, to be unmolested, stated their complaints, and devised means to ameliorate their condition. There is neither plot, conspiracy nor secrecy about this in Jericho. Your spies, desirous to make themselves important in your eyes, undoubtedly speak of shrewd conspiracies which they discovered."

"And why did you not apprise me of the fact?" Herod asked.

"Because you do not wish to know what your enemies say," Simon responded. "I am not hired as a spy. I speak and act from a free impulse."

"To morrow, I will hear it," said Herod. "I am tired. To morrow, I must hear you. One word more. What do you wish to prove by those two men from Jericho?"

"That Sabion is guilty of adultery, murder and high treason," said Simon.

"Then I do not wish to see them," said Herod. "I know the crimes of Sabion, but I also know his usefulness."

"Then I will go and tell those men to return to Jericho and say, there is no justice in Israel," Simon said; "tell them any crime is pardonable if the perpetrator is useful to Herod, or only understands the art to make him believe so."

"Yes, yes, tell them Herod reigns in Israel," he said; "and the greatest crime is not to obey him."

"I will," said Simon. "Farewell, my lord."

"Stay, traitor," Herod thundered. "None dare leave this saloon without my permission."

"If I was a traitor, I would be Herod's favorite," Simon responded. "But as I am not a traitor, and wish not to turn one, I must leave you. Forget not, I have your royal word, that under four eyes we are equals. My moral feelings are so much wounded, I feel the Deity himself so wickedly outraged by your impious words, that I can stay no longer. Once I thought, I can reform Herod, and it was a pleasing idea—but here I stand ashamed and corrected. Your wickedness is incurable."

"Let a thousand thunderbolts crush thy infamous tongue," Herod raged.

"God hears not the curses of the wicked," Simon replied.

"Forget not, young man, that you are in my power," Herod continued, furiously. "I might forget my royal word, and you are lost."

"You are lost, irrevocably lost," Simon said. "I am not in your power. Providence watches over the messengers of truth."

"I will prove you this is a lie," Herod cried, and with a dagger in his hand he quickly advanced toward Simon, who tore the clothes from his breast, and with a lion's power cried, "Strike the fatal blow if you dare!" Like marble statues, the two men stood opposite each other, each eyeing the other with looks of fire. "You are a man, I swear by the living God," said Herod, "not a feature of your countenance changed, not an idea of fear in your face. Aurion, your confidence in truth is great. The trial was hard, but you stood it manfully. It is not your life I want, but I wished to read in your heart, and I have read in it my own condemnation. Go! serious and stern disciple of truth, and remember, if thou canst not be Herod's friend, he will always be thine To morrow, more. Good night to you."

When Simon had left the saloon of Herod he met Sabion again. "I told the King, that your daughter did not run away with her lover. Next week by this time your spies must be able to tell where she is. You hear, my lord,—next week. I know you will oblige me." Without waiting for an answer Simon went away. He was accosted by the servants of Salome who told him, that she wished to see him immediately. He hesitated for a moment, but then he followed the servant to the apartment of the princess who received him with distinguishing kindness, and smilingly rebuked him for his long absence.

"I love the blossoming carpet of nature," said Simon, "the orchards studded with golden fruit, the vine-covered hills on the side of silvery streamlets. I love to hear the concert of merry birds, the bleating of the lamb, and the whistle of the wind when it plays musingly with the verdant leaves. I love all this, and still better do I love the people with their rosy cheeks, black eyes from which health, happiness, courage and innocence speak in open and amiable mien. I feel so happy and satisfied among the pure children of nature, that I could always be with them."

"Your description, sir, makes them delightful," said Salome, "although naturally they would not appear so to me. But tell me, what did you see and hear whilst roaming over the land? I like to listen to your descriptions, they are charming indeed."

"When walking one sultry day in the dark shade of a palm grove near Jericho," said Simon, "yielding to the amusing reveries of a playful fantasy, I was approached by a tender lad, whose fantastic costume and piercing looks attracted my attention. To my surprise he called me by name and invited me to sit down by his side. I did so. He told me a story without an introduction, which I must repeat to you, my lady; you might give me an interpretation to the waking dream."

"I am all ear for you," said Salome.

"Sabion, said he, has bad tricks in his head against you," Simon continued. "First he wanted to catch you in his net by the love of his only daughter. He gave her a ring, even the ring of Cleopatra, as a token of his wish, that she should love and marry you. But when he discovered your intimacy with Salome, and saw you rise steadily in the King's favor, he became so jealous and so apprehensive, that his crimes be exposed to the King and the people, that he resorted, in company with Castobarus, to the foul means of assassinating you. But this failed and so the evil had grown worse. Now he dreads your accusation before the King, and he removed your witnesses. His daughter Helen is gone, none knows whither, and the Greek ruffian is arrested in Jericho for the murder of Baruch ben Menahem. Be cautious, said the young man, every step of yours is watched. Then he went away without satisfying my curiosity as to his name or position."

"Do you believe all this?" Salome asked.

"It is not all, I believe," said Simon, earnestly. "I know, that you yourself, my lady, directed my attention to Helen; hence an understanding to this effect must have existed between you and Sabion. I know that Helen, in an unguarded moment, spoke too much in presence of her father, Castobarus and yourself, my lady, so that her father forcibly ejected her from the room. This violence was the voice of a revolting heart with which the father presumptuously played. You took it to be love. Was it not so, my lady? Helen must be put out of the way, thought Sabion and Castobarus, not to betray their villanies, and you gladly consented to it. Is it not so, my lady? You must know it best, and I beg you to tell me the truth in this matter."

"What do you care for that girl?" Salome asked. "You told me, you can not love, hence that girl can have no interest for you."

"She has much interest for me," said Simon. "I must prove by her, that Sabiou and Castobarus hired a ruffian to assassinate me. It is with her, that I must prove several other villanies of those two men, whom I am determined to expose. I will and I must know where she is; but as I believe you could tell me, and I wish to know you upright and honest, I come to ask you. Your jealousy which co-operated in this matter, you must comprehend, my lady, is too flattering to myself, that I should not be inclined to look on it with much pleasure, as a proof of your love. But truth, my lady, I expect of you stern and unexceptionable truth. This is the eve concluding the Day of Atonement. To day you and all Israel expected the remission of sins. You, my lady, if it was true what you told me last, especially must have expected to-day the grace of your God. Will you this very night soil your soul with a lie? Where is Helen, my lady?"

A painful pause ensued. Salome's looks were cast to the floor. Simon, standing before her, eyed her with the firm determination, not to let her escape by any trick. Neither of them appeared to be inclined to speak another word. Salome, observing the painful silence must be broken, stammered in a perplexed tone, "Speak, sir, what else have you to tell me?"

"I have spoken," said Simon, in a tone which penetrated every recess of Salome's heart. Finally, she broke the silence by accents of acute pain, "I can not, I dare not betray Sabion. Fettered by the chains of vice to his fate, I dare not offer my assistance to his ruin. In his fall he will expose me—and I am lost."

"Ah, is it thus, my lady," Simon said, "are you still kept in the bondage of vice and corruption? Then allow me to leave you, and weep a tear for the hapless daughter of Antipater who, thus deeply sunk in the mire of vice can rise no more. I dreamed a glorious dream, I hoped to see you restored to virtue and happiness; but your evil demon says, it shall not be, and no man is stronger than fate. Once, and if it should be in the moment of death, once you will remember the hour when I offered you the Balm of Gilead, and you refused it; when I offered you my assistance to break the horrid fetters which tie you to vice and vicious men, but you would not accept it. This remembrance will cause more agony to your wounded heart than all your sins. I am done. Farewell."

"Do you so hastily condemn me?" Salome asked. "O do not, I prithee. If you should know the real causes of my silence, you would pity me. But be sure, sir, I dare not be auxiliary to the fall of Sabion."

"He hired a ruffian to dispose of me, he is my deadly foe," said Simon, "and if I can I will avenge myself. I will render Herod the invaluable service of releasing him from his false friends. My lady, Sabion's fall would be a blessing to your royal house, and to this country. It would be the redemption of Herod from the clutches of the devil. Whether you assist me or not, Sabion will fall, and Helen will be found to testify before the King against her own father. But it is not Herod alone, I am anxious to serve, it is also you, my lady, to whom my best will is devoted. Sabion, the witness of your shame, the man who possesses the dreadful secret, that might ruin you—must be banished to a foreign land, to some distant province of the Roman empire, to a solitary island. He must be deposed and deported so suddenly and unexpectedly, that his words can not injure you. This man gone, and you will again breathe freely, the crushing weight of guilt and crime will be moved from your head, and you will commence a new life, a life over which the purest angels will rejoice, and make you forget its ignominious part. Remember the hour of repentance, and the promises you made me. Forget not the delight, the infinite pleasure you felt, when you thought your sins were forgiven, the past was drowned in oblivion. Salome, first be true and faithful to yourself!"

"And will you then love me, be mine, only mine?" she asked in a passionate tone. "Do tell me, I prithee, can you assure me, that then"—

"Where is Helen, my witness? Shall Sabion fall and be banished?" Simon interrupted.

"I am your witness," said she. "But tell me, speak, may I hope?"

"First convince me, that you can love," said Simon, "then speak of sacred affections. As long as your honor lies in Sabion's hands, we are too far apart to speak of love. As long as you heap vice upon crime, I do not, I dare not know you. You lent Sabiou a helping hand to dispose of his own daughter, such is the fact. First you must make this good, then you must assist to ruin Sabion, then we will speak of love. Once more, I ask you, madam, where is Helen? Shall Sabion fall?"

"Tyrant, reckon not too much upon the weakness of a loving woman?" she exclaimed; "I can not, I dare not do it. I am the mother of Sabicu's children, I dare not betray him. Here is the terrible secret of a woman frantic with love. Go and use it, if your honor allows "

This emotion in the debased heart of Salome had a violent effect on Simon. He was almost paralized. He changed his tone altogether, and in a compassionate manner he grasped the hand of Salome, and said, "I honor this maternal affection in you. But why do you wish to deceive yourself and me? If your affections for Sabion are still living, why do you wish to make me believe that you love me?"

"I hate, I despise him who robbed me of my innocence," said Salome. "I am his deadly enemy, with every fiber of my heart, every thought of my soul. I abhor the man who has placed the Cherub with the flaming sword between myself and the tree of life. But I am the mother of two children who are known now as the offspring of honest parents in Israel. My wealth and my tears bought them an honest name. If Sabion is driven to the utmost, he will betray the secret, and my children, the innocent offspring of sin and crime, will be stigmatized as bastards. Do you feel the crushing weight of this word, bastards, who dare not come in the congregation of the Lord, from whom every honest man turns with abhorrence? "No, no, no, do not ask of me, what I can not do, I can not expose Sabion. I, in an unguarded hour, revealed all these secrets in the presence of Helen, therefore she was sent away, that my children be no bastards."

"I am Sabion's deadly enemy as he is mine," said Simon. "Your honor is placed at his mercy. The fate of your children is in his hands. You must eradicate one name from your nomenclature—Sabion's or mine. Such is the case. You say, you love me and hate Sabion, then the choice is easy. Depose and deport Sabion before he can speak, send him to a place where his voice can not be heard, and the right remedy for your malady is found. Assist me, honestly and earnestly, and I will bring it about."

"You are mistaken in all this," said she. "Sabion is a cunning fox and too useful to my brother to be easily disposed of. The slightest move on my part, and he throws himself upon the mercy of Herod, who has an excuse for every crime, if the perpetrator is a useful instrument in his hands. This would only expose me to the anger of my brother, and my children to certain death. Herod would not have a bastard in our family, and my children—O, I can not, I dare not move."

"And you can not even tell me where Helen is?" Simon asked.

"No, she knows the whole secret and is so enraged, that she would betray it," was the answer.

"If I promise you to make her silent on this point, will you not tell me?" Simon asked.

"No, because it is not in your power to silence an enraged woman," she said.

"But your terrible secret is known to two competent witnesses," said Simon, "two besides me."

"You will not betray me, and the two men are dead," she replied.

"Sabion said so, but it is not true," said Simon. "I saw them and knew the fact before you told me."

"Then he spared them as his witnesses to ruin me and my children, if necessary," Salome lamented. "But they shall die, as sure as God lives."

"Do not blaspheme the Most High," Simon rebuked. "I tell you they shall not die by the hands of the assassin. Is this your repentance? this your idea of virtue? Ah, my lady, let us part forever, you deceived me. We have entrusted each other with terrible secrets, which each of us must conceal in his bosom, conceal for ever."

"I have not deceived you, I love you madly, passionately, as furiously, indeed, as I hate Sabion," she cried. "I can not live without your love. The secrets I entrusted to you, are the evidence of my boundless love and confidence. But I tremble for my innocent children, I turn an enraged lioness whenever danger threatens them. Ruin, destroy, annihilate foul, vile Sabion, if you can, I will thank you for it; but I dare not risk my own honor and the happiness of my children. Helen must speak no more in this country, and the two men of whom you speak can save their lives by silence only."

Like a madman, Simon left the saloon of Salome, without saying one word more. "Helen is lost," was all he could think or feel. For the rest of the night he ran about the park like a midnight specter, and cursed the hour when he first set his foot in this royal den of vice. A thousand schemes to save Helen flashed through his excited brains, but neither of them was practicable. When the morning dawned again on Mount Moriah, it found Simon as undecided as the night had made him. He sat like a mummy at the artesian well, and gazed at the spouting stream, as though he was to count its drops, when Elvira stepped cautiously to him and whispered "Baba ben Buta must see you." Without giving him time for reflection or question, she disappeared.

"Yes, I must see him," Simon murmured to himself, and left the park.

Salome was indignant at the strange conduct of Simon. He left her without any ceremony, left her excited as she had never seen him before. She understood him wrong. She believed he loved her, but could not bear the idea of seeing the honor of his bride or wife in the hands of so vile a man as Sabion. "Yet you shall be mine," she exclaimed, several times, "in defiance of every thing, you shall be mine. The world will envy me the possession of such a husband. I gladly sacrifice Sabion, Castobarus and ten more such vile creatures for this young Adonis." Like Simon, she walked her room all night to discover a proper plan, to put Sabion out of the way, without giving him time to betray her and her children. Then again she embraced the phantom of Simon which deluded her excited imagination, and swore to do any and every thing for the one prize, and that prize was Simon. She did not imagine, for a moment, that Simon cared for Helen more than because she was his best witness, and the best instrument to ruin Sabion. To ruin him without the aid of Helen was, after all, the same thing, she thought. So she reflected and schemed till morning dawn, when her servant came in and brought her an invitation to come early this morning to Herod in his private apartment.

CHAPTER X

THE CASTLE IN THE FOREST.

Where the southern end of the Valley of Sharon is bounded by the softly rising hills, there in the midst of a Sycamore grove was the country seat of Sabiou. It was the place of his birth; but since he rose so high at court, the little cottage had given way to a fine structure in the midst of a luxuriant park. The house was occupied by an old steward, his wife and two children, beside three servants. The oldest of the two children was a girl of about sixteen to eighteen years old, and the youngest was a lad of six years. The old couple were simple and good natured peasants and appeared to know no harm.

Besides the usual inmates of the house, which had not been visited for several years by its proud owner, several bearded men, of a martial appearance, and some ladies of delicate visages were visible about the house, who apparently had no other business than to while away their time with different games. In a shadowy arbor which afforded shelter against the rays of a tropic sun pouring down currents of heat at the noon of the day, Helen sat with the old steward's wife, and conversed a little louder than a whisper.

"I can not by any means," said the woman, "convey your letter to Jericho, nor dare I do any other thing for you, against the express command of your father. Our orders are to watch you closely, and allow no stranger to see you, or communicate with you directly or indirectly."

"Have these strict orders been explained to you?" Helen asked. "Why should I be thus buried alive in this lonely forest, where the hours grow into years and the days appear to last an eternity? Why must I be separated from all who are dear to my heart, and pine away in this dark grove? If you ever reflected on this subject, tell me the reason of all this and I will bear it patiently. But if you know no more than my father's command, then believe me, I am guilty of no crime, I suffer for no fault of mine, and assist me in escaping from this place, where I see but strange and suspicious countenances, and every one regards me with a watchful eye. Help me, good woman, and I will be grateful to you."

"I eat the bread of my lord Sabion, and shall obey his behests," said the woman. "This place is not half as lonely as it appears to you, nor the people half as bad as you imagine them. Be first used to them and soon you will find them tolerable. You speak against your own father who is a great man at the King's court, and that is wrong of you, it is wicked. I was told the cause of your being sent hither to lead a solitary life; but I have no reason to tell you your own faults."

"My faults?" Helen said, surprised. "Tell me what kind of faults did they invent to sully my name? O, I prithee, do tell me, of what misconduct am I guilty, to merit this painful seclusion from my friends? If your mouth is not sealed by the piece of bread which you eat, let me know what you have heard of me, let me hear it, that I might judge."

"It illy becomes me to speak of the faults of great Sabicu's only daughter," said the woman. "I obey his behests, because such is my duty. I eat his bread and do his work."

"I am Sabion's daughter, mark," said Helen, with much pathos, "I command you to tell me, what faults of mine you know."

"I know that you are a disobedient child who loves not her parent," the woman said, angrily. "I know that you attempted twice to run away with your lover, a vulgar shepherd. But you were caught and restored to your father. Now you are here to improve your conduct, become better and wiser."

"I do tell you by the honor of a virgin woman, by the grave of my deceased mother, by the shield of the Highpriest do I assure you, all you said is a malicious invention," Helen said. "I do tell, that dirty court intrigues required my absence and total disappearance; therefore I was deluded to this place, and am kept a prisoner here. I will not complain, but do me this one favor, let my friends in Jericho know where I am, so that they bewail me not as among the dead. I am Queen Mariamne's favorite lady; she will search after me, through the length and breadth of the country, and be sure, she will find me. Whenever I arrive back at court, I will richly pay your services. My diamonds are worth more than ten times this house and grove. You shall have half of them, if you carry this letter to Jericho."

"You can not bribe an honest woman," was the reply. "I eat the bread of Sabion and obey his behests, because such is my duty."

"Have you no duty to your God, none to your neighbor?" Helen asked, indignantly. "Know it, I am innocent and suffer for no fault of mine. But I will bear patiently my unfortunate lot. In Jericho, innocent people weep for me, because they think I am dead. Have you no heart to sympathize with the pain-stricken neighbor? Have you no duty to fulfil to those who suffer innocently? If you have, then do as I request you, convey this letter to Jericho."

"You wish to inform your lover where you are," she said, "and this is not necessary at all. He must forget you and you must forget him. You are here, that all communications between you and him might cease. None shall convey your letter to Jericho, till your father bids so to do."

"The Queen will find me, and home I will go," said Helen. "I will have opportunity to pay you for your unshaken fidelity, which I am forced to admire."

"I fear no menaces," the woman said. "The father will protect me against all the harm the daughter might contemplate."

"Will you go down with me to the next village, that I may gaze again on human countenances who are not the slaves of my father?" Helen asked with bitter sarcasm.

"No, I can not do that," said the woman, "it is against my orders. You must have no communications with anybody."

"Also not with your children?" Helen asked, with a peculiar emphasis.

The woman looked somewhat perplexed.

Collecting herself, she said, "You do not intend to seduce my children to disobedience against their own parents?"

"No, you need not fear that," said Helen. "But whenever I should return to court, I might take care of them, and do them much good."

"They stand in need of no favors," the woman said.

"I believe not," Helen remarked, "they have a mighty patron there. But I feel so much sympathy for your little boy, who looks exactly like my father. When I return I should like to take him with me."

The perplexity of the woman was so visible, that Helen easily observed it. She continued to tease her with the question, "Why does that boy favor my father so exactly?"

"I know not, surely, I know not," the woman stammered.

"But I do know," Helen said, angrily, "I know it, adulterous, fallen woman, why it is so. Now I understand your doggish servitude to my father. Now I know why you believe me to be a fallen woman. Go, scandalous woman, my mother curses you in her grave. Your own bastard child will curse his mother, when he will become conscious of her crimes. Go, and let me see you no more."

Deadly pale and quivering, the woman stood before Helen, and stared aghast. "It is not true, so help me God, it is not true," she exclaimed, pain-stricken and with a shrill voice. The noise attracted the attention of several men who came and inquired, "What is the matter here? What ails you?"

"Nothing that concerns you," Helen replied, harshly. The woman also recovering from her perplexity uttered some excuse; but the bearded men evinced no disposition to leave. Helen bid them leave and let her alone; but the Syrian Adarmelech stammered, in his broken dialect, that he would not go before he knew what had happened. Helen bid him again leave, but he refused. "I am here to watch you," the man said, "and I will do my duty."

Helen felt so mortified by the ruthless conduct of the rude man, that she could not reply, instantly. After awhile she rose, and there was a commanding dignity in her attitude, drew a dagger from its concealment, "I plunge this steel in your cowardly heart, if you do not leave immediately," she thundered. The Syrian laughed rudely, and casting a contemptuous look on her, he left.

"Am I thus sold a slave to slaves!" Helen cried. "Oh, my God, why have I so wicked a father, why am I the child of a monster?"

The Syrian returned with several other men, and demanded the dagger of Helen. She refused, indignantly. "Then I must use force," said the man, and on a given signal one pressed Helen in his arms, another held her hands, and the third took her dagger. "Tie her hands," the Syrian commanded, and they were tied fast. Laughing loudly, all left, also did the old woman, leaving Helen alone in a state of consternation and mortification. She could not even weep. For the first time in her life she felt the weakness of a frail woman, and the full wickedness of her father.

The little boy who looked so much like her father came toward her from the grove, she felt the blood rushing to her countenance on beholding him. "Why are your hands tied, lady?" the little boy asked, innocently.

"I know not," was Helen's short reply. "Shall I untie them?" he asked. "You can not," said Helen, "you must take the large slaughter knife of your father, and cut the cords."

The boy ran away, brought the large slaughter knife and cut the cords. Helen's hands were free again. She embraced and kissed the child. "It is not thy fault, thou child of sin," she murmured, and kissed the child again. "Tell none, that you did cut these cords," she said to the child, "your father would whip you."

The child appeared much frightened, but Helen gave him a few coins which made him forget the cords, knife and whipping. Helen took the knife, retired to her apartment which she kept locked for the rest of the day, reflecting on the sad and perilous condition in which she was placed.

Adarmelech walked through the grove with a man, whose rich dress was unusual in that part of the country. "Are we alone and undisturbed here?" the man asked. "You may speak," was the reply; when the stranger said: "You know the reward that awaits you, if you do precisely as you are instructed."

"Only one kind of reward will satisfy me," said the Syrian, "vengeance, bloody and black vengeance on Sabion."

"You shall have it," said the stranger, "and besides this your reward shall be great. Your duty now is to disgrace, defile the daughter of Sabion, then let her escape and return to her father with her despair, and let him always see the pale and withering countenance of his disgraced daughter."

"But what will lady Salome say to it?" the Syrian asked.

"It is her wish," said the stranger.

"I do not understand that," Adarmelech ejaculated. "Is not she Sabion's intimate friend?'

"Yes or no, just as you please," said the stranger. "The daughter of Sabion is her rival, and she must be ruined. You have seen the King's body physician, that young Apollo, he is the cause of all these troubles. Salome is passionately enamored with him, and he is supposed to be in love with Helen. The first plan was to get her out of the way; but this would enrage the lover and make the evil worse. Let her be dishonored, and the young physician will court her no longer. Thus a double purpose is achieved, the romance has an end, and you are avenged on Sabion."

"It is enough," said Adarmelech. "Give me the money and the letters. To-morrow she will escape, dishonored, disgraced, defiled, despairing, and return to her diabolic father. I go to Egypt to enlist under the Roman eagle."

Adarmelech, having received what he wanted, the man went away, and he returned to the house.

"God bless you, brave warrior," a man saluted Adarmelech. "Can you give shelter and a morsel of bread to a tired warrior?"

Adarmelech looked on the gigantic man before him, and after awhile he answered in the affirmative. "Whither do you go?"

"I go to Alexandria to enlist in the Roman army," said the man. "I last fought against the Arabs, in the ranks of Herod, now I desire to fight a few scores of Romans. Dogs, cowards, they are, those Romans, I will teach them to fight."

Adarmelech smiled about the foolish bragging of the stranger. Returned to the house he introduced him to his comrades. "In honor of our guest," said Adarmelech, "let us have the best wine from the cellar."

Plenty of wine was brought and drunk so rapidly, that the whole company was half drunk in a few minutes. Every body in the house was invited, the steward, his wife and children were called, and every body was forced to drink. The women no less than the little boy were made beastly drunk. Whoever refused to drink was forced to do it. When the night began to advance, a violent storm swept over the plain. The trees groaned heavily, as shaken by the wind. Thick clouds overhung the horizon. Not the voice of a living creature was audible in the vicinity. But the drunken company inside sang, screamed, laughed, shouted most hideously. The stranger among them appeared to be the most savage. He drunk, sung and cursed without intermission and broke one cup after the other, always upbraiding Adarmelech, that he could not drink like a man and warrior. Still wilder and noisier the company roared; still heavier grew the atmosphere, and the storm had increased into a hurricane.

Up stairs, Helen sat on a low sofa, mortified, disheartened and weeping. She imagined the agony of Simon and Elvira, and her tears flew rapidly. The howling storm, a strange muttering, sounding like distant thunder, and the groaning of the trees in the grove, sounded through the dark of a starless night. The rude voices of the inebriated multitude from below sounded to the wounded heart of Helen like a scoffing hell. Her agony gave way to the terror with which the hurricane-like storm surrounded the solitary room. The orgies in the lower part of the house filled her soul with disgust.

She sat and yielded to the most unhappy reveries. She frequently clasped the long knife before her, as though she had an omen of approaching danger. Again, she clasped it. for she heard knocking on her door. The knocking was repeated and Helen's name called.

"Who comes so late at night?" Helen asked, with a tremulous voice.

"Open; it is Adarmelech," a coarse voice responded outside.

Helen trembled on hearing the voice of that rude and gigantic man, her courage failed, she was undetermined what to do. Again, Adarmelech knocked and threatened to break the door, if it was not opened instantly. Helen clasped the knife with one hand, and a chair with the other, took a position near the door and thus was ready to receive the fiend. The door gave way, Ad armelech reeled into the room, and on beholding Helen in a position of defence, he laughed so diabolically wild, that Helen shuddered. "Poor little thing," said he, "your knife and chair are no arms against a man; lay them down, be amiable, capitulate with honor, and I will treat you right."

"You leave this room instantly," Hel en cried, "or I will teach you the strength of a desperate woman." A slight shock of earthquake was felt. Helen trembled. The drunken host below burst forth in a roar of wild laughter. Adarmelech laughed at the threats of Helen. "You are in my power, beautiful Helen," said he, "and I am determined to enjoy the prize of the happy moment."

"First, I will cleave thy intoxicated head," Helen cried. Adarmelech drew his sword, advanced upon her, laughing at her weakness. Helen fought and screamed with all her strength. The chair fell from her trembling hand, a blow of Adarmelech's sword broke the knife in two pieces. He clasped her right arm, threw his right arm round her waist, lifting her up high. "You shall not escape me," he cried, mad with passionate agitation, and dragged her toward the couch. Another shock of earthquake was felt, but it did not interrupt the fiend in the execution of his hellish plan. He succeeded in carrying her to the couch, when a voice well known to her sounded like thunder through the dark room, "Coward, hellish villain, fight for your life." Adarmelech turned round and the stranger stood before him with flaming eyes, armed to the teeth and apparently ready to grind him to atoms. But a few clashes of the sword had been heard, when another shock of earthquake threw them all on the floor. A current of fire issued from the troubled bosom of the earth, and lit the room for a moment. "It is Abba Shaul, my savior," Helen cried, frantic with joy. "Flee, immediately flee down to the village," Abba Shaul commanded, when both men wrestled on the floor. "I shall not leave you alone," she cried, "I rather will die with you." Adarmelech cried for help, but Abba Shaul run his knife through the throat of the coward. When the drunken multitude came with lights, Adarmelech wrinced himself in his blood. Helen seized Adarmelech's sword and, with Abba Shaul, confronted the drunken host. A sanguinary combat ensued.—The clash of arms re-echoed awfully from the halls of the house. They had reached the lower floor, the fury increased on both sides. Helen had succeeded in opening the outer door. "Fear not, Helen," Abba Shaul roared, so that the pillars trembled, "You are safe."—"Down to the village," he cried, and again the clash of swords was heard, furiously blow fell upon blow, curses, shouts of anger, the gnashing of the teeth, the groans of the wounded and dying and the howling storm sounded through the night like the awful voices of the condemned in hell.

Again a shock of earthquake, the house trembled, was shaken to its foundation—and another fearful shock, and its inmates were buried under the ruins of the castle. A current of fire swept rapidly over the scene, smoke and a sulphuric smell followed then the silence of the graveyard prevailed.

CHAPTER XI

THE KING'S TREACHERY.

The secret council in the private cabinet of Herod lasted many hours. Sabiou convinced Herod that the dissatisfied portion of the people prepared a heavy blow upon the government; but the conspiracy was kept so secret that it baffled detection. He furthermore convinced the King, that the revolutionists intended to dethrone Herod, and place the old and weak Hyrcan on the throne, with whom the Pharisees could do as they chose. He said the republican portion of the rebels would yield to the Asmonean party, as Hyrcan and no King was identical with them.

This having become clear to the mind of Herod, he came to the conclusion that the death of Hyrcan would rescue him from the dilemma, and deprive the Asmonean party of the last hope to realize their wishes. They must then cling to Mariamne, whose interests were too closely united with his to be dangerous to him. To all this there came the moral conviction, that one of the Asmoneans stood in close connection with the Queen of Egypt and the King of Arabia. He considered Mariamne innocent, and held Hyrcan responsible for the alleged treachery.

"Then Hyrcan must die," said Herod, after a long pause. These words produced a panic in the whole cabinet. Even the habitual rogues who counselled him to every wickedness, were amazed at the terrible thought, that the hoary King and high-priest, the last son of the Asmonean heroes, who just walked at the brink of the grave, should die by the hands of the executioner. A breathless silence brooded heavily upon the assembly, which was awful also to Herod. With looks of fire he regarded every man in the room, and then he said, "Why are you so astonished? I or Hyrcan must fall, let it be him and not me who takes leave from Israel and the world."

A savage joy flashed in the countenance of Sabion, when he said, "Herod is Israel's King," after which again a painful silence followed. Sohemus was the only man who ventured to say, "My lord, an insurrection of the people will and must be the result of Hyrcan's death. Hyrcan is eighty years old, he is known to be a quiet, mild and peacable man, who loves you as well as his own son. The people know the numerous blows of misfortune which fell on the head of that old prince, and sympathize with him. They know how you distinguished and honored him, how you called him your father and venerated him as such. His death must produce an immense insurrection. It is inevitable."

Herod regarded Sohemus with scrutinizing looks, and replied, with immense pride, "I am not afraid of my people. Hyrcan has received a present of Malchus, my deadly foe. He intends to fly to Petra, and return to this country at the head of an Arabian army, to support the rebels. We will prove this before the Sanhedrin, and this body must pronounce the sentence of death over Hyrcan. We are not concerned in the final action of the Sanhedrin."

The question was discussed for several hours. Sabion was victorious. The death of the old King was resolved upon, and the counsellors of the King were dismissed. Only Sabion remained in the saloon. The King clasped his hand and said to him: "Omniscient man, are you sure, that we are in possession of all the evidence we need before the Sanhedrin?"

"I am, my lord," said Sabion. "The Arabs who brought the animals to Hyrcan are in our power. Threats and promises will prompt them in communicating to the Sanhedrin the verbal message of the King of Arabia. The letter of Hyrcan to Malchus and the testimony of Dositheus must convict him. The captive Egyptian also will do us good services."

"What will the Queen say, if her grandfather falls!" Herod exclaimed, painfully. "I apprehend the family feuds will alarmingly increase."

"She will not deny her feminine nature," said Sabion, with a smile on his lips. "First she will weep and scold, then she will pout, and look sullen, one week over and all is forgotten."

"I hope it will be so," Herod said. "I fear much less my people than my family.

But, Sabion, are you positive, that our evidence is sufficient to convict Hyrcan ?"

"More than sufficient, my lord," he replied, "to convince *this* Sanhedrin of the guilt of any man *we* dislike. Be of good cheer, my lord; I will conduct the matter to your entire satisfaction."

"When Hyrcan is no more, the hopes of his party are gone," said Herod, "and with the hope the enterprise also expires. The Republicans must know well that they are unpopular in Rome, and dreaded by the Saducees, hence can not succeed. Let Hyrcan be no more, and I sit in peace on my throne. Let me have peace, and I will give it to my people and my family." A noise at the door interrupted Herod. The door was hastily opened and Salome rushed in, pale, quivering, distracted and exhausted; she fell down on a sofa. Both Herod and Sabion hastened to her assistance, and inquired after the cause of her alarm, but she could not answer till after a good while, when she stammered forth the words, "Sharon"—"Earthquake"—"Thousands killed."

Herod finally succeeded in getting out of her, that a courier arrived from the plain of Sharon, who brought the dreadful news of an earthquake. The courier was ushered into his presence, and told the terrific story of Sharon, where in a few minutes about thirty thousand people were buried under the roofs of their houses. "Also the castle of Sabion lies in ruins," the courier continued, "and none of its inmates escaped."

A shrill cry escaped the lips of Salome, while Sabion stood mummy-like before the King, and stared aghast. It appeared that none was prepared to say one word to the other. The courier was dismissed and Herod called his body physician to attend to Salome. Simon came. His presence exercised a magic influence on Salome. Inviting him to a seat by her side, she changed her visage at once, and when he extended his hand to her, she clasped it, passionately, and rose from her seat as Simon did. "You need rest and consolation, my lady," said the physician, "I will call your ladies and tell them to attend to you." The ladies were called, Salome was conveyed to her room, and Simon followed.

"This man is a magician," said Herod, after the others were gone. "He is an excellent man." Looking on Sabion, he found him standing yet in a state of consternation, which was so foreign to his nature, that Herod asked, astonished, "What ails you ?"

"I fear the worst has come to pass," said Sabion. "My only child, Helen, I fear"—here he stept, abruptly.

"Let me know fully what you fear," Herod bid.

Sabion was again himself. He had a ready lie to tell. "Before I came to this session," he said, "I received an account of my daughter. She absconded with one of my lord's officers, the Syrian Adarmelech. Fearing my anger, both returned to my country seat, and from thence they sent me a messenger to pray pardon of me."

"And now you fear both were killed by the earthquake," Herod inquired, "and you are left a childless man; is it not so?" Sabion answered in the affirmative, and Herod continued, "Be consoled, bereft father. It is better your daughter is dead than that she should tell us the stories of the assassin hired to kill my body physician, and several other amusing stories. Sabion, you are a great liar and villain, but your head is lost if you utter one lie to me in my own matters. I know that you have sent your daughter away with Adarmelech. I know that you are a scoundrel; but you are a faithful servant. Remain so or you are lost. Now go and weep for your daughter."

"One word more, my lord, and then I go," said Sabion. "I am Herod's most faithful servant, and his instrument in the execution of all his plans—Name me the crime I have not committed on your account, and I will be silent. Why then do you call ME a liar, villain or scoundrel? Know it, my lord, your body physician is a spy of your enemies, a tool of the rebels. He has entrapped you and Salome in his artful net, and none of you observe it; therefore I thought best to render him harmless. I failed, and you set it to the account of my sins. Had I succeeded, you would have set it to the account of my best services; for he is a spy."

"You lie again," Herod thundered, "he is an unpracticed, visionary man; but he is as virtuous as you are vicious. He is as useless to me as you are useful; but he is as honest as you are roguish; he is my only source of amusement; let him alone and unmolested. He lacks your prudence and shrewdness, but you lack his upright, bold and manly conduct. He is my man, when I wish to muse away an hour with a veracious man, and wo unto him, who molests my body physician. Now, go and weep for your daughter."

"My lord, remember I have experience enough to distinguish between the genuine, plain man of high virtues, and the comedian who plays the honest man for a certain purpose," said Sabion, "I caution you against your body physician."

"Go and weep for your daughter," said Herod, "I must think of the hapless people of Sharon." Sabion bowed and left. Herod stared after him. "What a contemptible fellow this is," he uttered, slowly, and after a pause he continued, "What a contemptible man must I appear to him, that I suffer him to be my counsellor." Running up and down the room for some time in rapid strides, and soliloquizing unintelligible words, he rung the bell, a chamberlain entered. "Call my body physician!" was the order. The man left, and Herod continued running about the room half mad with agitation. "If he also is a traitor," he burst forth, "then all mankind is a nest of serpents, a heap of basilisks, whom to kill with one blow is a virtue." Here Simon opened the door. "You have called me, my lord," said Simon, "called me away from the sick bed of your sister. It must be important."

"Very important," said Herod. "First I wish to know the cause of my sister's agitation. The mere information of an earthquake in Sharon could not excite her so violently."

"Your supposition is undoubtedly correct," said Simon; "but little as it behooves the physician to broach the secrets of his patients, still less it becomes a man to betray his neighbor. You are your sister's brother, she will tell you her secrets, if she considers them fit for your ears."

"I am the King, and she would not tell me, what she must reveal to her physician," said Herod; "therefore I ask you."

"Therefore I must observe profound silence," said Simon.

"I pray," said Herod.

"I have no right to grant," was the reply.

"I command," the King thundered.

"And I obey not," was the brief response.

"I will apply force," said Herod.

"Have you another dagger concealed somewhere, with which you intend to frighten a man?" Simon asked. "Ah, try it with your Sabions and your other creatures. I fear neither force nor violence."

"Because you know me to be your friend," said Herod smilingly

"Because I know I am right," Simon replied

"Is my sister very sick?" Herod inquired.

"She will recover in a few days; she is not actually sick," said Simon.

"How is the Queen?" Herod asked.

"I know not, my lord," he answered.

"Why do you not?" Herod continued.

"Because I have not seen her for some time," was the reply.

"Why do you neglect the Queen," said Herod, "when originally you were called to attend upon her?"

"Neglect a Queen?" Simon remarked. "A Queen is not neglected, if I do not wait upon her. Whenever she should need my services she will call me, till then I am of no use to her. Man's time must be applied usefully either to himself or to his fellow men."

"It appears you fear the scrutinizing looks of the Queen," said Herod; "for Sabion says you are a spy of my enemies."

"Then permit me to leave you," said Simon, "and command me to return no more, my lord. Why should you have a spy about you? You have so many excellent friends, Sabion, Castobarus, Sohemus and a host of others who are very faithful servants, wherefore should you be encumbered by a spy, a dry and serious Essence, who is dissatisfied with your system of government, and condemns your doings from the beginning to the end? Bid me go, and I will obey."

"I will do so forthwith," said Herod. "I will send you away, and you shall return only on your own account. Aurion, it behooves Kings to be magnificently charitable. I wish to be so, especially this time, beyond all comparison with former Kings, and you shall be my agent in this work of benevolence. Go to Sharon, carry comfort and consolation to every destitute widow and orphan. Carry aid and support to whomsoever needs it. Heal every wound and distil healing balm in every sore, in the name and in behalf of the King. My treasury is open to you."

Simon, overcome by this great and magnanimous offer of the King, fell down upon his knees before him and stammered his thanks. This was a proposal too congenial to the nature of Simon, and too highly honorable, that he should not consider it a token of the King's most distinguishing regard and kindness. "Rise and go," said Herod, "and when you are in Sharon let your actions be guided entirely by your generous impulses. Be a kind benefactor to the unfortunate of my people."

"Herod is a great King," said Simon, "he understands the great art to place the right man at the right spot. Sire, you could not confer on me a greater honor than this. I thank you for it. I will do honor to the magnanimity and generosity of him who sends me." "Farewell, farewell!" said Herod, and bowed Simon out of the saloon.

"Thank God that I have thus disposed of him for several weeks," Herod soliloquized, after Simon was gone, "and so I have none in my way, to rid myself of my last rival. As long as that young man is about me, I feel too virtuous to slay old Hyrcan"—"Hyrcan! Hyrcan! I must be King, and thou must die!" Herod exclaimed several times, running up and down the room like a madman. "Ah foolish Aurion," he then exclaimed, "you can not govern a nation, you can only be a good citizen and a happy man; but the King of a republican nation must be a bloody and reckless despot"—"And why should a man be a King," he soliloquized then, "if he must part with everything dear to the heart?" He crossed his arms over his breast, dropped his head and walked the room in silent meditation, from which the clash of arms woke him. A clash of arms in the royal palace is something so strange, that Herod could not pass it unnoticed. He went in the direction from which the sound came, until he stood before a barred door. Herod drew his sword and in a few moments the door was broken in. To his greatest surprise he found Simon and Sabion in a deadly combat. Sabion bled from several wounds, and Simon swung his sword with unabated fury. The King stepped between the combatants and stopped them. "Madmen, what do you do!" the King thundered. The trembling and bleeding Sabion bowed deeply before the King; Simon made no reply.

"Will you speak, sir?" the King asked Simon, angrily.

"I made use of my sovereign rights," said Simen. "If two Kings can not agree, and suppose to be wronged by each other, they appeal to arms. We appealed to arms to settle our difficulties."

"And so also Aurion is a weak man," said Herod, "I thought he can not thirst after vengeance. I thought justice, and nothing but justice and virtue are his guiding stars; but he breathes revenge. Go to Sharon, go. All men are weak."

"And why should I be better than a King?" Simon asked, proudly. "Yet I am no worse than a King. This monster occasioned his own daughter, his only child, to love me best of all men, and she did love me. Scarcely had he been convinced of her affections to me, when he sent her away in the silence of night and hired an assassin to slay the lover of his daughter. All ties of nature are dissolved. The sacredness of all affections is defiled. The evil demons, the envious devils of the lowest hell have taken possession of the human heart. He sent her to Sharon, to his own country seat and kept her a prisoner there. But ha, ha, ha, a host of malicious devils smile over the victory, the earthquake shook the house and buried Helen under it. I must send this monster to the eternal seat of justice, where his own daughter testifies against him; for there is no justice in Israel. But this is not all yet. This monster in human shape seduced the wife of an honest man, placed a raging hell in her bosom, exposed her to the torments of Satan in a wounded conscience. Two were the offspring of that black crime, which cost the life of the honest husband. This fallen, tormented, degraded woman lies in the clutches of this devil, for she fears he might expose her and her hapless children. The earthquake killed those two children, the woman is ravingly mad, and he laughs at the despair of a mother, at the torment of his own victim. I am the avenger of four innocent beings. Give way, my lord, I must slay the villain, that mankind be no longer outraged by such an accursed incarnation of Satan. Eternal justice itself strengthens my arm to punish the fiend. Give way, my lord, Sabion is ripe for hell."

"Your swords, gentlemen, I want your swords," the King commanded. Sabion obeyed, Simon hesitated. "Your sword, sir, or you are my prisoner," the King commanded

"Here is my sword and my solemn protest," said Simon. "I have not yielded my rights to anybody."

"Makes no difference," said Herod. "You dare not fight in my palace. I wish to know who the woman is of whom you speak."

"I betray none," said Simon.

"Sabion, who is the woman of whom he speaks?" the King thundered. "You speak immediately or you have breathed your last."

"Salome," Sabion stammered, and fell upon his knees before the King.

Herod pushed him back with a terrible curse. "Away, be out of my sight," he raged, and struck Sabion in the face. "Away, or I shall forget that I am a King." He was so agitated, that he embraced Simon, then again he cursed, laughed and wept in turn. "Go to Sharon," he finally exclaimed, "the matter is urgent, requires immediate attention. Go to Sharon. Farewell." Wildly laughing, Herod left the room after he had returned the sword to Simon.

For several days none was permitted to appear before Herod. He was agitated that none could speak to him on any public business. But Sohemus came one morning and insisted upon seeing the King, and he was admitted.

"My lord, this is a highly improper time for long meditations," said the soldier, "things have assumed a threatening aspect."

"What news do you bring us?" Herod asked. "Be brief. I am not in the humor to hear long orations,"

"Then I had better not begin at all," said, he, "for I have to say a great deal. The introduction is the threatening aspect of events."

"Speak, man of the sword," the King replied. "Is there no war, no combat, no battle on hand?"

"Plenty; more than required," said Sohemus. "Malchus, at the head of a large army, has appeared beyond Jordan, plunders, sacks, devastates and kills. The messengers from beyond Jordan, as in the days of Saul, cry for help. The rumor was spread in Arabia, that half of our country was destroyed by the late earthquake, so the Arabs come to take the rest."

"Then we will cross the Jordan and give them another defeat," Herod remarked, indifferently. "Go, Sohemus, give orders to my captains to be ready to leave the city tomorrow. You go with them. I follow you. Concentrate an army of 20,000 men north of the Jabek creek. We will show those Arabs, that we are not dead yet."

"One word more and I go to do my duty," said Sohemus. "The current of excitement runs very high in the city. The feeling is general, that all these miseries come on us on account of your sins. The pious men fast and implore the grace of the Most High to change your mind; but others curse instead of praying and drink wine instead of fasting, and they are quite dangerous fellows. They repeat in angry curses the substance of the pious men's prayers. If you with the garrison leave the city, they might play you foolish tricks."

"And which are the foremost of my sins in their estimation?" Herod asked, coolly.

"First and foremost, they say you are

guilty of two grievous sins," said Sohemus; "You tolerate the crimes of Sabion, altho' you know them, still treat him as your friend; and you keep the old Hyrcan in close quarters with the avowed intention to move him out of your way."

"Enough," interrupted the King, "I understand the plot." Walking the room for some time, he stopped before his general and, with a smile on his lips, he said, "Sohemus, you are an excellent soldier, but a poor statesman, if you can not see through this spider web of a plot."

"I profess my utter inability to discover any plot in these occurrences," said Sohemus.

"But I do," said Herod. "Malchus came with an army to restore Hyrcan to the throne But Sabion the most cunning man in Israel is in the way of the rebels, and they want me to remove him. Then they want the old Hyrcan to appear before the People to increase the excitement in his favor. An insurrection in Jerusalem, an Arabian army beyond Jordan, the Romans are otherwise engaged. The plot is well laid, but they broached it too early, that is all. Give my orders to my captains. Five thousand men and Sabion are sufficient to keep those scoundrels in their nests. Go, give my orders."

Sohemus went away, and Herod sent forthwith for Sabion. He appeared apparently bent down with grief, and fell down on his knee before the King. "Pardon me, my lord," he prayed, "I have brought disgrace on myself and your sister; but none knows it. She must have told the secret to Aurion. Pardon me, and while the silence of the grave now embraces the innocent offspring of my crime, while God has so sorely afflicted me, and has bereft me of all my children in one moment; let me not feel the crushing weight of your displeasure, my lord. Let the past be forgotten, and let me, in future, by my unshaken fidelity and untired exertion for you, my royal master, atone for my crimes. My life, the last drop of my blood are devoted to your service. I will live and die for you."

"Very good," said Herod, smilingly.—"You will henceforth live just to atone for old crimes, and hence you must grow very old. Rise, Sabion, and receive my pardon. But hear at the same time, and always bear in mind, your life is mine."

Sabion rose and bowed reverently, as a token of affirmation, when the King continued, "Are you informed of the state of affairs?"

"I am, my lord," said Sabion, "and am certain that the invasion of Malchus and the movements of the revolutionists stand in close connection. The object in view is to dethrone and exile you, and set Hyrcan on the throne."

"I must defeat Malchus," said Herod, "let it cost my throne, my life. None shall boast upon having attacked me without being chastised for it. Meanwhile, two objects must be accomplished. The city must be kept quiet and Hyrcan must be condemned and executed. Can you accomplish this, during my absence?"

"It is a difficult task, my lord," Sabion said, "but I believe I can accomplish it. One thing I promise you for certain, either I carry out your wishes to the very letter, or I die in your service."

"We are not at that point yet," said Herod. "Tell me how many men you want to keep the city quiet?"

"Five thousand soldiers, beside my secret officials," said Sabion, "are sufficient."

"And how will you proceed against Hyrcan?" was the next question.

"As soon as the first tidings of your victory over Malchus reach the city," said Sabion, "I will have the trial of Hyrcan begun. Reports from the seat of war, illuminations and festivities celebrating your brilliant victories, reports of your charities from Sharon, and accounts from the seat of the Roman war shall be subservient to our purposes, and Hyrcan will be dispatched before the people will awake from their enthusiasm. This is my plan."

"Suits me, exactly," said Herod. "So you will do, exactly so."

"But one thing more must be understood," said Sabion. "The presiding officers of the Sanhedrin are weak but pious men. I fear they will resign in preference of giving a verdict against Hyrcan. What must I do in this case?"

"Other officers must be appointed forthwith," said Herod, "such as will best suit our purpose. Think of the best men."

"I will, my lord," said Sabion. "The governor of the city, the governor of the palace and my treasurer will be instructed to obey you," said Herod. "Prevent every communication of the people with the Asmoneans, also with the Queen. No harm shall be done to them. If my body physician returns from Sharon send him with a safe escort to my head quarters; but be careful not to do him any harm."

Sabion was dismissed, arrangements were made accordingly, and in a few days the King followed his captains to the seat of war.

CHAPTER XII

THE ESCAPED.

Dumb, terror-stricken and overawed, Helen looked on the terrible scene, when before her eyes the edifice was crushed and buried its inmates. She heard the terrific shrieks, then the heavy groans, she felt the violent shock which threw her almost senseless to the earth, she saw the pillars of fire rising from the nether world and sweeping over the terrible scene; but she was incapable of uttering a sound or recognizing her position. Abba Shaul first recovered his senses, and several times, he called Helen, before he received an answer. When finally she gave an answer, the bold man groped through the dark of the night and succeeding in finding Helen. "Rise and follow me as fast as you can," he said, and raised her from the earth. She trembled, could not stand erect and fell again. "We are lost, if you do not master yourself," he said, raising her again, but finding her incapable to walk, he clasped her in his arms, and started off with her. Having proceeded but a few steps he fell over an uprooted tree. Again he rose and seized Helen, and pressed his course onward with due caution, until Helen fully recovered her self-possession.

"Let us not go from here before daybreak," she prayed, "let us render assistance to the unfortunate creatures, buried alive under yonder house. Let us return and try to assist them."

"Not I indeed," said Abba Shaul, "nor shall I permit you to return to those hellish, beastly hirelings. They are dead, we can do them no good." He seized Helen's arm and dragged her forward through the fragments of shattered trees and broken rocks, and she followed reluctantly. Having reached the end of the grove, they saw the next village and many others on fire. The shrieks of woe rent the air in all directions, still the muttering and violence of the earthquake and the rage of the hurricane had not subsided. Helen fell down upon her knees and cried, "Lord, this is a picture of thy fierce anger. Lord, destroy them not all, save the innocent." Abba Shaul also appeared to be overawed, for he halted a good while.

"Let us make haste," said he, "there in the village we could probably be of some use." They proceeded in rapid strides and reached the next village, where consternation ruled supreme. The presence of mind, the powerful voice and the natural strength of Abba Shaul rendered important services to the distracted villagers. "The sins of Herod and his vicious accomplices bring the punishment of the Lord on us," Abba Shaul vociferated, and in a few minutes it re-echoed from every breast of the wretched men, of whom one lamented the loss of his next relatives, while another groaned with bodily pain, a third lamented the loss of his home, his barn in which the provisions for the winter were stored away, and again another sat dumb with grief at the earthly remains of his children.

While Abba Shaul was engaged in rendering assistance where he could, and arresting the conflagration, Helen, with tears in her eyes, attended to the suffering and dying, and reached them the consolation at her command. Among those most severely wounded Helen found the chamberlain of Salome, whom we have seen before in conversation with Adarmelech. She recognised him instantly and calling his name he opened his eyes, and, beholding Helen, he sighed heavily and trembled violently. He closed and opened his eyes several times in quick succession, and, seeing Helen always before him, he cried with all his strength, "Away, spirit of vengeance, and let me die in peace."

"I am no spirit," Helen said, kindly laying her hand upon his forehead. "Can I do nothing for you?"

Again he opened his eyes and stared at her. Then he clasped her hand and asked her, "Did you escape?"

"I did, God protected me," said Helen.—"And Adarmelech did not succeed?"—the man asked, eagerly.

Helen blushed. "How do you know the schemes of that man?" she inquired.

"I brought him the command from Salome," the man stammered. "She insisted upon the violation of your person. She loves him who loves you. God has punished us all. The earthquake saved you. Return not to Jerusalem. Your ruin is inevitable. Pray for me, I die. I am a loathsome sinner." These were his last words, a few moments more and he was dead. Helen shuddered at the cold-blooded wickedness of Salome. A chill of terror and disgust coursed through her blood on looking at the dead man before her. She remembered the scene of scandal between her father, Salome and Castobarus, which nearly cost her liberty and life. She also remembered the wickedness of her father, and wretched, mortified and disgusted she pressed her hands upon her eyes, as though she could prevent herself from looking at all the scandal and wickedness, just passing before her agitated soul.

Two arms suddenly twined around her neck and a kiss pressed on her lips, roused Helen from her reveries. It was a female pressing herself closely to Helen's heart, with her face buried in the bosom of the surprised maiden. "Helen, my beloved, dearest, sweetest Helen," the girl cried, frantic with joy, "It is no dream, I have thee again." Recognizing the dear voice of Elvira, Helen dumb with rapture pressed the friend in her arms, and her tears gushed lightly on the head of Elvira. "I have no father, I have no mother," Helen cried, "but I have dear, beloved, faithful friends. My Elvira, faithful soul, how did you find your way to this solitary village?"

"I saw yonder monster prepare to leave the city," said Elvira, "and his preparations were so secret, that I knew he must be appointed to a wicked errand. I told it to the Queen, she gave me leave and protection to pursue the chamberlain of Salome. I followed his track unobserved, to this village. Here I learned that he went to the country house of your father, and intended to follow him instantly, when the earthquake grew so furious, that we could not leave. In the confusion here, I heard the voice of Abba Shaul, and he told me that you were here."

After an exchange of the fondest sentiments, Helen first communicated the story of the last day. Then she spoke of the former part of her story On coming to the wife of the steward, Elvira interrupted her, "Is she also, dead?" When Helen affirmed this, Elvira could not restrain her tears. On inquiry of Helen she said, that the woman was her nurse when she was quite young, but she remembered distinctly her kindness and fondness of her.

There was no time left for further explanation, for Abba Shaul came and urged them both to leave, which they did instantly. Elvira urged that all should return to Jerusalem, as the Queen would protect them against every harm. Abba Shaul, however, insisted, that Helen should go to Jericho, and wait there until Simon be informed of her fate, and he should tell where she should go.—Helen preferred the latter. Elvira was sent to Jerusalem with the instruction to inform none except the Queen and Simon of Helen's escape, and Helen followed Abba Shaul toward Jericho.

The sun rose that morning over a sad and melancholy scene. The whole plain of Sharon presented an awful picture of destruction, death and wretchedness. From every corner of the rich plain the voice of lamentation sounded in despairing accents. As Abba Shaul passed the desolate villages, he said, "The sins of Herod and his wicked accomplices brought this misery upon us," and before the evening shade again covered the wide plain, every child repeated the terrific sentence over Herod and his counsellors. In a few days the words of Abba Shaul, like the voice of an oracle, sounded from one end of the country to the other.—And as it traveled on the rushing pinions of rumor, it grew rapidly into a voice from heaven, into words spoken by terrific demons through the roar of the hurricane, and became an indisputable fact with all the opponents of Herod. It made its way to the humble cottage of the shepherd, to the temple and the royal palace in Jerusalem, and grew perpetually in its onward course.

When Simon left Jerusalem bending his steps toward the plain of Sharon, that voice of accusation almost arrested his progress; but his natural kindness maintained the superiority, and he proceeded to the place of his destiny. Wherever he came the same voice of complaint was heard. His eloquence was spent in vain, thousands said the same words, and thousands refused to accept anything of him in behalf of Herod. Still wherever he left, the blessings of the multitude followed him. Thousands of destitute widows and orphans enjoyed the gifts which he had brought them. He banished want and famine from the troubled plain of Sharon, brought consolation to many a cheerless heart, and his name was soon associated with those of the greatest benefactors in Israel; he appeared to many a grateful heart to be an angel sent by God in a human form to bring relief to the destitute and suffering. None thought of Herod, few believed that Simon was the messenger of the King.—Some said, he was a rich man who disliked to do such charity under his own name, therefore he said the King sent him. Others could not be caused to believe him a man, they took him to be an angel in the form of a man.

Simon had reached the ruins of Sabion's castle. With tears in his eyes he commanded the workmen he had brought to remove the shattered fragments, and find the dead bodies buried under it. Trembling and with a broken heart he looked on as the work progressed, expecting every moment to find the body of Helen. "They had a fight before they were buried under these ruins," some of the workmen exclaimed, on raising two dead bodies with their swords in their hands and several wounds on their bodies. They finally succeeded in excavating the whole body of men as we left them that memorable night. The combat was evident, but Simon had no mind to think of the causes. He looked eagerly at every stone they removed, and whenever a human form became visible he turned his eyes shily in another direction, fearing to see the mutilated body of Helen. "Females killed by the fall of the ceiling," said one of the workmen. Simon felt that his blood suddenly stopped its course and a cold perspiration forced itself through the pores. "An elderly woman and a young one and a little boy," said another of the workmen. His words pierced Simon's heart like a two-edged sword. He attempted in vain to move from the spot where he appeared to be rooted to the ground. In vain did he try to direct his eyes to the group of the excavated dead. His will was not strong enough to move his limbs, he was paralyzed. "And here is a man with a knife in his throat. They must have had a desperate fight," said one of the workmen. They brought the body so near to Simon, that he recognised Adarmelech, one of the infamous tools of Sabion. He examined the knife and, recognizing it as belonging to Abba Shaul, it fell from his hands. In the most painful accents he then exclaimed. "He kept his word and met with a horrible death." None of those present understood a word of what Simon said. They continued digging and removing the ruins.

It is with grief as with joy; if the heart is too full thereof, it becomes indifferent of either. The supposition that Abba Shaul also found his death in this house thus overwhelmed the heart of Simon with unutterable grief, that he indifferently inspected the dead bodies. It was evident to him that Abba Shaul was here and was the cause of the deadly combat, when the earthquake surprised them; but he could not find his body nor the body of Helen, and commenced to hope they might have escaped. The valuable articles found among the ruins were faithfully collected and deposited in a box. One of the workmen brought a bundle of manuscripts to Simon, which he gave to his servant for safe-keeping, supposing something might be in it to serve his own purpose. The whole house being made accessible, the dead bodies were buried, and Simon with the workmen hastened away from the scene of destruction tormented by uncertainty about the fate of Helen and Abba Shaul.

Returned to the village, Simon was received with the greatest enthusiasm by the inhabitants. The multitude crowded around him eager to catch a glance of the distinguished benefactor, or speak a word or two of praise to him, while the more superstitious portion, taking him to be a supernatural being, brought their children and prayed for a blessing. The sick waited impatiently for the marvelous physician, and not a few uttered the supposition, that the stranger was the Messiah, who had come to dethrone Herod and re-instate the golden age.

Simon had reached the apartments which the grateful villagers had prepared for him. Desiring to rest he begged his friends to admit none to his room, until he would permit it. Being alone he opened the bundle of manuscripts and began to examine its contents. Letters to the steward's wife by Sabion formed part of the contents. A letter about Helen, that she ran away twice with her lover, a simple shepherd, and must, therefore, be kept in close confinement, was the first he read. "Infernal liar!" Simon exclaimed, throwing the letter on the table.—Next he read a correspondence between the same parties about the boy, which the woman should adopt as her own. "That is Salome's child," he soliloquized. "But there are two children, where did he place the other?" He also found letters of Salome to the same woman, speaking of two children which she should adopt as her own, promising her a heavy reward. "Here is a mystery," Simon soliloquized, "one child is missing altogether." He continued reading, and there was another letter, signed by Baba ben Buta who assured the woman that the girl is well situated and will be educated to the best advantage. Then he found another letter of the same man, informing the woman that the girl is at Herod's court, in the immediate vicinity of Sabion and Salome; but they know not that she is their daughter.

"Then one of Salome's children lives," said Simon, "is at court, and she does not know it. What had Baba ben Buta to do with this affair?" Everything was a mystery to him. He looked over the other letters and found one of Salome's first husband threatening the woman with death and destruction, if she did not kill Salome's children. Then he found one of Salome informing the woman of the death of Joseph, Salome's husband. Searching among the costly things which were found in the house, he discovered a bracelet which he had seen on the arm of Helen, a purse and the letters of recommendation for Adarmelech signed by Salome, directed to Mark Antony. Then he discovered a copper box which he opened with difficulty. He was not a little surprised to find therein letters of Cleopatra to Sabion, proposing to make him the lord of Jericho and several other cities, if he succeeded in getting Herod out of the way. It appeared from the tenor of the letter that he had agreed to do so, and a written grant signed by Cleopatra and sealed with the grand seal of the Egyptian kingdom laid in the same box.

Simon lifted up the documents and exclaimed enthusiastically, "Now, infernal scoundrel, now thy doom is sealed.—How cunningly he did hide this precious parchment, but the earthquake brought it to light." He remembered the ring of Cleopatra, which he gave to Helen. If Helen and her uncertain fate had not occurred to his mind, he would have shouted with joy. But "where is Helen?"—"Where is Abba Shaul?" these questions produced a melancholy impression on his mind.

Here Jonathan ben Uziel opened the door, notwithstanding the loud protestations of the villagers, and the two friends sunk speechless into each other's embrace. "Thy fame is great in Sharon," said Jonathan, "and it is easy to find you. Every child knows where you are and whither you go. They say you are the Messiah, an angel, or at least an angelic u an."

"I am grateful to Herod for this opportunity," said Simon. "These are the greatest days of my life. But tell me what brings you to this place?"

"Baba ben Buta sends me to tell you, that Herod, on leaving Jerusalem appointed Sabion to manage his business. Sabion reigns supreme in Jerusalem," said Jonathan; "every honest man trembles. Such a reign of terror never was felt in Jerusalem. Hyrcan is accused before the Sanhedrin, in the name of the King, of high treason. According to our advice Hillel, our great teacher is his counsellor, and will appear for him before the Sanhedrin. Herod sent a written grant, that under no consideration should Hillel be harmed, and after the trial he should go back unmolested to Jericho. Although they have no men to oppose effectually the arguments of Hillel, we still apprehend fatal consequences, as almost the whole Sanhedrin consists of Herod's creatures. Still we shall be watchful on this point. The most important point of my mission is to inform you, that Sabicu has dispatched a body of men to bring you to Jerusalem alive or dead.—You are lost if you come to Jerusalem."

"I fear nothing for myself," said Simon. "I am prepared for all eventualities. But, my friend, have you no tidings of Abba Shaul, none of Helen?"

"None," said Jonathan with a sad look.—"None can imagine whither Abba Shaul has gone."

The conversation was interrupted by a noisy dispute at Simon's door. He opened to ascertain the cause. "The men of Sabion are here," Simon remarked. "Be ready for defence."

Both young men stepped out and attempted to stop the noise. "I must see the King's physician," one of the strangers said. "That is myself," said Simon, "what do you wish?" "You must follow me to Jerusalem. The King recals you from this mission. You are accused of high treason. Here is the order of the lower Sanhedrin of Jerusalem."

Simon read the order, examined the seal, and found all correct. "I am not an inhabitant of Jerusalem," said Simon, "that Sanhedrin has no jurisdiction over me. I shall lay down my commission in the hands of the King, who entrusted me with it. At my earliest convenience I will appear before the King in his camp. You are dismissed, sir, you have done your duty."

"Then you refuse to go with me?" the officer asked, significantly.

"You understood me right," Simon replied. Meanwhile hundreds of people had gathered about the house, listening impatiently to the conversation.

"Then it becomes my painful duty to apply force," said the officer; but seeing his men surrounded by a dense crowd, his courage failed, to assault Simon. He summoned him again to pay obedience to the laws of the country, but Simon insisted upon appearing first before the King. The officer then commanded the crowd to give way, that he might do his duty, in arresting a man who was accused of high treason, and place him before the tribunal of justice.—Hisses, groans and menaces were the replies of the people.

Simon retired to his room. Jonathan said to the people, "Know it, ye sons of Abraham, this is a treacherous design of Sabion, the King's vile spy, the bloody enemy of Israel. He wants to tear your benefactor from your midst and drag him to certain death."

Like the muttering of distant thunder an angry voice sounded from the crowd. It appeared as though the whole multitude had burst forth in one threatening curse. The officer remonstrated; but an old man stepped forward from the midst of the crowd and advised the officer to leave with his men, and not to irritate the people to the utmost

"After the King has been so graciously disposed toward you, and cared for you as a father does for his children, you will disobey his behests?" the officer asked.

"Away with him!" the people cried.

"God's anger has just passed most severely over your heads," the officer continued, "will you, ungrateful men, conjure down the King's wrath upon your heads, and destroy yourselves?"

"Away with him, instantly let him be gone!" the multitude cried, angrily.

The officer made some soothing remarks and went off with his men, followed by the hisses, curses, and groans of the multitude.

When Jonathan stepped into Simon's room, he led him to the window, and, pointing in a certain direction, he said to Jonathan, "Those men there come from the destroyed country-seat of Sabion. When they convey the tidings to that officer, that the documents of Sabion (now in my hands) are gone, they must return and try their utmost to obtain them. Such must be their order. Besides this Sabion hates half work. They will return to night with a strong force to surprise us."

Simon having shown the Egyptian correspondence to Jonathan, the latter left the room and apprized the crowd of Simon's fears.

When the people, outside of the house, were informed of the probable return of the officer with an increased force, they instantly dispatched messengers to the neighboring villages, and apprized their neighbors of what happened and what might yet occur. Before night had set in upon the plain, an armed multitude surrounded the house in which Simon tarried, and every one appeared to be ready for a deadly combat at any moment's notice. They had come so cautiously and from different sides, that their number could not be estimated. The hours of night advanced rapidly and without interruption. The people began to doubt the return of the officer. Simon, however, insisted that the officer must certainly return, and attempt to convey him to Jerusalem.

In the second hour after midnight, heavy steps were heard from a distance interrupted by an occasional clash of arms. "This is the step of a marching line of infantry," Jonathan said, "one man steps not so heavily, and the steps of many are not so regular unless they were regularly drilled soldiers." The sound of the steps became more distinct with every passing moment. The peasants posted themselves in front of the house and in several ambushes. Every body was ready for action. A line of soldiers arrived within sight. They were commanded by a stern voice to halt. The officer asked after the authority of the man who dared to command the King's troops, and he was told in a dignified manly tone: "I, sir, am the messenger of the Elders of this village and circuit. I, the chief authority of this district command you not to invade this village.—The people are agitated, they stand under arms. Every step you go forward will cost human blood, most likely human lives. Every drop of the blood thus shed will fall upon your conscience."

"In the name of the King, I command you and your people to desist," said the officer. "I am sent hither to arrest a man who is accused of high treason, and place him before the proper authorities. Whoever interferes with me in the discharge of my duty must bear the consequences. I command you and your people to retire."

"The people will not listen to your words, if you speak in the name of the King," said the man. "They know, that Jerusalem is defiled with innocent blood. I caution you not to advance. You are lost if you do.—The people are furiously enraged against you and your master, and well armed. I caution you not to advance."

"Tell your people," said the officer, "I am provided with a sufficient number of men and arms, to bring another earthquake over the plain of Sharon. I command them to desist or stand the consequence of their misplaced zeal."

"Then the will of the Lord be done," said the man, and turned to go.

"Stop, hoary rebel," the officer cried, "you are my prisoner and my hostage. You blasphemed God and insulted the King. You must go with me to Jerusalem. But if your accomplices refuse to surrender the other prisoner, I will massacre you before their very eyes."

"You are mistaken, rash man," said the man coolly, "I am not your prisoner; but you are mine. Or do you believe I entrusted myself to your magnanimity? Give me your sword, or you are lost."

"Take him!" the officer commanded.

A shrill whistle was the answer of the man who, having drawn his sword moved not one inch. A volley of arrows was showered on the soldiers from three different sides, and with the loud cries, "Down with Herod and his hirelings!" three different parties stormed upon the soldiers with furious vigor, and the man before them suddenly turned a military commander.

Those posted at the house and in the different ambushes were not a little astonished to see the soldiers fight, as they thought among themselves. Anyhow the signal was given and all rushed to the attack. The voice of Abba Shaul was heard above all as he commanded his men; for none else but him was the man who confronted the advancing troops of the King. The combat was brief and sanguinary. The soldiers were surrounded by an armed multitude. Their commanding officer did not yield, but the soldiers, one after the other, threw away their arms with the exclamation, "No honest man fights against his brothers." Abba Shaul summoned the officer again to yield, but he refused. "Better one dies than many," the gigantic man cried, and swinging his sword with rare vigor he cut his way through the remaining troops, and reached the officer who was again summoned to yield, and on refusing again, Abba Shaul's sword fell so heavily upon the helmet of the officer, that he fell bleeding from several wounds. In a few minutes the King's troops capitulated. The wounded were removed to the houses and the dead were placed on a hill, and sentinels left with them.

"Men and brethren," said Abba Shaul, to the people, "the cup of Herod's sin is full to its very brim. His iniquities brought misery on our country, such as our fathers never knew. Now is the time to chastise the tyrant. Organize forthwith into a company of volunteers, the Sharon Volunteers, and be ready for action by next Passover."

The people responded with thundering cheers. Messengers were dispatched to convoke all men of Sharon, and measures were adopted to complete the organization.

"And so you live, Abba Shaul, thank God that you live!" Simon exclaimed, enthusiastically, on approaching the warrior. "As you live Helen is not dead."

"She waits for you in Jericho, in the house of your mother," Abba Shaul said.

Simon's joy was boundless. He embraced Abba Shaul many times. His eyes radiated with rapture. "She lives, she lives!" he burst forth. "Hear it thou midnight sky, hear it silvery moon, glittering stars, she lives, she was not buried under yonder ruins. My God, I thank thee for this grace, the mercy thou hast bestowed upon me.—She lives, I defy Herod and his wrath, the prayer of that angel will shield me, shield thee, Abba Shaul, shield all Israel. Abba Shaul, you are a great man, I am your debtor. I have no words of thanks good enough for you. Command me to go to death for you and I will cheerfully obey. My indebtedness to you is so great, that I fear I must be ungrateful."

"Folly, nothing but folly," said Abba Shaul. "A friend must be willing to do something for a friend without expecting thanks."

"But how in God's name did you come here at such an opportune time?" Jonathan asked.

"On hearing that Sabion is lord in the absence of Herod, I knew that it must result so," said Abba Shaul. "I knew that bloody man's schemes. I left Jericho instantly to follow Simon. By the way, I collected a small body of men around me. To-day I met the messenger sent out from this village. I ascertained the whereabouts of the enemy, when night set in I took my position, and when they came I was prepared for them."

After the necessary conversation was had, the three men spoke of the steps to be taken next. "Sabion must receive false reports of this affair," was the opinion of all. Jonathan and several others were appointed to assume the uniforms of the soldiers, and convey such information to Sabion as was subservient to the revolutionary cause. Abba Shaul preferred to travel and be where he could do most. But Simon insisted upon going to Herod and producing before him the manuscripts he had found, that he be convinced of the character of Sabion.—All the others remonstrated, they attempted to convince Simon, that he would expose himself to almost certain death, especially if Herod should learn the attack made on his troops; but in vain, Simon insisted on his plan to ruin Sabion, save Herod if possible, and convince him of his own innocence and Sabion's scandalous wickedness. "I can not stand it, that Herod should consider me a traitor. Let him kill me, but first he must confess, that I am right and he is wrong with his slaves."

The words of his friends were wasted and in vain, Simon insisted upon going to Herod, notwithstanding threatening dangers. He was the first to leave the plain.

"Yet he is right," said Jonathan, after Simon was gone. "Herod entrusted him with this commission which he must appear to have used against the King. It looks too much like a breach of confidence, Simon must do as he says."

CHAPTER XIII

UNEXPECTED VISITS.

Salome sat before her writing desk, reading over the lines which she had written on a neat piece of parchment. "So, that will set him right," she soliloquized. "He is accused of high treason, can not escape the grasp of Sabion. He is lost if I do not help him. But I will help him only on the one condition, that in his very prison we must be married. He can not escape this time.—He must become a great man, the King's brother in-law." While still contemplating over her scheme, she was surprised with a visit by Castobarus. She welcomed him coolly, and listened, apparently absent-minded, to his flattering words. Castobarus construed her silence to suit himself best. He fell down upon his knees before her, and prayed in the most affectionate terms, not to torment him any longer, to hear his request and be his. Salome laughed uncourteously at her ardent lover, and told him that she had not resolved yet upon giving up her liberty, and be again a man's wife. Castobarus doubled his affectionate words, but they were in vain, she refused, most unceremonily, to give him any hope.

"The King, my gracious lady, the King promised me your hand, in grateful remembrance of my humble services," Castobarus imprudently remarked.

"Then go to the King and accept what he promised you," she said, and turned from him.

"And you do not hear me?" Castobarus asked.

"Nor do I wish to see you," she replied, firmly.

"And let me despair?" he continued.

"If you choose, yes," was the answer.

"I feel that I must venture the utmost," said Castobarus.

"Anything to suit yourself, when you are gone," she replied, drily

Castobarus went off, Salome laughed at his ugly face, ill-shaped body, and coarse manners.—"I would not have him for my servant," she ejaculated. "He and Aurion!—Nature is fond of contrasts, but I love him only." Again she cast a glance over the lines she had written, and then she smiled complacently. "You can not escape this time," she soliloquized, "You must yield, you must be mine."

"A Greek, my lady, insists upon a private interview with you," said the chamberlain, "he says, he brings important news from the plain of Sharon."

"Admit him," she replied, hastily, "and guard the door of the anti-room, that none listen."

The chamberlain retired, a tall Greek was ushered into her presence, who bowed reverently, but said nothing. "Who sent you to me?" she asked, quickly.

"Myself," was the answer. Beard and wig being taken off, Simon stood before the surprised lady. Salome stretched out her arms and ran to embrace him.

"Desist," Simon said, so frigidly, that she staggered and sunk back upon the sofa.—"We are strangers to each other, and I trust we shall remain so."

"Cruel, monstrous man!" she cried, violently. "For weeks past the happiness of this moment was my only consolation, and now—begone, sir. Who told *you, you* to come in?"

"My duty, madam," was the reply. "In two minutes, I am done, then I shall go."

"Nay, nay, stay, I prithee! let me gaze one moment longer at that heartless, still beloved countenance," she said, and tears gushed from her eyes. "I am so lonely, so desolate, so utterly forsaken and forlorn when you are gone. Stay a little while longer, I prithee."

"As you command, madam," Simon said. "But now to my business. Here, I give you the letters which I found. You, Sabion and your deceased husband wrote them to the woman who was the nurse of your children. These letters, in other hands, might be injurions to you." She grasped them, eagerly. "I know one important fact, to which I must call your attention. Only one of your children is dead, your daughter lives"

"Speak, by the love of your own mother, I entreat you, speak. What do you know of my daughter?" she asked.

"I ascertained beyond the shadow of a doubt," Simon continued, "that your daughter was taken from that nurse, placed under the care of a man who brought her to this court the first month after Herod had taken Jerusalem."

"Then it is Helen, and none but Helen," Salome exclaimed, "For she was born the same hour and in the same house where I was confined. O speak, where is she! she is my daughter. Where, where is she?—Speak, in the name of God and his mercy, speak."

Simon laughed so furiously that Salome shuddered. "Adarmelech would not let her die before he had violated her person, as her unnatural raven mother commanded," Simon vociferated, with gnashing teeth. "Despair in raving madness, satanic woman, thou art ripe for hell."

Pale, shivering and dumb, Salome reclined on the sofa. Covering her eyes with both her hands she was so perfectly paralyzed, that she could not move her hands from her eyes for a good while; when she again regained dominion over herself and removed her hands from her eyes, Simon was gone.—She stared about the room like a maniac, then she struck herself with her own fists, and cursed herself and all mankind. "My own daughter dishonored, and he is gone," were all the words she could utter in her rage, for a long time. But finally love triumphed over all other sentiments of her black heart. Again her eyes glowed with passion and her bosom heaved violently.—"Mine he must be, let it cost half of my days," she cried, "mine he must be or die a wretched, miserable death." Then she rang the bell so violently, that the chamberlain came hurrying into the saloon. "The Greek who was here just now," she said, "must be arrested forthwith and conducted to Sabion. He is a spy. Do you hear, you arrest him, or you will leave this palace forever."

The chamberlain left; carried the orders of his lady to the proper officers, and started off in search of the Greek.

"Helen a bastard, the daughter of Salome and Sabion! It can not, it dare not be, nature can not so contradict itself," was all Simon could think, and this was almost sufficient to break his heart in agony. He reeled into the private apartment of Elvira, and, almost mad with excitement, he asked her, "How can I reach the house of Baba ben Buta? he must know all about it." She could not understand these words, and her questions remained unanswered. In two minutes Simon was changed into a soldier of the guard, with a long beard and long locks, and started off as Elvira directed him.

Simon had reached the summit of Mount Olive. Here he stood and gazed down upon the proud city of the great Kings with its hundred palaces, overtowered by the gigantic temple on Mount Moriah. He cast a look upon the picturesque sceneries unrolled under his feet, as it were. A landscape full of villages, towns, gardens, orchards, vineyards and rich fields losing itself in the southern desert stretched before his eyes into a grand panorama. He followed the winding course of the Cedron as like a silvery thread it makes its way to the Jordan, and gladdens the roots of many willows and palm trees, the habitations of a thousand variegated minstrels of the air. There he stood and gazed on one side on the proud Queen of Palestine, the finest specimen of human architects; while on the other hand the work of the Supreme architect excited his admiration.

"How beautiful and blessed is this land!" Simon exclaimed. "Nature and nature's God, art and industry have lavished on it their costliest treasures. O, thou art the most precious jewel of all lands!" Here he stopped abruptly, as though an evil omen had crept over his soul, and casting a look heavenward he cried, "God! must this beautiful land be the prey ef ravens that feed on our living bodies? So beautiful a land, and so misruled by a despotic hand; so fine a country, and so exposed to a system of espionage, such as God has not destined it to bear. Land of my fathers, graves of our prophets, I feel your woe, I weep your tears." Again he stopped, overpowered with painful emotions. "And must thy dust be again hallowed by the blood of thy champions," he continued, after awhile with a sobbing heart, "this shall be my last essay to prevent it—then the will of the Lord be done. Better a few of us die than all be dead.—Better our blood flows, than our liberty, our law take wings. It is by far better that the number of our widows and orphans be increased, than all of us be demoralized and deadened by this system of oppression and espionage. Thy will, O God, be done."

"What ails you, Essence, that you pray so seriously and devoutly at this unusual hour of the day?" one of the three peasants asked,who had,unnoticed,approached Simon.

"My father remained behind in Jerusalem," said Simon, "and Jerusalem is a dangerous place in our days. I prayed for him."

"Truly, a dangerous plaee," the peasant ejaculated. "Almost every day somebody is found slain in the street, and the perpetrators are scarcely ever detected."

"That is Sabion's work!" Simon inadvertautly exclaimed.

"What do you say, Essence?" the peasant asked, evincing no little curiosity.

Simon, on scrutinizing their countenances closer, considered it best to be careful with his words. "I mean, since Sabion is the principal man in the absence of the King," he said, "it is his duty to prevent such atrocities; but he does not."

"Permit me, my friend," said another of the company, "is not your name Aurion?"

"My name is Simon," was the answer.

"Anyhow, I believe it is best, you return with us to the city," said one of them to Simon, "if your name is not Aurion, no harm shall be done you."

"I have long been desirous," said Simon, "to form the acquaintance of Sabicu's spies. I see, I have now unexpectedly the honor. I am altogether disappointed; for you look like other human beings. I thought you must look like foxes, hungry wolves, bloodthirsty tigers, or something like it. I am altogether disappointed; for I believed you are shrewd, cunning devils, but I see you are fools, since you think I would return to Jerusalem with you."

"Makes not the slightest difference how we look or how wise we are," said one of the three, "we will convey you back to Jerusalem, and there we will teach you courtesy."

"And I say you will not," said Simon.—"I am going to the King to tell him, how you catch people and butcher them in the dark of night, and throw them in the street, that they be found in the morning. Ah, ye hissing scorpions, murderous, vile tools of Satan, I am about exposing your hellish work to the King, to the people if he refuses to hear me."

One of the three evinced a disposition to attack Simon. "Beware, heedless man, or it will cost your life," Simon said, calmly. He pointed back on the road toward the city, and to their dismay they saw several men driving their animals very fast behind them. "These are our friends," one of them exclaimed. "You are mistaken, they are mine," said Simon, smilingly. As they came to a stand still, the men behind them drove furiously and came with lightning speed upon them.

"Cut off their hair and beards," said Simon, "that they utter no lies to anybody, and let them return to Jerusalem, to be a reproach to every man who serves in the rank of Sabien."

"Why should not we cut their ears off, and their noses too," said the Greek proselyte, who was among the arriving party, "that it be known for ever, that these scoundrels were once the servants of a slave, of a dog?"

The stern remonstrance of Simon saved the poor fellows' ears and noses, but their hair and beards were cut so short, that they could not show their faces for the next four weeks to any man.

"Let us travel somewhat faster," said the Greek, after the spies were dispatched, "or else we will be obliged to fight a host of them."

"In one hour we will be beyond the reach of Sabion," said Simon; "for the country people about here, clear to the Jordan, are all antagonists of Herod."

The rage of Sabion on hearing of the escape of Simon and the treatment of his servants was outdone only by the fury of Salome, who struck her servants, cursed her ladies of honor, sent her first chamberlain to jail, accused Sabion of conspiracy with Simon against herself, and refused to listen to anybody. After she was exhausted by the furious rage, she reclined, sobbing and groaning on her sofa, and schemed new designs to capture the lover she could not forget.

Simon arrived safely in the camp of the King, but the King was reported sick, and none was admitted into his presence. "Tell the King his body physician has arrived," he said to the chamberlain, "who must see him on important business." He was admitted instantly.

Stepping into the tent, the King cast a long and scrutinizing look on Simon. Then he said, "Your audacity is nearly as great as your villainy, artful man. How dare you appear again before me? Go, our contract is broken, you broke it violently. Go, I do not wish to forget that I am a King."

"I am prepared to hear you speak thus, sire," said Simon, so calmly, that it almost perplexed the King; "for I know the false reports you have received concerning me. If I beg leave to defend myself against those reports, it is only not to let you believe all men are impostors and villains; it is only not to appear as such in your eyes. Here I am in your power, sire, helpless like a new born child in the midst of your army.—Here I am ready to die, if heaven so decrees. But first I will perform a threefold sacred duty. I must prove to you, that there are also honest men in this world, that I always attempt to be one of them, and that you are deceived, betrayed, sold by your slaves.—But you are sick, I must not speak to day."

The King stared into the open countenance of Simon, as though he was to read his own future in it. "What have you to tell me?" he asked, hastily. "Be quick, I am sick."

"I can not be quick," said Simon, "I have too much to say. But here is a box containing valuable manuscripts. I found it under the ruins of Sabion's house. Read them, they are very important. Meanwhile, I am your prisoner. Then I will speak."

"Your word of honor, that you will stay in the camp till I ordain otherwise," said the King, harshly.

"So it is, sire," Simon replied, bowed and retired.

Simon was not long gone when an officer of the guard called him back to the King. He found Herod in a condition in which he never before had seen him, pale with rage and madness. He trembled with agitation, foamed savagely, and laughed at intervals so furiously, that his servants trembled.—"My lord, you have called me," said Simon, after he stood long enough before Herod, without hearing an articulate sound.

"I have called you to laugh me to scorn," said Herod, with gnashing teeth and a hoarse voice. "I have called you to name me a fool, a maniac, a credulous boy, a thoughtless baby. Why do you not scold? why do you not laugh? the story is so amusing, so ridiculous, so laughable. Ha, ha, ha, help me laugh, that Satan be ashamed of his mewing. Laugh, in God's name laugh, scold as much as you can." Then Herod made such wild gestures and roared forth inarticulate sounds with such a violence, that Simon began to fear for his intellect.

"My lord, do please to hear me," Simon begged; "you are now seriously sick. I pray you, hear me. You must take some sedative, and if this will not restore the normal circulation of your blood, you must bleed. You are very sick, indeed."

"Let us have your drugs, but put no poison to it," Herod ejaculated. "Let us have it, I am sick; but I would not die just now to save all mankind. Let us have the drug without poison."

"My lord, your words are very harsh," said Simon, "I am no poisoner. Take this at once," Simon said on reaching the medicine to Herod, who immediately swallowed it. Simon insisted upon the King to be alone and recline on his couch, and Herod obeyed. Having slept awhile he awoke very much exhausted. Finding Simon at his bedside, he asked him where he found the manuscripts he brought. Simon described time and place, with the other circumstances which brought him in possession of the manuscripts. He also told the King the story of Cleopatra's ring which was in possession of the Queen, as he ascertained she was too magnanimous to speak of it.

The King well comprehended, that the documents before him were no forgery, and that the intention of Sabion to dethrone him in favor of Cleopatra was evident from the documents. "But how could he, so doggishly faithful, do what I commanded?" the King asked. "How could he thus lay at my feet like a slave, and, like an automaton, be moved by any words?"

"Herod is so wise and can not explain this!" Simon said, much astonished. "He attempts successfully to render your government so odious to the people, that they must prefer Cleopatra, anybody to yourself. He first tries to move out of the way all the Asmoneans, then leave you exposed to the hatred of an infuriated, down-trodden, desperate people. Then Cleopatra can easily step in. Is not this a fine scheme? My lord, you must understand it; it can not be otherwise."

"I commence to believe," said the King, "that you are not altogether wrong. There is something self-evident in what you say, although I can not yet account for it. But, before we continue, you must render me account for your own conduct. I sent you to Sharon to look after the hapless and miserable, but you used my kindness for revolutionary purposes, made the people believe they were punished for my sins, and allowed them to deify you almost. This is ingratitude, the vileness of a demagogue, a breach of promise, a violation of sacred obligations, the vile intention to kill a man with the very knife which he gave you to cut from his bread for your hungry children. Speak! if you can, if you dare."

"I can and I dare," Simon said, calmly. "The cry that your sins were the efficient cause of the misery that came over them, was started long before I arrived there, and I have no doubt Sabion himself started it, with the malicious intention to render your benevolence odious and effectless. I opposed it successfully in one place, and without success at other places. But when I was just in a fair way to overcome that prejudice, Sabion sent his troops to arrest me and place me before the Sanhedrin of Jerusalem. This confirmed the people in their preconceived notions, and like furies they rose to protect me. So Sabion did succeed and your benevolence is not known, not acknowledged. I could have gone to another place, but I came to you, to convince you, that there are also honest men in the world. I came because I could not bear the idea of appearing a traitor in your eyes. I appeared before you to hand you these documents and be exonorated; then I will go far, far beyond the reach of your soulless slaves. I have done my duty."

"There is something in the sound of your voice," said the King, "so round, soft and sonorous, which speaks to the heart. I have no evidence, that what you say is true, yet I believe it." He paced the tent in rapid strides and was lost in deliberation. "I thank you, my friend Aurion," the King said, in a kind tone, "I thank you for the discovery of these documents, for they unmask a dangerous serpent. Still more I thank you for the conviction that you are an honest man. I despaired of humanity. I was afraid all are thieves, robbers, scoundrels and traitors. I am better satisfied now than I ever was. Aurion, I can not be your debtor. Although I can not pay you this service, yet I must pay part of it.—Speak what shall I do for you."

"For me?—Nothing," Simon said. "I am satisfied with my lot."

"Proud Diogĕnes, do you know nothing which appears to you worth possessing?" the King said. "Whatever thou wishest shall be granted."

"Ah, I wish many things," said Simon. "I wish you first to change your government, and treat this people becoming a magnanimous King, befitting men born free. I wish you to be relieved of your slaves, traitors and smooth villains who surround your person, fill your court and hold the highest offices. But above all things I wish just now, that the old, weak still amiable Hyrcan be saved, saved through your interference in his favor. Nothing short of this will satisfy me."

"Aurion, you ask what is not in my power to grant," the King said. "Hyrcan is guilty of conspiracy with the enemies of my country; the law of my country dare not be set at nought by the King."

"Hyrcan is innocent," Simon interrupted, hastily. "Sabion has a double purpose in view in this matter—to render Hyrcan harmless to Cleopatra, and conjure up against you the most intense hatred of the people. Sabion and none else made you believe Hyrcan, the weak and peaceable man, conspired against you with the enemies of your country. My lord, save Hyrcan, and you save yourself. Hyrcan's life shall be my reward, and this I must see saved, or you remain in my debt forever."

"If you was not Aurion I would consider you a co-laborer of Hyrcan and Malchus in this treachery," said the King. "I am certain, that Hyrcan, by his weakness of mind, turned a traitor. Let us speak of something else. You return directly to Jerusalem, take the place of Sabion, if you can promise me to keep the city quiet until my return. Let this be the proof of my confidence in you, and the first step to a high position, which you shall occupy hereafter."

"Shall Hyrcan live?" was the answer of Simon.

"Now, about your office," said the King. "You keep the city quiet, and on my return I will dispose of Sabion and elevate you to a high position."

"Shall Hyrcan live, my lord?" Simon asked again.

"We will speak about this some other time," the King said. "Now, I want to know of you, whether you can keep the city quiet to my return."

"If Hyrcan lives, yes," said Simon; "but if Hyrcan dies none can do it."

"Consider, young man," said the King, "I entrust you with an important commission. If you prove faithful and efficient, the way to the highest dignities of the state is open and leveled to you."

"I am well satisfied with what I am," said Simon. "I would not for any price in the world be an officer in a state built upon the murdered bodies of innocent men, cemented with the blood of its best citizens, cursed by the thousand widows and orphans, hated by its patriots, and feared, dreaded by its own King. My lord, I have a conscience of which I can not dispose."

"And so you will not accept the appointment?" Herod asked.

"If Hyrcan lives, yes," said Simon, "otherwise, no."

"Are you a personal friend of Hyrcan," the King asked.

"I never saw him," was the answer.

"Why do you thus pray for him?" the King inquired

"Because his death will be a deep-dyed crime, an everlasting stain on your history," said Simon. "Because his death must excite the people to furious madness, and call upon you the vengeance of heaven. Because it tears asunder forever the family ties of your own house. Because you will repent, too late, this horrid action. Or, do you believe Kings are not accountable to Providence? If you do, let me inform you, that you are grossly mistaken. As you do, even so will be done to you. Crime has its thousand tongues, and each cries perpetually. Take care, my lord, when the cry grows too mighty, none is heard, none seen any longer. The sea breaks its dam and the inundation is master."

"But Hyrcan is my enemy, and the enemy of the country," said Herod.

"So Sabion says, and nobody else," said Simon, "everybody else knows the old King is a quiet, peace-loving and kind man, notwithstanding his weakness of mind. He is old and harmless. My lord, do not soil your name with that blood. My lord, do not inscribe your name in history with the blood of Hyrcan."

"Will you keep the city quiet to my return?" Herod asked.

"If Hyrcan lives, yes," said Simon.

"Then Hyrcan shall live," said Herod, "you have conquered me."

"Hear it, God and ye angels of peace and love," Simon exclaimed, "and bring the glad tiding to the tormented man." Simon was about to give utterance to his sentiments; but the King would not hear him. "In half an hour your letters will be prepared," said the King, "Sohemus will hand them to you. Be faithful, prudent. Your future greatness depends on this first and important post entrusted to your care. Farewell."

Simon was not gone more than one hour, when Salome reeled into the tent of the King. He received her with much surprise. "The battle of Actium is lost. Antony is completely defeated. Octavius hotly pursues him into Egypt," Salome said. "The news is not known yet in Jerusalem, but if spread we are lost. The friends of Hyrcan are prepared to strike a desparate blow."

Herod acted like a madman. He could not master his agitated feelings. He broke every thing in the tent and struck himself with both his fists.

"I congratulate you, my King," said Sohemus. "Petra is ours. It capitulates.—You are lord of Arabia."

"Just in time," said the King. "Where is Aurion?"

"He is gone, this good while. You was so much in a hurry about him," said Sohemus.

"He must be stopped. No. He must be brought back. No, that will not do. My royal word. Now Hyrcan must die. Sohemus, that Aurion must be detained on the road as long as possible; but none shall do him the least harm. Do you hear, your honor as a pledge, that he will be detained and not harmed. He must arrive too late. Now, be quick, Sohemus. We must be able to return to Jerusalem with our army in the shortest time possible. Farewell." Turning to Salome, he said, "What do you think of that Aurion, can I entrust him with a high post in this crisis?"

"My lord, this Aurion is a great man," said Salome, "but I know not whether he is loyal. Give him to me, let him be my husband, and you are sure of his fidelity."

"This is not your own thought, sister," the King cried, "an angel, a God speaks through you. Yes, let him be my brother-in-law, and I am certain of his faith."

CHAPTER XIV

THE TRIAL.

The city of Jerusalem presented for weeks the most peculiar picture of hilarity, excitement, enthusiasm, murder and violence.—Such was the policy of Sabion to govern the people. Every day new triumphs of Herod over the Arabs were celebrated by illuminations, public banquets, and other festivities of the most exciting nature. Half of the population was continually held in a state of intoxication by false reports and grand festivities. Whoever was in the way of Sabion fell a victim to his blood-thirsty disposition. Daily almost dead bodies were found in some part of the city, and none knew how they came to their death. Consternation and terror reigned supréme and formed a bloody contrast to the hilarity and merriment, which were visible everywhere. Every body trembled for his own safety, until finally a total indifference to death seized upon all, and all appeared to have yielded to the intoxicating hilarity of the endless public feasts, which soon reached a high degree of self-forgetfulness and madness.

This was the very state of mind which Sabion wished to see in Jerusalem. Now was his time to carry out his schemes. He sat in his easy chair one morning and heard the several reports of his servants with a self-complacent air. After he was through and the servants were dismissed, he called Elvira. She appeared. Sabion asked her, "Will you now tell me all you know about Helen and Aurion?"

"You know more than I do, sir," said Elvira. "I can tell you nothing. But if I could, I would not do it."

"Ah, I know of proper means to bend the obstinacy of such creatures," said Sabion. "The torture, Miss, the torture will teach you to speak." Elvira made no reply.—"Will you answer my questions?"

"No," was the brief answer. "Your contemptible menaces frighten me not. Since you threaten I shall not speak at all."

"Then I will not threaten," said Sabion, "I will promise. If you tell me what you know, I will elevate you to the first lady of the court. The women shall envy, the men shall respect you, as the most powerful, most influential, most happy lady at court. Every look of yours shall set a host of servants in motion. The finest silks of Damascus, the linen of Egypt, the purple of India, the pearls of Persia, the costliest diamonds, the most precious rubies shall be yours. I will make you my wife."

Elvira laughed so heartily that Sabion stopped abruptly. "This is a most cruel torture you have invented," she said; "indeed if I fear anything, it is certainly this torture. Your wife? What a hell there is in these two words! O, do not deceive yourself, my lord, you are so old and ugly, so despicable and monstrous, that to be your wife is to be wedded to hell and the prince of darkness."

"Never mind, Elvira," Sabion ejaculated. "First, tell me what you know of Helen, then you will be my wife. I am lord, supreme ruler of this city, and I am not such a fool, as to sigh, groan and beg. I command, and you must obey."

"I rather would bite off my own tongue and spit it in your face than tell you one word," said Elvira. "I rather would destroy myself with pins than be your wife. You are too mean a man to know what a woman can do, if despair drives her to it."

"You shall stay in your room for three days," said Sabion; "some gentlemen and ladies are appointed to keep you safely. I have urgent business just now. After three days, I will marry you. Farewell."

"During three days it might please his Satanic majesty to recall his representative on earth to the hellish palace," said Elvira, when she retired.

"Then I will take you along," said Sabion. When Elvira was gone he soliloquized, "She must know more than I do; for she was in Sharon and that hellish Aurion came with her, or soon after her from there. They must know whether she is dead."

Knocking on the secret door was heard; Sabion opened and admitted a man. "Ah, you returned quickly. What news do you bring from the plain of Sharon?"

"Disastrous, very disastrous," said the stranger. "I had a narrow escape. All the peasants are under arms. Not a man of your soldiers sent there will ever return. Some are killed, and the rest fraternized with the people."

"And they did not return with you?"—Sabion asked.

"Return? there was none there to return," said the man; "for their defeat occurred just when they arrived on the plain and attempted to arrest Aurion."

"And all the reports I received afterwards?" Sabion asked.

"Were lies, mere fabrications of your enemies," said the man. "The people of Sharon are prepared for a general insurrection. They talk of marching to Jerusalem."

"Our walls are strong enough, to make us laugh at a hundred thousand such fools," said Sabion. "But I will have vengeance, bloody satisfaction.—How many men are under arms in the plain?"

"I do not know," said the man. "It appears to me, that Sharon is the center of a great commotion which spreads far and wide. There must be ten thousand armed men there, rather more than less."

"Then we can do nothing immediately,"

said Sabion. "First we must settle our difficulties here, then we go to Sharon."

The man being dismissed, Sabion rubbed his hands and ran about the room. "It comes all right," he soliloquised. "The revolution is at the door. Hyrcan will fall. Is Herod victorious, I am his savior. If he falls, Cleopatra is Queen and I am the richest man in Judah. Let me have money enough, influence enough, and I am King; let name and title have who is pleased with such shadows. I am King.—But who are the scoundrels in Sharon, that deceived me? who stands at the head of that work? I must know this. Hum, if I fraternize with them in favor of Cleopatra — this is the shortest way.—But if Herod is victorious and Autony falls, what then? Now I can not depend on the whims of Mars. I would rather play through my safe game.—But then I must do something against the rebels of Sharon."—Thus soliloquizing he went down to the park to scheme new plans.

Meanwhile a scene of quite a different character was enacted in the hall of the Sanhedrin, the *Lishath-Hagazith*. The Sanhedrin were assembled. Each member sat in his chair in a semi-circle. The *Nassi*, the *Ab-Beth-Din* on one side and the *Hacham* on the other, with the two scribes, sat on the platform. The officers were posted at a distance from the chairs, guarded every door that no stranger might come in on this solemn and sad occasion. A silence, painful and solemn reigned in the hall. None appeared desirous to say anything to his neighbor. Expectation and apprehension brooded heavily upon the whole assembly.

When the officers opened the door all the senators turned to look at the comer. They evidently expected some extraordinary affair this day. The silence was interrupted by the sound of heavy steps which were heard upon the marble pavement approaching the Principal entrance to the hall. This being opened twelve men of the royal guard entered. Behind them the hoary and outworn Hyrcan, the King and Highpriest of Israel, the son of the Asmonean heroes, entered the hall. His pale countenance framed in a long white beard, with two large blue eyes under thin eyebrows, looked sad, weary of life, and furrowed by the misfortunes of many unhappy years. Few were the white locks which hung from the bald head. His tall form was bent, leaning on the arm of a servant; his looks were sad and a melancholy smile played around his lips. His faint steps on the marble pavement sounded plaintively through the spacious hall. All eyes were directed upon the old King as he advanced to the judgment seat, where Hillel, surrounded by his most eminent scholars, among them both Jonathan ben Uziel and Akabiah ben Mehalalel, rose to salute the unfortunate King.

The impression made on the Sanhedrin by the appearance of Hyrcan was so great, that none in the hall could speak. After a long and painful silence the Nassi rose and addressed Hyrcan thus: "Hyrcan, son of Alexander, King of Israel, Highpriest of the Most High, thou art accused before the Sanhedrin, the supreme tribunal of justice, of high treason against thine own country and her King. Hyrcan, son of Alexander, art thou guilty of the said crime?"

"No," said the faint old man with a firm voice.

"Then stand and hear the evidence of the witnesses who testify against thee," said the Nassi. "Then let us also hear the witnesses who are in thy favor, that this venerable Sanhedrin be enabled to judge correctly, and render judgment in justice, for justice is the will of our God." Turning toward the Sanhedrin the Nassi continued: "Venerable Sanhedrin, with the permission of the heavenly tribunal I admonish you to remember, that you are the agents of God Almighty in Israel, to dispense justice in the manner as Moses our great teacher said: 'Hear the cause between your brethren, and judge them with justice, between a man, and between his brother, and between his stranger. 'Ye shall not respect any countenance in judgment, the small as the great ye shall hear, ye shall not dread any man; for the judgment is God's.' Therefore I cause you to swear, that you will also in this case against Hyrcan, son of Alexander, hear all the witnesses and render judgment in justice as God commands you to do."

"Amen, amen, amen," it resounded from all lips. Hyrcan on account of his old age and weakness was permitted to sit down.—Then a side door was opened, the witnesses were admitted, and after the law concerning false witnesses was read before them, the *Ab-Beth-Din* read the judicial oath to the witnesses, which they repeated and concluded with a firm Amen. The witnesses with the exception of one retired to the room from which they came. Hyrcan, being asked whether he wished to have an advocate, and whom he would select to this function, pointed to Hillel. This being announced to the Sanhedrin, Castobarus rose and said, it would be nothing but justice to give a competent advocate to Hyrcan, as the importance of the momentous case required a learned, distinguished and competent man. Hyrcan insisting upon his choice, Castobarus continued to oppose it on the ground, that it offended the dignity of the late Highpriest and King, as well as the dignity of the Sanhedrin, that an unknown stranger should act in the capacity to which Hillel was thus appointed.—He considered this an insult to all sages of Israel.

Next to Castobarus a man rose and said, Hillel was not an unknown stranger. He recollected well when the choice advocate of Hyrcan did saw and split wood in his house for a scanty pay. The friends of Hillel were enraged by the indignity thus offered to their great teacher; but he would not allow them to demonstrate their displeasure in any shape or form.

"And what have you to say, Hillel?" the *Ab-Beth-Din* asked in a mild tone.

"Nothing," said Hillel; "for our sages of blessed memory said, 'Those who are insulted and insult none, who hear their own reproach and answer not, are understood under the word of God, which says, And His beloved are like the sun rising in strength.' If this conduct is prescribed in case of actual insult and reproach, I certainly must be silent when I hear the truth. I wish to God, nothing but truth were spoken here on this occasion. Our sages also said, to assault one publicly is a crime equal to murder; therefore I believe, it is better to split wood than to pierce hearts. Shemaiah and Abtalion in a solemn congregation laid their hands upon my head and declared me a judge and teacher in Israel. If my presence is unbecoming the dignity of this venerable Sanhedrin, the fault is not mine but theirs who authorized me. But judges who advise their culprit what he must do or omit, violate the law; hence let that man speak no more."

The *Ab-Beth-Din* looked with admiration on the old sage whose temper was not the least roused by the insulting remarks of the others. Then he ruled that the defendant was entitled to be represented by Hillel.—By his orders the trial commenced. The first witness of the prosecution was Dositheus. He said he was an intimate friend of Hyrcan and governor of the royal palace. Hyrcan had given him a letter to Malchus, King of Arabia, in which Hyrcan stated his resolution to leave Jerusalem, join him in Petra, and give him seven cities and their districts for his services in dethroning Herod and setting him (Hyrcan) upon the throne of Judah. Dositheus said, that a copy of the letter was sent to Malchus and the original was retained. He exposed the original to the Sanhedrin. It was shown to Hyrcan; he declared it a skilful forgery. Cross examination was in vain with the shrewd courtier. He maintained his position to the utmost.

Next an Arab was heard. He said he was an Arabian proselyte to Judaism. When Malchus, his King, invaded the country beyond Jordan, he was dispatched with fifty men, dressed like horse traders who go to Egypt, having two hundred horses with them. He was instructed by Malchus to leave the horses in Hebron, send ten of them to Hyrcan as a present of his old friend, and accompany him in the dark of night to Hebron, and from thence to Beersheba and over to Arabia. But he was arrested in Jerusalem and confessed all about his mission.

Then an Egyptian and Syrian were introduced after each other. Both said they were the body servants of Hyrcan. He ordered them to pack his baggage and escape with him. He promised them heavy rewards for their fidelity and bid them to say nothing of his plan, not even to his daughter. After them a host of witnesses were introduced who said they had been promised high offices by Hyrcan, whenever he should be King, which he promised to be the ease in a few months.

One of Herod's advocates rose and said the testimony on the part of the prosecution was closed, because it was considered complete. The crime of high treason could be made no clearer to the Sanhedrin, than the present testimony did. The connection of Hyrcan with the enemy of the country in time of actual war, the acceptance of the horses sent by Malchus, the orders to his servants to prepare speedily to leave the city, the promise of office to so many of his friends, and the assurance that he would be King in a few months, leave no room to doubt the guilt of Hyrcan.

Hillel rose and said, that the argument just heard would be conclusive, if the premises were true. He proposed to prove, that not one of the premises was t. ue. The private scribe of Hyrcan testified, that the old King was incapable to write, more than three years past, partly on account of his weak eyesight, and partly on account of trembling hands. The letter to the King of Arabia must have been written years ago. Upon investigation it was found by many witnesses that names and date were skilfully changed in the letter. Another witness stated, that the Arab was a horse trader, commonly known as such in Jerusalem, and never was an agent of the King of Arabia. Next an Arabian Israelite was heard who stated that his brethren, residents of Arabia, sent Hyrcan a present of several horses through the very man, who says he is an agent of Malchus. The two chamberlains of Hyrcan stated, that his body servants were suspected of evil intentions toward Hyrcan, and being removed from their functions, six months ago, received a pension, but were never again admitted into the presence of the old King. His body servants now attending on him were then introduced to the Sanhedrin.—Next, a large number of intimate friends of the old King testified, that they often conversed with him on his former difficulties, when he still was the reigning head of Israel, and he often thanked God, that he now was free of all the troubles and anxiety of public affairs. They testified, that he never evinced the least ambition to be King once more, but on the contrary he always expressed his utmost satisfaction with his present retired life.

Baba ben Buta, the blind president of the peeple's council was introduced. On examination he stated, that he was an opponent of Hyrcan ever since Herod was tried before the Sanhedrin for acts committed in Galilee. But on being appointed by his friends to ascertain the sentiments of Hyrcan as to the future government of Israel, because the witness and his friends consider the present government a violent and unjust imposition on the people, he did not directly offer to Hyrcan the aid of his friends in again mounting the throne of his fathers, but would first ascertain his sentiments on the subjects. Hyrcan, however, expressed such an aversion to public life, and considered himself so happy that he could conclude his days in the peace of private life, that witness could not propose the wishes of his friends to the old King. Several interviews leading to the same result, witness advised his friends to try no more, as Hyrcan had grown too old and weak to be a King.

The advocates of Herod examined the blind man for hours. But it was in vain; he could not be confused. He said the same thing always again. Without the least token of fear he stated his objections to the government of Herod and his wish to see him dethroned. Hillel declared the evidence on the part of the defence as concluded.—Every word of the testimony was known in Jerusalem, notwithstanding the closed doors of the Sanhedrin. Baba ben Buta was borne in triumph from the Temple to his house. The forged letter, the hired proselytes and creatures of Sahion formed the common theme of conversation. There was an indignation audible in the community, which was threatening. The public feasts and hilarities, the rumors of Herod's brilliant victories, of Mark Antony's success over his opponent, and subsequent illuminations did not silence the threatening voice of indignation. The reign of terror was defied, and Sabion found it extremely difficult to maintain the peace of the city.

Long and vehement were the debates before the Sanhedrin, before Hillel spoke.— He hoped the evidence in the case would convince the Sanhedrin of Hyrcan's innocence, and observed profound silence. The good man could not even think, that the large majority of the Sanhedrin were so much guided by political motives, personal interest, and the will of Herod, that the plainest evidence in favor of Hyrcan was perverted by shrewd sophistry. Mortified, and after a serious struggle against his own feelings, Hillel rose, and having obtained permission to speak he said:

"It is probably impertinent that I, an humble stranger, should oppose the wise judgment of so many learned and distinguished men. I feel my incapacity just now more than ever before. But there is a God in heaven who commands that justice should be done to the lowest and to the highest, and here sits a hoary, unhappy and crushed man who demands justice from your hands, justice for the sake of his life, of your honor and reputation, of Israel and its laws, justice for the sake of justice.— There is a God in heaven who has placed a conscience in the heart of man which revolts and prompts him to speak and act, when violence and injustice rear their destructive heads. Man's intellect is so frail, that the wisest and best may err; therefore I must speak. However crude or childish my words may be, I must speak.

"To a better understanding of the testimony before you, I must refresh your memory in regard to historical facts. After the battle of Jericho between the Asmonean princes Aristobul and Hyrcan, peace returned to Israel; for Aristobul, according to his inclinations, was King and Highpriest, and Hyrcan, according to his inclinations, retired in to private life. But the ambition of Antipater to be King of Israel, leaving to Hyrcan the name thereof as he had no inclination to govern, could not rest, did not care for the weal of Israel. After a long and artful attempt, he succeeded in persuading Hyrcan, to write a letter to Aretas, then King of Arabia, requesting his friendship and protection. This letter was brought to Aretas by Antipater, and this is the very same letter which, dates and names intentionally changed, is now laid before you, as being of a recent date. We have proved that the document is several years old and bears traces of eradication just at the spots of names and date; so skilful scribes have stated before you.— Hence no further evidence is necessary to prove the document a malicious forgery.

"You ask who is capable to commit such a crime, such a despicable treachery? Dositheus presented the document to you.— Dositheus says Hyrcan handed it to him with the direct command to convey it to Malchus. Hence Dositheus is the man who stands accused of this low crime, or at least of an intimate knowledge of the perpetrator. But Dositheus is a great man and a favorite of the King; he must not be accused of a crime so deep-dyed, so villanous; it is too great a crime for Dositheus—still it was committed, and the proof is in your hands.

"Two servants who have not seen Hyrcan for the last six months, as the chamberlains tell us, testify to what they never heard or saw; to that which is evidently not true.— Who are those suspected servants? None knows them, none can tell us why they come here to testify against their own master.— Hired they must have been, for the purpose; for they eat the bread of Hyrcan, and they will eat it no longer. They must have been hired and well paid. Who hired and paid those men? The same man undoubtedly who falsified the letter; for the testimony of the servants was intended to corroborate the fact to be established by said letter. Can you suppose for a moment that a falsifier, a base forger would hire honest witnesses to testify to a lie? Still the shrewd servants would not tell us why they came to testify against their own master, or who hired and paid them.

"If there was a word of truth, a spark of sincerity in this accusation, why did our adversaries resort to a falsified document and to lying witnesses? If one thousand witnesses and more should now testify against Hyrcan, their words could not be considered; for the accusers began with a lie, with forgery and two false witnesses, and the accusers must know that the document is falsified, and the servants have not seen their master within six months.

"But then the prosecution brings a host of witnesses who testify, that Hyrcan promised them offices whenever he should be King which, they say, he thought should be soon. They asked no favors of him, they say, but he, in order to seduce them, promised them high and remunerative offices. There stands a host of other witnesses opposed to the former and testify, that Hyrcan dreads the idea of public functions, and feels highly satisfied with his private life. In conclusion, comes the bold man, the blind Baba ben Buta and tells you, that he was sent to Hyrcan to offer him the assistance of a powerful faction in Israel; but Hyrcan would not hear anything of public life. If he had the remotest idea of again mounting the throne of his fathers, would not he have entrusted his secret to the enemies of Herod? must he not have initiated Baba ben Buta into his secrets, as Baba whom Herod deprived of his eyes, is a known enemy of the King? Or do you suppose the old King has not wisdom enough to prefer the enemies of Herod to his friends, if he intended hostilities against the King?—Or do you believe you can impeach the testimony of Baba ben Buta, the unbent oak, the gigantic cedar? There is not a man or woman in Israel who doubts the veracity of Baba.

"But we will suppose the evidence is balanced only, and this would be enough to dismiss the case. But we may justly look back upon the history of Hyrcan to decide the conflicting statements of the witnesses you have heard. Hyrcan's biography proves two things; first that he never wished to be a King, and secondly that he fondly loved Herod. Who reigned in Israel after Pompey decided in favor of Hyrcan, he or Antipater? After Antipater was dead, did Hyrcan rule in Israel or Phesael and Herod?—You know fully well that Antipater first, Phesael and Herod then, governed the people. Was Hyrcan opposed to their governing the land in his name, or did he favor it? You know that he wanted it so, defended Herod before the Romans against the accusations of the people, and preferred an easy, retired life to all public affairs. He never had the inclination to govern. When the power was in his hands he gave it to others, why then should it be believed, that now when he is old and feeble, he should long after a troublesome crown?

"And Hyrcan loved Herod, as a father loves his son. When Herod executed many men in Galilee who were accused of robbery, when he executed them without the permission of the law, without the verdict of a Sanhedrin, this body then consisting of other men, summoned him before the supreme tribunal of justice. He defied the highest authority of the country, appeared before the Sanhedrin in purple and state jewels, girded with his sword and surrounded by a strong body guard. The Sanhedrin was dumb, and Hyrcan so fondly loved the son of Antipater, that he would not punish him even for the defiance of the highest tribunal of justice, an open revolt against the laws.

"Herod and his brother Phesael were every thing to Hyrcan. He gave them the best proof of his love. The brighest jewel in the diadem of the Asmoneans, the most precious treasure in the gift of the King, Mariamne, the wisest, most virtuous and most beautiful of women, the grand daughter of two Kings, was given to Herod.—Hyrcan gave Mariamne to Herod. Can the fondest love invent a clearer demonstration, a more truthful exhibition of itself? Could Hyrcan more effectually prove his love of Herod? O, I beg you to consider, is not this of itself a conclusive evidence of the old King's innocence?

"The love of a man then nearly sixty years old changes no more. The inconsisteney of youth being passed, whatever the old man loves he loves forever. Behold, when Hyrcan had been retained in Babylon a captive of the Parthians, the Israelites of Persia and Media as far as India and China honored the old Asmonean as their chief and provided for him with royal generosity. He was happy, respected and beloved.—Knowing as he did that Herod sat upon his throne, his love for his favorite prompted him to leave his new and happy home and return to Jerusalem. Herod called him his father, and he called him his son; because Hyrcan loved Herod before all men and had no ambition to be King. When at the pool of Jericho the youthful highpriest Aristobul, the brother of Mariamne, the grand son of Hyrcan and his brother, the only legal heir to the throne of the Asmoneans was drowned, in a manner unknown to you—every man suspected Herod to have caused the death of the young highpriest, even Mark Antony and Cleopatra suspected him. But not a word of accusation or suspicion passed the lips of Hyrcan. 'Love covers every transgression,' not a word was heard of him; because Hyrcan loves Herod as never one man loved another.

"I need say no more, you can not believe Hyrcan guilty of conspiracy and treason against Herod. You must be convinced that this is a malicious plot of the enemies of a man who should have none. All those who now testify against him, once were his most obedient servants, his echo, his shadow. They trembled when he spoke, danced when he smiled, and wept when he looked sad. Now they sell Joseph for twenty silver pieces, and tell the father, a wild beast has devoured him. For humanity's sake let this foul ingratitude not go unpunished. For justice's sake expose this malicious conspiracy. Behold, here sits a hoary man, born a King in the sunshine of happiness, rocked in the cradle of fortune, and nursed with the sweets of life. Here sits the son of heroic and glorious ancestors, who redeemed Israel from the yoke of Syria. His claims on the happiness of life were great and just. But mild and peaceable as he always was, still all the billows of misfortune passed over his head. His family once so glorious, slumbers in the dust. His kingdom is his prison. Dashed is his crown, and his throne is occupied by another. Once he ministered before the living God in his temple; now he is your prisoner. Once he was the pride of a royal mother, and the hope of his nation, now he is accused of treason.—He saw his whole family perish, and the husband of his only grand daughter, upon whom he lavished all his affections, permits him now to stand like a low criminal before you. There, in Parthia, his own nephew bit off his ears that he be highpriest no more, and here his own friends whom he elevated to the highest offices, testify to a lie to deliver his grey head bloody to the grave. Lions, tigers and hyenas must feel compassion with the old man. Malice itself, one should think, must be moved to tears on beholding the unfortunate man, and must allow him to conclude his days in peace. A man too old and feeble to be dangerous to a child, should not be accused of a crime which he is incapable of committing.

"But worse than all this is the onslaught, the despicable scheme to turn this Sanhedrin into a soulless tool of a political party, to become the dagger in the hands of the assassin. Israel's Sanhedrin is the defence of our laws, our rights, our liberties. How mean must the enemies of Hyrcan think of this Sanhedrin, if they think their spider-web of lies and forgery should not be exposed here? How mean must those men think of Israel if they thus think of its Sanhedrin?

"I caution you in behalf and in the name of the God of justice, not to let those false witnesses escape unpunished. Set an example of the wisdom and justice of this Sanhedrin. Permit none to insult this body with malicious lies, to depreciate Israel by thus disrespecting the supreme tribunal of justice, to blaspheme God with lies and forgery in the presence of His temple, on the side of the sacred altar, in the hall where Esra and the prophets sat, here on Mount Moriah where the God of truth is worshipped and rules supreme."

When Hillel was done it appeared as tho' the consciences of all revived; for the silence of the grave ruled supreme in the hall. But in a short time the debate was resumed. The friends of Herod insisted upon the guilt of Hyrcan, and the opponents of Herod were overruled by the majority. When the *Nassi* observed the state of affairs, he rose and told the Sanhedrin, that he was no longer Nassi. All the presiding officers formally and solemnly resigned, and left the hall The creatures of Sabion, prepared for the emergency, filled the vacancies immediately, and continued the matter. Having the field all for themselves they rendered the judgment of "guilty," in the usual solemn manner, and pronounced the sentence of death upon the hoary man, who listened to it with indifference almost. Hillel rose and exclaimed, "Lord! this innocent blood soils not my hands. Let not thy fierce anger be kindled against all thy people." He and his friends left the hall. Outside they were received by a strong escort of citizens, who followed Hillel to the house of Baba ben Buta.

Like thunder, it roared through the whole city, Hyrcan is condemned to die, the best men of the Sanhedrin have resigned, Hillel is the greatest man in Israel, still he could not prevent the foul crime. The people ran by thousands to the temple; but Hyrcan had been led away through the subterranean hall to the palace of the Kings. Before the military came on the ground in sufficient force, several of the senators who had left the temple, were killed, or rather torn in pieces by the excited populace. The military made a terrible carnage among the multitude, dispersed them and restored the appearance of quietude and peace. Actually, however the whole city appeared to rest on a volcano. Every sense of justice was outraged, every heart rebelled in its bosom.—There was a defiance, an angry hatred visible on every countenance.

Hillel by the advice of his friends returned to Jericho. Hundreds of the foremost men of the city went with him. As he passed through the streets of the city the exclamations, "Long live Hillel,"—"Hillel should be Nassi"—"Hillel is the friend of the people," and similar exclamations saluted him everywhere. His way from Jerusalem to Jericho was a triumph. Everywhere he was greeted with the utmost enthusiasm, and the most respected of the towns and villages through which he passed followed him to Jericho. His reception in Jericho was princely. The good man was so overwhelmed with honor and distinction, that he was glad to be again in his humble cottage in the bosom of his family.

When Sabion received the news of the verdict given by the Sanhedrin, he immediately commanded the arrest of the officers and senators who had resigned; but it was too late. They had left the city with Hillel. Also Baba ben Buta was gone. The conduct of the people terrified him somewhat; but he soon recovered and acted with despotic energy. The whole city was filled with armed men, and none was permitted to speak a loud word. The gates were closed, the forts locked, terror and dismay ruled supreme.—Immediately Sabion dispatched a courier to Herod, to inform him of the state of affairs in Jerusalem and Sharon.

"We are lost," Castobarus cried, reeling into the room of Sabion. "Mark Antony is utterly defeated. Octavius hotly pursues him. Rumors are afloat that Antony and Cleopatra committed suicide."

CHAPTER XV.

A FRIDAY NIGHT IN JERICHO.

The enthusiasm with which Hillel was received in Jericho would not subside for many days. Hillel should, he must be Nassi in Israel, was the cry of the vast multitude, of which he had not the remotest idea. He sat again in his low cabin, attended again to his garden, and studied in the scrolls before him. The Greek proselyte, whom Simon had sent back home, kept faithful watch at the door of the venerable savan, that no harm might befal him.

It was Friday afternoon. The busy and bustling commotion in the lanes of Jericho showed the end of the week. Each man appeared to have yet some important business to transact before the close of the week.—Each woman seen in the street was in a hurry to finish her work in time for the Sabbath. Hillel, according to an old custom, had retired to his bath-room, to prepare himself for the reception of the *Sabbath queen*.—Everything was so still and quiet in the whole house, that it sounded peculiar and strange, when a stout, robust man with a strong, shrill and disagreeable tenor voice, reeled into the house, and notwithstanding all the remonstrations of the Greek proselyte, he cried, "Where is Hillel? Where is Hillel?" so loud and shrill, that everybody in the house must have heard it. Wrapped in a cloak Hillel came forth from his bath-house. "What wishest thou, my son?" he asked, calmly.

"Art thou Hillel?" the stranger vociferated, without any demonstration of respect

"I am, my son," said Hillel, "what wishest thou?"

"Why are the heads of the Babylonians oval, and not round as ours?" the stranger asked.

"Thou hast asked a great question, my son," said Hillel. "This is the fault of their midwives; but God has made all men alike."

Without another word the stranger hurried away; but scarcely had Hillel retired to his bathroom, when the fantastic stranger's shrill voice again resounded, "Where is Hillel? Where is Hillel?" The Greek proselyte was so angry at the man's total want of courtesy and propriety, that he was just about scolding him, when the door of the bath room opened and Hillel, wrapped in his cloak, came through it. Friendly and kind as ever he asked, "What wishest thou, my son?"

"Why have the people of Tadmor eyes so weak and red?" he asked.

"Thou hast asked, a great question, my son," said Hillel. "Because the wind blows the fine sand of the desert in their eyes.—Still they can see and admire the beauties of God's creation."

Without a word of thanks or excuse, the stranger disappeared, and Hillel returned to his bath. But in a few moments the annoying stranger was again in the house, and as rude as ever, he cried, "Where is Hillel? Where is Hillel?" The proselyte closed his fist and showed an angry face to the man; but he could not speak, for, with a smile on his lips, Hillel instantly made his appearance. "What wishest thou, my son," he asked, as mildly and kindly as before.

"Why have the east Africans broad feet?" the stranger asked.

"Thou hast asked a great question," said Hillel. "Because they live on swamp land. Still they can walk erect before God."

"I should have to ask thee many more questions," said the stranger; "but I fear to provoke thee to anger."

Hillel sat down, invited the stranger to a seat opposite himself, and encouraged him to ask him all the questions he wished to have answered.

"Art thou Hillel, whom the people call Nassi of Israel?" the stranger asked.

"I am Hillel," was his answer, "but I know not what the people call me."

"Then I wish that no more like thee be born in Israel," said the stranger, angrily.

"Why my son," Hillel asked, "have I done thee any harm?"

"Yes, yes," the stranger vociferated. "I wagered four hundred Sus, that I would provoke thee to anger. But I see I can not do it. I lose four hundred Sus."

"Better thou losest other four hundred Sus," said he, "than Hillel should be angry one moment only."

The stranger, thus disappointed, left the house, and told his story everywhere, to the greatest praise of the sweet temper of the old sage. Hillel soon appeared in the circle of his family to bless each of them, as the Sabbath approached. Also Helen rose and approached the venerable patriarch, "Bless me also, my father," she said.

Hillel laid his hands upon her head and said, "May God silence thy sighs and dry up thy tears, my daughter. Heaven's Sabbath rest and Seraphic bliss may fill thy heart."—"Amen," said Helen, with tears in her eyes, and kissed vehemently the border of his cloak.

Hillel regarded her closely, and on beholding tears in her eyes, he said: "Weep not, on Sabbath, it is a day of holiness.—Why art thou not happy among us, we love thee so well?"

"Happy, as happy as I can be, I am in the bosom of your family," Helen said. "I can say much more than this. I have learned here what true happiness is. The wealth, luxury and hilarity of a royal court are like the glowing rays of the sun at noon. Splendid, beauteous, charming are the colors reflected in its glaring flood of light; but the sweetest blossoms wither, the fragrant roses melancholy recline their heads, and Flora mourns over her children. There is splendor and death, honey and poison, in one cup. But joy, true happiness is enthroned among the good and innocent, under the silent roof of virtuous inmates. You, my good father, have taught me happiness, real bliss; but my heart is not susceptible of happiness. May I not mourn for a lost father? not weep a tear after him who roams over the country and throws himself in the embrace of danger, to destroy my parent? Is the Sabbath so holy, that I may not mourn for the one, and pray for the other? Can I reconcile my love with the voice of nature? O, my father, I feel how happy I could be with you, if I could be happy."

"Be as happy, my daughter, as thou art virtuous," Hillel said. "Confide in God, and the sun of happiness will soon return to thy heart." Hillel would have said more, if he had not been interrupted by the unexpected arrival of Simon. "It is he, my life, my love, my only hope!" Helen exclaimed, and sank in the open arms of Simon, who pressed her in silent rapture on his high beating heart. Smilingly, Hillel said, "the sun of happiness has returned already to her heart."

"And so you are yet mine, all mine, so lovingly, so faithfully mine!" Simon exclaimed, fervently, gazing enrapturedly upon the blushing countenance and radiating black eyes of Helen. "A world of happiness, a paradise speaks through thy looks, my only love. Speak, speak, my dearest life, what hast thou to tell me?"

"Everything, nothing," Helen stammered. "My soul is full of divine music, I can speak no words."

"I feel the angelic accords, as they reecho in my heart," said Simon. Turning to his parents he kissed them and said: "I can stay only a few short moments with you.—A sacred mission entrusted to my care urges me onward and forward. I must be in Jerusalem to-morrow."

"The mission must be very important, indeed," said Hillel, "if my son thinks to desecrate the Sabbath by traveling."

"My venerable father and teacher," said Simon, "you taught me, to save a human life is a more sacred duty than to observe all the Sabbaths of a lifetime. You taught me that even in case of doubt—man may violate the Sabbath, if he believes thus to save the life of a human being."

"I did say so, and this is the meaning of the Law: 'What man should do to live by it,' and not to die with it. Self-preservation is man's first duty. 'Love thy neighbor as thyself,' implies first the duty to preserve the life of our fellow men as well as ours. Hence the perservation of life is man's first duty. But tell me, my son, whose life art thou to save?"

"Hyrcan's, my father," said Simon. "I prevailed so long on Herod until he appointed me governor of Jerusalem and pardoned Hyrcan. I bear the documents. I can save the life of Hyrcan and of many others who die now in Jerusalem almost every day, for no offence of theirs."

"Then go, travel fast, be in time in Jerusalem, and may God speed thee," Hillel exclaimed, joyfully. "All good men in Israel will bless thee, and Herod's name might yet be saved from perdition." Instantly Hillel looked serious and deliberating. After a moment of reflection, he asked, "But why didst thou not go the straight rout from Petra to Jerusalem?"

"Notwithstanding the decrees of the King, signed by him, and bearing his seal," said Simon, "nothwithstanding my traveling with a strong escort of the royal guard, I was so much molested and delayed at each military post, that I determined upon chosing this byway, where no military posts are, and I may arrive much sooner at Jerusalem."

"This is suspicious my son," Hillel said. "I fear thou art deceived. I know the perfidy and inconsistency of Herod. It looks to me, as though Herod could not resist thy prayers. But he sent the command before thee to delay thee on the road, till it is too late, till Hyrcan is no more. How in the world dared the officers of the different posts delay thee, if thou carriest the King's orders? Hyrcan was condemned to death by an outrageous and presumptuous body of men, who evidently obeyed the behests of Herod. I fear my son, thou art deceived."

Like a flash of lightning it rushed through the soul of Simon. He rose from his seat and looked about like one who feels the approach of insanity. "Is it possible that Herod is so perfidious, so outrageously satanic, such a feeble, weak, hellish liar!" Simon exclaimed, furiously. "Yet it appears to be as my sagacious father says. Herod, then, dig thy grave, thou art a lost man. This pardon alone could save him. O, my father, my kind father, you know not how my soul mourns over that Herod, how I dread the idea of the bloody revolution, that must ensue. O, I hoped to save him, to spare my people the lives of the thousand patriots.—It was a sweet, pleasant dream. If Herod is a liar, then the dream is over, and the sword, the bloody sword will decide the fate of Israel." Simon covered his face with his hands and wept so loud, that all in the room wept with him. Painful was the silence that followed, and the emotions that appeared to dominate every heart. Then he burst forth violently, "Israel, curse the infamous seducers of Herod! Israel, curse Salome, Dositheus, Castobarus, curse Sabion"——

The shrill and painful cry of Helen, "Hold on, for God's sake, hold on, he is my father!" directed every look to her. "Simon, save him, I prithee, save his life, he is my father. What love can invent to please, to bring down the bliss of heaven upon thee, to enrapture thee with feelings divine, I will do, I will cheerfully do; nay, nay, nay, it shall be my only study, my sole thought to make thee so happy as no other mortal can be; when thou sleepest my love shall rock thee in paradisian dreams, when thou wakest my fiery passions shall change the dust under thy feet into fragrant roses; I will wrestle with the stars for their diadem of light to crown thy brow; O, I will conjure up love and joy from barren deserts to make thee smile in happiness—but save, save, man, save the life of my father!"

"Poor woman, thy father is lost," said Simon, as monotonous and slow, as though a marble statue spoke. "I found a correspondence between him and Cleopatra, from which it is evident that he conspired with her against Herod. I found the documents under the ruins of his house in Sharon, and gave them to the King. His doom is sealed. If the people or Herod rule, his doom is sealed."

"And the beloved of my heart is the murderer of my father," Helen lamented, "how unhappy a girl am I!"

"Murderer? No!" Simon said, emphatically. "The man who murdered thousands, he who exposed his own child to disgrace and death, is condemned to death. The King and the people condemned him, and I was one of the witnesses when that villain was tried for his crimes. Helen, my virtuous Helen, speak no more, pray no more for him who happens to be your father. He is guilty enough to die a thousand deaths if he could, and you know it; hence pray no more."

Helen embraced Hillel and his wife. "Be you my father, be my mother, woman with the great looks," she implored. "I will warm my soul at the fire of your virtues, and be worthy to be your child."

"So may God bless thee, as I love thee," said Hillel. "Helen, we are thy parents, thou our child."

"Ah, how it rolls, how it ebbs and floods through the heart like a current of bliss!" Helen exclaimed, and embraced her parents.

"Now let us part," said Simon, "my duty calls me hence. Perhaps I can yet save Hyrcan, and give a favorable turn to the state of affairs. If it is too late, Abba Shaul is just in time. Things are pressed to a fearful crisis. The moment of final decision is nigh. The Passover week draws near.—When we meet again the iron dice are cast. The fate of Herod and Israel is decided. I go to co-operate with my people in a great and sacred work, if my negotiations fail. I feel the solemnity of the cause, and its importance. Therefore before I leave, Father, Mother, give me your blessing, that it strengthen my will and support my energies."

"No, no, no, do not go from hence," Helen cried, "death, death, death, I see nothing but death before me. Wild is my fantasy, black my omens, dreadful my presentiments Simon, leave us not. You can not save the King, and in the revolution—O leave us not, I fear we will see you no more."

"And if I can not save the life of Hyrcan, not rescue Herod from the claws of his friends," said Simon, "should he boast upon my cowardice to carry out my mission, and tell him to his face, that I go to those who will do him justice? If my people appeal to arms to redress their grievances, dare I stand aloof and rejoice in the embrace of love? This is not your wish; your affections, Helen, spoke too loudly. If I fall, here are your parents; and there, in a better world, Helen, we meet again." He pointed aloft, and after a pause, he continued, "But you shall not remain in this world as the daughter of Sabion, you shall be known as Hillel's daughter. Here in presence of my mother and thine, of my beloved ones and thine, our father shall join our hands in the sacred bonds of matrimony. Here and now, Helen, my only love, here and now let us be united for ever. If I return, thy husband returns; if I return not Hillel is thy father, and thy husband will stand at the gates of paradise and wait for thy arrival. Suffering here will be everlasting triumph there. Love and fidelity here will be the glorious crown of victory in the home of angels. Come, Helen, dear, be mine before God and man."

Helen sank in the outstretched arms of Simon. She did not speak, and what woman under the influence of such sentiments could have spoken? Simon, pressing her closely to his heart, addressed his father and mother in touching words. All rose and Hillel filled two goblets with wine and pronounced the solemn benediction over the lovers. Then Simon took a ring and placed it on Helen's finger while saying, "Thus shalt thou be sanctified to me by this ring, as I am to thee."—"Amen, amen," it sounded from every lip. Hillel stretched out his hands and blessed his loving children, while Helen clung to the lips of Simon in a long kiss. Not an eye was tearless, every heart was moved with the most conflicting sentiments of joy and pain, happiness and apprehension.

Simon, having regained his presence of mind, brought Helen to his mother who clasped her in her arms, then turning to his father he stammered, "My time is over, I must go. Father, bless me."

Hillel laid his hands upon Simon's head and said, "Remain firm in the path of godliness and virtue, true to thy God and thy people, and the God of Abraham, Isaac and Jacob will watch over thee. He has commanded his angels to guard thee on all thy ways. Go with God and return in peace, Amen."

"Now I feel an army in my breast, a host of heroes in my soul," Simon exclaimed.—"Helen, Father, mother, farewell. Israel calls, I come. Israel weeps, I am prepared, ready to die or be victorious with Israel.—Farewell, farewell"

"Stay, one moment longer, stay," Helen cried, but he was gone, and she sunk back in the embrace of her mother.

CHAPTER XVI.

THE ARRESTS.

In the royal palace of Jerusalem a sudden change had taken place. The hilarious festivities were over. An awful silence, mournful and eloquent, like heavy and dark clouds, overhung the luxurious saloons. It appeared as though suddenly every tongue was lamed, every smile banished, and happiness was exiled. The servants and courtiers ran quickly and dumb through the apartments. Herod had returned from the Arabian expedition. Returned from the field of battle as a signal victor, still no voice of enthusiasm received him, no demonstration of joy remunerated the fatigued and victorious warrior. Unregarded, noticed only to go out of his way, the King traveled through the country, entered the capital and his palace, and everywhere gloomy, melancholy and sad countenances stared on him a short time, and then turned aside to curse him, as it were. Only his court creatures and servants were in attendance, and also they appeared to regret the past and apprehend the future. Only one smiled, and that was Sabion, as he received the King in the palace.

Without another word of reply to Sabion's

compliments, the King asked, "And Hyrcan?"

"Is dead and buried," Sabiou replied, with a malicious smile on his lips. Herod started back, like one who dreads his own shadow. He appeared to shudder at his own black deed. "And the people?" he continued, interrogating. "Are quiet," said Sabion, "I have kept my word."

"Quiet, very quiet," said Herod, "not one of them has a word of joy to speak to the returning victor."

"My lord, none knew of your arrival," Sabion excused himself, "or else"——

"You would have hired some criers to give me an enthusiastic reception," the King interrupted. "It is well, as it is. What says the Queen?"

"I can not tell, my lord," said Sabion, "none is permitted to see her. She is sick I presume."

"Yes, yes, she is sick, I presume," said the King, "and could not receive her royal husband in due form. Her children, chamberlains, courtiers, officers, servants all sick, I presume, only Sabiou and myself are well. Ha, ha, ha, this is a sickly season.— But what is the latest news from Egypt?"

"Melancholy intelligence," said Sabion.— "Antony and Cleopatra are dead, they ended in suicide."

Thunderstruck, Herod looked on Sabicn, without saying one word. The wild gestures of the King and his rapid strides were the only demonstration of his emotions. Gradually he wrought himself into a frantic excitement, pushed his head against the wall, struck himself with his own fists, and made dreadful gesticulations. He did not hear what Sabion said, and raged on for a good while. Sabiou begged leave to retire, but Herod ejaculated like a madman: "Ah, you faithless dog of a friend, not even a tear you can weep for Cleopatra who promised you a fortune. Ah, you are a faithless dog."

The remonstrance of Sabion was in vain. The King, in his violent rage, did not listen to what he said. Again and anon he bowed to attract the attention of the King, but in vain. The Chamberlain also stood a good while in the saloon, without being able to obtain a hearing of the King. He behaved like a maniac and none could bring him to his senses. Sabion commenced to feel that it was unsafe to stay any longer in his presence, and without the King's permission he went toward the door. "Stay, traitor, faithless dog, miserable wretch," the King cried, madly, "you can not sell me any more to Cleopatra; that vile woman is dead. Why are you in such a hurry, your business is done? Call Sohemus and Castobarus."

Both appeared instantly. "Sohemus! take Jericho as quick as possible," the King commanded, "drive out the Egyptians, and leave a garrison there." Sohemus bowed and left. "Castobarus, Sabiou is your prisoner. Your honor and your head are forfeited if he escapes."

Sabion fell upon his knees before the King. "My lord, my gracious King," he begged, "do not abandon your most faithful servant. I have done my duty at the risk of my own life."

"Yes, yes, you have done your duty, as well as any other executioner," the King replied; "but your work is done. Cleopatra is dead, you can not sell me and Judea to her. You are at the end of your race. Begone. To-morrow your trial shall be."

Sabion attempted to speak again, but the King moving his hand, Castobarus took the sword of Sabiou and bade him follow, when suddenly the door was opened and Salome came in. "My lord, hear your faithful sister," she cried, "commit no rash act against Sabion. The documents handed to you may be forged after all. Your enemies are shrewd. They may have placed the documents in the hands of Aurion, without his knowledge of their being spurious. Be not too hasty. I suspect the people of Sharon, who are under arms against you."

"You pray for your seducer?" the King asked, with gnashing teeth. "What means this?"

"Your interest, your safety, my royal lord, and not my hatred," said Salome, "prompt me to this step. Consider well before you act."

"To-morrow shall be his trial," the King said, "All my courtiers shall decide whether the documents in my possession are forged." The King left the saloon, and Salome assailed Sabion like a fury, "Speak, satanic monster, where is my daughter, where is Helen?"

"Helen is not your daughter," said Sabion.

"You see, infamous devil, your life is in my hands, I alone can save you," said Salome. "Aurion found your treacherous correspondence with Cleopatra and handed it to the King. You are a dead man. Give me my daughter and I shall be your advocate before the King. Give me my child, and I will attempt to save you."

"Your children are dead," said Sabion, "the earthquake killed them."

"You lie, one of them lives," Salome cried, "and you must know where she is. I believe Helen is my child. If so, speak, tell me where she is, and I will save you."

"You have promised so much, and kept so little, that I would not trust you with the offiee to plead my cause before the King," said Sabion. "You wish to have your daughter, and then deliver me into the hands of the executioner. No, if I must die, you shall at least mourn the loss of your children."

"I entreat, I beseech you, Sabion," she prayed, "give me my daughter, give me my child, and I will forget all the wrong you have done me. I will forget that you are a devil, a traitor, a hangman, my curse, my hell, I will forget it and pray upon my knees to save you. Monster give me my child."

"If Castobarus swears to send me safely to Arabia," said Sabion, "in case the King condemns me, I shall tell you all I know."

Salome's prayers did not move Castobarus. He insisted upon his duty. "If you swear to marry me," he said, finally, to Salome, "I will do as you wish." After her tears and prayers were wasted in vain, Salome swore a solemn oath to marry Castobarus, who also promised under oath to send Sabion safely to Arabia, if the King condemned him.

Sabion then said: "Helen is your daughter. I took her from the nurse when I came to Jerusalem. She was born in the same hour with my other daughter and in the same house. I changed the children without the knowledge of my wife, and gave my other daughter to another nurse. She died soon after. Helen is your daughter. But I know not whether she escaped, or where she is.—Only two persons can know it, Aurion and Elvira, they were at the spot right after the earthquake. Elvira is in my power. Examine her, perhaps she will tell you what she knows."

Castobarus and Sabicu left the saloon.—Salome stared a good while after them. "A hell if you wish, but Salome you shall not have for a spouse," she vociferated. "I will send you to my first husband if it must be, and let Sabion give you company.—But does that man not tell me a lie to save his life? Is Helen my daughter? Is she disgraced? knows she that I commanded it? If she is and knows it, must she not curse, hate, despise me; why do I wish to see her? How foolish I am. Still I must know it, and if she is my daughter, I must see and love her. I am a mother, I can not divest myself of my love. Aurion knows where she is, he loves her, and I—No, she shall die—Die? my own child? I must have certainty on all these questions, then I will act speedily."

A violent roar, like that of a madman sounding dreadfully through the arched halls of the palace, made Salome listen. "Hark! is this not the voice of Herod?" she soliloquized, when he, like a fury, reeled into the room with a sword in his hand. "Leave me, instantly, venomous serpent," he cried. "Lost, dead, gone, everything is lost, all dead, gone. You, hellish monsters, you have caused me to slay Hyrcan, you have poisoned my soul with suspicion against him. Go, let me alone with my grief."

"I go, if you command," Salome said. "But I can not imagine, why you now, in this dangerous crisis, repent the death of Hyrcan. I wish you my royal brother, to come to your senses."

"Foul, vile, disgraced woman," Herod thundered, "is there yet so much womanhood left in your degraded soul, that you can feel the pain, the burning torment of a father, a husband, who comes after months of separation to embrace his wife and his children; but she, ha, ha, ha, laugh yourself mad, but she, and she is the most beauteous of women, she closes her doors, sends me my ring, the token of my love, sends me my ring, and the message, that she swore a solemn oath never to allow me to see her or embrace her children. That is your work, hellish fiend; for she says, the blood of Hyrcan quenched every spark of love in her heart, she hates and abhors me. Ha, ha, ha, Sabiou's prostitute! laugh yourself mad, this is your hellish work."

Salome quivered with anger. Not being able to give vent to her rage, she fainted away, falling down senseless before Herod. "Die, worthless creature," he roared, when she fell. She groaned heavily and appeared to die. Herod lifted her up, laid her on a sofa, called his servants who administered restoratives to her. She revived without Herod's looking at her. The servants, obeying her command, left the saloon; she was again alone with Herod. "If you wish me to die, kill me," she said, in a cool and cutting tone; "dispatch me quickly, you are master in the art of assassination, kill me at once."

"Be dumb, worthless woman," he cried.

"So every maniac treats his faithful friends," she continued, calmly. "Better Hyrcan lives and Herod dies than Herod lives and Mariamne plays the impotent despot against him. It is not worth while to be Herod's friend, it is a crime to be his faithful sister; for he is the admirer of his enemies."

"I command you to be silent, and leave this room," he thundered.

"I am none of your obedient slaves," she said, "first I must tell you what I have to say, then I shall leave you. You are blind with passion, and I see. Know it, Herod, Mariamne is now more dangerous than all your enemies living or dead."

"May the thunder crush thy infamous tongue," he raged, while running about the room in perfect madness. "Am I a King, when I can not protect myself against the tongue of a woman?"

"O, you can, you can kill me even," she said, ironically. "You are a heroic, powerful warrior, you have a sword, and I am a feeble, defenceless woman. But if you do not kill me, I will speak, because I must.—Antony is dead. Octavius is your enemy. The people are infuriated. Mariamne hates, abhors you. A revolution in her favor is at your door. Your fall, your death is certain almost. Hyrcan is disposed of, but Mariamne steps in his place, leads the revolution, and avenges her brother and grand-father on you, while you sigh after her love. If you are a man, crush this scheme in time. Send her away to a place where the rebels can not reach her, and she can not communicate with them. Send her away in the silence of night, under the veil of darkness, and let her be there till the storm is over, and she repents her harsh conduct against you. If you are a man, reflect and act."

"You are right, by the honor of a man you are right," said Herod, much pacified. "Sister, forgive my harsh words. I know how to value your sagacity and attachment to me. Come, let us speak wisely. What do you think about the present crisis?"

"I think it will take all your wisdom and power to avoid serious consequences," said she, "even if Octavius undertakes nothing against you. Therefore you should not divide your forces at present. On the contrary, you should attempt to concentrate all the mental and physical forces at your command, and meet your enemies in full vigor."

"I do not understand you," said Herod.—"Speak more intelligibly."

"My advice is this," she continued; "Mariamne and her children, together with her mother, must be sent to a castle, where she can hold no communication with the rebels. Nay, they must not even know where she is. Sabion's cunningness and experience is now necessary to serve your interests. Therefore he must be discharged, exonerated and used to the best advantage, till the storm is over. Aurion must reach here to-day or to-morrow. You insist upon our marriage. As soon as he is thus connected with us, appoint him governor of the city, his influence is better here than an army, and his connection with our house is the best guarantee for his fidelity. Jericho and the other cities held by Cleopatra must be retaken as quick as possible. An army must be sent to the plain of Sharon to disperse the rebels. All this will easily be accomplished, if the city remains quiet. This effected, you may fearlessly appear before Octavius as the popular and strong King of Judea, and he can not say anything against you. This would be my plan of action in this crisis"

"You are the most sagacious counsellor of my court," said Herod. "I will reflect on everything you said. I will have decided in a few hours. Let me be alone now: in a few hoors I will be decided,"

Salome left; Herod was alone. Looking on the ring which Mariamne had returned him, he fell again into a fit of violent passions, sent one messenger after another to Mariamne; none of them, however, was admitted into her presence. Now he wept after his wife and children, and cursed his friends and counsellors; then again he swore to avenge himself on his disobedient wife and all the rest of the Asmoneans. So he raged for several hours, when the chamberlain came in and announced Aurion who wished to see the King. Being commanded to admit him, Simon was ushered into his presence.

"You are a slow messenger," the King said. "Do you thus carry out the command of your King?"

"Of the King? No. Of Herod? Yes," Simon replied, while he laid down all the documents before the King. "I have not done my duty," he continued, "I return my commission into your hands, with the only request to be dismissed forthwith. My destiny calls me hence."

"You think to excuse your sloth by obstinate language?" Herod said. "You shall not get away here so easy. It appears to me, you extorted the pardon of me, that I should send none else, that you linger on the road till it be too late, that the death of Hyrcan, my benefactor, my father, fall upon my head. You, you are the murderer of Hyrcan. If you had not been commissioned with my pardon, I would have sent one who would have arrived in due time. You shall give me good cause for your neglect of duty."

"Sohemos is an honest man and a warrior," Simon said. "Sohemus deals in no ambiguities, my lord; and Sohemus testifies that Herod is lost, morally lost, sunk into the lowest mire of perfidy and corruption.—You have extorted these words of me.—Farewell. My destiny calls me hence."

"And my authority commands you to stay," Herod said. "You add insult to neglect of duty, and think to extricate yourself from this dilemma by impertinence. I have had much more patience with you than I would have with my children. But you go too far. You shall give me full account of your neglect of duty, or I will let you feel my authority."

"Ah, I should not wonder if you attempt to get me out of your way, as you did with Hyrcan," said Simon; "for it appears you can not bear an honest man about you. My lord, we are done, I have nothing to request of you, nothing to fear, nothing to hope.—The last request I prefer to you is, let me go from hence, go instantly, without the loss of another word."

"I am not accustomed to excuse so easily a gross neglect of duty," Herod said, "especially if it engenders such disastrous and sad consequences. You are responsible for the death of Hyrcan, responsible to me, to the Queen, the people, to the world you are responsible for the death of a King. Speak in your own defence and I will listen."

"Now I understand you," said Simon.—"You know that your command to detain me on the road until it be too late, must fill my soul with indignation, with disgust. Ah, and now you see the revolution at your door; now you fear, you dread the consequences; now your own conscience haunts you; now you fear I will join the revolution, and you throw the blame on me, to justify your murderous schemes, your unparalleled perfidy. Sir, I look through your treacherous designs, and am ready to stand the consequences.—Sir, I despise you."

"Dare you speak thus to a King," Herod cried. "Are you mad? Ah, you are a fantastic man. You intend to irritate me, that I kill you, in order to give the rebels another pretext to an insurrection, so that you be a martyr. Very noble, but not noble enough for me. You can not escape with accusations and offensive words. I hold you to account for the death of Hyrcan."

No answer being given, Herod commenced again and anon to speak, but he could get no answer of Simon. He was determined to speak no more, and so he did. "You give me your word of honor, that you will keep your room till I command otherwise."

"I promise nothing," said Simon.

"Then I must have you arrested," Herod said. Simon made no reply. Herod called Dositheus, gave him orders to place a guard of honor at the door of Aurion. Both retired without a word from Simon. Herod informed Salome of Simon's arrest, and then sent a message to Mariamne, informing her of Simon's neglect to bring Pardon to Hyrcan in time, and of his arrest in consequence thereof.

Salome on hearing of the arrest of Simon hastened into the King's apartment. "My lord, why did you arrest my favorite friend," she asked, "who could be so useful to you in this crisis?"

"He might become as dangerous as you imagine him to be useful," said Herod. "He is indignant to the utmost at the death of Hyrcan and my orders to detain him on the road. I arrested him to prevent rash acts, and I will keep him in close confinement till he joins our ranks, er till this storm is over. My friends now give currency to the report, that I dispatched him with a pardon for Hyrcan, but he lingered on the road till it was too late, in order to arouse a rebellion against me. You know what influence this exercises on the people. Hence one way or the other Aurion must be useful to me. Anyhow he must remain in my hands, until I can conveniently restore him to liberty."

"But you intend not to do him any harm," Salome said, in an imploring tone.

"No," said Herod. "Go, take proper care that the Queen learn why Aurion and Sabion are arrested. Sabion, because he commanded the execution of Hyrcan before I returned, and Aurion on account of his calculated, preconcerted sloth in this affair. You hear, the Queen must know it, exactly as I say so she must know it."

Salome bowed and left the saloon hastening at once into Simon's room. He did not rise when she entered, and responded not to her salutation. There was a determined obstinacy visible in the stare and oblique looks darting like pointed arrows from his black eyes. His countenance somewhat unusually pale and, therefore, the more interesting, was so smooth, and looked so calm, that not the slightest emotion of the heart was betrayed. Only a characteristic furrow on his prominent and white forehead betokened profound thought in which he was disturbed, and the acute angle of his mouth expressed the dissatisfaction he felt at his unwelcome visitor.

After Salome had gazed at him for some time without receiving a look in return, she said in plaintive notes, "Has Aurion not a word to say to her who loves him so dearly?"

A sarcastic smile moved his lips. He crossed his arms over his breast, rose and looked firmly into her eyes. "Do you believe you can deceive me again?" he said. "The children of darkness know not what love is. Wild lust and burning passions like impetuous billows ebb and flood in your bosom between the rocks of crime, vice and iniquity. You call this wild, unnatural state of emotion love, I call it animal lust. I cast a deep glance into your black heart. I read an abhorrable chapter in your benighted soul. Satan himself must be ashamed of your fall. Salome, after she knelt before me in profound repentance and shame of her inhuman crime, after she conjured God and his angels to witness her return to the path of virtue, again associated with Sabion and plotted with the father the cruel scheme to dispose of his own daughter. Yes, she, the degraded daughter of Antipater, commanded Adarmelech to violate the chastity of a spotless virgin, the sacred laws of nature, the holiest sentiments of womankind are desecrated, defiled, set at naught, a woman commanded the violation of virgin chastity. This you have done after you feigned repentance at my feet, after you wringed yourself in the dust before me. But as tho' this was insufficient to fill your hellish cup of crime and Satanic malice, you planned the hellish scheme to assassinate Hyrcan, and after Herod had granted him pardon through my hands you arrived in the camp and frustrated the King's good design.—You, daughter of hell, you speak of love?—Ah, do not deceive yourself, I hate, I abhor you as you deserve it. Nay, not as you deserve it, for I can not hate so radically, so furiously, so hellishly as your deep-dyed crimes deserve it. I have but one word more to tell you, then I am done. Leave me forever, do not rob me of life's precious moments by your intolerable presence.—Curse, hate, kill me, if you please, only do not love me. The idea of being loved by so profligate a woman is sufficient to set an honest man mad."

Simon turned away from her with looks of contempt which pierced through her heart. Agonized, tormented, crushed, she uttered inarticulate sounds like an excited savage, which ended in a deep groan. Simon appeared to take no notice of it. In her madness she lifted up her hand to strike him. "Beware, profligate," Simon thundered, "or you have committed your last crime." The roaring voice and tremendous looks of the indignant man fell on her heart like a thunder-clap. Shuddering, she started back several paces, and reaching the sofa she fell back on it crying violently for help. The guards rushed in the room and asked after her command. Meanwhile she recovered her senses, and observing the stern calmness in the countenance of Simon, she said, "It is nothing, I am sick, and the King's physician considers my disease incurable. I was so frightened. But it is all over. Go! I do not need you." The guard withdrew, and the silence of the grave reigned in the the room.

After awhile Salome rose, came up to the seat of Simon who had turned to the window and addressed him in a plaintive and tremulous voice: "Aurion, will you hear me, once more hear me?" No answer being received she implored again, "Aurion, are you deaf to my tormenting pain, are you blind to my tears? Only once more do hear me." Simon appeared to be deaf to her words, but again, and with tears in her eyes, she implored, "O, hear an unfortunate, tormented woman who stands begging before you. Only once more do hear me." Simon yielded. He turned to her and, in a pacified and solacing tone, he told her to speak.

"Who told you that I commanded the violation of Helen's chastity?" she asked.

"The chamberlain, who conveyed your orders to Adarmelech, confessed it in the agony of death," was the reply.

"And does Helen know it?" she asked, eagerly.

"I can not tell," was the short reply.

"Does she live?" she continued, interrogating. No answer followed. She repeated the question several times, but Simon, fearing harm for Helen did not answer. On being pressed by her urgent requests, he said, "She is dead for you." Salome misunderstood Simon, and on hearing the word "dead," she covered her face with her hands and cried violently, "And I am her murderer." Simon was on the point to tell her, that she was mistaken, when one of her servants came in the room and said, "My lady, she died under the torture, but would not confess where Helen is."

"Who died?" Simon asked hastily, while Salome nearly fainted away.

"That obstinate servant," said the man, "they called her Elvira, she was Helen's servant."

Dumb, pain-stricken, pale and motionless, Simon stood several moments and stared at the furious woman before him, while the servant retired. Then his eyes began to roll wildly in their sockets. He cried like a madman, "Awake, fury, kneel in the dust crushed, annihilated, and admire the punishing, just hand of the Almighty Ruler of human destinies. Hear it, bloody woman, and hide your face before the light of the day; hear it, monstrous profligate, you have murdered your own child—she—Elvira—she is your daughter."

One cry was heard shrill and painful, and Salome laid senseless on the sofa. Simon would not even look at her, when the door opened, and Herod entered. Without perceiving his sister he said, "The King comes to inquire after his prisoner."

Without looking on him Simon, pointing to Salome said, "And to see his dying sister."

Herod on observing Salome, asked, surprised, "What means this?"

"Nothing unusual in Herod's palace," Simon, coolly and monotonously, replied.—"Remorse and shame overpowered her, and she fainted away. But she will soon recover to endure a thousand deaths." The King busying himself to restore her, Simon said: "For mercy's sake do not recall her to consciousness. Let her sleep without a dream. If you restore her suddenly her heart might break under the crushing weight of her guilt. Behold, King of Judea, here lies your sister, your vile counsellor, here she lies crushed with remorse; for she killed her own daughter, and her daughter was an angel. Behold, King of Judea, she is a vile, degraded, dishonored woman, still she is an angel in comparison with you, even you. She fainted on hearing that she murdered her own child, and you remained unshaken when you heard of the death of your own father, through your hands."

"Irritate not my anger," Herod roared, foaming with rage. Salome groaned heavily, and the King attended to her. Simon continued: "Your anger is quite harmless. You can only kill me, dispatch me to those whose blood boils upon your guilty heart.—Ah, Sire, there are moments in every man's life when death loses its terror and life its charms, before another all-absorbing passion. I feel now this very inclination. I must tell you, what no other mortal can or dare, so that my voice re-echo in your heart when I am no more, when this form of clay decays in the dust—that my form haunt you with terror and dismay through all scenes of your life. Hear me, King of Judea, wretched, miserable, bent with grief, remorse and self-contempt as your sister lies here, you will be crushed under the oppressive weight of your guilt. You will curse the day of your birth, curse yourself and every day of your life. The blood of a King and two highpriests stains your guilty soul. The blood of your own brother-in-law crimsons your fingers. Thousands of widows and orphans, an oppressed, outraged nation, an enslaved, fettered people curse you whenever your name is mentioned, an offended wife, a down trodden angel weeps over your fall.—Your own children must hate you. In remorse and despair you will die, haunted by the shadows of those you murdered, scalded by the hot tears of your enemies, suffocated with the sighs of your foes, whom you outraged, and haunted by my spirit. Thus will be your end, for there is a justice in heaven, there is a God who avenges the innocent and oppressed. Now, Herod, I am ready to die."

Herod raged furiously; but Salome having somewhat recovered clung so closely to him that he could not give vent to his wrath. "Let me go, sister, that I may kill that infernal liar," he ejaculated, hoarse and foaming with anger; but Salome minded him not, she clung so firmly around his neck that he could not move. Simon hastened to his rescue, opened the arms of Salome and cried: "Now, Herod, your hands are free. Kill me, to fill the cup of your crimes to its very brim. Tyrant, despot, inhuman murderer, kill me!"

Herod clasped his sword, hesitated, the cries of Salome, the firmness of Simon, the fiery looks of the young enthusiast paralized his arms. They fell straight, his head dropped, his anger was gone. "Aurion, Aurion, you are a cruel man," he cried. "Your words are worse than the fire of hell. I would dismiss you in peace; but I know you will join the rebels. Therefore I must secure your person, till we are capable to see each other in better humor. Here you must stay and expect your fate."

Herod offered his arm to Salome, and both left the room, before which a double guard was placed.

CHAPTER XVII.

THE IMPORTANT SESSION.

The secret hall under the temple was crowded with bearded, robust men and arms of all descriptions. Swords, spears, helmets and shields, bows, arrows and slings were towered into artificial pyramids. In the midst of the capacious hall there was erected an artificial column of the ancient implements, the relics of the place, which had been used by the workmen of King Solomon and Zerubabel to build the temple, beneath which the secret hall was. On the top of the pillar was a representation of the ark, the Cherubim and the two tables of stone. Next to the first, another pillar was constructed of twelve large shields, bearing the names of the twelve sons of Jacob, said to be the same shields which the princes of the twelve tribes bore when coming with Joshua to the land of Canaan. The lion of Judah, the mighty *Ariel* rested upon this pillar and was represented to watch over the rod of Moses Seventy chairs stood in the midst of the hall in a semicircle before a platform covered with significant symbols, upon which a chair resembling a throne was placed. The purple robe and the semi-crown laid on a velvet cushion on a table.

The chair was occupled by the blind president Baba ben Buta who rose and said to the multitude assembled in the hall: " Bro thers and friends. This is the last time I will preside over your meetings; for you will now organize your Sanhedrin, over which the great and learned Hillel and Menahem will preside. With armed hands you will leave this subterranean sanctuary and take possession of the temple, the city, the throne and the crown. Herod's cup of crimes is filled to its brim, his verdict is rendered, his doom is sealed. You have resolved to place him before Israel's Sanhedrin and have him tried according to our laws for the usurpation of our crown, the murder of two high priests, the violation of our laws, the oppression of our people, the illegal dissolution of our Sanhedrin, the protection of Rome's interests inimical to our own, and the introduction of pagan rites and customs. You are just and your cause is sacred, therefore God will protect you, and you will be victorious. Abba Shaul promised to be here with Hillel and our friends from Jericho before the first watch of the night is closed, and he keeps his word. Let us, before we go to the organization of the Sanhedrin, deliberate on ways and means to save Queen Mariamne from the fury of Herod. I fear he will kill her as soon as he perceives our strength."

Here a Shamaite rose, and, having respectfully bowed to the assembly, he said: " I wish to call your attention to a rumor current in Jerusalem, that Simon ben Hillel is a traitor. He received a grant of pardon for Hyrcan from the hands of Herod; but he lingered so long on the road until the pardon came too late. Herod's anger was so great on this occasion, that he threw Simon in a prison; but on mature reflection he pardoned him. Simon married the sister of Herod, the bloody Salome, and is governor of Jerusalem, and successor to Sabion in the King's confidence. Sabion is in prison for a treachery of his which Simon discovered. Every child of Jerusalem tells this story. If this is so, we can not elevate Hillel to the dignity of Nassi in Israel, this must be clear to every unprejudiced mind. Therefore I say, we must wait, for we must be cautious, until we know for certain, that this story is not true; we can not till then appoint Hillel to the highest dignity in Israel."

The sensation excited by these remarks was great and painful. None could contradict the rumor, and every one appeared to feel, that under such circumstances, Hillel could not be elevated to the highest dignity of the people. The father of a traitor could not be entrusted with the presidency over the highest juridical and legislative tribunal. Still it was the ardent wish of the vast multitude to place the integral, upright and learned Hillel at the head of that body. Jonathan ben Uziel was the only man in the assembly who had the courage to rise and contradict the rumor. He said: "Does not our sacred law ordain 'The parents shall not die on account of their children, and the children shall not die on account of their parents,' why then should we punish Hillel for the sin of Simon? Even if Simon is a traitor to the sacred cause of Israel, Hillel can never be. He would rather reject all his children and die under the executioner's hands, than betray the cause of his people; for life has but one object in his estimation; it is granted to man to prepare here for a life hereafter, to gather here for a self-support hereafter, to be an agent of divine good ness here, in order to be an angel hereafter. He is incapable of being wicked.—As for Simon, the son of Hillel, my school mate and friend, I discredit that rumor, entirely. I know the generous and patriotic heart of Simon. There glows but one passion in his great soul, all others are subjected to this which fills his whole mind—and this passion is to rescue Israel from its tyrants. I pledge my life and honor for the integrity of Simon. I will die the death of a wretch before your eyes, nay still more and worse than all tortures, I will live an outcast in Israel, if that rumor is not a falsehood, a base invention of Herod and his wicked counsellors to deceive the people, and counteract the influence of Simon on Israel's myriads."

None replied. None could reply; for both the accusation and the defence were based on mere suppositions. Still every body felt instinctively that Hillel should not be entrusted with so responsible an office, if his son turned a traitor to the people. One wrapped in a black cloak was admitted in the hall after signs and countersigns were correctly exchanged and the passwords given. The stranger eagerly examined every countenance in the hall, went from one place to the other and nowhere found the desired rest. The restless search of the stranger attracted attention, and one asked him, "Do you seek any man?"

"I do," the stranger replied, in a tremulous, feminine tone, "I seek Simon ben Hillel."

"He is not here," was the reply, "nor will he come hither; for he is with Herod."

"Then it is true, merciful God," the stranger cried, so shrill and painful, that every body in the capacious hall looked surprised, at the stranger. But, before any question could be asked, Helen threw off her cloak and mask, and cried in heart piercing accents, "Men of Israel, save my husband, rescue Simon from the clutches of the devil.—Have mercy with the tears, the breaking heart of a helpless woman, save my husband?"

Baba ben Buta listened attentively to the prayer of Helen. He bade her approach him nearer, and Jonathan ben Uziel supported her to do so. "Art thou, my daughter, the wife of Simon ben Hillel?" he asked.

"I am, my gracious lord," she replied.—"Hillel himself blessed our covenant of love."

"And where is your husband, my daughter?" he continued, "Speak without fear."

"He is imprisoned in the royal palace," Helen lamented, "and a dreadful end awaits him. Rescue my husband, save Simon, he is the noblest in Israel!"

"How do you know of his fate?" the blind sage asked."

"I remained in Jericho when he came to Jerusalem with a grant of pardon to Hyrcan," said Helen. "The soldiers of Herod had everywhere detained him on the road, so that he should come too late, and too late he came. Dreadful were my omens, terrible my dreams, I could rest no longer in Jericho There came Sohemus with his host to capture Jericho. The men of Jericho bade all women and children to leave the city, as they were determined to resist to the last. I embraced this opportunity and in the garb of a man I hastened to Jerusalem. In vain I attempted to enter into the palace, as no stranger is now admitted. To day, I heard a rumor in the city, that Simon proved a traitor to his country and his wife.—Madness seized me, my brain was heated, delirious, my eyesight was gone, I could hear no longer. I ran toward the gate of the palace without knowing what I wished to do there. There came Marcus, the servant of my unhappy sister, and told me, that the Queen and her children were sent away in the dark of night to an unknown spot; that Elvira, my half sister was tortured to death by orders of Salome; that Simon is imprisoned in a subterranean prison, ostensibly because he arrived too late with the pardon, but in reality because he would not accede to the wishes of Herod and Salome. Marcus, having learned this, risks his life to inform the friends of Simon of his real condition. I hastened to the house of Hillel's wealthy brother, told him all I knew. He informed me of your session this evening, and advised me to come hither and inform you of the perilous state of Simon.—

Here I am with my tears, my trembling heart, my despairing soul: here I am and beseech, implore you, save my husband, give me my husband, he sacrifices himself for his people. Here I kneel before you, and in the name of the God of love I beg, I entreat you, give me my husband!"

"Let us storm the palace," many thundered, in an excited tone. "Let us beat the tyrant at once."

"Do, for God's sake do," Helen cried, "and give me a sword, a heavy sharp sort, that I may fight in the ranks of the brave. Death and destruction to the breed of scorpions, the children of hell. Death and destruction to all tyrants. Go on men, with the steel decked hearts, fight for your country, and let me fight among you. Strike the fatal blow at once, and return crowned with victory to your wives and children."

With lightning speed the swords rushed from the sheaths, under the thunder like exclamation: "Death and destruction to all tyrants. Forward, onward to combat and victory!"

"Not without me," Abba Shaul roared, that every one of the excited multitude heard it.

The enthusiastic reception of Abba Shaul subsided not for some time. Order being restored he reported himself to Baba ben Buta: "I have carried out the wishes of the People," said Abba Shaul. "I went to Jericho and there met Sohemus with his host, dispatched by Herod to take Possession of the city. The Egyptian garrison and the citizens were prepared to offer strong resistance and Sohemus made preparations for an assault. I arrived in time. We attacked them and they retreated. The people inside supported our movements, and Sohemus betook himself to disorderly flight."

A thunder of cheers and hurrahs interrupted the speaker. When he could continue, he said: "When Sohemus was gone, followed by half of my men, I went to the city, made arrangements for the return of the Egyptians by Arabia to their own country, saw them leave Jericho, organized the people for the coming events and returned with Hillel, Menahem and the other members of the Sanhedrin in Jericho, who are here and wait for your further orders."

While the deafening applause resounded in the subterranean hall, Helen approached Abba Shaul, and, in the anguish of her heart, addressed him, "Thou who hast saved me from infamy and death, rescue my husband, thy friend, the friend of the people—rescue Hillel's son from the iron grasp of Herod."

"Be of good cheer, Helen," said Abba Shaul, "I know every thing, and have dispatched men of the right cast to rescue Simon."

The multitude. insisted on proceeding at once to the capture of the temple and the fort of Antonio, and appeal to the people for aid. But Abba Shaul opposed it. He said: "Everything is prepared for the attack.—Fifty thousand of our brethren are under arms and posted not far from Jerusalem.—They approach in forced marches. It would be extremely easy for us to take the city and drive Herod to despair. But we must spare bloodshed as much as possible. We must spare the city. Therefore let us be wise in all we do. The gates are closed, none is admitted except unarmed pilgrims with their paschal lambs. But they come by innumerable thousands, and plenty of arms are stored in the city to make them formidable to Herod, and force him to surrender, without much bloodshed, and without damage to the city.

"Before we dispose of the old government, the new must be completely organized.—Therefore first of all organize the new Sanhedrin and charge them with the sole government of the people. This done we will take possession of the temple and place the Sanhedrin at its proper place, to begin its functions forthwith."

All were satisfied and preparations were made forthwith to receive the members of the Sanhedrin. The chairs were evacuated and Hillel, followed by the seventy senators, entered the hall under the loud demonstrations of joy and satisfaction. Arrived between the two pillars, Hillel halted and Baba ben Buta in a slow and sonorous tone said: "Behold Sampson between the pillars of Israel, not to break but to support them that they support him. Thou Hillel, art the giant in the Law of God, thou art chosen by Israel's myriads to watch over these pillars that they support thee and thy people."—Then all the senators passed between the pillars with their right hands uplifted to a sacred oath. Undisturbed silence reigned among the multitude, when Baba ben Buta again begun: "Three crowns were given to Israel—the King's crown, the crown of the highpriest, and the glorious diadem of the Law. The last is the most sacred, for it is our inheritance from Sinai, it is ours and our descendants forever. Ye nobles of Israel, ye chosen of the Lord, your people entrust you with this holiest of our possession, to watch over the Law and the people of God." Two men led Hillel to his chair amid the loud exclamations of joy. One clad him in the purple cloak, and when Baba said, "Behold the prince of Israel," all exclaimed, "Long live Hillel, Israel's prince." Another placed the diadem upon his head and gave the golden staff in his hand.—"This is the diadem of Israel's law, and this is the staff of Moses. The people bow before this diadem and, with this staff, lead them as their father, teacher and judge, as once Moses led them from Egypt, through the wilderness to the land beyond Jordan." All bowed before the new Nassi. Then Baba gave the scroll of the Law to Hillel and said: "This is the Law which Moses laid before the children of Israel. This is your sole guide and teacher, and you are its guardian and expounder. The eyes of all Israel are directed toward you, you must provide them with the pure water of the Law of God. Sacred is the most holy place of the temple; for the ark of the covenant was deposited there. Sacred is the ark; for the word of God, written on two tables of stone, was preserved therein. Most, sacred, however, is Israel's Sanhedrin, the bearers of God's law and the expounders of His divine will. The crowns of the King and High priest will pass away, and the crown of the Law will remain forever." Silver staffs were then given to all the Sanhedrin, Menahem was dressed in the attire of his office and all were led to their seats amid the exclamations of joy and satisfaction.

"Brethren, it is the will of the nation," said Abba Shaul, "that this Sanhedrin should be supreme until another government is organized by the will of the people, and with the consent of the Sanhedrin.—Therefore let us kneel down and swear allegiance to the Sanhedrin."

All swords rushed from their sheaths, all men fell upon their knees, lifting up their right hands and, holding up the sword with their left hands, they exclaimed: "We swear allegiance, strict and unexceptional obedience to the mandates of the Sanhedrin.—We swear to fight for our rights and liberties and protect this Sanhedrin with our lives, and enforce its decrees faithfully. In the name of the God of Israel. Amen."

All rose, and the clash of arms and outbursts of enthusiasm only gave way when Hillel rose from his chair and addressed the assembly thus:

"I render thanks and glory to the God of Israel 'who elevateth the poor from the dust, lifteth up the needy from the dung hill, to set him with the nobles, even the nobles of his people.' I wish to express my thanks to my people for the confidence reposed in my humble qualities, the dignity to which they have elevated the son of an unnoticed family; for my family is the youngest in Israel. Not words but my whole life shall be an eloquent expression of gratitude to my people. You know that I am no man of many words; but my heart and my soul are devoted to Israel and its sacred cause. My actions will speak better than I can at this moment of strong and unutterable emotions.

"Brethren: Israel's greatness and protection, its glory and divine mission is its Law, the greatest the world has seen or will ever see; for it is of divine origin. We are the chosen guardians of truth and justice; and truth and justice, even God himself, are our protectors. This Law, this sacred inheritance, is entrusted to the hands of your Sanhedrin, to expound, teach and enforce it.—We will do our duty before God and Israel, let it cost our lives.

"This is a time of particular tribulation

in Israel. Two enemies are against us, Rome and Herod. It requires double courage to maintain our rights Yours is the sword and the valor, ours is the word and the moral fortitude to check the progress of usurpation, despotism and violence. You are ready to fight, conquer or die, we are prepared to shield our rights with our breasts, in behalf of God, justice and Israel. Justice, the will of God, must return and remain in Israel, justice at any price, any risk.

"Our functions can not commence here and now. The work of the Sanhedrin must be done in the broad light of the day, so the law commands; for the spread of divine light is the duty of this body, and its actions must be far from obscurity and night. The law points out the place where the Sanhedrin should meet, the spot which the Lord has chosen by His prophets, in the temple next to the altar, the *Lishkhath Hagazith*, in the presence of God's sanctuary. There and then our functions begin.

"But, as your brother, allow me to advise you thus: Send a deputation to Octavius who tarries on the Isle of Rhodes, and inform him of the causes that brought about this revolution. Let him be prayed not to attempt an undue interference in Judea.—Then let us proceed and take possession of the temple, appeal to the people and trust in God.

"I need not admonish you to be valorous and prudent, for your past conduct testifies to your excellent qualities. Obey your leader, Abba Shaul, for he is a whole-souled patriot and warrior. I need promise nothing, for I am the most humble servant of my God and His people; I must obey their orders and decrees. I need not encourage you, for you fear nothing. I need not pray for you, for God watches over his messengers. You need not encourage us, for we know our duty and your faithfulness, your determination and decision. In the name of God and in behalf of Israel let us lay hand on the great work."

The unsheathed swords glittered like starlight in the subterranean hall, while the thunder of applause and the outbursts of enthusiasm rolled like muttering cataracts. "For God and Israel!" it resounded from every mouth, and the mute walls re-echoed a solemn Amen. "To arms, companions," Abba Shaul commanded, and the multitude dressed with lightning speed in the iron armament ornamenting the hall. In a few moments every breast was iron-decked, the helmet of brass covered every head, the shield was fastened to the left arm, the spear was held with the right. Again the voice of Abba Shaul was heard, and the men formed into a column six abreast. Two doors were thrown open, and a wide subterranean passage opened to their gaze. "This is the way to the temple," said Abba. "Forward! follow me." With a sword in one hand and the banner in the other, Abba Shaul preceded and the multitude followed in the best order.

The Sanhedrin left their places to follow last behind the warriors. Hillel observed Helen and came up to her. "My daughter, why are you here?"

"O my father, my beloved father," she lamented, "Simon is in the hands of Herod. This revolt will cost his life."

"Associate not with the wicked," Hillel said, "this is the adage of the savans.—But fear not my daughter, no harm will befal him. God watches. My heart tells me God watches. Follow me to the temple, when the morning dawns I will care for the rescue of my son." Helen seized arms, dressed in the warrior's brass habiliment, and followed the marching men.

CHAPTER XVIII.

THE CATASTROPHE.

The inmates of the royal palace were in a state of consternation. Night had spread her benign shade over the earth, but no repose, no sleep refreshed the weary eyelids of Herod and his courtiers. Like an infuriated tiger Herod ran through the apartments and halls of the palace. "Sohemus defeated, my soldiers defeated by the rebels, this disgrace upon the arms of Herod! Defeated by a grave digger, by the lowest rabble of my people!" were all the words that could be heard of him. He would not allow anybody to sleep, nor could any speak to him.

Castobarus was the only man, who had

the courage to speak to him; but even he but seldom received an answer. "Where is Joseph my treasurer?" the King asked, suddenly.

"My lord, you sent him away with the Queen and the royal princes to Alexandra," Castobarus replied. "He is gone as you commanded."

"Then she is gone?" he asked.

"The Queen, my lord, her mother and the royal princes are gone, as you commanded," said Castobarus. "They started exactly three hours ago."

"Did you see them leave?" Herod asked. "How did the Queen behave? What did she say? Did she not inquire after me?—Speak, did she not mention my name, not a word, not a single word did she say?"

"Not a word, my lord," said Castobarus. "She mounted the carriage, took her children in her arms, kissed them and away the chariot rolled."

"Not a single word she said?" Herod asked again. "Speak, man, did she not weep, not sigh, not request you to see me only for a moment?"

"She said nothing, did not weep nor sigh," Castobarus replied. "When I handed her your decree she bowed slightly, and said, 'I am ready to depart.' Since then I have not heard her speak."

"Castobarus, have you a wife and children?" the King asked, suddenly.

"No, my lord," was the courtier's reply.

"Then go, you do not understand me," the King said. "Go send me a man who is a husband and a father. But no, stay. I have dark omens. Call Aurien, I am sick. —No, call him not. Give me a cup of wine —No, I mean call Salome —Hark, what is this? Armed men go through the hall. Pst, they approach the door."

"I hear nothing, my lord," said Castobarus. "It is the wind that whistles through the leaves."

Herod appeared to be totally absent minded and wandering. He paced the room rapidly, stared through the window into the dark, and struck frequently the handle of his sword, and exclaimed, "I am King, I will teach the rebels that I am."

Suddenly he turned to Castobarus with the command "Call Sabion hither, I must see him." Sabion was ushered into his presence.

"You are an obstinate sinner," said Herod, "you intended to sell me and Judea to Cleopatra. But she is dead and you repent. Is it not so, Sabien?"

"My lord, I am yours with all my life," said Sabion, kneeling before the King.—"Command and I will die for you, without a groan."

"Sabien, have you heard of the defeat of Sohemus, by the rebels?" the King asked.

"I have, my lord," was the reply.

"Sohemus says their number is formidable," the King quothed. "An attack upon Jerusalem is in contemplation. They can not take Jerusalem. But they might do us much harm in the country. What is your advice, shall I wait until they attack Jerusalem, or shall I go out in person to meet them in open battle before they concentrate their forces?"

"It would not do for the King to fight his own people," said Sabien. "Your enemies in the country are so very few, that they can not even bring together men enough to be called an army. Sohemos went with a few men to Jericho, and being defeated he considers the numbers of the enemy formidable. You are too much feared and respected in the country to be betrayed by the multitude. Keep the city safe, concentrate your army around it, and watch their movements, is my advice."

"So is my inclination," said Herod.—"But if they besiege the city, what then?"

"Then you have more than the required forces to drive them to pairs," said Sabien. "Now, they dare not think of besieging the city, for the pilgrims coming by the thousand would insist upon raising the siege, nor would they hem in the pilgrims. Till after passover you have your forces concentrated and they are lost if they attempt to approach the city."

"But the pilgrims; have we not to fear the worst of the pilgrims themselves?" Herod exclaimed.

"They are harmless, because there are

too many women and children among them," said Sabion, "besides this they are unarmed."

"Sabion, you are a wise man," said the King. "Your life is forfeited, but no harm shall be done you, you shall have one of the cities now belonging to Cleopatra, if you succeed in exciting a counter-revolution among the pilgrims. Tell them Sabion and Aurion are arrested on account of Hyrcan's death. The Queen left the city from fear of the rebellious people. You are the messenger of the Queen and complain in her behalf of the conduct of the rebels. Tell them yourself or by your agents anything to please them, just excite a counter-revolution, and your reward shall be great."

Dositheus reeled into the King's apartment pale with excitement. "My lord, the temple and the fort of Antonio——"

"What of them?" the King asked.

"Are in the hands of the rebels, without resistance—treachery—the garrison, priests, Levites, all must be traitors," Dositheus stammered. None could speak. Every one stared aghast. "Did you see and hear right?" the King asked.

"I saw too well only," said Dositheus.—"The bridge is broken down, no communication is left between the city and the temple."

Herod laughed savagely, and ran about like a madman. After a while he turned to Sabion and bade him, "Fifty howling Pharisees must be hired to lament over the sinfulness of those who prevent the pious pilgrims from making their paschal sacrifices and appear before the Lord. Lamentations must be heard in every corner of the city, and inflammatory speeches made against the impiety of the rebels. Sohemus must besiege the temple forthwith from all sides.—Castobarus is entrusted with the city affairs. Now, call Aurion into my presence. I must see him instantly."

Notes, melancholy and sad, like those of a wandering demon resounded in the hall.—A female sung the names of Joseph, my husband, Aristobul, Hyrcan, Baruch ben Menahem, Elvira. Herod drew his sword and opened the door. There stood before him dressed in black, Salome, his sister, who went slowly and madly singing through the hall. He seized her by the arm and led her into his apartment. "What ails thee, sister?" he asked, hastily.

"I sat all night by the dead body of my child," she said, monotonously and feebly, "my child Elvira whom I have killed; and there came the spirits of the murdered men to me. Do you not see them? There they go; there they are. I must sing, cry, weep, despair. Aurion said I must despair."

Herod felt his blood congeal in his veins. He looked fearful in the direction his sister pointed, but observing nothing, he said, "You are sick, my sister, you want rest, you are too much agitated, over-excited. I will send for a physician. I will send for Aurion."

"No, for God's sake not," she cried, "let that man not drive me to despair with his rigid virtue.—Yes, send for him, his presence will heal me.—No, no, no, let me not again see his tremendous, cold, heartless looks. Contempt is in his words, eternal damnation darts from his eyes—O, let me see him once more my horrid lover. Elvira, my murdered child, thy mother—curse thy mother! Elvira was an angel, and I—O let him not come, he will drive me to madness. King, beware, that man will make a fool, a maniac of you."

The chamberlain returned with the report: "The room of Aurion is empty, I found nothing in it except this letter addressed to my lord. Herod eagerly seized the letter and read: "Herod, by the power of Rome, King of Judea. I have loved you as none else does, because I admired in you the hero and the man, and pitied you for your vices. I hoped to be of service to you and my people; but you have not listened to my advice, you have degraded royalty to brutality, and majesty to perfidy. You have told me a lie in the camp, I can be no longer with you. Herod, you are lost. Speedy flight alone can save your life, to spend it in repentance of your grievous sins. I will always mourn your loss, for I loved you.—Farewell. My Gentile name is Aurion, but my Hebrew name is Simon ben Hillel."

The gesticulations and inarticulate sounds of Salome were so wild and disorderly, that Herod nearly wept with her. "Give me Aurion," she cried, "King of Judea, give me Aurion or speedy death."

Herod called several officers and commanded them: "Go immediately, and bring me back my physician. He ran away. He can not be gone far; for he was here yet last evening. Whoever brings him before me shall be to-morrow one of the richest men of Judea, he shall have the finest palace in Jerusalem, and the world shall envy him, sound and uninjured he must be brought before me."

Every one of the officers promised to bring Aurion and place him before the King. When they were gone Herod soliloquized, "Also Herod had a friend, but he is gone."

Whenever the door of Herod's apartment was opened, his question always was: "Did they find Aurion?" When this was answered in the negative, he sent away other officers with the strictest orders to bring Aurion instantly into his presence. Then again he paced his room in the most agitated state of mind.

"My lord, three men with a truce are at your door," said Dositheus, "shall they be admitted into your presence?"

"Where do they come from?" Herod asked. "From the temple," was the answer.

"Do they sue for mercy?" Herod asked.

"I know not, my lord," said Dositheus, "they would not speak; they insist upon presenting their message to you personally, and to none else."

"Admit them," said Herod, and Jonathan ben Uziel, in company of two other men bearing a flag of truce, was ushered into the presence of the King.

"In the name of the God of Israel and His divine law, I bring you a message of the Sanhedrin," said Jonathan.

"The Sanhedrin is not in session," Herod replied, drily.

"Two witnesses are with me," said Jonathan, "to testify that the Sanhedrin is in session in their apartments prescribed by law, that I was charged with the duty to bring to you the message of which I inform you."

"Who presides?" Herod asked.

"Hillel and Menahem," was the reply.

"Who appointed them?" was the question.

"The people and the people's savans," was the response.

"I have appointed the sons of Bethera to preside over the Sanhedrin," said Herod. "They must be respected as the heads of that body."

"The sons of Bethera resigned, Hillel and Menahem were appointed," said Jonathan.

"They had no right to resign in my absence," said Herod.

"Not knowing the law as well as Hillel and Menahem they were obliged to resign," said Jonathan. "Beside the trial of Hyrcan, where it became evident that Hillel is more competent than Joshua ben Bethera, another question was laid before the old Sanhedrin, and they could not answer. The eve of passover being this year on a Sabbath, the question was whether the paschal lamb may be brought on the Sabbath-day. Hillel, the pupil of Shemaiah and Abtalion, was the only man who could expound the law in this particular case. The sons of Bethera themselves acknowledge his superiority and agree, that Hillel and Menahem should preside over the Sanhedrin."

"And what is the message you have to bring me?" Herod asked.

"Herod, son of Antipater, the Sanhedrin of Israel assembled in the temple of the Lord command thee to appear before them," Jonathan said.

"Not a word more," Herod interrupted. "I command you to be silent, and the self-constituted Sanhedrin to disband forthwith, or else each of them pays with his life for this rebellious conduct."

"I am the messenger of the Sanhedrin, and must do my duty," said Jonathan, coolly. "I must bring you the message. You are accused of usurpation, high treason, wilful murder and"—

"Be dumb, lest I forget that I am a King and you bear a flag of truce," Herod bade.

But Jonathan continued: "And theft committed on the people's property." Herod's rage was boundless; but Jonathan did not mind it and, after a short pause, he continued: "Thou shalt appear before them forthwith to be held in custody until the cases will be tried."

"Go back to the rebels and tell them," Herod vociferated, "I give them 24 hours time to disband in peace. But if they fail to do so, within the given time, none of them shall escape alive."

"I am the messenger of the Sanhedrin," said Jonathan, "I can not and will not convey to them your message."

"Then begone, as quick as possible," said Herod. "If you are found here after the lapse of one hour, death is your penalty."

Jonathan, without showing the least reverence to Herod by either words or motions, turned to go, when Herod stopped him with the question, "What is your name?"

"Jonathan ben Uziel," was the answer.

"Your behavior as an official is commendable," said Herod. "Pity, that you are on the wrong side. Be wise, then come again."

"The messenger of the Sanhedrin can not enter upon any conversation with you," said Jonathan, and left the room.

"What a hell of pride there is in the deportment of this young man; he is an Aurion, number two!" Herod exclaimed, in the midst of his furious rage. "Let Sohemus make preparations to take the temple by assault," the King commanded. "Let every man be on his post. None shall be permitted to leave his ranks. The strictest vigilance must be kept. Did they find Aurion?" he asked again.

The commotion in the city was of an extraordinary character. The oldest men did not remember ever to have seen such a crowd in Jerusalem. The streets and lanes were in some spots so densly crowded that they were impassable. Houses, squares and parks were filled with strangers. Yet the largest number of the pilgrims still sojourned in the suburbs of Jerusalem. At the upper Market a large crowd congregated to listen to the arguments of a public speaker who denounced in the most reckless terms those who hold the temple in their possession, and prevent the pilgrims from appearing before the Lord and making the sacrifices as the law ordains.

"Falsehoods, falsehoods! he utters falsehoods," one of the multitude cried: "It is Sabion, the chief of the spies, the satanic counsellor of Herod."

"Down with him! Kill him!" it sounded from a thousand manly lips, and down he was pulled from the platform, and a thousand daggers were pointed toward his heart. "Brethren and friends," Sabion cried, in the anguish of his soul, "you are mistaken, you kill an innocent man, I am not Sabion, I am a friend of the people."

"He is Sabion," it resounded again from the crowd, "I know him well. I have seen him often enough."

"Kill him! Tear him in pieces! Drag out his satanic heart!" the multitude vociferated, fiercely, and Sabion fell upon his knees and prayed for his life. "I am not Sabion," he cried desperately. "I am an innocent man. Have mercy with my wife and children, I have six innocent children at home."

"A lie, it is a lie," another said, "he has neither wife nor children. It is the very devil who killed a thousand innocent men. He is the murderer of those who are found dead in the streets of Jerusalem; he is the plague of this city, of this land; he schemed and carried out the death of Hyrcan. It is black-souled Sabion."

"Death be his penalty," it resounded like the muttering thunder from the crowd, and a hundred daggers were lodged in the body of the terrible man. He cried desperately, cursed Herod, himself, and the world at large, and expired with the most terrible curses upon his lips. When the military guards arrived at the spot, it was too late. Sabion was dead. The crowd had dispersed, and none could say who killed Sabion.

Herod, on hearing of the unexpected death of Sabion by the hands of an excited people, was so infuriated, that he gave orders to catch and execute forthwith anybody who is in the least suspected to have co-operated in the murder of Sabion. "Where is Aurion?" Herod asked a returning officer.

"He it was that delivered Sabion into the

hands of the excited populace," the officer said; "but it is impossible to catch him.—Wherever a public speaker appears, Aurion is present, and denounces him as the slave of Sabion; and several of them were killed already. I hunted after him from spot to spot, but could not reach him."

"Let it cost half of my kingdom," Herod cried, "I must have him to day, I must have him, living and well. Whoever brings him to me, brings him living and well, shall have what his heart desires, let it be half of my kingdom. Go, tell all the officers that I command them to bring my physician before me. Tell them the reward I have promised. Go, be in a hurry, lose no time."

When the officer was gone Herod cried, violently: "No friend, no honest heart mourns with a King over the wounds which false friends inflict on him. Sabion is executed as he deserved to be; but I stand alone in this crisis. Where is Salome, where is my sister?" the King asked, and she was ushered into his presence. "Brother," she cried, "I fear we are lost; for the revolt has spread into the very heart of the city. Who can manage this immense crowd?"

"I can and I will," Herod exclaimed.—"Dositheus, take as many of my troops as may be necessary and drive every stranger, every suspicious citizen out of Jerusalem. Whoever refuses, let him die, no matter how many lives it costs. Send my command to my officers who command outside of the city gates, to disperse the crowd ejected from the city, pursue them as far as possible and send them home terror-struck and dismayed, that they revolt no more." When Dositheus was gone, Herod cried, "Terror must reign in Jerusalem, and teach this spiteful people, that Herod is King in Israel! What have you now to say, sister?"

"Energy and determination alone can save us," she said. "Let them pay with their lives for their disobedience."

Castobarus reeled in the King's room.—"My Lord and King," said he, "The combat at the fort of Antiochus is terrible. The carnage is awful. The people sternly refuse to leave the city, and attack your troops most recklessly."

"They must leave the city or die," Herod cried. "It is high time to quench this revolt."

"Blood and despair only can subdue it," Salome coolly added.

"My Lord and King," said Sohemus, "the rebels appeal to the people, from the hight of the temple, and the armed bands appear to spring from the earth as it were, and engage us on all sides."

"Show no mercy, give no quarters," Herod thundred, "kill every one who is found with arms, or refuses to leave the city."

"The combat is fierce and doubtful," Dositheus said. "I fear we have lost the fort of Antiochus. Three heavy columns storm in from the north, on the three roads from Anathoth, Ramah and Gibeon, and in the city the armed rebels are innumerable."

"Castobarus will receive the storming columns and throw them back," said Herod.—"Keep yourself on the defensive till I change orders. The garrison from the House of the Mighty support the soldiers in the fort of Antiochus."

The revolt had assumed such an alarming aspect that, like wild-fire, it spread over all parts of the city. The trumpets and horns resounded everywhere with martial vigor. The commanding voices of officers, the cries of attacking bands, the exclamations of furious combatants, the cries of rage and hatred, the terrific voice of vengeance and death rolled like a roaring ocean over the whole city, and was heard distinctly in the apartments of the King. Adjutants came and left in the greatest hurry, Salome cried vehemently, for fear; but Herod remained calm. He appeared to be in his right element. An officer covered with blood entered the King's room and brought the tidings, that Abba Shaul had crossed over by Bezetha, and was joined by a storming column from the tombs of the Kings. Upon which the garrison of fort of Antiochus fraternized with the people. "Salem, Bezetha and the Temple are as good as lost," said he, "the soldiers retreat across the ravine in good order."

Herod cursed audibly, but did not lose for a moment his presence of mind, while

Salome appeared to be altogether deranged with fear. One adjutant after the other brought new reports of new defeats and before the evening approached Herod was besieged on Mount Zion. A heavy shower of rain, a dark night and a terrific thunderstorm suspended the actions of the combatants. Herod held a council in his palace, to determine upon the steps to be taken the next day. They deliberated for several hours and came to the conclusion, that Zion could be effectually defended and the rebels could be subdued yet, to which end a plan was adopted. The King, however, insisted upon commanding in person and be prepared for all eventualities. He commanded Sohemus to leave the city with an adequate force and go to the fort of Alexandrium, where the Queen and her children were. He commanded Sohemus to hold the fort at any risk. As soon as he should be convinced of the King's death, he should kill Mariamne, her children and her mother. Sohemus knelt down and swore a solemn oath to carry out punctually the command of the King. Before the morning dawned Sohemus with his men had left the city, unobserved by the enemy.

Then the King called Castobarus and charged him with the duty to convey his mother Cyprus and his sister Salome to the fort of Masado, to keep that fort at any risk, protect the royal family, and in case of the King's death to proclaim Antipater, the King's son by his first wife Doris, King of Israel.

"I will faithfully perform my duties," Castobarus said. "But I pray you, my lord, you have promised me the hand of your royal sister; now is the time to redeem your pledge."

"Salome is yours!" the King said.

Ravingly mad Salome fell down before the King, "Give me Aurion or kill me," she cried; but the King insisted that she be the wife of his most faithful friend Castobarus. Salome seized her dagger and attempted to kill Castobarus, and when she was prevented from it, she attempted to commit suicide. It was necessary to tie her hands, but then she cried so violently and cursed Castobarus so loudly, that she could not safely be conveyed away from the city. When hastily the arrangements had been completed to convey the royal family out of the city to the appointed fort, and Salome continued raging most furiously and crying most violently, "Give me Aurion or death," the King, her mother begged and threatened in vain, she only became more desperate and furious with every passing moment. The hours of the night passing away rapidly, the morning was fast approaching, no time was to be lost. Herod commanded to gag her; her hands tied, her mouth gaged, three men seized the furious woman, placed her in the carriage at the side of her mother, and the whole train, commanded by Castobarus, started off with the utmost speed, and escaped without being noticed by the enemy.

Herod almost wept over the agony of his sister, but he could not help her. Circumstances required, that Castobarus should be tied closely to the royal family, whose chief interests were placed in his hands. While he was still lost in a train of painful tho'ts a servant opened the door and asked shily, "My lord, what shall be done with the body of Elvira, your sister left no orders?"

Herod shuddered. He covered his eyes with his left hand and exclaimed, "She is avenged." Turning after awhile to the servant he said, "Bury her by the side of Sabion in his family sepulcher." Two large tears glittered in the eyes of Herod. When the servant was gone he inadvertantly exclaimed, "There is a God of justice, but Herod is lost." Frightened as it were at his own words he violently struck the handle of his sword. Dositheus, understanding this to be a signal, entered the room and said, "My lord, what is your command."

"It is my command to prepare every thing for our speedy departure," said Herod, calmly. "I have come to the conviction, that we shed blood in vain. We go directly to Rhodes. I must see Octavius. If I fail with him, I can reign no longer. My people hate me, and my soldiers disobey. Prepare quickly, we must be off in less than an hour."

Dositheus was astonished, but he ventured no remark. When the morning dawned on Mt. Zion, the gates of the city were all opened, the soldiers fraternized with the people, and Herod was gone, none knew whither. The people shouted with joy, but the joy was not without tears. In the fort of Antiochus a guard of honor surrounded a dead man. He bled from many wounds, and closing his eyes in death he shouted yet, "We are victorious." With awe and reverence the warriors looked at the dead Hero, and many a tear coursed down hardy and sun burnt cheeks. It was the dead body of Abba Shaul, who fell during the storming of the fort, pierced by the arrows of the enemy. He died the death of a hero, with the words of "onward for God and Israel" on his lips.

In the midst of the excited and joyful crowds, Helen ran from street to street in search of Simon, but found him not. Despairing and tearless, she arrived at the royal palace where she found the dead bodies of Elvira and her father. She covered the countenances of both with tears and kisses, and lamented over them in mute pain. The thundering shouts of joy and victory resounding through the streets disturbed her not. The warbling of the trumpets to signalize the people's victory alleviated not her pain. The outbursts of an unlimited enthusiasm which rent the air of Jerusalem reached not Helen's suffering heart. "My father, my sister," were the only words she could utter. A voice was heard in the arched halls of the palace, a voice so well known to Helen. She listened. Again he spoke. She opened the door and cried "Simon, Husband, here, here is your wife," and Simon heard it, he came and seized her as a hungry lion grasps after the prey. "Then you live yet, my dearest, only beloved Helen," Simon cried. "In vain have I sought thee, in vain sent twenty messengers to find thee; all said you fell on the side of Abba Shaul. Thank God you live, you are here, and mine."

Mute Helen pointed to the dead lying in the room. Simon pressed Helen on his heart, and wept with her. Then he commanded the servants of Sabion to remove the bodies to the very sepulchre which Herod had ordained.

The Passover was a feast of joy and victory for the people. The happiest days of Israel appeared to have returned. Also Helen was healed from her grief by the enthusiasm generally prevailing, the love and tenderness of Simon, who was overhappy at the side of his beloved wife, and the pious consolation of Hillel who, notwithstanding the numerous congratulations he was obliged to receive, had yet time enough to attend sometimes to his family.

We may meet again with Simon, Helen and Jonathan ben Uziel in another story; but for this time we must part with them, and bid our readers FAREWELL.

THE AUTHOR.

2

M. B. Levy

HISTORY OF THE JEWS.

THE Jews, without reference to their religious belief, are among the most remarkable people in the annals of mankind. Sprung from one stock, they pass the infancy of their nation in a state of servitude in a foreign country, where, nevertheless, they increase so rapidly, as to appear on a sudden the fierce and irresistible conquerors of their native valleys in Palestine. There they settle down under a form of government and code of laws totally unlike those of any other rude or civilized community. They sustain a long and doubtful conflict, sometimes enslaved, sometimes victorious, with the neighboring tribes. At length, united under one monarchy, they gradually rise to the rank of a powerful, opulent, and commercial people. Subsequently weakened by internal discord, they are overwhelmed by the vast monarchies which arose on the banks of the Euphrates, and transplanted into a foreign region. They are partially restored, by the generosity or policy of the Eastern sovereigns, to their native land. They are engaged in wars of the most romantic gallantry, in assertion of their independence, against the Syro-Grecian successors of Alexander. Under Herod, they rise to a second era of splendor, as a dependent kingdom of Rome: finally, they make the last desperate resistance to the universal dominion of the Cæsars. Scattered from that period over the face of the earth--hated, scorned, and oppressed, they subsist, a numerous and often a thriving people; and in all the changes of manners and opinions retain their ancient institutions, their national character, and their indelible hope of restoration to grandeur and happiness in their native land. Thus the history of this, perhaps the only unmingled race, which can boast of high antiquity, leads us through every gradation of society, and brings us into contact with almost every nation which commands our interest in the ancient world; the migratory pastoral population of Asia; Egypt, the mysterious parent of arts, science, and legislation; the Arabian Desert; the Hebrew theocracy under the form of a federative agricultural republic, their kingdom powerful in war and splendid in peace; Babylon, in its magnificence and downfall; Grecian arts and luxury endeavoring to force an unnatural refinement within the pale of the rigid Mosaic institutions; Roman arms waging an exterminating war with the independence even of the smallest states; it descends, at length, to all the changes in the social state of the modern European and Asiatic nations.

The religious history of this people is no less singular. In the narrow slip of land inhabited by their tribes the worship of one Almighty Creator of the Universe subsisted, as in its only sanctuary. In every stage of society, under the pastoral tent of Abraham, and in the sumptuous temple of Solomon, the same creed maintains its inviolable simplicity. During their long intercourse with foreign nations in Egypt and Babylon, though the primitive habits and character of the Hebrew nation were greatly modified, and perhaps some theological notions engrafted on their original tenets, this primary distinction still remains; after several periods of almost total apostacy, it revives in all its vigor. Nor is this merely a sublime speculative tenet, it is the basis of their civil constitution, and their national character. As there is but one Almighty God, so there is but one people under his especial protection, the descendants of Abraham. Hence their civil and religious history is inseparable. The God of the chosen people is their temporal as well as spiritual sovereign; he is not merely their legislator, but also the administrator of their laws. Their land is his gift, held from him, as from a feudal liege-lord, on certain conditions. He is their leader in war, their counsellor in peace. Their happiness or adversity, national as well as individual, depends solely and immediately on their maintenance or neglect of the divine institutions. Such was the common popular religion of the Jews, as it appears in all their records, in their law, their history, their poetry, and their moral philosophy. Hence, to the mere speculative inquirer, the study of the human race presents no phenomenon so singular as the character of this extraordinary people; to the Christian, no chapter in the history of mankind can be more instructive or important, than that which contains the rise, progress and downfall of his religious ancestors.

Abraham, the Father of the Faithful, holds an eminent place in all oriental tradition, not only among the Jews, but likewise among the Persians, Arabians, and perhaps the Indians,

It is difficult to say how far these legends may have been propagated by the Mahometan conquests, for our knowledge of the history and literature of Eastern nations, anterior to the Hegira, is still limited and unsatisfactory. The Arabian accounts of Abraham, adopted into the Koran, are no doubt much older than Mahomet; but whether they were primitive traditions, or embellishments of their authentic history, originating among the Jews themselves, is a question perhaps impossible to decide. The simplicity of the narrative in the Book of Genesis affords a remarkable contrast to the lofty pretensions which the patriarch assumes in these legends, as the teacher not merely of religious truth, but of science, arithmetic, mathematics, and astronomy, to the Egyptians. Abraham was the son of Terah, the head of a pastoral family, consisting of three sons, Abram, Nahor, and Haran. Haran, probably the eldest, died early, leaving a son named Lot. Abram was married to Sarah, daughter of Terah by another wife; Nahor married Milcah, a daughter of Haran. Their native place was Ur, a district to the northeast of that region, which lies above the confluence of the Tigris and Euphrates, and became afterward the seat of the great Babylonian monarchy. About Ur the country is open, dry, and barren, well suited for pasture, but not for tillage. In the spacious and level plains of Chaldea, where the nights are delightfully cool and serene, a pastoral people would naturally be led to contemplate the heavenly bodies with peculiar attention. To this country the first rudiments of astronomy are generally ascribed, and here the earliest form of idolatry, the worship of the host of heaven, usually called Tsabaism, began to spread. The Arabian traditions suppose that a farther step had been already taken, and represent Terah, the father of Abram, as a maker of images, called from his name Teraphim. Other legends attribute to this period the origin of fire worship. But, whatever the signs or systems of religion, in whatever manner he acquired his purer notions of the Deity, Abram stood alone in a tribe and family of idolaters, as a worshiper of the one great Creator.* According to the usage of nomadic tribes, the family of Terah broke up from their settlement at Ur, and migrated to Carrhan, a flat barren region lying west of Ur, and celebrated in later history for the defeat of Marcus Crassus, near Carrhæ. After a residence of some years in Carrhan, the pastoral horde divided, and Abram set forth to establish an independent tribe in a remote region. Lot, the son of his brother Haran, followed his fortunes. Nahor remained with Terah his father, the hereditary chieftain of the settlement in Carrhan. This separation of Abraham, as the single stock from which a new tribe was to trace its unmingled descent, is ascribed to the express command of God. Already while in Ur, Abram had received some communication from the Deity; to his departure into Canaan he was incited by a direct promise, the most splendid which could be offered to the ambition of the head of a nomadic tribe, in which numbers constitute power and wealth: His seed was to become hereafter a great nation. A more obscure and mysterious intimation was added, that some part of his future race should exercise a most important influence on the destinies of mankind. The family of Abram, already grown into a petty clan, moved with all their flocks and slaves across the Euphrates; according to a tradition preserved by Justin and by an ancient author quoted in Josephus, dwelt some time near Damascus, and arriving at length in Palestine, settled first at Sechem, a valley between the mountains Ebal and Gerizim; then in a hilly region to the north of Jericho, afterward called the Desert of Quarantania. As the pastures were exhausted, the tribe moved southward, till a famine again drove them forth, and Egypt, probably the earliest, certainly the most productive country of the ancient world, became as at a later period, the only place of refuge.

Except as showing that the valley of the Nile was already occupied by an industrious agricultural population, the visit of Abram throws little light on the existing state of Egypt. The monarch seems to have lived in considerable state, and possessed a numerous seraglio, which was supplied by any means, however lawless or violent. This was so notorious, that Abram, though an independent Sheik or Emir, if his fair complexioned Mesopotamian wife should excite the cupidity of the swarthy Egyptians, might apprehend the worst consequences. He ran the risk, not only of losing his wife, but of being murdered for the sake of so valuable a prize. He took the precaution, therefore, to make Sarai assume the name of his sister, (she was in fact his father's daughter, though not by the same mother,) perhaps hoping that, if sought in legitimate marriage, he might protract the espousals till the famine would permit him to make his escape from the country. The event justified his apprehensions, Sarai was seized and transferred to the harem of the sovereign, who was so proud of his acquisition as to make magnificent presents to Abram, intended, it may seem, as a dowry for his sister.

In a short time a pestilence broke out in the royal family, the king, having discovered

*The most pleasing of the traditionary fictions is the following: "As Abraham was walking by night from the grotto where he was born, to the city of Babylon, he gazed on the stars of heaven, and among them on the beautiful Venus. 'Behold,' said he within himself, 'the God and Lord of the Universe!' but the star set and disappeared, and Abraham felt that the Lord of the Universe could not thus be liable to change. Shortly after, he beheld the moon at the full: 'Lo,' he cried, 'the Divine Creator, the manifest Deity!' but the moon sank below the horizon, and Abraham made the same reflection as at the setting of the evening star. All the rest of the night he passed in profound rumination; at sunrise he stood before the gates of Babylon, and saw the whole people prostrate in adoration. 'Wondrous orb,' he exclaimed, 'thou surely art the Creator and Ruler of all nature! but thou, too, hastest like the rest to thy setting!—neither then art thou my Creator, my Lord, or my God.'"

the relationship between Abram and Sarai, attributed the visitation to the God of the stranger, who thus revenged his breach of hospitality. Abram received back his wife, and returned to Canaan loaded with possessions suitable to his habits of life—"sheep and oxen, and he asses, and men servants and maid servants, and she asses and camels," a curious picture of the wealth of a pastoral chieftain. In Canaan, Abram is described, as not merely rich in these simpler commodities, but in silver and gold, obtained, probably, in exchange for the produce of his flocks and herds, from the settled native population of the towns. Abram first re-occupied his former encampment near the site where Bethel subsequently stood, and offered sacrifice for his safe return from Egypt, on an altar, which he had before built on one of the adjacent hights. There the pastures proving insufficient for the great stock of cattle, which the tribe possessed, dispute arose between the herdsmen of Abram and Lot. The chieftains, dreading lest the native clans should take advantage of their divisions, and expel or plunder both, agreed to part amicably, and thenceforth inhabit independent settlements.

Lot departed eastward into the rich and blooming valley of the Jordan, then abounding in flourishing towns.

This separation still farther secured the unmingled descent of the Abrahamitic family; and the Almighty renewed the promise of a race, countless as the dust of the earth, the future possessors of Palestine, which Abram was commanded to survey from its northern to its southern, its eastern to its western extremities, as the inalienable patrimony of his descendants. In pursuance of this command, Abram again moved his encampment, and the tents of his tribe were pitched in the southern plain of Mamre. But the more fertile district, which had attracted the choice of Lot, exposed him to perpetual dangers. The rich valley of the Jordan was invaded by a confederacy of the kingdoms on the Euphrates and Tigris, headed by Cedor-Laomer, king of Elam (Elymais.) His subordinate allies were Amraphel, king of Shinaar (the Babylonian plain,) Arioch, king of Ellasar (perhaps Thelassar,) and Tidal, king of Nations. Whether a considerable monarchy had already grown up on the banks of the Tigris, or whether this was a league of several small predatory tribes, does not appear from the Hebrew annalist. The independent princes in the valley of the Jordan, the kings of Sodom, Gomorrah, Admah, Tseboim, and Tsoar, submitted to pay tribute. Thirteen years after, they endeavored to throw off the yoke, but Cedor-Laomer advanced into the country, subdued all the neighboring tribes, some of whom were of gigantic stature, and at last found battle with the princes of the Jordan in the vale of Siddim. There the ground was broken with deep pits and fissures caused by the bituminous nature of the soil; the troops of the five confederates were routed, two of the kings fell among the pits, the rest of the army dispersed, and Lot, among others, was seized as a captive. A fugitive brought the intelligence to Abram, who hastily collected three hundred and eighteen of his own clan, called some of the neighboring tribes to his assistance, and pursued the enemy to a place near the fountains of the Jordan. He fell on their camp by night, dispersed them, rescued Lot, with the rest of the prisoners, and recovered the booty. The defeat, by so small a force, is thought to give but a mean notion of the strength of the invading army, yet among undisciplined troops of different nations, the panic from an unexpected night attack is often so great that the inference can scarcely be considered decisive.

This bold exploit ensured the admiration and gratitude of all the native chieftains. The king of Salem (by some thought to be Jerusalem, by others a town near Scythopolis, where a ruin, called Melchizedeck's palace, was shown in the time of Jerom) met him at a place called the King's Vale (identified sometimes with the valley of Jehosaphat.) Melchi-Zedeck, the King of Justice (such was his honorable title,) united in his own person, like the monarchs of the heroic ages in Greece and Rome, and indeed of most among the early oriental tribes, the office of king and priest. Like Abram he worshiped the one Great God, in whose name he blessed the deliverer of his country from foreign invaders, and refreshed his troops with bread and wine.

On his part, Abram, according to general custom, consecrated a tenth part of the spoil to their common Deity. As he rivalled Melchi-Zedeck in piety, so Abram equaled the king of Sodom in generosity, he refused to retain any part of the spoil, not so much as a shoe-latchet, he only reserved a portion for the young native sheiks, Aner, Eshcol, and Mamre, who had joined him in his expedition. But the pious conqueror returned to a childless tent and a barren wife. The name, the chieftainship of his clan, would pass away into the line of a stranger, Eliezer of Damascus, who held the next rank in the tribe. Yet the divine promise was repeatedly renewed, and under the most striking circumstances.

One night as Abram gazed on the cloudless heavens, the Celestial Voice commands him to count the stars of the firmament, for even so numerous should be his descendants. The aged and childless man yielded up his soul to perfect reliance on his Almighty Benefactor. The promise was further ratified by a covenant, transacted in the primitive form of federal compact, which subsisted among various nations to a late period. A sacrifice was offered, the victims exactly divided, and the contracting parties passed between the two halves, which lay opposite each other. Abram offered a heifer of three years old, a turtle dove, and a young pigeon. These he divided, except the birds, and sat watching till the evening, lest the fowls of prey should stoop upon them. As the sun declined, a deep sleep fell upon him, and more than common darkness spread around. A voice announced the fate of his posterity, their servitude of four centuries in a foreign land, their return, their possession of the whole territory from the Euphrates to the sea. As the sun set, the symbol of the Deity, a cloud of smoke like that of a furnace, a flashing fire like that of a lamp, passed between the severed victims, and thus solemnly ratified the covenant. Still the tent of Abram resounded not with the welcome cry of infancy. At length Sarai, despairing of issue from her own body, had recourse to a custom, still known in the East, particularly in China. The chief or lawful wife substitutes a slave in her own place, the children born in this manner have the rank and privilege of legitimacy, and are considered in every respect as the offspring of the mistress of the establishment. In this manner Hagar, an Egyptian slave, bore a son to Abram, he was named Ishmael. Fourteen years after, when Abram was a hundred, Sarah ninety years old, a new revelation from the Divinity announced the surprising intelligence that Sarah herself was to bear a son. There is something singularly beautiful in the attachment of Abram to the first child, who had awakened the parental feeling in his bosom. He would fain transfer the blessing to Ishmael, and is reluctant to sacrifice the earliest object of his pride and joy to the unborn son of Sarah. But the race of Abram is to be beyond every possible impeachment on its legitimacy; Abram is commanded to assume the mysterious name of Abraham, (the father of a multitude) as the ancestor of a great and numerous people, who were to descend from Sarah, and become lords of all Palestine. The tribe were to be distinguished by the rite of circumcision, perhaps before, certainly afterward, common to many people of the East; a rite of great utility, as conducing, in southern climates, both to health and cleanliness.

During this time Abraham had occupied his former encampment near Hebron. Here, as he sat in the door of his tent, three mysterious strangers appeared. Abraham, with true Arabian hospitality, received and entertained them. The chief of the three renewed the promise of a son to be born from Sarah, a promise which the aged woman received with laughter. As they pass forth toward the valley of the Jordan, the same Divine Being, for so he manifestly appears to be, announces the dreadful ruin impending over the licentious cities among which Lot had taken up his abode. No passage, even in the sacred writings, exhibits a more exalted notion of the Divinity, than that in which Abraham is permitted to expostulate on the apparent injustice of involving the innocent in the ruin of the guilty. "Shall the city perish, if fifty, if forty-five, if forty, if thirty, if twenty, if ten righteous men be found within its walls?" "Ten righteous men shall avert its doom." Such was the promise of the Celestial Visitant—but the guilt was universal, the ruin inevitable. The horrible outrage attempted against the two inferior of these preternatural beings, who descended to the city; the violation of the sacred laws of hospitality and nature, which Lot in his horror attempted to avert by the most revolting expedient—confirmed the justice of the divine sentence

The valley of the Jordan, in which the cities of Sodom, Gomorrah, Adma, and Tseboim, were situated, was rich and highly cultivated. It is most probable that the river then flowed in a deep and uninterrupted channel down a regular descent, and discharged itself into the eastern gulf of the Red Sea. The cities stood on a soil broken and undermined with veins of bitumen and sulphur. These inflammable substances, set on fire by lightning, caused a tremendous convulsion; the water courses, both the river and the canals by which the land was extensively irrigated, burst their banks; the cities, the walls of which were perhaps built from the combustible materials of the soil were entirely swallowed up by the fiery inundation; and the whole valley which had been compared to Paradise, and to the well-watered cornfields of the Nile, became a dead and fetid lake. The traditions of the country, reported by Strabo, Tacitus, and other ancient writers, kept alive the remembrance of this awful catastrophe. In the account of the latter, the number of cities destroyed is magnified to thirteen. The whole region is described by modern travelers as a scene of gloomy desolation, precipitous crags hanging over dull and heavy waters; not, indeed, as the local superstitions have asserted, devoid of life, for the lake abounds in fish, nor fatal to the birds which fly over it; but the specific gravity of the water is so great, that those who can not swim float on the top; and it is bitterly salt to the taste. Unwholesome fogs hang perpetually over the lake, and the stagnant surface is broken by clots of asphaltus, which are constantly bubbling up from the bottom. A distinguished modern geographer thus describes the present indications of the physical agency, by which Divine Providence brought about this memorable destruction: "The valley of the Jordan offers many traces of volcanoes; the bituminous and sulphurous water of Lake Asphaltites, the lavas and pumice thrown out on its banks, and the warm baths of Tabarieh, show that this valley has been the theater of a fire not yet extinguished. Volumes of smoke are often observed to escape from Lake Asphaltites, and new crevices are found on its margin."

Lot, warned of the impending ruin, fled with his daughters. His wife, in contempt of repeated warnings, lingering behind, was suffocated by the sulphurous vapors, and her body incrusted with saline particles which filled the atmosphere. Later tradition, founded on a literal interpretation of the Mosaic account, pointed to a heap or column of salt, which bore perhaps some resemblance to a human form, and was believed, even by the historian Josephus, who had seen it, to be the pillar into which she was transformed. Lot fled first to Zoar, at the end of the present lake, then into the mountains. The tribes of Ammon and Moab, famous in the Jewish history, were derived from an incestuous connexion, into which he was betrayed by his daughters, who, according to Josephus, supposing themselves and their father the only surviving remnants of mankind, the rest having perished in the recent catastrophe, did not scruple to violate the laws of nature.

While these rival tribes were thus born of incest, amid all the horrors of convulsed nature, the legitimate parent of the numerous offspring promised to Abraham is at length born. He is named Isaac, from the laughter of Sarah when the birth was announced. But now the jealous apprehensions of the mother are directed against Hagar and her child. Usage, stronger than written law, gives the chief wife in the tent of wandering pastoral people unlimited authority over her female slaves. Hagar had already been exposed to the jealousy of Sarah when, previous to the birth of Ishmael, she had been treated with such harshness, as to fly into the wilderness, whence she had returned by the direction of an angel. Sarah now insists, and Abraham, receiving a divine intimation as to the destiny of the elder born, complies with her demand, that Hagar and Ishmael should be sent forth to seek their fortune in some of the unoccupied and uncultivated districts which lay around. The supply of provisions which they carried from the tent of Abraham soon failed, and the mother and the youth wandered into a district which was destitute of water. History or poetry scarcely presents us with any passage which surpasses in simple pathos the description of Hagar, not daring to look upon her child, while he is perishing with thirst before her face. "And she went and sat down over against him a good way off, as it were a bow-shot; for she said, Let me not see the death of the child. And she sat over against him, and lifted up her voice and wept." But Ishmael likewise was to become the father of a great people; by divine interposition Hagar discovered a well, the water restored them to life. Ishmael either joined some horde of Arabs, or maintained himself in independence by his bow, till his mother obtained him an Egyptian wife. The wandering Arabs to this day, by general traditions adopted into the Koran, trace their descent to the outcast son of Abraham. "The wild man, whose hand is against every man, and every man's hand against him," still waylays the traveler by the fountain, or sweeps his rapid troop of horse across the track of the wealthy caravan.

The faith of Abraham was to pass through a more trying ordeal. He was suddenly commanded to cut off that life on which all the splendid promises of the Almighty seemed to depend. He obeys, and sets forth with his unsuspecting child to offer the fatal sacrifice on Mount Moriah. The immolation of human victims, particularly of the most precious, the favorite, the first-born child, appears as a common usage among many early nations, more especially the tribes by which Abraham was surrounded. It was the distinguishing rite among the worshipers of Moloch; at a later period of the Jewish history, it was practised by a king of Moab; it was undoubtedly derived by the Carthaginians from their Phœnician ancestors on the shores of Syria. The offering of Isaac bears no resemblance, either in its nature, or what may be termed its moral purport, to these horrid rites. Where it was an ordinary usage, as in the worship of Moloch, it was in unison with the character of the religion, and of the deity. It was the last act of a dark and sanguinary superstition, which rose by regular gradation to this complete triumph over human nature.

The god, who was propitiated by these offerings, had been satiated with more cheap and vulgar victims; he had been glutted to the full with human suffering and with human blood. In general it was the final mark of the subjugation of the national mind to an inhuman and domineering priesthood. But the Mosaic religion held human sacrifices in abhorrence; the God of the Abrahamitic family, uniformly beneficent, imposed no duties which entailed human suffering, demanded no offerings which were repugnant to the better feelings of our nature. Where, on the other hand, these filial sacrifices were of rare and extraordinary occurrence, they were either to expiate some dreadful guilt, to avert the imminent vengeance of the offended deity, or to extort his blessing on some important enterprise. But the offering of Isaac was neither piacular nor propitiatory; Abraham had committed no guilt, and apprehended no danger; the immolation of his only son seemed for ever to deprive him of that blessing which was nearest to his heart, the parentage of a numerous and powerful tribe. It was a simple act of unhesitating obedience to the divine command; the last proof of perfect reliance on the certain accomplishment of the divine promises. Isaac, so miraculously bestowed could be as miraculously restored. Abraham, such is the comment of the Christian Apostle, believed that God could even raise him up from the dead. Still, while the great example of primitive piety appears no less willing to offer the most precious victim on the altar of his God, than the idolaters around him, the God of the Hebrews maintains his benign and beneficent character. After every thing is prepared, the wood of the alter laid, even the sacrificial knife uplifted, the arm of the father is arrested; a single ram, entangled by his horns in a thicket, is substituted, and Abraham called the name of the place Jehovah Jireh, the Lord will provide. This last trial of his faith thus passed, the promise of the divine blessing was renewed to Abraham in still more express and vivid terms. His seed were to be numerous as the stars of heaven, and as the sands of the sea shore; their enemies were to fall before them; and the whole world was to receive some remote and mysterious blessing through the channel of this favored race.

After this epoch the incidents in the life of Abraham are less important, yet still characteristic of the age and state of society. He lived on terms of amity with the native princes. particularly with Abimelek, the king of Gerar, on whose territories his encampment at one time bordered. With Abimelek an adventure took place, so similar in its circumstances with the seizure and restoration of Sarah in Egypt, as almost to excite a suspicion that it is a traditional variation of the same transaction, more particularly as it is unquestionably related out of its place in the Mosaic narrative, and again repeated in the life of Isaac. Abimelek permitted the stranger Shiek to pitch his tent, and pasture his flocks and herds in any part of his domains. The only dispute related to the valuable possession of a well, and this was prudently and amicably arranged.

The death of Sarah gave occasion for another friendly treaty with the native princes. Every independent tribe has its separate place of burial. The patriarch or parent of the tribe has the place of honor in the common cemetery, which is usually hewn out of the rock, sometimes into spacious chambers, supported by pillars, and with alcoves in the sides, where the coffins are deposited. Each successive generation, according to the common expression, is gathered to their fathers. On Abraham's demand for permission to purchase a place of sepulture, the chiefs of the tribe of Heth assemble to debate the weighty question. The first resolution is to offer the rich and popular stranger the unusual privelege of interring his dead in their national sepulchres. As this might be misconstrued into a formal union between the clans, Abraham declines the hospitable offer. He even refuses as a gift, and insists on purchasing, for four hundred pieces of silver, a field named Machpelah, surrounded by trees, in which stood a rock well suited for sepulchral excavation. Here, unmingled with those of any foreign tribe, his own remains, and those of Sarah, are to repose.

In another important instance the isolation of the Abrahamitic family, and its pure descent from the original Mesopotamian stock are carefully kept up. The wife of Isaac is sought not among their Canaanitish neighbors, but among his father's kindred in Carrhan. At a later period the same feeling of attachment to the primitive tribe, and aversion from mingling with the Canaanites, is shown in the condemnation of Esau, for taking his wives from the inhabitants of the country, which were a grief of mind unto Isaac and to Rebekah, while Jacob is sent to seek a wife in the old Mesopotamian settlement. So completely do the seclusion and separation of Abraham and his descendants run through the whole history. Abraham solemnly adjures his most faithful servant, whom he despatches to Carrhan on this matrimonial mission for his son, to discharge his embassage with fidelity. Having sworn by the singular ceremony of placing his hand under his master's thigh, a custom of which the origin is unknown, the servant sets off with his camels, and arrives in safety near the old encampment of the tribe. At the usual place of meeting, the well, he encounters Rebekah, the beautiful daughter of Bethuel, the son of Abraham's brother Nahor. The courteous maiden assists him in watering his camels; her relations receive him with equal hospitality. The intelligence of Abraham's wealth, confirmed by the presents of gold and jewels which he produced, made them consent with alacrity to the betrothing of the damsel to the son of Abraham. The messenger and Rebekah reached in safety the encampment of Abraham; and Isaac when he hears the sound of the returning camels beholds a fair maiden modestly veiled, whom he conducts and puts in possession of his mother Sarah, that which belonged to the chief wife of the head of the tribe.

After the death of Sarah, Abraham took another wife Keturah, by whom he had many children. Isaac, however, continued his sole heir, the rest were sent away into the east country; their descendants are frequently recognized among the people noticed in the Jewish annals, but always as aliens from the stock of Abraham. At length the Patriarch died, and was buried in Machpelah, by Ishmael and Isaac, who met in perfect amity to perform the last duty to the head and father of their tribes.

Such is the history of their great ancestor, preserved in the national records of the Jewish people, remarkable for its simplicity and historic truth, when compared with the mythic or poetic traditions of almost all other countries. The genealogies of most nations, particularly the eastern, are lost among their gods; it is impossible to define where fable ceases, and history begins; and the earlier we ascend the more indistinct and marvellous the narrative. In the Hebrew record it is precisely the converse, God and man are separated by a wide and impassable interval—Abraham is the Emir of a pastoral tribe, migrating from place to place, his stations marked with geographical accuracy, and with a picturesque simplicity of local description; here he pitches his tent by some old and celebrated tree, there on the brink of a well-known fountain. He is in no respect superior to his age or country, excepting in the sublime purity of his religion. He is neither demi-god nor mighty conqueror, nor even sage, nor inventor of useful arts. His distinction is the worship of One Great God, and the intercourse which he is permitted to hold with this mysterious Being. This is the great patrimonial glory which he bequeathed to his descendants; their title to be considered the chosen people of the Almighty, was their inalienable hereditary possession. This is the key to their whole history, the basis of their political institutions, the vital principle of their national character.

The life of Isaac was far less eventful, nor is it necessary for the right understanding of the Jewish history, to relate its incidents so much at length as those of the great progenitor of the Jewish people. At first, the divine promise of a numerous posterity proceeds very slowly toward its accomplishment. After some years of barrenness Rebekah bears twins, already before their birth seeming to struggle for superiority, as the heads and representatives of two hostile people. They were as opposite in their disposition as in their way of life. The red-haired Esau was a wild hunter, and acquired the fierce and reckless character which belongs to the ruder state of society to which he reverted; Jacob retained the comparative gentleness of the more thoughtful and regular pastoral ocenpation. It is curious to observe the superior fitness in the habits and disposition of the younger, Jacob, to become the parent of a united and settled people. Though the Edomites, the descendants of Esau, ranked in civilization far above the marauding Bedouins, who sprung from Ishmael; though Esau himself possessed at a later period considerable wealth in flocks and herds, yet the scattered clans of the Edomites, at perpetual war with each other and their neighbors, living, according to the expression of the sacred writer, by the sword, retain as it were the stamp of the parental character, and seem less adapted to the severe discipline of the Mosaic institutions, or to become a nation of peaceful husbandmen. The precarious life of the hunter soon laid him at the mercy of his more prudent or rather crafty brother. After a day of unsuccessful hunting, Esau sold his right of primogeniture for a mess of herbs. The privilege of the first-born seems to have consisted in the acknowledged headship of the tribe, to which the office of priest and sacrificer was inseparably attached. Esau, therefore, thus carelessly threw away both his civil and religious inheritance, and abandoned all title to the promises made to his tribe.

Whether the parental blessing was supposed of itself to confer or to confirm the right of primogeniture, is not quite clear; but the terms in which it was conveyed by Isaac, "Be lord over thy brethren, and let thy mother's sons bow down before thee," seem to intimate a regular investiture with the supreme authority as head of the tribe. This blessing, couched in these emphatic words, which Isaac evidently doubted his power to retract, was intercepted, with the assistance of his mother, by the subtle and unscrupulous Jacob. These repeated injuries roused the spirit of revenge in the indignant hunter; he only waits the decease of his father that he may recover his rights by the death of his rival. But Rebekah anticipates the crime. Jacob is sent to the original birthplace of the tribe, partly to secure him from the impending danger, partly that, avoiding all connexion with the Canaanites, he may intermarry only with the descendants of his forefathers. On his way to Mesopotamia, the promise made to Abraham is renewed in that singular vision—so expressively symbolical of the universal providence of God—the flight of steps uniting earth and heaven, with the ministering angels perpetually ascending and descending. In commemoration of this vision, Jacob sets up a sort of primitive monument—a pillar of stone. The adventures of Jacob among his nomadic ancestors present a most curious and characteristic view of their simple manners and usages. His meeting with Rachel at the well, the hospitality of Laban to his sister's son; his agreement to serve seven years* to obtain Rachel in marriage; the public ceremony of espousals in the presence of the tribe; the stratagem of Laban to substitute his elder for his younger and fairer daughter, in order to bind the enamored stranger to seven years' longer service; the little jealousies of the sisters, not on account of the greater share in their husband's affections, but their own fertility, the substitution of their respective handmaids; the contest in cunning and subtlety between Laban and Jacob, the former endeavoring to defraud the other of his due wages, and at the same time to retain so useful a servant, under whom his flocks had so long prospered—the latter, apparently by his superior acquaintance with the habits of the animals which he tended, and with the divine sanction, securing all the stronger and more flourishing part of the flocks for his own portion; the flight of Jacob, not as so rich a resident ought to have been dismissed with mirth and with songs, with tabret and with harp; Laban's religious awe of one so manifestly under the Divine protection; Rachel's purloining and concealment of her father's teraphim; above all, their singular treaty, in which Laban at length consents to the final separation of this great family, with which he had expected to increase the power and opulence of his tribe;—all these incidents throw us back into a state of society different not merely from modern usages, but from those which prevailed among the Jews after their return from Egypt. The truth and reality of the picture is not more apparent than its appropriate locality in the regions which it describes:—it is neither

*"I once met with a young man who had served eight years for his food only; at the end of that period he obtained in marriage the daughter of his master, for whom he would otherwise have had to pay seven or eight hundred piastres. When I saw him he had been married three years: but he bitterly complained of his father-in-law, who continued to require of him the performance of the most servile offices, without paying him any thing; and that prevented him from setting up for himself and family."—*Burckhardt's Travels in Syria*, p. 297. This was in the Haouran, the district south-east of Damascus.

Egyptian nor Palestinian, nor even Arabian life; it breathes the free air of the wide and open plains of inland Asia, where the primitive inhabitants are spreading, without opposition or impediment, with their flocks, and herds, and camels, over unbounded and unoccupied regions.

Isaac, in the mean time, had continued to dwell as a husbandman towards the southern border of the promised land. Early in life he had begun to cultivate the soil, which amply repaid his labors. He seems to have been superior to the native population in one most useful art, not improbably learned by his father in Egypt, that of sinking wells. The manner in which the native herdsmen drove him from place to place as soon as he had enriched it with that possession, so invaluable in an arid soil, indicates want of skill, or at least of success, in providing for themselves. Perhaps it was as much by ignorant neglect as by wanton malice, that the Philistines suffered those formerly sunk by Abraham to fall into decay and become filled with earth. Jacob had crossed the Jordan with nothing but the staff which he carried in his hand; he returned with immense wealth in cattle, flocks, asses, and camels, male and female slaves, and with the more inestimable treasure of eleven sons, born to him in Mesopotamia. But before he could venture to return to his father, he must appease the resentment of his injured brother. Upon the borders of the land of Canaan, at a place called Mahanaim (from a vision of angels seen there) he sends messengers to announce his approach as far as Seir, a district extending from the foot of the Dead Sea. There Esau was already established as the chieftain of a powerful tribe, for he sets forth to meet his brother at the head of 400 men. The peaceful company of Jacob are full of apprehension; he sends forward a splendid present of 200 she-goats 20 he-goats 200 ewes and 20 rams, 30 milch camels, with their colts, 40 kine, 10 bulls, 20 she-asses, and 10 foals, he likewise takes the precaution of dividing his company into two parts, in order that if one shall be attacked the other may escape. Having made these arrangements, he sends his family over a brook, called the Jabbok, which lay before him. In the night he is comforted by another symbolic vision, in which he supposes himself wrestling with a mysterious being, from whom he extorts a blessing, and is commanded from thenceforth to assume the name of Israel (the prevailing): for having prevailed against God, so his race are to prevail against men.* Yet he does not entirely relax his caution; as he and his family advance to meet the dreaded Esau, the handmaids and their children are put foremost, then Leah with hers, last of all, as with the best chance of escape, should any treachery be intended, the favorite Rachel and her single child Joseph. But the hunter, though violent, was nevertheless frank, generous, and forgiving. While Jacob approaches with signs of reverence, perhaps of apprehension, Esau ran to meet him, and embraced him and fell on his neck, and kissed him, and they wept.

At first he refuses the offered present, but at length accepts it as a pledge of fraternal amity, and proposes that they should set forward together, and unite their encampments. The cautious Jacob, still apprehensive of future misunderstandings, alleges the natural excuse, that his party, encumbered with their cattle, their wives, and children, must travel more slowly than the expiditious troop of the Edomites; and immediately on his brother's departure, instead of following him to Seir, turns off toward the Jordan; encamps first at Succoth, then crosses the Jordan, and settles near Shalem. Here he purchases a field of the inhabitants, and resides in security, until a feud with the princes of the country drives him forth to seek a safer encampment. Sechem, the son of Hamor, the great chieftain of the tribes which occupied that part of Canaan, violated Dinah, the daughter of Jacob.

In all Arabian tribes, the brother is most deeply wounded by an outrage on the chastity of the females, (a part of Spanish manners, no doubt inherited from their Arabian ancestry,) on him devolves the duty of exacting vengeance for the indignity offered to the tribe or family. Simeon and Levi, without consulting their father, take up the quarrel. Sechem offers to marry the damsel, his father and his people, not averse to a union with the wealthy strangers, consent to submit to circumcision, as the condition of the marriage, and as a solemn pledge to the union of the clans. While they are disabled from resistance by the consequences of the operation, Simeon and Levi, with their followers, fall on the city, put the inhabitants to the sword, and pillage the whole territory. The sense of this act of cruelty to his allies, and disregard to his own authority, sank deep into the heart of the peaceful Jacob. In his last vision, Simeon and Levi are reprobated as violent and bloodthirsty men, and, as if this dangerous disposition had descended upon their posterity, they are punished, or rather prevented from bringing ruin upon the whole race, by receiving a smaller and a divided portion of the promised land. Jacob retreats to Luz, where he had formerly parted from his brother Esau. Here the family was solemnly dedicated to God, all the superstitious practices which they had brought from Mesopotamia were forbidden; the little images of the tutelar deities, even the earrings, probably considered as amulets or talismans, were taken away and buried. On the other hand, the magnificent promise, repeatedly made to Abraham and Isaac, was once more renewed to Jacob. An altar was raised, and the place called

* An awful respect for the divine nature induces us to adopt, with some learned writers, the notion, that this contest took place in a dream, as Josephus says, with a phantasm. It should be added, that whether real or visionary, Jacob bore an outward mark or memorial of this conflict, in the withering of the back sinew of the thigh. His decendants abstained till the time of Moses, and still abstain, from that part of every animal slain for food.

Beth-el, the house of God. From Luz, Jacob removed to Ephrath or Bethlehem, the birthplace of Jesus. There his favorite wife Rachel died in childbed, having given birth to his youngest son, called by the expiring mother Ben-oni, the child of her sorrow, by the father Ben-jamin, the son of his right hand. Having raised a sepulchral pillar over her remains, he sets forth to a new settlement near the tower of Edar, the site of which is unknown.

Here his domestic peace is disturbed by another crime, the violation of his concubine, Bilhah, by Reuben, his eldest son. At length he rejoins his father Isaac in the plain of Mamre, where the old man dies, and is honorably buried by his two sons. But henceforward the two branches of Isaac's family were entirely separated. The country about Mount Seir became the permanent residence of the Edomites, who were governed first by independent shieks or princes, afterward were united under one monarchy.

Jacob continued to dwell in Canaan, with his powerful family and ample possessions, until dissensions among his sons prepared the way for more important changes, which seemed to break forever the connexion between the race of Abraham and the land of Canaan, but ended in establishing them as the sole possessors of the whole territory.

Here let us pause, and, before we follow the family of Jacob into a country where the government and usages of the people were so totally different, look back on the state of society described in the Patriarchal History. Mankind appears in its infancy, gradually extending its occupancy over regions, either entirely unappropriated, or as yet so recently and thinly peopled, as to admit, without resistance, the new swarms of settlers, which seem to spread from the birthplace of the human race, the plains of Central Asia. They are peaceful, pastoral nomads, traveling on their camels, the ass the only other beast of burthen; the horse appears to have been unknown — fortunately, perhaps, for themselves and their neighbors — for the possession of that animal seems fatal to habits of peace.

The nomads, who are horsemen, are most always marauders. The power of sweeping rapidly over a wide district, and retreating as speedily, offers irresistible temptation to a people of roaming and unsettled habits. But the unenterprising shepherds, from the Hebrew tribe descended, move onward as their convenience or necessity requires, or as richer pastures attract their notice. Wherever they settle, they sink wells, and thus render districts habitable.

It is still more curious to observe how the progress of improvement is incidentally betrayed in the summary account of the ancient record. Abraham finds no impediment to his settling wherever fertile pastures invite him to pitch his camp. It is only a place of burial, in which he thinks to obtain a proprietary right. Jacob, on the contrary, purchases a field to pitch his tent. When Abraham is exposed to famine, he appears to have had no means of supply but to go down himself to Egypt. In the time of Jacob a regular traffic in corn existed between the two countries, and caravansaries were established on the way. Trading caravans had likewise begun to traverse the Arabian deserts, with spices and other produce of the east, and with slaves, which they imported into Egypt. Among the simpler nomads of Mesopotamia, wages in money were unknown; among the richer Phœnician tribes, gold and silver were already current.

It has been the opinion of some learned men that Abraham paid the money for his bargain by weight, Jacob in pieces, rudely coined or stamped. When Abraham receives the celestial strangers, with true Arabian hospitality he kills the calf with his own hands, but has nothing more generous to offer than the Scythian beverage of milk; yet the more civilized native tribes seem, by the offering of Melchisedek, to have had wine at their command. Isaac become more wealthy, and having commenced the tillage of the soil, had acquired a taste of savory meats, and had wine for his ordinary use. The tillage of Isaac bespeaks the richness of a virgin soil, as yet unbroken by the plough—it returned a hundred for one. These primitive societies were constituted in the most simple and inartificial manner. The parental authority, and that of the head of the tribe, was supreme and without appeal—Esau so far respects even his blind and feeble father, as to postpone the gratification of his revenge till the death of Jacob. Afterward the brothers who conspire against Joseph, though some of them had already dipped their hands in blood, dare no perpetrate their crime openly. When they return from Egypt to fetch Benjamin in order to redeem one of their company, left in apparent danger of his life, they are obliged to obtain the consent of Jacob, and do not think of carrying him off by force. Reuben, indeed, leaves his own sons as hostages, under an express covenant that they are to be put to death if he does not bring Benjamin back. The father seems to have possessed the power of transferring the right of primogeniture to a younger son. This was perhaps the effect of Isaac's blessing; Jabob seems to have done the same, and disinherited the three elder sons of Leah. The desire of offspring, and the pride of becoming the ancestor of a great people, with the attendant disgrace of barrenness, however in some degree common to human nature, and not unknown in thickly peopled countries, yet as the one predominant and absorbing passion (for such it is in the patriarchal history) belongs more properly to a period, when the earth still offered ample room for each tribe to extend its boundaries without encroaching on the possessions of its neighbor.

These incidents, in themselves trifling, are

not without interest, both as illustrative of human manners, and as tending to show that the record from which they are drawn was itself derived from contemporary traditions, which it has represented with scrupulous fidelity. Even the characters of the different personages are singularly in unison with the state of society described. There is the hunter, the migratory herdsman, and the incipient husbandman. The quiet and easy Isaac adapts himself to the more fixed and sedentary occupatiou of tillage. Esau the hunter is reckless, daring, and improvident. Jacob the herdsman, cautious, observant, subtle, and timid. Esau excels in one great virtue of uncivilized life, bravery; Jacob in another, which is not less highly appreciated, craft. Even in Abraham we do not find that nice and lofty sense of veracity which distinguishes a state of society where the point of honor has acquired great influence. It is singular that this accurate delineation of primitive manners, and the discrimination of individual character in each successive patriarch, with all the imperfections and vices, as well of the social state as of the particular disposition, although so conclusive an evidence to the honesty of the narrative, has caused the greatest perplexity to many pious minds, and as great triumph to the adversaries of revealed religion. The object of this work is strictly historical, not theological; yet a few observations may be ventured on this point, considering its important bearing on the manner in which Jewish history ought to be written and read.

Some will not read the most ancient and curious history in the world, because it is the Bible; others read it in the Bible with a kind of pious awe, which prevents them from comprehending its real spirit. The latter look on the distinguished characters in the Mosaic annals as a kind of sacred beings, scarcely allied to human nature. Their intercourse with the Divinity invests them with a mysterious sanctity, which is expected to extend to all their actions. Hence when they find the same passions at work, the ordinary feelings and vices of human nature prevalent both among the ancestors of the chosen people, and the chosen people themselves, they are confounded and distressed. Writers unfriendly to revealed religion, starting with the same notion, that the Mosaic narrative is uniformly exemplary, not historical, have enlarged with malicious triumph on the delinquencies of the patriarchs and their descendants. Perplexity and triumph equally groundless! Had the avowed design of the intercourse of God with the patriarchs been their own unimpeachable perfection; had that of the Jewish polity been the establishment of a divine Utopia, advanced to premature civilization, and overleaping at once those centuries of slow improvement, through which the rest of mankind were to pass, then it might have been difficult to give a reasonable account of the manifest failure. So far from this being the case, an ulterior purpose is evident throughout. The patriarches and their descendants are the depositaries of certain great religions truths, the unity, omnipotence, and providence of God, not solely for their own use and advantage, but as conservators for the future universal benefit of mankind. Hence, provided the great end, the preservation of those truths, was eventually obtained, human affairs took their ordinary course; the common passions and motives of mankind were left in undisturbed operation. Superior in one respect alone, the ancestors of the Jews, and the Jews themselves, were not beyond their age or country in acquirements, in knowledge, or even in morals; as far as morals are modified by usage and opinion. They were polygamists, like the rest of the Eastern world; they acquired the virtues and the vices of each state of society through which they passed. Higher and purer notions of the Deity, though they tend to promote and improve, by no means necessarily enforce moral perfection; their influence will be regulated by the social state of the age in which they are promulgated, and the bias of the individual charaeter to which they are addressed. Neither the actual interpositiou of the Almighty in favor of an individual or nation, nor his employment of them as instruments for certain important purposes, stamps the seal of divine approbation on all their actions; in some cases, as in the deception practiced by Jacob on his father, the worst part of their character manifestly contributes to the purpose of God: still the nature of the action is not altered; it is to be judged by its motive, not by its undesigned consequence. Allowance, therefore, being always made for their age and social state, the patriarchs, kings, and other Hebrew worthies, are amenable to the same verdict which would be passed on the eminent men of Greece or Rome. Excepting where they act under the express commandment of God, they have no exemption from the judgment of posterity; and on the same principle, while God is on the scene, the historian will write with caution and reverence; while man, with freedom, justice, and impartiality.

BOOK II.

ISRAEL IN EGYPT.

THE seed of Abraham had now become a family; from the twelve sons of Israel it was to branch out into a nation. Of these sons the four elder had been born from the prolific Leah, Reuben, Simeon, Levi and Judah. The barren Rachel had substituted her handmaid, Bilhah, who gave birth to Dan and Naphtali. Leah, after her sister's example, substituted Zilpah; from her sprang Gad and Asher. Rachel, for the sake of some mandrakes, supposed among eastern women to act as a love philter and remove barrenness, yielding up her right to her sister, Leah again bore Issachar and Zebulun, and a daughter, Dinah. At length the comely Rachel was blessed with

Joseph; and in Canaan, Benoni or Benjamin completed the twelve.

The children of the handmaidens had no title to the primogeniture. Reuben had forfeited the esteem of his father by incest with his concubine, Simeon and Levi by their cruelty towards the Sichemites. Judah, the next brother, was inadvertently betrayed into a serious crime. There was a singular usage afterward admitted into the Mosaic law, that in case a married man died without issue, his next brother was bound to take his wife, in order that his line might not become extinct. The perpetuation of their name and race through their offspring being then, as it is still in some countries of the East, the one great object to which all moral laws, even those generally recognized, were to give away. The eldest son of Judah, Er, died; the second, Onan, was guilty of a criminal dereliction of that indispensable duty, and was cut off for his offence. Judah, neglecting his promise to bestow the widow, Tamar, on his third son, Shelah, was betrayed into an unlawful connexion with her, and became the incestuous father of two children.

But Joseph, the eldest born of the beloved Rachel, had always held the first place in the affections of his father. He was a beautiful youth, and it was the pride of the fond father to behold him in a dress distinguished from the rest of his sons—*a coat of many colors.* The envy of his brothers was still farther excited by two dreams seen by Joseph, which, in the frankness of his disposition, he took no pains to conceal. In one, the brothers were binding sheaves of corn (a proof that they were advancing in the cultivation of the soil), the sheaves of the brothers bent, and did homage to that of Joseph. In the other, the sun and the moon and the eleven stars seemed to make obeisance to Joseph. Each of these successive visions intimated his future superiority over all the family of Israel.

One day, when Joseph had set forth to the place where his brothers were accustomed to feed their flocks, they returned to their father's tent without him, bearing that very dress, on which Jacob had so often gazed with pleasure, steeped in blood. The agony of the old man cannot be described with such pathetic simplicity as in the language of the Sacred Volume,—*He refused to be comforted, and he said I will go down into the grave with my son, mourning.* But before he went down to the grave he was to behold his son under far different circumstances. His brothers, at first, notwithstanding the remonstrances of Reuben, the eldest born, a man of more mild and generous disposition, had determined to put their hated rival to death. With this intention they had let him down into a pit, probably an old disused well. A caravan of Arabian traders happening to pass by, they acceded to the more merciful and advantageous propositiou of Judah to sell him as a slave. Though these merchants were laden only with spicery, balm and myrrh, commodities in great request in Egypt, all of them being used in embalming the dead, they were sure of a market of such a slave as Joseph, and in that degraded and miserable character he arrived in Egypt. But the Divine Providence watched, even in the land of the stranger, over the heir to the promises made to Abraham, Isaac and Jacob. The slave rose with a rapidity surprising, though by no means unparalleled in eastern kingdoms, to be the all-powerful vizier of the king of Egypt. He was first bought by Potiphar, a chief officer of the king, the captain of the guard, by whom he was speedily promoted to the care of the whole household. The entire confidence of his master in the prudence and integrity of the servant is described in these singular terms,—*He left all that he had in Joseph's hand, and he knew not aught he had, save the bread which he did eat.* The virtue of Joseph in other respects was equal to his integrity, but not so well rewarded. Falsely accused by the arts of his master's wife, whose criminal advances he had repelled, he was thrown into prison. The dungeon opens a way to still farther advancement. Wherever he is, he secures esteem and confidence. Like his former master, the keeper of the prison entrusts the whole of his responsible duties to the charge of Joseph. But the chief cause of his rapid rise to fortune and dignity is his skill in the interpretation of dreams. Among his fellow-prisoners were the chief cup-bearer and chief purveyor of the king. Each of these men was perplexed with an extraordinary vision. The interpretation of Joseph was justified by the event of both; one, as he predicted, was restored to his honors, the other suffered an ignominious death. Through the report of the former, the fame of Joseph, in a character so important among a superstitious people, reached the palace, and when the king himself is in the same manner disturbed with visions which baffle the professed diviners of the country, Joseph is summoned from the prison. The dreams of the king, according to the exposition of Joseph, under the symbolic forms of seven fat and fleshy kine followed by seven lean and withered ones, seven good ears of corn by seven parched and blasted with the east wind, prefigured seven years of unexampled plenty, to be succeeded by seven of unexampled dearth. The advice of Joseph being demanded how to provide against the impending calamity, he recommends that a fifth part of the produce during the seven abundant years, shall be laid up in granaries built for the purpose. The wisdom of this measure was apparent; and who so fit to carry such plans into effect as he whose prudence had suggested them? Joseph, therefore, is at once installed in the dignity of chief minister over the whole of this great and flourishing kingdom.

The information we obtain from the Mosaic narrative, concerning the state and constitution of Egypt during this period, is both valuable in itself, and agrees strictly with all the knowledge which we acquire from other sources. Egypt had long been the great corn country of the ancient world, now in a high state of cultivation, but dependent for its fertility on the overflow of the river on whose banks it lay. Should the annual increase of the Nile be interrupted, the whole valley would remain a barren and unvegetating waste. The cause of the long period of famine is nowhere indicated, but it was by no means a local calamity, it extended to all the adjacent countries. A long and general drought, which would burn up the herbage of all the pastoral districts of Asia, might likewise diminish that accumulation of waters which at its regular period pours down the channel of the Nile. The waters are collected in the greatest part from the drainage of all the high levels in that region of central Africa where the tropical rains, about the summer solstice, fall with incessant violence. But whatever might be its cause, Egypt escaped the famine which pressed so severely on other countries, only through the prudent administration of Joseph. It is necessary, however, before we describe the policy which he adopted, or the settlement of the family of Israel in this country, to give some insight into the state of the Egyptian government and people; for without this we shall neither be able to comprehend the transactions which relate to the Israelites in Egypt, nor the degree of originality to be assigned to the Mosaic institutions. Egypt, before this period, had enjoyed many centuries of civilization, most likely of opulence and splendor. Whether she had already reared her vast and mysterious pyramids, commenced the colossal temples of Ipsambul and Thebes, or excavated those wonderful subterraneous sepulchral palaces for her dead kings, can not at present be decided with certainty. But of her singular constitution we have distinct indications in the Mosaic narrative. The people were divided into castes, like those of India, as they exist to the present day, and as they formerly prevailed among many other oriental nations. At the head of these castes stood that of the priesthood. From this order the king was usually selected; if one of the warriors, the next class in rank, should attain to that eminence, he was always installed and enrolled in the superior order. The priestly caste, in rank and power, stood far above the rest of the people. In each name of district (if indeed these divisions were of so early a date) stood a temple and a sacerdotal college. In them one-third of the whole land of the country was inalienably vested. The priests were not merely the ministers of religion, they were the hereditary conservators of knowledge. They were the public astronomers, by whom all the agricultural labors of the people were regulated; the public geometricians, whose service was indispensable, since the Nile annually obliterated the landmarks of the country; in their hieroglyphical characters the public events were recorded; they were the physicians, in short, to them belonged the whole patrimony of science, which was inseparably bound up with their religion. The political powers of this hereditary aristocracy were unbounded; they engrossed apparently both the legislative and judicial functions; they were the farmers, the conservators, the interpreters of the laws. As interpreter of dreams, Joseph, no doubt, intruded into the province of this all-powerful caste, and the king, not improbably with a view to disarm their jealousy, married his new vizier to the daughter of the Priest of the Sun, who dwelled in On, called afterward by the Greeks Heliopolis (the City of the Sun). Moreover, in the great political measure of Joseph, the resumption of all the lands into the hands of the crown, the sacred property of the priests was exempted from the operation of the law, and the whole class supported, during the famine, at the royal charge. The next caste in dignity was that of the warriors, called by Herodotus, Hermotybies or Kalasyries. The lower classes of the people constituted the rest of the orders; according to Herodotus five, to Diodorus three more. The latter reckons husbandmen, artisans, and shepherds; Herodotus, shepherds, swineherds, manufacturers and shopkeepers, interpreters, and mariners, that is, the boatmen of the Nile. The boundaries of these castes were unalterably fixed, the son held forever the same rank, and pursued the same occupation with his father. The profession of a shepherd, probably the lowest of these castes, was held in particular discredit. "Every shepherd was an abomination to the Egyptians." Several reasons have been assigned for this remarkable fact. A German writer of great ability supposes, that when the first civilizers of Egypt, whom, from reasons, which every accession to our knowledge of ancient Egypt seems to confirm, he derives from Ethiopia, directed the attention of the people to tillage, for which the country was so admirably adapted, in order to wean the rude people from their nomadic habits, they studiously degraded the shepherds into a sort of Pariah caste. Another and a more general opinion derives this hostility to the name of shepherd from a recent and most important event in the Egyptian history. While Egypt was rapidly advancing in splendor and prosperity, a fierce and barbarous Asiatic horde burst suddenly upon her fruitful provinces, destroyed her temples, massacred her priests, and, having subdued the whole of Lower Egypt, established a dynasty of six successive kings. These Hyksos, or royal shepherds, with their savage clans, afterward expelled by the victorious Egyptians, Monsieur Champollion* thinks, with apparent reason, that he recognizes on many of the ancient monuments. A people with red hair, blue eyes, and covered only with an undressed hide, loosely wrapped over them, are painted, sometimes struggling

* Lettre a Mons de Blacas, p. 57

in deadly warfare with the natives, more usually in attitudes of the lowest degradation which the scorn and hatred of their conquerors could invent. They lie prostrate under the footstools of the kings, in the attitude described in the book of Joshua, where the rulers actually set their feet on the necks of the captive kings.* The common people appear to have taken pride in having the figures of these detested enemies wrought on the soles of their sandals, that they might be thus perpetually trampled on: even the dead carried this memorial of their hatred into the grave; the same figures are painted on the lower wrappers of the mummies, accompanied with similar marks of abhorrence and contempt. It would be difficult to find a more apt illustration of the phrase in the book of Genesis, "every shepherd was an abomination to the Egyptians." Several other incidents in the Mosaic history seems to confirm the opinion, that these invaders had been expelled, and that but recently, before the period of Joseph's administration.

The seven years of unexampled plenty passed away exactly as the interpreter of the royal dreams had foretold. During all this time Joseph regularly exacted a fifth of the produce, which was stored up in granaries established by the government. The famine soon began to press heavily, not merely in Egypt, but on all the adjacent countries: among the first who came to purchase corn, appeared the ten sons of Jacob. It is no easy task to treat, after the Jewish historian, the transactions which took place between Joseph and his family. The relation in the book of Genesis is, perhaps, the most exquisite model of the manner in which history, without elevating its tone, or departing from its plain and unadorned veracity, assumes the language and spirit of the most touching poetry. The cold and rhetorical paraphrase of Josephus, sometimes a writer of great vigor and simplicity, enforces the prudence of adhering as closely as possible to the language of the original record. The brothers are at first received with sternness and asperity, charged with being spies come to observe the undefended state of the country. This accusation, though not seriously intended, in some degree confirms the notion that the Egyptians had recently suffered, and therefore constantly apprehended, foreign invasion. They are thrown into prison for three days, and released on condition of proving the truth of their story, by bringing their younger brother Benjamin with them. Their own danger brings up before their minds the recollection of their crime. They express to one another their deep remorse for the supposed murder of their elder brother, little thinking that Joseph, who had conversed with them through an interpreter, (perhaps of the caste mentioned by Herodotus), understood every word they said. And Joseph turned about from them and wept. Simon being left as a hostage, the brothers are dismissed, but on their way they are surprised and alarmed to find their money returned. The suspicious Jacob will not at first intrust his youngest and best-beloved child to their care; but their present supply of corn being consumed, they have no alternative between starvation and their return to Egypt. Jacob reluctantly and with many fond admonitions commits the surviving child of Rachel to their protection. On their arrival in Egypt they are better received, the Vizier inquires anxiously about the health of their father. Is your father alive, the old man of whom ye spoke, is he yet alive? The sight of his own uterine brother Benjamin overpowers him with emotion. He said, "God be gracious unto thee, my son; and Joseph made haste, for his bowels did yearn upon his brother; and he entered into his chamber and wept there." They are feasted, (and here again we find a genuine trait of Egyptian manners,) Joseph must not eat at the same table with these shepherd strangers. Benjamin is peculiarly distinguished by a larger portion of meat. The brothers are once more dismissed, but are now pursued and apprehended on a charge of secreting a silver cup, which had been concealed in the sack of Benjamin, and at length the great minister of the king of Egypt makes himself known as the brother whom they had sold as a slave. "Then Joseph could not refrain himself before all them that stood by him; and he cried, Cause every man to go out from me; and there stood no man with him, while Joseph made himself known unto his brethren. And he wept aloud, and the Egyptians and the house of Pharaoh heard. And Joseph said unto his brethren, Come near to me, I pray you. And they came near. And he said, I am Joseph; doth my father yet live? And his brethren could not answer him, for they were troubled at his presence. And Joseph said unto his brethren, Come near to me, I pray you. And they came near. And he said, I am Joseph your brother, whom ye sold into Egypt. Now therefore be not grieved nor angry with yourselves that ye sold me hither: for God did send me before you to preserve life; and he hath made me a father to Pharaoh, and lord of all his house, and a ruler throughout the land of Egypt." He sends them, with great store of provisions, and with an equipage of wagons to transport their father and all their family into Egypt, for five years of the famine had still to elapse. His last striking admonition is, "See that ye fall not out by the way." When they arrived in Canaan, and told their aged father, "Joseph is yet alive, and he is governor over all the land of Egypt, Jacob's heart fainted, for he believed them not." Convinced at length of the surprising change of fortune, he said, "It is enough, Joseph my son is yet alive; I will go and see him before I die."

Thus all the legitimate descendants of Abra-

*Joshua x. 24.

ham with their families, amounting in number to seventy, migrate into Egypt. The high credit of Joseph ensures them a friendly reception, and the fertile district of Goshen, the best pasture land of Egypt, is assigned by the munificent sovereign for their residence. But if the deadly hostility borne by the native Egyptians to foreign shepherds really originated in the cause which has been indicated above, the magnanimity of Joseph in not disclaiming his connection with a race in such low esteem, and his influence in obtaining them such a hospitable reception, must not escape our notice. Their establishment in Goshen, coincides in a remarkable manner with this theory. The last stronghold of the shepherd kings was the city of Abaris. Abaris must have been situated either within or closely bordering upon the district of Goshen. The expulsion of the shepherds would leave the tract unoccupied, and open for the settlement of another pastoral people. Goshen itself was likewise called Rameses, a word ingeniously explained by Jablonski, as meaning the land of shepherds, and contained all those low, and sometimes marshy meadows on the Pelusiac branch of the Nile, and extending very considerably to the south. Here, says Maillet, the grass grows to the height of a man, and so thick that an ox may browse a whole day lying on the ground.

Joseph pursued the system of his government with consummate vigor and prudence. His measures, however calculated to raise the royal authority, seem to have been highly popular with all classes of the nation. It is difficult precisely to understand the views or the consequences of the total revolution in the tenure of property, which he effected. During the first years of the dearth, all the money of the country found its way into the royal treasury; in a short time after, all the inhabitants hastened to part with their stock; and at length were glad to purchase subsistence at the price of their lands: thus the whole territory, except that of the priests, was vested in the crown. Whether the common people had any landed property before this period; and whether that triple division of the lands, one-third to the king for the expenses of the court and government; one-third to the priests, and the other third to the military class, existed previous to this epoch, we have no means of ascertaining. The Mosaic history seems to infer that the body of the people were the possessors of the soil. If, however, the state of property, described above from Diodorus, was anterior to this period, the financial operation of Joseph consisted in the resumption of the crown lands from the tenants, with the reletting of the whole on one plain and uniform system, and the acquisition of that of the military. In either case the terms on which the whole was relet, with a reservation of one-fifth to the royal exchequer, seem liberal and advantageous to the cultivator, especially if we compare them with the exactions to which the peasantry in the despotic countries of the East, or the miserable Fellahs who now cultivate the banks of the Nile, are exposed. Another part of Joseph's policy is still more difficult clearly to comprehend, his removing the people into the cities. This has been supposed by some an arbitrary measure, in order to break the ties of attachment, in the former possessors to their native farms; by others a wise scheme, intended to civilize the rude peasantry. A passage in Belzoni's travels may throw some light on the transaction. He describes the condition of the poor cultivators in Upper Egypt, as wretched and dangerous. Their single tenements or villages are built but just above the ordinary high-water mark, and are only protected by a few wattles. If the Nile rises beyond its usual level, dwellings, cattle, and even the inhabitants are swept away. The measure of Joseph may have been merely intended to secure the improvident peasantry against these common, but fatal accidents.

Among the fertile pastures of Goshen, enjoying undisturbed plenty and prosperity, the sons of Jacob began to increase with great, but by no means incredible, rapidity. The prolific soil of Egypt not merely increases the fertility of vegetable and animal life, but that of the human race likewise. This fact is noticed by many ancient writers, particularly Aristotle, who states that women in Egypt sometimes produce three, four, or even seven at a birth! Early marriages, polygamy, the longer duration of life, abundance and cheapness of provisions, would tend under the divine blessing, still further to promote the population of this flourishing district. At the end of 17 years, Jacob died, aged 147. Before his death he bestowed his last blessing on Joseph, and solemnly adjured him to transfer his remains to the cemetery of the tribe in Canaan. The history of his life terminates with a splendid poetical prophecy, describing the character of his sons, and the possessions they were to occupy in the partition of the promised land. This poem was no doubt treasured up with the most religious care among the traditions of the tribes. One curious point proves its antiquity. The most splendid destiny is awarded to Judah and the sons of Joseph, but Jacob had never forgotten the barbarity of Simeon and Levi. These two families are condemned to the same inferior and degraded lot, as divided and scattered among their brethren. Yet how different their fate! The tribe of Levi attained the highest rank among their brethren, scattered indeed they were, but in stations of the first distinction, while the feeble tribe of Simeon, soon dwindled into insignificance, and became almost extinct. A later poet, certainly Moses himself would not have united these two tribes under the same destiny. The funeral procession of Jacob was conducted with Egyptian magnificence to the sepulchre of his fathers, to the great and lasting astonishment of the native Canaanites. The protecting presence of their father being withdrawn, the brothers began again to apprehend the hostility of Joseph; but his favor still watched over the growing settlement, and he himself at length, having seen his great grandchildren upon his knees, died at the age of 110 years. He left directions that his body should be embalmed, and put into a coffin; on the return of his kindred to Canaan, to be transported to the grave of his forefathers.

How long a period elapsed* between the migration into Egypt under Jacob, and the Exodus or departure, under Moses, has been a question debated from the earliest ages by Jewish, no less than Christian writers. While some assign the whole duration of 430 years to the captivity in Egypt, others include the residence of the patriarchs, 215 years, within this period. The vestiges of this controversy appear in all the earlier writings. The Hebrew and Samaritan texts, the different copies of the Greek version of the Scriptures, differ. St. Stephen, in the Acts, seems to have followed one opinion. St. Paul, in his epistle to the Galatians, the other. Josephus contradicts himself repeatedly. The great body of English divines follow the latter hypothesis; the great modern scholars of Germany generally prefer the former. The following brief statement may throw some light on this intricate subject. The Jews were firmly and religiously persuaded that their genealogies were not merely accurate, but complete. As then only two names appeared between Levi and Moses, those of Kohath and Amram, and the date of life assigned to these two seemed irreconcilable with the longer period of 430 years, they adopted very generally the notion that only 215 years were passed in Egypt.† They overlooked, or left to miraculous intervention to account for a still greater difficulty, the prodigious increase in one family during one generation. In the desert the males of the descendants of Kohath are reckoned at 8609. Kohath had four sons, from each son then, in one generation, must have sprung on the average 2150 males. On this hypothesis the alternative remains, either that some names have been lost from the genealogies between Kohath and Amram, or between Amram and Moses, a notion rather confirmed by the fact that in the genealogy of Joshua in the book of Chronicles, he stands twelfth in descent from Joseph, while Moses is the fourth from Levi: or, as there are certain grounds for suspecting, some general error runs through the whole numbering‡ of the Israelites in the desert.

*Some curious particulars of this period may be gleaned from the genealogies in the book of Chronicles. Some intercourse with the native country was kept up for a time Certain sons of Ephraim were slain in a freebooting expedition to drive the cattle of the inhabitants of Gath. Chron. vii. 21. Another became ruler of the tribe of Moab. Chron. vii. 22. Some became celebrated in Egypt as potters, and manufacturers in cotton (byssus). Chron. iv. 21.

† On account of this uncertainty we have omitted the dates till the time of the Exodus, when chronology first seems to offer a secure footing.

‡ Some observations on this subject will subsequently be offered.

At what period in Egyptian history the migration under Jacob took place; and which of the Pharaohs perished in the Red Sea, may possibly come to light from the future investigation of the hieroglyphic monuments by Mons. Champollion. One point appears certain from the Mosaic history, that the patron of Joseph was one of the native sovereigns of Egypt, not, as Eusebius supposes, one of the foreign shepherd dynasty. The flourishing and peaceful state of the kingdom; the regularity of the government; the power of the priesthood, who were persecuted and oppressed by the savage shepherds; the hatred of the pastoral race and occupation; all these circumstances strongly indicate the orderly and uncontested authority of the native princes.

In process of time, such is the lot of the greatest of public benefactors, the services of the wise and popular vizier were forgotten. A new king arose,† who knew not Joseph, and began to look with jealous apprehension on this race of strangers, thus occupying his most open and accessible frontier, and able to give free passage, or join in a dangerous confederacy with any foreign invader. With inhuman policy he commenced a system of oppression, intended at once to check their increase, and break the dangerous spirit of revolt. They were seized, and forced to labor at the public works in building new cities, Pithom and Raamses,‡ called treasure cities. Josephus employs them on the pyramids, on the great canals, and on vast dams built for the purpose of irrigation. But tyranny, short-sighted as inhuman, failed in its purpose. Even under these unfavorable circumstances, the strangers still increased. In the damp stone-quarry, in the lime-pit and brick-field, toiling beneath burthens under a parching sun, they multiplied as rapidly as among the fresh airs and under the cool tents in Goshen; and now instead of a separate tribe, inhabiting a remote province, whose loyalty was only suspected, the government found a still more numerous people, spread throughout the country, and rendered hostile by cruel oppression. Tyranny having thus wantonly made enemies, must resort to more barbarous measures to repress them. A dreadful decree is issued; the midwives, who in this land of hereditary professions, were most likely a distinct class under responsible officers, were commanded to destroy all the Hebrew children at their birth. They disobey or evade the command, and the king has now no alternative, but to take into his own hands the execution of his exterminating project, which, if carried into effect, would have cut

* The change of dynasty and accession of the shepherd kings during this interval, is liable to as strong objections as those above stated. The inroad of this savage people which must have passed, in all its havoc and massacre, over the land of Goshen, would hardly have been forgotten or omitted in the Hebrew traditions. The great architectural and agricultural works bespeak the reign of the magnificent native princes, not that of rude barbarians. Mr. Faber's ingenious theory, which assigns the building of the pyramids to the shepherds, is, in our opinion, highly improbable.

† It is curious that Mons. Champollion assigns to this period, a king called Rhamses, however, was not an uncommon name in the Egyptian dynasties.

short at once the race of Abraham. Every male child is commanded to be cast into the river, the females preserved, probably to fill in time the harems of their oppressors.

But Divine Providence had determined to raise u that man, who was to release this oppressedppeople, and after having seen and intimately known the civil and religious institutions of this famous country, was deliberately to reject them, to found a polity on totally different principles, and establish a religion, the most opposite to the mysterious polytheism of Egypt; a polity and a religion, which were to survive the dynasty of the Pharaohs, and the deities of their vast temples, and exercise an unbounded influence on the civil and religious history of the most remote ages. Amram, if the genealogies are complete, the second in descent from Levi, married in his own tribe. His wife bore him a son, whose birth she was so fortunate as to conceal for three months, but at the end of this period she was obliged to choose between the dreadful alternative of exposing the infant on the banks of the river, or of surrendering him to the executioners of the king's relentless edict. The manner in which the child in its cradle of rushes, lined with pitch, was laid among the flags upon the brink of the river, forcibly recalls the exposure of the Indian children on the banks of the holy Ganges. Could there be any similar custom among the Egyptians, and might the mother hope, that if any unforeseen accident should save the life of the child, it might pass for that of an Egyptian? This however was not the case. The daughter of the king, coming down to bathe in the river, perceived the ark, and, attracted by the beauty of the infant, took pity on it, and conjecturing that it belonged to one of the persecuted Hebrews, determined to preserve its life. By a simple and innocent stratagem, the mother was summoned, her own child committed to her charge, and as it grew up it became the adopted son of the princess, who called it Moses, from Egyptian words signifying drawn from the water. The child received an excellent education, and became trained in all the wisdom of the Egyptians. This last fact rests on Jewish traditions reported by St. Stephen; but it is highly curious to contrast the other romantic fictions of the later writers, probably the Alexandrian Jews, with this plain narrative. These fables have no appearance of ancient traditions, but all the exaggeration of rabbinical invention. The birth of Moses was prophetically foreshown. The sacred scribe announced to the king that a child was about to be born among the Israelites, who was to bring ruin on the power of Egypt, and unexampled glory on the Hebrew nation; he was to surpass all the human race in the greatness and duration of his fame. To cut short this fatal life, not with the design of weakening the Jewish people, this elder Herod issues out his edict for the first massacre of the innocents. Amram the father of Moses, is likewise favored with a vision, foretelling the glory of his son. Thermutis, the daughter of Pharaoh (the manners having become too refined to suppose that a king's daughter would bathe in the river,) is more elegantly described as amusing herself on the banks. Seeing the basket floating on the water, she orders certain divers, ready of course at her command, to bring it to her. Enchanted by the exquisite beauty of the child she sends for a nurse; but the infant patriot indignantly refused the milk of an Egyptian; nurse after nurse is tried and rejected; nothing will satisfy him but the breast of his own mother. When he was three years old, he was such a prodigy of beauty that all who passed by would suspend their work to gaze upon him. The princess adopts him, shows him to her father, and insists on his being recognized heir to the kingdom.

The king places the diadem on his head, which the child contemptuously seizes and tramples under his feet. The royal scribe in vain attempts to awaken the apprehensions of the monarch. The youth grows up in such universal esteem and favor, that when the Ethiopians invade the country, he is placed at the head of the army. The district through which he chooses to march, rather than ascend the Nile, being full of noxious reptiles, he presses a squadron of tame ibises, lets them fly at the serpents, and thus speedily clears his way. By this extraordinary stratagem, he comes unexpectedly upon the enemy, defeats and pursues them to their capital city, Meroe. Here the daughter of the king falls in love with him, and the city is surrendered on condition of his marrying the Ethiopian princess; a fiction obviously formed on the Cushite or Arabian, translated in the LXX Ethiopian, wife of Moses. Jealousy and hatred, the usual attendants on greatness, endanger his life; the priests urge, and the timid king assents to the death of the stranger, who with difficulty makes his escape into the desert. But, as is usual with those who embellish genuine history, the simple dignity of the Jewish patriot is lowered rather than exalted. The true greatness of Moses consists in his generous indignation at the oppressions under which his kindred were laboring; his single-minded attachment to the poor and degraded and toil-worn slaves from whom he sprung; his deliberate rejection of all the power, wealth and rank, which awaited him if he had forsworn his race, and joined himself to the people who had adopted him. An accident discovered his impatience of the sufferings inflicted on his brethren. As he saw them laboring under their burthens, he saw one of the Egyptian officers (such is the probable supposition of a late writer) exercising some great personal cruelty on one of the miserable slaves under his inspection. He rose up in defence of his countryman, slew the officer, and hid his body in the sand. No Egyptian had witnessed what he had done, and on the fidelity of his brethren he supposed that he might fairly calculate. The next day, when he took upon himself the office of reconciling two of the Israelites, who had accidentally quarreled, he found that his secret was not safe. The whole transaction certainly gives ground for the supposition, that an unformed notion of delivering his countrymen from their bondage, was already brooding in the mind of Moses.* His courage in avenging their wrongs, and his anxiety to establish good-will and unity among the people, were the surest means he could adopt to secure confidence, and consolidate their strength. If this were the case, the conduct of his countrymen, ready to betray him on every occasion in which their passions or fears were excited, instead of encouraging, was likely to crush forever his ambitious hopes, and sadly convince him that such a design, however noble, was desperate and impracticable. At all events he had been guilty of a crime, by the Egyptian law, of the most enormous magnitude; even if his favor at the court might secure him from the worst consequences of the unpardonable guilt of bloodshed, the example of revolt and insurrection precluded all hope of indulgence.

A lonely exile, Moses flies beyond the reach of Egyptian power, to the tents of the nomadic tribes which lie on the borders of Palestine and Arabia. Here for forty years the future lawgiver of the Jews follows the humble occupation of a shepherd; allied in marriage with the hospitable race who had received him, he sees his children rising around him, and seems as entirely to have forgotten his countrymen and their oppression, as, in all probability, he was forgotten by them; so entirely did he seem alienated from his own people, that he had neglected to initiate his children into the family of Abraham, by the great national rite of circumcision. On a sudden, when eighty year old, an age which according to the present proportion of life may be fairly reckoned at sixty or sixty-five, when the fire of ambition is usually burnt out, and the active spirit of adventure subsided, entirely unattended, he appears again in Egypt, and either renews, or first boldly undertakes the extraordinary enterprise of delivering the people of Israel from their state of slavery, and establishing them as a regular and independent commonwealth. To effect this, he had first to obtain a perfect command over the minds of the people, now scattered through the whole land of Egypt, their courage broken by long and unintermitted slavery, habituated to Egyptian customs, and even deeply tainted with Egyptian superstitions; he had to induce them to throw off the yoke of their tyrannical masters, and follow him in search of a remote land, only known by traditions many centuries old, as the residence of their forefathers. Secondly, he had to overawe, and induce to the surrender of their whole useful slave population, not merely an ignorant and superstitious people, but the king and the priesthood of a country where science had made considerable progress, and where the arts of an impostor would either be counteracted by similar arts, or instantly detected, and exposed to shame and ridicule.

*Compare Acts vii. 23—25.

What then were his natural qualifications for this prodigious undertaking—popular eloquence? By his own account, his organs of speech were imperfect, his enunciations slow and impeded; he was obliged to use the cold and ineffective method of addressing the people through his more ready and fluent brother Aaron. Had he acquired among the tribes, with whom he had resided, the adventurous spirit and military skill, which might prompt or carry him through such an enterprise? The shepherds, among whom he lived, seem to have been a peaceful and unenterprising people; and far from showing any skill as a warrior, the generalship of the troops always devolved on the younger and more warlike Joshua. His only distinguished acquirements were those which he had learned among the people, with whom he was about to enter on this extraordinary contest; all the wisdom he possessed, was the wisdom of the Egyptians.

The credentials which Moses produced in order to obtain authority over his own people, and the means of success on which he calculated, in his bold design of wrestling these miserable Helots from their unwilling masters, were a direct commission from the God of their fathers, and a power of working preternatural wonders. His narrative was simple and imposing. The Sea of Edom, or the Red sea, terminates in two narrow gulfs, the western running up to the modern Isthmus of Suez, the eastern extending not quite so far to the north. In the mountainous district between these two forks of the sea, stands a remarkable eminence with two peaks, higher than the neighboring ridge, the south-eastern, which is much the loftiest, called Sinai, the north-western Horeb. Into these solitudes Moses had driven his flocks, when suddenly he beheld a bush kindling into flame, yet remaining unconsumed. A voice was next heard, which announced the presence of the God of Abraham, Isaac, and Jacob, and declared the compassion of the Almighty toward the suffering race of Israel, their approaching deliverance, their restoration to the rich and fruitful land of Canaan; designated Moses as the man who was to accomplish this great undertaking, and ended by communicating that mysterious name of the great Deity, which implies in its few pregnant monosyllables, self-existence and eternity. "I am that I am." Moses, diffident of his own capacity to conduct so great an enterprise, betrayed his reluctance. Two separate miracles, the transformation of his rod or shepherd's staff into a serpent, the immediate withering of his hand with leprosy, and its as immediate restoration; the promise of power to effect a third, the change of water into blood, inspired him with courage and resolution to set forth on his appointed task. Such was his relation before the elders of the people; for even in their bondage this sort of government by the heads of families seems to have been retained among the descendants of Jacob. Aaron, his brother, who had gone forth by divine command, as he declared, to meet him enters boldly into the design. The people are awed by the designs which are displayed, and yield their passive consent. This is all that Moses requires; for while he promises deliverance, he does not insist on any active co-operation on their part; he enjoins neither courage, discipline, enterprise, nor mutual confidence, nothing which might render insurrection formidable, or indicate an organized plan of resistance.

The king of Egypt probably held that sort of open court or divan, usual in oriental monarchies, in which any one may appear who would claim justice or petition for favor. Moses and Aaron stand before this throne, and solicit the temporary release of all their people, that they may offer sacrifice to their God. The haughty monarch not only rejects their demand, but sternly rebukes the presumptuous interference of these self-constituted leaders. The labors of the slaves are redoubled; they are commanded not merely to finish the same portion of work in the brick-field, but to provide themselves with straw; they are treated with still greater inhumanity, and severely chastised because they can not accomplish the impracticable orders of their taskmasters. The wretched people charge the aggravation of their miseries on Moses and Aaron, whose influence, instead of increasing rapidly, declines, and gives place to aversion and bitter reproaches. Yet the deliverers neither lose their courage nor depart from their holy assurance of success. The God of their fathers assumes that ineffable name, Jehovah (the Faithful and Unchangeable,) which the Jews dare not pronounce. That release, which they can not obtain by the fair means of persuasion, Moses and Aaron assert that they will extort by force from the reluctant king. Again they appear in the royal presence, having announced, it should seem, their pretensions to miraculous powers; and now commenced a contest, unequal it would at first appear, between two individuals of an enslaved people, and the whole skill, knowledge, or artifice of the Egyptian priesthood, whose sacred authority was universally acknowledged; their intimate acquaintance with all the secrets of nature extensive, their reputation for magical powers firmly established with the vulgar. The names of the principal opponents of Moses, Jannes and Jambres, are reported by St. Paul from Jewish traditions; and it is curious that in Pliny and Apuleius the names of Moses and Jannes are recorded as celebrated proficients in magical arts.

The contest began in the presence of the king. Aaron cast down his rod, which was instantaneously transformed into a serpent. The magicians performed the same feat. The dexterous tricks which the eastern and African jugglers play with serpents will easily account for this without any supernatural assistance. It might be done, either by adroitly substituting the serpent for the rod; or by causing the serpent to assume a stiff appearance like a rod or staff, which being cast down on the ground might become again pliant and animated. Aaron's serpent swallowed up the rest—a circumstance, however extraordinary, yet not likely to work conviction upon a people familiar with such feats, which they ascribed to magic.

Still the slaves had now assumed courage, their demands were more peremptory, their wonders more general and public. The plagues of Egypt, which successively afflicted the priesthood, the king, and almost every deity honored in their comprehensive pantheon,—which infected every element, and rose in terrific gradation, one above the other, now began. Pharaoh was standing on the brink of the sacred river, the great object of Egyptian adoration, not improbably in the performance of some ceremonial ablution, or making an offering to the native deity of the land. The leaders of the Israelites approached, and renewed their demand for freedom. It was rejected; and at once the holy river, with all the waters of the land, were turned to blood. The fish, many of which were objects of divine worship, perished. Still the priesthood were not yet baffled. The Egyptians having dug for fresh and pure water, in some of these artificial tanks or reservoirs, the magicians contrived to effect a similar change. As their holy abhorrence of blood would probably prevent them from discharging so impure a fluid into the new reservoirs, they might, without great difficulty, produce the appearance by some secret and chymical means. The waters of the Nile, it is well known, about their period of increase, usually assume a red tinge, either from the color of the Ethiopian soil, which is washed down, or from a number of insects of that color. Writers, who endeavor to account for these miracles by natural means, suppose that Moses took the opportunity of this periodical change to terrify the superstitious Egyptians. Yet, that Moses should place any reliance on, or the Egyptians feel the least apprehension at an ordinary occurrence which took place every year, seems little less incredible than the miracle itself. For seven days the god of the river was thus rebuked before the God of the stranger, instead of the soft and delicious water, spoken of by travelers as peculiarly grateful to the taste, the fœtid stream ran with that of which the Egyptians had the greatest abhorrence. To shed, or even to behold blood, was repugnant to all their feelings and prejudices. Still the king was inflexible, and from the sacred stream was derived the second plague. The whole land was suddenly covered with frogs. The houses, the chambers, even the places where they prepared their food, swarmed with these loathsome reptiles. It is undoubtedly possible that the corrupted waters might quicken the birth of these creatures, the spawn of which abounded in all the marshy and irrigated districts. Hence the priests would have no difficulty in bringing them forth in considerable numbers. The sudden cessation of this mischief at the prayer of Moses is by far the most extraordinary part of this transaction,—in one day all the frogs, except those in the river, were destroyed. So far the contest had been maintained without manifest advantage on either side. But the next plague reduced the antagonists of Moses to a more difficult predicament. With the priesthood the most scrupulous cleanliness was inseparable from their sanctity. These Bramins of Egypt, so fastidiously abhorrent of every kind of personal impurity that they shaved every part which might possibly harbor vermin, practised ablutions four times a-day, wore no garments but of the finest linen, because woollen might conceal either filth or insects, heard with the greatest horror, that the dirt had been changed into lice, and that this same vermin, thus called into existence, was spreading over the whole country. After a vain attempt, notwithstanding their prejudices, to imitate their opponent, they withdrew for the present from the contest. But the pride of the king was not yet broken, and the plagues followed in rapid and dreadful succession. Swarms of flies, or rather musquitoes, in unusual numbers covered the whole land: by the intercession of Moses they were dispersed. Next, all the cattle, of every description, were smitten with a destructive murrain, all but those of the Israelites, who were exempt from this as from the former calamity. This last blow might seem to strike not merely at the wealth, but at an important part of the religion of Egypt, their animal worship. The goat worshiped at Mendes, the ram at Thebes, the more general deity, the bull Apis, were perhaps involved in the universal destruction. Still this is by no means certain, as the plague seems to have fallen only on the animals which were in the open pastures; it is clear that the war-horses escaped. If this plague reached the deities, the next was aimed at the sacred persons of the priesthood, no less than at the meaner people. Moses took the ashes of the furnace, perhaps the brick-kiln in which the wretched slaves were laboring, cast them into the air, and where they fell the skin broke out in boils. The magicians, in terror and bodily anguish, fled away. It is impossible to read the following passage from Plutarch without observing so remarkable a coincidence between the significant action of Moses and the Egyptian rite, as to leave little doubt that some allusion was intended. "In the city of Eilithuia," as Manetho relates, calling them Typhonian, (as sacrificed to Typhon) "they burned men alive, and winnowing their ashes, scattered them in the air and dispersed them." The usual objects of these sacrifices were people with red hair, doubtless their old enemies the shepherds. Had any of the Israelites suffered in these horrid furnaces, it would add singular force and justice to the punishment inflicted on the priests and people. It would thus have been from the ashes of their own victims, that their skins were burning with insufferable agony, and breaking out into loathsome disease. The next plague, though in most tropical climates it would have been an ordinary occurrence, in Egypt was an event as unusual as alarming. All ancient and modern writers agree that rain, though by no means unknown, falls but seldom in that country. It appears to be rather less uncommon now than formerly. According to Herodotus it rained once at Thebes, and the circumstance excited general apprehension. "There, at present," says Belzoni, "two or three days of moderate rain generally occur during the winter." But lower down, in the part of the valley where these events took place, it is still an uncommon, though not an unprecedented phenomenon. Hasselquist saw it rain at Alexandria and other parts of the Delta: Pocock saw even hail at Faiume. Ordinarily however the Nile, with its periodical overflow and constant exhalations, supplies the want of the cool and refreshing shower. Now, according to the prediction of Moses, a tremendous tempest burst over the country. Thunder and hail, and fire mingled with the hail, "that ran upon the ground," rent the branches from the trees, and laid prostrate the whole harvest. From the cultivation of flax, Egypt possessed the great linen manufacture of the ancient world; on the barley the common people depended for their usual drink, the rich soil of Egypt in general being unfit for the vine. Both these crops were totally destroyed. The rye and the wheat, being later, escaped. This tempest must therefore have taken place at the beginning of March. By this time the inflexible obstinacy of the king began to fail; on the deliverance of the country from this dreadful visitation, he engaged to release the bondsmen. At the word of Moses the storm ceased. Still, to deprive the whole land of so valuable a body of slaves seemed too great a sacrifice to the policy, and too humiliating a concession to the pride of the monarch. To complete the desolation of the country, the corn lands were next laid waste by other means of destruction. The situation of Egypt usually secures the country from that worst enemy to the fertility of the Asiatic provinces, the locusts. As these insects fly in general from east to west, and can not remain on the wing for any length of time, the width of the Red Sea presents a secure barrier to their invasions.

Their dreadful ravage is scarcely exaggerated by the strong images of the prophets, particularly the sublime description in Joel. Where they alight, all vegetation at once disappears; not a blade of grass, not a leaf escapes them; the soil seems as if it were burnt up by fire; they obscure the sun as with a cloud; they cover sometimes a space of nine miles, and thus they march on in their regular files till "*the land which was as the garden of Eden before them, behind them is a desolate wilderness.*" Such was the visitation which came to glean the few remaining signs of the accustomed abundance of Egypt, spared by the tempest. A strong and regular east wind brought the fatal cloud from the Arabian shore, or, according to the Septuagint translation, a south wind from the regions of Abyssinia. The court now began to murmur at the unbending spirit of the king; on the intimation of this new calamity he had determined to come to terms. He offered to permit all the adults to depart, but insisted on retaining the children, either as hostages for the return of the parents, or in order to perpetuate a race of slaves for the future. Now he was for an instant inclined to yield this point; but when the west wind had driven these destroying ravagers into the sea, he recalled all his concessions, and continued steadfast in his former resolutions of resistance to the utmost. At length, therefore, their great divinity, the Sun, was to be put to shame before the God of the slave and the stranger. For three whole days, as Moses stretched his hand toward heaven, a darkness, described with unexampled force as a DARKNESS THAT MIGHT BE FELT, overspread the land; not merely was the sun unable to penetrate the gloom, and enlighten his favored land, but they could distinguish nothing, and were constrained to sit in awe-struck inactivity. The king would now gladly consent to the departure of the whole race, children as well as grown-up men; yet, as all the latter plagues, the flies, the murrain, the hail, the locusts, the darkness had spared the land of Goshen, the cattle of that district, in the exhausted state of the country, was invaluable; he demands that these should be surrendered as the price of freedom. "Our cattle also shall go with us, not a hoof shall be left behind," replies his inexorable antagonist. Thus, then, the whole kingdom of Egypt had been laid waste by successive calamities; the cruelty of the oppressors had been dreadfully avenged; all classes had suffered in the undiscriminating desolation. Their pride had been humbled; their most sacred prejudices wounded; the Nile had been contaminated; their dwellings polluted by loathsome reptiles; their cleanly persons defiled by vermin; their pure air had swarmed with troublesome insects; their cattle had perished by a dreadful malady; their bodies broken out with a filthy disease; their early harvest had been destroyed by the hail, the later by the locusts; an awful darkness had enveloped them for three days, but still the deliverance was to be extorted by a calamity more dreadful than all these. The Israelites will not depart poor and empty-handed; they will receive some compensation for their years of hard and cruel servitude; they levy on their awe-struck masters contributions in gold, silver, and jewels. Some, especially later writers, have supposed that they exacted these gifts by main force, and with arms in their hands. Undoubtedly, though the Israelites appear to have offered no resistance to the Egyptian horsemen and chariots which pursued them in the desert, they fight with the Amalekites, and afterward arrive, an armed people, on the borders of Canaan.

Josephus accounts for this, but not quite satisfactorily, by supposing that they got possession of the arms of the Egyptians, washed ashore after their destruction in the Red Sea. But the general awe and confusion are sufficient to explain the facility with which the Israelites collected these treasures. The slaves had become objects of superstitious terror; to propitiate them with gifts was natural, and their leader authorized their reception of all presents which might thus be offered. The night drew on, the last night of servitude to the people of Israel, a night of unprecedented horror to the ancient kingdom of Egypt. The Hebrews were employed in celebrating that remarkable rite, which they had observed for ages down to the present day. The Passover, the memorial that God passed over them when he destroyed the first born of all Egypt, has been kept under his significant name, and still is kept as the memorial of their deliverance from Egypt by every faithful descendant of Abraham. Each family has to sacrifice a lamb without blemish, to anoint their door-posts and the lintels of their houses with its blood, and to feast upon the remainder. The sacrifice was over, the feast concluded, when that dreadful event took place, which it would be presumptuous profanation to relate except in the words of the Hebrew annalist. "And it came to pass, that at midnight the Lord smote all the first-born in the land of Egypt, from the first-born of Pharaoh that sat on the throne, unto the first-born of the captive that was in the dungeon, and all the first-born of the cattle. And Pharaoh rose up in the night, he and all his servants, and all the Egyptians; and there was a great cry in Egypt, for there was not a house where there was not one dead." The horrors of this night may be better conceived, when we call to mind that the Egyptians were noted for the wild and frantic wailings with which they lamented their dead. Screaming women rush about with disheveled hair, troops of people assemble in tumultuous commiseration around the house, where a single corpse is laid out—and now every house and every family had its victim. Hebrew tradition has increased the horror of the calamity, asserting that the temples were shaken, the idols overthrown, the sacred animals, chosen as the first-born, involved in the universal destruction. While every household of Egypt was occupied in its share of the general calamity, the people of Israel, probably drawn together during the suspension of all labor, caused by the former calamities, or assembled in Goshen to celebrate the new national festival already organized by a sort of discipline among the separate tribes; with all their flocks and herds, with sufficient provisions for an immediate supply, and with the booty they had extorted from their masters stood prepared as one man for the signal of departure. During the night the permission, or rather entreaty, that they would instantly evacuate the country, arrived, yet no one stirred before the morning, perhaps apprehensive lest the slaughter be attributed to them, or in religious fear of encountering the angel of destruction. The Egyptians became only anxious to accelerate their departure, and thus the Hebrew people set forth to seek a land of freedom, bearing with them the bones of their great ancestor, Joseph. Their numbers not reckoning the strangers who followed them, most of whom probably fell off during the march, amounted to 600,000 adults, which, according to the usual calculations, would give the total sum of the people at 2,500,000 or 3,000,000*

From the point of reunion, at which the several bodies had collected, Rameses, probably another name for Goshen, the borders of Canaan might have been reached, even by so great a multitude, in a few weeks. Two routes led to Canaan; one northward near the sea, but this was occupied by the Philistines, a very warlike people, with whom the Israelites were not yet sufficiently disciplined to contest their passage. The other passed immediately round the head of the western branch of the Red Sea, coming upon part of the modern track of caravans from Cairo to Suez.

Their first march was to Succoth, originally a place of tents, and which probably afterward grew up into a village. Josephus considers it the same with Latopolis. From Succoth they advanced to Etham, by some supposed to be a castle or small town at the extreme point of the Red Sea, by Jablonski derived with great probability from an Egyptian word signifying the termination of the sea. Here they were on the borders of the desert; should they once advance to any distance in that sandy and barren region they were safe from pursuit; the chariots of Egypt, or even the horsemen, would scarcely follow them far on a track only suited for the camel, and where the want of water, the fountains being already consumed by the flying enemy, would effectually delay the advances of a large army. On a sudden the march of the Israelites is altered; instead of pressing rapidly onward, keeping the sea on their right hand, and so heading the gulf, they strike to the south, with the sea on their left, and deliberately encamp at no great distance from the shore, at a place called Pi-hahiroth, explained by some the mouth or opening into the mountains. This, however, as well as much more learned etymology, by which the site of Migdol and Baalzephon, as well as Pi-hahiroth, has been fixed, must be considered very uncertain. The king, recovered from his panic, and receiving intelligence that the Israelites had no thoughts of return, determined on pursuit: intelligence of this false movement, or at least of this unnecessary delay on the part of the Israelites, encouraged his hopes of vengeance. The great caste of the warriors, the second in dignity, were regularly quartered in certain cities on the different frontiers of the kingdom, so that a considerable force could be mustered on any emergency. With great rapidity he drew together 600 war chariots, and a multitude of others, with their full equipment of officers. In the utmost dismay the Israelites beheld the plain behind them glittering with the hostile array; before them lay the sea, on the right impracticable passes. Resistance does not seem to have entered their thoughts; they were utterly ignorant of military discipline; perhaps unarmed, and encumbered with their families and their flocks and herds. *Because there were no graves in Egypt*, they exclaimed, in the bitterness of their despair, *hast thou taken us away to die in the wilderness?* Their leader alone preserved his calmness and self-possession, and an unexpected incident gave temporary relief to their apprehensions. A remarkable pillar, of cloud by day and fire by night, had preceded their march; it now suddenly shifts its position, and stations itself in the rear, so as to conceal their movements from the enemy, showing the dark side to them, while the bright one gave light to the Hebrew camp. But this could not avail them long; they could hear, at still diminishing distance, the noise of the advancing chariots, and the cries of vengeance from the infuriated Egyptians. On a sudden Moses advances toward the sea, extends his rods, and a violent wind from the east begins to blow. The waters recede on both sides, a way appears; at nightfall, probably about eight o'clock, the caravan begins to defile along this awful pass. The wind continued in the same quarter all the night; but immediately they had passed over, and while the Egyptians, madly plunging after them, were in the middle of the passage, the wind as suddenly fell, the waters rushed back into their bed, the heavy chariot-wheels of the pursuers sank into the sand, broke and overthrew the chariots, and in this state of confusion the sea swept over the whole host, and overwhelmed the king and all the flower of the Egyptian army. Such is the narrative of Moses, which writers of all ages have examined, and, according to the bias of their minds, have acknowledged or denied the miraculous agency, increased or diminished its extent. At an early period, historians (particularly in Egypt) hostile to the Jews, asserted that Moses, well acquainted with the tides of the Red Sea, took advantage of the ebb, and passed over his army, while the incautious Egyptians, attempting to follow, were surprised by the flood and perished. Yet, after every concession, it seems quite evident that, without one particular wind, the ebb tide, even in the narrowest part of the channel, could not be kept back long enough to allow a number of people to cross in safety. We have then the alternative of supposing, that a man of the consummate prudence and sagacity, and the local knowledge, attributed to Moses, altered, suspended, or at least did not hasten his march, and thus deliberately involved the people, whom he had rescued at so much pains and risk, in the danger of being overtaken by the enemy, led back as slaves, or massacred, on the chance that an unusually strong wind would blow at a particular hour, for a given time, so as to keep back the flood, then die away and allow the tide to return at the precise instant when the Egyptians were in the middle of their passage.

Different opinions, as to the place where the passage was effected, have likewise been supported with ingenuity and research. The one carries the Israelites nearly seventy miles down the western shore of the sea, to Bedea, where it

*The question of the numbers will be discussed in a future note.

is said that an inlet, now dry, ran up a defile in the mountains; that in this defile, the opening of which was the Pihahiroth of Moses, and which ended in this inlet of the sea called, according to the advocates of this hypothesis, Clusma, the Israelites were caught as in what is commonly called a cul-de-sac. Here, however, the sea is nearly twelve miles broad, and the time is insufficient to allow so great a multitude to pass over, particularly if they did not, as some Jewish writers suppose, send their families and cattle round the head of the gulf. The other hypothesis rests chiefly on the authority of the Danish traveler Niebuhr, who had investigated the question on the spot. He supposes that the passage was effected near the modern Suez, which occupies the site of an old castle, called by the Arabians al Kolsum, a name apparently derived from the Greek Klusma. Here Niebuhr himself forded the sea, which is about two miles across, but he asserts confidently that the channel must formerly have been much deeper, and that the gulf extended much farther to the north, than at present. The intelligent Burckhardt adopts the views of Niebuhr. Here besides that the sea is so much narrower, the bottom is flat and sandy; lower down it is full of sharp coral rocks, and sea-weed in such large quantities, that the whole gulf is called by a name, *Al Souf*, which signifies the weedy sea. Still, wherever the passage was effected, the Mosaic account cannot fairly be made consistent with the exclusion of preternatural agency. Not to urge the literal meaning of the waters being a wall on the right hand and on the left, as if they had stood up sheer and abrupt, and then fallen back again; the Israelites passed through the sea with deep water on both sides; and any ford between two bodies of water must have been passable only for a few people at one precise point of time. All comparisons, therefore, to marches like that of Alexander, cited by Josephus idly, and in his worst spirit of compromise, are entirely inapplicable. That bold general took the opportunity of the receding tide to conduct his army round a bluff headland in Pamphylia, called Climax, where, during high water, there was no beach between the cliffs and the sea. But what would this or any other equally daring measures in the history of war, be to the generalship of Moses, who must thus have decoyed his enemy to pursue him to the banks of the sea, and so nicely calculated the time, that the lowest ebb should be exactly at the hour of his greatest danger, while the whole of the pursuing army should be so infatuated, and so ignorant of the tides, as to follow them without any apprehension of the returning flood? In this case Moses would appear as formidable a rival to the military fame of Alexander, as to the legislative wisdom of Solon or Lycurgus.

This great event was not only preserved in the annals of the Jewish people, it was likewise, as might be expected, the great subject of their national poetry. But none of their later bards surpassed, or perhaps equaled, the hymn which Moses, their bard as well as their leader and lawgiver, composed on the instant of their deliverance, and which was solemnly chanted to the music of the timbrel. What is the Roman arch of triumph, or the pillar crowded with sculpture, compared, as a memorial, to the Hebrew song of victory, which, having survived so many ages, is still fresh and vivid as ever; and excites the same emotions of awe and piety in every human breast susceptible of such feelings, which it did so many ages past in those of the triumphant children of Israel.

Local traditions have retained the remembrance of the same memorable catastrophe, if not with equal fidelity. The superstitious Arabs still call fountains or wells by the names of Moses and Pharaoh. The whole coast is looked on with awe. Whenever, says Niebuhr, you ask an Arab where the Egyptians were drowned, he points to the part of the shore where you are standing. There is one bay, however, where in the roaring of the waters they pretend to hear the cries and wailings of the ghosts of Pharaoh's army. If these were mere modern notions, they would be of little value; but Diodorus Siculus states as a tradition derived by the Icthyophagi (the people who live on fish), from their remote forefathers, that once an extraordinary reflux took place, the channel of the gulf became dry, the green bottom appearing, and the whole body of water rolling away in an opposite direction. After the dry land in the deepest part had been seen, an extraordinary flood tide came in, and restored the whole channel to its former state.

The history of the Jewish Exodus, or deliverance from Egypt under the directions of Moses, was undoubtedly preserved in the Egyptian records, and from thence was derived the strange and disfigured story which we read in Diodorus, Strabo, Justin, and Tacitus. Unfortunately, the ancient enmity between the Egyptian and Hebrew people was kept alive by the civil, religious, and literary dissensions and jealousies under the reign of the Ptolemies in Alexandria. Josephus, in his treatise against Apion, has extracted the contradictory accounts of his ancestors, from three Egyptian historians, Manetho, Chæremon, and Lysimachus. In each of these there is the same attempts to identify or connect the Jews with the earlier shepherd-kings, the objects of peculiar detestation to the Egyptian people. So much is their history interwoven, that some learned writers, probably Josephus himself, considered the whole account of the fierce and conquering shepherds a fable, built on the history of the Israelites. He states, though in somewhat ambiguous terms, that in another copy of Manetho the word Hyksos, usually translated shepherd-kings, was also rendered shepherd-captives. Yet the Egyptian monuments seem conclusively to prove the existence of this distinct and savage race of conquerors. In other points the Egyptian accounts are equally contradictory, they confound or associate together at one time Osarsiph (Joseph) and Moses. All agree in describing the Jews as a people of lepers, a disease to which, notwithstanding the indignation of Josephus, they were in all likelihood very subject. The wise precautions of the Lawgiver against the malady prove its prevalence. Quarantine laws are only strictly enforced where there is great danger of the plague.

There are other points of Jewish history where their ignorance or misrepresentation is unquestionable. They ascribe to Moses, or even to the earlier shepherds, the foundation of Jerusalem and its temple. The testimony of the Jews, unsuspicious at least on this point, shows that they were not in possession of Jerusalem till the reign of David, and that down to that period it was nothing more than a hillfort, inhabited by the Canaanites. In short, the whole history betrays the controversialist of a much later period, working on materials so obscure and imperfect, as easily to be disfigured and distorted by national animosity. Still these traditions are not without their value; they confirm the plain leading facts of the Mosaic narrative, the residence of the Hebrews in Egypt, their departure under the guidance of Moses, and the connexion of that departure with some signal calamity, at least for a time, fatal to the power and humiliating to the pride of Egypt.

BOOK III.

THE DESERT.

The March—Mount Sinai—Delivery of the Law—The Tabernacle.—The Law

THUS free and triumphant the whole people of Israel set forth upon their pilgrimage toward the promised land, a land described in the most glowing language as flowing with milk and honey. But at present an arid and thirsty desert lay before them, long levels of sand or uneven stony ground broken by barren ridges of rugged mountains, with here and there a green spot where a few palm-trees overshadowed a spring of running water. Extraordinary as it may seem, we can almost trace their march, at least in its earlier stations; for, while the face of cultivated countries and the manners of civilized nations are in a perpetual state of change, the desert and its inhabitants are alike unalterable. The same wild clans pitch their tents in the same valleys, where waters which neither fail nor increase give nourishment to about the same extent of vegetation. After three days' march through the wilderness of Shur, the Israelites reached the well of Marah, but here a grievous disappointment awaited them. As they rushed to slake their burning lips in the stream, they found it, unlike the soft and genial waters of the Nile, so bitter that it could not be drunk. From Ajoun Mousa (the wells of Moses), near the part of the sea where Niebuhr supposes that the passage was made, the observant and accurate Burckhardt traveled in 15 hours and a quarter (a good three days' march for a whole people like the Israelites) to a well called Howara, "the water of which is so bitter, that men cannot drink it: and even camels, if not very thirsty, refuse to take it." The spring was sweetened by the branch of a tree, which Moses, by divine direction, cast into it, whether from the natural virtue of the plant seems uncertain. A plant with this property is indicated in the papers of Forskal, who traveled with Niebuhr as botanist, and is said to be known in the East Indies. Burckhardt suggests the berry of the Gharkad, a shrub which grows in the neighborhood.* From hence the caravan passed on to Elim, which all travelers place in the valley of Girondel or Gharondel. Here they rested under the shade of seventy palm-trees, with twelve springs of water bubbling up around them. Nine out of the twelve wells still remain, and the palm-trees have spread out into a beautiful grove. The natives pointed out to Shaw a spot called Hummun Mousa, where the household of Moses are said to have pitched their tents. In this delightful resting-place, the nation reposed for a month; and then set forth again, not in the direction of Palestine, but towards that mysterious mountain where the Almighty had first made himself known to Moses. Their route lay at no great distance from the sea, several of the valleys which it crossed led down to the shore; at the end of one of these, probably that called by Burckhardt the Wady Taybe, they halted on the beach. From thence they struck into the wilderness, but by this time their provisions totally failed, and the dreadful prospect of erishing by famine in this barren and thirsty desert arose before their eyes. Of all human miseries, both in apprehension and reality, to die slowly of hunger, and to see others, to whom we can afford no assistance, die around us, is undoubtedly the worst. The Israelites began to look back to Egypt, where, if they suffered toil and oppression, at least they never wanted food. All was forgotten, the miracles wrought in their favor, the promises of divine protection, the authority of their leader. Murmurs of discontent spread through the camp, till at length the whole body broke out into open remonstrances. But their Almighty Protector had not abandoned them; and in his name, without hesitation, Moses promised an immediate and plentiful supply. In the spring of the year, quails, migratory birds, pass in large flocks over the Arabian peninsula; they are very heavy on the wing, and their line of flight depends much on the direction of the wind. A cloud of these birds was suddenly wafted over the camp of the Israelites, and fell around them in immense numbers. Nor was this all, in the morning, exactly as Moses had foretold, the ground was covered with manna. This is now clearly ascertained by Seetzen and Burckhardt, to be a natural production; it distils from the thorns of the tamarisk, in the month of June. It is still collected by the Arabs before sunrise, when it is coagulated, but it dissolves as soon as the sun shines upon it. "Its taste is agreeable, somewhat aromatic, and as sweet as honey. It may be kept for a year, and is only found after a wet season." It is still called by the Bedouins "mann." The quantity now collected, for it is only found in a few valleys, is very small; the preternatural part therefore of the Mosaic narrative consists in the immense and continual supply, and the circumstances under which it was gathered; particularly its being preserved firm and sweet only for the Sabbath-day. The regulation that enough, and only enough for the consumption of the day should be collected at a time, seems a prudent precaution, enforced by the remarkable provision that no one found that he had collected more or less than an omer, lest the more covetous or active should attempt to secure an unfair proportion, and deprive the rest of their share.

After two other resting-places, at Dophkah and Alush, the Israelites arrived at the foot of that awful mountain already sanctified by the presence of their Almighty Creator. But a new calamity, not less insupportable than famine, the want of water, called forth new discontents and murmurs. So great was the excitement that the life of Moses was endangered. He cried unto the Lord, saying, "What shall I do unto this people, they be almost ready to stone me."

By the divine command, in the presence of the assembled elders, and with the rod with which he before struck the Nile, Moses smote the rock, and water flowed forth; the place was called Massah and Meribar, from the discontents of the people. Here, likewise their fortitude, as well as their faith and patience, was put to the trial. The camp was suddenly surrounded by one of the wild, marauding clans, the Amalekites or, according to Josephus, by a confederacy of all the sheiks of the desert, determined to exterminate these invaders of their territory.

Moses delegates the military command to Joshua who afterward conducted their armies to the conquest of Canaan. He himself, with his brother Aaron and Hur, takes his station on an eminence; there, in the sight of the entire army, he raises his hands in earnest supplication to heaven. The Israelites, encouraged by their trust in Divine protection, fight manfully. Still the attack is fierce, long, and obstinate. The strength of Moses fails, and the Israelites behold with alarm and trepidation his arms hanging languidly down, and their courage too begins to give way. His companions, observing this, place him on a stone, and support his hands on each side. The valor of the people revives, and they gain a complete victory. This wanton and unprovoked aggression gave rise to a perpetual hereditary feud between the tribes; the Amalekites were devoted to eternal and implacable hostility.

The fame of these successes reached the pastoral chieftain whose daughter Moses had married. Jethro joins the camp with Zipporah the wife, and Gershom and Eliezer the sons of Moses. He is received with great respect, and by his prudent advice the Jewish leader proceeds to organize the body of his people under more regular and effective discipline. Hitherto the whole burden of the religious and civil affairs had rested on himself: he had been the sole leader,, sole judge, and sole interpreter of the Divine will. He withdraws into the more remote and sacred character, leaving the common and daily affairs to be administered by the officers, appointed in regular subordination over the subdivisions of the whole people, into tens, fifties, hundreds, and thousands. These arrangements completed, the Israelites wind along the defiles of this elevated region, till at length they come to the foot of the loftiest peak in the whole ridge, that of Sinai. Here, after the most solemn preparations, and under the most terrific circumstances, the great lawgiver of the Jews delivered that singular constitution to his people, which presupposed their possession of a rich and fertile territory in which as yet they had not occupied an acre, but had been wandering in an opposite direction, and not even approached its borders.

The laws of a settled and civilized community were enacted among a wandering and homeless horde who were traversing a wilderness, and more likely, under their existing circumstances, to sink below the pastoral life of their forefathers, than advance to the rank of an industrious agricultural community. Yet, at this time, judging solely from its internal evidence, the law must have been enacted. Who but Moses ever possessed such authority as to enforce submission to statutes so severe and uncompromising? yet as Moses incontestibly died before the conquest of Canaan, his legislature must have taken place in the desert. To what other period can the Hebrew constitution be assigned? To that of the judges? a time of anarchy, warfare or servitude! To that of the kings? when the republic had undergone a total change! To any time after Jerusalem became the metropolis? when the holy city, the pride and glory of the nation, is not even alluded to in the whole law! After the building of the temple? when it is equally silent as to any settled or durable edifice! After the separation of the kingdoms? when the close bond of brotherhood had given place to implacable hostility! Under Hilkiah? under Ezra? when a great number of statutes had become a dead letter!

The law depended on a strict and equitable partition of the land. At a later period it could not have been put into practice without the forcible resumption of every individual property by the state; the difficulty, or rather impossibility, of such a measure, may be estimated by any reader, who is not entirely unacquainted with the history of the ancient republics. In other respects, the law breathes the air of the desert. Enactments intended for a people with settled habitations, and dwelling in walled cities, are mingled up with temporary regulations, only suited to the Bedouin encampment of a nomad tribe. There can be no doubt that the statute book of Moses, with all his particular enactments, still exists, and that it recites them in the same order, if it may be called order, in which they were promulgated.

First, however, must be related the circumstances under which the Hebrew constitution was enacted. The Israelites had been accustomed only to the level of the Egyptian valley, or to the gentle slopes which skirted the pastures of Goshen; they had been traveling over the flat sands or moderate inequalities of the desert; the entrance into a wild and rugged mountainous region, the peaks of which were lost in the clouds, must in itself have excited awful and appalling emotions. How much more so, when these high and frowning precipices had been haunted by the presence of their God! Their leader departs alone to the unseen, and apparently inaccessible, summit of the mountain. He returns bearing a message from their God, which, while it asserts his universal dominion over the earth, proclaims his selection of the Israelites from all the nations, as his peculiar people; they were to be to the rest of mankind what the great caste of the Egyptian priesthood was to the other classes of that community. The most solemn purifications are enjoined, a line is drawn and fenced at the foot of the mountain, which, on pain of death, they are not to transgress. It is announced, that on the third day the presence of the Almighty will display itself. On the third day the whole people are assembled in trembling expectation; the summit of the mountain appears clothed in the thickest darkness, tremendons thunders and lightnings, phenomena new to the sheperds of Goshen, whose pastures had escaped the preternatural tempest in Egypt, burst forth, and the terrors are heightened by a wild sound, like that of a trumpet, mingling with, and prolonging, the terrific din of the tempest. The mountain seems to have shown every appearance of a volcanic eruption; blazing fires, huge columns of smoke, convulsions of the earth. Yet a most philosphical observer has decided, from the geological formation of the mountain, that it has never been subject to the agency of internal fire. The dauntless leader takes his stand in the midst of this confusion of the elements; the trumpet peals still louder, and is answered by a voice distinct and audible, but from whence it proceeded no man knew. It summons Moses to the top of the mountain; he returns, and still more earnestly enjoins the people not to break through the prescribed limits. Immediately on his dsecent, the mysterious voice utters those ten precepts usually called the Decalogue, a summary, or rather the first principles, of the whole law. The precautions of Moses to restrain the curiosity or presumption of the people were scarcely necessary. Their fears are too highly excited; instead of approaching the sacred summit of the mountain, they retire in terror from the place where they were assembled, and entreat that from henceforth they may receive the will of God, not directly, but through Moses, their acknowledged representative. Moses again enters into the darkness, and returns with another portion of the law. The assent of the people to these leading principles of their constitution is then demanded, religious rites are performed, twelve alters raised, one for each tribe; sacrifice is offered, the law read, and the covenant between God, the lawgiver, and the whole people, solemnly ratified by sprinkling them with the blood of the sacrifice. Moses again ascends the mountain, accompanied this time by Aaron, Nadab, and Abihu, who were selected for the priestly office, and by seventy elders of Israel. All these remained at a respectful distance; yet, it is said, they saw the God of Israel; it should seem, the symbolic fire which indicated his presence, beneath which was what appeared like a pavement of lapis-lazuli, or sapphire, or the deep blue of the clearest and most cloudless heaven. Delegating the charge of the people to the elders, to Aaron, and Hur, Moses once more ascended into the cloud, which was now at times illuminated with the glory of the Lord, *like a devouring fire*. Forty days he remained on the mountain, neither appearing nor holding any communication with the people. Day after day they expected his return: the gloom and silence of the mountain remained unbroken. Had he perished? Had he abandoned the people? Aaron himself is in the same total ignorance as to the designs and the fate of his brother. Whither shall they wander in the trackless desert? Who shall guide them? Their leader and their God seem equally to have deserted them. Still utterly at a loss to comprehend the sublime notions of the Deity, which their leader would inculcate, they sink back to the superstitions of the country which they had left. They imperiously demand, and Aaron consents to cast an image of gold, similar to the symbolic representation of the great god of the Egyptians, under the form of an ox or calf, and they begin to celebrate this new deity with all the noise, tumult and merriment of an Egyptian festival. When their leader descends he sees the whole people dancing in their frantic adoration around the idol. In the first excess of indignation he casts down and breaks the stone tablets, on which the law was inscribed. He seizes the image, which was most likely of small dimensions, though raised on a lofty pole, commands it to be ground or dissolved to powder, throws it into the neighboring fountain, and forces the people to drink the water impregnated with its dust. A more signal punishment awaits this heinous breach of the covenant. The tribe of Levi espouse the cause of God, fall upon the people, slay the offenders, without regard to kindred or relationship, till 3,000 men lie dead upon the field. The national crime thus dreadfully atoned, the intercourse between the law-giver and the Deity is renewed.* Yet the offended God still threatens to withdraw his own visible presence, during their approaching invasion of Canaan, that presence which he had before promised should attend on their armies, and discomfit their enemies; he disclaims them as his people, and gives them over to the tutelar protection of *his angel*.

* Josephus jealous of the national character, omits this hole scene.

Already, before the construction of the great tabernacle, there had been a tent set apart for public urposes; where the councils of the leaders had been held, and, most probably, sacrifices performed. This tent Moses removed beyond the polluted precincts of the camp: no sooner had this been done, than the Deity appeared suddenly to return; the people, standing before their tents, beheld the cloud of glory taking up its station at the door of the tabernacle into which Moses had entered. They bowed down at once in awe-struck adoration, while their God and their leader held their secret council within the tent. Within the tent a scene took place which it is best to relate in the language of the sacred writer. Moses, having obtained the promise of divine protection for the people, addresses the Almighty visitant—"I beseech thee show me thy glory," that is, make me acquainted with the essence of the divine nature. And God said, "I will make all my goodness pass before thee, and I will proclaim the name of the Lord before thee." "And he said, Thou canst not see my face: for there shall no man see me, and live." Mortal man cannot comprehend the divine nature; but afar off, and overshadowed by my protection, thou shalt be favored with some farther revelation of the great Creator. On the re-ascent of Moses to the mountain with two new tablets of stone, this promise is thus fulfilled,—"The Lord passed by before him, and proclaimed,—the Lord, the Lord God, merciful and gracious, long-suffering and abundant in goodness and truth, keeping mercy for thousands, forgiving iniquity and transgression and sin, and that will by no means clear (the guilty), visiting the iniquity of the fathers upon the children, and upon the children's children unto the third and to the fourth generation." Such were the notions of the Divinity, taught to a barbarous nation in that remote period of the world! Forty days longer the lawgiver remained in secret conference with God upon the mountain. On his descent with new tables of stone, the awe-struck people beheld his countenance so radiant and dazzling that he was obliged to cover it with a veil; but it is not quite clear, whether or not after that period, like several of the oriental conquerors, he was constantly shrouded with this veil, excepting when he went into the tabernacle to communicate with God.

These pure and abstract notions of the Divinity were beyond the age and the people of Moses. No religious impressions would be lasting which were not addressed to the senses. With this view is commenced the sacred tabernacle or pavilion-temple, which hereafter is to occupy the central place of honor, that usually assigned to the king or chieftain of a nomadic horde. The whole nation is called upon to contribute to its construction and ornament. The riches which they brought from Egypt, and the arts which some of them had learned, now come into request. From all quarters offerings pour in; brass, silver, gold, jewels, fine linen, embroidered stuffs of all colors, valuable skins, spices, oils, and incense, in such profusion that they can not all be brought into use. The high district immediately around Sinai, extending about thirty miles in diameter, is by no means barren, the vegetation is richer than in other parts of the desert, streams of water flow in the valleys, date and other trees abound, and groves, chiefly of the black acacia (the shittim.) These latter were speedily felled, all the artificers set to work, the women were employed in weaving and spinning, and the whole camp assumed a busy appearance. The construction of the tabernacle was intrusted to the superintendence of two skilful workmen, Bezaleel and Aholiab. The area, or open space in which the tabernacle stood, was an oblong square, 175 feet long by 87½ wide. The enclosure was made by twenty brazen pillars on the north and south sides, ten to the west, and six to the east, where the gate of entrance stood. The capitals of these pillars were of silver; the hooks and the rods, from which the curtains hung, of silver. The curtains were of fine linen or cotton, woven in a kind of network; the curtain before the entrance was of richer materials and more brilliant colors, blue, purple, and scarlet, supported by four pillars, which do not seem to have been different from the other six that formed the eastern line of the court. Within the court before the tabernacle stood a great laver of brass, for the purpose of ablution, and the altar of burnt-offerings, measuring eight feet and three quarters each way, five feet and a quarter high. The altar was overlaid with brass, and had a grate of brass in the centre. It stood before the gate of the tabernacle.

The tabernacle itself was fifty-two feet and a half long, seventeen and a half wide, and the same high. It was made with planks of shittim wood, skilfully fitted and held together by poles which ran the whole length through golden rings. The planks were overlaid with gold. To defend it from the weather it was hung without with curtains of a kind of canvass, made of goat's hair, and over the whole was thrown an awning of skins.

The interior of the tabernacle was hung with curtains of the finest linen and the richest colors, embroidered with the mysterious figures called cherubim. The tabernacle was divided into two unequal parts: the first, or holy place, thirty-five feet long; in this stood the golden candlestick, the golden altar of incense, the table of show bread. The second, or Holy of Holies, seventeen feet and a half in length, was parted off by a veil of the same costly materials and splendid colors with the rest of the hangings, and suspended by hooks of gold from four wooden pillars likewise overlaid with gold.

A solemn gloom, unless when the veil was partially lifted, prevailed in the Holy of Holies; in the holy place the altar was constantly fed with costly incense, and the splendid chandelier with seven branches, wrought with knosps and flowers, illuminated the chamber, into which daylight never entered.

Within the most sacred precinct, which was

only entered by the High Priest, stood nothing but the Ark or coffer of wood, plated all over with gold, and surmounted by two of those emblematic figures, the cherubim, usually represented as angels under human forms, but more probably, like the Egyptian sphinx, animals purely imaginary and symbolic, combining different parts, and representing the noblest qualities of the man, the lion, the eagle, and the ox. They stood face to face at each extremity of the ark, and spread their golden wings so as to form a sort of canopy or throne. In the ark were deposited the two tablets of stone, on which the law was written.

The priests, who were to minister in this sumptuous pavilion-temple, were likewise to have *holy garments for glory and for beauty.* Aaron and his sons were designated for this office. The High Priest wore, first a tunic of fine linen, which fitted close, and without a fold, to his person, with loose trousers of linen; over this is a robe of blue, woven in one piece, without sleeves, with a hole through which the head passed, likewise fitted close round the neck with a rich border, and reached to the feet, where the lower rim was hung with pomegranates and little bells of gold, which sounded as he moved. Over this again was the ephod, made of blue, purple, and scarlet thread, twisted with threads of gold. It consisted of two pieces, one hanging behind, the other before, perhaps like a herald's tabard. From the hinder one, which hung much lower, came a rich girdle, passing under the arms and fastened over the breast. It had two shoulder-pieces, in which were two large beryl stones, set in gold, on which the names of the twelve tribes were engraved. From these shoulder-pieces came two gold chains, which fastened the pectoral or breast-plate; a piece of cloth of gold a span square, in which twelve precious stones were set in four rows, each engraved with the name of one of the tribes. Two other chains from the lower corners fastened the breast-plate to the lower part of the ephod.

In the breast-plate was placed the mysterious Urim and Thummim, the nature of which was so well known to the Jews as to require no explanation—to us remains mere matter of conjecture. The most probable opinion seems, that the two words mean Light and Perfection, and were nothing more than the twelve bright and perfect stones set in the breast-plate, emblematic of the union and consent of the whole nation, without which the high priest might not presume to interrogate the oracle of God. If the oracle was given by the Urim and Thummim itself, it seems not improbable, that the stones appearing bright or clouded might signify the favor or disfavor of the Almighty; but it is more likely that the oracle was delivered by a voice from the sanctuary. It is a remarkable coincidence, that the Egyptian high priest, according to Diodorus and Ælian, wore round his neck, by a golden chain, a sapphire gem, with an image representing truth. The head-dress of the priest was a rich turban of fine linen, on the front of which appeared a golden plate, inscribed "Holiness to the Lord."

Such were the first preparations for the religious ceremonial of the Jews. As this tall and sumptuous pavilion rose in the midst of the coarse and lowly tents of the people, their God seemed immediately to take possession of the structure raised to his honor. All the day the cloud, all the night the pillar of fire rested on the tabernacle. When the camp broke up, it rose and led the way; when the people came to their resting place, it remained unmoved.

Thus the great Jehovah was formally and deliberately recognised by the people of Israel as their God—the sole object of their adoration. By the law, to which they gave their free and unconditional assent, he became their king, the head of their civil constitution, and the feudal lord of all their territory, of whom they were to hold their lands on certain strict, but equitable terms of vassalage. Hence the Mosaic constitution, of which we proceeded to give a brief outline, was in its origin and principles entirely different from every human polity. It was a federal compact, not between the people at large and certain members or classes of the community designated as the rulers, between the Founder of the state, the proprietor of the land which they were to inhabit, and the Hebrew nation, selected from the rest of the world for some great ulterior purpose. The Hebrews were not a free and independent people entering into a primary contract in what manner their country was to be governed, they had neither independence nor country but as the free gift of their sovereign. The tenure by which they held all their present and future blessings, freedom from bondage, the inheritance of the land flowing with milk and honey, the promise of unexampled fertility, was their faithful discharge of their trust, the preservation of the great religious doctrine, the worship of the one great Creator. *Hear, therefore, O Israel, and observe to do it that it may be well with thee, and that ye may increase mightily, as the Lord God of thy fathers hath promised thee, in the land flowing with milk and honey. Hear O, Israel,* THE LORD OUR GOD IS ONE LORD. Thus the rights of the sovereign, not merely as God, but as the head of the state, or theocracy, were anterior to the rights of the people—the well-being of the community, the ultimate end of human legislation, was subordinate and secondary to the great purpose for which the Jews existed as a separate community.

Hence, any advantage to be derived from foreign commerce, or a larger intercourse with the neighboring tribes, wealth, or the acquisition of useful arts, could not for an instant come into competition with the danger of relapsing into polytheism. This was the great national peril, as well as the great national crime. By this they annulled their compact with their sovereign, and forfeited their title to the promised land. Yet by what legal provisions was the happiness of any people, *suasi bona nôrint,* so bountifully secured as by the Jewish constitution? A country under a delicious climate, where the corn-fields, the pastures, the vineyards, and olive-grounds vied with each other in fertility; perfect freedom and equality; a mild and parental government, the administration of justice by local authorities according to a written law; national festivals tending to promote national union;—had the people duly appreciated the blessings attached to the strict and permanent observance of their constitution, poets might have found their golden age in the plains of Galilee and the valleys of Judea.

The fundamental principle of the Jewish constitution, the purity of worship, was guarded by penal statutes; and by a religious ceremonial, admirably adapted to the age and to the genius of the people, and even accommodated, as far as possible, to their previous nomadic and Egyptian habits and feelings. The penal laws were stern and severe, for idolatry was two-fold treason—against the majesty of the sovereign, and the well-being of the state. The permanence of the national blessings depended on the integrity of the national faith. Apostacy in the single city, or the individual, brought, as far as was in their power, the curse of barrenness, defeat, famine or pestilence, on the whole land. It was repressed with the most unrelenting severity. If any city was accused of this anti-national crime, and after strict and diligent investigation was found guilty of setting up false gods for public worship, the inhabitants were to be put to the sword; no living thing, not even the cattle, spared; the whole spoil was to be collected in a heap and burned, (a wise regulation, lest an opulent community should be unjustly accused and laid waste for the purpose of plunder,) the whole city to be set on fire, razed to the ground, and the strongest anathema pronounced against any one who should attempt to rebuild it.—Deut. xiii. 13—18. To convict an individual of idolatry, the testimony of two witnesses was required; if condemned, he was publicly stoned to death—the two witnesses were to cast the first stone. Idolatry was of two kinds: 1st, image worship, or the representation of the one great Creator under the similitude or symbolic likeness of any created being. The history of all religion shows the danger of this practice. The representative symbol remains after its meaning is forgotten; and thus the most uncouth and monstrous forms, originally harmless emblems of some attribute belonging to the divinity, become the actual deities of the vulgar worship.

2d. The substitution, or what was more usual, the association of other gods with the one great God of their fathers. The religion of the natives, in whose territory the Israelites were about to settle, appears to have been a depravation of the purer Tsabaism, or worship of the host of heaven. On this primitive form of idolatry had gradually been engrafted a system of rites absurd, bloody, or licentious. Among the Canaanites human sacrifices were common—babes were burnt alive to Moloch. The inland tribes, the Moabites and Midianites, worshiped that obscene symbol, which originally represented the generative influence of the sun, but had now become a distinct divinity. The chastity of their women was the offering most acceptable to Baal Peor, or the Lord Peor. It was this inhuman and loathsome religion which was to be swept away from the polluted territory of Palestine by the exterminating conquest of the Jews; against the contagion of these abominations they were to be secured by the most rigid penal statutes, and by capital punishments summary and without appeal.

All approximation to these horrible usages was interdicted with equal severity. The Canaanites had no enclosed temples, their rites were performed in consecrated or open spaces on the summits of their hills, or under the shade of groves devoted to their deities. The worship of God on mountain-tops, otherwise a sublime and innocent practice, was proscribed. No grove might be planted near the altar of the Holy One of Israel, the strictest personal purity was enjoined upon the priests; the prohibition against prostituting their daughters, as well as that which forbids the woman to appear in the dress of the man, the man in that of the woman, are no doubt pointed against the same impure ceremonies. Not merely were human sacrifices expressly forbidden, but the animals which were to be sacrificed, with every particular to be observed, were strictly laid down. All the vulgar arts of priestcraft, divination, witchcraft, necromancy, were proscribed. Even a certain form of tonsure, certain parti-colored dresses, and other peculiar customs of the heathen priesthoods, were specifically forbidden.

But while this line of demarcation between the worshipers of one God and the worshipers of idols, was so strongly and precisely drawn, a rude and uncivilized horde were not expected to attain that pure and exalted spirituality of religion, which has never been known except among a reasoning and enlightened people. Their new religion ministered continual excitement; a splendid ceremonial dazzled their senses, perpetual sacrifices enlivened their faith, frequent commemorative festivals not merely let loose their gay and joyous spirits, but reminded them of all the surprising and marvelous events of their national history. From some of their prepossessions and habits they were estranged by degrees, not rent with unnecessary violence. The tabernacle preserved the form of the more solid and gigantic structures of Egypt; their priesthood were attired in dresses as costly, in many respects similar; their ablutions were as frequent; the exclusion of the daylight probably originated in subterranean temples hewn out of the solid rock, like those of Ipsambul and the cave temples of India; the use of incense seems to have been common in every kind of religious worship. Above all, the great universal right of sacrifice was regulated with the utmost precision. It is unnecessary to enter into all these minute particulars, still less into the remote and typical meaning of the

Jewish sacrificial law. Suffice it to say, that sacrifices were either national or individual. Every morning and every evening the smoke from the great brazen altar of burnt-offerings ascended in the name of the whole people—on the Sabbath two animals instead of one were slain.

From particular sacrifices or offerings no one, not even the poorest, was excluded. A regular scale of oblations was made, and the altar of the common God of Israel rejected not the small measure of flour which the meanest might offer. The sacrifices were partly propitiatory, that is, voluntary acts of reverence, in order to secure the favor of God to the devout worshiper: partly eucharistic, or expressive of gratitude for the divine blessings. Of this nature were the first fruits. The Israelite might not reap the abundant harvest, with which God blessed his fertile fields, or gather in the vintage, which empurpled the rocky hill-side, without first making an oblation of thanksgiving to the gracious Being, who had placed him in the land flowing with milk and honey. Lastly, they were piacular or expiatory; every sin either of the nation or the individual, whether a sin committed in ignorance, or from wilful guilt, had its appointed atonement; and on the performance of this condition the priest had the power of declaring the offender free from the punishment due to his crime. One day in the year, the tenth day of the seventh month, was set apart for the solemn rite of national expiation. First a bullock was to be slain, and the blood sprinkled, not only in the customary places, but within the Holy of Holies itself.

Then two goats were to be chosen, lots cast upon them, the one that was assigned to the Lord was to be sacrificed, the other, on whose head the sins of the whole people were heaped by the imprecation of the high priest, was taken beyond the camp and sent into the desert to Azazel, the spirit of evil, to whom Hebrew belief assigned the waste and howling wilderness as his earthly dwelling. An awful example confirmed the unalterable authority of the sacrificial ritual At the first great sacrifice after the consecration of the priesthood, on the renewal of the national covenant with the Deity, fire flashed down from heaven and consumed the burnt offerings. But Nadab and Abihu, the sons of Aaron, kindled their censers with fire, obtained from some less pure and hallowed source; and, having thus acted without command, were struck dead for the offense.

The ordinary festivals of the Jewish nation were of a gayer and more cheerful character. Every seventh day was the Sabbath: labor ceased throughout the land, the slave and the stranger, even the beast of labor and burden, were permitted to enjoy the period of ease and recreation; while the double sanction, on which the observance of the day rested, reminded every faithful Israelite of his God, under his twofold character of Creator and Deliverer. All creation should rest, because on that day the Creator rested; Israel more particularly, because on that day they rested from their bondage in Egypt. In later times, as well as a day of grateful recollection, it became one of public instruction in the principles of the law, and of social equality among all classes. Rich and poor, young and old, master and slave, met before the gate of the city, and indulged in innocent mirth, or in the pleasures of friendly intercourse.

The new moon of the seventh month was appointed as the Feast of Trumpets; it was, in fact, the beginning of the old Hebrew, and remained that of the civil year. The new moon, or the first day of the lunar month, was not commanded by positive precept, but recognised as a festival of established usage. But if those weekly or monthly meetings contributed to the maintenance of the religion, and to the cheerfulness and kindly brotherhood among the separate communities, the three great national festivals advanced those important ends in a far higher degree. Three times a year all the tribes assembled wherever the tabernacle of God was fixed; all the males, for the legislator carefully guarded against any dangers which might arise from a promiscuous assemblage of both sexes; besides that the women were ill qualified to bear the fatigue of journeys from the remote parts of the land, and the household offices were not to be neglected. This regulation was a master-stroke of policy, to preserve the bond of union indissoluble among the twelve federal republics, which formed the early state. Its importance may be estimated from the single fact, that, on the revolt of the ten tribes, Jeroboam did not consider his throne secure as long as the whole people assembled at the capital; and appointed Dan and Bethel, where he set up his emblematic calves, as the places of religious union for his own subjects.

The first and greatest of these festivals, the Passover, or rather the first full moon, the commencement of the religious year, was as it were the birthday of the nation, the day of their deliverance from Egypt, when the angel of death passed over their dwellings. The festival lasted seven days, and every ceremony recalled the awful scene of their deliverance. On the first evening they tasted the bitter herb, emblematic of the bitterness of slavery: they partook of the sacrifice, with their loins girded, as ready for their flight: they eat only unleavened bread, the bread of slavery, prepared in the hurry and confusion of their departure. During the fifty days, which elapsed after the Passover, the harvest was gathered in, and the Pentecost, the national harvest home, summoned the people to commemorate the delivery of the law and the formation of the covenant, by which they became the tenants of the luxuriant soil, the abundance of which they had been storing up. The gladness was to be as general as the blessing. *Thou shalt rejoice before the Lord thy God, thou and thy son, and thy daughter, and thy man servant, and thy maid servant, and the Levite that is within thy gates and the stranger, and the fatherless, and the widow.* The third of these feasts, that of tabernacles, took place in autumn, at the end of the vintage, in all southern climates the great time of rejoicing and merriment.

If more exquisite music and more graceful dances accompanied the gathering in of the grapes on the banks of the Cephisus; the tabret, the viol, and the harp, which sounded among the vineyards of Heshbon and Eleale, were not wanting in sweetness and gayety, and instead of the frantic riot of satyrs and bacchanals, the rejoicing was chastened by the solemn religious recollections with which it was associated, in a manner remarkably pleasing and picturesque. The branches of trees were woven together in rude imitation of the tents in which the Israelites dwelt in the desert, and within these green bowers the whole people passed the week of festivity. Yet however admirably calculated these periodical solemnities for the maintenance of religion and national unity, they were better adapted for the inhabitants of one of the oases in the desert, or a lonely island in the midst of the ocean, than a nation environed on all sides by warlike, enterprising, and inveterate enemies. At each of these festivals, the frontiers were unguarded, the garrisons deserted, the country left entirely open to the sudden inroad of the neighboring tribes. This was not unforeseen by the lawgiver, but how was it provided against? by an assurance of divine protection, which was to repress all the hostility and ambition of their adversaries. *I will cast out the nations before thee, and enlarge thy border; neither shall any man desire thy land when thou shalt go up to appear before the Lord three times in every year.** The sabbatic year was another remarkable instance of departure from every rule of political wisdom, in reliance on divine Providence. The whole land was to lie fallow, the whole people was given up to legalized idleness. All danger of famine was to be prevented by the supernaturally abundant harvest of the sixth year; but it is even more remarkable, that serious evils did not ensue from this check on the national industry. At the end of seven periods of seven years, for that number ran through the whole of the Hebrew institutions, the jubilee was appointed.† All the estates were to revert to their original owners, all burthens and alienations ceased, and the whole land returned to the same state in which it stood at the first partition. A singular Agrarian law, which maintained the general equality, and effectually prevented the accumulation of large masses of property in one family, to the danger of the national independence, and the establishment of a great landed oligarchy.

Such was the religious constitution of the Hebrew nation. But if the lawgiver, educated in all the wisdom of the Egyptians, departed most widely from the spirit of Egyptian polytheism in the fundamental principle of his religious institutes, the political basis of his state was not less opposite to that established in the kingdom of the Pharaohs. The first, and certainly the most successful legislator of antiquity, who assumed the welfare of the whole community as the end of his constitution, Moses annihilated at once the artificial and tyrannical distinction of castes, and established political equality as the fundamental principal of the state. The whole nation was one great caste, that of husbandmen cultivating their own property. Even the single privileged class, that of Levi, stood on a totally different footing from the sacerdotal aristocracy of Egypt. With a wise originality, Moses retained all that was really useful, and indeed, under the circumstances of the age and people, absolutely necessary, in a priestly order, and rejected all that might endanger the liberties of the people, through their exorbitant wealth or power.

In a constitution, founded on a religious basis, sacred functionaries set apart from the mass of the people were indispensable; where the state was governed by a written law, minute and multifarious in its provisions, conservators and occasional expositors of the law were equally requisite; a people at first engaged in ferocious warfare, afterward engrossed by agricultural labors, without an exempt order, which should devote itself to higher and more intellectual studies would soon have degenerated into ignorance and barbarism. Besides the officiating priesthood, the Levitical class furnished the greater number of the judges, the scribes, the genealogists and registers of the tribes, the keepers of the records, the geometricians, the superintendents of weights and measures: and Michaelis thinks, from the judgment in cases of leprosy being assigned to them, the physicians. Their influence depended rather on their civil than on their ecclesiastical functions. They were not, strictly speaking, religious teachers; they were bound to read the whole law before the people once in seven years; but in other respects their priestly duties consisted only in attendance in the tabernacle or the temple in their appointed courses. There were no private religious rites in which they were called on to officiate. Circumcision was performed without their presence, marriage was a civil contract, from funerals they were interdicted. They were not mingled up with the body of the people, they dwelt in their own separate cities.

Their wealth was ample, but not enormous. Instead of the portion in the conquered land, to which they had a claim, as one of the twelve tribes, a tenth of the whole produce was assigned for their maintenance, with forty-eight cities, situated in different parts of the territory, and a small domain surrounding each. These were the possessions of the whole tribe of Levi.

The officiating priesthood received other contributions, portions of the sacrifices, the redemption of the first born, the first fruits, and every thing devoted by vow: yet most of these last were probably laid up in the public

*Exod. xxxiv. 24.

†This institution, as well as the last, was perhaps rather of a civil than religious character.

religious treasury, and defrayed the expenses of the rich and costly worship, the repair and ornament of the tabernacle, the vestments of the priests, the public sacrifices, the perpetual oil and incense. The half-shekel poll-tax was, we conceive,only once levied by Moses,and not established as a permanent tax till after the captivity.

Such were the station, the revenue, and the important duties assigned to his own tribe by the Hebrew legislator, a tribe, as one of the less numerous, most fitly chosen for these purposes. On the departure from Egypt, the first born of each family were designated for these sacred duties; but the difficulties and inconveniences which would have attended the collecting together the representatives of every family into one class, the jealousies which might have arisen from assigning so great a distinctton to primogeniture, and many other obvious objections, show that the substitution of a single tribe was at once a more simple and a more effective measure.

The superiority of Moses in all other respects to the pride of family, particularly where hereditary honors were so highly appreciated, is among the most remarkable features in his character. The example of Egypt and of all the neighboring nations would have led him to establish an hereditary monarchy in his own line, connected and supported, as it might have been by the sacerdotal order; but though he made over the high-priesthood to the descendants of his brother Aaron, his own sons remained without distinction, and his descendants sank into insignificance. While he anticipated the probability that his republic would assume hereafter a monarchical form, he designated no permanent head of the state, either hereditary or elective. Joshua was appointed as military leader to achieve the conquest, and for this purpose succeeded to the supreme authority. But God was the only king, the law his only vicegerent.

Did Moses appoint a national senate? if so, what was its duration, its constitution, and its powers? No question in Jewish history is more obscure. At the delivery of the law on Mount Sinai, Moses was attended by seventy elders; during a rebellion in the wilderness (Numb. xi.) he established a great council of the same number. This latter the Jewish writers suppose to have been a permanent body, and from thence derive their great Sanhedrim, which took so important a part in public affairs after the captivity. But this senate of seventy is not once distinctly named in the whole intervening course of Hebrew history. Joshua twice assembled a sort of diet or parliament, consisting of elders, heads of families, judges, and officers, who seem to have represented all Israel. On other occasions the same sort of national council seems to have met on great emergencies. But most probably neither the constitution, nor the powers, nor the members of this assembly were strictly limited. Moses left the internal government of the tribes as he found it. Each tribe had itsacknowledged aristocracy and acknowledged chieftain, and governed its own affairs as a separate republic. The chieftain was the hereditary head of the whole tribe, the aristocracy the heads of the different families; these with the judges, and perhaps the shotcrim, the scribes or genealogists, officers of great importance in each tribe, constituted the provincial assembly. No doubt the national assembly consisted of delegates from the provincal ones; but how they were appointed, and by whom, does not appear. In short, in the early ages of the Hebrew nation, the public assemblies were more like those of our German ancestors or a meeting of independent septs or clans, where general respect for birth, age, or wisdom, designated those who should appear and those who should take a lead, than the senate of a regular government, in which the right to a seat and to suffrage is defined by positive law. The ratification of all great public decrees by the general voice of the people (the congregation) seems invariably to have been demanded, particularly during their encampment in the desert. This was given, as indeed it could not well be otherwise, by acclamation. Thus in the ancient Hebrew constitution we find a rude convention of estates, provincial parliaments, and popular assemblies; but that their meetings should be of rare occurrence, followed from the nature of the constitution. The state possessed no legislative power; in peace, unless on very extraordinary occasions, they had no business to transact; there was no public revenue except that of the religious treasury; their wars, till the time of the kings, were mostly defensive. The invaded tribe summoned the nation to its assistance; no deliberation was necessary; the militia, that is, all who could bear arms, were bound to march to the defense of their brethren. Such was the law: we shall see hereafter that the separate tribes did not always preserve this close union in their wars; and, but for the indissoluble bond of their religion, the confederacy was in perpetual danger of falling to pieces.

The judges or prefects, appointed according to the advice of Jethro, seems to have given place to municipal administrators of the law in each of the cities. The superior education and intelligence of the Levitical order pointed them out as best fitted for these offices, which were usually intrusted, by general consent, to their charge. Of their numbers, or mode of nomination, we know nothing certain. They held their sittings, after the usual Oriental custom, in the gates of the cities.

The people were all free, and excepting this acknowledged subordination to the heads of their families and of their tribes, entirely equal.

Slavery, universal in the ancient world, was recognized by the Mosaic institutions; but of all the ancient lawgivers, Moses alone endeavored to mitigate its evils. His regulations always remind the Israelites, that they themselves were formerly bondslaves in Egypt.

The freeborn Hebrew might be reduced to slavery, either by his own consent, or in condemnation as an insolvent debtor, or as a thief unable to make restitution. In either case he became free at the end of seven years' service. If he refused to accept his manumission, he might remain in servitude. But to prevent any fraudulent or compulsory renunciation of this right, the ceremony of reconsigning himself to bondage was public; he appeared before the magistrate, his ear was bored, and he was thus judicially delivered back to his master; but even this servitude expired at the Jubilee, when the free-born Hebrew returned into the possession of the patrimonial estate. The law expressly abhorred the condemnation of an Israelite to perpetual servitude. As a punishment for debt, slavery, at least under its mitigated form, may be considered as merciful to the sufferer, and certainly more advantageous to the creditor and to the public, than imprisonment. The Israelite sold to a stranger might at any time be redeemed by his kindred on payment of the value of the service that remained due. He who became a slave, being already married, recovered the freedom of his wife and family as well as his own; he who married a fellow slave, left her and her children as the property of his master. The discharged slave was not to be cast forth upon society naked and destitute; he was to be decently clothed, and liberally furnished *out of the flock, and out of the floor, and out of the wine-press.*

A parent in extreme distress might sell his children; if male, of course the slave recovered his freedom at the usual time; if female, the law took her under its especial protection. By a mitigation of the original statute, in ordinary cases, she regained her freedom at the end of seven years. But if the master took her himself, or gave her to his son, as an inferior wife, she was to receive the full conjugal rights of her station; if denied them, she recovered her freedom. If he did not marry her, she might be redeemed, but on no account was to be trafficked away into a foreign land.

After all, slavery is too harsh a term to apply to this temporary hiring, in which, though the master might inflict blows, he was amenable to justice if the slave died under his hands, or within two days, from the consequences of the beating; if maimed or mutilated, the slave recovered his freedom. The law went farther, and positively enjoined kindness and lenity; *Thou shalt not rule over him with rigor, but thou shalt fear the Lord.*

The condition of foreign slaves was less favorable; whether captives taken in war, purchased, or born in the family, their servitude was perpetual. Yet they too partook in those indulgences which in a spirit very different from that which bestowed on the wretched slaves in Rome the mock honors of their disorderly Saturnalia, the Jewish law secured for the slave, as well as for the poor, the orphan, the widow, and the stranger. The Sabbath was to them a day of rest; on the three great festivals they partook of the banquets which were made on those occasions. All that grew spontaneously during the sabbatical year belonged to them, in common with the poor. Besides these special provisions, injunctions perpetually occur in the Mosaic code which enforce kindness, compassion, and charity, not merely toward the native poor, but to the stranger. Far from that jealous inhospitality and hatred of mankind of which the later Jews were not altogether unjustly accused, the stranger, unless a Canaanite, might become naturalized, or if he resided in the land without being incorporated with the people, he was not excluded from the protection of the law. He was invited to the public rejoicings; he was to be a witness in the bounties of the God who blessed the land.

Such were the political divisions among the Hebrew people, but over all classes alike the supreme and impartial law exercised its vigilant superintendence. It took under its charge the morals, the health, as well as the persons and the property, of the whole people. It entered into the domestic circle, and regulated all the reciprocal duties of parent and child, husband and wife, as well as of master and servant. Among the nomadic tribes, from which the Hebrews descended, the father was an arbitrary sovereign in his family, as under the Roman law, with the power of life and death. Moses, while he maintained the dignity and salutary control, limited the abuse of the parental authority. From the earliest period the child was under the protection of the law. Abortion and infanticide were not specifically forbidden, but unknown among the Jews. Josephus, appealing in honest pride to the practice of his countrymen, reproaches other nations with these cruelties. The father was enjoined to instruct his children in all the memorable events and sacred usages of the land. In extreme indigence, we have seen, the sale of children as slaves was permitted, but only in the same cases, and under the same conditions, that the parent might sell himself, to escape starvation, and for a limited period. The father had no power of disinheriting his sons; the first-born received by law two portions, the rest shared equally. On the other hand, the Decalogue enforced obedience and respect to parents under the strongest sanctions. To strike, or to curse a parent, was a capital offense. On parricide, the law as if, like that of the Romans, it refused to contemplate its possibility, preserved a sacred silence. Though the power of life and death was not left to the caprice or passion of the parent, the incorrigible son might be denounced before the elders of the city, and, if convicted, suffered death. It is remarkable that the father and mother were to concur in the accusation, a most wise precaution where polygamy, the fruitful source of domestic dissension and jealousy, prevailed.

The chastity of females was guarded by statutes, which, however severe and cruel according to modern notions, were wise and merciful in that state of society. Poems and travels have familiarized us with the horrible atrocities committed by the blind jealousy of eastern husbands. By substituting a judicial process for the wild and hurried justice of the offended party, the guilty suffered a death probably less inhuman; the innocent might escape. The convicted adulterer and adulteress were stoned to death. Even the incontinence of a female before marriage, if detected at the time of her nuptials, which was almost inevitable, underwent the same penalty with that of the adulteress. Where the case was not clear, the female suspected of infidelity might be summoned to a most awful ordeal. She was to be acquitted or condemned by God himself, whose actual interposition was promised by his daring lawgiver. The woman was led forth from her own dwelling into the court of the Lord's house. In that solemn place she first made an offering of execration; not entreating mercy, but imprecating the divine vengeance if she should be guilty. The priest then took some of the holy water, and mingled it with some of the holy earth: as he placed the bowl of bitter ingredients in her hand, he took off the veil in which she was accustomed to conceal herself from the eyes of man, and left her exposed to the public gaze: her hair was loosened, and the dreadful form of imprecation recited. If innocent, the water was harmless, if guilty, the Lord would make her a curse and an oath among the people: she was to be smitten at once with a horrid disease; *her thigh was to rot, her belly to swell.* To this adjuration of the great all-seeing God, the woman was to reply *Amen, Amen.* A solemn pause ensued, during which the priest wrote down all the curses, and washed them out again with the water. She was then to drink the water, if she dared; but what guilty woman, if she had courage to confront, would have the command of countenance, the firmness and resolution to go through all this slow, searching, and terrific process, and finally expose herself to shame and agony far worse than death? No doubt cases where this trial was undergone were rare; yet the confidence of the legislator in the divine interference can hardly be questioned; for had such an institution fallen into contempt by its failure in any one instance, his whole law and religion would have been shaken to its foundation.

Marriages were contracted by parents in behalf of their children. A dowry or purchase-money was usually given by the bridegroom. Polygamy was permitted rather than encouraged: the law did not directly interfere with the immemorial usage, but, by insisting on each wife or concubine receiving her full conjugal rights, prevented even the most wealthy from establishing those vast harems which are fatal to the happiness, and eventually to the population, of a country. The degrees of relationship, between which marriage was forbidden, were defined with singular minuteness. The leading principle of these enactments was to prohibit marriage between those parties among whom, by the usage of their society, early and frequent intimacy was unavoidable, and might lead to abuse.

Having thus secured the domestic happiness of his people, or at least moderated, as far as the times would allow, those lawless and inordinate passions which overbear the natural tenderness of domestic instinct and the attachment between the sexes—guarded the father from the disobedience of the son, the son from the capricious tyranny of the father—secured the wife from being the victim of every savage fit of jealousy, while he sternly repressed the crime of conjugal infidelity, the lawgiver proceeded, with the same care and discretion, to provide for the general health of the people. With this view he regulated their diet, enforced cleanliness, took precautions against the most prevalent diseases, and left the rest, as be safely might, to the genial climate of the country, the wholesome exercise of husbandry, and the cheerful relaxations afforded by the religion. The health of the people was a chief, if not the only object of the destinction between clean and unclean beasts, and the prohibition against eating the blood of any animal. All coarse, hard, and indigestible food is doubly dangerous in warm climates. The general feeling of mankind has ordinarily abstained from most of the animals proscribed by the Mosaic law, excepting sometimes the camel, the hare, and the swine. The flesh of the camel is vapid and heavy; the wholesomeness of the hare is questioned by Hippocrates; that of the swine in southern countries tends to produce cutaneous maladies, the diseases to which the Jews are peculiarly liable; besides that the animal being usually left in the East to its own filthy habits, is not merely unwholesome, but disgusting; it is the scavenger of the towns. Of the birds, those of prey were forbidden; of fish, those without fins or scales. The prohibition of blood (besides its acknowledged unwholesomeness, and in some instances fatal effects) perhaps pointed at the custom of some savage tribes, which, like the Abyssinians, fed upon flesh torn warm from the animal, and almost quivering with life. This disgusting practice may have been interdicted not merely as unwholesome, but as promoting that ferocity of manners which it was the first object of the lawgiver to discourage.

Cleanliness, equally important to health with wholesome diet, was maintained by the injunetion of frequent ablutions, particularly after touching a dead body, or any thing which might possibly be putrid; by regulations concerning female disorders, and the intercourse between the sexes; provisions which seem minute and indelicate to modern ideas, but were doubtless intended to correct unseemly or unhealthful practices, either of the Hebrew people or of neighboring tribes. The leprosy was the dreadful scourge which excited the greatest apprehension. The nature of this loathsome disease is sufficiently indicated by the expressive description—*a leper as white as snow*. In its worst stage the whole flesh rotted, the extremities dropped off, till at last mortification ensued, and put an end to the sufferings of the miserable outcast; for as the disease was highly infectious, the unhappy victim was immediately shunned, and looked on with universal abhorrence. The strict quarantine established by Moses provided for the security of the community, not without merciful regard to the sufferer. The inspection of the infected was committed to the Levites; the symptoms of the two kinds of disorder accurately pointed out; the period of seclusion defined; while all, if really cured, were certain of readmission into the community, none were readmitted until perfectly cured. Clothes, and even houses which might retain the infection, were to be destroyed without scruple; though it does not seem quite clear whether the plague, which lurked in the plaster of houses, was the same leprosy which might become contagious, or a kind of mildew or worm, which might breed some other destructive malady.

Human life, in all rude and barbarous tribes, is of cheap account; blood is shed on the least provocation; open or secret assassination is a common occurrence. The Hebrew penal law enforced the highest respect for the life of man. Murder ranked with high treason (i. e. idolatry, blasphemy), striking a father, adultery, and unnatural lust, as a capital crime: the law demanded blood for blood. But it transferred the exaction of the penalty from private revenge, and committed it to the judicial authority. To effect this, it had to struggle with an inveterate though barbarous usage, which still prevails among the Arabian tribes. By a point of honor, as rigorous as that of modern duelling, the nearest of kin is bound to revenge the death of his relation: he is his Goel or blood-avenger. He makes no inquiry; he allows no pause; whether the deceased has been slain on provocation, by accident, or of deliberate malice, death can only be atoned by the blood of the homicide. To mitigate the evils of a usage too firmly established to be rooted out, Moses appointed certain cities of refuge, conveniently situated. If the homicide could escape to one of these, he was safe till a judicial investigation took place. If the crime was deliberate murder, he was surrendered to the Goel; if justifiable or accidental homicide, he was bound to reside within the sanctuary for a certain period: should he leave it, and expose himself to the revenge of his pursuers, he did so at his own peril, and might be put to death. Where a murder was committed, of which the perpetrator was undetected, the nearest city was commanded to make an offering of atonement. With the same jealous regard for human life, a strict police regulation enacted that the terrace on the top of every house should have a parapet. In one case inexcusable carelessness, which caused death, was capitally punished. If an ox gored a man so that he died, the beast was put to death: if the owner had been warned, he also suffered the same penalty; but in this case his life might be redeemed at a certain price.

While the law was thus rigorous with regard to human life, against the crime of theft it was remarkably lenient. Man-stealing, as the kidnapped person could only be sold to foreigners, inflicted political death, and was therefore a capital offense; but the ordinary punishment of theft was restitution. Here personal slavery was a direct advantage, as it empowered the law to exact the proper punishment without touching the life. No man was so poor that he could not make restitution; because the labor of a slave being of higher value than his maintenance, his person could be sold either to satisfy a creditor or to make compensation for a theft.

The law of property may be most conveniently stated after the final settlement of the country.

In all the foregoing statutes we see the legislator constantly, yet discreetly, mitigating the savage usages of a barbarous people. There are some minor provisions to which it is difficult to assign any object, except that of softening the ferocity of manners, and promoting gentleness and humanity. Kindness to domestic animals—the prohibition to employ beasts of unequal strength, the ox and the ass, on the same labor (unless this is to be classed with those singular statutes of which we have no very satisfactory explanation, which forbade wearing garments of mixed materials, or sowing mixed seeds)—the prohibition to seeth a kid in its mother's milk (though this likewise is supposed by Spencer to be aimed at a religious usage)—or to take the young of birds and the dam together. Toward all their fellow-creatures the same kindly conduct was enjoined on the Hebrew people, both by general precept and by particular statute. The mildness of their slave-law has been often contrasted to their advantage, with that of those ancient nations which made the loudest boast of their freedom and civilization. The provisions for the poor were equally gentle and considerate; the gleanings of every harvest field were left to the fatherless and widow; the owner might not go over it a second time: the home of the poor man was sacred; his garment, if pledged, was to be restored at nightfall. Even toward the stranger oppression was forbidden; if indigent, he shared in all the privileges reserved for the native poor.

The general war-law, considering the age, was not deficient in lenity. War was to be declared in form. The inhabitants of a city, which made resistance, might be put to the sword; that is, the males; but only after it had been summoned to surrender. Fruit-trees were not to be destroyed during a siege. The conduct toward female captives deserves particular notice. The beautiful slave might not be hurried, as was the case during those ages falsely called heroic, in the agony of sorrow, perhaps reeking with the blood of her murdered relatives, to the bed of the conqueror. She was allowed a month for decent sorrow: if after that she became the wife of her master, he might not capriciously abandon her, and sell her to another; she might claim her freedom as the price of her humiliation.

To the generally humane character of the Mosaic legislation there appears one great exception, the sanguinary and relentless conduct enjoined against the seven Canaanitish nations. Toward them mercy was a crime—extermination a duty. It is indeed probable that this war-law, cruel as it seems, was not in the least more barbarous than that of the surrounding nations, more particularly the Canaanites themselves. In this the Hebrews were only not superior to their age. Many incidents in the Jewish history show the horrid atrocities of warfare in Palestine. The mutilation of distinguished captives, and the torture of prisoners in cold blood, were the usual consequences of victory.

Adonibezek, one of the native kings, acknowledges that seventy kings, with their thumbs and toes cut off, had gathered their meat under his table. The invasion and conquest once determined, no alternative remained but to extirpate or be extirpated. The dangers and evils to which the Hebrew tribes were subsequently exposed by the weakness or humanity which induced them to suspend their work of extermination before it had been fully completed, clearly show the political wisdom by which those measures were dictated: cruel as they were, the war once commenced, they were inevitable. Their right to invade and take possession of Palestine depended solely on their divine commission, and their grant from the sovereign Lord of heaven and earth; for any other right—deduced from the possession of the patriarchs, who never were owners of more than the sepulchers they purchased, and, if they had any better title, had forfeited it by the abeyance of many centuries—is untenable and preposterous. Almighty Providence determined to extirpate a race of bloody, licentious, and barbarous idolaters, and replace them by a people of milder manners and purer religion. Instead of the earthquake, the famine, or the pestilence, the ferocious valor of this yet uncivilized people was allowed free scope. The war in which the Hebrew tribes were embarked was stripped of none of its customary horrors and atrocities; nor was it till these savage and unrelenting passions had fulfilled their task that the influence of their milder institutions was to soften and humanize the national character. Such was the scheme, which, if not, as we assert, really authorized by the Supreme Being, must have been created within the daring and comprehensive mind of the Hebrew legislator. He undertook to lead a people through a long and dreadful career of bloodshed and massacre. The conquest once achieved, they were to settle down into a nation of peaceful husbandmen, under a mild and equal constitution. Up to a certain point they were to be trained in the worst possible discipline for peaceful citizens; to encourage every disposition opposite to those inculcated by the general spirit of the law. Their ambition was inflamed; military habits formed; the love of restless enterprise fostered; the habit of subsisting upon plunder encouraged. The people, who were to be merciful to the meanest beast, were to mutilate the noblest animal, the horse, wherever they met it: those who were not to exercise any oppression whatever toward a stranger of another race, an Edomite, or even toward their ancient enemy—an Egyptian; on the capture of a Canaanitish city, were to put man, woman, and child to the sword. Their enemies were designated; appointed limits fixed to their conquests: beyond a certain boundary the ambitious invasion, which before was a virtue, became a crime. The whole victorious nation was suddenly to pause in its career. Thus far they were to be like hordes of Tartars, Scythians, or Huns, bursting irresistibly from their deserts, and sweeping away every vestige of human life: at a given point their arms were to fall from their hands, the thirst of conquest subside; and a great unambitious agricultural republic—with a simple religion, an equal administration of justice, a thriving and industrious population, brotherly harmony and mutual good-will between all ranks, domestic virtues, purity of morals, gentleness of manners—was to arise in the midst of the desolation their arms had made, and under the very roofs—in the vineyards and corn-fields—which they had obtained by merciless violence.

The sanction on which the Hebrew law was founded, is, if possible, more extraordinary. The lawgiver, educated in Egypt, where the immortality of the soul, under some form, most likely that of the metempsychosis or transmigration of the soul, entered into the popular belief; nevertheless maintained a profound silence on that fundamental article, if not of political, at least of religious legislation—rewards and punishments in another life. He substituted temporal chastisements and temporal blessings. On the violation of the constitution followed inevitably blighted harvests, famine, pestilence, barrenness among their women, defeat, captivity; on its maintenance, abundance, health, fruitfulness, victory, independence. How wonderfully the event verified the prediction of the inspired legislator—how invariably apostacy led to adversity—repentance and reformation to prosperity—will abundantly appear during the course of the following history.

BOOK IV.

THE INVASION.

Advance to the Holy Land—Repulse—Residence in the Desert—Second Advance—Conquests to the East of the Jordan—Death and Character of Moses.

At length the twelve tribes broke up their encampment in the elevated region about Mount Sinai. A year and a month had elapsed since their departure from Egypt. The nation assumed the appearance of a regular army: military order and discipline were established; each tribe marched in succession under its own leaders, with its banner displayed, and took up its position in the appointed quarter of the camp. When the silver trumpets sounded, the tribe of Judah, mustering 74,600 fighting men, defiled forward from the east side of the camp, and led the van, followed by Issachar, with 54,400, and Zebulun, 57,400. Then came a division of the tribe of Levi, the descendants of Gershom and Merari, bearing the tabernacle, which was carefully taken down, and, thus moving after the advanced guard might be set up, ready for the reception of the ark. Then Reuben, numbering 46,500, Simeon, 59,300, Gad, 45,650, broke up, and advanced from the southern part of the encampment. The second division of the Levites, the family of Kohath, next took their station, bearing the sanctuary and the ark, and all the sacred vessels, with the most religious care, lest any hands but those of Aaron and his assistants should touch a single part. All the males of the house of Levi amounted only to 22,000. Ephraim 40,500, Manasseh 32,200, Benjamin 35,400, defiled, and formed the western wing of the encampment. Dan 62,700, Asher 41,500, Napthali 53,400, brought up the rear. The whole number of fighting men was 603,550.* This formidable army set forward, singing, "*Rise up, O Lord, and let thine enemies be scattered;*" and thus—already furnished with their code of laws, irresistible both in their numbers and the promised assistance of their God—they marched onward to take possession of the fruitful land which had been promised as the reward of their toils. The cloud still led the way; but their prudent leader likewise secured the assistance of Hobab, his brother-in-law, who, at the head of his clan, had been accustomed to traverse the desert, knew intimately the bearings of the country, the usual resting-places, the water-springs, and the character and habits of the wandering tribes.

Their march was not uninterrupted by adventures.

At Taberah a fire broke out, which raged with great fury among the dry and combustible materials of which their tents were made. The people trembled before the manifest anger of the Lord: the destructive flames ceased at the prayer of Moses. Not long after (at a place subsequently called Kibroth Hattaavah) discontent and mutiny began to spread in the camp. The manna, on which they had long fed, began to pall upon the taste. With something of that feeling which reminds us of sailors who have been long at sea, they began to remember the flesh, the fish, and particularly the juicy and cooling fruits and vegetables which abounded in Egypt; a species of lotus, a favorite food among the lower orders; and the watermelon, the great luxury of southern climates. The discontent rose so high that, to strengthen the authority of the leader, a permanent council of seventy elders was appointed; the model, and, as the Jews assert, the origin, of their famous Sanhedrin. Still Moses doubted whether it might not be necessary to satisfy the mutinous spirits by slaying all the flocks and herds, which had hitherto been religiously reserved for sacrifices. By divine command he promised an immediate supply of food, but at the same time warned them of the fatal consequences which would attend the gratification of their appetites. Quails again fell in great abundance around the camp; but immediately on this change of diet, or even before, if we are to receive the account to the strict letter a dreadful pestilence broke out. It has been suggested that quails feed on hellebore and other poisonous plants, and may thus become most pernicious and deadly food. The place was called Kibroth Hattaavah, the graves of the greedy after food. During the height of this mutiny the leader received unexpected assistance from two of the seventy, Eldad and Medad, who of their own accord began to prophesy, to speak in the name of God, or to testify their religious zeal by some peculiar and enthusiastic language. Far from reproving with jealous indignation these intruders on his own spiritual function, the prudent leader commended their zeal, and expressed his desire that it might spread throughout the nation.

At their next stage new difficulties arose—jealousy and dissension within the family of the lawgiver. Miriam, the sister of Moses, who, from the prominent part she took in the rejoicings on the shore of the Red Sea, seems to have been the acknowledged head of the female community, found, or supposed, herself supplanted in dignity by the Arabian (Ethiopian) wife of Moses—whether Zipporah or a second wife is not quite clear. Aaron espoused her quarrel; but the authority of Moses and the impartiality of the law were at once vindicated. The offenders were summoned before the tabernacle, and rebuked by the voice from the cloud. The

* Of the difficulties and discrepances which occur in the sacred writings of the Hebrews, perhaps two-thirds are found in passages which contain numbers. Of the primitive Hebrew system of notation we are most likely ignorant; but the manner in which the numbers are denoted in the present copies of the sacred boo[k] is remarkably liable to error and misapprehension. (See dissertation in the last edition of Calmet.) It is by no means easy to reconcile the enormous numbers contained in the census with the language of other passages in the Scriptures, particularly that of the seventh chapter of Deuteronomy. The nation which could arm 600,000 fighting men is described as "the fewest of all people," as inferior in numbers, it should seem, to each of the seven "greater and mightier nations" which then inhabited Canaan. And it is remarkable, that while there has been much controversy, whether the whole area of Palestine could contain the Hebrew settlers, the seven nations are "to be put out by little and little, lest the beasts of the field increase upon" the new occupants. The narrative of the campaign in the book of Joshua is equally inconsistent with these immense numbers; *e. g.*—the defiling of the whole army of 600,000 men, seven times in one day, round the walls of Jericho; the panic of the whole host at the repulse of 3,000 men before Ai. The general impression from this book is, that it describes the invasion of nations, at once more warlike and numerous, by a smaller force, which, without reliance on divine succor, could not have achieved the conquest; rather than the irruption of the host, like that of Attila or Zengis, which might have borne down all opposition by the mere weight of numerical force. We have not, however, thought fit to depart from the numbers as they stand in the sacred writings; though, if we might suppose that a cipher has been added in the total sum, and throughout the several particulars: or if we might include men, women, and children under the 600,000, the history would gain, in our opinion, both in clearness and consistency. It may be added, that the number of the first-born [Num. iii. 43] is quite out of proportion to that of the adult males.

mutinous Miriam was smitten with leprosy, and cast, like a common person, out of the camp, till she should have completed the legal term of purification.

At length the nation arrived on the southern frontier of the promised land, at a place called Kadesh Barnea. Their wanderings are now drawn to an end, and they are to reap the reward of all their toil and suffering, the final testimony of the divine favor. Twelve spies, one from each tribe, are sent out to make observations on the fruitfulness of the land, the character of the inhabitants, and the strength of their fortifications. Among these the most distinguished are Caleb, of the tribe of Judah, and Joshua, of Ephraim. During the forty days of their absence the assembled people anxiously await their return; and at length they are seen advancing toward the camp, loaded with delicious fruits, for it was now about the time of the vintage. In one respect their report is most satisfactory: Canaan had undergone great improvement since the time when Abraham and Jacob had pastured their flocks in the open and unoccupied plains. The vine, the olive, the pomegranate and the fig, were cultivated with great success; and the rich sample which they bare—a bunch of grapes, almost as much as two men can carry, suspended from a pole, with figs and pomegranates—confirms their cheering narrative. But, on the other hand, the intelligence, exaggerated by the fears of ten out of the twelve spies, overwhelms the whole people with terror. These treasures were guarded by fierce and warlike tribes, not likely to abandon their native plains without an obstinate and bloody contest. Their cities were strongly fortified; and, above all, nearly the first enemies they would have to encounter would be men of colossal stature, the descendants of the gigantic people celebrated in their early national traditions, people before whom they would be *as grasshoppers*. The inhabitants of Egypt are in general of small stature; and the same causes which tended to the rapid increase of the Jewish people in that country were unfavorable to their height and vigor. But, worse than this, their long slavery had debased their minds: the confidence in the divine protection gave way at once before their sense of physical inferiority, and the total deficiency of moral courage. *"Back to Egypt"* is the general cry. The brave Joshua and Caleb in vain reprove the general pusillanimity; their own lives are in danger; and, in bitter disappointment, the great law-giver perceives that a people accustomed to the luxuries of a relaxing climate, and inured to slavery from their birth, are not the materials from which he can construct a bold, conquering, and independent nation. But his great mind is equal even to those dispiriting circumstances; and in all the wonderful history of the Jews, perhaps nothing is more extraordinary, or more clearly evinces his divine inspiration and confident reliance on the God in whose name he spoke, than his conduct on this trying occasion. The decision is instantaneously formed: the plan of immediate conquest at once abandoned; the people are commanded, on the authority of God, to retreat directly from the borders of the promised land. They are neither to return to Egypt, nor assail an easier conquest; but they are condemned to wander for a definite period of forty years in the barren and dismal regions through which they had marched.

No hope is held out that their lives shall be prolonged; they are distinctly assured that not one of them shall receive those blessings on the promise of which they had surrendered themselves to the guidance of Moses, abandoned Egypt and traversed the wilderness. Even Moses himself, at the age of eighty, acquiesces in the discouraging apprehension, that he never shall enjoy the reward of his honorable and patriotic ambition—the pride and satisfaction of seeing his republic happily established in the land of Canaan. A desperate access of valor, or an impatient desire of beholding once at least the pleasant land, in vain repressed by their leader, brought the Hebrews into collision with their enemies. Those who ascended the hill were fiercely assailed by the native warriors, and driven back to the main body with great loss. All the spies, except the faithful two, were cut off by an untimely death, a pestilence sent from God. Nothing remained but in sullen resignation to follow their inexorable leader into that country in which they were to spend their lives and find their graves—the desert.

Yet, however signal this evidence of the authority acquired by Moses over the minds of the people, the first incident during the retreat showed a dangerous and widely-organized plan of rebellion. A formidable conspiracy was made to wrest the supreme civil power from Moses, and the priesthood from his brother. Korah, a Levite of the race of Kohath, announced himself as the competitor of the latter: Dathan, Abiram, and On, all descended from Reuben, rested their claim to pre-eminence on the primogeniture of their ancestor—the forfeiture of whose title they did not acknowledge: 250 of the chieftains engaged in the rebellion. Moses confidently appealed to God, and rested his own claim and that of his brother on the issue. The earth suddenly opened, and swallowed up the tents of the Ruebenite mutineers. Korah and his abettors were struck dead by fire from heaven. The people, instead of being overawed and confounded by these dreadful events, expressed their pity and indignation. The plague immediately broke out, by which 14,700 perished. Another miracle left Aaron in undisputed possession of the priestly office. Twelve rods, one for the prince of each tribe, were laid up in the tabernacle; that of Aaron alone budded, and produced the flowers and fruits of a living branch of the almond tree.

Of the Hebrew history during the period of thirty-eight years, passed in the wilderness, nothing is known except the names of their stations. Most of these probably were in the elevated district around Mount Sinai, which is about thirty miles in diameter, the most fruitful and habitable part of the peninsula. There the tribes would find water, and pasture for their flocks and cattle. Their own labors and traffic with the caravans, which crossed this region, would supply most of their wants. In short, their life was that of the Bedouins of the desert.

An opinion, advanced by Eusebius, has been recently revived—that, during this time, the great Egyptian conqueror, Sesostris, mounted the throne, and extended his victorious arms over a great part of the world. Should future discoveries in the hieroglyphical literature of Egypt throw light on this subject, it would be a remarkable fact, that the Israelites should have escaped, in the unassailable desert, the conquering and avenging power of their former masters.

At length, when the former generation had gradually sunk into the grave, and a new race had sprung up, trained to the bold and hardy habits of the wandering Arab—when the free air of the desert had invigorated their frames, and the canker of slavery had worn out of their minds—while they retained much of the arts and knowledge acquired in Egypt; the Hebrew nation suddenly appeared again at Kadesh, the same point on the southern frontier of Palestine from which they had retreated.

At this place Miriam died, and was buried with great honor. The whole camp was distressed from want of water, and was again miraculously supplied. Here likewise Moses himself betrayed his mistrust in the divine assistance, and the final sentence was issued, that he should not lead the nation into the possession of the promised land. Many formidable difficulties opposed their penetrating into Canaan on this frontier. The country was mountainous, the hills crowned with strong forts, which, like Jerusalem, then Jebus, long defied their arms, and were not finally subdued till the reign of David. It was not the most fruitful or inviting district of the land: part of it was the wild region where David afterward maintained himself with his freebooting companions, when persecuted by Saul. The gigantic clan about Hebron would be almost the first to oppose them; and the Philistines who occupied the coast, the most warlike of the tribes, might fall on their rear. They determined, therefore, to make a circuit; to pass round the Dead Sea, and, crossing the Jordan, proceed at once into the heart of the richest and least defensible part of the land. To affect this march they must cross the deep valley which, under the name of El Ghor and El Araba, extends from the foot of the Dead Sea to the gulf of Elath. On the eastern side of this valley rises a lofty and precipitous ridge, Mount Seir, still called Djebal Shera, traversed only by a few narrow defiles; one only, called El Ghoeyr, passable by a large army. This ridge was occupied by the Edomites; and Moses sends to demand free passage through the country under a strict promise to keep the highway (the Ghoeyr), and commit no ravage or act of hostility. While this negotiation was pending, one of the Canaanitish chieftains, Arad, made a bold and sudden attack on their outposts. He was repulsed, pursued into his own country, and some of his towns taken. But this advantage did not tempt them to alter their plan; and when the Edomites not merely refused, but appeared in great force to oppose their passage, no alternative remained but to march southward along the valley of El Araba, and turn the ridge where it is very low, close to the branch of the Red Sea. Before they commenced this march Aaron died, and was buried on Mount Hor. His place of burial is still pointed out by the natives with every appearance of truth. Josephus fixes the position of Mount Hor a short distance to the west of Petra, the capital of the Nabathean Arabs. The ruins of this city were discovered by Burckhardt, and, exactly in the position pointed out by the Jewish historian, he was shown the burying-place of Aaron. Marching along the valley, due south, the Israelites arrived at a district dreadfully infested by serpents, "sent among them," in the language of the sacred volume, "as a punishment for their renewed murmurs." An adjacent region, visited by Burckhardt, is still dangerous on this account. Moses caused a serpent of brass to be made: by steadfastly gazing on this mysterious emblem, whoever had been bitten was miraculously restored to health.

From the end of the ridge, near the gulf of Elath, their march turned northward. The Edomites, taken in flank on the open side of their country, offered no resistance, and the army advanced into the territory of the Moabites. This tribe had been weakened by an unsuccessful war against the Amorites, their northern neighbors, who had pushed their own frontier to the river Arnon. The Israelites passed without opposition through the district of Moab, till they reached that stream now called the Modjeb, which flows in a deep bed with steep and barren banks. Before they violated the territory of the Amorites, they sent a peaceful message to Sihon, their king, requesting free passage on the same terms offered the Edomites. The answer was warlike: a bloody battle took place, which decided the fate of the Amorish kingdom; and the victorious Israelites advanced to the brook Jabbok, which divided the Amorites from the Ammonites, who lay to the eastward, and Bashan which extended along the banks of the Jordan, and the lake of Gennesareth. Og, the chieftain of the latter district, was of a gigantic stature. His iron bedstead, or the iron framework of the divan on which he used to recline, was nine feet long.* But the terror of these formidable antagonists had now passed. Og was defeated, his cities were taken, Argob, his capital, fell: and thus two decisive battles made the Israelites masters of the whole eastern bank of the Jordan, and of the lake of Gennesareth. Still the

* The cubit here is not the sacred cubit, one foot nine inches long, but the natural cubit.

promised land remained unattempted, and the conquerers drew near the river, at no great distance above its influx into the Dead Sea, in a level district, belonging to the Moabites, nearly opposite to Jericho.

The Moabites hitherto had made no resistance: now, in the utmost apprehension, they sent to entreat succor from their more powerful neighbors, the tribes of Midian; who were scattered in different parts of northern Arabia, but lay in the greatest strength to the south-east of Moab, beyond the line on which the Israelites had advanced. Their messengers recounted the fearful numbers of the invaders in language singularly expressive to a people of herdsmen. *They shall lick up all that is round about us, as the ox licketh up the grass.* But they looked for more effective succor than the armed squadrons of Midian. The march of the Israelites had rather the appearance of a religious procession than of a warlike invasion. In the center of the camp, instead of the sumptuous pavilion of their emir or king, arose the consecrated tent of their God. Their leader openly avowed a sacred and inspired character. Their battle-cry denounced their adversaries as the enemies of their God, who was to arise and scatter them. Would the Gods of Moab and Midian, who seem to have been closely connected in their religious belief, interfere in their behalf? Could not some favorite of heaven be found who might balance the fortunes of the Hebrew chieftain, and rescue the natives from their otherwise inevitable servitude? There lived near the river Euphrates a religious man, whose reputation for sanctity extended through all the tribes between that river and the Jordan. The imprecations of Balaam might arrest that tide of victory, which the prayers and sacrifices of Moses had obtained for his people; the disheartened warriors. under the influence of their own prophet, would take courage to encounter again the fierce enthusiasm of the invaders; and in the strength and under the protection of their own deities, the contest might be renewed with confidence of success. But Balaam at once rejects the invitation of Balak king of Moab, and declares that the God of the Israelites forbade him to take part against them. Again, the Moabites send a more urgent request by ambassadors of still higher rank, accompanied with gifts far more costly than they had offered, as the customary present, on the former occasion. At first Balaam refuses, alleging the same insuperable reason, the interdiction laid upon him by the powers of heaven. At length he consents to set forth, and Balak, king of Moab, receives him with the highest honor in one of his frontier cities. But the prophet came not with a lofty mien and daring language of an interpreter of the Divine Will, confident in the success of his oracular predictions.

Strange prodigies, he related, had arrested him on his journey; an angel had appeared in his way; the beast on which he rode had spoken with a human voice, and whether favorable or unfavorable to the cause of Balak, he could only utter what he was commanded from on high. Balak first led him to an eminence sacred to the God of the country; here the king and the prophet built seven altars, a mystical number, sacred among many people, and on each altar offered a bullock and a ram. Balaam then retired apart to another holy and perhaps more open eminence, to await the inspiration. He cast his eyes below; he saw the countless multitudes of the Israelitish tents whitening the whole plain to an immense distance. Awe-struck, he returned to the king, and in wild oracular poetry, began to foretell the splendid fortunes of the people whom he was called upon to curse. Balak carried him to another eminence, where, as if he apprehended that the numbers of the enemy had appalled the mind of the prophet, he could only see a part of their camp. Again the sacrifice is offered, again the prophet retires, and comes back unfolding, in still more vivid strains, the irresistible might of the people whose cause God so manifestly espouses. A third time the trial is made. On the mountain, which was the sanctuary of Peor, or from which, as his most sacred place, the great national God received his name, a third sacrifice is offered. But here the prophet did not, as before, retire to perform his private rites of divination. The trance fell on him at once, and he broke out in admiration of the beautiful order in which the tents of Israel were arrayed, magnified their force, and foretold their uninterrupted career of victory. In vain the king remonstrated. The language assumed a still higher strain and a more mysterious import, the glory of Israel, the total discomfiture of all their adversaries, was the burden of his song. On the one side he beheld the mighty and regular army of Israel, on the other the few and scattered troops of some of the native tribes. On the latter he denounced ruin and destruction, on the former the most splendid destiny which prophetic language could unfold. The general belief of the Jews has dwelt on these mysterious words, "I shall see him, but not now, I shall behold him, but not nigh; there shall come a star out of Jacob, and a scepter out of Israel," as foretelling that great king and conqueror, the Messiah, who was to discomfit the enemies of the Jewish people, and establish their universal and permanent dominion.

But the perverse and venal mind of Balaam was little affected by his own predictions; he gave advice to the native princes more fatal than all his imprecations could have been. While the Israelites lay still encamped under the acacia groves in the plains near the Jordan, the festival of the Midianites approached, in which their maidens were accustomed to prostitute themselves, like the Babylonians and others of the eastern tribes. in honor of their deity. To these impure and flagitious rites, celebrated probably with voluptuous dances and effeminate music, the Israelites are invited: they fall into the snare, they join in the idolatrous sacrifices, partake of the forbidden banquets, worship the false gods, even their princes are corrupted, and the contagion reaches the camp. Zimri, a Simeonite of high rank, publicly leads to his tent the daughter of a Midianitish chieftain. In this dangerous emergency, the conduct of the lawgiver is, as usual, prompt and decisive. The judges are commanded to pronounce the capital sentence enacted in the law. Phineas, the son of Eleazar, the High Priest, seized with holy indignation, transfixes the Simeonite and his mistress in each other's arms. No sooner had this been done, than the pestilence ceased which had broken out in the camp, and by which 24,000 persons had died.

The tribes of Midian paid a dreadful penalty for this insidious and unprovoked attempt on the prosperity of the Israelites. 12,000 chosen warriors, 1,000 from each tribe, made a rapid descent on their country, carried fire and sword into every quarter, destroyed their towns, slew their kings, cut off all their males with the sword, not sparing those of their women who had been the cause of the war, and reserving only the young female virgins, as slaves. In the general massacre fell Balaam the prophet. The booty in cattle and slaves was immense; 675,000 sheep, 72,000 beeves, 61,000 asses, 32,000 female slaves. This was divided into two equal portions, one half assigned to the combatants, the other to the rest of the people. From the share of the combatants a five hundredth part, a fiftieth part from that of the people, was deducted for the sacred treasury committed to the care of the priests and Levites.

After this conquest some of the Israelites began to think they had done enough. The tribes of Reuben and Gad, addicted to a pastoral life, and rich in flocks and herbs, could desire no fairer possession than the luxuriant meadows of Bashan, and the sloping pastures of Gilead. They demanded their portion of the land on the east of the Jordan. The lawgiver assented to their request on the condition that the warriors, leaving their women and their flocks behind, should cross the river, and assist their brethren in the conquest of Palestine. Accordingly the whole conquered territory was assigned to Reuben, Gad, and half the tribe of Manasseh.

At length the termination of the forty years approached, the appointed period at which the Israelites were to enter into the promised land. But the triumph of the people was to be preceded by the death of the lawgiver. He was to behold, not to enter the promised land. Once he had sinned from want of confidence in the Divine assistance; the penalty affixed to his offense was now exacted. As his end approached, he summoned the assembly of all Israel to receive his final instructions. His last thoughts were the welfare of the commonwealth, and the permanence of their constitution. Already the people had been numbered for the third time, they were found not to have increased or decreased very materially since the departure from Egypt. Moses recounted their whole eventful history since their deliverance, their toils, their dangers, their triumphs; he recapitulated and consolidated in one brief code, the book of Deuteronomy, the whole law in some degree modified, and adapted to the future circumstances of the republic. Finally he appointed a solemn ratification of the law, which, although it was not to take place, nor did take place, till after the conquest; yet it is so deeply impressed with the genius and lofty character of the lawgiver, that it may be better to relate it here, than at the time, when it was fulfilled under the direction of Joshua.

Never did human imagination conceive a scene so imposing, so solemn, so likely to impress the whole people with deep and enduring awe, as the final ratification of their polity as commanded by the dying lawgiver. In the territory, afterward assigned to the tribe of Ephraim, a central region, stand two remarkable mountains, separated by a deep and narrow ravine, in which the ancient Sechem, the modern Naplous, stands. Here all Israel was to be assembled, six tribes on one height, six on the other. In the open day, and in a theater, as it were, created by the God of nature for the express purpose, after a sacrifice offered on an altar of stones, the people of Israel testified their free and deliberate acceptance of that constitution, which their God had enacted. They accepted it with its inseparable conditions, maledictions the most awful, which they imprecated on their own heads, in case they should apostatize from its statutes—blessings, equally ample and perpetual, if they should adhere to its holy and salutary provisions.

The type of either destiny lay before them: Mount Ebal was a barren, stony, arid, and desolate crag; Gerizim, a lovely and fertile height, with luxuriant verdure, streams of running water, and cool and shady groves* As God has blasted Ebal, so he would smite the disobedient with barrenness, hunger, and misery; as he crowned Gerizim with beauty and fruitfulness, so he would bless the faithful Israelites, with abundance, with peace, with happiness. On mount Ebal—as the Levites read the heads of the prohibitory statutes, and denounced the curse against the idolator, the oppressor, the adulterer, the unnatural son, the incestuous, the murderer—the tribes of Reuben, Gad, Asher, Zebulun, Dan, and Napthali, with one voice, which was echoed back from the opposite height, responded Amen, so be it. On Gerizim stood the tribes of Simeon, Levi, Judah, Issachar, Joseph, and Benjamin; as the blessings of the law were recited, to give the same unreserved assent

Having thus appointed all the circumstances of this impressive scene; the lawgiver himself enlarged on the blessings of obedience; but with a dark and melancholy foreboding of the final destiny of his people, he laid before them still more at length the consequences of apostacy and wickedness. The sublimity of his

*Whether the sacrifice was offered on Ebal or Gerizim was a question long contested with the greatest acrimony by the Jews and Samaritans, each appealing to their own copy of the law.

denunciations surpasses any thing in the oratory or the poetry of the whole world. Nature is exhausted in furnishing terrific images; nothing, expecting the real horrors of the Jewish history—the miseries of their sieges, the cruelty, the contempt, the oppressions, the persecutions, which for ages this scattered and despised and detested nation have endured—can approach the tremendous maledictions which warned them against the violation of their law. "The Lord shall smite thee with a consumption, and with a fever, and with an inflammation, and with an extreme burning, and with the sword, and with blasting, and with mildew; and they shall pursue thee until thou perish. And the heaven that is over thy head shall be brass, and the earth that is under thee iron. The Lord shall make the rain of thy land powder and dust; from heaven shall it come down upon thee till thou be destroyed..... And thou shalt become an astonishment, and a proverb, and a byword among all nations whither the Lord shall lead thee. A nation of fierce countenance. . . . . . shall besiege thee in all thy gates, ... and thou shalt eat the fruit of thine own body, the flesh of thy sons and thy daughters, which the Lord thy God hath given thee, in the seige and in the straitness wherewith thine enemies shall distress thee. . . . . . And among the nations shalt thou find no ease, neither shall the sole of thy foot have rest; for the Lord shall give thee there a trembling heart, and failing of eyes, and sorrow of mind; and thy life shall hang in doubt before thee, and thou shalt fear day and night, and shalt have none assurance of thy life. In the morning thou shalt say, Would God it were even! and at even thou shalt say, Would God it were morning! for the fear of thine heart wherewith thou shall fear, and for the sight of thine eyes which thou shalt see." The sequel of our history must furnish a most awful comment on these terrific denunciations.

And now closing at length his admonitions, his warnings, and his exhortations to repentance—having renewed the covenant with the whole nation, from the highest to the lowest, *from the prince to the hewer of wood and the drawer of water*—having committed the law to the custody of the Levites, and appointed the valiant Joshua as his successor—finally, having enriched the national poetry with an ode worthy of him who composed the hymn of triumph by the Red Sea—Moses ascended the loftiest eminence in the neighborhood, in order that he might once behold, before his eyes closed for ever, the land of promise.

From the top of Mount Abarim; or Nebo, the former of which names may perhaps be traced in Djebel Attarous, the highest point in the district, the lawgiver, whose eyes were not yet dimmed, and who had suffered none of the infirmities of age, might survey a large tract of country. To the right lay the mountain pastures of Gilead, the romantic district of Bashan; the windings of the Jordan might be traced along its broad and level valley, till, almost beneath his feet, it flowed into the Dead Sea. To the north spread the luxuriant plains of Esdraelon, the more hilly yet fruitful country of Lower Galilee. Right opposite stood the city of Jericho, imbowered in its groves of palms—beyond it the mountains of Judæa, rising above each other till they reached the sea. Gazing on this magnificent prospect, beholding in prophetic anticipation his great and happy commonwealth occupying its numerous towns and blooming fields, Moses breathed his last. The place of his burial was unknown, lest perhaps the impious gratitude of his followers might ascribe divine honors to his name, and assemble to worship at his sepulcher.

Such was the end of the Hebrew lawgiver—a man who, considered merely in an historical light, without any reference to his divine inspiration, has exercised a more extensive and permanent influence over the destinies of his own nation and mankind at large, than any other individual recorded in the annals of the world. Christianity and Mohammedanism alike respect, and, in different degrees, derive their origin from the Mosaic institutes. Thus throughout Europe, with all its American descendants—the larger part of Asia and the north of Africa—the opinions, the usages, the civil as well as religious ordinances—retain deep and indelible traces of their descent from the Hebrew polity. To his own nation Moses was chieftain, historian, poet, lawgiver. He was more than all these—he was the author of their civil existence. Other founders of republics, and distinguished legislators, have been, like Numa, already at the head of a settled and organized community; or have been voluntarily invested with legislatorial authority, like Charondas, Lycurgus, and Solon, by a people suffering the inconveniences of anarchy. Moses had first to form his people, and bestow on them a country of their own, before he could create his commonwealth. The Hebrews would either have been absorbed in the population of Egypt, or remained a wretched Pariah caste, had Moses never lived, or never received his divine commission. In this condition he took them up, rescued them from captivity; finding them unfit for his purpose, he kept them for forty years under the severe discipline of the desert; then led them as conquerors to take permanent possession of a most fruitful region. Yet with singular disregard to his own fame, though with great advantage to his design, Moses uniformly referred to an earlier and more remote personage the dignity of parent of his people. The Jews were children of Abraham, not of Moses; they were a distinguished nation as descendants of the patriarch, not as compatriots of the lawgiver. The virtue of pure and disinterested patriotism never shone forth more unclouded. He nobly declined the offer made to him by the Almighty, to substitute his own family for the offending race of Israel. The permanent happiness of the whole people was the one great object to which the life of Moses was devoted; so that, if we could for an instant suspect that he made use of religion for a political purpose, still that purpose would entitle him to the highest rank among the benefactors of mankind, as having been the first who attempted to regulate society by an equal written law. If God was not the sovereign of the Jewish state, the law was: the best and only safe vicegerent of Almighty Providence, to which the welfare of human communities can be intrusted.

If the Hebrew commonwealth was not a theocracy, it was a nomocracy. On the other hand, if, as we suppose in the Mosaic polity, the civil was subordinate to the religious end, still the immediate well-being of the community was not sacrificed to the more remote object. Independent of the temporal blessings promised to the maintenance of the law, the Hebrew commonwealth was so constituted, as to produce (all circumstances of the times, the situation and character of the people considered) as much or more real happiness and independence than any existing or imaginary government of ancient times. Let, Moses, as contrasted with human legislators, be judged according to his age; he will appear, not merely the first who founded a commonwealth on just principles, but a lawgiver who advanced political society to as high a degree of perfection as the state of civilization which his people had attained, or were capable of attaining, could possibly admit. But if such be the benign, the prematurely wise, and original character of the Mosaic institutions, the faith of the Jew and the Christian in the divine commission of the great legislator is the more strongly established and confirmed.

BOOK V.

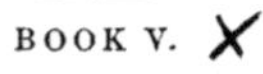

THE CONQUEST.

Joshua assumes the Command—Passage of the Jordan—Capture of Jericho—War with the Canaanites of the South—and of the North—Partition of the Land—Law of Property.

THE lawgiver had done his part, the warrior succeeded to the administration of affairs, and to the directing intercourse with Divine Providence. For thirty days Israel lamented the death of Moses, and then prepared themselves to fulfill his dying instructions. The first military operation of Joshua was to send spies to gain intelligence, and to survey the strength of Jericho, the most powerful city near the place where he proposed to cross the Jordan. The spies entered the city, and took up their lodgings in the house of a woman who kept a public caravansary. The king sent to apprehend them; but Rahab, the mistress of the house, struck with religious terror at the conquests of the Jews, and acknowledging the superiority of their God, concealed them, and provided them with means of escape, letting them down the city wall, on which her house stood, and directing them to fly by the opposite road to that which their pursuers had taken. She received a promise, that on the capture of the city the lives of herself and her family should be spared. She was commanded to mark her house by a scarlet line hanging from the window. The spies brought word that the success of the Hebrew arms had struck terror into the native princes; and Joshua immediately gave orders to effect the passage of the river. The entrance into the promised land was made with suitable solemnity, not in the usual order of march. Instead of occupying its secure central position, the ark of God, borne by the Levites, advanced to the van. This was a bold and dangerous measure. Joshua had no security against a sudden movement or secret ambush of the enemy, which might surprise the sacred coffer, and thus annihilate the hopes, by extinguishing the religious courage of the people. The ark moved forward to the bank of the river; the whole army—for the warriors of Reuben, Gad, and half Manasseh, leaving their families and flocks behind, assembled in the common enterprise—followed at the distance of more than three-quarters of a mile. In the spring, the Jordan is swollen by the early rains, and by the melting of the snow on Mount Lebanon. In its ordinary channel, it is described by Pococke as about as broad as the Thames at Windsor, deep and rapid; but, during its inundation, it forms a second bed, of much greater width, the boundaries of which, according to Maundrell, may be distinctly traced. It was now the season of the flood; but no sooner had the priests, bearing the ark, entered the river, than the descending waters were arrested, the channel became dry, and the whole army passed in safety to the western bank. They encamped in a place named Gilgal; there they kept the fortieth passover since its first institution in Egypt. A rude monument, formed of twelve stones from the bed of the river, was set up to commemorate their wonderful passage; all who had not undergone circumcision were initiated by that rite into the commonwealth; and here the manna, on which they had fed in the desert, entirely failed.

Palestine was by this time governed by a multitude of petty independent kings, who were appalled by this sudden invasion, not of a hostile tribe in quest of plunder, or of a neighboring monarch with the design of reducing the country to a tributary province; but of a whole people advancing with the obvious and avowed intention of obtaining a permanent settlement. The extraordinary circumstances, which attended the march of the Israelites, did not abate their fears. But their fears neither taught them prudence nor unanimity. At first they entered into no league to resist the common enemy, each kingdom or city was left to make the best defense in its power. The storm first broke upon Jericho, a city standing at the extremity of a plain which slopes to the Jordan encircled on every side by an amphitheater of hills, which almost overhang it with their precipitous cliffs. The inhabitants of Jericho prudently awaited behind their walls the approach of the enemy. To their surprise, no attempt was made to scale the walls, or force the gates. They saw what might seem a peaceful procession going regularly round the walls of the city. The army marched first, in total silence. In the rear came the ark, escorted by seven priests blowing seven trumpets, made of rams' horns. For six successive days this mysterious circuit took place; no voice was heard from the vast and breathless army--nothing but the shrill wailing of the trumpet. On the seventh day, this extraordinary ceremony was repeated seven times. At the close of the last round the whole army on a sudden set up a tremendous shout, the walls of the city fell, and the defenseless people found the triumphant enemy rushing along their streets. The slaughter was promiscuous and unsparing, not merely human life, but the beasts of labor were destroyed. Rahab alone escaped. The city was devoted to perpetual desolation, and a malediction imprecated upon the head of him who should attempt to rebuild it.

The capture of Jericho was of great importance, for the art of besieging towns, however rudely fortified, was yet in its infancy. The cities to the east of the Jordan had surrendered in consequence of pitched battles in the open field. Some of the hill fortresses, like Jerusalem, were not taken till the reign of David.

In their next expedition the Israelites suffered a sudden check. Three thousand men marched against the neighboring city of Ai, but were repulsed with loss. The discomfiture implied the abandonment of their cause by the great Giver of victory—their abandonment, guilt. The lots were cast to discover the offender. The lot of condemnation fell on the tribe of Judah. Among the families of Judah it fell on the family of the Zarhites—of that family on the household of Zabdi—of that household on Achan, the son of Carmi.

The criminal confessed that he had purloined from the part of the booty consecrated to God, a rich garment of Babylonian work, and some silver. He was stoned, and his remains burned with fire.

After this signal proof that no crime could escape detection, the army set forth, and by a stratagem became masters of Ai. The main body approached the city, and, when the enemy, emboldened by their former success, sallied forth against them, the Israelites, pretending a sudden panic, fled on all sides. The warriors of Ai pursued, but turning back, saw in utter amazement their city in a blaze. Joshua had placed 5,000 men in ambush, who, rising at an appointed signal, rushed on the town, and, having set it on fire, advanced to attack the enemy in the rear, while Joshua, facing about, attacked them in front. The whole people were exterminated, their king hanged.

The great body of the Israelites remained encamped at Gilgal, a central position. Hither in a short time came some travel-tainted men, with mouldy provisions, their wine-skins full of rents, their shoes worn through. They described themselves as coming from a distant country, where the fame of the Jewish conquests had reached them, to tender their humble submission. The Israelites incautiously consented to a treaty, but found shortly that they had been outwitted by the inhabitants of Gibeon (a Canaanitish city) and its dependant villages which lay at no great distance. The treaty was held sacred, the lives of the Gibeonites spared; but they were degraded into a sort of slaves to the officiating priesthood, in which humble condition we find their descendants at a late period in the history.

A league was now formed among the southern princes of the Amoritish race, five in number, headed by Adonibezek, King of Jerusalem, to revenge the defection of Gibeon, and to arrest the farther progress of the invaders. They attacked the Gibeonites, who sent in all haste to demand assistance. Joshua, by a rapid night-march, fell on the Canaanites, defeated, and pursued them with immense slaughter, while a tremendous hail-storm increased the panic and destruction of the flight. During this pursuit, took place that memorable event, the arresting the sun and moon in their respective courses, at the prayer of Joshua, in order that he might complete the extermination of his flying enemies. Many learned writers, whom to suspect of hostility to revealed religion would be the worst uncharitableness, have either doubted the reality or the extent of this miracle. Some have supposed the miracle only apparent, and have imagined a preternatural refraction of the sun's rays after it had really sunk below the horizon. The words "about a whole day," during which the sun hastened not to go down, they translate, "after the day was finished." Others conceive that the whole is a highly-wrought poetical passage from the book of Jasher, (which there is good reason to believe was the great collection of national lyrics), and hence abounding, according to the genius of Hebrew poetry, with the most daring apostrophes, and delighting in figures drawn from the heavenly bodies. Those who contend for the literal acceptation of the miracle, urge as its obvious purpose, the giving a death-blow to the prevailing superstition of the country, the worship of the sun and moon. Nor can it be denied that there is something astonishingly sublime in supposing the deities of the conquered people thus arrested in their career, and forced to witness the discomfiture and contribute to the extirpation of their worshipers.

After this victory the conquest was rapid and easy: the five kings had fled for refuge to a cave, from which they were taken and put to death; city after city fell, tribe after tribe was exterminated. Joshua returned to Gilgal, having completed the subjugation of the south as far as Gaza, with the exception of some of the strong fortresses.

The northern chieftains had looked on with impolitic indifference during the subjugation of the south; they now saw the tide of conquest roll back upon themselves, and too late began to prepare for their defense. They organized a powerful confederacy, and pitched their camp near the waters of Merom, probably the Samachonite lake, the first into which the Jordan flows. Their strength lay in their cavalry and chariots, which in the central plains and valleys of Palestine could act with greater effeet than in the more mountainous district of the south. Joshua suddenly fell upon them, and one battle decided the fate of the whole region. The conqueror deliberately destroyed all the chariots, and maimed the horses; thus wisely incapacitating the people from extending their conquests beyond the borders of Canaan. The war lasted, on the whole, seven years, the latter part of which was consumed in the reduction of the cities. During this period the seven nations—the Canaanites properly so called, the Amorites, the Hittites, the Hivites, the Girgashites, the Perizzites, and the Jebusites—were entirely subdued, though not extirpated; thirty-one kings had fallen under the sword. At the end of the seven years the Israelites grew weary of the war; they longed to enjoy the fruits of their victories. The tribes of Reuben, Gad, and half Manasseh, impatiently demanded to be dismissed to their families and possessions on the east of the Jordan. Fatally for the future peace of the commonwealth the war was suspended; the conquest remained unfinished; many of the Canaanites remained within the Jewish territory, ready on all occasions to wreak their vengeance on their conquerors, and perpetually weaning the Israelites from their own pure and spiritual faith to the barbarous or licentious rites of idolatry.

The first two objects after the conquest were, first, the solemn recognition of the law on Mount Ebal and Gerizim, according to the last instructions of Moses. This scene took place with all its imposing circumstances. Secondly, the survey and division of the land, with the location of the tribes.

It is almost impossible to calculate with accuracy the area of a country, the frontier of which is irregular on every side. Lowman has given three different estimates of the extent of territory occupied by the twelve tribes, the mean between the two extremes approaches probably the nearest to the truth. According to this computation, the Jewish dominion, at the time of the division, was 180 miles long, by 130 wide, and contained 14,976,000 acres. "This quantity of land will divide to 600,000 men, about 21½ acres, assigned to each household, of course a larger proportion of pasture must have been given to those tribes who subsisted on their herds and flocks, than of arable to those who lived by tillage, the portions of the latter, therefore, must be considerably reduced. On the other hand, the extraordinary fertility of the whole country must be taken into the account.

No part was waste; very little was occupied by unprofitable wood; the more fertile hills were cultivated in artificial terraces, others were hung with orchards of fruit-trees; the more rocky and barren districts were covered with vineyards. Even in the present day, the wars and misgovernment of ages have not exhausted the natural richness of the soil. Galilee, says Malte Brun, would be a paradise were it inhabited by an industrious people, under an enlightened government. No land could be less dependant on foreign importation; it bore within itself every thing that could be necessary for the subsistence and comfort of a simple agricultural people. The climate was healthy, the seasons regular; the former rains, which fell about October, after the vintage, prepared the ground for the seed, the latter, which prevailed during March and the beginning of April, made it grow rapidly. Directly the rains ceased, the grain ripened with still greater rapidity, and was gathered in before the end of May. The summer months were dry and very hot, but the nights cool and refreshed by copious dews. In September, the vintage was gathered. Grain of all kinds, wheat, barley, millet zea, and other sorts, grew in abundance; the wheat commonly yielded thirty for one. Besides the vine and the olive, the almond, the date figs of many kinds, the orange, the pomegranate, and many other fruit trees, flourished in the greatest luxuriance. Great quantities of honey were collected. The balm tree, which produced the opo-balsamum, a great object of trade, was probably introduced from Arabia in the time of Solomon. It flourished about Jericho and in Gilead.

By giving a rapid sketch of the territory assigned to each tribe, we shall be enabled to show the political divisions, the boundaries, the most remarkable features in the general surface of the country, and the productions most abundant in each district. Commencing, from the Transjordanic possessions, the Israelites' southern border was the river Arnon, which divided the land of the Hebrews from that of Moab. Here the tribe of Reuben received their allotment—the northern bank of the Arnon up to Aroer. It comprehended a large portion of the Ghor, or valley of the Jordan. Its chief cities Heshbon, Eleale, and Sibmah, were famous for their vines. All these towns stood inland in the more mountainous district. The ruins of many of them are still visible, and retain their ancient names, Aroer, (Arayr), Heshbon (Hesbon), Eleale (El Aal), Baal Meon (Myoun), Medeba (Madeba). The whole district is called the Belka. The superiority of its pasturage over that of all southern Syria, is the cause that its possession is still fiercely contested by the Arabs. The Bedouins have a saying, "Thou canst not find a country like the Belka." The beef and mutton of this district are preferred to all others. The tribe of Gad was placed to the north of the Reubenites. It is almost impossible to trace their boundary to the south. Their land lay on both sides of the Jabbok(the modern Zerka). On the east it extended as far as Rabbath Ammon, afterward Philadelphia.

It contained all the east side of the valley of the Jordan up to the foot of the sea of Gennesareth, and the southern part of the mountain range called Gilead, the name of which, Djelaad, is still found belonging to a ridge south of the Jabbok; formerly, however, it extended to the whole range from Lebanon to the land of Reuben. Mr. Buckingham was struck with the romantic scenery of this district. Gilead was celebrated for its flocks, and for goats with remarkably fine hair, to which the tresses of the bride, in the Song of Solomon, are compared. North again of Gad, was settled the half tribe of Manasseh, occupying the eastern shore of the lake of Gennesareth, the whole of Bashan, famous for its vigorous breed of cattle, and probably some part of the fertile corn-lands of the ancient and Auronitir, the modern Haouran. This part of the tribe was under the command of Machis, the eldest descendant of Manasseh.

Within the borders of the promised land, the most northern point, at the foot of Lebanon, and near the fountain of the Jordan, was occupied by part of the tribe of Dan, who, finding themselves straitened in their quarters, migrated and took the town of Laish, which assumed the name of their tribe. Next came Napthali, its possessions probably running up into the delightful valleys of the Anti-Libanus. To Asher was assigned the sea coast, a long and narrow slip of land, from the frontiers of Sidon, all round the noble bay of Ptolemais, excepting where it was broken by a part of the territory of Zebulun, to Carmel, including the mountain and part of the rich valley at its foot. But the sea ports, Achzib (Ecdippa) and Acco, (the celebrated Ptolemais, the key of the country during the Crusades), remained in the power of the old inhabitants. The tribe of Zebulun stretched across the land, with one extremity resting on the lake of Gennesareth, the other on the sea in some part of the bay of Acco. Issachar, the other half of Manasseh, and Ephraim, lay in the same manner, one below the other, extending from the Jordan to the Mediterranean.

On the borders of Zebulun and Issachar, rose the Mount Tabor, standing quite alone, on the edge of the great plain of Jezreel (Esdraelon), which is described, even in the present day, as spreading out a boundless expanse of the most luxuriant grain, waving like the sea. The portion of Manasseh became more hilly. Ephraim lay below a fertile, but uneven, and in some parts mountainous territory. On its northern extremity rose Ebal and Gerizim, and to the south the Mount of Ephraim, a district in which were several passes of great importance in the military history of the Jews Ephraim ranked as the most numerous and powerful of the northern tribes. Southward the sea coast and the western part of the inland district fell to the lot of Dan. Benjamin took possession of the palm groves and fertile plain of Jericho, spread over part of the valley of the Jordan and the head of the Dead Sea, and extended westward as far as Jebus, then a fortress in possession of the enemy, afterward Jerusalem. The rest of the south, to the borders of Edom, excepting a district on the south-west about Gaza, assigned to Simeon, made the large and opulent domain of the great tribe of Judah, to whom the first lot had fallen. On the whole, the best pastures were on the east of Jordan, the central plains were the most productive corn lands, the hills of Judah and Benjamin had the richest vineyards and olive grounds.

The assignment of the different estates, the average of which we will assume at about twenty acres, as a farther deduction should be made at this period on account of the unconquered parts of the territory, seems to have been left to the local government of each tribe. Certain distinguished persons, as Joshua and Caleb, received grants of land larger than ordinary; perhaps the heads of the tribes enjoyed a similar privilege; but the whole land was subject to the common law of property. The great principle of this law was the inalienability of estates. Houses in walled towns might be sold in perpetuity, if unredeemed within the year; land only for a limited period. At the jubilee, every estate reverted, without repurchase, to the original proprietor.

Even during this period it might be redeemed should the proprietor become rich enough, at the value which the estate would produce during the years unelapsed before the jubilee. This remarkable Agrarian law secured the political equality of the people, and anticipated all the mischiefs so fatal to the early republics of Greece and Italy, the appropriation of the whole territory of the state by a rich and powerful landed oligarchy, with the consequent convulsions of the community, from the deadly struggle between the patrician and plebeian orders. In the Hebrew state, the improvident individual might reduce himself and his family to penury or servitude, but he could not perpetuate a race of slaves or paupers.

Every fifty years God, the King and Lord of the soil, as it were resumed the whole territory, and granted it back in the same portions to the descendants of the original possessors. It is curious to observe in this earliest practical Utopia, the realization of Machiavelli's great maxim, the constant renovation of the state according to the first principles of its constitution. The outline of this plan may have been Egyptian. The king of that country, during the administration of Joseph, became proprietor of the whole land, and leased it out on a reserved rent of one-fifth, exactly the two-tenths or tithes paid by the Israelites. Thus the body of the people were an independent yeomanry, residing on their hereditary farms, the boundaries of which remained for ever of the same extent; for the removal of a neighbor's landmark was among the crimes against which the law uttered its severest malediction; an invasion of family property, that of Naboth's vineyard, is selected as the worst crime of a most tyrannical king; and in the decline of the state, the prophets denounce, with their sternest energy, this violation of the very basis of the commonwealth. In this luxuriant soil, each man had the only capital necessary to cultivate his property to the highest degree of productiveness, the industry of himself and his sons. Hence large properties would by no means have increased the general wealth, while they might have endangered the independence of the people. The greater danger to be apprehended in so populous a country, might seem to have been the minute subdivisions of the estates, as all the sons inherited; the eldest had a double portion. Females succeeded only in default of males, and then under the restriction that they might not marry out of their own tribe. Yet this inconvenience seems never to have been practically felt, the land, though closely, was never overpeopled. Periods of famine are by no means common.

The law against usury must not be omitted. It is well known how much the exactions from the poor, through the enormous rate of interest added to the political inequalities, evils and jealousies, which distracted Rome and Athens. The Hebrew lawgiver anticipated this evil likewise. He positively prohibited, not merely usury, but all interest whatever on money lent to a Hebrew. A loan was a charitable accommodation due from a brother to a brother. Money might be lent with profit or advantage only to a foreigner. Even pledges, or goods taken in pawn, were under strict regulations. Nothing absolutely necessary to life was to be retained; on no account both the upper and lower stones of the hand-mill in common use. Raiment was to be restored before nightfall; the raiment of a widow was not to be taken at all in pledge. The house was sacred, and could not be entered to seize the goods in pawn.

Each estate was held on the tenure of military service; all Israel was one standing army. Some curious exemptions were made, which show the attention of the lawgiver to the agricultural habits and domestic comfort of his people—the being just married, or having newly taken a piece of land into cultivation.

The only taxes were the two-tenths and the other religious offerings. The first tenth was assigned to the tribe of Levi, as we have before observed for the maintenance of this learned nobility, and in return for the surrender of their right to a twelfth portion of the land. The Levites had likewise forty-eight cities, each with a domain of between eight and nine hundred acres. Thirteen of these cities were in the northern provinces of Napthali, Issachar Asher, and the half of Manasseh beyond Jordan. Twelve in Reuben, Gad, and Zebulun. In Ephraim, half Manasseh, and Dan, ten. In Judah, Benjamin, and Simeon, thirteen.

The second tenth was called the Tithe of Feasts, or the Tithe of the Poor. For the first and second year, in the place where the nation assembled for divine worship, *in the presence of the Lord;* every third year in the chief town of the district, public tables were opened, at which all ranks and classes feasted together at the common expense of the richer proprietors. An institution, simple and béautiful, securing the advantages of brotherhood and kindly feeling, while it avoided that too great interference with the private and domestic habits which arose out of the public tables in some of the Grecian republics. The Hebrew was reminded sufficiently often that he was a member of a larger national, and a smaller municipal community, but his usual sphere was that of private life. The Greek was always a public man, the member of the family was lost in the citizen.

The only public revenue of the Hebrew commonwealth was that of the sacred treasury, the only public expenditure that of the religious worship. This was supported by a portion of the spoils taken in war; the first fruits, which in their institution were no more than could be carried in a basket, at a later period were rated to be one part in sixty; the redemption of the first born, and of whatever was vowed to the Lord. Almost every thing of the last class might be commuted for money according to a fixed scale. The different annual festivals were well calculated to promote internal commerce; maritime or foreign trade, is scarcely mentioned in the law, excepting in two obscure prophetic intimations of advantages, which the tribes of Dan and Zebulum were to derive from their maritime situation.

On this subject the lawgiver could have learned nothing in Egypt. The commerce of that country was confined to the inland caravan trade. The Egyptians hated or dreaded the sea, which they considered either the dwelling of the evil principle, or the evil principle itself. At all events, the Hebrews, at this period were either blind to the maritime advantages of their situation, or unable to profit by them. The ports were the last places they conquered. Sidon, if indeed within their boundary, never lost its independence; Tyre, if it existed, was a town too obscure to be named Ecdippa and Acco remained in the power of the Canaanites; Joppa is not mentioned as a port till much later.

The manufactures of the people supplied their own wants; they brought from Egypt the arts of weaving woollens and linens, stuffs made of fine goat's hair, and probaly cotton; of dying in various colors, and bleaching, and of embroidering; of many kinds of carpenter's work; of building, some of the rules of which were regulated by law; of making earthenware vessels; of working in iron, brass, and the precious metals, both casting them and forming them with the tool; of gilding, engraving seals, and various other kinds of ornamental work, which were employed in the construction of the altars and sacred vessels of the Tabernacle.

Thus the posterity of Abraham, Isaac, and Jacob, were permanently established in the promised land, each man, according to the picturesque language of the country, dwelt under his own vine or his own fig-tree. No accident disturbed the peace and harmony of the state before the death of Joshua, excepting a dispute between the tribes within and those beyond the Jordan. The Transjordanic tribes raised a public altar to God; this was resented by the rest of the nation as a signal of defection from the national religion and national confederacy. But before they resorted to violent means, they tried an amicable remonstrance.

The conference was conducted with temper and moderation, the tribes beyond the river disclaimed all intention of derogating from the dignity of the single national place of divine worship, and protested that they had raised the altar, not for the purpose of offering rival sacrifices, but only to commemorate to their posterity the signal mercies of their God. The explanation was considered satisfactory, and peace restored.

A short time after this event Joshua, whose military prowess and experience had directed the conquest of the country, died. He appointed no successor to the supreme authority, and the separate republics, under the control of their own chieftains, and other local officers, assumed the administration of affairs.

The Utopia of the lawgiver commenced its political existence; the land of milk and honey began to yield its fruits to a simple, free, and pious race of husbandmen, people worthy of its blessings: but one fatal act of disobedience, the desisting from the war before their enemies were rooted out, prevented its permanence; and the land which was intended to be a scene of peace and freedom, before long became that of war and servitude.

BOOK VI.

THE JUDGES.

Authority of the Judges—Destruction of the Tribe of Benjamin—Othniel—Deborah—Gideon—Jephthah—Samson—Eli—Samuel—Nomination of Saul as King.

THE PERIOD FROM THE EXODUS TO THE BUILDING OF THE TEMPLE.

According to Josephus and St. Paul, 591 *yrs.* 6 *m.*	
The desert	40
Conquest and partition	7
To first servitude	20
Mesopotamian servitude	8
Othniel to second servitude	40
Moabite servitude	18
Ehud and Shamgar	80
Canaanitish servitude	20
Deborah and Barak	40
Midianitish servitude	7
Gideon	40
Abimelech	3
Tola	22
Jair	22
Ammonitish servitude	18
Jephthah	6
Ibzan	7
Elon	10
Abdon	8
Philistine sevitude-Samson and Eli	60
Anarchy	20.6
Samuel	12
Samuel and Saul	40
David	40
Solomon	3
	591.6

According to the Vulgar Bible Chronology, 478 *yrs.* 6 *m.*	
The desert	40
Conquest and partition	6.4
Mesopotamian servitude and Othniel	40
Moab and Ehud	80
Canaanites and Deborah	40
Midian and Gideon	40
To Abimelech	9.2
Abimelech—Tola—Jair	48
Jephthah	6
Ibzan—Elon—Abdon	25
Eli and Samson	40
Samuel	21
Saul	40
David	40
Solomon	3
	478.6

According to the shorter scheme, the Exodus took place about 1490, B. C.; according to the longer, about 1600, B. C.

The period of the Judges is the heroic age of Hebrew history. It abounds in wild adventure, and desperate feats of individual valor. Personal activity, daring, and craft, were the qualifications which raised the judges to their title and eminence. They appear in their history as gallant insurgents or guerilla leaders, rather than as grave adminstrators of justice, or the regular authorities of a great kingdom. The name by which they are called, Sophetim, derived from a word signifying "to judge," bears remarkable resemblance to the Suffetes of the Carthaginians. The office of the Hebrew judge was rather that of the military dictator, raised on an emergency to the command of the national forces. What his judicial functions could have been, seems very doubtful, as all ordinary cases would fall under the cognizance of the municipal judicatures. Nor do we find the judges exercising authority, or even engaged in war, beyond the boundaries of their own tribe; unless perhaps Deborah, who sate under her palm-tree judging the tribes of Israel. Yet even this convention bears the appearance rather of an organized warlike confederacy, to break the yoke of the Canaanites, than of a peaceful judicial assembly; and some of the tribes took no share in her gallant enterprise, nor, as far as appears, rendered any allegiance to her authority. In fact, the want of union among the tribes arose naturally out of their disobedience to the commands of their lawgiver, and brought with it the punishment of that disobedience, not merely in the abandonment of protecting Providence, but in the ordinary course of events. The neighborhood of the idolatrous tribes led to apostacy, apostacy to weakness and servitude. For, as the national strength depended on the national union, and the only bond of the national union was the national religion, that bond weakened or dissolved, the tribes remained a number of scattered cantons each entirely dependant on its own internal resources to resist foreign invasion, or the insurrection of the Canaanites.

The imperfect conquest had left formidable enemies, not only on the frontier, but in the heart of the land. The necessity of taking up those arms which they had so rashly laid down, speedily became urgent. It was no longer, however, a national war, but a war of the separate tribes against their immediate enemies. The Danites were driven into the mountains by the revolt of the Amorites, and part of the tribe was obliged to seek a settlement by force of arms on the extreme northern frontier. The town of Laish was hence called Dan. Judah and Simeon attacked Bezek, a powerful king, of Jebus or Jerusalem—defeated him with great loss—treated him as he had been accustomed to treat the other kings whom he had subdued, by the mutilation of his extremities. They burned the lower part of Jerusalem; then, turning their arms southward, expelled the gigantic inhabitants of Hebron.

But Gaza, Askelon, and Ekron, still defied their power; and though they starved many of the mountain fortresses to surrender, they dared not encounter the iron chariots of the inhabitants of the southern valleys. Ephraim took the town of Bethel; but the other tribes seem to have adopted the dangerous measure of entering into terms with their enemies, and permitting them to reside in the land on the payment of tribute. Intermarriages soon followed, and led to community of religious rites. The Israelites strayed without scruple into the shady groves, where the voluptuous rites of the Canaanites were held, or attended at their gay and splendid festivals. By degrees they began to incorporate the two religions, and to pay indiscriminate homage to the symbolic representations of the powers of nature, particularly of the sun and moon, as well as to their own peculiar God, the Creator of the Universe.

The decline of the national faith, and the dissolution of manners, were fearfully exemplified in certain other transactions which occurred before the time of the Judges. Part of the Danites, on their way to their conquest of the northern border, took violent possession of a silver idol, the property of an individual named Micah, and set it up, with a wandering Levite for its priest, as an object of religious worship. The crime of Benjamin was of a more cruel nature, and as directly opposite to the principles of the moral law, as to the spirit of the national union. It led to a bloody civil war, and almost to the total annihilation of the guilty tribe. It is a history of bloody crime, wild justice, and still wilder mercy. A Levite returning to his home with his concubine, or inferior wife, entered, to pass the night, the city of Gibeah, in the territory of Benjamin. The dissolute inhabitants abused the wretched woman till she died. The Levite cut the body into pieces, and sent a portion to each of the tribes.

The whole of Israel assembled as one man at Mizpeh, heard with indignation the appeal to their justice, and sent to demand the surrender of the delinquents. The proud and powerful tribe refusing satisfaction, the rest declared war, and invaded their territory. Twice they were defeated with great slaughter: on the third attack, employing a common stratagem, they enticed their enemies, by a pretended flight, to leave the strong walls of Gibeah, and follow them into the plain. An ambush rose up behind and surprised the city. Benjamin was defeated with the loss of 25,000 men—the guilty city razed—the whole land laid desolate—men, women, and children put to the sword: 600 men alone remained strongly posted on the rock of Rimmon. But even in the pride of triumph, and the stern satisfaction of just revenge, Israel could not behold the extermination of their tribes without the deepest sorrow and repentance. Yet they had sworn at Mizpeh never to give their daughters in marriage to the unnatural and rebellious race.

How then shall the families of Benjamin be renewed, and the twelve tribes of Jacob again meet in their solemn assemblies? Strange situations lead to strange expedients. One city, Jabesh in Gilead, had been guilty of that most heinous crime, the desertion of the common cause at a time of danger and distress. The city was devoted. All the men were slain; the women given to the survivors of Benjamin. The number not being sufficient, the rest of the Benjamites were permitted to surprise the damsels dancing at a festival without the gates of Shiloh; and by these Sabine marriages the tribe of Benjamin gradually recovered its strength and consideration.

The generation which had entered the land with Joshua, is said to have passed away before the declension of the people from the national faith led to servitude; but not entirely, for the first deliverer of the people was Othniel, the nephew and son-in-law of Caleb, whose name occurs as a brave warrior during the conquest.

A powerful monarchy had now grown up in Mesopotamia; the king, Chushan-rishathaim, extended his conquests at least as far as the Jordan. The federal leagues between the tribes was not yet so far relaxed but that Othniel, of Judah, took up their defense. At the end of eight years the Mesopotamian was entirely defeated, and the whole land remained in peace for forty more. The eastern tribes were then assailed by a confederacy of the Ammonites,—Malekites, and Moabites, under Eglon, king of the latter tribe. Jericho, the city of palms, or its site, was also taken, perhaps from the tribe of Benjamin not having yet recovered its strength. This oppression lasted eighteen years. The deliverance was effected by a desperate enterprise of Ehud, a Benjamite. Ehud was a man ambi-dexter, who could use his left hand as well as his right.

He obtained an audience of Eglon, a remarkably fat man, struck his dagger into his body, escaped, and flying to the mountainous part of the land of Ephraim, roused that powerful tribe, and totally defeated the Moabites. Eighty years of peace were the fruit of this hazardous adventure. The only exploit recorded of the next judge, Shamgar, is the slaughter of 600 Philistines with an ox-goad, a formidable weapon, if like that described by Maundrell—a strong pike, eight feet long, and pointed with iron. By this time, the Canaanites, in the north, had grown into a powerful people. Hazor, the capital of Jabin their king, was on the shore of the Samachonite Lake, and his general, Sisera, was a man terrible for his valor and conduct. For twenty years he oppressed the northern tribes. Deborah a high born woman of the tribe of Ephraim, richly endowed, at least, with the poetic part of the character of a prophetess, was inspired with the noble design of freeing her brethren from the yoke. She sat in the open air, under a palm-tree, reminding us of the Velleda of ancient Germany, and organized a strong confederacy. Ephraim, Benjamin, and Manasseh, as well as the northern tribes, obeyed her call. She commanded Barak to draw up the forces of Issachar, Zebulun and Naphthali on the summit of Mount Tabor.

The vast army of the Canaanites, 900 chariot strong, covered the level plain of Esdraelon at its foot. Barak burst suddenly from the mountain—the Canaanites were broken, and fled. The river Kishon, which bounded the plain was swollen, and multitudes perished in the waters. But for the criminal inactivity of the inhabitants of Meroz, an adjacent town, who did not join in the pursuit, few would have escaped. Sisera fled, and took refuge in the tent of Jael, a woman of the Kenite tribe, the descendants of Hobab, Moses' brother-in-law. She received him hospitably, entertained him with the pastoral refreshment of milk, and left him to repose. In his sleep she drove one of the iron pegs of the tent into his head and killed him. Deborah's hymn of triumph was worthy of the victory. The solemn religious commencement—the picturesque description of the state of the country—the mustering of the troops from all quarters—the sudden transition to the most contemptuous sarcasm against the tribes that stood aloof—the life, fire and energy of the battle—the bitter pathos of the close—lyric poetry has nothing in any language which can surpass the boldness and animation of this striking production. But this hymn has great historic as well as poetic value. It is the only description of the relation of the tribes to each other, and of the state of society during the period of the Judges. The northern tribes—Zebulun, Issachar, Naphthali—appear in a state of insurrection against their oppressors; they receive some assistance from Ephraim, Manasseh, and Benjamin. The pastoral tribes beyond Jordan remain in unpatriotic inactivity. Dan and Asher are engaged in their maritime concerns; a curious fact, for we have no other intimation of any mercantile transactions of the Hebrews—as these expressions seem to imply—earlier than the reign of Solomon. Of Judah and Simeon there is no notice whatever, as if they had seceded from the confederacy, or were occupied by enemies of their own.

Thus sang Deborah and Barak, son of Abinoam,
In the day of victory thus they sang:
That Israel hath wrought her mighty vengeance,
That the willing people rushed to battle,
O, therefore, praise Jehovah!

Hear, ye kings! give ear, ye princes!
I to Jehovah, I will lift the song,
I will sound the harp to Jehovah, God of Israel!

Jehovah! when thou wentest forth from Seir!
When thou marchedst through the fields of Edom,
Quaked the earth, and poured the heavens,
Yea, the clouds poured down with water:
Before Jehovah's face the mountains melted,
That Sinai before Jehovah's face,
The God of Israel.

In the days of Shamgar, son of Anath,
In Jael's days, untrodden were the highways,
Through the winding by-path stole the traveler;
Upon the plains deserted lay the hamlets,

Even till that I, till Deborah arose,
Till I arose in Israel a mother.

They chose new gods;
War was in all their gates!
Was buckler seen, or lance,
'Mong forty thousand sons of Israel?

My soul is yours, ye chiefs of Israel!
And ye, the self-devoted of the people,
Praise ye the Lord with me!
Ye that ride upon the snow-white asses;
Ye that sit to judge in rich divans;
Ye that plod on foot the open way,
Come meditate the song.

For the noise of plundering archers by the wells of water,
Now they meet and sing aloud Jehovah's righteous acts;
His righteous acts the hamlets sing upon the open plains,
And enter their deserted gates the people of Jehovah.

Awake, Deborah! awake!
Awake, uplift the song!
Barak, awake! and lead thy captives captive,
Thou son of Abinoam!

With him a valiant few went down against the mighty,
With me Jehovah's people went down against the strong.

First Ephraim, from the Mount of Amalek,
And after thee, the bands of Benjamin!
From Machir came the rulers of the people,
From Zebulun those that bear the marshal's staff;
And Issachar's brave princes came with Deborah,
Issachar, the strength of Barak:
They burst into the valley on his footsteps.

By Reuben's fountains there was deep debating—
Why sat'st thou idle, Reuben, 'mid thy herd-stalls?
Was it to hear the lowing of thy cattle.
By Reuben's fountains there was deep debating—

And Gilead lingered on the shores of Jordan—
And Dan, why dwelled he among his ships?—
And Asher dwelled in his sea-shore havens,
And sat upon his rocks precipitous.
But Zebulun was a death-defying people,
And Naphthali from off the mountain heights.

Came the king and fought,
Fought the kings of Canaan,
By Taanach, by Megiddo's waters,
For the golden booty that they won not.

From the heavens they fought 'gainst Sisera,
In their courses fought their stars against him:
The torrent Kishon swept them down,
That ancient river Kishon.
So trample thou, my soul, upon their might.

Then stamped the clattering hoofs of prancing horses
At the flight, at the flight of the mighty.

Curse ye Meroz, saith the angel of the Lord,
Curse, a twofold curse upon her dastard sons:
For they came not to the succor of Jehovah,
To the succor of Jehovah 'gainst the mighty.
Above all women blest be Jael,
Heber the Kenite's wife,
O'er all the women blest, that dwell in tents.

Water he asked—she gave him milk,
The curded milk, in her costliest bowl.

Her left hand to the nail she set,
Her right hand to the workman's hammer—

Then Sisera she smote—she clave his head;
She bruised—she pierced his temples.
At her feet he bowed; he fell; he lay;
At her feet he bowed; he fell;
Where he bowed, there he fell dead.

From the window she looked forth, she cried,
The mother of Sisera, through the lattice;
"Why is his chariot so long in coming?
Why tarry the wheels of his chariot?"
Her prudent women answered her—
Yea, she herself gave answer to herself—
"Have they not seized, not shared the spoil?
One damsel, or two damsels to each chief?
To Sisera a many-colored robe,
A many-colored robe, and richly broidered,
Many-colored, and broidered round the neck."

Thus perish all thine enemies, Jehovah;
And those who love thee, like the sun, shine forth,
The sun in all its glory.*

At the end of forty years of peace new enemies appeared—the wild hordes of the desert, Midianites, Amalekites, and other nomadic tribes, swept over almost the whole land, pitched their tents, and fed their camels in the midst of the rich corn-fields of Israel. This was the most extensive and destructive servitude the nation had yet suffered. The people fled to mountain fastnesses, and hid themselves in caves. The land lay uncultivated, the cattle were destroyed, and a grievous famine ensued. The miserable Israelites called upon their God for succor, and Gideon, of the tribe of Manasseh, received the divine commission as the deliverer of his country. An angel appeared to him while he was thrashing corn by stealth in an underground winepress; preternatural signs convinced him of the celestial nature of his visitant. Gideon had offered as a present to this superior being, a kid and a small portion of flour: he laid them on a rock. The angel touched them, and fire arose from the rock and consumed them. His first exploit, after having built an altar, and, according to divine command, offered sacrifice, was to overthrow at midnight the altar of Baal in the city of Ophrah. His father Joash was commanded by the indignant citizens to bring forth his son to be punished for this offense. *Will ye plead for Baal?* said the old man: *let Baal plead for himself.* And Gideon thence was called Jerub-baal—let Baal plead. The whole host of the invaders lay encamped on the plain of Jezreel. Gideon demanded a sign from heaven; it was granted. One night, the dews which fall so copiously in those regions, fell only on a fleece which he had spread; the next night the ground was steeped with moisture—the fleece remained dry. Gideon now prepared for a vigorous attack; 22,000 men, from Manasseh, Zebulun, Naphthali, and Asher, rallied at the sound of his trumpet—but the victory was to be achieved by a much smaller band. The army was first diminished to 10,000, all whose valor could not be relied on being allowed to return home. These were again reduced by a singular process, of which it is difficult to discover the meaning. They were led to the water side: those who knelt down to drink, were dismissed; those who stood up, and lifted the water to their lips with their hands, were retained. Thus 300 of the bravest were chosen for a night attack. Each of these had a trumpet, a concealed lamp and an earthen pot. At the onset, each crashed his pot in pieces, and blew his trumpet with all his might. The wild and mingled tribes awoke, and, in their panic and confusion, turned their arms upon each other. The herds, and particularly the camels, affrighted at the lights, ran wildly about and added to the tumult. The fugitives were slain by the rest of Gideon's troops. The Ephraimites now joined the insurrection, pursued the remnant of the Midianites beyond Palestine, and slew two of their princes, Oreb and Zeb! Their indignation against Gideon at not being earlier summoned to the war, was soothed by the courtesy of the leader. Gideon took a dreadful revenge on the inhabitants of Succoth for having refused refreshment to his famishing warriors—he scourged their elders to death with thorns. He inflicted as dreadful a chastisement on the surviving princes of Midian, Zebah and Zalmuna, who had slain his kindred: he put them to death without mercy; and thus the war ended with the loss of 120,000 men to the Midianites. The gratitude of his compatriots induced them to make an offer of royal authority to Gideon, but his ambition was satisfied with the deliverance of his country; he returned to dwell in quiet in his native city. Yet even Gideon fell into a direct violation of the law. From the spoil of the Midianites, who, like all the inhabitants of those regions, wore enormous golden earrings, and from the splendid raiment of the kings, he made an ephod or priestly garment; and set up a worship distinct from the one sacred place in Shiloh, where the ark rested.

After the death of Gideon, his bastard son Abimelech, a daring and bloody man, determined to attain the crown which his father had rejected. He formed a conspiracy with his mother's kindred at Shechem; with a band of adventurers fell unexpectedly on Ophrah; seized his father's seventy sons, slew them all; and, in a great convention of the Shechemites and the inhabitants of the neighboring towns, was elected king by acclamation. Of all Gideon's sons, Jotham alone, the youngest, had escaped. On the summit of Gerizim, which overlooked Shechem he denounced the usurper, and reproved the people in the well-known parable: "The olive tree and the vine refused to assume the royal dignity, but the worthless bramble accepted at once the first offer of a tyrannous superiority over the trees of the forest." The authority of Abimelech seems to have been confined to Shechem and its neighborhood; the other tribes neither contributed to his rise or

* In the above translation an attempt is made to preserve something like a rythmical flow. It adheres to the original language, excepting where an occasional word is, but rarely, inserted, for the sake of perspicuity.

downfall. But the fickle Shechemites, after three years, began to be weary of their king, and attempted to throw off the yoke. The usurper was not wanting in vigor and promptitude; he took the city, razed it to the ground, and burned the citadel, on which they seem to have relied as a place of strength. Pursuing his conquests, he was accidentally wounded by a woman during an attack on Thebez, but disdaining to die by so ignoble a hand, he commanded his armor-bearer to pierce him with his sword.

Two undistinguished names follow in the list of judges: Tola, of the tribe of Issachar, who nevertheless, dwelt at Shamir in the mountainous country of the Ephraimites; and Jair, a Gileadite, whose thirty sons were masters of thirty cities, *and rode on thirty ass colts.* A new apostacy led to a new invasion. The Philistines attacked the southern border; and a more formidable enemy, the Ammonites, not merely subdued the tribes beyond Jordan, but crossed the river, and engaged the combined forces of Ephraim, Judah, and Benjamin.

Jephthah, a bastard son of Gilead, having been wrongfully expelled from his father's house had taken refuge in a wild country, and become a noted captain of freebooters. His kindred, groaning under foreign oppression, began to look to their valiant, though lawless compatriot, whose profession however, according to their usage, was no more dishonorable than that of a pirate in the elder days of Greece. They sent for him, and made him head of their city. Jephthah's first measure was to send an embassy to the Ammonitish king, remonstrating on his unprovoked aggression. The Ammonite demanded the formal surrender of the transjordanic provinces, as the patrimony of his own ancestors and of those of his allies. Negotiations being fruitless, Jephthah prepared for war. But before he set forth he made the memorable vow, that, if he returned victorious, he would sacrifice as a burnt offering whatever first met him on his entrance into his native city, Mizpeh. He gained a splendid victory; but it was neither one of those animals appointed for sacrifice, nor even an unclean beast, an ass, or camel, prohibited by the law, which was destined for the burnt offering of Jephthah. At the news of her father's victory, his only daughter came dancing forth in the gladness of her heart, and with the most jocund instruments of music, to salute the deliverer of his people. The miserable father rent his clothes in agony, but the noble-spirited maiden would not hear of the evasion or disregard of the vow, she only demanded a short period to bewail upon the mountains, like the Antigone of Sophocles, her dying without hope of becoming a bride or mother of Israel, and then submitted to her fate. Many learned writers have labored to relieve the Jewish annals and the character of the judge from the imputation of human sacrifice, and have supposed that Jephthah's daughter was consecrated to the service of the tabernacle, and devoted to perpetual virginity.

But all these expedients are far more improbable than that a fierce freebooter, in a period of anarchy, should mistake an act of cruel superstition for an act of religion; and it is certain that vows of celibacy were totally unknown among the Hebrews, and belong to a different stage of society. Another objection of Michaelis is fatal to these views. The daughter could not be consecrated to the service of the high-priest, for the high-priest and the ark were then at Shiloh, in the Territory of Ephraim, with whom Jephthah was at deadly war. The haughty and overbearing character of this tribe resented, as usual, their not being summoned to take the lead in the Ammonitish war. They threatened to wreak their vengeance on Jephthah and his adherents; but the Gileadite chieftain defeated them, and at the passage of the Jordan, distinguishing the Ephraimites by a peculiar pronunciation, (Shibboleth, water streams, they sounded as Sibboleth), put them to the sword without mercy to the number of 42,000. Jephthah enjoyed his dignity for seven years; then follow a list of undistinguished names; of their actions, or against whom they waged war, the record is silent. Ibzan of Bethlehem judged seven; Elon of Zebulun ten; Abdon, an Ephraimite, eight years.

The oppressions of the foreign powers which had hitherto overrun or subdued Palestine, had been heavy and debasing while they lasted, but once repelled, the invaders retired within their own frontiers; the Philistines on the southern borders were more dangerous and implacable enemies to the peace of Israel. They had subdued apparently the whole allotment of Simeon; this tribe was annihilated, or scattered for refuge among the rest. Gaza and Ashkelon were in the power of the conquerors, and their frontier extended to that of Dan. At this juncture the most extraordinary of the Jewish heroes appeared; a man of prodigious physical power, which he displayed not in any vigorous and consistent plan of defense against the enemy, but in the wildest feats of personal daring. It was his amusement to plunge headlong into peril, from which he extricated himself by his individual strength. Samson never appears at the head of an army, his campaigns are conducted in his own single person. As in those of the Grecian Hercules, and the Arabian Anter, a kind of comic vein runs through the early adventures of the stout-hearted warrior, in which love of women, of riddles, and of slaying Philistines out of mere wantonness, vie for the mastery. Yet his life began in marvel, and ended in the deepest tragedy. An angel announced to the wife of Manoah, a man of eminence in the tribe of Dan, that her barrenness should be removed, and that she should become the mother of a wonderful child. The child was to be a Nazarite from the womb, that is, dedicated by vow to the Lord; he was, therefore, to allow his hair to grow, and preserve the most rigid abstinence. A second time the angel appeared to Manoah and his wife, renewed the command and the promise, and mounting with the smoke of the sacrifice they had offered, ascended into heaven. When Samson grew up, his first demand was, that he might marry a Philistine woman, whom he had seen and fallen in love with at Timnath. With reluctance his parents consented, for they suspected some latent design against the oppressor. As he went down to Timnath, a young lion roared at him; Samson tore him asunder with his hands. The next time he passed that way bees had hived in the lion's carcass, and at his bridal feast he gave this riddle to the thirty youths who attended him, if they found it out he was to forfeit to each a sheet and a garment, if they did not, they were to pay the same to him.

"Out of the eater came forth meat, and out of the strong came forth sweetness." At the entreaty of his wife, he betrayed the secret to her, and she to her countrymen. "Had ye not ploughed with my heifer, ye had not found out my riddle," replied the indignant bridegroom, and immediately set out and slew thirty Philistines, in order to make good his promise. He then returned home in anger, but, in a short time, visiting his wife again, he found her married to another. To revenge himself he caught three hundred jackals, tied them tail to tail with a fire-brand between them, and turned them loose into the dry corn-fields of the Philistines. In return they burned his wife and her father to death. Samson immediately fell on them, and slew great numbers; he then took refuge on a rock called Etam.

The Philistines were assembled in a narrow pass, from some fanciful resemblance to the jaw-bone of an ass, or more probably from the adventure of Samson, called Lehi. So completely were the valiant tribe of Judah disheartened by the Philistine oppression, that, to appease their wrath, they determined to surrender Samson. They seized and bound him, and brought him to the pass. There the spirit of the Lord came upon him, he burst the bonds like flax, seized the jaw-bone of an ass that lay in the way, and with this strange weapon slew a thousand men. But exhausted with fatigue and thirst, he began to faint, the ground was suddenly cloven, and a spring of water flowed before his feet. His next exploit was to visit a harlot in Gaza, the capital city of his enemies. They closed their gates, and waited quitely to seize their formidable foe. At midnight Samson arose, burst the gates, took them on his shoulders, and left them on a hill near twenty miles distant. He then fell into the more fatal snares of Delilah.

The Philistine chieftains bribed her to obtain the secret of his prodigious strength. Twice he eluded her; the third time he betrayed himself into her power. It lay in the accomplishment of his Nazaritish vow, part of which was never to permit his hair to be shorn. In his sleep she deprived him of his hair and of his strength. The Philistines siezed him, put out his eyes, bound him with brazen fetters, and set him to the servile task of grinding at the mill. The grave and solemn mind of Milton has seized upon the history of Samson at this point, and arrayed the close of his life in all the grandeur of heroic patience and resignation. The insults of the Philistines did not end with the prison; savages delight in making a public exhibition of distinguished captives, and this barbarous people sent for their prisoner to contribute to their diversion in a kind of rude amphitheater, in the area of which stood the captive; the roof, which formed the seats, was crowded with spectators.

But the strength of Samson had now returned; the whole building was supported by two pillars, which he grasped, and leaning himself forward, dragged down the whole building, burying himself and all his enemies in one common ruin.

While Samson was thus wasting his prodigal strength, not altogether uselessly, for, without doubt, the terror of his name retarded the progress of the Philistine conquests, and inspired courage into the disheartened Israelites; still without that permanent advantage to the liberty of his countrymen which might have been expected from such preternatural powers, regulated by prudence and self-restraint; a wiser and more useful head of the state was growing up within the sacred precincts of the tabernacle. Hannah, one of the wives of Elkanah, a Levite who resided in Rama-Zophim, a city in Mount Ephraim, made a vow, that if the curse of barrenness were removed from her, she would devote her first-born to the service of God.

Samuel, her son, was thus educated in the service of the high-priest Eli. It was to be expected that the high-priest would obtain great weight and authority in the Hebrew constutition. Wherever the ark resided, might be considered the temporary capital of the state. The present circumstances of the Hebrew history contributed to exalt still higher the sacerdotal power. The tabernacle and the ark were at Shiloh in the territory of Ephraim, from its fortunate central position the most powerful, as the least exposed to foreign invasion, of all the provinces. The northern and eastern tribes had enough to do to defend their frontiers; Judah, the great rival of Ephraim, now tamely acnowledged the Philistines as their masters. Hence the uncontested pre-eminence of the Ephraimities led to a temporary union of a civil as well as religious supremacy in the high-priest Eli. But Eli was now old and almost blind, his criminal indulgence to his sons Hophni and Phineas had brought disorder and licentiousness into the sacred ceremonies. The priests had become overbearing and tyrannical; instead of taking the portions of the sacrifices assigned by the law, they selected all the better parts for their own use; and Hophni and Phineas had introduced still worse abuses, those which disgraced the voluptuous rites of the heathen deities. They debauched the women who assembled before the tabernacle, and the worship of Jehovah was thus in danger of becoming as impure, as that of Baal Peor, or the

Babylonian Mylitta. In the midst of this corruption the blameless Samuel grew up to manhood. Already in his early youth he had received divine intimations of his future greatness; the voice of God, while he slumbered within the area where the tabernacle stood, had three times called upon his name; and at length aroused him, and commanded him to communicate to the aged Eli the fate which awaited his family. the war between the Philistines and Israelites broke out anew; whether the Israelites, encouraged by the destruction of so many of the Philistine chieftains in the fall of the temple at Gaza, had endeavored to throw of the yoke, or whether the Philistines seized the op portunity of Samson's death to extend their dominion, does not appear. A bloody battle took place at Aphek, in the northern part of Judah, in which the Israelites were totally defeated, and in their desperation they determined to resort to those means of conquest which had proved irresistible under the direction of Joshua. They sent to Shiloh for the ark of God, and placed it in the center of their forces. But the days were gone when the rivers dried up, and the walls of cities fell down, and the enemy fled at once before the symbol of the presence of Israel's God. The measure was unauthorized by the Divine command. Yet even the victorious Philistines were not free from hereditary apprehension of the mighty God, who had discomfited the Egyptians, and subjugated the whole land of the Canaanites. They exhorted each other to maintain their character for valor. The Israelites fought with desperate but unavailing resolution—the iron chariots of the Philistines triumphed.

Thirty thousand Israelites perished, and the ark of God fell into the hands of the uncircumcised—the guilty sons of Eli were slain in its defense. The aged high-priest sat by the wayside in dreadful anxiety for the fate of the ark. A messenger rushed in, bearing the sad intelligence; a wild cry ran through the whole city, the blind old man, now ninety-eight years of age, fell from his seat, broke his neck, and died. The wife of Phineas was seized with the pains of premature labor; the women around her endeavored to console her with the intelligence that she had borne a male child; she paid no attention to their words, and only uttered a passionate exclamation by which we may judge how strongly the religious reverence for the divine worship was rooted in the hearts of the Israelites.

The pride and exultation of maternal tenderness, the grief for her father-in-law and her husband were absorbed in a deeper feeling. She said, *the ark of God is taken*; and she called her child Ichabod, the glory is departed from Israel.

Nothing now remained to the race of Abraham but the prospect of hopeless and irremediable servitude. Their God had abandoned them—perhaps might appear on the side of their enemies. Not merely the glory, and the independence, even the political existence of Israel seemed departed with the ark, departed for ever. With what amazement and joy must the extraordinary intelligence have been received, that after seven months, the Philistines were sending back the ark of God, not in contempt of his power, but with signs of reverential terror. They had sent the strange deity from city to city, every where their own gods had been rebuked, the statutes had fallen prostrate, their harvests had been wasted by mice, their persons afflicted by a loathsome disease. They yoked two milch kine to the car, and loaded it with propitiatory offerings. Instead of lingering near their calves, the kine had set off on the direct road to Bethshemesh, within the border of the Israelites. There the Levites received it, and sacrificed the kine to the Almighty. The profane curiosity of the inhabitants of Bethshemesh was punished, seventy men were struck dead for presuming to look within the ark, which was soon after solemnly removed to the city of Kiriathjearim.

Yet twenty years longer the Israelites groaned under the yoke of the Philistines; but Samuel was now grown to manhood, and was established not merely with the authority of a judge, but likewise of a prophet. The high priesthood had passed into the next branch of the family of Eli, and sunk into comparative insignificance before the acknowledged weight of the new leader. Samuel, having labored with success to extirpate the idolatrous practices which had grown up among the people, summoned a general assembly at Mizpeh. The Philistines took alarm, and put their forces in motion to suppress the insurrection. The Israelites were full of terror, but too far engaged to recede: their confidence in the favor of God toward their righteous judge, induced them to risk their safety on the acceptance of his prayers. The event was a victory so complete, caused partly by a tremendous storm, that the Philistines were forced to evacuate the whole country, and to accept of equitable terms of peace.

The civil administration of Samuel was equally prosperous. He united at least all the southern tribes under his authority; he held three annual sessions of justice at Bethel, Gilgal, Mizpeh: his residence he fixed in hi native city of Ramah. But his sons, who in his old age were installed in the judicial office, did not follow the example of their upright father; they were venal and corrupt. The people therefore, having seen the superior efficacy of the monarchical government, which prevailed in the neighboring countries, by a formal representation of their elders, demanded that their republican polity should be changed into an hereditary kingdom. It is most remarkable that Moses had anticipated this resolution; and, providing against the contingency of kingly government, had laid down regulations for the election of a sovereign and the administration of regal power. The king was not to be a foreigner, lest the independence of the country should be lost, and the Israelitish commonwealth sink into a province of some great empire. He was prohibited from maintaining any force of cavalry, lest he should attempt foreign conquest, to the neglect or danger of the internal strength and security of the kingdom. The lawgiver either perceived that a free republic, or rather a federal government of twelve distinct republics, was an experiment in the constitution of society, or that the external relations of the commonwealth might so far change as to require a more vigorous executive.

The avowed objects of the people in demanding a king were, the more certain administration of justice, and the organization of a strong and permanent military force; *that our king might judge us, and go out before us, and fight our battles.* The national militia, untrained and undisciplined, might be sufficient to repel the tumultuary invasions of the wandering tribes; but they had now to resist powerful monarchies, and the formidable league of the Philistine chieftains, who could bring into the field an overwhelming power of chariots and cavalry. The prosperity of the state under David and Solomon amply justifies the deviation from the original constitution. The conduct of Samuel on this occasion was prudent and moderate: he fairly laid before the people the dangers of an oriental despotism, the only monarchy then known, with all the exactions and oppressions of arbitrary power; and left them to make their choice. The popular feeling was decided in favor of the change. The next object therefore was the election of the king. The nomination took place by divine instruction, but may be admired on the plainest principles of human policy. The upright and disinterested Samuel showed no favor to his own family, kindred, or tribe. It was expedient that the king should be chosen from the southern tribes, as more immediately exposed to the most dangerous and implacable enemy. A prince of Asher or Napthali might have neglected the interests of Judah and Benjamin. An election from the great rival tribes of Ephraim or Judah might excite mutual jealousy, or dread of a domineering influence among the weaker clans. A youth of singularly tall and striking person, an eminent distinction in the East, arrived at Ramah. He was the son of a Benjamitish chieftain, and had been wandering in search of some asses, a valuable property, which his father had lost. Him Samuel is directed to nominate and receive with regal honors. Giving him the chief seat and distinguished portion at a feast where thirty persons were present, he proceeds privately to anoint him as the future king. But the youth was to be prepared for his high office by a course of religions instruction; and his mind imbued with deep and powerful enthusiasm for the national law and national faith. He was sent to one of those schools of the prophets, most likely instituted by Samuel, where the pupils were initiated in the circle of Hebrew education, religions knowledge, religious music, and religious poetry. Here the character of the youth was totally changed: he mingled in the sacred dances; his spirit became full of lofty and aspiring thoughts. So totally were the former levity and carelessness of his youth cast off, that his wandering compatriots exclaimed, *Is Saul also among the prophets?* Thus qualified for the royal dignity, at a solemn assembly at Mizpeh, Saul is designated by lot and received as king, not indeed without murmur or opposition from some few factious spirits, but by the unanimous consent of the great majority. His first measure was bold, and answerable to the public expectation, as showing that the strength and vigilance of the royal power would extend its protection to the remotest part of the commonwealth. Nahash king of the Ammonites, had invaded the Transjordanic tribes, and now besieged the town of Jabez, in Gilead. He demanded that the inhabitants should submit to have their eyes put out; a revolting act of cruelty, which he had exacted, as a sign of subjection, from all the people he had subdued. The inhabitants sent in all haste to the king for succor. Saul instantly hewed a yoke of oxen to pieces, and sent this sign, like the fiery cross of the Highlanders, to summon all the tribes of Israel. The army mustered to the number of 330,000 men.

The Ammonites were totally defeated and dispersed. The young king signalized his victory by an act of mercy; though persuaded to use his power to revenge himself on the factious persons who had opposed his elevation, he refused and declared that the life of no Israelite should be sacrificed at such a period of public rejoicing.

Encouraged by this prosperous commencement, Samuel assembled the people at Gilgal. Here the upright magistrate solemnly appealed to the whole assembly to bear witness to the justice and integrity of his administration, invited their scrutiny, and defied their censure; and, thus, having given a public account of his charge, rebuked the people, both by his own words and a sign from heaven, a thunderstorm at the unusual time of the wheat-harvest, for their innovation on the established constitution without direct preinstruction from heaven, he surrendered his judicial authority, and proceeded to the formal inauguration of the king elect.

Thus ended the period of the Judges; a period, if carelessly surveyed, of alternate slavery and bloody struggles for independence. Hence may rashly be inferred the total failure of the Mosaic polity in securing the happiness of the people. It has already been shown that the views of the legislator were not completely carried into effect, and that the miseries of the people were the natural consequences of their deviation from the original statutes. But, in fact, out of this period of about 460 years, not one fourth was passed under foreign oppression, and many of the servitudes seem to have been local, extending only over certain tribes, not over the whole nation.

Above 300 years of peaceful and uneventful happiness remain, to which history, only faithful in recording the crimes and sufferings of man, bears the favorable testimony of her silence. If the Hebrew nation did not enjoy a high degree of intellectual civilization, yet as simple husbandmen, possessing perfect freedom, equal laws, the regular administration of justice—cultivating a soil which yielded bountifully, yet required but light labor—with a religion strict, as regards the morals which are essential to individual, domestic, and national peace, yet indulgent in every kind of social and festive enjoyment—the descendants of Abraham had reached a higher state of virtue and happiness than any other nation of the period. A uniform simplicity of manners pervaded the whole people; they were all shepherds or husbandmen.

Gideon was summoned, to deliver his country, from the thrashing-floor; Saul, even after he was elected king, was found driving his herd; David was educated in the sheep-fold. But the habits of the people are nowhere described with such apparent fidelity and lively interest as in the rural tale of Ruth and her kinsman—a history which unites all the sweetness of the best pastoral poetry with the truth and simplicity of real life. Now, however, we must turn to the rise, the greatness, and the fall of the Hebrew monarchy.

BOOK VII.

THE MONARCHY.

Reign of Saul—David—Death of Saul—Union of the whole Kingdom under David—His conquests—Occupation of Jerusalem His crime—Expulsion—Restoration Death—Solomon—The Building of the Temple—Magnificence and Commerce of Solomon.

Some time must have elapsed between the nomination of Saul and his active and regular administration of the kingly office: he was a youth when nominated, his son Jonathan now appears grown up, a gallant and daring warrior. The monarch's first care was to form a regular and disciplined army: for the Philistines were mustering the most numerous and overpowering host they had ever brought into the field. Jonathan began the war by attacking a garrison at Geba, before the preparations were complet d. The Philistines broke into the country, and, with 3,000 chariots and 6,000 horse, swept the whole region. The panic-stricken Israelites fled on all sides: the few troops which obeyed the trumpet of Saul met at Gilgal. Here Saul, in direct violation of the Hebrew constitution and the express command of Samuel, took upon himself the priestly function, and offered sacrifice. The union of these two offices in one person, would either have given an overweening weight to the kingly authority; or the religious primacy, instead of maintaining its independent dignity, would have sunk into a subordinate branch of the royal office. Samuel, who, if he offered sacrifice, probably assumed that right as belonging to the prophetic function, denounced, as the penalty of Saul's offense, that the kingdom should not be hereditary in his line, but pass into that of a man more obedient to the divine institutions.

In the meantime the Philistines overrun the territory; part turned southward to the valley near the Dead Sea, part to the mountainous country of Ephraim, part toward the Jordan as far as Ophrah. They seized all the arms, and carried away all the smiths in the country, forcing the inhabitants to go to their towns to get all their larger implements of husbandry ground. Saul occupied the strong fortress of Gibeah with 600 ill-armed men. From this critical situation he was delivered by an adventurous exploit of Jonathan. This daring youth, unknown to his father, and accompanied only by his armor-bearer, scaled a rock which was an outpost of the enemy, slew twenty men, and threw such confusion into the camp that the army, most likely formed of different tribes, fell upon each other. Saul, perceiving this from the height of Gibeah, rushed down, and increased the tumult. The Philistines fled on all sides: the Israelites sallied forth from their hiding-places in the woods and rocks, and slew them without mercy. The blow would have been more fatal but for an impolitic vow of Saul, who had adjured the people not to taste food till the close of the day. Many evils ensued from this rash oath. The weary soldiers could not pursue their advantage: when they came to eat, they seized the spoil, and, in direct violation of the law, eat the meat while the blood was still in it. Saul hastened to prevent this crime, and commanded a large stone to be rolled forward, on which the cattle might be slain, and the blood flow off. Worse than all, Jonathan was found to have violated the vow, of which he was ignorant, by tasting a little wild honey. Saul was about to sacrifice his noble and victorious son for this breach of discipline, and the Hebrew annals might have anticipated the glory or the crime of the Roman Torquatus, but the people, with more humane feeling, interfered, and forbade the execution.

Saul continued to wage a successful war with the enemies on all quarters: the most harrassing and unconquerable were the wild tribes of the desert, called the Amalekites. These fierce marauders constantly hovered on the borders, swelled the Philistine armies, or followed in the rear, like Tartan hordes, pillaging and massacreing; and, as the Israelites had no cavalry, retreated without loss to the security of their deserts. It was a cruel but inevitable policy to carry a war of extermination into their country. T ere was an old feud of blood between the nations, since their first attack on the Israelites near Sinai. The war-law of nations, and necessity, as well as the divine command, justified this measure. Even the flocks and herds were to be involved in the general destruction, lest the scattered fugitives (for the tribe were not so entirely annihilated but that it appeared again in force during David's residence at Ziklag), should reassemble, and form a new settlement on the Israelitish frontier. In the conduct of this expedition Saul again transgressed the divine commandment: he reserved the best part of the spoil, under pretext of offering it in sacrifice, and spared the life of the king. There seems to be an obvious policy in this command to destroy all plunder, lest the Israelites should have been tempted to make marauding excursions upon their neighbors, and by degrees be trained up as an ambitious and conquering people. This danger the lawgiver clearly foresaw, if they should fall under a monarchy. Agag the king of the Amalekites, to whom the Jews owed long arrears of vengeance for his cruelties to their countrymen, was hewn to pieces before the altar by the command of Samuel—a fearful example to the merciless chieftains of the wild tribes: *As thy sword hath made women childless, so shall thy mother be childless among women.* But his repeated acts of disobedience had destroyed all hopes of finding in Saul a religious and constitutional king, punctual in his conformity to the law of the land and to the divine commandment. Another fatal objection to his sovereignty, and that of his race, began to display itself: he was seized with the worst malady to which mankind is subject; and as the paroxysms of his insanity became more frequent and violent, the brave though intractable warrior sank into a moody and jealous tyrant.

The early history of David is involved in considerable difficulty. The events are here related in what appears the most easy and natural order. Samuel, by the divine command, went down to Bethlehem to sacrifice, and there selected and anointed as king the youngest of the eight sons of Jesse; a beautiful youth, then employed in his father's pastures, where he had already signalized his bravery by combatting and slaying two wild beasts, a lion and a bear. A short time after, in the course of the Philistine war, the whole army of the Israelites was defied by a gigantic champion, Goliath of Gath, who was almost cased in a brazen armor. Notwithstanding a splendid reward offered by Saul, no warrior dared to confront this terrible foe Suddenly a youth, of modesty and piety equal to his beauty and valor, appeared; accepted the combat, slew the insulting Philistine with a stone from his sling, and returned in triumph, with the head of the enemy, to the camp. This bold achievement endeared David to the kindred spirit of Jonathan, the son of Saul, and proved the commencement of a romantic friendship, one of the most beautiful incidents in the Jewish annals. But in their triumphant songs the maidens of Israel had raised the fame of David above that of Saul: deep and rankling jealousy sank into the distempered mind of the monarch. For several years the increasing malady preyed upon his spirit, till it was thought that the power of music (in modern times, and among nations less susceptible of deep emotions from sound, employed not without success in cases of derangement), might sooth him to composure.

David, who may have passed the intermediate time in a prophetic school, had attained that exquisite skill in music and poetry which appears in the energy and tenderness of his Psalms. He was summoned to attend upon the king. At first the wayward spirit of Saul is allayed; but the paroxysms return: twice he attempts the life of David; but his trembling hand can not direct the spear with fatal force. In his lucid interval he promotes David to a military command, in which the future king acquires universal popularity. A short time after, Saul promises him his daughter in marriage, on the invidious condition that he should bring the foreskins of a hundred Philistines. David and his troop slew two hundred; and received not Merab, the daughter of Saul, who had been promised to him at first, but Michal, who loved him tenderly, as his reward. In a conference with the Philistine chieftains he acquired great reputation, even among the enemy, for his wisdom in council. The jealousy of Saul again broke out, but was allayed by the friendly interference of Jonathan. New triumphs of David excited new hostility; and hardly saved by a stratagem of his wife, who placed an image in his bed, he fled to Samuel, at Ramah. Officers were despatched to seize him: they found him employed among the sacred choir, who, with Samuel at their head, were chanting some of their solemn religious hymns. The messengers were seized with the same enthusiasm, and mingled their voices with those of the prophets. Three times the awe of the inspired prophets thus prevented the officers of Saul from executing his command. At length Saul himself set forth with the same hostile design; but his melancholy spirit was not proof against the sacred contagion; the early and gentle associations of his youth arose within him; he too cast off his royal habits, and took his former place in the devotional assembly.

After this reconciliation, David was rescued from new danger by the generous intervention of Jonathan. This noble youth not merely sacrificed his hopes of a kingly succession to his friend, the designated heir of the throne; but, confronting the worst paroxysm of his father's frenzy, had nearly lost his life. The lance aimed at him missed its blow. David was made acquainted with the failure of his friend's interference by a concerted signal, and after taking a long farewell of Jonathan, he made his escape to Nob, a sacerdotal city in the tribe of Benjamin. Here he pretended a secret mission from the king; deceived by his plausible story, in order to hasten him on his way, the priest bestowed on him a part of the bread-offering, which it was profanation in any but those of Levitical race to touch; and the more valuable present of Goliath's sword, which had been laid up as a trophy. David then fled to Gath; but mistrusting the hospitality of the Philistine king, he feigned idiocy, and escaped to a wild cave, that of Adullam, where he became the captain of an independent troop of adventurers, composed of the discontented and distressed from all quarters. He was joined by some marauders, warriors of remarkable bravery, from the tribe of Gad, who crossed the Jordan and placed themselves under his banner. The devoted attachment of these men to their chieftain was shown in a gallant exploit performed by three of them, who broke through the Philistine army to procure water for David, which he had earnestly wished to have from his native fountain in Bethlehem. But David would not taste water purchased at such a risk as the lives of three brave men—*he poured it out to the Lord.* This gallant troop undertook no enterprise against their native country, but they fell on the Philistine army, who were besieging some valuable corn magazines at Keilah, and defeated them with great slaughter.

Saul, in the meantime, had wreaked dreadful vengeance on the priesthood. From the information of Doeg, an Edomite he had been apprised of the service rendered to David at Nob, by Abimelech. His jealous nature construed this into a general conspiracy of the whole order. He commanded their indiscriminate slaughter; his awe-struck followers refused to imbrue their hands in holy blood; and Saul was forced to employ the less scrupulous arm of an alien, the sanguinary Doeg. Eighty-five of the sacred order were slain, Abiather, the son of Abimelech, fled to David. After this atrocity, Saul set out in pursuit of David, and had almost surprised him at Keilah. The fugitive, having intrusted his family to the generous protection of the king of Moab, fled from cave to rock, from desert to fastness, perpetually making hair-breadth escapes, yet disdaining to make use of any advantage or to commit any violence against the person of his royal enemy who was twice within his power.

Once the king retired to sleep in a cave at Engedi, the inner part of which was the lurking place of David. He cut off the skirt of his robe, and then making himself known, expressed his repentance for having so far ventured to desecrate the royal person. The better spirit of Saul revived, and a temporary accommodation took place. A second time David, by the negligence of his guard, surprised the king sleeping as before in his tent; he repressed the murderous intentions of his companion, Abiathar; but, to show what he might have done, carried away a spear and a cruise of water that stood by his bed side. He then, from the top of a hill reproved Abner, Saul's general, for keeping so negligent a watch over the sacred person of the monarch. The magnanimity of David was equaled by the generous fidelity of Jonathan, who, regardless of his own advancement, the great object of his father's jealousy, expressed his anxious desire that David might succeed to the throne of Israel, and he himself fill the subordinate place of his *vizier.*

But the resentment of Saul is implacable; he gives to another Michal, David's wife; and David himself, like Themistocles or Coriolanus, takes refuge in the capital of his country's enemy; but with no design either of hostility to his native land, or even of revenge against the ungrateful king. Achish assigns him to the town of Ziklag for his residence, where he dwells with his two wives, Ahinoam and Abigail, the widow of the churlish Nabal, from whom, during his freebooting life, he had demanded a supply of provisions, in return for the protection which his troops had afforded to the pastures of the Israelites. Abigail had arrested his wrath from her parsimonious husband, who refused the succor required, by propitiatory gifts; and Nabal, dying of drunkenness and terror, David took her as his wife. Thus an involuntary exile, David found himself in great difficulty to avoid embarking in hostilities against his native land.

For some time he deceived the Philistine king by making inroads on the wild tribes of the desert, while he pretended that his troops had been employed in ravaging Judea. His embarrassment increased when the king of the Philistines seized the favorable opportunity to renew the war; and he was formally summoned to range his forces under the banner of his new liege lord. He appeared at the rendezvous; but he was fortunately relieved from this difficult position by the jealous mistrust of the Philistine chieftains. Dismissed from the invading army, he found on his return to Ziklag that his old enemies, the Amalekites, had made a sudden descent on his residence, burned the city, and carried off all the women and children. David pursues, overtakes, falls on them by night, slaughters them without mercy, and having rescued the captives, returns laden with booty.

The end of the unhappy Saul drew near. Ill supported by his subjects, many of whom, even in the remotest districts, seem to have maintained a friendly correspondence with David, he determined to risk his crown and kingdom on a great battle with the Philistines. Still, however, haunted with that insatiable desire of searching into the secrets of futurity inseparable from uncivilized man, he knew not to what quarter to turn. The priests, who had escaped the massacre, outraged by his cruelty, had forsaken him; the Urim and Thummim was with Abiathar, he knew not where. The prophets stood aloof: no dreams visited his couch; he had persecuted even the unlawful diviners. He hears at length of a female necromancer, a woman with the spirit of Ob: strangely similar in sound to the Obeah women in the West Indies.

To the cave-dwelling of this woman, in Endor, the monarch proceeds in disguise. The woman at first alleges her fears of the severity with which the laws against necromancy were then executed. Saul promises her impunity. He commands her to raise the spirit of Samuel. At this daring demand of raising a man of such dignity and importance, the woman first recognizes, or pretends to recognize, her royal visitant. "Whom seest thou?" says the king.

"Mighty ones ascending from the earth." "Of what form?" "An old man covered with a mantle." Saul in terror bows his head to the earth, and, it should seem, not daring to look up, receives from the voice of the spectre the awful intimation of his defeat and death. On the reality of this apparition, we presume not to decide: the figure, if figure there were, was not seen by Saul; and, excepting the event of the approaching battle, the spirit said nothing which the living prophet had not said before repeatedly and publicly. But the fact is curious, as showing the popular belief of the Jews in departed spirits to have been the same with that of most other nations.

The prophecy, like others, may have contributed to its own accomplishment. In the bloody battle of Gilboa, the Israelites were totally defeated. Jonathan and the other sons of Saul were slain; and the desperate monarch, determined not to outlive his fall, commanded his armor-bearer to pierce him with his sword. The faithful servant refused to obey. His master then fell on his own sword, but the wound not being mortal, he called on a youth, an Amalekite, to drive the weapon home. The faithful armor-bearer slew himself on his master's corpse. The bodies of Saul and Jonathan were taken by the Philistines, treated with great indignity, and that of Saul hung on the walls of the city of Beth-Shan, afterward Scythopolis. It was soon after rescued by a daring incursion made by the inhabitants of Jabesh, a city beyond Jordan, who, remembering how Saul had rescued their city from the cruelty of the Ammonites at the commencement of his reign, displayed that rarest of virtues, gratitude to a fallen monarch; and adorned the annals of their country with one of its most noble incidents.

The news of the battle of Gilboa soon reached David. The young Amalekite took possession of the bracelet and ornaments of Saul, and carried them with all possible speed to his designated successor: but David ordered him to execution for thus assisting in the death and plundering the person of the king. He expressed the deepest sorrow, not merely for the defeat of Israel and the death of his dear friend Jonathan, but also for that of the gallant monarch, whose early valor demanded unmixed admiration, whose malady might extenuate much of his later aberrations. During David's wild and adventurous life, his poetic faculty had been constantly kept alive. Many of his most affecting elegies receive a deeper interest when read in connection with his personal history; but none is more touching than that which he composed on the death of Saul and Jonathan—lovely and pleasant in their lives, in their death not divided.

But David did not waste the time in lamentation; he suddenly appeared at Hebron, was welcomed by the tribe of Judah, and immediately raised, by common acclamation, to the vacant throne. Abner, the most powerful of the military leaders in the army of Saul, and his near relative, appealed to the jealousy of the northern tribes against Judah, and set up Ishbosheth, Saul's only surviving son, as king. Ishbosheth was totally unfit for the high situation; and after Abner had supported the contest for more than two years by his personal weight and activity, on some disgust he fell off to David. But unfortunately in a battle which had taken place at Gibeon, he had slain Asahel, the brother of Joab, David's most powerful follower. Joab in revenge assassinated him with his own hand. David was deeply grieved, and as well to show his regret, as to remove all suspicion of participation in the crime, Abner received an honorable burial, and the king appeared as chief mourner. The loss of Abner was fatal to the party of Ishbosheth, and as the falling never want enemies, he was put to death by some of his own followers. Rechab and Baanah, the murderers, instead of meeting with a welcome reception and reward from David, were executed for their crime.

The power and character of David, now thirty years old, triumphed over all the jealousies of the tribes. The whole nation received him as their king; their united forces ranged themselves under his banner, their most valiant captains took pride in obeying his commands. The Philistines, who, from the terror of his name, seem immediately to have withdrawn within their own frontier, were defeated in all quarters. Yet the exterminating character of the former wars with this people may be estimated from the number of troops contributed from the several tribes, if indeed the numbers are correct, Judah musters only 6,000 men; Ephraim, 20,800; Zebulun, 50,000; the powerful tribes beyond Jordan, 120,000 men.

After residing seven years and a half at Hebron, David determined to found a capital city, which should thenceforth be the seat of the government and the religion. Josephus asserts that the foundation of Jerusalem and the building of the temple, were expressly enjoined by Moses, and that he even anticipated the nature of the hill, on which the latter was to stand, and the size of its stones. But, except in one obscure prophetic passage, there is no allusion to Jerusalem in the writings of the lawgiver. The German writer, Herder, has drawn an ingenious inference from a verse in the same last prophecy of Moses, where the passage is found, in which Jerusalem is supposed to be designated. It is said of Zebulun, they shall call the people into the mountain, there they shall offer sacrifices of righteousness. This mountain he supposes to be Tabor, on the borders of Issachar and Zebulun, which stands alone at the edge of a vast plain, with a fine level space on its top, admirably calculated for the site of a city; while the sides are richly clothed with wood, and capable of a high degree of cultivation. Herder dwells with great eloquence on the commanding majesty and the strength of a situation which is seen on all sides from an immense distance, and overlooked by no neighboring eminence. It is an obvious objection to this hypothesis that Tabor fell early, in the days of Joshua, into the power of the Israelites, but no attempt was made either to found a city, or transfer thither the tabernacle and the ark of God.

But Jerusalem was destined to become the seat of the Hebrew government, and the scene of more extraordinary events, more strange and awful vicissitudes, than any city in the universe, not excepting Rome. There stood on the borders of Judah and Benjamin a strong fortress, which had remained in the possession of the native inhabitants, the Jebusites, since the conquest of Canaan.

The natural strength and long security of the citadel tempted the Jebusites to treat a summons to surrender with insolent defiance. David, however, took both the town and the citadel, which stood on Mount Sion, and there established his royal residence. The situation of Jerusalem is remarkably imposing, it stands on several eminences of unequal heights, some parts of which slope gradually, on others the sides are abrupt and percipitous. All around, excepting in the north, run deep ravines or valleys, like intrenchments formed by nature, beyond which arise mountains of greater height, which encircle and seem to protect the city. It is open only to the north, as if the way had been leveled, for the multitudes from the rest of the tribes to arrive at the holy city without difficulty or obstacle. The hill of Sion, on which David's city stood, rose to the south, it was divided by a deep and narrow ravine from the other hills, over which the city gradually spread .

The next great step of David was the re-establishment of the national religion with suitable dignity and magnificence. Had David acted solely from political motives, this measure had been the wisest he could adopt. The solemn assembling of the tribes would not only cement the political union of the monarchy, but increase the opulence of his capital, and promote the internal commerce of the country; while it brought the heads of the tribes, and indeed the whole people, under the cognizance and personal knowledge of the sovereign, it fixed the residence of the more eminent among the priesthood in the metropolis.

The ark, after the restoration by the Philistines, had probably remained at Kirjath Jearim; from thence it was moved with the greatest state, attended by David, at the head of 30,000 men. It was placed on a car; Uzzah, who presumed to touch it, was struck dead. Wherever it moved, it was escorted with instruments of music and hymns, which recalled all the former wonders of the Jewish history, the triumphs of God over his enemies. That noble ode, the 68th Psalm, Let God arise, and let his enemies be scattered, is generally supposed to have been written on this occasion. The ark remained for three months in the house of Obed-Edom, while preparations were making for its solemn reception within the city. When the pavilion was ready, David made a feast for the whole people, and himself having cast off his royal robes, and put on a simple linen tunic, joined the procession, which was conducted with that dramatic union of music, singing, and dancing, common to the festal worship of all southern nations. On the second removal the 105th and 106th Psalms were sung. Michal alone, the daughter of Saul, the wife of David's youth, whom on his accession he had taken back, entered not into the general enthusiasm; she rebuked her husband for thus derogating from the royal dignity, of which she seems to have entertained truly Oriental notions. David, offended by her presumption and irreligion, from that time abstained from her bed.

David had already built a royal palace, with the assistance of Hiram, king of Tyre, of whom he received cedar timber from Lebanon, and experienced artisans. This was the commencement of that amity between the Tyrians and the Hebrews so mutually advantageous to the two nations, the one agricultural, and the other commercial. The religious king, in pursuance of the wise policy which led him to found a capital, and reinstate the religion in its former splendor, determined to build a permanent temple. The tabernacle might be suitable to the God of the wandering Israelites, but a more solid and durable edifice seemed accordant to the Deity of a settled people. See, now, says the king to the prophet Nathan, I dwell in an house of cedar, but the ark of God dwelleth within curtains.

The prophet at first highly approved of this pious design; but shortly after, the divine commandment was proclaimed, that David was to desist from the great national enterprise, and leave the glory of it to his son, who was to inherit his throne. The reason of the prohibition is most remarkable, entirely in unison with the spirit of the Mosaic institutions, which aimed at forming a peaceful, not a warlike or conquering people. Thou hast shed blood abnndantly, and hast made great wars; thou shalt not build a house unto my name, because thou hast shed much blood upon the earth in my sight. From whence could so sublime a precept descend, amid a people situated as the Jews then were, unless from the great Father of love and mercy.

The sanguinary career of David's victorious arms was not yet terminated. On every side he extended his frontier to the furthest limits of the promised land, and secured the whole country by the subjection or unrelenting extermination of its restless enemies. He defeated the Philistines, and took Gath and a great part of their dominion. He conquered and established garrisons in the whole territory of Edom: Hadad, the last of the royal race, fled to Egypt. He treated the Moabites with still greater severity, putting to the sword a great part of the population. He overthrew the Syrians of Zobah (supposed by Michaelies to be the kingdom of Nisibis, bordering on Armenia, which was famous for its breed of horses); Zobah lay between the Transjordanic tribes and the Euphrates: they were routed with a loss of 1,000 chariots, 700 horsemen, and 20,000 foot. Faithful to the law he mutilated all the horses, except a certain number reserved for state and splendor. The Syrians of Damascus marched to the defense of their kindred, but retreated, having suffered the loss of 22,000 men. The kingdom of Hamath entered into a strict alliance with the conqueror. Thus the Euphrates became the eastern boundary of the Hebrew kingdom; the northern was secured by the occupation of the fortresses in the kingdom of Damascus, and by the friendly state of Tyre; the southern by the ruin of the Philistines and the military possession of Edom.

In the height of his power, David did not forget his generous friend, Jonathan. One of his sons, Mephibosheth, a lame youth, still survived. He was sent for, kindly received, and assigned a maintenance at the royal table. David soon after restored to him the personal estate of Saul, which was intrusted to the management of his adherent, Ziba. The estate must have been considerable, much larger than the patrimonial inheritance of Saul: perhaps, increased by confiscation during his possession of royal authority. A new war broke out shortly against the Ammonites, who had entered into a defensive alliance with several of the Syrian princes The war originated in this manner. On the accession of Hanun, the son of Nahash, to the throne, David, who had been on friendly terms with the father, sent an embassy of congratulation. The Ammonites suspecting the ambassadors to be spies, treated them with the greatest contumely; shaved their beards, the worst insult that can be inflicted in the East, cut their garments short, and dismissed them. The forces of David marched immediately into the country, commanded by Joab and Abishai, who totally defeated the Ammonites and their allies. Another formidable army of Syrians making its appearance, David took arms in person, and discomfited them with the loss of 700 chariots.

So far unexampled splendor and prosperity had marked the reign of David; the remainder was as gloomy as disastrous. His own crime was the turning point of his fortunes. Walking on the terrace roof of his palace, he looked down on the bath of a neighboring harem, in which he saw a beautiful woman, Bathsheba, the wife of Uriah, a man of Canaanitish descent, but one of his bravest soldiers. He became enamored of her, and sent for her to his palace. To cover the consequences of his crime, her husband was summoned from the army, then occupied with the siege of Rabbah, the capital of the Ammonites. But Uriah, either from secret suspicion, or mere accident, avoided the snare: the brave warrior refused to enjoy the comforts and luxuries of his home, while his companions in arms were sleeping in the open air. Foiled in his purpose, David plunged headlong down the precipitous declivity of guilt: he sent secret orders that Uriah should be exposed on a post of danger, where death was inevitable. He did not perpetrate this double crime without remonstrance. The prophet Nathan addressed to him the beautiful and affecting apologue of the rich man who, while possessed of abundant flocks, took by force the one ewe lamb of the poor man to feast a stranger. The bitterness of the king's repentance may be estimated by his own sad and pathetic expressions in the poems, particularly the 51st Psalm, composed on this humiliating subject. But henceforth the hand of God was against him.

The Ammonitish war, indeed, was brought to a favorable termination; Joab, after wasting the whole country, pressed the siege of Rabbah. David joined the army, and took the city; where he wreaked the most dreadful vengeance on the inhospitable people. All, those at least, who were found in arms, were put *under saws and under harrows of iron, and under axes of iron, and made to pass through the brick kiln.* The long hostilities of the nations around Palestine were not likely to mitigate the ferocity of the usages of war; and the Ammonites seem to have been the most savage people of the whole region, and were, for this reason, as well as on account of their conduct to the embassadors, whose persons are sacred among the fiercest tribes, selected as fearful examples to the enemies of Israel. But now the life of David began to darken, a curse, fatal as that which the old Grecian tragedy delights to paint, hung over his house. Incest, fratricide, rebellion of the son against the father, civil war, the expulsion of the king from his capital —such are the crimes and calamities which blacken the annals of his later years. The child, of which Bathsheba was pregnant, died; but its loss was replaced by the birth of the famous Solomon. Worse evils followed. Ammon the eldest born son of David, committed an incestuous rape on Tamar, the sister of Absalom. Absalom (for in many eastern nations, as has before been observed, the honor of the brother is wounded more deeply even than that of the parent, by the violation of an unmarried female) washed out the stain in the blood of his brother. The murderer fled, but by the intervention of Joab, David's faithful captain, he was permitted to return; and at length, by a singular artifice, admitted to his father's presence. A woman of Tekoah was directed to appear in mourning apparel before the king. Of her two sons, one had slain the other in an accidental quarrel, the family sought to put the survivor to death, and leave her alone in her childless house. The analogy of her situation with his own, struck the mind of David; though he detected the artifice, in evil hour he recalled his offending and exiled son to Jerusalem; but still refused him permission to appear in his court. Before long, the daring youth set fire to a field of barley belonging to Joab, declaring that he had rather appear before his father as a criminal, than be excluded from his presence. An interview followed, in which the parental feeling of David triumphed over his justice and his prudence. Absalom was a youth of exquisite beauty, remarkable for his luxuriant hair; his manners were highly popular, and by consummate address and artful impeachments of his father's negligence in the administration of justice, he gradually won the hearts of the whole people.

He was aided by Ahitophel, a man of the most profound subtlety, and acute political foresight. Having thus prepared the way, he suddenly fled to Hebron, raised the standard of revolt, and in a short time the conspiracy grew so formidable that David was obliged to fly from his capital. He went forth from the eastern gate, crossed the brook Kidron, and ascended the Mount of Olives, from whence he looked back upon the city which he had founded, or the ornamented abode for many years of all his power, his glory, and his happiness. He was leaving it in his old age, perhaps forever, a miserable fugitive, driven forth by a people, whose independence as a nation he had established, and by an unnatural son, whose life had been his gift. He did not attempt to disguise his sorrow: with his head covered and his feet bare, he began his melancholy pilgrimage, amid the tears and lamentations of the people, who could not witness without commiseration this sad example of the uncertainty of human greatness. Yet the greatness of David did not depend upon his royal state; it was within his lofty soul, and inseparable from his commanding character. Neither his piety, nor his generosity, nor his prudence deserted him. The faithful priests, Zadok and Abiathar, followed him with the ark; he sent them back, unwilling that the sacred treasures of God should be exposed to the perils and ignominy of his flight. He remonstrated with Ittai, a stranger, on the imprudence of adhering to his fallen fortunes. At the same time, he left Hushai, a man of great address, to counterwork the intrigues of the crafty Ahitophel. He had more trials to endure; as he passed Bahurim, a man named Shimei loaded him with the bitterest and most contemptuous execrations. David endured his reproaches with the humblest resignation as punishments from the Almighty, nor would he permit his followers to attempt the chastisement of the offender. Absalom in the mean time entered Jerusalem without resistance. It is a singular usage in the East that he who assumes the crown of a deceased or dethroned monarch, becomes master of his harem. Absalom, by Ahitophel's advice, took public possession of that of David. Ahitophel urged the immediate pursuit of the fugitive monarch, but Hushai, having insinuated himself into Absalom's counsels, insisted on the danger of driving so brave a warrior to desperation. "They be mighty men, and they be chafed in their minds like a bear robbed of her whelps." He advised, as a more prudent course, the assembling an army from the whole nation. The counsel of Hushai prevailed; and during the time thus gained, David escaped beyond Jordan, where he was hospitably received, particularly by the wealthy Barzillai. The crafty politician, Ahitophel, saw at once the failure of his scheme, and to anticipate the vengeance of his enemies, destroyed himself. The event justified his sagacity. A powerful army assembled round David, and the termination of the contest depended on a decisive battle to be fought beyond the Jordan. Amasa commanded the troops of Absalom, Joab those of David. Before the conflict began, the fond father gave the strictest charge, that the life of his rebellious son should be respected. The battle took place on ground encumbered with wood; and Absalom, riding at full speed, got entangled in the bows of an oak. Thus, suspended by his beautiful hair, the relentless Joab found him and transfixed his body with three darts. David awaited the issue of the conflict in the city of Mahanaim. The messengers came rapidly one after the other to announce the victory. The king only answered with the question, "Is the young man Absalom safe?" His conduct, when the fatal tidings at last arrived, can be described in no other language than that of the sacred historian. "The king was much moved, and went up to the chamber over the gate and wept, and as he wept, thus he said, O my son, Absalom! my son, my son, Absalom! would God I had died for thee, O Absalom, my son, my son!"

This ill-timed, though natural grief, roused the indignation of the hardy Joab, and David was constrained to repress it. On the death of Absalom, the nation returned to its allegiance, the king, with humane policy, published a general amnesty, from which, not even the insulting Shimei was excepted. Among the faithful adherents of David, the aged Barzillai declined all reward, his advanced age was incapable of any gratification from honor or pleasure, his son Chimham was advanced to the highest dignity. Ziba, the faithless steward of Mephibosheth, endeavored to implicate his master in the conspiracy, in order to secure the confiscated estate. He succeeded at first, but Mephibosheth, exculpating himself, proved that he deeply mourned the expulsion of David, and had only been prevented following his fortunes by his infirmity and the craft of Ziba. The decree was revoked.

But at this period the seeds of fatal jealousy between the northern tribes and that of Judah were sown. The northern tribes were exasperated because the men of Judah took upon themselves to reinstate the king without their assent and concurrence. An adventurer named Sheba put himself at the head of a revolt. Amasa, the general of Absalom, suspected of traitorous dealings with the insurgents, was barbarously despatched by Joab; and Sheba shut up the city of Abel, where he was put to death by his own party, and his head thrown over the wall. These two rebellions were followed (if the order of events be observed by the sacred historian), or long preceded (if we are to judge from probability), by a famine, attributed to some obscure crime of Saul and his bloody family, in slaying the Gibeonites, the attendants on the priesthood. Seven descendants of Saul were put to death: but the barbarity of the transaction is relieved by the tender fidelity of Rizpah, one of Saul's concubines, who watched for months the remains of her unhappy children, lest the vultures or wild beasts should destroy them. David afterward gave honorable burial to their bones, as well as to those of Saul and Jonathan. The civil wars, perhaps the three years' famine, had so enfeebled the strength of the kingdom, that the restless Philistines began to renew hostilities. Four gigantic champions, one of whom had put the life of David into peril, having been slain by his valiant chieftains, the war terminated.

David, now reinstated in all his strength and splendor, determined to take a census of his vast dominions, which extended from Lebanon to the frontiers of Egypt, from the Euphrates to the Mediterranean. The numbers differ, but the lowest gives 800,000 men fit to bear arms in Israel, 500,000 in Judah. Benjamin and Levi were not reckoned. Whether in direct violation of the law, David began to contemplate schemes of foreign conquest, and to aspire to the fame of a Sesostris; or whether the census exhibited the relative strength of Judah, so weak at the commencement of David's reign, as become formidable to the rest of the tribes; this measure was reprobated by the nation in general, as contrary to the Divine command, and as impolitic, even by the unscrupulous Joab. It called down the anger of Providence. The king was commanded to choose between seven years' famine, three months of unsuccessful war and defeat, or three days' pestilence. David, with wise humility, left the judgment in the hand of God. The pestilence broke out, 70,000 lives were lost; the malady spread to Jerusalem, but the king was commanded to build an altar on Mount Moriah, the site of the future temple, then occupied by the thrashing-flood of Araunah, one of the old Jebusite race. Araunah offered to make a gift of the place, and all the utensils, to be burnt for sacrifice; but David insisted on paying the full price of the ground. There the altar was built, and the plague immediately ceased.

The remaining years of David were spent in making the most costly preparations for the building of the temple, and in securing the succession to his son Solomon, to whom this great trust was to be bequeathed. As his time drew near, those evils began to display themselves, which are inseparable from Oriental monarchies, where polygamy prevails; and where among children, from many wives, of different ranks, no certain rule of succession is established. Factions began to divide the army, the royal household, and even the priesthood. Adonijah, the brother of Absalom, supported by the turbulent Joab, and by Abiathar, the priest, assembled a large body of adherents, at a festival. When this intelligence was communicated to David, without the slightest delay he commanded Nathan, the prophet, and Zadok, the priest, with Benaiah, one of his most valiant captains, to take Solomon down to Gihon, to anoint and proclaim him. The young king re-entered the city amid the loudest acclamations; the party of Adonijah, who were still at their feast, dispersed and fled. Adonijah took refuge at the altar: his life was spared. David, after this success, assembled first the great body of leading men in the state, and afterward perhaps a more extensive and popular convention of the people, before whom he designated Solomon as his successor, commended to the zeal and piety of the people the building of the temple, and received their contributions toward the great national work.

As his death approached, he strictly enjoined his son to adhere to the Mosaic laws and to the divine constitution. He recommended him to watch with a jealous eye the bold and restless Joab; a man who, however brave and faithful, was dangerous from his restless ambition, and from the savage unscrupulousness with which he shed the blood of his enemies. Abner and Amasa had both fallen by his hand, without warrant or authority from the king. Solomon, *according to his wisdom*, on the first appearance of treasonable intention, was to put him to death without mercy. Shimei was in the same manner to be cut off, if he should betray the least mark of disaffection. But to the sons of Barzillai the Gileadite, the successor of David was to show the utmost gratitude and kindness.

Thus, having provided for the security of the succession, the maintenance of the law, and the lasting dignity of the national religion, David breathed his last, having reigned forty years over the flourishing and powerful monarchy of which he may be considered the founder. He had succeeded to a kingdom distracted with civil dissension, environed on every side by powerful and victorious enemies, without a capital, almost without any bond of union between the tribes. He left a compact and united state, stretching from the frontier of Egypt to the foot of Lebanon, from the Euphrates to the sea. He had crushed the power of the Philistines, subdued or curbed all the adjacent kingdoms: he had formed a lasting and important alliance with the great city of Tyre. He had organized an immense disposable force: every month 24,000 men, furnished in rotation by the tribes, appeared in arms, and were trained as the standing militia of the country. At the head of his army were officers of consummate experience, and, what was more highly esteemed in the warfare of the time, extraordinary personal activity, strength, and valor. His heroes remind us of those of Arthur or Charlemagne, excepting that the armor of the feudal chieftains constituted the superiority; here main strength of body and dauntless fortitude of mind. The Hebrew nation owed the long peace of the son's reign to the bravery and wisdom of the father. If the rapidity with which a kingdom rises to unexampled prosperity, and the permanence, as far as human wisdom can provide, of that prosperity, be a fair criterion of the abilities and character of a sovereign, few kings in history can compete with David.

His personal character has been often discussed; but both by his enemies, and even by some of his learned defenders, with an ignorance of, or inattention to, his age and country, in writers of such acuteness as Bayle, as melancholy as surprising. Both parties have been content to take the expression of the *man after God's own heart*, in a strict and literal sense. Both have judged by modern European and Christian notions, the chieftain of an eastern and comparatively barbarous people. If David in his exile became a freebooter, he assumed a profession, like the pirate in ancient Greece, by no means dishonorable. If he employed craft or even falsehood in some of his enterprises, chivalrous or conscientious attachment to truth was probably not one of the virtues of his day. He had his harem, like other eastern kings. He waged war, and revenged himself on his foreign enemies with merciless cruelty, like other warriors of his age and country. His one great crime violated the immutable and universal laws of morality, and therefore admits of no excuse. On the other hand, his consummate personal bravery and military talent—his generosity to his enemies—his fidelity to his friends—his knowledge of, and steadfast attention to, the true interests of his country—his piety and gratitude to his God, justify the fervent attachment of the Jewish people to the memory of their great monarch.

The three most eminent men in the Hebrew annals, Moses, David, and Solomon, were three of their most distinguished poets. The hymns of David excel no less in sublimity and tenderness of expression than in loftiness and purity of religious entiment. In comparison with them the sacred poetry of all other nations sinks into mediocrity. They have embodied so exquisitely the universal language of religious emotion, that (a few fierce and vindictive passages excepted, natural in the warrior poet of a sterner age), they have entered with unquestioned propriety into the ritual of the holier and more perfect religion of Christ. The songs which cheered the solitude of the desert caves of Engedi, or resounded from the voice of the Hebrew people as they wound along the glens or the hill-sides of Judea have been repeated for ages in almost every part of the habitable world, in the remotest islands of the ocean, among the forests of America or the sands of Africa. How many human hearts have they softened, purified, exalted!—of how many wretched beings have they been the secret consolation!—ou how many communities have they drawn down the blessings of Divine Providence, by bringing the affections into unison with their deep devotional fervor.

Solomon succeeded to the Hebrew kingdom at the age of twenty. He was environed by designing, bold, and dangerous enemies. The pretensions of Adonijah still commanded a powerful party: Abiathar swayed the priesthood; Joab the army. The singular connection in public opinion between the title to the crown and the possession of the deceased monarch's harem, has been already noticed. Adonijah, in making request for Abishag, a youthful concubine taken by David in his old age, was considered as insidiously renewing his claims to the sovereignty. Solomon saw at once the wisdom of his father's dying admonition: he seized the opportunity of crushing all future opposition, and all danger of a civil war. He caused Adonijah to be put to death; suspended Abiathar from his office, and banished him from Jerusalem: and though Joab fled to the altar, he commanded him to be slain, for the two murders of which he had been guilty, those of Abner and Amasa. Shimei, another dangerous character, was commanded to reside in Jerusalem, on pain of death if he should quit the city. Three years afterward he was detected in a suspicious journey to Gath, on the Philistine border; and having violated the compact, he suffered the penalty.

Thus secured by the policy of his father from internal enemies, by the terror of his victories from foreign invasion. Solomon commenced his peaceful reign, during which Judah and Israel dwelt safely, every man under his vine and under his fig-tree, from Dan to Beersheba. His justice was proverbial. Among his first acts after his succession, it is related that after a costly sacrifice at Gibeon, the place where the tabernacle remained, God had appeared to him in a dream, and offered him whatever gift he chose: the wise king had requested an understanding heart to judge the people. God not merely assented to his prayer, but added the gift of honor and riches. His judicial wisdom was displayed in the memorable history of the two women who contested the right to a child. Solomon, in the wild spirit of Oriental justice, commanded the infant to be divided before their faces: the heart of the real mother was struck with terror and abhorrence; while the false one consented to the horrible partition; and by this appeal to nature the cause was instantaneously decided.

The internal government of his extensive dominions next demanded the attention of Solomon. Besides the local and municipal governors, he divided the kingdom into twelve districts: over each of these he appointed a purveyor, for the collection of the royal tribute, which was received in kind; and thus the growing capital and the immense establishments of Solomon were abundantly furnished with provisions. Each purveyor supplied the court for a month. The daily consumption of his household was 300 bushels of finer flour, 600 of a coarser sort; 10 fatted, 20 other oxen; 100 sheep; besides poultry and various kinds of venison. Provender was furnished for 40,000 horses, and a great number of dromedaries. Yet the population of the country did not, at first at least, feel these burthens. Judah and Israel were many, as the sand which is by the sea in multitude, eating and drinking, and making merry.

The foreign treaties of Solomon were as wisely directed to secure the profound peace of his dominions. He entered into a matrimonial alliance with the royal family of Egypt, whose daughter he received with great magnificence; and he renewed the important alliance with the king of Tyre. The friendship of this monarch was of the highest value in contributing to the great royal and national work, the building of the temple. The cedar timber could only be obtained from the forests of Lebanon: the Sidonian artisans, celebrated in the Homeric poems were the most skillful workmen in every kind of manufacture, particularly in the precious metals. Solomon entered into a regular treaty, by which he bound himself to supply the Tyrians with large quantities of corn; receiving in return their timber, which was floated down to Joppa, and a large body of artificers. The timber was cut by his own subjects, of whom he raised a body of 30,000; 10-000 employed at a time, and relieving each other every month; so that to one month of labor they had two of rest. He raised two other corps, one of 70,000 porters of burthens; the other of 80,000 hewers of stone, who were employed in the quarries among the mountains. All these labors were thrown, not on the Israelites, but on the strangers, who, chiefly of Canaanitish descent, had been permitted to inhabit the country. These preparations, in addition to those of King David, being completed, the work began. The eminence of Moriah, the Mount of Vision; *i. e.* the height seen afar from the adjacent country; which tradition pointed out as the spot where Abraham had offered his son; where recently the plague had been stayed by the altar built in the thrashing-floor of Ornan, or Araunah, the Jebusite; rose on the east side of the city. Its rugged top was leveled with immense labor; its sides, which to the east and south were precipitous, were faced with a wall of stone, built up perpendicular from the bottom of the valley, so as to appear to those who looked down of most terrific height; a work of prodigious skill and labor, as the immense stones were strongly mortised together and wedged into the rock. Around the whole area or esplanade, an irregular quadrangle, was a solid wall of considerable height and strength: within this was an open court, into which the Gentiles were either from the first or subsequently admitted. A second wall encompassed another quadrangle, called the court of the Israelites. Along this wall, on the inside, ran a portico or cloister, over which were chambers for different sacred purposes. Within this again, another, probably a lower, wall, separated the court of the priests from that of the Israelites. To each court the ascent was by steps, so that the platform of the inner court was on a higher level than that of the outer. The temple itself was rather a monument of the wealth than the architectural skill and science of the people. It was a wonder of the world, from the splendor of its materials more than the grace, boldness, or majesty of its height and dimensions. It had neither the colossal magnitude of the Egyptian, the simple dignity and perfect proportional harmony of the Grecian, nor perhaps the fantastic grace and lightness of modern oriental architecture. Some writers, calling to their assistance the visionary temple of Ezekiel, have erected a most superb edifice; to which there is this fatal objection, that if the dimensions of the prophet are taken as they stand in the text, the area of the temple and its courts would not only have covered the whole of Mount Moriah, but almost all Jerusalem. In fact, our accounts of the temple of Solomon are altogether unsatisfactory. The details, as they now stand in the books of Kings and Chronicles, the only safe authorities, are unscientific, and, what is worse, contradictory. Josephus has evidently blended together the three temples, and attributed to the earlier all the subsequent additions and alterations. The temple, on the whole, was an enlargement of the tabernacle, built of more costly and durable materials. Like its model it retained the ground plan and disposition of the Egyptian, or rather of almost all the sacred edifices of antiquity; even its measurements are singularly in unison with some of the most ancient temples in Upper Egypt. It consisted of a propylæon, a temple, and a sanctuary; called respectively the porch, the Holy place, and the Holy of Holies. Yet in some respects, if the measurements are correct, the temple must rather have resembled the form of a simple Gothic church. In the front to the east stood the porch, a tall tower, rising to the height of 210 feet. Either within, or, like the Egyptian obelisks, before the porch, stood two pillars of brass; by one account 27, by another above 60 feet high; the latter statement probably including their capitals and bases. These were called Jachin and Boaz (Durability and Strength). The capitals of these were of the richest workmanship, with net-work, chain-work, and pomegranates. The porch was the same width with the temple, 35 feet; its depth 17½. The length of the main building, including the holy place, 70 feet, and the holy of holies, 35, was in the whole 105 feet, the height 52½ feet. Josephus carries the whole building up to the height of the porch; but this is out of all credible proportion, making the height twice the length and six times the width. Along each side, and perhaps at the back of the main building, ran an aisle, divided into three stories of small chambers: the wall of the temple being thicker at the bottom, left a rest to support the beams of these chambers, which were not let into the wall. These aisles, the chambers of which were appropriated as vestiaries, treasuries, and for other sacred purposes, seem to have reached about halfway up the main wall of what we may call the nave and choir: the windows into the latter were probably above them; these were narrow, but widened inwards.

If the dimensions of the temple appear by no means imposing, it must be remembered that but a small part of the religious ceremonies took place within the walls. The Holy of Holies was entered only once a year, and that by the high-priest alone. It was the secret and unapproachable shrine of the Divinity.

The Holy Place, the body of the temple, admitted only the officiating priests. The open courts, called in popular language the temple, or rather the inner quadrangle, was in fact the great place of divine worship. Here, under the open air, were celebrated the great public and national rites, the processions, the offerings, the sacrifices; here stood the great tank for ablution, and the high altar for burnt offerings. But the materials, the richness and variety of the details, amply compensated for the moderate dimensions of the building. It was such a sacred edifice as a traveler might have expected to find in El Dorado. The walls were hewn stone, faced within with cedar, which was richly carved with knosps and flowers; the ceiling was of fir-tree. But in every part gold was lavished with the utmost profusion; within and without, the floor, the walls, the ceiling, in short, the whole house is described as overlaid with gold. The finest and purest—that of Parvaim, by some supposed to be Ceylon—was reserved for the sanctuary. Here the cherubim, which stood upon the covering of the ark, with their wings touching each wall, were entirely covered with gold. The sumptuous vail, of the richest materials and brightest colors, which divided the Holy of Holies from the holy place, was suspended on chains of gold. Cherubim, palm-trees and flowers, the favorite ornaments, every where, covered with gilding, were wrought in almost all parts. The altar within the temple, and the table of the show-bread, were likewise covered with the same precious metal. All the vessels, the 10 candlesticks, 500 basins, and all the rest of the sacrificial and other utensils, were of solid gold. Yet the Hebrew writers seem to dwell with the greatest astonishment and admiration on the works which were founded in brass, by Huram, a man of Jewish extraction, who had learned his art at Tyre. Besides the lofty pillars above mentioned there was a great tank, called a sea, of molten brass, supported on twelve oxen, three turned each way, this was seventeen and a half feet in diameter.

There was also a great altar, and ten large vessels for the purpose of ablution, called lavers, standing on bases or pedestals, the rims of which were richly ornamented with a border, on which were wrought figures of lions, oxen, and cherubim. The bases below were formed of four wheels, like those of a chariot.

All the works in brass were cast in a place near the Jordan, where the soil was of a stiff clay suited to the purpose.

For seven years and a half the fabric arose in silence. All the timbers, the stones, even of the most enormous size, were hewn and fitted, so as to be put together without the sound of any tool whatever: as it has been expressed, with great poetical beauty,

"Like some tall palm the noiseless fabric grew."

At the end of this period, the temple and its courts being completed, the solemn dedication took place, with the greatest magnificence which the king and the nation could display. All the chieftains of the different tribes, and all of every order that could be brought together, assembled. David had already organized the priesthood and the Levites; assigned to the 38,000 of the latter tribe, each his particular office. 24,000 were appointed for the common duties, 6,000 as officers, 4,000 as guards and porters, 4,000 as singers and musicians. On this great occasion, the dedication of the temple, all the tribe of Levi, without regard to their courses, the whole priestly order of every class, attended. Around the great brazen altar, which arose in the court of the priests before the door of the temple, stood—in front the sacrificers, all around the whole choir, arrayed in white linen. 120 of these were trumpeters, the rest had cymbals, harps, and psalteries. Solomon himself took his place on an elevated scaffold, or raised throne of brass. The whole assembled nation crowded the spacious courts beyond. The ceremony began with the preparation of burnt offerings, so numerous that they could not be counted. At an appointed signal commenced the more important part of the scene the removal of the ark, the installation of the God of Israel in his new and appropriate dwelling, to the sound of all the voices and all the instruments, chanting songs of those splendid odes, the 47th, 97th, 98th, and 107th, psalms. The ark advanced, borne by the Levites, to the portals of the temple. It can scarcely be doubted that the 24th Psalm, even if composed before, was adopted and used on this occasion.

The singers, as it drew near the gate, broke out in these words: "Lift up your heads, O ye gates, and be ye lifted up, ye everlasting doors, that the King of Glory may come in." It was answered from the other part of the choir—"Who is the King of Glory?"—the whole choir responded—"The Lord of Hosts, he is the King of Glory." When the procession arrived at the Holy Place, the gates flew open; when it reached the Holy of Holies, the vail was drawn back. The ark took its place under the extended wings of the cherubim, which might seem to fold over, and receive it under their protection. At that instant all the trumpeters and singers were, at once, "to make one sound to be heard in praising and thanking the Lord; and when they lifted up their voices, with the trumpets and cymbals, and instruments of music, and praised the Lord, saying, For he is good, for his mercy endureth for ever, the house was filled with a cloud, even the house of the Lord, so that the priests could not stand to minister, by reason of the cloud; for the glory of the Lord had filled the house of God." Thus the Divinity took possession of his sacred edifice. The king then rose upon the brazen scaffold, knelt down, and spreading his hands toward heaven, uttered the prayer of consecration.

The prayer was of unexampled sublimity; while it implored the perpetual presence of the

Almighty, as the tutelar deity and sovereign of the Israelites, it recognized his spiritual and illimitable nature. "But will God, in every deed, dwell with men on earth? Behold, heaven and the heaven of heavens can not contain thee, how much less this house which I have built." It then recapitulated the principles of the Hebrew theocracy, the dependance of the national prosperity and happiness on the national conformity to the civil and religious law. As the king concluded in these emphatic terms: "Now, therefore, arise, O Lord God, into thy resting-place, thou and the ark of thy strength; let thy priest, O Lord God, be clothed with salvation, and thy saints rejoice in goodness. O Lord God, turn not away the face of thine anointed; remember the mercies of David, thy servant"—the cloud which had rested over the Holy of Holies, grew brighter and more dazzling; fire broke out and consumed all the sacrifices; the priests stood without, awe-struck by the insupportable splendor; the whole people fell on their faces, and worshiped and praised the Lord, "for he is good, for his mercy is for ever."

Which was the greater, the external magnificence, or the moral sublimity of this scene? Was it the temple, situated on its commanding eminence, with all its courts, the dazzling splendor of its materials, the innumerable multitudes, the priesthood in their gorgeous attire, the king with all the insignia of royalty on his throne of burnished brass, the music, the radiant cloud filling the temple, the sudden fire flashing upon the altar, the whole nation upon their knees? Was it not, rather, the religious grandeur of the hymns and of the prayers; the exalted and rational views of the Divine Nature, the union of a whole people in the adoration of the one great, incomprehensible, almighty, everlasting Creator?

This extraordinary festival, which took place at the time of that of Tabernacles, lasted for two weeks, twice the usual time; during this period, 22,000 oxen, and 120,000 sheep were sacrificed, every individual probably contributing to the great propitiatory rite; and the whole people feasting on those parts of the sacrifices which were not set apart for holy uses.

Though the chief magnificence of Solomon was lavished on the temple of God, yet the sumptuous palaces which he erected for his own residence, display an opulence and profusion which may vie with the older monarchs of Egypt or Assyria. The great palace stood in Jerusalem; it occupied thirteen years in building. A causeway bridged the deep ravine, and leading directly to the temple, united the part either of Acra or Sion, on which the palace stood, with Mount Moriah.

In this palace was a vast hall for public business, from its cedar pillars, called the House of the Forest of Lebanon. It was 175 feet long, half that measurement in width, above fifty feet high; four rows of cedar columns supported a roof made of beams of the same wood; there were three rows of windows on each side, facing each other. Besides this great hall, there were two others, called porches, of smaller dimensions, in one of which, the throne of justice was placed. The harem, or women's apartments, joined to these buildings; with other piles of vast extent for different purposes, particularly, if we may credit Josephus, a great banqueting hall. The same author informs us, that the whole was surrounded with spacious and luxuriant gardens, and adds, a less credible fact, ornamented with sculptures and paintings. Another palace was built in a romantic part of the country for his wife, the daughter of the king of Egypt; in the luxurious gardens of which we may lay the scene of that poetical epithalamium, or collection of idols, the Song of Solomon.

The descriptions in the Greek writers of the Persian courts in Susa and Ecbatana; the tales of the early travelers in the East about the kings of Samarcand or Cathay; and even the imagination of the Oriental romancers and poets, have scarcely conceived a more splendid pageant than Solomon, seated on his throne of ivory, receiving the homage of distant princes who came to admire his magnificence, and put to the test his noted wisdom. This throne was of pure ivory, covered with gold; six steps led up to the seat, and on each side of the steps were twelve lions carved. All the vessels of his palace were of pure gold, silver was thought too mean: his armory was furnished with gold; 200 targets, and 300 shields of beaten gold were suspended in the house of Lebanon. Josephus mentions a body of archers who escorted him from the city to his country palace, clad in dresses of Tyrian purple, and their hair powdered with gold dust. But enormous as this wealth appears, the statement of his expenditure on the temple, and of his annual revenue, so passed all credibility, that any attempt at forming a calculation on the uncertain data we possess, may at once be abandoned as a hopeless task. No better proof can be given of the uncertainty of our authorities, of our imperfect knowledge of Hebrew weights of money, and, above all, of our total ignorance of the relative value which the precious metals bore to the commodities of life, than the estimate, made by Dr. Prideaux, of the treasures left by David, amounting to eight hundred millions.

Our inquiry into the sources of the vast wealth which Solomon undoubtedly possessed, may lead to more satisfactory, though still imperfect results. The treasures of David were accumulated rather by conquest than by traffio. Some of the nations he subdued, particularly the Edomites, were wealthy. All the tribes seem to have worn a good deal of gold and silver in their ornaments and their armor; their idols were often of gold, and the treasures of their temples perhaps contained considerable wealth. But during the reign of Solomon almost the whole commerce of the world passed into his territories. The treaty with Tyre was of the utmost importance: nor is there any instance in which two neighboring nations so clearly saw, and so steadily pursued, without jealousy or mistrust, their mutual and inseparable interest. On one occasion only, when Solomon presented to Hiram twenty inland cities which he had conquered, Hiram expressed great dissatisfaction, and called the territory by the opprobrious name of Cabul. The Tyrian had perhaps cast a wistful eye on the noble bay and harbor of Acco, or Ptolemais, which the prudent Hebrew either would not, or could not—since it was part of the promised land—dissever from his dominions. So strict was the confederacy, that Tyre may be considered the port of Palastine, Palastine the granary of Tyre. Tyre furnished the shipbuilders and mariners; the fruitful plains of Palastine victualed the fleets, and supplied the manufacturers and merchants of the Phœnician league with all the necessaries of life.

This league comprehended Tyre, Aradus, Sidon, perhaps Tripolis, Byblus and Berytus; the narrow slip of territory which belonged to these states was barren, rocky, and unproductive. The first branch of commerce, into which this enterprising people either admitted the Jews as regular partners, or at least permitted them to share in its advantages, was the traffic of the Mediterranean. To every part of that sea the Phœnicians had pursued their discoveries; they had planted colonies, and worked the mines. This was the trade to Tarshish, so celebrated, that ships of Tarshish seem to have become the common name for large merchant vessels. Tarshish was probably a name as indefinite, as the West Indies in early European navigation; properly speaking, it was the south of Spain, then rich in mines of gold and silver, the Peru of Tyrian adventure. Whether or not as early as the days of Solomon, without doubt in the more flourishing period of Phœnicia; before the city on the mainland was destroyed by Nebuchadnezzar, and insular Tyre became the emporium—the Phœnician navies extended their voyages beyond the pillars of Hercules, where they founded Cadiz. Northward they sailed along the coast of France to the British isles: southward along the African shore; where the boundaries of their navigation are quite uncertain, yet probably extended to the Gold Coast.

The second branch of commerce was the inland trade with Egypt. This was carried on entirely by the Jews. Egypt supplied horses in vast numbers, and linen yarn. The valleys of the Nile produced flax in abundance; and the yarn, according to the description of the prudent housewife in the Proverbs, was spun and woven by the females in Palestine.

The third, and more important branch, was the maritime trade by the Red Sea. The conquests of David had already made the Jews masters of the eastern branch of this gulf. Solomon built or improved the towns and ports of Elath and Ezion-geber. Hence a fleet, manned by Tyrians, sailed for Ophir, their East Indies, as Tarshish was their West. They sailed along the eastern coast of Africa, in some part of which the real Ophir was probably situated.

When the Egyptians under Necho, after the declension of the Israelitish kingdom, took possession of this branch of commerce, there seems little reason to doubt the plain and consistent account of Herodotus, that the Tyrians sailed round the continent of Africa. The whole maritime commerce, with eastern Asia, the southern shores of the Arabian peninsula, the coasts of the Persian gulf, and without doubt some parts of India, entered, in the same manner, the Red Sea, and was brought to Elath and Ezion-geber. Yet even this line of commerce was scarcely more valuable than the inland trade of the Arabian peninsula. This was carried on by the caravans of the native tribes, who transported on camels, the spices, the incense, the gold, the precious stones, the valuable woods, particularly the almug, thought to be the sandal—and all the other highly prized productions of that country; perhaps also the foreign commodities which were transported across the Persian gulf, or which were landed, by less adventurous traders from the east, in the Arabian ports on that sea. Both these lines of commerce flowed directly into the dominions of Solomon. Those goods which passed on to Tyre were, not improbably, shipped at Joppa. Two of the towns which Solomon built, Gezer and lower Beth-boron, were nearly on the line from the Red Sea to that haven. This traffic was afterward recovered by the Edomites, under the protection, or sharing its advantages with the Egyptians; still, however, the Tyrians were most likely both the merchants who fitted out the enterprises, and the mariners who manned the ships.

The goods, intended for Tyre, were then most probably shipped at Rhinocorura. Under the Romans the Nabathean Arabs carried on the same traffic, of which their great city, Petra, was the inland emporium; at least that by the caravans, for the Ptolemies had diverted a great part of the Red Sea trade to their new port of Berenice. A fifth line of commerce was that of inland Asia, which crossed from Assyria and Babylonia to Tyre. In order to secure and participate in this branch of traffic, Solomon subdued part of the Syrian tribes, and built two cities, as stations, between the Euphrates and the coast. These were Tadmor and Baalath, one the celebrated Palmyria, the other Baal-bec. After the desolating conquests of Assyria, and the total ruin of old Tyre, this line of trade probably found its way to Sardis, and contributed to the splendor of Crœsus and his Lydian kingdom. It was from these various sources of wealth, that the precious metals and all other valuable commodities were in such abundance—that, in the figurative language of the sacred historian, *silver was in Jerusalem as stones, and cedar trees as sycamores.*

Solomon was not less celebrated for his wisdom than his magnificence. The visits of the neighboring princes, particularly that of the Queen of Sheba, (a part of Arabia Felix), were to admire the one, as much as the other. Hebrew tradition, perhaps the superstitious wonder of his own age, ascribed to Solomon the highest skill in magical arts, and even unbounded dominion over all the invisible world. Tadmor, in the wilderness, was said to have been built by his enchantments. More sober history recognizes in Solomon the great poet, naturalist, and moral philosopher of his time. His poetry, consisting of 1005 songs, except his epithalemium, and perhaps some of the Psalms, has entirely perished. His natural history of plants and animals has suffered the same fate. But the great part of the book of Proverbs and Ecclesiastes, (perhaps more properly reckoned as a poem), have preserved the conclusions of his moral wisdom.

The latter book, or poem, derives new interest, when considered as coming from the most voluptuous, magnificent, and instructed of monarchs, who sums up the estimate of human life in the melancholy sentence—*Vanity of vanities! vanity of vanities!* It is a sad commentary on the termination of the splendid life and reign of the great Hebrew sovereign. For even had not this desponding confession been extorted by the satiety of passion, and the weariness of a spirit, over-excited by all the gratifications this world can bestow—had no higher wisdom suggested this humiliating conclusion—the state of his own powerful kingdom, during his declining years, might have furnished a melancholy lesson on the instability of human grandeur. Solomon, in his old age, was about to bequeath to his heir, an insecure throne, a discontented people, formidable enemies on the frontiers, and perhaps a contested succession. He could not even take refuge in the sanctuary of conscious innocence, and assume the dignity of suffering unmerited degradation ; for he had set at defiance every principle of the Hebrew constitution. He had formed a connection with Egypt—he had multiplied a great force of cavalry—he had accumulated gold and silver—he had married many foreign wives. His seraglio was on as vast a scale as the rest of his expenditure—he had seven hundred wives, and three hundred concubines. The influence of these women, not merely led him to permit an idolatrous worship within his dominions ; but even Solomon had been so infatuated, as to consecrate to the obscene and barbarous deities of the neighboring nations, a part of one of the hills, which overlooked Jerusalem ; a spot almost fronting the splendid temple which he himself had built to the one Almighty God of the universe.

Hence, clouds on all sides gathered about his declining day. Hadad, one of the blood-royal of the Edomite princes, began to organize a revolt in that province, on which so much of the Jewish commerce depended. An adventurer seized on Damascus, and set up an independent sovereignty, thus endangering the communication from Tadmor. A domestic enemy, still more dangerous, appeared in the person of Jeroboam, a man of great valor, supported by the prophet Abijah, who foretold his future rule over the ten tribes. Though forced to fly, Jeroboam found an asylum with Shishak, or Sesac, the Sesonchosis of Manetho, who was raising the kingdom of Egypt to its alarming grandeur; and, notwithstanding his alliance with Solomon, made no scruple against harboring his rebellious subject.

Above all, the people were oppressed and dissatisfied ; either because the enormous revenues of the kingdom were more than absorbed by the vast expenditure of the sovereign; or because the more productive branches of commerce were interrupted by the rebellions of the Edomites and Damascenes. At this period likewise, Solomon departed from the national, though iniquitous policy of his earlier reign, during which he had laid all the burdens of labor and taxation on the strangers, and exempted the Israelites from every claim, but that of military service.

The language held to Rehoboam, on his accession, shows that the people had suffered deeply from the arbitrary exactions of the king, who, with the state of splendor, had assumed the despotism of an Oriental monarch. Hence, the decline of the Jewish kingdom, supported rather by the fame of its sovereign, than by its inherent strength, was as rapid as its rise. Solomon died after a reign of forty years, and with him expired the glory and the power of the Jewish empire.

BOOK VIII.

KINGDOMS OF JUDAH AND ISRAEL

Accession of Rehoboam—Jeroboam—Separation of the Two Kingdoms—Asa—House of Ormri—Building of Samaria—Ahab—The prophets Elijah—Elisha—Jehoshaphat—Hostilities with Syria—House of Jehu—Athaliah Uzziah—Hazael—Jeroboam the Second—Ahaz.

Fall of Samaria—Captivity of the Ten Tribes—Hezekiah—Manasseh—Josiah—Assyrian Conquests—First—Final Capture of Jerusalem.

KINGS OF JUDAH.	Yrs.		KINGS OF ISRAEL.	Yrs.
Rehoboam......reigned	17.	B.C. 979.	Jeroboam......reigned	22
Abijah	3	B.C. 962.		
Asa	41.	B.C. 959.		
		B.C 957	Nadab	2
		B.C. 955.	Baasha	23
		B.C. 932.	Elah	2
		B.C 930.	Zimri, Omri	11
		B.C. 919.	Ahab	22
Jehoshaphat	25.	B.C. 918.		
		B.C. 897.	Ahaziah	2
		B.C. 895.	Jehoram	12
Jehoram	8.	B.C. 893.		
Ahaziah	1.	B C. 885.		
Athaliah	6.	B.C. 884—3.	Jehu	28
Jehoash	40.	B.C. 878.		
		B.C. 855.	Jehoahaz	17
Amaziah	29.	B.C. 838.	Jehoash	16
		B.C. 822.	Jeroboam 2d	42
Uzziah or Azariah	51.	B.C. [illegible]		
		B.C. 781.	Inter genum.	11
		B.C. 770	Zachariah & Shallum.	1
		B.C. 769.	Menahem	10
		B.C. 759.	Pekahia	2
Jotham	16.	B.C. 758.	Pekah	20
Ahaz	16.	B.C. 742.		
		B.C. 737.	2d Interregnum	9
		B.C. 728.	Hoshea	9
Hezekiah	29.	B.C. 726.		
		B.C. 719.	Samaria taken.	
Manasseh	55.	B.C. 697.		
Amon	2.	B.C. 642.		
Josiah	31.	B.C. 640.		
Jehoahaz.... 3 months—		B C. 609.		
Jehoiachim	11			
Jehoiachin or Coniah 3 months—		B.C. 598.		
Zedekiah	11			
Jerusalem destroyed		B.C. 587.		

Rehoboam, the son of Solomon, was received as king by the whole nation. But his title, though recognized at Jerusalem, seemed insecure without the formal adhesion of the other tribes. An assembly therefore was summoned at Shechem; but instead of adopting the wise and conciliatory language recommended by the older counsellors of Solomon, Rehoboam followed the advice of the young and violent; and when the assembly, headed by the popular Jeroboam, who made his appearance from Egypt, demanded an alleviation of the public burthens, the rash and inconsiderate king, not merely refused compliance, but in the true character of Eastern monarchy, threatened them with still heavier exactions. "My father made your yoke heavy, and I will add to your yoke; my father chastised you with whips, but I will chastise you with scorpions." "To your tents, O Israel," was the instantaneous cry; the ten tribes unanimously renounced their allegiance, raised Jeroboam to the throne, forced the son of Solomon to fly to his native kingdom of Judah, and stoned Adoram the collector of his tribute. Thus the national union was for ever dissolved, and the Hebrew Kingdom never recovered this fatal blow.

Rehoboam had recourse to arms, and raised a host of 180,000 men. But the authority of the prophet Shemaiah, prevented the civil war, and Rehoboam was obliged to content himself with fortifying and securing his own dominions. In the mean time the politic and unscrupulous Jeroboam pursued every measure which could make the breach irreparable, and thus secure his throne. As long as Jerusalem was the place of national worship, it might again become the centre of the national union. The Levitical class, who constantly went up to the temple in their courses, and the religion itself, were bonds which must be dissolved: a separate kingdom must have a separate priesthood, and a separate place and establishment for sacred purposes. To this end Jeroboam caused two golden calves to be made, and consecrated some ignoble persons, not of the Levitical tribe, as the priesthood. These calves were set up, the one in the remote city of Dan. They were speciously contrived as symbolical representations, probably preserving some resemblance to the churbim, of which the ox was one of the four constituent parts. Still they were set up in no less flagrant violation of the law, than if they had been the deities of Egypt, to which they bore a great likeness. This heinous deviation from the Mosaic polity, was not carried into effect without remonstrance on the part of the prophets. As Jeroboam stood by the altar to burn incense, one of the seers made his appearance, denounced a curse, and foretold the disasters that would inevitably ensue. The king attempting to seize him, his hand was suddenly withered, but restored at the prayer of the prophet. The prophet himself, not strictly complying with the divine command, was destroyed on his return home by a lion, an awful example to all those who should exercise that function, so important in the later period of the Jewish kingdom. But Jeroboam was not satisfied with thus securing his throne against the influence of the national religion. It may be assumed, that not without his suggestion or connivance, his patron Shishak, king of Egypt, made a descent on the kingdom of Judah, now weakened by the corrupt morals of the people. Rehoboam offered no effectual resistance to the invader: the treasures of the temple and palace of Solomon were plundered; the golden shields carried away, and replaced by others made of the baser metal, brass.

After a reign of seventeen years Rehoboam was succeeded on the throne of Judah by Abijah, his son, (B. C. 962,) who immediately raised a great force to subdue the kingdom of Israel. The armies of Abijah and Jeroboam met in Mount Ephraim. Jeroboam had on his side both numbers (800,000 men to 400,000) and military skill, which enabled him to surround the forces of Judah. But Abijah had the religious feelings of the people. The presence of the priesthood, and the sound of the sacred trumpets inspirited Judah, as much as they disheartened Israel. Jeroboam was totally defeated with the loss of 500,000 men; the disaster preyed on his mind, and he never after recovered his power or enterprise.

After a short reign of three years Abijah died, and was succeeded by his son Asa, (B.

C. 959,) a prudent and religious prince. He pursued the wiser policy of establishing the national religion in all its splendor and influence, encouraging those who came up to the feasts from the neighboring kingdom, and checking idolatry, which he punished even in the person of Maachah the queen-mother, whom he degraded and banished. Asa strengthened his army and fortified his cities, and thus was enabled to repel a most formidable invasion headed by Zerah, the Ethiopian, some suppose Arabian, or, more probably, either Osorchon, the king of Egypt, or his general, at the head of a million of men, and 300,000 chariots.

But while, from the sacred reverence in which the lineage of David and Solomon was held, the throne of Judah passed quietly from son to son, the race of Jeroboam, having no hereditary greatness in their favor, was speedily cut off from the succession, and adventurer after adventurer contested the kingdom of Israel. During the illness of his elder son Abijah, Jeroboam had sent his wife in disguise to consult the prophet Abijah upon his fate. The prophet not only predicted the death of this promising youth, on the immediate return of his mother to the capital city of Tirzah, but also the total extermination of his race. At the death of Jeroboam the fatal prophesy immediately came to pass. Nadab, his son and successor, (B. C. 957,) was dethroned and put to death, and his whole lineage put to the sword by Baasha, (B. C. 955,) who filled the throne for twenty-four years. Baasha endeavored to counteract the prudent policy of Asa, by building a city (Ramah) on the frontier, to intercept those who deserted the old kingdom and to the purer religion of Jerusalem. In the war that ensued, the king of Judah carried off the materials collected for building the city. Asa adopted a more unprecedented measure, a league with a foreign potentate, the king of Syria, against his Israelitish brethren ; a league which he purchased by a considerable present, taken from the treasures of the temple. The zeal of the prophets took fire, and Hanani, in the name of God, remonstrated against the unnatural alliance. The house of Baasha, after his death, suffered the same fate with that of Jeroboam ; his son Elah was overthrown by Zimri, Zimri in his turn by Omri; who, finally prevailing over another antagonist, Tibni, transferred the royal residence from Tirzah, a beautiful city, where Zimri had set fire to the royal palace, and burned himself and all the treasures in the flames, to Samaria, so long the hatred rival of Jerusalem.

The apostacy of the ten tribes and wickedness of their kings did not reach their heights till the accession of Ahab, the son of Omri (B. C. 919); this prince married Jezebel, the fierce and cruel daughter of the king of Sidon. Under her influence the Sidonian worship of Baal, the Sun, was introduced; his temples were openly built and consecrated ; and this fierce and persecuting idolatry threatened to exterminate the ancient religion. The prophets were put to death, 100 escaped by lying concealed in a cave; yet these intrepid defenders of the God of their fathers still arose to remonstrate against these fatal innovations; till at length Elijah, the greatest of the whole race, took up the contest, and defied and triumphed over the cruelty, both of the king, and his blood-thirsty consort.

At this period the prophets act their most prominent and important part in Jewish history, particularly in that of Israel, where the Levites having been expelled, and the priesthood degraded, they remained the only defenders of the law and religion of the land. Prophecy, it has been observed before, in its more extensive meaning, comprehended the whole course of religious education; and as the Levitical classes were the sole authorized conservators and interpreters of the law, the prophets were usually of that tribe, or at least persons educated under their care. Now, however, they assume a higher character, and appear as a separate and influential class in the state. They are no longer the musicians, poets, and historians of the country, but men full of high and solemn enthusiasm, the moral and religious teachers of the people. The most eminent are described as directly, and sometimes suddenly, designated for their office by divine inspiration, endowed with the power of working miracles, and of foretelling future events. But, setting aside their divine submission, the prophets were the great constitutional patriots of the Jewish state, the champions of virtue, liberty, justice, and the strict observance of the civil and religious law, against the iniquities of the kings of the people. In no instance do they fall beneath, often they rise above, the lofty and humane morals of the Mosaic Institutes. They are always on the side of the oppressed; they boldly rebuke but never factiously insult their kings; they defend, but never flatter the passions of the people. In no instance does one of the acknowledged seers, like the turbulent demagogues of the Grecian or the Roman republics, abuse his popular influence for his own personal aggrandizement or authority. Sometimes the Hebrew prophets ventured beyond the borders of their own land, and were universally received with honor and with awe; for in fact most of the Eastern nations treat with reverence all pretentions to divine afflatus; so as to respect even madness or idiocy as possibly partaking of that mysterious influence. Hence, the appearance of Elisha at Damascus, or even of Jonah at Nineveh, is by no means incredible. Nevertheless, the exercise of public function was attended with the greatest danger, particularly in their native country. The Mosaic law, while it promised an uninterrupted line of prophets, provided by the enactment of the severest penalties, and by the establishment of a searching test, against the unwarranted assumption of the holy office. If the prophet's admonitions were not in accordance with the law, or if the event answered not to his predictions, he was to be put to death. Hence, though false prophets might escape by dexterously flattering the powerful, the bold and honest discharge of the office demanded the highest zeal and intrepidity. Of all the prophets, none united such distinguished qualifications, or was so highly gifted as Elijah, who appeared at this disastrous juncture, when the abrogation of the ancient religion, and the formal establishment of the Sidonian worship, were subtly and deliberately attempted. At his first appearance before Ahab, Elijah denounced as imminent and immediate one of those penalties, with which, according to the first principles of the Mosaic law, the land was threatened on the desertion of the national worship, a long and distressing drought of many years. Having delivered his message, he concealed himself near a brook which ran into the Jordan; there he was fed, as some translate the word, by ravens, as others, by traveling merchants or Arabians. At length the brook dried up, and Elijah fled into Sarepte, a town within the dominions of his Sidonian enemies. Here he was entertained by a charitable widow, whose services were rewarded by the miraculous repletion of her cruse of oil, and the restoration of her son to life.

Still the drought continued; the fruitful plains and the luxuriant valleys of Ephraim and Zebulun lay parched and crumbling with heat; the fountains, the wells, the rivers were all dried up, there was not herbage enough to feed the royal horses and cattle. At this juncture, Elijah suddenly appeared before the king, having previously sent him a message by the reluctant Obadiah. He demanded to put the truth of the two religions to the test of a public and splendid miracle. The scene took place on the summit of that lofty mountain, Carmel, which on one side commands a view of the boundless ocean, on the other of the richest valleys of the promised land. The priests of Baal, the Sun, assembled to the number of 450: Elijah stood alone. All the people awaited the issue in anxious expectation. Whichever sacrifice was kindled by fire from heaven was to decide the cause.

The priests of Baal, having selected their victim, placed it on the altar. As their god began to arise above the eastern horizon, they hailed his appearance with the smoke of their incense, and the loud sound of their orisons. They continued their supplications till he reached the height of his noonday splendor; then with frantic cries, wild dances, cutting their flesh with knives and lancets, they summoued their god to reveal his power. All above was mute and still, the altar cold and unkindled. Elijah began to taunt them. Cry aloud, (he said) for he is a god, either he is talking, or he is pursuing, or he is on a journey, or peradventure he sleepeth and must be awaked. Still as the orb began to descend, they continned to chant their hymns, till at length it sank into the waves of the sea. Elijah then raised an altar of twelve stones, filled the trench around it with water, placed his victim upon it, uttered a brief and simple prayer to the God of his fathers.

Instantaneously the fire flashed down, and consumed both the sacrifice and the altar, and licked up the water in the trench. The people at once recognized the hand of God; the law was put in force against the idolatrous priests, they were taken down and put to death on the banks of the Kishon. Immediately the curse was removed from the land: Elijah saw a small cloud, the usual forerunner of rain, arise as from the sea, and the whole country was refreshed by abundant showers. Elijah entered Jezreel with Ahab, but was soon obliged to fly from the vengeance of the queen; he passed first to Beersheba, the southern extremity of Judah, then into the desert to Horeb, the scene of the delivery of the law. Here he received a divine commission to anoint a new king of Syria, Hazael; a new king of Israel, Jehu; a new prophet in his own place, Elisha. The circumstances of the divine communication are remarkable, as apparently designed to impress the mind with notions of the greatness and goodness, rather than the terror and wrath of God. God appears neither in the earthquake nor the fire, but in the still small voice behind; behold the Lord passed by, and a great and strong wind rent the mountains, and break in pieces the rocks before the Lord, the Lord was not in the wind; after the wind an earthquake; the Lord was not in the earthquake; and after the earthquake a fire, the Lord was not in the fire; and after the fire, a still small voice.

In the meantime the affairs of Israel, after the restoration of the ancient religion, had prospered. A great confederacy of the Syrian kings, headed by Benhadad, a name common to the kings of Damascus, after an insolent command of unconditional surrender, besieged Samaria. As the Syrian troops were negligently feasting in their camp, certain of the youth of high rank fell upon them, and discomfited them with great slaughter. The Syrians consoled themselves by the notion that the God of Israel was the God of the Hills: on the plain their superior numbers and immense force in chariots would regain their superiority.

A second total defeat destroyed their confidence, though the Israelites were described as two little flocks of kids in comparison with their vast army. The fugitives took refuge in Aphek, and great numbers were crushed by the falling of the walls of that city. Benhadad and his leaders had no other course than to surrender. Ahab received them honorably, spared their lives on condition that all the conquests of the Syrians should be restored, and that the Israelites should have a quarter in the city of Damascus assigned for their residence. This unusual lenity, and the neglect to secure the inviolability of the Holy Land by the exemplary punishment of foreign invaders, roused the indignation of the prophets, one of whom appeared wounded, and with ashes on his head, and rebuked the king for this, according to the existing notions, most criminal weakness.

The providential success of Ahab's arms, neither reconciled him to the worship of the true God, nor taught him reverence for the institutes of his country. The law of property was still in full force; but a piece of land occupied by a vineyard, lying conveniently near that of the king, he desired to purchase it. Naboth, the owner, refused to alienate the inheritance of his family. By the advice of his crafty queen, Ahab caused the unhappy man to be accused of blasphemy. Through the subornation of witnesses, and the corruption of the municipal court of judicature, he procured his condemnation: Naboth was stoned to death. The crime was no sooner committed than the king was startled by the sudden reappearance of Elijah. He denounced divine vengeance, and proclaimed aloud, that the dogs should lick the blood of Ahab as they had licked the blood of Naboth; that a terrible fate awaited his queen, Jezebel, near the walls of Jezreel; and that his whole family should perish by a violent death.

All this time the kingdom of Judah had enjoyed an interval of peace and prosperity. After a reign of forty-one years, Asa was succeeded (B. C. 918) by his son Jehoshaphat. The new king pursued the prudent and religious course of his father, fortified his kingdom, maintained a powerful army, established public teachers of the law, and organized the courts judicature in all the cities of Judah. The kingdom was in a high state of prosperity; the Philistines and the Arab tribes paid tribute to the king of Jerusalem. By this time, the bitter animosities which arose out of the separation of the two kingdoms, had subsided. Jehoshaphat entered into an alliance with the King of Israel, and in an evil hour, he married his son, Jehoram, to the cruel and ambitious daughter of Ahab, Athaliah, who introduced the crimes and calamities of the Israelitish dynasty into the royal house of Judah. Ahab had determined to wrest the important town of Ramoth, in Gilead, from the power of the Syrians, and summoned his ally, Jehoshaphat, to his assistance.

But, before the expedition set forth, the prophets had to be consulted. Ahab had, however, taken a sure way of ridding himself of their importunate admonitions, by raising a prophetic fraternity in his own interests. The honest Micaiah, who alone foretold calamity and ruin, was insulted, and thrown into prison; and Ahab, persuaded by his own prophets, who were filled with lying spirits, went boldly out to the war. In the onset, the troops of Syria avoided the king of Judah, and centered their whole attack against the person of the king of Israel. Ahab, shot through by a random arrow, was brought to Samaria, his armor and chariot were washed in the pool of Samaria, where, according to the predictions of Elijah, the dogs licked his blood.

Jehoshaphat, on his return to his own kingdom, was threatened by a formidable confederacy of Ammonites, Moabites, and other predatory tribes, who appeared among the rich gardens of Engedi, west of the Dead Sea.

But while the army of Judah remained motionless, engaged in their religious rites, and joining in their hymns of battle, some misunderstanding or dissention broke out among the troops of the enemy; the different tribes fell upon each other, and Judah had only to share the rich booty of the abandoned camp.

The alliance between the two Hebrew kingdoms lasted during the short and uneventful reign of Ahaziah, (B. C. 891,) the son and successor of Ahab. This prince, having met with an accident which endangered his life, sent to consult Baalzebub, the god of Ekron, whom perhaps the Philistines endowed with some of the powers of healing, attributed by the Greeks to Apollo. Elijah was commanded to rebuke this idolatrous disparagement of the God of Israel; twice, a troop of fifty men sent to seize him were struck with lightning; the third time he came boldly down from the hill on which he stood, and foretold the king's death, which almost immediately took place. Jehoram, his brother, ascended the throne. His first measure was the organization of a confederacy between the kings of Israel, Judah and Edom, to chastise the revolted king of Moab, who had refused his accustomed tribute of 100,000 sheep and 100,000 lambs. Their united forces marched round the foot of the Dead Sea, but found themselves bewildered in an arid desert without water. By the advice of Elisha, who had now assumed the prophetic office, they dug deep trenches along the plain, down which the waters from the mountainous district of Edom flowed rapidly and abundantly. The Moabites in the morning, mistaking the waters reddened by the rising sun for pools of blood, supposed that the common fate of confederate armies had taken place, that they had quarrelled and mutually slaughtered each other. They sallied down to plunder the camp, but, meeting with unexpected resistance, were defeated on all sides; the king in his despair, after having in vain attempted to break through the hostile forces, and having seen his whole country cruelly devastated, offered his eldest son as a sacrifice to his gods. Yet he seems to have been saved from total ruin by some dissension among the allies, which led to the withdrawing of their forces.

On the death of Jehoshaphat, his son Jehoram succeeded, and thus we have a prince of the same name on each of the thrones, increasing the difficulty of relating the parallel history of the two kingdoms with perspicuity. In the first measure of Jehoram king of Judah, the fatal consequences of the connection with the sanguinary house of Ahab began to appear; all his brethren were put to death without remorse. The reign which began in blood, proceeded in idolatry and defeat, till the fearful doom, denounced in a letter sent by the prophet Elisha, was entirely fulfilled. The kingdom suffered a fatal blow in the revolt of Edom, and the loss of their remaining seaport on the Red Sea. Jehoshaphat had continued this commerce in conjunction with Ahaziah king of Israel; he had fitted out a large fleet at Ezion-geber, which was wrecked on a ledge of rocks near that incommodious harbor. He then transferred his marine to Elath, and fitted out another expedition on his own account with better success. But Elath now also fell into the hands of the rebellious Edomites, and all commerce was entirely cut off. Nor was this the end of Jehoram's calamities: the Philistines and Arabians invaded the country, surprised his palace, captured his seraglio, and slew all his sons but one. Jehoram himself died of a painful and loathsome disease, so little honored that he was not buried in the sepulchre of the kings; Ahaziah his son succeeded.

We now return to the kingdom of Israel, where we find the king Jehoram engaged in a new war with his inveterate enemy, the Syrian king of Damascus. The hopes of the country rested on the prophet Elisha. Elijah had been wrapt to heaven in a car of fire, but had bequeathed his mantle, his office, and a double portion of his spirit, to his successor. This took place beyond the Jordan. Elisha, in possession of the miraculous mantle, divided the waters and passed over; he was received and recognized by the prophetic school at Jericho, though originally an uneducated husbandman. The early period of his prophetic office is described as a succession of miracles; he purified the waters of Jericho, to which was attributed the singular property of causing women to miscarry: he laid his curse on forty-two youths in Bethel, who had mocked his bald head; they were devoured by bears; he multiplied a widow's vessel of oil, and restored to life the child of an opulent woman in the town of Shunam; he destroyed the poisonous qualities of a mess of herbs, and fed 100 men with twenty loaves. He had contributed to gain the victory over the Moabites. His fame spread into Syria. Naaman, one of the great military leaders of that kingdom, was a leper. Elisha cured him by commanding him to wash in the Jordan; but to avoid the least suspicion of venality, he not merely refused all remuneration, but his servant Gehazi was punished by the same disease for fraudulently obtaining gifts in his name, from the grateful stranger. As the Syrians pressed the war with greater vigor, their king, Benhadad, found all his measures anticipated, and attributed his want of success to the presence of Elisha. He sent an army to surprise him in the city of Dothan, at no great distance from Samaria. The troops were all smitten with blindness, conducted to Samaria, but released by the merciful intervention of the prophet.

But the city of Samaria was now environed on all sides, and endured the first of those dreadful sieges, by which the two capitals of the Jewish kingdoms appear, through some awful fatality, to have been distinguished beyond all the other cities of the world. The most loathsome food, an ass's head and the dung of pigeons, were sold at enormous prices. Two women had made an agreement to kill their children for food, and one of them called upon the king to enforce her reluctant copartner to fulfill her share in this horrible compact. The king rent his clothes, and was discovered to have sackcloth next his skin. Jehoram, for some reason which does not appear, determined to wreak vengeance on Elisha: when on a sudden the prophet announces the speedy discomfiture of the Syrian army, and unexampled abundance and cheapness of provisions. First, some lepers, desperate from their wretched condition, sally forth: they find the camp totally deserted. Wild noises of arms and chariots had been heard on all sides. The Syrians, supposing that the Egyptians, or some other powerful allies had marched to the relief of Samaria, had been seized with a sudden panic and dispersed. The greatest plenty, and an immense booty, rewarded the Samaritans for their dreadful sufferings. One of their officers, who had presumed to doubt the truth of Elisha's prophecies, according to his prediction, saw, but did not partake of the abundance; he was trampled to death in the press at the gate.

The prophetic fame of Elisha was now at its height; he entered the metropolis of the Syrians, where the king lay dangerously ill (as Josephus says) of a deep melancholy, occasioned by his defeat. He was met by Hazael, an eminent officer of the court, with a sumptuous present, borne on forty camels. *Will the king recover?* demands the Syrian. The prophet returns an enigmatical, yet significant answer, that the disease is not mortal, but that the monarch's end is approaching.

With these words he burst into tears; for he knew that Hazael entertained designs against his master's life; and that the bold and unprincipled usurper would be a more formidable enemy to his native country than had yet sat upon the throne of Syria. The fatal prediction is accomplished in every point. Hazael smothers his master with a wet cloth, seizes the throne, and his first measure is a battle at Ramoth, against the combined forces of both the Jewish kingdoms under Jehoram, king of Israel, and Ahaziah, who had just succeeded his father, Jehoram of Judah. In this calamitous field, Jehoram was wounded, and retreated to Jezreel, where Ahaziah came to meet him. But the dynasty of the sanguinary Ahab was drawing to a close. Elisha commanded a young prophet to anoint Jehu, a valiant officer, as king of Israel. The army at Ramoth revolted, and espoused the cause of Jehu: he advanced rapidly on his chariot on Jezreel, for he was noted for his furious driving.

Jehoram and Ahaziah went forth from the city against Jehu: they met in the fatal vineyard of Naboth. Jehoram attempted to parley; but he was reproached with his own crimes, and with the idolatries of his mother, Jezebel. The king shrieked aloud, "There is treachery, O, Ahaziah," and fled. The bow of Jehu was strung, and the arrow pierced the unfortunate monarch through the heart. His body was taken up, and cast into the vineyard of Naboth. Ahaziah fled with no better fortune. He received a mortal wound, and died at Megiddo; his body was carried to Jerusalem. Jehu entered Jezreel in triumph. As he passed through the gate, the haughty Jezebel, "who had painted her face and tired her head," looked forth from a window, and reproached him with the murder of the king: "Had Zimri peace, who slew his master?" Jehu lifted up his head, and exclaimed, "Who is on my side, who?" Some of the perfidious eunuchs of the queen immediately appeared. "Throw her down," was the stern command of Jehu.

They obeyed: her blood fell upon the wall, and the horses trampled over her body; and when, at length, the unrelenting conqueror consented to permit her body to be buried, because, "though a cursed woman, she was a king's daughter," nothing but the miserable remains of her corpse were found, the skull, the feet, and the palms of the hands; for "the dogs"—according to the words of Elijah—"had eaten the flesh of Jezebel in the portion of Jezreel." Thus, by the death of Jehoram and Ahaziah, both the thrones of Judah and Israel were vacant. Jehu hastened to secure the latter. There were seventy sons of Ahab in Samaria. Jehu sent to command the elders of the city, which was strongly fortified, and well provided with arms, to set the best of Ahab's sons upon the throne. The elders apprehended that they might perform a more acceptable service; they made known their ready subservience to the views of the usurper.

An indiscriminate slaughter of the seventy sons, the friends and kindred of Ahab took place; the heads were sent, in the modern Turkish fashion, to Jehu, at Jezreel. The subtle usurper ordered them to be placed by the gate; and addressed the assembled people, obliquely exculpating himself from the guilt of the massacre: "Behold, I conspired against my master, and slew him; but who slew all these?" He proceeded to attribute their death to the inscrutable decrees of the Almighty, who had determined on the extirpation of the whole guilty house of Ahab.

The crafty Jehu continued his successful, though bloody career. The house Ahaziah met with no better fate than that of Ahab: Jehu put to death forty-two of them, whom he encountered on his way to Samaria, obviously with a view to popularity. He entered Samaria with Jonadab, the son of Rechab, the founder of an austere ascetic sect, who abstained from the use of wine, seated by his side in his chariot.

He concluded his terrible work of vengeance by the total extermination of the priests of Baal, which he conducted with his usual subtlety. He avowed himself an ardent worshiper of that idolatry; and summoned a general assembly of the priesthood. The temple was crowded: he commanded all the worshipers to put on splendid and distinguishing apparel; and ordered strict search to be made whether any of the worshipers of Jehovah were present. He then, having encircled the building with his guard, gave the signal of an unsparing massacre. Not one escaped: the idols were destroyed, the temples razed. Jonadab, the ascetic, countenanced and assisted this dreadful extirpation of idolatry. Yet even Jehu adhered to the symbolic worship established by Jeroboam.

Thus Israel was finally delivered from the fatal house of Ahab; but Athaliah, the queen mother of Judah, showed herself a worthy descendant of that wicked stock, and scenes as bloody, and even more guilty, defiled the royal palace of Jerusalem. She seized the vacant throne, massacred all the seed royal, excepting one child, Joash, who was secreted in the temple by his father's sister, Johosheba, the wife of the High Priest. Athaliah maintained her cruel and oppressive government for six years, during which the temple was plundered, and the worship of Baal established. In the seventh a formidable conspiracy broke out, headed by the High Priest.

As Athaliah entered the courts of the temple, she beheld the young and rightful heir of the kingdom, crowned, and encircled by a great military force, who with the assembled priesthood, and the whole people, joined in the acclamation, "God save the King." She shrieked aloud, Treason, treason! but her voice was drowned by the trumpets, and the cries of the multitude. Incapable of resistance, she was seized, dragged beyond the precincts of the temple, and put to death. (B. C. 878). Jehoiada, the High Priest, who assumed the control of public affairs, the king being only seven years old, commanded Mattan, the priest of Baal, to be slain in his temple, and totally suppressed the religion.

The reign of Joash began under favorable auspices: the influence of the High Priest, and the education of the king himself in the temple, promised the restoration of the national worship. Large contributions were made for the repair of the sacred edifice, which at first, it appears, were diverted by the priests to their own purposes. But a check having been devised to their fraudulent and irreligious proceedings, the fabric was restored in all its splendor, its services reorganized, and the sacred vessels, which had been profaned by Athaliah, replaced. But the peace of Judah, as well as of Israel, was threatened by the increasing power and ambition of Habael, the ambitious and formidable usurper of the Syrian throne. During the latter part of the reign of Jehu, he had severed from the kingdom of Israel all the Transjordanic provinces; and during that of Jehoahaz, the successor of Jehu, reduced Samaria almost to a tributary province; ten chariots, fifty horsemen, and 10,000 infantry, were all the remaining force of that once powerful kingdom.

Hazael having taken Gath, now advanced

against Jerusalem. The unwarlike Joash purchased his retreat at the price of all the sacred treasures of the temple: and in every respect the latter part of the reign of Joash belied the promise of the former. After the death of the High Priest Jehoiada, idolatry, which before, excepting the worship on high places, had been entirely suppressed, began to spread again among the higher ranks. Zachariah, the son of Jehoiada, both as priest and prophet, resisted with the strongest denunciations the prevailing apostacy. The King, forgetful of his father's services, and the people, weary of his remonstrances, conspired together to stone him.

Defeat and death followed hard on the ingratitude and apostacy of Joash. The Syrians again appeared with a small force, but totally discomfited the Jewish army; and his own officers revenged the disgrace of the nation on the person of the king, by murdering him in his bed. Nor was he thought worthy of a place in the sepulchers of the great kings of Judah.

The first act of Amaziah, the son and successor of Joash, was to do justice on the murderers of his father; but with merciful conformity to the law, unusual in such times, he did not involve the children in the treason of their fathers.

Amaziah (B. C. 838) raised 300,000 men in Judah, and hired 100,000 from Israel, but the latter, by command of a prophet, he dismissed. With his own great army he invaded the revolted kingdom of Edom, gained a signal victory in the Valley of Salt, and took Selah, the rock, probably the important city of Petra. The Israelites whom he had sent back, surprised on their return some of the cities of Judah; and Amaziah, flushed with his conquests over Edom, sent a defiance to the king of Israel. Jehoash, who now filled that throne, was a politic and successful prince; after the death of the formidable Hazael, he had reinstated his kingdom in its independence, and reconquered great part of his territory by three victories over the Syrians, which took place according to the prediction of the dying Elisha.

Three times, according to the prophet's injunction, he had smote on the ground with certain arrows. Had he not paused, he had gained more than three victories. He treated the defiance of Amaziah with contempt. The two armies met at Bethshemesh; Judah was totally routed, Jerusalem pillaged, and the treasures of the temple carried away to Samaria. Fifteen years after the death of his rival, Amaziah, like his father, fell a victim to a conspiracy within the walls of his palace; he fled to Lachish, but was slain there.

In neither case was the succession altered; his son Azariah, or Uzziah, assumed the royal power, (B. C. 809,) and commenced a long, religious, and therefore prosperous reign of fifty-two years. The great warlike enterprise of Azariah was the subjugation of the Philistines, and others of the adjacent tribes; but his more important conquest was the recovery of Elath, the port of the Red Sea. Azariah provided with equal success for the internal prosperity of the country by the encouragement and protection of husbandry. He kept on foot a powerful army, strongly fortified Jerusalem, and endeavored to make himself master of all the improvements in armor, and in the means of defending walled towns, then in use.

But this good and prudent king was guilty of one great violation of the law; he began to usurp the office of the priests, and offer incense. While he was offering, he was suddenly struck with leprosy; and in rigid conformity to the law of Moses, he was set aside, and the administration of public affairs intrusted to his son Jotham. The kingdom of Israel, or Ephraim as it is now often called, regained a high degree of prosperity during the early period of Azariah's reign in Judah.

Jeroboam the Second, an able prince, had succeeded Jehoash (B. C. 825), and pursuing his father's successes, re-established the frontier from Hamath to the Dead Sea; even Damascus, the Syrian capital, surrendered to his forces. But the kingdom which was to remain in the line of Jehu to the fourth generation, at the death of Jeroboam fell into a frightful state of anarchy. At length, after eleven years of tumult (B. C. 770), his son Zachariah obtained the scepter, but was speedily put to death by Shallum; Shallum, in his turn, by Menahem.

Menahem (B. C. 769), a sanguinary prince, reigned ten years; during which the fatal power of the great Assyrian empire was advancing with gigantic strides to universal conquest. Pul, the monarch, who ruled at Nineveh, was rapidly extending his conquests over Syria, and began to threaten the independence of Israel.—Menahem only delayed the final servitude by submission and tribute, which he wrung from his people by heavy exactions. Menahem was succeeded by his son Pekahiah, (B. C. 758,) who, in ten years after, was put to death by a new usurper, Pekah, the son of Remaliah. In the second year of Pekah began the reign of Jotham, (B. C. 757,)—who took the reins of government during the lifetime of his father. Jotham strengthened the kingdom of Judah, made the Ammonites tributary, and, after an able, but not very eventful reign, left the throne to his son Ahaz, the worst and most unfortunate monarch who had ruled in Judah.

As the storm darkened over the Hebrew kingdom, the voices of the prophets became louder and more wild; those, whose writings have been preserved in our sacred volume, now come upon the scene. In their magnificent odes, we have a poetical history of these momentous times, not merely describing the fall of the two Hebrew nations, but that of the adjacent kingdoms likewise. As each independent tribe or monarchy was swallowed up in the great universal empire of Assyria, the seers of Judah watched the progress of the invader; and uttered their sublime funeral anthems over the greatness, the prosperity, and independence of Moab, and Ammon, Damascus and Tyre.—

They were like the great tragic chorus to the awful drama, which was unfolding itself in the eastern world. Nor did they confine their views to their own internal affairs, or to their own immediate neighborhood. Jonah appeared as a man under divine influence at Nineveh; and Nahum described the subsequent fate of that spacious city in images, which human imagination or human language have never surpassed.

Still, in general, the poets of Judæa were pre-eminently national. It is on the existing state, the impending dangers, and future prospects of Ephraim and Judah, that they usually dwell. As moral teachers, they struggle with the noblest energy against the corruptions which prevailed in its ranks and classes. Each kingdom had its prophets; in that of Israel, the obscure and sententious Hosea reproved the total depravation. The rustic and honest Amos inveighed against the oppressions of the wealthy, and the corruptions of the judges. In Judah, Joel described the successive calamities which desolated the country. But Isaiah, not only took a great share in all the affairs of the successive reigns from Azariah to Hezekiah; described or anticipated all the wars, conquests and convulsions, which attended the rise and fall of the Assyrian and Babylonian dynasties; but penetrated still farther into futurity. To Isaiah may be traced the first clear and distinct intimations of the important influence to be exercised by the Jews on the destiny of mankind —the promise of the Messiah; and the remote prospects of future grandeur, which tended so strongly to form their national character, and are still the indissoluble bond which has held together this extraordinary people through centuries of dispersion, persecution and contempt. Still blind to the fulfillment of all these predictions in the person and spiritual kingdom of Christ, the Jew, in every age and every quarter of the world, dwells on the pages of his great national prophet, and with undying hope looks forward to the long-delayed coming of the Deliverer, and to his own restoration to the promised land in splendor and prosperity, far surpassing that of his most favored ancestors.

The dissensions between the two kingdoms led to their more immediate ruin. Ahaz succeeded to the throne of Judah in the seventeenth year of Pekah, (B. C. 742,) the last able or powerful monarch of Israel. Pekah entered into a confederacy with Rezin, king of Damascus, to invade Judæa. Their first expedition did not meet with much success; a second descent was more fatal. On the retreat of the Syrians, Ahaz ventured on a battle. In this bloody field Judah lost 120,000 men; Zichri, a valiant chieftain of the Israelites, slew with his own hand Maaseiah, the king's son, and some of his household. Two hundred thousand men, women, and children, were led away into captivity. The sight of their brethren in this miserable condition aroused the better feelings of the Israelites: they refused to retain them in servitude; forced the army into milder measures; treated the prisoners with great kindness; gave them food, raiment, and the means of returning home: a beautiful and refreshing incident in this gloomy and savage part of their annals; and, as usual, to be ascribed to one of their prophets. Rezin, in the meantime, the ally of Pekah, seized Elath. The Edomites and Philistines revolted; and Ahaz, attacked on all sides, in his desperation threw himself under the protection of Tiglath Pileser, the Assyrian king, who had already subdued all the Transjordanic tribes, and advanced his frontier to the banks of the river. This treaty led to the usual results, where a weaker state enters into an alliance with a stronger. The Assyrian lent his aid as far as suited his own views of conquest; invaded Syria, took Damascus, led the people away captive, and slew the king. But against the more immediate enemies of Ahaz, the Edomites, he sent no succors, and exhausted the kingdom of Judah by the exaction of a heavy tribute.

It was not from want of base subservience to his protector, that Ahaz suffered this ungenerous treatment. Ahaz revolted entirely from the national faith; he offered public worship to the gods of Syria; constructed a new altar on the model of the one he saw at Damascus, where he went to pay homage to the Assyrian; and robbed the treasury to pay his tribute. He defaced many of the vessels and buildings of the temple. No superstition was too cruel for Ahaz; he offered incense in the valley of Hinnom, and made his children pass through the fire. In short had not his death relieved his people, Jerusalem seemed rapidly following the example, and hastening toward the fate of Samaria. For now the end of that kingdom drew on. The unprincipled, though able Pekah, was assassinated; another period of anarchy lasted for several years, till at length the sceptre fell into the feeble hands of Hoshea, who had instigated the murder of Pekah. A new and still more ambitious monarch, Shalmaneser, now wielded the power of Assyria; Hoshea attempted to avert the final subjugation of his kingdom by the payment of tribute, but being detected in a secret correspondence with the king of Egypt, called So, the Sevechus of Manetho, the Assyrian advanced into the kingdom, besieged Samaria, which, after an obstinate resistance of three years, surrendered, and thus terminated for ever the independent kingdom of Israel or Ephraim.

It was the policy of the Assyrian monarchs to transplant the inhabitants of the conquered provinces on their borders, to the inland districts of their empire. Thus they occupied their outposts with those on whose fidelity they might rely; and, with far wiser and more generous views, by introducing agricultural colonies among the ruder and nomadic hordes, as the Russians have done in their vast dominions, carried culture and civilization into wild and savage districts. Pul and Tiglath Pileser had already swept away a great part of the population from Syria, and the Transjordanic tribes:

and Shalmaneser, after the capture of Samaria, carried off vast numbers of the remaining tribes to a mountainous region between Assyria and Medea, who were afterward replaced there by colonies of a race called Cuthæans.

From this period, history loses sight of the ten tribes as a distinct people. Prideaux supposes that they were totally lost and absorbed in the nations among whom they settled; but imagination has loved to follow them into remote and inaccessible regions, where it is supposed that they still await the final restoration of the twelve tribes of their native land; or it has traced the Jewish features, language, and religion, in different tribes, particularly the Afghans of India, and in a still wilder spirit of romance, in the Americans. How far the descendants of the Israelites constituted the mingled people of the Samaritans,, whose history has come down to us only as it is colored by irreconcilable Jewish hostility, is a question hereafter to be discussed.

While the kingdom of Israel was rarely blessed by a permanent, vigorous, and prudent administration, and frequently endured all the evils of a contested and irregular succession, which placed adventurer after adventurer, or short and precarious dynasties upon the throne: while the best of their kings only so far returned to the national faith, as to extirpate foreign idolatry, but remained true to the separate, symbolic, and forbidden worship of Jeroboam—the hereditary succession of Judah remained unbroken in the line of David, and a period of misrule and irreligion was almost invariably succeeded by a return to the national faith. Accordingly, six years before the final destruction of Samaria, one of the best and wisest of her kings, Hezekiah, replaced his father Ahaz on the throne of Judah (B. C. 726) Hezekiah carried the reformation much farther than his most religious predecessors. The temple was cleansed—the rites restored with more than usual solemnity—the priesthood and Levites reinstated in their privileges—every vestige of idolatrous superstition eradicated—the shrines of false gods demolished—the groves levelled—the high places desecrated: even the brazen serpent made by Moses in the wilderness, having been abused to superstitious purposes, was destroyed. Having thus prepared the way, Hezekiah began still farther to develop his plans, which tended to the consolidation of the whole Hebrew race under their old religious constitution. He determined to celebrate the passover (that which was called the second passover) with all its original splendor and concourse of people. He sent messengers into the neighboring kingdom of Israel, to summon the ten tribes, then under the feeble rule of Hoshea. The proud Ephraimites treated his message with contempt; but from the smaller tribes multitudes flocked to Jerusalem, where the sacrifices were offered with something like the ancient state and magnificence. On their return, the religious zeal of those who had visited Jerusalem, had great effect on their kindred; idolatry was put down by force, the temples and altars destroyed. How far, if the Jewish constitution had existed in its original vigor, and the whole of Palestine remained one great consolidated kingdom, it could have offered an effectual resistance to the vast monarchies which now began to spread the shadow of their despotism over the East—how far the kingdoms of David and Solomon might have held the balance between the rival empires of Egypt and Assyria, in whose collision it was finally crushed—must be matter of speculation. But from this fatal period, Palestine was too often the debatable ground, on which rival kingdoms or empires fought out their quarrels. On this arena, not only the monarchs of Nineveh and Babylon, and the ancient Egyptian sovereigns, but subsequently also the Ptolemaic and Syro-Grecian dynasties, the Romans and Parthians—we may add the Christian and Mahommedan powers during the crusades—strove either for ascendency over the eastern world or for universal dominion.

The wise policy of Hezekiah, if his views led to the union of the kingdoms, came too late.—He himself threw off the yoke of Assyria, and gained important advantages over the Philistines. But divine Providence had ordained the fall of Israel, and after the capture of Samaria, Jerusalem might tremble at the approach of the victor. Shalmaneser, however, was allured by the more tempting conquest of opulent Tyre. The princely merchants of that city resisted vigorously a siege of five years; though their aqueducts were broken, and the population reduced to great distress. The besieged were at length relieved by the death of the invader. The hereditary power and ambition of his conquering ancestors descended into the vigorous hand of Sennacherib. An immense army made its appearance in Judæa, and sat down before Lachish. The dismay can scarcely be conceived with which, after the total destruction of the sister kingdom by these irresistible invaders, and the transplantation of the people to distant regions, the inhabitants of Jerusalem expected the approach of the hostile forces to the walls. There is a passage in the book of Isaiah descriptive of their terrors, most probably, on this occasion: "What aileth thee now that thou art wholly gone up to the housetops; thou that art full of stirs, a tumultuous city, a joyous city: .... for it is a day of trouble and of treading down, and of perplexity by the Lord God of hosts in the valley of vision, breaking down the walls, and of crying to the mountains. And Elam bare the quiver, and Kir uncovered the shield. And it shall come to pass that thy choicest valleys shall be full of chariots, and the horsemen shall set themselves in array in the gates." The prophet goes on to describe the preparations for defense made by Hezekiah, who strengthened the walls, added to the fortifications, laid in a great store of arrows and other ammunition, deepened the trenches, and cut off all the waters which might have supplied the besieging army.

The wilder and voluptuous desperation of others is, if possible, more striking. It reminds us of the frantic revelry among the Athenians, during the time of the plague, described by Thucydides. "And in that day did the Lord God of hosts call to weeping, and to mourning, and to baldness, and to girding with sackcloth: but behold joy and gladness, slaying oxen and killing sheep, eating flesh and drinking wine: let us eat and drink, for to-morrow we die."—The submission of Hezekiah, and the payment of an enormous tribute, for which he was obliged to strip the gold from the walls and pillars of the temple, for the present averted the storm; and Sennacherib in person marched onward to a much more important conquest, that of the great and flourishing kingdom of Egypt. His general, Tartan, had already taken Azotus, and Sennacherib in person formed the siege of Libnah or Pelusium, the key of that country. But he left behind him a considerable force under Tartan, Rabsaris and Rabshakeh, who advanced to the walls of Jerusalem, and made a demand of unconditional surrender. Hezekiah sent three of the chief officers of his palace to negotiate. Rabshakeh, as Prideaux conjectures, an apostate Jew or one of the captivity, delivered his insulting summons in the Hebrew language, with the view of terrifying the people with the menace of total destruction. He contemptuously taunted them with their confidence in their God. "Hath any of the gods of the nations delivered at all his land out of the hand of the king of Assyria. Where are the gods of Hamath and of Arpad? where are the gods of Sepharvaim, Hena and Ivah? have they delivered Samaria out of mine hand?" The people listened in silence. The king clothed himself in sackcloth, and with his whole court and the priesthood, made a procession to the temple, in that sad and humiliating attire.—But Isaiah encouraged them in their defiance of the enemy, and Rabshakeh marched away to the army before Pelusium.

This city made a most vigorous resistance; and Sennacherib received intelligence of the march of Terhakah, king of Ethiopia, (no doubt Taraco, a king of Egypt, who appears in the Ethiopian dynasty of Manetho,) to relieve this important post. The conquest of Judea, and the surrender of Jerusalem, became almost necessary to his success. He sent a second summons by letter, more threatening and peremptory than the former, describing the nations who, notwithstanding the vaunted assistance of their gods, had fallen before the power of Assyria. Hezekiah again had recourse to the temple, and in a prayer, unequaled for simple sublimity, cast himself on the protection of the God of his fathers. Isaiah at the same time proclaimed, that the Virgin of Zion might laugh to scorn the menaces of the invader.

The agony of suspense and terror, which prevailed in Jerusalem, was speedily relieved by the surprising intelligence that the army of Sennacherib had experienced a fatal reverse, that all which survived had dispersed, and that the monarch himself had fled to his capital, where he was slain by his own sons, while offering public sacrifice. The destruction of Sennacherib's army is generally supposed to have been caused by the Simoon, or hot and pestilential wind of the desert, which is said not unfrequently to have been fatal to whole caravans. The Arabs, who are well experienced in the signs which portend its approach, fall on their faces, and escape its mortal influence. But the foreign forces of Sennacherib were little acquainted with the means of avoiding this unusual enemy, and the catastrophe taking place by night, (the miraculous part of the transaction, as the hot wind is in general attributed to the heat of the meridian sun,) suffered immense loss.

Herodotus relates a strange story of this ruin of Sennacherib's army: A number of field mice gnawed asunder their quivers, their bow-strings and shield straps: upon which the army took to flight. Has Herodotus derived this from the misinterpretation of a hieroglyphic, in which the shield, the quiver, and the bow, the usual symbols, by which as in Hebrew poetry, the might of a great army is represented, were destroyed by some secret and unseen or insignificant instrument of the divine power typified by the field mouse.*

At the latter end of the same year, the fourteenth of his reign, Hezekiah fell dangerously ill. His earnest prayer for the prolongation of his life was accepted at the throne of mercy. Isaiah foretold his recovery, and the grant of fifteen years of life, and likewise of children; for the good king was leaving the kingdom without legitimate heir. The prophet directed the means of his cure, by laying a plaster of figs on the boil from which he suffered; and proved his divine mission by the sign of the shadow retrograding ten degrees on the dial of Ahaz. On this sign, and on the dial, volumes have been written. It is not necessary to suppose that the sun actually receded, but that the shadow on the dial did; a phenomenon which might be caused by a cloud refracting the light.

Whether the Jews possessed sufficient astronomical science to frame an accurate dial, can neither be proved nor disproved; still less the more rude or artificial construction of the instrument itself; for as the dial was probably set up by Ahaz, who was tributary to the Assyrians, it might have come originally from Chaldea. Immediately indeed after this event, Hezekiah received an embassy from Merodach Baladan, the independent king of Babylon, for the ostensible purpose of congratulating him on his recovery; some suppose for that of inquiring into the extraordinary astronomical phenomenon, the intelligence of which had reached that seat of Oriental science; but more probably with the view of concerting measures

*According to Horapollo, total destruction was represented, in Egyptian hieroglyphics, by the symbol of a mouse.

for an extensive revolt from the Assyrian yoke.

Hezekiah made a pompous display of his treasures, very likely much enriched by the plunder of Sennacherib's broken army. For this indiscreet ostentation, so calculated to excite the cupidity of a foreign invader, the king was reproved by the more prudent Isaiah. Internal convulsions in the kingdom of Assyria permitted Hezekiah to pass the rest of his reign in peace and opulence. His public treasury was full; the husbandry and pasturage of the country returned to their former productiveness. He strengthened the cities, ornamented Jerusalem with a new aqueduct, and at length went down to the grave, honored and regretted by the whole people. He was succeeded by Manasseh, a king to whose crimes and irreligion the Jews mainly attribute the dreadful evils which shortly after consigned them to ruin and slavery.

Manasseh ascended the throne at the age of twelve: the administration fell into the hands of unworthy ministers, of whom Shebna is represented, by Isaiah, as the most haughty and violent. But with his years the evil dispositions of the king came to maturity. Idolatry was restored; every kind of superstition, witchcraft, and divination practiced; altars to idols were raised even within the sacred precincts; the temple itself was defiled by a graven image. The irreligion of Manasseh was only equalled by his tyranny. The city ran with innocent blood; the sacred persons of the prophets were violated. Tradition ascribes the horrid martyrdom of Isaiah, who was sawn asunder, to this relentless tyrant. His vices brought their own punishment in the contemptible weakness to which the state was reduced. When the army of Esarhaddon, the new sovereign of Assyria, made its appearance under the walls, Jerusalem offered no resistance, and the unworthy heir of David and Solomon was led away to learn wisdom and piety in the dungeons of Babylon. Esarhaddon completed the plan of colonization commenced by his predecessors, and established bodies of his own subjects in the desolated provinces of Israel. So frightful had been the ravages inflicted on these beautiful and luxuriant plains, that the new colonists found themselves in danger from beasts of prey. The strangers had brought their own religious rites with them. The Babylonians had set up the pavilions of Benoth, the Cuthites, the settlers from Hamath and the Avites, and the Sepharvites, had each their separate divinity. They trembled before the lions, which infested their territory; and looked on them not only with terror, but with religious awe, as manifest instruments of divine wrath.

The remaining Israelites, no doubt, proclaimed that they were sent by their God; and the strangers, in the true spirit of polytheism, recognized the anger of the local deity, whom they supposed offended by the intrusion of their national gods into his territory. They appealed in haste to Esarhaddon, by whose command an Israelitish priest was sent to propitiate the God of the land, whom they readily admitted to a participation in divine honors with their native deities; and thus a mingled worship of idolatry and true religion grew up in these provinces.

The lessons of adversity were not lost on Manasseh: he was restored to his throne, and the end of his long reign of fifty-five years, past in the observance of law and religion, in some degree compensated for the vices of his youth. His son Amon, who succeeded, following the early career of his father, fell a victim to a conspiracy among his own officers.

At the age of eight years (B. C. 640) Josiah came to the throne. The memory of this prince is as deservedly dear to the Jews, as that of Manasseh is hateful.

Josiah surpassed even his most religious predecessors, Asa, Jehoshaphat, Azariah, or Hezekiah, in zeal for the reformation of the national religion. His first care was to repair the temple. While the work was proceeding, the king and the whole nation heard, with the highest exultation, that Hilkiah, the high priest, had discovered the original copy of the law. But so little were its real contents known, that, on its first reading, the king was struck with terror at its awful denunciations. The book was read in public; Josiah and all the nation renewed the solemn covenant with their God.

The king proceeded to carry into execution the divine precepts of the Law. He began by the total extirpation of idolatry, not merely in Judea, but throughout all the holy land. The vessels of the temple, which had been abused to unhallowed uses, were burned to ashes: all the high places levelled—the worship of the host of heaven suppressed—the filthy and sanguinary rites of the Sodomites and worshipers of Moloch forbidden—the sacred places defiled. The horses dedicated to the sun—the altars which Ahaz had built on the top of the royal palace—the high places which Solomon had consecrated to the deities of his foreign wives—the altar raised by Jeroboam at Bethel—were not merely destroyed, but defiled with that from which Jewish feelings revolted with horror, as the foulest contamination, the ashes and the bones of dead men.

The authority of Josiah was acknowledged, and his orders fulfilled to the most remote part of Palestine; an apparent proof that, notwithstanding the numbers that had been carried away into the foreign colonies, the ten tribes were not so entirely exterminated, but that their descendants, at least of the lower orders, were still the predominant population of the country. Josiah completed his reform by the celebration of the great national festival, the passover, on a scale of grandeur and magnificence unknown to the later ages of the Jewish kingdom. Yet the virtues of Josiah delayed only for a time the fate of Jerusalem. The hopes of re-uniting the dominions of David and Solomon into one powerful kingdom, animated with lofty religious zeal, and flourishing under the wise and beneficent constitution of

Moses, were cut short, so Divine Providence ordained, by the unfavorable circumstances of the times, and the death of the wise and virtuous king.

A monarch of great power and abilities, Necho, was now the Pharaoh of Egypt. He determined to act on the offensive against the rival empire of Assyria, at this time, probably, weakened by internal dissensions among the different kingdoms of which it was composed. His design was to gain possession of Carchemish, a city which commanded the passage of the Euphrates, and make that river his frontier. Josiah was bound to the Assyrian interest by the terms of his vassalage, by treaty, by gratitude for the permission to extend his sovereignty over Samaria. From one, or all of these motives, or from a desire of maintaining his own independence, instead of allowing free passage to the army of Necho, he determined on resistance. A battle took place, in which Josiah was unfortunately shot by an arrow. On the scene of the battle it is difficult to decide. The sacred writers place it at Megiddo, in the district of Manasseh, to reach which the Egyptian army must have passed through the whole of Judæa, and almost under the walls of Jerusalem. Herodotus, with greater local probability, fixes the scene of action at Magdolum, on the frontier of Egypt—Josephus at Mendes. The Jewish copyists may have substituted the more familiar name, Megiddo, for the more remote Magdolum.

At this period of the approaching dissolution of the Jewish state, appeared the prophet Jeremiah, a poet, from his exquisitely pathetic powers, admirably calculated to perform the funeral obsequies, over the last of her kings, over the captive people, the desolate city, the ruined temple. The prophet himself, in the eventful course of his melancholy and persecuted life, learned that personal familiarity with affliction which added new energy to his lamentations over his country and his religion. To our great loss his elegy on the death of Josiah, in which the nation joined with heartfelt anguish, is not now extant among his prophecies. Necho, after his victory over the Assyrians and the capture of Carchemish, took possession of Jerusalem, where, by a hasty choice, Jehoahaz, a younger son of Josiah, had been raised to the throne.

The capture of the city under the name of Kadutis (the holy city) is related by Herodotus. In the celebrated royal tomb, discovered by Belzoni, in the valley of Beban el Malook, near Thebes, the name of Necho was thought to be distinctly deciphered.* A painting, on the same walls, exhibited a procession of captives, some of whom, from their physiognomy and complexion, were clearly distinguished as Jews. The conqueror deposed and imprisoned Jehoahaz, after a reign of three months; exacted a heavy fine from the kingdom, and placed Eliakim (Jehoiakim) on the throne. From this period the kingdom of Judæa fell into a state of alternate vassalage to the two conflicting powers of Egypt and Assyria. The shadows of kings, who were raised to the throne, were dismissed at the breath of their liege lord. It is a deplorable period of misrule and imbecility. Without ability to defend them, these unhappy kings had only the power of entailing all the miseries of siege and conquest on their people, by rebellions which had none of the dignity, while they had all the melancholy consequences of a desperate struggle for independence.

In the fourth year of Jehoiakim (B. C. 604), the mightiest monarch who had wielded the Assyrian power, Nebuchadnezzar, was associated in the empire with his father, and assumed the command of the armies of Nineveh. The prophetic eye of Jeremiah foresaw the approaching tempest, and endeavored to avert it by the only means which remained in the empoverished and feeble state of the kingdom, timely submission. Long had he struggled, but in vain, to restore the strength of the state by the reformation and religious union of the king and the people. In the royal palace and in the temple, he had uttered his solemn warnings. His honest zeal had offended the priesthood. He had been arraigned as a false prophet before the royal council, where, by the intervention of powerful friends, he had been acquitted.

Uriah, another prophet, who had boldly exercised that unwelcome office, after having fled in vain to Egypt, had been seized and put to death. At this juncture, Jeremiah again came forward. In opposition to a strong Egyptian faction, he urged the impracticability of resistance to the Assyrian forces, already on their march. But he spoke to deaf and heedless ears. He then denounced an impending servitude of the whole people, which was to last for seventy years, and to give farther publicity to his awful remonstrances, he commanded Baruch, a scribe, to write on a roll the whole of his predictions. The roll was read, during a general fast, in the most public place, before the gate of the temple. The chief nobility of the city were strongly affected, but the headstrong king cut the roll to pieces, cast it into the fire, and Jeremiah and Baruch were obliged to conceal themselves from his vengeance. The event soon justified the wisdom of the prophet. Nebuchadnezzar, having re-taken Carchemish, (B. C. 601,) passed the Euphrates, and rapidly overran the whole of Syria and Palestine. Jerusalem made little resistance. The king was put in chains to be carried as a prisoner to Babylon. On his submission, he was reinstated on the throne, but the temple was plundered of many of its treasures, and a number of well born youths, among whom were Daniel, and three others, best known by their Persian names, Shadrach, Meshech, and Abednego. From this date commence the seventy years of

*A strong objection has been raised to this supposition; Necho was of the Saitic dynasty of kings; and Herodotus clearly asserts that the burial-place of that whole race was in Lower Egypt. The tomb was certainly not that of Necho.

the captivity. Jehoiakim had learned neither wisdom nor moderation from his misfortunes. Three years after, he attempted to throw off the yoke of Assyria. Nebuchadnezzar, occupied with more important affairs, left the subjugation of Palestine to the neighboring tribes, who for three years longer ravaged the whole country, shut up Jehoiakim in Jerusalem; and at length this weak and cruel king was slain, (B. C. 598,) perhaps in some sally. His unhonored remains were buried, "with the burial of an ass."

Jehoiachin (Jecomas or Coniah), his son, had scarcely mounted the throne, when Nebuchadnezzar himself appeared at the gates of Jerusalem. The city surrendered at discretion. The king and all the royal family, the remaining treasures of the temple, the strength of the army and the nobility, and all the more useful artisans, were carried away to Babylon. Over this wreck of a kingdom, Redekiah (Mattaniah), the younger son of Josiah, was permitted to enjoy an inglorious and precarious sovereignty of eleven years, during which he abused his powers, even worse than his imbecile predecessors. In the ninth year, notwithstanding the remonstrances of the wise Jeremiah, he endeavored to assert his independence; and Jerusalem, though besieged by Nebuchadnezzar in person, now made some resistance. The Egyptian faction in the city were encouraged by the advance of Hophra (Apries), the reigning Pharaoh, into Palestine. This march suspended for a time the operations of the Assyrians.

The Jews, released from the pressing danger, recanted all the vows of reformation, which they had begun to make. But Hophra and the Egyptian army were defeated; and the toils closed again around the devoted city. Jeremiah, undaunted by his ill-success, still boldly remonstrated against the madness of resistance. He was thrown into a foul and noisome dungeon, on an accusation of treasonable correspondence with the enemy. At length famine reduced the fatal obstinacy of despair. Jerusalem opened its gates to the irresistible conqueror. The king, in an attempt to break through the besieging forces, was seized, his children slain before his face, his eyes put out, and thus the last king of the royal house of David, blind and childless, was led away into a foreign prison.

The capture of Jerusalem took place on the ninth day of the fourth month: on the seventh day of the fifth month, (two days on which Hebrew devotion still commemorates the desolation of the city by solemn fast and humiliation,) the relentless Nabuzaradan executed the orders of his master, by leveling the city, the palaces, and the temple, in one common ruin. The few remaining treasures, particularly the two brazen pillars which stood before the temple, were sent to Babylon; the chief priests were put to death, the rest carried into captivity.

Jeremiah survived to behold the accomplishment of all his darkest predictions. He witnessed all the horrors of the famine, and, when that had done its work, the triumph of the enemy. He saw the strong hold of the city cast down, the palace of Solomon, the temple of God, with all its courts, its roof of cedar and of gold, leveled to the earth, or committed to the flames, the sacred vessels, the ark of the covenant itself, with the cherubim, pillaged by profane hands. What were the feelings of a patriotic and religious Jew at this tremendous crisis he has left in record in his unrivalled elegies. Never did city suffer a more miserable fate, never was ruined city lamented in language so exquisitely pathetic.

Jerusalem is, as it were, personified, and bewailed with the passionate sorrow of private and domestic attachment: while the more general pictures of the famine, but common misery of every rank, and age and sex, all the desolation, the carnage, the violation, the dragging away into captivity, the remembrance of former glories, of the gorgeous ceremonies, and the glad festival, the awful sense of the Divine wrath heightening the present calamities, are successively drawn with all the life and reality of an eyewitness. They combine the truth of history with the deepest pathos of poetry.

How solitary doth she sit, the many-peopled city!
She is become a widow, the great among the Nations;
The Queen among the Provinces, how is she tributary!

Weeping—weeps she all the night; the tears are on her cheeks;
From among all her lovers, she hath no comforter;
Her friends have all dealt treacherously; they are become her foes.—i. 1, 2.

The ways of Sion mourn: none come up to her feasts,
All her gates are desolate; and her Priests do sigh;
Her virgins wail! herself, she is in bitterness.—i, 4.

He hath plucked up his garden-hedge. He hath destroyed His Temple;
Jehovah hath forgotten made the solemn feast and Sabbath;
And in the heat of ire He hath rejected King and Priest.

The Lord his altar hath disdained, abhorred his Holy place,
And to the adversary's hand given up his palace walls;
Our foes shout in Jehovah's house, as on a festal day.
ii. 7, 8.

Her gates are sunk into the earth, he hath broke through her bars;
Her Monarch and her Princes are now among the Heathen:
The Law hath ceased; the Prophets find no vision from Jehovah.—ii. 10.

My eyes do fail with tears; and troubled are my bowels
My heart's blood gushes on the earth, for the daughter of my people;
Children and suckling babes lie swooning in the squares—

They say unto their Mothers, where is corn and wine?
They swoon as they were wounded, in the city squares;
While glides the soul away into their Mother's bosom.
ii. 11, 12.

Even dragons, with their breasts drawn out, give suck unto their young;
But cruel is my people's daughter, as the Ostrich in the desert;
The tongue of sucking infants to their palates cleave with thirst.

Young children ask for bread, and no man breaks it for them;
Those that fed on dainties are desolate in the streets;
Those brought up in scarlet, even those embrace the dunghill.—iv. 3, 4, 5.

Behold, Jehovah, think to whom thou e'er hast dealt thus?
Have women ever eat their young, babes fondled in their hands?
Have Priest and Prophet e'er been slain in the Lord's Holy place?

In the streets, upon the ground, lie slain the young and old;
My Virgins and my youth have fallen by the sword;
In thy wrath thou'st slain them, thou hast had no mercy.

Thou hast summoned all my terrors, as to a solemn feast;
None 'scaped, and none were left in Jehovah's day of wrath;
All that mine arms have borne and nursed, the enemy hath slain.—ii. 20. 1, 2.

Remember, Lord, what hath befallen.
Look down on our reproach
Our heritage is given to strangers,
Our home to foreigners,
Our water have we drunk for money.
Our fuel hath its price.—v. 1, 2, 3.

We stretch our hands to Egypt,
To Assyria for our bread.
At our life's risk we gain our food,
From the sword of desert robbers.
Our skins are like an oven, parched,
By the fierce heat of famine.
Matrons in Sion have they ravished,
Virgins in Judah's cities.
Princes were hung up by the hand,
And age had no respect.
Young men are grinding at the mill.
Boys faint 'neath loads of wood.
The elders from the gate have ceased,
The young men from their music.
The crown is fallen from our head,
Wo! wo! that we have sinned.
'Tis therefore that our hearts are faint,
Therefore our eyes are dim.
For Sion's mountain desolate,
The foxes walk on it

The miserable remnant of the people were placed under the command of Gedaliah, as a pasha of the great Assyrian monarch: the seat of government was fixed at Mizpeh. Yet ambitiou could look with envy even on this eminence. Gedaliah was assassinated by Ishmael, a man of royal blood. Johanan attempted to revenge his death. Ishmael, discomfited, took refuge with the Ammonites, but Johanan and the rest of the Jews, apprehensive lest they should be called in question for the murder of Gedaliah, fled to Egypt, and carried Jeremiah with them. There the prophet died; either, according to conflicting traditions, put to death by the Jews, or by King Hophra.

Thus closes the first period of the Jewish History; and, in the ordinary course of human events, we might expect, the national existence of the Israelitish race. The common occupancy of their native soil seems, in general, the only tie that permanently unites the various families and tribes, which constitute a nation. As long as that bond endures, a people may be sunk to the lowest grade of degradation; they may be reduced to a slave-caste under the oppression of foreign invaders; yet favorable circumstances may again develop the latent germ of a free and united nation; they may again rise to power and greatness, as well as to independence. But, when that bond is severed, nationality usually becomes extinct.

A people, transported from their native country, if scattered in small numbers, gradually melt away, and are absorbed in the surrounding tribes: if settled in larger masses, remote from each other, they grow up into distinct commonwealths; but in a generation or two theprinciple of separation, which is perpetually at work, effectually obliterates all community of interest or feeling.

If a traditionary remembrance of their common origin survives, it is accompanied by none of the attachment of kindred; there is no family pride or affection; there is no *blood* between the scattered descendants of common ancestors. For time gradually loosens all other ties; habits of life change; laws are modified by the circumstances of the state and people; religion, at least in all polytheistic nations is not exempt from the influence of the great innovator.

The separate communities have outgrown the common objects of national pride; the memorable events of their history during the time that they dwelt together; their common traditions, the fame of their heroes, the songs of their poets, are superseded by more recent names and occurrences: each has his new stock of reminiscences, in which their former kindred can not participate. Even their languages have diverged from each other. They are not of one speech, they have either entirely or partially ceased to be mutually intelligible. If, in short, they meet again, there is a remote family likeness, but they are strangers in all that connects man with man, or tribe with tribe.

One nation alone seems entirely exempt from this universal law. During the Babylonian captivity, as in the longer dispersion under which they have been for ages afflicted, the Jews still remained a separate people. However widely divided from their native country, they were still Jews; however remote from each other, they were still brethren. What then were the bonds by which Divine Providence held together this singular people? What were the principles of their inextinguishable nationality? Their law and their religion.

THE END.

M. B. Levy

LETTERS

OF

Benjamin Dias Fernandez,

ON THE

EVIDENCES OF CHRISTIANITY.

BLOCH & CO., PUBLISHERS AND PRINTERS. CINCINNATI, O.,

1869

LETTERS
OF
BENJAMIN DIAS FERNANDEZ,
ON THE
EVIDENCES OF CHRISTIANITY.

LETTER I.

DEAR FRIEND: About the year 1740, the maternal grandfather of the well-known Grace Aguilar, Mr. Benjamin Dias Fernandez, a retired merchant in England, wrote a series of letters on the gospels to a friend in Jamaica. They were not intended for publication, but were privately preserved by his descendants, and were only given to the public in 1842 by the late Rev. Leeser of Philadelphia. A revision of the work will undoubtedly be of interest to you as well as to the public, as the questions and subjects treated in these letters are of importance to every inquiring mind.

To prevent mistakes and confusion which are unavoidable when terms are made use of that have no well defined meaning, or have no proper ideas annexed to them, I shall take care to settle and fix the proper meaning of the terms; and to use them according to their true sense and signification. Neither shall I assert anything but such truths as I am convinced of, and for which there is either a "thus saith the Lord," or good literary authority. He that holds an honestly acquired opinion will not be offended if opinions are expressed that may differ from his own. The time is past when the overawed Jew could but suffer and die for his convictions; on the contrary he is expected to state the reasons why during nineteen centuries he has held fast to his own opinion in spite of all outside pressure.

Our first inquiry, therefore, must be into the authority of the New Testament; for no person can have the least right over our understanding or demand our assent to any proposition contrary to our conviction, and we may be sure that we can not offend, when we make inquiries into the nature of the evidence produced for our conversion, since it is the only method we have to arrive at the knowledge of truth in any matter. Besides in so doing we avoid being imposed upon as much as possible, and act as reasonable beings, according to the dignity of our natures.

"God himself," says the judicious Mr. Chandler, "who is the object of all religious worship, to whom we owe the most absolute subjection, and whose actions are all guided by the discerned reason and fitness of things, can not, as I apprehend, consistent with his own perfect wisdom, require of his creatures the implicit belief of, or actual assent to any proposition which they do not, or can not, either wholly, or in part understand; because it is requiring of them a real impossibility, no man being able to stretch his faith beyond his understanding."* Therefore our inquiry into the nature of any proposition is absolutely necessary; particularly in matters offered for our conversion. And it is a very just observation of Mr. Basnage, when he says, "We must prove the divine authority of the Gospel (to the Jews) before we engage in the particulars of other controversies."† And I add, till this is done, and the Jews admit the divine authority of the New Testament, nothing can be urged from it

*Introduction to his History of the Inquisition.
†History of the Jews. B. 7, C. 34.

or their conversion; for, in controversies, neither party can, with the least shadow of reason, make use of any authority which is not admitted or granted by the other. A Mohammedan might as consistently urge the authority of the Koran for the conviction of the Christian, as a Christian make use of or urge anything from the New Testament for the conviction of the Jew. The absurdity of such a method in either case is equally plain and obvious; for, as the Christian does not admit the infallibility or divine inspiration of the Koran, what force or validity could any argument drawn therefrom have, or what regard would the Christian pay to such authority? So, in like manner, what regard can it be expected the Jew will pay to any proof drawn from the New Testament, the authority or infallibility of which they do not admit? Can conviction be reasonably expected upon such grounds?

Whoever now believes, or is persuaded of the divine inspiration, or infallibility of the writings of the New Testament, must, I apprehend, have his evidence and conviction from one of the following means:

1. The immediate inspiration of the writer.
2. The immediate evidence of God's influence.
3. Immediate tradition from the inspired writer.
4. Distant tradition.
5. Education or authority.
6. Evidence arising from examination.

Firstly—By inspiration I mean, "God communicating His will, and inciting a person to publish, by writing, or proclaiming by words, such matters as are dictated to him." A person thus actuated either in his writings or words is properly inspired and whatever he writes, or says, under such circumstances, must be infallible, or true because, being under the immediate influence or guidance of God, he can not be liable to error or deception. But the person so actuated or influenced must necessarily lose his own free agency; because he thereby becomes an instrument which God makes use of, under whose direction he acts, for otherwise he would not be infallible. Therefore when I speak of the infallibility of any book or writing, I mean thereby that its author was under the circumstances afore-mentioned at the time of writing; for if he was not under those circumstances, then can not his writings be infallible, because he, like other free agents, must be liable to deception, and may mistake things concerning which he writes, or may impose upon others. Not one of the authors of the four gospels claims in his writings that he was thus irresistibly influenced, and if they do not inform us of the fact, what right have we to suppose that they were so, and claim them to be infallible. That not every word could be dictated by God is plain from the contradictions they contain; and if only some part or parts of these writings should be thought infallible, such difficulties must necessarily arise in settling what part is so, and what part is not so, that it would be impossible to come to any tolerable agreement concerning it. And I am sure that nothing less than an inspired person could make that discrimination; for otherwise there would be as many different opinions as persons employed in the selection, and we should hear one person give as fallible what another asserted to be infallible.

Secondly—The evidence to that which the writer himself has, is, when God is pleased to impress on, or influence the mind of a person by irresistibly forcing him, by some supernatural means, to believe such and such writings to be inspired. It is very certain that God may do this, but it is a question if He ever did; for no person did ever pretend to these supernatural illuminations, without being suspected by the more cool and sedate; and all pretending to such a gift never met with any credit from the more discerning who generally ascribe it to a distempered imagination. However, they, like the writer, may very consistently believe such writings to be infallible. But then neither the writer nor the person so influenced can be any evidence to me, unless I attain to the certainty of it by the same supernatural means.

Thirdly—Immediate tradition from the inspired writer. This can not be *to me* any thing but mere human fallible tradition; for if a person, whether really or pretendedly inspired, publishes a book or writing, and declares that it contains doctrines dictated by God to himself, his evidence to me is at least but human evidence, and therefore uncertain and precarious;

for if I believe it written by inspiration, it is self authority, which is both human and fallible.* This being the case, how or in what manner shall I be able to distinguish the truly inspired writer from the impostor, who should pretend to the like privilege? And if we take the writers' words in all cases, or give heed to their own testimony, we shall be liable to be deceived and imposed upon by every pretender to revelation; and the want of a certain criterion, I apprehend, was the occasion that in the first ages of the church so many different gospels appeared, which by many were received with veneration, while others rejected them as false and spurious: so that this immediate tradition can be no evidence at all of the divine inspiration or infallibility of any book or writing.

Fourthly—As to distant tradition, this evidence must be less the farther it is removed from the original; and if immediate tradition be but human fallible evidence, and a true revelation can not by it be distinguished from a false one, how can it be the better ascertained by being more distant from the original tradition, for the farther it is removed the more it is weakened.

Fifthly—The evidence arising from education or authority, if it proves anything, proves that all the different books which give rise to the different religions in the world, are all inspired; for on this footing each person believes his to be so, and therefore this can be no evidence at all.

Sixthly—Evidence arising from examination. This is the only one to be depended on; but then it is entirely personal, and can never extend farther than the person who examines: that is, it may appear probable to me, on examination, that such a book was written under God's immediate influence and direction; but if a book appears to me to be probably divinely revealed, this is no reason why another person should believe the same, or that it should appear to him in the same light, unless he likewise find it to be so on his own examination.

*Joe Smith's or Brigham Young's claims to inspiration, for instance, rest but on their own evidence.

LETTER II.

Having myself examined the writings of the New Testament, and likewise what is generally offered to support the opinion of their inspiration, I declare it to be altogether insufficient to me; for there does not appear any one circumstance, whether alleged by others, or contained in the writings themselves, sufficient to prove that any of the writers, at the time of writing, was under the unerring guidance or special influence of God.

We are unfortunately without any contemporaneous records whatever in regard to the events narrated in the Gospels. The casual allusion to Christ in Pliny's letters X, 97. *Lamprid. vit. Alex Sever.* 29, 43. *Lucian. de. mort. Perger.* 11, 13, is of no historical value; there are but two passages in the writings of earlier non-Christian historians generally brought forward with some effect. The one occurs in Josephus' Jewish Antiquities xviii, 3, 3, but all impartial and even many partial critics have acknowledged that this passage* was not written by Josephus, but interpolated by a later writer. For, although even Eusebius quotes this passage, it must be remembered that he lived from 267—340 C. E., and there was sufficient reason up to his time for interpolating such a passage into the work of Josephus, which was then extensively known, so that such a reliable witness could be referred to. But, as it always happens, whoever intends to prove too much testifies against himself. Both external and internal evidence prove that this passage was *not* composed by Josephus. As to external evidence, it is introduced in a manner that it interrupts the context, being connected with neither the preceding nor the following passages. In the preceding paragraph mention is made of a sedition of the Jews at Jerusalem which Pilate suppressed by cunningness and violence. In the following the offence of some wicked

*The passage reads as follows: "Now, there was about this time Jesus, a wise man, if it be lawful to call him a man; for he was a doer of wonderful works, a teacher of such men as receive the truth with pleasure. He drew over to him both many of the Jews and many of the Gentiles. He was the Christ. And when Pilate, at the suggestion of the principal men among us, had condemned him to the cross, those that loved him at the first did not forsake him; for he appeared to them alive again on the third day, as the divine prophets had foretold these and thousand other wonderful things concerning him. And the tribe of Christians, so named from him, are not extinct at this day.

persons at Rome is related, in consequence whereof many Jews were expelled from that city. The preceding narrative concludes with the words, "And thus was an end put to this sedition," and the following begins thus, "About the same time also another sad calamity befell the Jews." Now, any one reading the intervening passage, quoted in the note, will at once perceive that the thread of the historical narrative is thereby completely broken.

"Another sad calamity" of §4 can refer only to the "sedition and its violent overthrow" of §2, and thus completely excludes the contents of §3. The internal evidences are still stronger. It is impossible that Josephus should have said, "He was the Christ," for he must have then professed himself a Christian, of which profession there is not the least trace in his works. On the contrary, every expression of Josephus, in matters of religion and law, is in such direct conflict with that assumption, (Josephus proves himself to be such a faithful votary of Jewish faith and Jewish law,) that it must be evident, even to the most prejudiced, that his sentiments can not be reconciled with such an allegation.

The other passage† occurs in Tacitus (born 54, consul 97 C. E.) *Annal.* xv, 44, 4, and merely states in explanation of the name of Christians that Christ had been executed through the procurator Pontius Pilate, under the reign of Tiberius.

This will be sufficient to show that all outside historical evidence for the life of Jesus is wanting. All later writers draw exclusively from Christian sources, which again are based upon the Gospels alone. We are thus reduced to the necessity of taking every particular from such as were deeply engaged, or whose interest must naturally have led them to relate things which, perhaps, never happened, and many others in which they might be deceived. Yet none of these writers lay any claim to inspiration, nor indeed could such a prerogative be consistently ever allowed to them; for if every one of them, at the time of writing, had been under the immediate guidance of God, they would all have given us the very same account of things, without the least difference or variation; for it is impossible, if God dictated to them all the same history, that any variation or difference should be found. But that there are frequent contradictions is evident.

From this circumstance, and many others, I conclude that the writers of the New Testament could not be under the infallible guidance of God; neither do I find that they published their writings as such. And if they did not declare themselves inspired, what authority or foundation could any one else have to declare them so? On the contrary, it very evidently appears that there were no writings deemed canonical in what is called the first ages of Christianity, but the Old Testament. The famous Dodwell says,‡ "We have at this day certain most authentic ecclesiastical writers of the times, as Clemens, Romanus, Barnabas, Hermas, Ignatius, and Polycarpurs, who wrote in the same order wherein I have named them, and after all the writers of the New Testament, except Jude and the two Johns, but in Hermas you will not find a passage, nor any mention of the New Testament; nor in all the rest is any one of the Evangelists named; and if sometimes they cite any passages like those we read in our Gospels, you will find them so much changed, and for the most part, so interpolated, that it can not be known whether they produced them out of our, or some other apocryphal Gospels; nay, they sometimes cite passages which most certainly are not in the present Gospels." Another writer‖ states as the result of his investigations, "Thus the review of the evidence with regard to the first three Gospels gives this result, That, soon after the beginning of the *second century*, certain traces are found of their existence, not indeed in their present form, but still of a considerable portion of their contents, and with every indication that the source of these contents is derived from the country which was the theater of the events in question. On the other hand the issue of the examination with regard to the fourth Gospel (John) is far less favorable, and goes to prove that

†*Ergo abolendo rumori Nero subdidit reos, et quaesitissimis poenis affecit, quos per flagitia invisos, vulgus Christianos appellabat. Auctor nominis ejus Christus, qui Tiberio imperitante, per procuratorem Pontium Pilatum supplicio affectus erat.* Therefore in order to remove the rumor (that he had himself caused the conflagration of the city,) Nero accused and punished with the most exquisite penalties those who, hated on account of their Vices, were commonly called Christians. The author of this name was Christus who was executed through the procurator Pontius Pilate, during the reign of Tiberius.

‡Dissert. 1, In Iren.

‖Strauss, the Life of Jesus, p. 70.

it was not known until after the middle of the century (the second,) and bears every indication of having arisen on a foreign soil, and under the influence of a philosophy of the time, unknown to the original circle in which Jesus lived. In the first case, it is true that the period between the occurrence of the events and the recording of them in their present form, amounts to several generations, and the possibility is not excluded that what is legendary and unhistorical may have crept in; but in the latter there is every probability of an admixture of philosophical combination and designed fiction."

The Gospel bearing the name of Matthew is generally supposed to have been written before the others, but its date is uncertain; some fixing its date of writing at one time, and some at another. Again, some think the original was composed in the Hebrew or Jerusalem dialect, but has disappeared. What is still more extraordinary, the Judaizing Christians (for whose use it is said he wrote) had a Gospel under his name, but its authenticity was not admitted by the other sects; not because they found, on comparing their version with the original, that it was corrupted, (for this they could not do for want of the original,) but because it differed from or was contradictory to the many other spurious Gospels which they had received, or to the opinion which the majority of that council which settled the canon had embraced. But what will appear still more surprising to you, is, that the Christian should offer to the world for acceptance, inspired and infallible, a Greek version, which is the one now existing, and which most readers mistake for the original of Matthew's Gospel, without any person comparing this version with the original, or indeed without knowing any thing either of the original or the author of the version. Should they not, in an affair of such importance, and before they pretend to fix on it the stamp of infallibilty, be certain that it was at least a true version? But nothing of this kind is done, which appears to me such a proceeding as nothing can justify.

To give it all authority possible under the circumstances, some ascribe the version to St. Matthew himself; others ascribe it to St. James; others to St. John; others to St. Paul; others to St. Luke; others to St. Barnabas; and others again ascribe the translation to the joint labor of the apostles, so that these many different opinions prove nothing but their entire ignorance in this matter. But can people be serious in persuading others to admit as infallible the version of a book, without any knowledge of the original, or without knowing whether it be a true version? In the seventeenth century an Armenian translation was discovered, which a doctor in the Sorbonne thought to be of great antiquity, and was of the opinion that it might be very useful in correcting the Greek text. This shows that they do not think it infallible, for if it were, it would require no correction.*

Of as little authority is the Gospel under the name of Mark. Some take this Evangelist to be the disciple of Peter, and his interpreter; others take him to be the same as John Mark, mentioned in the Acts; some think him to have been a priest, while others say he was Peter's nephew. And as regards his Gospel there are a great many different opinions concerning its authorship, the time and place of writing, that these differences merely prove the want of knowledge of its infallibility or inspiration.

The third Evangelist is Luke, who, as he declares in his introduction to his Gospel, wrote only by hearsay and according to information given him by others; he makes not the least pretension to supernatural illumination or information; neither does he pretend to be an original evidence of the facts which he relates: so that it will be hard to say how infallibility came to be ascribed to his writings; for it was even impossible for him ever to vouch for the truth of the facts which he relates; neither would his evidence, being only hearsay, be admitted in any court of law or justice. I can not here forbear noticing how useless and how little known must the Gospels which were published, have been, when the writer or author of one, knew not of the publication or writings of the others, as is plainly demonstrable from the following: Matthew published his Gospel many years before Luke; yet when Luke published his, he took no notice of Matthew's; for it is certain he thought no Gospel authentic when he wrote; for if he had, he

*See all the particulars in Calmet's Dictionary on the word Matthew.

would not have been under the necessity of collecting his materials from others, having an infallible guide in Matthew; so that either he knew not that Matthew had written an infallible relation of those facts, or he confounds the Gospel of Matthew amongst the spurious ones that were abroad in those days; none of which he admitted as true and authentic.

Now, how a person of Luke's character should be ignorant of the infallibility of Matthew's Gospel; or how, if he was not ignorant of it, he should not make use of it, or send it to his friend, rather than his own, is, what I confess I can not comprehend.

"The Gospels," says a well known author,* "continued so concealed in those corners of the world where they were written, that the latter Evangelists knew nothing of what the preceding wrote, otherwise there could not have been so many apparent contradictions, which, almost since the first constitution of the canon, have exercised the wits of learned men. Surely, if St. Luke had seen that genealogy of our Lord which is in St. Matthew, he would not himself have produced one wholly different from the other, without giving the least reason for the diversity; and when in the preface to his Gospel he tells the occasion of his writing, which is, that he undertook it from being furnished with the relation of such as were eye witnesses of what he writes, he plainly intimates that the authors of those Gospels which he had seen were destitute of that help; so that neither having seen themselves what they relate, nor consulted with diligence and care such as had seen them, their credit was therefore dubious and suspected."

To the foregoing observations I shall only add, that there are the same doubts as to his person and character, profession and writings, as the others; for it is not known whether he was a Jew or a heathen, a physician or a painter; and as to his Gospel, some think it properly St. Paul's, while others say that Luke only digested what Paul preached to the Gentiles; and others, again, that he wrote with the help of St. Paul.†

The last is St. John; and it is plain, that he wrote only for the purpose of establishing the divinity of Jesus, which particular is not contained in the Gospels then extant; he, for this reason, goes on a very different plan from the other Evangelists. "His principal care in this undertaking," says Calmet,‡ "was to relate such things as might be of use in confirming the divinity of the son; and to this purpose says many things which the others are silent on, and omits such matters in which the others are very particular, and which we reckoned very essential and necessary in the history. Thus, considering his very great care and tenderness for Mary, the mother of Jesus, he does but little honor to her memory, in not relating those most remarkable and wonderful transactions mentioned by Matthew and Luke (though with a wide difference), concerning the miraculous conception of Mary, and the birth of Jesus. And as Mary continued to live with him from the time of Jesus' death, (John xix, 25—27,) surely he must have had many opportunities of informing himself of those extraordinary affairs, from her own mouth, with much more certainty than the others; for it must be thought very extraordinary that the Evangelist under the circumstances aforementioned, should make no mention at all of such an essential article as the most wonderful conception of a virgin, and the birth of the person who was the subject of his history. How far his neglect of relating so important a matter, and likewise those extraordinary dreams and visions which the others mention, weakens the authority of their relation, or of his own, I shall not determine; but certain it is, that his Gospel met not with that reception which one would think was due to a person of his authority; for many rejected his Gospel; the Alogians in particular, though they admitted the three others, yet rejected this; and others believed a heretic was its author, one Cerenthius; and no doubt but the difference in the point of doctrine might be the occasion of it, or the want of sufficient evidence of his being the author."

The difficulties which must arise from the aforesaid considerations are such, in respect to the proof of the inspiration or infallibility of the Gospels, as can not be got

*Dodwell. Dissert. in Iren.

†For particulars, see Calmet on the word Luke.

‡I prefer quoting eminent Christian authors, as their opinion must give additional strength to what I assert.

over; and yet this is not all; for whoever is in any way acquainted with the history of the ancients and the observations of the moderns, must be convinced of the many additions, alterations and interpolations which the writings of the New Testament have undergone, of which I shall collect some accounts for your information.

LETTER III.

Even in the first ages of Christianity there was not any one sect but complained of interpolations and additions made to the Gospels; nay, some sects or parties went so far as to reject some one or other of the Gospels, now received as authentic; and others the whole of the New Testament.* Eusebius (about the year 300,) states, that the story of the woman taken in adultery to be only in the Gospel according to the Hebrews; and consequently must have been inserted after his time into the Gospel of John; and St. Jerome declares that, in his time, the story was only to be found in some copies. Both St. Jerome and St. Austin complain of the great variety of the Latin copies of the Evangelists, and how widely they differed from each other;† and they likewise declare the same difference in the Greek copies. St. Ambrose says of the Greek copies that they were so different as to give rise to many controversies; (and these different copies must as naturally have occasioned different opinions and doctrines.) St. Jerome declares that he found as many different versions as books.‡ Now, as there could not be any possibility of distinguishing the true copy or version (had there been one), so every one followed that which either suited his interests or opinions; and to this end, every one added, omitted, or altered whatever he thought most conducive to his purpose.

In the controversies between the Unitarians and Trinitarians, the latter interpolated the text about the "three in heaven" into John's letter (I. John, 5, 7,) and this same verse is missing in *all* the oldest and fairest manuscripts.§

*Eccles. Hist. lib. III., ch. 39.
†See Calmet on the word Bible.
‡Calmet on the word Vulgate.
§Gibbon's Rome.

Origen (about 200 A. C.) says: "We found great differences in the copies, and made use of what was convenient out of the Old Testament, making use of our judgment in such things, as out of the Septuagint (the Greek version of the Old Testament) seemed doubtful, and were not to be found in the Hebrew." You see, even he inserted what he thought necessary, and used only what suited his notions. Thus also Grotius declares he made use of the Vulgate (the Latin version); because the author delivers no opinions contrary to the (Romish) faith.‖ Now, if liberty has been taken of correcting, interpolating, and altering the New Testament, what person is there who can assert and prove that these are the genuine writings of those persons whose names they bear? If it should be said that this was done only in matters of small importance, I ask, what certainty have we that any thing was left untouched? In Origen's time, Celsus exclaims against the liberty which Christians took of changing the first writing of the Gospel, three, four, or more times.* The Manicheans denied the genuineness of the whole present New Testament, and showed others books of their own. Faustus, their bishop, says: "You think, that of all the books in the world, the Testament of the Son only, could not be corrupted; and that it alone contains nothing which ought to be disallowed, especially when it appears it was written neither by himself, nor his apostles, but a long time after, by certain obscure persons, who, lest no credit should be given to the stories they told, did prefix to their writings partly the names of the apostles, and partly of those who succeeded the apostles—affirming that what they wrote themselves was written by these, wherein they seem to have been more injurious to the disciples of Christ, by attributing to them what they wrote themselves, so dissonant and repugnant, pretending to write those Gospels under their names, which are so full of mistakes and of contradictory relations and opinions, that they are neither coherent with themselves, nor consistent with one another."† Again the same bishop says: "Many things were foisted by your

‖Grot. Pref. Annot. in Vet. Test.
*Origen, lib. II., Contr. Cels.
†Augustin con. Faust. lib. XXXV, c. 1, and XXXVI, c. 3.

ancestors into the Scriptures of our Lord, which, although marked with his name, agree not with his faith." The learned Doctor Mills gives an account of a general alteration of the Gospels, as late as the sixth century.§ He likewise with great labor published all the readings of the New Testament, which are so numerous and so different, that the learned Dr. Whitby declares, that "The vast quantity of various readings collected must, of course, make the mind doubtful or suspicious, that nothing certain can be expected from books where there are various readings in every verse, and almost in every part of every verse."* Mr. Gregory of Christ Church in Oxford, England, declares, that "There is no profane author whatever, other things being equal, that has suffered so much by the hand of time as the New Testament has done."† How willing and ready the priests have been at all times to encourage pious frauds need not be mentioned. One fact, however, I can not pass in silence, and that is a letter of Cardinal Belarmine, who, with the other divines, attended the correction of the Vulgate, in which he acknowledges that there are still several faults which for good reasons the correctors did not think proper to remove.‡ I shall make no remark on this passage, but shall proceed to a short account of the rest of the writings of the New Testament.

The book of Acts, which is said to be the work of St. Luke, was rejected by many sects. St. Chrysostom complains that this book was little known, and that it was little read, which shows that even in his time it was not held in any degree of authority. In this book Paul is said to have gone to Jerusalem from Damascus, and to have seen the other apostles (IX, 26—30), while he solemnly declares in the Epistle to the Galatians that after his conversion he did not confer with any body, but went to Arabia, where he remained three years (Galat. I, 17—22). But there have also been many debates concerning the authenticity of the Epistles, particularly St. Paul's Epistle to the Hebrews, the Epistle of St. James, the second Epistle of Peter, the second and third Epistles of John, and the Epistle of Jude. As to the authority of the Apocalypse, or Revelations, since its author can not be ascertained, how is it possible that its inspiration should? For "Cajus, priest of the Church of Rome, who lived at the end of the second age, seems to assure us that the Apocalypse, or Book of Revelations, was written by the arch-heretic Cerinthus; and Deonylas, bishop of Alexandria, says that some, indeed, thought Cerinthus to be the author of it, but that for his own part, he believed it to be written by a holy man, named John, but he would not take it upon himself to affirm that it was really the work of the apostle or evangelist of that name. The Apocalypse has not at all times been owned to be canonical. Jerome, Amphilocus, and Sulpitius Severus remark that in their time there were many churches in Greece that did not receive this book."§ The Protestants retained it because they turned its prophecies against the Church of Rome, and did not want to lose so good and useful a weapon.

Thus, on investigation, the writings of the New Testament appear to me to be far from being infallible, being even destitute of proof that they were written by the persons whose names they bear. The uncertainty of their authorship, together with the continual alterations they have undergone, makes it impossible to credit them even as histories. Moreover, it appears highly improbable that any of the Gospels we now have should be the genuine works of the apostles; the writers of the different epistles neither allude to them, nor seem to be aware of their existence, as there can not be found any mention of them in the epistles said to be written by the apostles. Besides, there is no corroborating evidence to be found in any of the cotemporaneous historians to the marvelous events related therein. It is true, common and usual facts, such as may happen in the common course of things, may, and do generally receive credit on the evidence of the historian; but it would not be the same, were he to relate things out of the common course of probability, or what appeared improbable; for the more extroardinary the facts are which he relates, the more extraordinary ought the evidence to be. But this evidence is nowhere to be had but in these writings themselves, which is no evi-

§Mill's Prolegom. p. 98.

*Whitby's Ex. Var Lect Milli, p. 3, 4.

†Pref. to his posthum. works.

‡Calmet on the word Vulgate.

§Calmet on the word Apocalypse

dence at all, they being destitute of proof, and therefore can not be admitted or allowed.

The only thing which seems probable, from the accounts transmitted to us, is, that there were many who wrote; that as Christianity developed itself gradually its preachers published a Gospel suited to the new change. Thus, in answer to a Pharisee's question, the Gospel of Mark (XII, 29,) has Jesus saying: "Hear, O Israel, the Lord our God is One Lord," being the Jewish idea of God's Unity; while Luke's Gospel, being composed much later when the deification of Jesus had begun, and a second person had been added to the Divinity, omits this expression of God's Unity entirely. John's Gospel, being written still later, begins with the principal idea of the Jewish Alexandrian Philosophy. To give these writings greater authority, they published them under the names they now bear, but of their followers each one only accepted such Gospels as agreed with his individual opinion. These books being also in private hands (long before the invention of printing), and being only multiplied by the laborious process of copying, the possessors did not want for opportunities of changing, interpolating, adding, and curtailing whatever they thought convenient, or was agreeable to the opinion they had embraced. Under these circumstances it was impossible to know, in the course of time, what was, and what was not original in the Gospels, and even if the apostles had written any Gospels they fared no better than those published by others.

LETTER IV.

Our next inquiry is, who were the persons that met in council to establish a new canon, and what authority they had for so doing?* In answer to this, we find that they plainly appear to have been a set of men entirely unqualified for such an undertaking; for, according to the best authorities we may collect, a majority in these councils was always formed by faction and intrigue; that the members were led by interest, prejudice and passion; and that they were contentious, ambitious, ignorant and wicked. The judicious Mr. Chandler gives such a character to the Fathers,† and such a description of all general councils, as must be very convincing how improper they were, and what little authority their determinations ought to have. He says,‡ "It is infinite, it is endless labor to consult all that the Fathers have written; and when we have consulted them, what one controversy have they rationally decided? how few texts of Scripture have they critically settled the sense and meaning of? how often do they differ from one another, and in how many instances from themselves? Those who read them, greatly differ in their interpretation of them, and men of the most contrary sentiments all claim them for their own. Athanasians (Trinitarians,) and Arians (Unitarians), all appeal to the Fathers, and support their principles by quotations from them. And are these the venerable gentlemen, whose writings are to be set up in opposition to the Scriptures? Are creeds of their dictating to be submitted to as the only criterion of orthodoxy, or esteemed as standards to distinguish between truth and error? Away with this folly and superstition! the creeds of the Fathers and councils are but human creeds, that have marks in them of human frailty and ignorance."

Another eminent person§ declares, "The Fathers, you say, whom you regard as the propagators of the Christian religion, must necessarily have been men of true piety and knowledge; but it has been maintained and proved to you by a great number of instances, that the Fathers have not only fallen into very gross errors, and been most profoundly ignorant of many things which they ought to have known; but farther, that most of them have more or less suffered themselves to be led by passion; so that their conduct has been found frequently to be such as is neither regular nor justifiable. In the first ages of Christianity, and those that followed after, the men most applauded, and who bore the

*The Council of Laodicea was the first that selected the present Gospels from the many then extant, and declared them inspired, and Scripture; about the end of the fourth century.

†The Bishops, Preachers, and religious writers of the first six centuries, after the time of the apostles, are called Fathers (of the church).

‡Introduct. to History of the Inquisition, p. 111.

§Barbeyr. Hist. and Crit. Account of the Science of Morality, chap. IX and X.

greatest character in the church, were not always those that had the greatest share of good sense, or were the most eminent for learning and virtue."

As to general councils, "I think it will evidently follow from this account," says Mr. Chandler,‡ "that the determinations of councils and decrees of synods as to matters of faith are of no manner of authority, and carry no obligation upon any Christian whatsoever. I will mention here one reason which would itself suffice if all others were wanting, viz: that they have no power given them, in any part of the Gospel revelations, to make these decisions in controverted points, and to oblige others to subscribe to them; and that therefore the pretence to it is an usurpation of what belongs to the great God who only has, and can have a right to prescribe to the conscience of men. But, to let this pass, what one council can be fixed upon that shall appear to have been composed of such persons as upon impartial examination might be deemed fit for the work of settling the faith, and of determining all controversies relating to it? I mean, in which the majority of the members may in charity be supposed to have been disinterested, wise, learned, peaceable and pious men. Will any man undertake to affirm this of the council of Nice? Can any thing be more evident, than that the members of that assembly came, many of them, full of passion and resentment; and others were crafty and wicked; and others ignorant and weak? Did their meeting together in a synod immediately cure them of their desire of revenge, make the wicked virtuous, or the ignorant wise? If not, their joint decree as a synod could really be of no more weight than their private opinions, nor perhaps of so much; because it is well known that the great transactions of such an assembly are generally managed and conducted by a few; and that authority, persecution, prospect of interest, and other temporal motives are commonly made use of to secure a majority. The second general council were plainly the creatures of the emperor Theodosius, all of his party, and convened to do as he bid them. The third general council were the creatures of Cyril, who was their president, and the inveterate enemy of Nestorius, whom he condemned for heresy, and was himself condemned for rashness in this affair. The fourth met under the awe of Emperor Marcian, managed their debates with noise and tumult, were formed into a majority by the intrigues of the Legates of Rome, and settled the faith by the opinions of Athanasius, Cyril and others. I need not mention more; the farther they go the worse they will appear. As their decisions in matters of faith were arbitrary and unwarranted, as the decisions themselves were generally owing to Court practices, intriguing statesmen, the thirst for revenge, the management of a few crafty interested bishops, to noise and tumult, the prospects and hopes of promotions and translations, and other like causes, the reverence paid them by many Christians is truly surprising."

"All the world saw," says Barbeyrac,* who quotes an author who can not be suspected of any ill will toward the Fathers, "the dreadful cruelties that were committed in these unhappy centuries: they maintained sieges in their monasteries; they battled in their councils; they treated with the utmost cruelty all whom they but suspected to favor opinions which too often proved to be such as nobody understood, not even those that defended them with the greatest zeal and obstinacy." "These," says he, "are the great lights of the church! These are the holy Fathers whom we must take for men of true piety and knowledge."

"One council," says another historian,† "was summoned to annul what another had done, and all things were managed with that faction, strife and contention, as if they labored to quench the spirit of meekness and brotherly love, so often recommended in the Gospel. Some were banished, some were imprisoned, and against others they proceeded with more severity, even to the loss of their lives."

This character which even the most partial defenders of the Fathers are forced to admit leads us naturally to ask, whence such men had the authority to establish a new canon. They produced no authority, from Jesus, none from the apostles, nothing was even said in the writings about

‡Introduct. to the Hist. of the Inquisition, sec. iii, p. 100–102.

*Histor. Acct. of the Science of Morality, sec. 10.
†Echard, Rom. History, vol. III, 57.

which they decided, so they were reduced to claim a traditional right, supported only by their own word, which, considering what men they were, will never be allowed to be any authority at all. We do not hear of any pretension to extraordinary assistance or revelation to these councils from God, so that the authority which they attach to these writings appear to have been entirely accidental. Of this opinion is also Mr. Collins (in Grounds and Reasons, p. 13), he says: "Jesus and his apostles do frequently and emphatically style the books of the Old Testament 'the Scriptures,' and refer men to them as their rule and canon; but no new books are declared by them to have that character. Hence if Jesus and his apostles have declared no books to be canonical: I would ask who did, and who could afterward declare or make any books canonical? If it had been deemed proper and suited to the state of Christianity to have given or declared a new canon or digest of laws: it would seem most proper to have been done by Jesus or his apostles, and not left to any after them to do, but especially not left to be settled long after their times, by weak, fallible, factious and interested men who were disputing with one another about the genuineness of all books bearing the names of the apostles, and contending with one another about the authority of every different book."

It would be tedious to continue this subject. If you wish to learn farther particulars, I refer you to any history of the church, or of the Roman Empire. I shall in my next proceed to the examination of the internal evidence of the Gospel writings.

LETTER V.

Before we proceed further, it is necessary to explain the word Messiah. משיח Meshiach, pronounced Messias by the Greeks, means "the anointed one," (Greek: Christos) from a verb (mashach) that signifies to anoint. Anointing being in ancient times among the Jews a ceremony performed on kings and priests on first entering upon the duties of their office. The term Messiah, Christ, or the anointed one, is therefore frequently used instead of king or priest; and the ancient Jews, by way of eminence and emphasis, called or designated by this appellation a man who, as certain prophecies particularly describe, should deliver their nation from foreign oppression, and establish a universal kingdom of righteousness and peace in the world.

The writers of the Gospels claim that Jesus fulfilled these prophecies, and the only sure guide we have, to come at the truth of this assertion, is to examine the prophecies in the Old Testament which they cite and apply as fulfilled by and accomplished in him. It is by such an examination only that a true judgment can be formed of the validity of their application and accomplishment—the prophecies being the only criterion by which the Messiah is to be known, since it is from them alone that his character can be proved; and we may be most certain that such evidence must be not only superior, but most sure, as Peter (Pet. i. 19) expresses it. For what in nature can be superior to plain and clear prophecies delivered to different persons and at different times, all unanimously and uniformly foretelling so long before, that which should happen or come to pass—being transactions so very extraordinary that, when duly attended to, the prophecies compared to the events, evidently, obviously, and literally fulfilled and accomplished, must be the highest testimony any thing can possibly be capable of. This task is, therefore, absolutely necessary, and I with pleasure undertake the examination.

1. The first prophecy taken from the Old Testament and applied in the New, is that which concerns the conception of Mary and the birth of Jesus from a virgin, which St. Matthew tries to prove by applying a passage out of Isaiah:* "Now all this was done (says he) that it might be fulfilled which was spoken of the Lord by the prophet, saying, Behold a virgin shall be with child, and shall bring forth a son, and they shall call his name Emanuel."† Now it happens that this passage cited from Isaiah, according to its plain and obvious meaning, concerns neither the birth of Jesus from a virgin, nor the birth of the Messiah at all; and its citation by the Evangelist can not prove any thing. This

*Isaiah vii. 14.
†Matthew i. 23.

will plainly and evidently appear from an examination of the entire chapter of Isaiah vii. In the days of Ahaz, king of Judah, the kings of Syria and Israel made war against Jerusalem, and after one failure to take the city, return again to besiege it. King Ahaz and the royal family (the house of David) are in great consternation. On this occasion, Isaiah was sent by God to comfort Ahaz, and to assure him in His name that the allied kings should not prevail in their design; and in order to convince Ahaz of this, the prophet, in God's name, tells him to ask a sign of him. The incredulous king excuses himself, under pretence of not tempting God. The prophet, after complaining of the king's behavior, tells him that God Himself will give him a sign—no doubt such a clear, indisputable, immediate sign—such a one as would convince Ahaz and his people of the truth of Isaiah's assertion, and inspire them with confidence; viz: that a young woman (for so the word *Almah*, used in the Hebrew text, signifies) which he points out among the bystanders (the Hebrew text has the definite article) should be delivered of a son; that before the child should know good from evil, that is in a short time, both kings of whom Ahaz was afraid should be no more; that after the child's birth butter and honey and every thing else which during the siege was scarce would be plenty. Now, it is plain as words can make it, that this sign was given to Ahaz as a proof to convince him of the truth of the prophet's prediction, and so it effectually was; and it must have been the greatest absurdity, and contrary to the very intention of the sign, to have understood the prophet as St. Matthew does, describing here the conception of Mary, and the birth of her son Jesus—an event which was not to happen till seven or eight hundred years after. For how could a sign or event happening eight hundred years after have confirmed Ahaz in the hope and expectation of the destruction of his two powerful enemies within a short time? But the certain foretelling of the birth of a male child by a designated woman, and the declaring that before it should have any knowledge both the kings, his enemies, should be destroyed, appears a proper and well adapted sign, because it must have shortly verified the prophet's prediction. But a sign which was not to come to pass till eight hundred years after could never answer the purpose; for how could it be a sign to the incredulous king to prove that which was immediately to happen? On the other hand, nothing can be clearer than that the whole transaction was plainly fulfilled in the days of Ahaz, within the time limited by the prophet, before the child which was born could distinguish good from evil, or in about two years, as is evident from sacred history; for within that time the king of Syria was slain after the taking of Damascus;‡ and the king of Israel was killed by Hosea, who rebelled against him,* by which means the land which Ahaz abhorred was bereft of both her kings, which event fulfilled the prophet's prediction, for which the prophet's own child (and not Jesus as it is pretended) was given the sign. The birth of the child is described in the next (the viii) chapter of Isaiah, where the prophet himself declares (v. 18,) "Behold, I and the children whom the Lord has given me are for signs and for wonders in Israel from the Lord of Hosts." Thus was the sign given to convince Ahaz fulfilled, and the whole prophecy accomplished at that very time, and consequently it excludes all their pretenses. The word *Almah*, rendered "virgin" in the English Bible, signifies no more than a young woman, whether maid, married, or widow. When a virgin is intended, it is always expressed by the word *Bethulah*, which is the proper term for virgin; this is evident from the word *Bethulah* being used for virgin throughout the Scriptures.†

I can not here forbear observing how cautiously Calmet treats and explains the word *Almah*. He trifles and imposes on his readers and endeavors to hide from them, as much as lies in his power, its true meaning by declaring that the Hebrews had no term that more properly signifies a virgin than *Almah*; for though he at last contrary to his inclination, is forced to confess the contrary, he does it in a manner that discovers his glaring chicanery; for he says, "It must be confessed, without lessening, however, the certainty of Isaiah's prophecy, that sometimes by mistake any young woman, whether virgin or not, is

‡ II Kings xvi, 9.
* II Kings xi, 30.
†See Gen. 14, 16; Lev. xxi, 3 & 13; Deut. xxii, 28 & 28.

called *Almah*." Now observe, first he assures you that the Hebrews have no term that more signifies a virgin than *Almah*, which is evidently false; secondly, when he brings himself to the confession that any young woman whatsoever is called by this name, he will have it to be by mistake, which is also false. How vain, nay, how frivolous are such shifts and evasions.

There are many Christian commentators, both ancient and modern, who do justice to this passage of Isaiah, and acknowledge that the whole must be understood of his own son who was made the sign to Ahaz; and then content themselves with making Isaiah's son a type of Jesus. The Evangelist here in proof cites a passage taken out of all connection, which on inspection shows not to refer to his subject at all. What would be thought of a scholar, or a lawyer, making quotations and citing proof that does not exist at all or does not bear on the subject. But all Evangelists and apostles, down even to Paul, are guilty of this unfair proceeding, as I will show you.

2. The next prophecy cited by Matthew, as fulfilled in Jesus, is concerning the place of his birth and greatness; the passage referred to is in Micah v, 2: "And thou Bethlehem in Judah art not the least among the princes of Judah: for out of thee shall come a governor that shall rule my people Israel."‡ This is said to be the answer made to Herod by the chief priests and scribes when he inquired of them concerning the place of the Messiah's birth; both he and all Jerusalem being troubled, at the news published by the Eastern wise men, of having seen his star in the East, by which they knew of the birth of the king of the Jews.§ That is according to Matthew's account of this affair. But in this whole transaction there seem some things not only very improbable, but even incredible; such as that Herod should ask the priests and scribes such a question, and that they should give him such an answer—that an extraordinary star should appear in the East; or that its appearance should be known to be a notification of the birth of a child in Judea; that the wise men should take a long journey to no purpose; that the star should make its appearance to people who were nowise concerned in the birth of a king of the Jews, and not to the Jews themselves who were the people chiefly interested; that the inhabitants of Jerusalem should be troubled at an event which must have been a matter of great joy and comfort to them;‖ that an assembly of priests and scribes should fix the place where their king should be born when it seems to have been an established principle among them (according to John vii, 27,) that they were not to know the place of the Messiah's birth, since there have followed many pretenders to that character, without being born at Bethlehem; and lastly that the star which the wise men had seen in the East should again appear to them when they had parted from Herod, march before them, and make a stand "Over where the child was" for manner of purpose; since we hear no more of these wise men, nor of any use that was made of their journey; all of which seems to be a piece of extravagance, and a continual series of impossibilities and incredibilities. For how could people, acquainted with the vast magnitude of the stars (for wise they were,) think that one went before them to show the way from house to house? And since the star must necessarily have traveled from the East, where it first appeared, to Jerusalem, where the wise men again found it—for it was the same star (Matthew ii, 9) which guided them to the place where the child was—why did not the star guide them directly from the place they set out from to Bethlehem? for the guidance of the star from Jerusalem appears needless as Herod had directed them before. Besides so extraordinary a phenomenon must have drawn the attention of the whole city, and numbers of other people would have it as well as the wise men, had it really been seen; but of this the story takes no manner of notice. All these considerations make it more than probable that the whole was invented to make way for the application of this and two other passages as fulfilled; for, as the Gospel of Matthew was written to convince the Jews of the Messiahship of Jesus, and they believing that the character of the Messiah was clearly described by the prophets, the writer not being able to produce passages fitting to his purpose, according to their plain, obvious

‡ The proper translation from the Hebrew would be: "among the clans of Judah," which also restores the sense of the passage. David was of the clan Bethlehem.

§ Matthew ii, 1–4.

‖ Luke ii, 10.

meaning, invented facts to have an opportunity of introducing something as having been fulfilled. The whole passage, as it is in Micah, can not be applied to Jesus, since the person there spoken of was to be a "ruler" in Israel and a protection against the Assyrian. See the whole chapter, and the impossibility of applying it to Jesus literally. For unless it be so, according to its primary sense and meaning, it can neither be deemed to be fulfilled, nor produced to prove anything.

3. One of the passages, or prophecies, which is cited by Matthew, and said by him to be fulfilled, in consequence of the needless discovery made to Herod by the wise men, is the following and is the next which the Evangelist cites. It is from that discovery that he tells us how that Joseph dreamed that an angel appeared to him, and ordered him to flee with the child and its mother into Egypt, which being done, he says, "that he was there till the death of Herod, that it might be fulfilled what was spoken of the Lord by the prophet, saying, Out of Egypt have I called my son." You will see by the marginal note, or reference, that this passage is taken from Hosea ix, 1, but it evidently and plainly appears on examination not to be prophetical, but to have reference to a long past action, viz: the call of the children of Israel out of Egypt. The prophet's words are, "When Israel was a child (when the nation was young,) then I loved him, and I called my son out of Egypt,"* so that this passage could not be in Jesus' return, since it is no prediction. Please to notice that *Luke in all these things plainly contradicts Matthew;* for according to him, they brought Jesus to Jerusalem to present him to the Lord, and to offer the appointed sacrifice,† whence "when they had performed all things according to the law of the Lord they returned into Galilee, to their own city of Nazareth," which if true, puts Matthew out with his whole narration.

4. The other passage or prophecy which I think to be cited by Matthew, and said by him to be fulfilled, in consequence of the discovery which the wise men made to Herod, is brought in on the occasion of the slaughter which, he says, Herod made of the babes in Bethlehem. "Then (says he) was fulfilled that which was spoken by Jeremiah, the prophet, saying, In Rama was there a voice heard, lamentations, and weeping and great mourning, Rachel weeping for her children, and would not be comforted, because they are not."‡ Please turn in your Bible to Jeremiah xxxi, 12, and you will find that it evidently and plainly relates to the sufferings of the ten tribes and their glorious return. The strongest confirmation that the whole story of the wise men was invented to usher in the accommodation of the three cited passages is, that Luke is silent about it, and gives an entire different relation of the circumstances of his birth. He substitutes the story of the shepherds who kept watch (ii, 8-20.) I have observed before his differing also concerning the journey to Egypt. So neither does he mention the massacre of the babes by Herod, but places the birth of Jesus at the time when Cyrenius (lat. Quirinius) was made Governor of Syria, which was several years after King Herod's death, Judea being annexed to Syria (Josephus Antiq. xviii, 1.) "For it was Cyrenius' province to tax and assess those people, and make seizure of the moneys and moveables of Archelaus," who had succeeded his father Herod, but was deposed by the Roman Emperor. It was on occasion of this tax that Joseph and Mary went to Bethlehem. "And so it was, that, while they were there, the days were accomplished that she should be delivered; and she brought forth her first-born son." (Luke ii, 4-8.) But had he been born in Herod's time, it must appear very surprising and incredible that none but Matthew should relate this most barbarous and inhuman act. Josephus is very circumstantial and very particularly describes the cruelties which this barbarous king committed; and yet says not a word concerning this bloody deed, which he would most certainly have related had it been true; for he was not sparing of his character. It is mere trifling to pretend, as some do, that Josephus purposely concealed this butchery to avoid giving countenance to the Evangelist. For even if true, and related as such by Josephus, it could only prove the jealousy of Herod, but never that another king was really born. But surely

*Moses calls Israel God's son in his demand before Pharaoh. Exod.

† Luke ii, 21--39.

‡ Matthew ii, 16—18.

they can not and dare not tax Luke with any such design; yet it is plain from his placing the birth of Jesus when Cyrenius was Governor of Syria, an event that happened after the death of Herod, that Jesus could not be born during his reign. The agreement of Josephus and Luke in this particular, and Luke's silence in these affairs and never mentioning any thing to have happened under Herod, is equal to a demonstration against the facts as recorded by Matthew.

LETTER VI.

5. The next citation made by Matthew, and said by him to be fulfilled, is the following: "And he came and dwelt in a city, called Nazareth, that it might be fulfilled, which was spoken by the prophets, He shall be called a Nazarene." (ii, 23.) But as Matthew unfortunately omits to say which of the prophets foretell this, and no one of the numerous commentators of the Bible has been able to find the prediction in the Scriptures, I feel tempted to think the passage, like a good many others, to be invented for the edification of the ignorant and credulous. The marginal references point us to Judges, but we only find there a command from the angel announcing Sampson's birth to his parents to bring the boy up as a Nazarite, which means a person under a vow of abstinence, the particulars whereof you may read in Numbers, chap. xvii. If Matthew meant this he only shows his entire ignorance of the Hebrew language by confounding the word Nazarene, signifying an inhabitant of Nazareth, with Nazarite. From this and further quotation of Matthew which I shall consider in its proper order, it is almost proved to a certainty, that the writer did not understand Hebrew, and compiled his narrative long after the custom of the Nazarite with his vows had ceased with the destruction of the temple, and had been nearly forgotten. For that any one having even but a superficial knowledge of Hebrew should mistake one for the other of these terms, so widely differing in their meaning, appears altogether incredible.

As I am only showing that the passages, or prophecies, said to be fulfilled in Jesus, are not properly applied, and none pretend that this is literally fulfilled, it is not my place to take notice, or make any remarks on what they say concerning this passage. But the solution of Dr. Echard* is certainly very curious, who, after relating Jesus' return to his former habitation, adds, "which being a mean and despicable place, it afterward gained Jesus the reproachful title of a Nazarene, according to the aim and turn of several prophecies, as St. Matthew observes." But here the Doctor is mistaken, for the title of Nazarite was honorable, and was never given by way of reproach; the term Nazarene was long after the time of Jesus turned from its first meaning of an inhabitant of Nazareth to denote Christians in general. As usual the Doctor omits to produce the "several prophecies."

6. The next citation made by Matthew concerns the preaching of John. "For this is that was spoken of by the prophet Esaias, saying, The voice of one crying in the wilderness, prepare ye the way of the Lord and make His paths straight." (iii, 3.) But the context of the chapter (Is. xlix) whence this citation is taken, very evidently shows that John was not the person spoken of. For it says, "Comfort, comfort ye my people, saith your God. Speak ye comfortably to Jerusalem, and cry unto her, that her warfare is accomplished, that her iniquity is pardoned; for she has received of the Lord's hand double for her sins," which verses precede the one quoted by Matthew. What comfort it was now that John brought to the Jews and Jerusalem has not yet been made out. How could their warfare be accomplished, when the greatest vengeance was at that time to be poured out? how could their iniquities be said to be pardoned, when they are accused to have contracted the highest guilt at that very time? or how could the prophet declare that they had received double for all their sins, when the greatest punishment was still to be inflicted on them? from which circumstances in the prophecy it is plain that this passage is not properly cited, and not literally fulfilled. The prophecy is, according to its plain, obvious meaning, declarative of times and circumstances entirely different from those which

*Eccles. Hist. vol. I, p. 7.

came to pass at that time, therefore it could not relate to John.

7. The next citation made by Matthew is to prove that Jesus' removal from Nazareth and settling at Capernaum was foretold. This Jesus did that it might be fulfilled which was spoken by Esaias, the prophet saying:

Matthew iv, 15, 16.	Isaiah ix, 1, 2.
"The land of Zebulon, and the land of Nepthalim by the way of the sea, beyond Jordan, Galilee of the Gentiles; the people which sat in darkness saw great light; and to them which sat in the region and shadow of death light is sprung up."	"Nevertheless, the dimness shall not be such as was in her vexation, when at first he lightly afflicted the land of Zebulon, and the land of Naphtali, and afterward did more grievously afflict her by the way of the sea, beyond Jordan, in Galilee of the nations. The people that walked in darkness have seen a great light; they that dwell in the land of the shadow of death upon them has the light shone."

I have put the citation and text in different columns, that you may see the difference. The seventh chapter of Isaiah with the five succeeding ones forms a continuous poem in which are described the reign of Ahaz, the punishment for his want of faith by the Assyrians, Hezekiah's birth and promising youth, and the destruction of Sennacherib. In the verses above quoted, the prophets' plain meaning is, to declare the joy which the inhabitants of those regions should have, in the midst of their sorrow and affliction, occasioned by the army of the King of Assyria which was to be totally destroyed, and they were thus to be delivered from this dreadful enemy. This event and prophecy relates no more to the removal of Jesus from one place to another, than it does to your removal from New York to Richmond.

8. The next prophecy cited by Matthew, and said to be fulfilled by Jesus, is "that it might be fulfilled what was spoken by Esaias, the prophet, saying, Himself took our infirmities and bore our sicknesses," (Matth. viii, 16, 17,) which citation thus said to be fulfilled is in Isaiah liii, 4: "Surely he hath borne our grief, and carried our sorrows." Now, whoever can, from this passage of the prophet, draw a sense importing the casting out of devils out of men's bodies and the healing of diseases, must do it by the help of some uncommon rule, or art, to us unknown; for literally it can not mean any such thing. Curing or removing a disease is not bearing it. But even supposing it would mean this, and that it was really fulfilled by Jesus in performing these cures bodily, must it not upset some person's deductions who explain this passage by the cure of sin and spiritual infirmities by his death? The pretense that it means spiritual cures must of course be contrary to Matthew, who says the passage was fulfilled by those bodily cures. As I intend to write to you in full on the fifty-third chapter of Isaiah, whence this citation is taken, I will pass it now without further comment.

9. The next citation by Matthew is, when Jesus, in order to persuade the people to believe that John was Elias, says: "And if ye will receive it, this was Elias which was to come." (Matth. xi, 14.) Elias is the Greek pronunciation and spelling of Elijah, which was the name of a prophet in King Ahab's time, and who is said to have mysteriously disappeared (II. Kings). The prophet Malachi promises his re-appearance (Mal. ii, 5, 6,) in the following words: "Behold, I will send you Elijah the prophet before the coming of the great and dreadful day of the Lord, and he shall turn the heart of the fathers to the children, and the heart of the children to the fathers, lest I come and smite the earth with a curse." This is certainly a great and glorious work which that great prophet was to be sent to do; and it should not be wondered that the Jews, on a promise so plainly expressed, should found the hope of Elias' or Elijah's coming for so desirable and beneficent a purpose; at least those who, on another occasion, do firmly believe that not only Elias, but Moses, too, did really come down from heaven in a bodily shape (for how otherwise could the disciples know it was they, or to what end should they desire to build a tabernacle for their abode?)* to answer no purpose at all that we know of, ought not to be surprised at their having such hopes. But be that as it may, thus much is certain, Elias or Elijah was promised to be sent, that is, a person who bore that name; and John's coming can not be deemed a literal fulfilling of the promise.

10. The next citation made by Matthew, and said by him to be fulfilled by Jesus, is on occasion of the cures that he wrought on the multitude of his followers, and his charging them not to make it known.

*Matth. xvii, 1–4; Mark ix, 4, 5; Luke ix, 30–33.

"All this happened," says Matthew, "that it might be fulfilled, which was spoken by Esaias, the prophet, saying, Behold my servant whom I have chosen; my beloved, in whom my soul was well pleased: I will put my spirit upon him, and he shall show judgment to the Gentiles. He shall not strive nor cry; neither shall any man hear his voice in the streets. A bruised reed shall he not break, and smoking flax shall he not quench, till he send forth judgment unto victory. And in his name shall the Gentiles trust" (Matth. xii, 15—21). This citation is made from Isaiah, (xlii, 1—4) with some difference, particularly the last sentence, "And in his name shall the Gentiles trust," which is an addition of the evangelist's. I confess, that considering the citation and what is said thereby to be fulfilled, I can not see the least resemblance, nor find the least connection to the matter intended; for how can the passage cited said to be fulfilled, either by the multitudes following Jesus, or by his healing them, or by his charging them not to make him known? I know that it is pretended "that by the secrecy which Jesus imposed on those he cured, (but for which we have only the evangelist's word) the passage is fulfilled, because it represents his quiet, humble, and meek temper."† To this I answer, that his imposing silence on those he cured, did not proceed from his quiet, humble, and meek disposition, but from altogether different motives; and for the truth of this I appeal to Dr. Echard himself,‡ to Mr. Locke§, and to many others, who assign other motives for his imposing secrecy; therefore this citation neither proves one thing nor the other to be thereby fulfilled.

11. Matthew's next citation is occasioned by Jesus' speaking in parables, that he might not be understood by the people he spoke to, lest otherwise they should understand him, and be by that means converted and healed, for though it is pretended that he came to save, yet, as St. John says, they were to have their eyes blinded, and their hearts hardened "that they should not see with their eyes, nor understand with their heart." (John xii, 40.) "Therefore (says Matthew xiii, 13, 14) speak I to them in parable; because seeing they see not, and hearing they hear not, neither do they understand. And in them is fulfilled the prophecy of Esaias, which saith, By hearing ye shall hear, and shall not understand, and seeing ye shall see, and shall not perceive." The prophet (Isaiah ii, 9 to the end) speaks in perfectly plain terms about the obstinacy of the people of his own time, consequently the passage has not the least relation to those who lived in the time of Jesus, and is therefore no literal fulfilling about it. Matthew makes yet another citation about Jesus' speaking in parables: "All these things (says he) spake Jesus unto the multitude in parable, and without a parable spake he not unto them."

Matthew xiii, 35.	Psalm lxxviii, 2, 3.
"That it might be fulfilled which was spoken by the prophet, saying, I will open my mouth in parables: I will utter things which have been kept secret from the foundation of the world."	"I will open my mouth in a parable; I will utter dark sayings of old which we have heard and known, and our fathers have told us."

You have in different columns the citation, and the place from which it is cited, by which it appears, that nothing is thereby fulfilled, neither does the psalm contain any thing which can be extended or made in any way applicable to a Messiah; besides this the evangelist has adulterated the text, and qualified it to his purpose, which, to say the least, is unfair. You will pardon here a short digression. Speaking in parables is not peculiar to Jesus, or the New Testament. The preachers and teachers of the Talmudical times very frequently illustrate their doctrines by parables, of which a very great number has reached us in the Talmudical writings. You may enjoy them by the dozens, every one as good and frequently superior to those related in the Gospels as proceeding from Jesus. Herder has collected and published some of them. I may possibly translate some for you if I have leisure, and you should desire to see any. The aphorisms and maxims of Jesus and Paul are also equalled and excelled by Jewish post-Biblical writers, many of whom lived before the time of Jesus.

12. The next prophecy, said by Matthew to be fulfilled by Jesus, concerns his entry into Jerusalem. It is also mentioned by the other three evangelists, who refer to the same prophecy cited from Zechariah (ix, 9), which Matthew (xxi, 5) quotes in the following words: "Tell ye the daughter of Zion, Behold, thy King cometh unto

†Echard's Eccles. Hist. vol. I, pages 96 and 97.
‡Ibid, 89—90.
§Reason. of Chris., vol. II p. 522.

thee, meek, and sitting upon an ass, and a colt, the foal of an ass." Now here the evangelist's ignorance of the Hebrew language leads him into a ridiculous blunder. Tautology, or repetition of the same idea in different words, is a peculiarity of Hebrew poetry, as you may notice in thousands of passages of the Bible. The writer of Matthew in his endeavor to prove Jesus the very Christ (Messiah) mistakes the tautological expression, "sitting upon an ass, even a colt, the foal of an ass" for a peculiar prophecy, and relates as a literal fulfillment, "the disciples went, and did as Jesus commanded them, and brought the ass and the colt, *and put on them their clothes, and they set him thereon.*" I think it is not of much importance to settle on what sort of a beast it was that Jesus made his triumphant entry into the capitol of Judea; you may, if you like, follow Matthew, and believe he sat both on the colt and the ass: or you may follow Mark and Luke who say it was on a colt; or if you prefer, let it be, with John, the ass alone. You may also believe this evangelist when he tells you that the beast was found by Jesus, and not sent for as the others. John makes a remark on this occasion from which you may draw your own inferences concerning this and other transactions related as having taken place; he says (John xii, 16): "These things understood not his disciples at the first: but when Jesus was glorified, *then remembered they that these things were written of him, and that they had done these things unto him.*" A person's riding upon an ass, or any other beast can never be a sure mark of a Messiah, because this would be within any pretender's power to fulfill. Moreover, the passage as it stands in Zechariah, describes the entry of Zerubbabel, is no prophecy of a future event, and can not be literally fulfilled, since Jesus was no king, neither was his appearance any matter of rejoicing to Jerusalem, as they pretend, for instead of the promised victory and defense, war and desolation followed.

13. The next citation made by Matthew, and said by him to be fulfilled, concerns Judas returning the thirty pieces of silver with which was bought the potter's field. "Then (says he) was fulfilled that which was spoken by Jeremy the prophet, saying, And they took the thirty pieces of silver, the price of him that was valued, whom they of the children of Israel did value, and gave them for the potter's field as the Lord appointed me." (Matth. xxvii, 3—10.) It happens somewhat unluckily, that the book of Jeremy does not contain this passage; neither is any such saying to be found in all the prophets. In Zechariah (xi, 13) there is a passage concerning thirty pieces of silver given to the prophet as a recompense when he asked the officers of the people for a reward in return for God's care of the nation, and which he, by God's command, returned to the treasurer (potter) of the temple. The commentators of the New Testament refer to this passage; but this is contrary to the thing intended by the evangelist, for he represents it as a prophecy foretold, which the passage in Zechariah is not, since it relates to us an act performed there and then. There is no such prophecy in the whole Bible, and therefore none can be said to be fulfilled.

14. The next citation, and the last contained in Matthew's Gospel (xxvii, 35) said by him to be fulfilled, is on the circumstance of dividing Jesus' vestments; "that it might be fulfilled which was spoken by the prophet, They parted my garments amongst them, and upon my vesture did they cast lots," alluding to one of the Psalms (xxii, 18) which, as plainly appears from its contents, seems to have been composed by David under the utmost affliction and distress, probably on his flight from Jerusalem during Absalom's rebellion. His expressions are adapted throughout his Psalms to the circumstances he was then in, describing at the same time his trust in God, and his prayer to be delivered. Therefore, to imagine that on such an occasion, he prophesied or foretold how the Roman soldiers were to divide Jesus' garments, appears not only very absurd, but quite foreign and trifling, and can not be made to answer any end at all; for surely none will place the proof of a Messiah on such a circumstance, as the Roman law gave the clothing worn by any person adjudged unto death to the executioner. Besides, the whole Psalm having relation to David himself, no part can by any circumstance be literally fulfilled.

LETTER VII.

Having in my two last letters examined all the quotations produced by the writer of the Gospel called Matthew's, and said by him to be fulfilled in Jesus, and found them not to be so in their plain, proper and literal sense, you will, I am sure, excuse my not doing the like by the other quotations in the remaining Gospels, as it would only be tedious; yet I can with truth assure you that, having carefully examined every one of them, they all appear to me such as either have no reference to any Messiah, and are torn from all connection in the chapters whence they are taken, or are qualified and adulterated to the writer's purpose. Paul in particular is guilty of the latter artifice in his epistles. This you will find, if you will go to the trouble of comparing the passages, said to be fulfilled, with their plain meaning in the Bible.

Being in an historical mood to-day let us sift the trial and execution of Jesus; for on account of the hatred and bloody persecutions which this part of the Gospel narrative has caused, it deserves the attention of every thinking mind.

As an historical fact only the execution of Christ by Pontius Pilate, under the reign of Tiberius, is established, as related by Tacitus, and cited to you in a former letter.* On examining the accounts of the Evangelists, we arrive at this result: *That it was the Romans alone who, for political reasons, executed Jesus, because he presented himself as the Messiah among the Jews.* If we strike from the Gospels the account of the trial of Jesus before the Sanhedrin, and of the influence of the Jewish people upon his execution, all connection and natural course of the events is restored, and the contradictions are removed. This assertion is fully proven by the following *facts:*

Crucifixion was no Jewish death penalty, either according to Biblical or Talmudical law. *It did not exist at all among the Jews,* and considering the tenacity with which the Jews adhered to their law, no Jewish tribunal could pronounce the punishment of crucifixion, nor have it carried into execution. The Jewish lawful manners of executing criminals were by the sword, by stoning, and by strangulation; and the sufferings of the death penalty—being only inflicted, in the language of the Bible, "to put away the evil from amongst you, and not for revenge and torture"—were mitigated by administering to the culprit a soporific medicine, a humane provision which even our much boasted modern civilization lacks.

On the contrary, crucifixion was in use among the Greeks; and the Roman law provided crucifixion as the greatest punishment for the crime of *perduellio,* which comprised all offenses against the peace and security of the commonwealth, such as treason, rebellion, conspiracy, usurpation of political power and authority, &c., (*Pauli,* sent. rec. lib. V. tit. 17 §3. *Summa supplicia sunt cruce, &c.*) Even at a later period, when the term *crimen majestatis* was used in law for all political offenses, the crime of *perduellio* was still retained as distinct from the whole class. (l. ii, D. xlviii, 4.) To perfect the crime it was not a necessary condition that an overt act should have been committed; mere treasonable language, disclosing the intention of the person, was sufficient to render him guilty of the crime. (*Pauli,* sent. lib. C., tit. 19 §1; lib. IV., §1, 10 D. l. 7 §3; D. 48, 4; l. 11 cit: *Hostili animo adversus rem publicam vel principem animatus.*) Whoever was found guilty of *perduellio* was bound, scourged, and hanged (crucified) with his head covered. It was of this crime of *perduellio* of which Jesus was tried and convicted before Pilate, and for which he was crucified according to the Roman law. While in Rome certain officers—the *duumvari, quaestores, &c.*—superintended executions, this task was committed in the provinces to a *centurio;* the execution itself was performed by a *speculator,* (Sen. *deira* i, 16, Dion. lviii, 14, l. 6, D. 48, 20) or by assistants—*optiones*—such as soldiers, &c., chosen by the *centurio* (l. 6, cit. Varro, L. L. v, 16). We find the *centurio* and his soldier assistants at the execution of Jesus; the *speculator* is mentioned in Mark vi, 27. The garments with which a culprit was clothed when he was carried to his execution—*spolia*—could be kept by the executioner, whereas all other effects that he had with him—*paunicularia*—were either delivered to the *fiscus,* or employed by the *praeses* for other purposes. Lastly, the

*I use here Philippson's "Crucifixion and the Jews."

body of an executed criminal was delivered to his relatives, or to any other person that demanded it. (Dig. 48, 24 *de cadav. punit.*)

From these particulars you will see that the mode and manner of the execution of Jesus was in full keeping with Roman law and usage. We are further told by the Evangelists, that after his condemnation by Pilate, the Roman soldiers put on him a scarlet or purple robe, placed a crown of thorns on his head, and a reed in his right hand, bowed the knee before him, and mocked him, saying: "Hail, King of the Jews!" But when they had crucified him they "set up over his head his accusation, written, "This is Jesus, the King of the Jews." (Matth. xxvii, 27—37; Mark xv, 16—20; Luke xxiii, 38; John xix, 2.) According to John (xix, 19) Pilate himself "wrote a title and put it on the cross, and the writing was, Jesus of Nazareth, the King of the Jews." The Jews demurred to this inscription, but "that he had said, I am King of the Jews", whereupon Pilate answered, "What I have written, I have written." What conclusion can we derive from all this? Undoubtedly no other than that the Romans, with Pilate at their head, executed Jesus as a political offender against the Roman rule. They crucified him as "King of the Jews:" they mocked him as such by a purple robe, by a crown and a sceptre; they thus gave vent to their hatred, not alone against Jesus, but also against the Jewish people. Nay, the inscription composed by Pilate himself, and the obstinacy with which he insisted upon it, clearly show that Pilate thereby intended to represent the Jews as accomplices in the political crime; whereas they desired every allusion to their complicity removed. (Pilate attempted the same thing before, and the Jews demurred to it. [John xix, 14, 15.])

But it might be asked, was there sufficient reason to induce Pilate to regard Jesus as a king, and was he the man capable of ordering an execution on that accusation?

For three years and a half, as the scanty fragmentary Gospel narratives inform us, *Jesus traveled about in Galilee, teaching without serious interruption from the Jews;* he did and said all he pleased, without being actually persecuted by them. On the contrary, he found many adherents among the people, (so they relate) and those that were hostile to him only sought to render him suspicious before the people by putting captious questions to him. He goes to Judea. He approaches Jerusalem completely undisturbed; he enters the city in solemn procession. Great multitudes come to meet him, spread their garments in the way, &c.; the whole city is thrown into commotion and pay him homage. He goes into the Temple and drives out all who sold objects of sacrifices, money changers, and venders of doves. He harangues the multitude, chastises the Scribes and Pharisees, and encourages the people to proclaim him king, in opposition to the warning words of some Pharisees (Luke xix, 39, 40). The people believe him, "for," says Luke (xix, 48), "all the people were very attentive to hear him," and although "the chief priests, and the scribes, and the chiefs of the people sought to destroy him, yet they feared the people;" they did not therefore venture to touch him (Luke xix, 47, 48; xx, 19). Considering the manner of his conduct in general, the proclamations and opinions of his disciples and followers (Luke xix, 39; Acts i, 6), his entrance into Jerusalem, (whatever opinion [*cum grano salis*] we may entertain of the *related particulars*) the commotion and excitement of the people, it was but a natural consequence that the Roman procurator or governor interfered, secured the person of Jesus, and condemned him on his own confession. (Matth. xxvii, 11; Mark xv, 2; Luke xxiii, 3; John xviii, 37.) A trial before the Sanhedrin was by no means required to bring about such an issue.

I need not relate to you, who are acquainted with history, all the events that preceded the administration of Pilate as governor of Judea; you may read the full particulars in Josephus; suffice it to say that the Jews endured the Roman yoke with reluctance. They were extremely irritated and sensitive, ready for revolt and resistance. Pilate himself had, from the beginning of his appointment, refused to spare the feelings of the Jews, nurtured their indignation, and, ever on the alert for new pretexts for interference, was at any moment ready to use the sword against them and cut them down. (How much his right, according to Roman law, to dispose of the effects of the executed rebels, had to do with this, you may judge for yourself.) Speaking of an event, not at all connected with our subject, Philo gives us a description of his character. "Pilate," he tells us, "was by nature inflexible and cruel, as well as relentless." *Legat. ad Caj.*) Among other acts of violence, Pilate seized the Temple treasure, under the pretext to use it for the construction of an aqueduct. The people assembled and raised a loud clamor; Pilate sent a large number of soldiers, dressed in Jewish garments, with clubs concealed beneath, and these ferociously fell upon the complaining populace, and slew a large number. "This atrocity," says Josephus, "brought the Jews to silence." (Antiqu. xviii, 3 §2; Jew. W. ii, 9 §2.) Among the Samaritans a great commotion was stirred up by an impostor who induced them to dig after some sacred vessels which, as he stated, had been buried by Moses on Mount Gerizzim. Pilate anticipated them, stationed troops, horse and foot, on the road to the mountain. These cut down a portion, dispersed others, and made many prisoners, of whom Pilate had the most distinguished put to death. This massacre afforded the cause for his dismissal. The Samaritans proved to Vitellius, the governor of Syria, that they had no intention to rebel against the Romans, and he at once ordered Pilate to repair to Rome to defend himself against the charges made against him by the Jews. (Antiq. xviii, 4, §1.) To these actions the conduct of Pilate, as described by John on the occasion of the inscription above the cross, agrees very well.

For a man of such a character, suspicion and a popular commotion already commenced were a sufficient pretext for ordering the execution of a man accused of seeking to usurp the rule over the people; and, indeed, the Roman governors were very watchful of every attempt to claim the Messiahship among the Jews. Wherever and whenever such an attempt was made, they suppressed it with relentless rigor. Thus, a certain *Theudas* represented himself, in the year 46, as the Messiah, and with four hundred followers went to the banks of the Jordan which he had promised to divide; but the Roman governor *Fadus* sent a troop of cavalry after them. They beheaded Theudas, and killed his adherents. (Jos. Antiq. xx, 5, §1.) During the administration of Felix, an Egyptian Jew called upon the people to go with him upon the Mount of Olives, where he would show them how, upon his command, the walls of Jerusalem would fall down. Felix ordered his troops to attack the people; four hundred were cut down, but the Egyptian escaped. (Antiq. xx, 8, 6.) Thus, there was sufficient pretext for Pilate, as shown from his character, and the tendency of the Roman rule in general, to condemn and execute Jesus for political reasons.

On the other hand the Evangelists relate very fully (though with a wide difference) the repeated efforts of Pilate to save Jesus, and the persistent demands of the Jews for his execution.

However changeable the temperament of a populace may be in general, does it seem probable that the same people that a day before had received Jesus with a festive procession and paid him the highest homage; that gave him the power to act the part of a master in the Temple, does it seem likely that these same people on the day following clamor for the blood of Jesus, refuse all requests, repudiate all compassion, prefer the release of a notable robber, and even invoke the curse upon their own heads and the heads of their children? Still greater is the contradiction, that Pilate, who, as we have seen, was inflexible, cruel and relentless, even in matters of little account, who hated and despised the Jewish people, and most cruelly treated them on every occasion, who punished and suppressed with the severest atrocity every popular commotion and riot, all at once appears as the weakest coward, and delivers a man, whom he publicly declares innocent and whom he makes every exertion to save, to his soldiers for the most atrocious indignities and the most agonizing execution, simply because the congregated rabble clamored for his death. Nay, if Pilate had indeed been such a contemptible coward, how could he have *thus* compromised the dignity of his office, the authority of the Roman rule? If he would, indeed, yield to the populace from fear, must he not at least have saved the appearance, so that he did not make the weakness of his own power, and that of the Romans, still more manifest by his repeated attempts to change the determination of the multitude, and his frequent protestations of the innocence of Jesus? He thus appears not only as the most miserable coward who from fear makes himself the executioner of an innocent man, but also as the most contemptible representative of the Roman power. Had Pilate met the Jewish people with vigorous resistance to avoid the charge of weakness, he would undoubtedly have been justified by the Roman authorities, even on the accusation of having spared the life of a rebel. But what are the historical facts? Was he not, shortly after the execution of Jesus, accused of precisely the reverse, of relentless severity against the Jews, and for that reason sent to Rome by Vitellius, who acted with indulgence and consideration for the Jews? (Jos. Ant. xviii, 4, 3.)

We find here what generally happens—men go too far in their zeal to strengthen the belief in a cause, and thus refute it themselves.

As it became more and more evident in the course of the development of Christianity, that the Jews could not be won for it, that the Graeco-Roman world was the proper field for its propagation, the manipulators of the Gospels sought to represent the execution through the Roman governor in a way as to clear him as much as possible, and to heap all of it on the Jews. It was of vital importance for the preachers to controvert the belief that Jesus had been executed by Roman authorities as a political offender and public enemy; they had to present it, on the contrary, as a false insinuation by the Jews, and to show that the Roman judge was fully convinced of the innocence of the accused, but was forced to yield to the obstinate clamors of the Jews. The more the attempts of the Romans to save Jesus were prolonged, the more innocent did *they* appear, and the more guilty the Jews. Dreams, washing of hands, imprecations were invented to emphasize the innocence of the Romans and the guilt of the Jews. But the narrators did not see that, while they made themselves more credible in the eyes of those who *wanted* to find the Jews guilty, they entangled themselves in contradictions which rendered the fiction evident and their motives manifest to all who will and can see clearly. Who, then, will hesitate to erase this whole scene from history

LETTER VIII.

A trial of Jesus before the Sanhedrin,* as fictitiously related by the Evangelists, never took place. Such a proceeding, and the demand of his death by the Jewish people, lack every historical authority, and even the circumstances of historical credibility.

1. First of all, such a trial, with a sentence of death resulting therefrom on account of *religious opinions*, is without parallel in the history of the Jews, and it can not be shown the Jewish Sanhedrin thus made themselves judges of faith. The divers religious views of the then existing parties, of the Pharisees, Sadducees, and Essenes, and their manifold branches, the ofttimes diametrically opposed interpretations of the academies of Shamai and Hillel had produced such a spirit of toleration in matters of creed, that it ended only at a point where flagrant violations of the law commenced. Especially the Messianic idea, however powerfully it moved the popular heart, never caused judicial proceedings, and the men who presented themselves as Messiahs were never persecuted by the Jewish authorities, but always by the Roman governors, as the examples cited in my last letter. Even the (*ex parte*) history of the Apostles furnish a proof for this statement. The Acts (v, 34) relate that, when Peter and John were made prisoners and brought before the Sanhedrin on account of their addresses to the people, the court released them upon the protest of Gamaliel, that religious opinions must not be made the subject of judicial cognizance and decision, but be left to the judgment of God. Compare also the account of the condemnation of James in Josephus. (Antiq. xx, 9, 1.)

2. The Gospel, according to John, knows nothing at all of the judicial proceedings, of the examination of witnesses, of the interrogatories put to the accused and his condemnation, of all of which the other Evangelists present such a full account. After having related (xi, 47) that the high

* Sanhedrin (Gr. Synhedrion) were the Jewish Supreme Court, composed of seventy scholars from the people. They were admitted to power by Prince Hyrcanus, during the long struggle between the Zadokites (Gr. Sadducees) or Priest-Nobility, and the purely Jewish people that had separated themselves from the mixed multitude and Samaritans, and were therefore called Pharisees (Separationists). (Comp. Geiger's Hist. of Judaism.)

priests and Pharisees had first counseled together to put Jesus to death, it gives an account of the arrest of Jesus (xviii), tells us that Jesus was at first led to Annas, the former high priest, who asked him "of his disciples and of his doctrines," whereupon Jesus pointed to the fact that he had openly taught in the synagogue and in the temple; hereupon Jesus was brought before Caiaphas who sent him before Pilate. With the exception of the account of Peter's denial of Christ, this is all that John narrates until his appearance before Pilate; hence there is not the least trace to be found in his Gospel of a judicial proceeding before the Sanhedrin. If the other three Gospels did not exist, we could derive no other conclusion from John than this, that a number of Pharisees, in connection with the high priest, had secretly conspired against Jesus, and then delivered him up to the Roman Governor. His silence on such an important act is of the greatest weight in an examination of the life and death of Jesus, and must essentially strengthen our doubts of the real occurrence of the facts related. This silence of John justifies our assumption that the accounts given by the other Gospels are but embellishments without any historic value whatever.

3. The accounts contain a number of contradictions in themselves, with each other, and with the Jewish law. Even the arrest of Jesus presents some doubts. The band commissioned with his execution is said to have consisted of servants of the high priest and the Sanhedrin, and, nevertheless, to have found it necessary to employ a traitor, not alone to designate the place where Jesus had spent the night, but also to point him out among his disciples. According to the three Evangelists, Judas kissed Jesus to give them a sign: "Whomsoever I shall kiss that same is he; hold him fast." According to John, Jesus went to meet them, and asked them: "Whom seek ye?" And when they assured him by calling out his name, he continued: "I am he;" whereupon they repeatedly "fell to the ground." Can it be imagined that the servants and messengers of the priests and Sanhedrin should not have known the man whose preaching in the Temple and whose public acts and appearance before the eyes of the people had created such great commotion? Is it possible that there was not even one among all the servants of the High Court of the Jews who should have known him, so that a paid traitor and such special proceedings were required to effect his arrest? These questions become the more emphatic and important when we consider that, but a little after, two maid servants of the house of the high priest recognized Peter as one of Jesus' disciples, and designated him as such in spite of his repeated denial. If the disciple of Jesus was thus generally known as such, how can it be possible that his master was not equally generally known? This contradiction vanishes when we recognize the band who arrested him, not as servants of the Jewish authorities, but as Roman soldiers, who, indeed, required a Jewish guide, as whom the traitor Judas presented himself. And John actually designates them as (Roman) soldiers (xviii, 3): "Judas then received the band of men and officers from the chief priests and Pharisees," and verse 12: "Then the band and the captain, and officers of the Jews took Jesus." Thus, then, the captain and the band were Roman soldiers (there were no Jewish troops at that time) who were accompanied by several Jewish officials, so that the arrest of Jesus was an act of the Roman Governor, and not of the Jewish court. The mention of *high priests*—in the plural number—is in conflict with the Jewish institutions. Matthew (xxvii, 1) speaks even of "all" the high priests. John repeatedly speaks of the high priest of "that same year;" for instance, xviii, 13, he says: "who was the high priest that same year," as though there had been an annual rotation in the office of the high priest, whereas the tenure was generally during life, and Caiaphas held that office without interruption during the whole administration of Pilate, that is to say, ten years. These expressions show a great ignorance of the Jewish institutions which, it is easy to explain, existed a century after the discontinuation of that office.

But the greatest objections grow out of the dates given, the variety of which creates various doubts when compared with the customs and laws of the Jews. All four Evangelists state that the resurrection of Jesus took place on a Sunday, and that his body rested in the grave on the Sabbath (Saturday) preceding; but how do they represent all the rest? In the first consultation, the Sanhedrin are said to have agreed not to proceed against Jesus "on a feast day, lest there be an uproar among the people." (Mat. xxvi, 5, Mark xiv, 2.) Did they thus seek to avoid all commotion of the people, or did they fear the people might rebel against them, for a violation by them of a solemn feast? And should they have, nevertheless, proceeded against Jesus on the feast day, and thus stirred up a commotion of the people? Matthew (xxvi, 17) relates that the Passover meal was prepared for Jesus "on the first day of the feast of unleavened bread;" that he celebrated it "when the even was come;" that in the night he was arrested, tried, and sentenced; that in the morning he was carried before Pilate and executed, and in the evening laid into the grave. In this account there is a double inconsistency: first, that the day preceding the feast is called "the first of the feast of unleavened bread;" and second that his trial and condemnation took place on the first day of Passover, which is in conflict with the Jewish law (*Mishnah, Sanhedrin*, 32): "Whenever a man was tried for his life, a verdict of not guilty could be pronounced on the same day; but if he was to be condemned, the decision had to be postponed until the day after. For this reason such a case could not be tried on the eve of Sabbath, or of a festival. A criminal case could never be decided at night."

Mark (xv, 42) and Luke (xxiii, 54) state that the trial and execution took place on the day of preparation for the Sabbath, viz: Friday, which was also the first day of Passover, being the day after the preparation for that feast. (xxii, 7.) Luke relates further, that on the same day women prepared spices and ointments for the corpse to use them on Sunday, and that they "rested on the Sabbath day, according to to the commandment" (56). The inconsistencies of all these proceedings on the feast of Passover, which was celebrated with great distinction, are thus increased by another, to-wit: that the women prepared ointments on a feast day in violation of the law, whereas they observed the Sabbath conscientiously. John does not at all agree with the three other Evangelists. John dates the last supper on the evening before the preparation day for Passover (xiii, 1 and 29) the arrest, trial and execution on the preparation day (xviii, 28, xix, 31), or the day before the feast, so that the first day of Passover occurred on the Sabbath. Thus the supper loses the character of a Passover meal on which the other three Evangelists tenaciously insist; and hence another contradiction is presented: the latter give a full narrative of the Passover supper at the house of a man in the city; whereas, according to the account of John, who makes the last supper an ordinary meal, with the washing of feet preceding it, the Passover meal did not take place at all.*

But this is not all yet. The Passover was and is in latitude and climate of Palestine the beginning of harvest and during the warm season. Mark (xiv, 67), Luke (xxii, 55, 56), and John (xviii, 25), say, that Peter went to warm himself by the fire, which circumstance points the time of Jesus' execution to have been winter. I am of the opinion that this was the case, and that Paul who founded Christianity on allegory, and made the facts to conform to his preaching, after allegorizing Jesus into the Passover lamb of the Gentiles, transferred the season of the execution from winter to the Passover feast, to which change the Gospel writers of course conformed. Hence all the contradictions.

* Please notice the marks of development of Christianity and its rites in the words which each Evangelist records as spoken by Jesus at the last supper. Mark (xiv, 24, 25) makes him say: "This is my blood of the New Testament which is shed for many. Verily I say unto you I will drink no more of the fruit of the vine, until that day I drink it new in the kingdom of God," which expresses plainly the hopes and ideas then prevalent of a sudden catastrophe (end of the world) inaugurating a millennial state, or the kingdom of God, and has no trace of the communion table. Matthew (xxvi, 26, 29) adds "the remission of sins," and says "my Father's kingdom" after the Passover-sacrifice-idea and the divine sonship had been adopted. Luke (xxii, 15-20), writing still later, adds: "this do in remembrance of me," to authorize the last supper which—grown out of the *Agapae* or love feasts which in their turn had arisen out of the social gatherings at the sacrifices, and had supplanted them—had become a fixed ceremony at the Christian Worship.

LETTER IX.

Moses and the prophets are in several instances appealed to in the Gospels as testifying of Jesus as the Christ; but only one passage from the books of Moses is brought forward to support this assertion. It is in Acts (iii, 22) from Deuteronomy (xviii, 15): "I will raise them up a prophet from among their brethren, like unto thee, and will put my words into his mouth, and he shall speak unto them all that I shall command him." From these words Dr. Leland* concludes that "Moses tells the people that God would raise up from among them a prophet like unto him; that is, not an ordinary prophet, but one of peculiar eminence, that should like Moses give them laws in the name of God Himself, and to whom they were indispensably obliged to hearken and to pay an entire obedience." Had this learned divine pointed out the particulars by which Jesus distinguished himself to be this eminent person, prophet and lawgiver like Moses, he had done something to the purpose; and then we should be enabled to judge of their exact correspondence and likeness. This he has not done; but this is what I shall now examine, and as we have the principal actions of both on record, it is not difficult to make the comparison.

Moses discovers his commission to those to whom he was sent; in confirmation of his assertions he works sundry miracles. and at last happily executes his promise in delivering the Israelites from the Egyptian bondage. Then it was, and not until then, that the people were convinced that he was a person sent from God for that purpose. It was his performing this essential part of his commission and promise that wrought in them this belief. "Thus the Lord saved Israel that day out of the hand of the Egyptians; and Israel saw the Egyptians dead upon the sea shore; and Israel saw that great work which the Lord did upon the Egyptians, and the people feared the Lord, and believed in the Lord, and Moses His servant." (Exod. xiv, 30, 31.) Now has Moses failed in the essential part of his commission, could or would any of his miracles, however stupendous, have proved him to have been sent from God with such a commission? Certainly not. And as it was absolutely necessary to produce conviction that Moses should accomplish the delivery of the Israelites according to his promise: So it would be necessary that a Messiah should perform those things which are foretold concerning him; the prophecies being, as even the Evangelists by their reference to them prove, the test, or touchstone, by which alone we could judge, if he were the person therein described or not. The most stupendous wonders and splendid miracles would not, in this case, afford any proof of his character, because it has no dependence on them. It must stand or fall, according as his actions would agree, or disagree, with the prophecies, or as he did, or did not fulfill them.

*Divine Authority, vol. I, p. 100.

If Jesus' pretensions were true, he ought to have performed and done those things which were foretold, and in so doing, have given an undeniable proof. This would have convinced the people that he was the promised person, beyond all objections, and he would then have acted consistently. I will here transcribe a few of those prophecies.

1. "And I will gather the remnant of my flock out of all countries whither I have driven them and will bring them again to their folds, and they shall be fruitful and increase. And I will set up shepherds over them who shall feed them; and they shall fear no more nor be dismayed; neither shall they be lacking, saith the Lord. Behold, the days come, saith the Lord, that I will raise unto David a righteous branch, *and a king shall reign and prosper, and shall execute judgment and justice in the earth.* In his day Judah shall be saved, and Israel shall dwell safely; and this is his name whereby he shall be called, THE LORD OUR RIGHTEOUSNESS. Therefore, behold, the days come, saith the Lord, that they shall no more say the Lord liveth which brought up the children of Israel out of the land of Egypt; but the Lord liveth which brought up and which led the seed of the house of Israel out of the north country, and from all countries wherein I have driven them; and they shall dwell in their own land." (Jer. xxiii, 3—8.)

2. "And I will make with them a covenant of peace, and will cause the evil beasts to cease out of the land, and they shall dwell safely in the wilderness, and sleep in the woods. And I will make them, and the places round about my hill, a blessing; and I will cause the shower to come down in its season; there shall be showers of blessing. And the tree of the field shall yield her fruit, and the earth shall yield her increase, and they shall be safe in their land, and shall know that I am the Lord, when I have broken the bands of their yoke, and delivered them out of the hand

of those that served themselves of them." (Ezek. xxxiv, 24, &c.)

I will not tire you with any more, as you can find them easily in the prophets. Had Jesus fulfilled any of these prophecies, he would then have proved himself to be the Messiah, or person meant by that designation. How it came to pass that he did not prove himself by doing so, is not my business to inquire; that he did not is very evident. The names of Judah or Israel can not be usurped here for the church; nor can the plain term, "A king shall reign and prosper, and shall execute judgment and justice IN THE EARTH," be applied to a pretended establishment of a kingdom in heaven. How could Jesus be the king "in whose days shall Judah be saved and Israel dwell safely," when the very reverse happened in his time?

Here, then, we have a very material difference between Moses and a Messiah: The one had no character or description to answer, the other has. But it is plain that Jesus did not answer it; and in order to show that Jesus was not the prophet like Moses, let us make a short comparison. Moses was prepared by God with a sign when the Israelites should demand it; but Jesus constantly refused any sign. (Mat. xii, 39.) Moses did mighty wonders, and wrought such stupendous miracles, as convinced those that beheld them; these he did not do after the manner of jugglers, before chosen witnesses, or in corners, but in public, and in the presence of all the people whom he assembled for that purpose; he performed them in the presence of his very opponents, who were sometimes made to feel the truth and the effects of them. The magicians who endeavored to rival him confessed that it was the hand of God. Thus acted Moses. But Jesus took quite a different method; those miracles which are related of him were wrought in secret, performed before chosen witnesses, and on believers only, in corners and by-places; the very persons who partook of the benefits were hindered from mentioning them and were enjoined secrecy; his very brethren and relations disbelieved them. (Mat. xiii, 54.) The difference is manifest; for one convinced his enemies and rivals, the other could not even convince his brethren and nearest relatives. The more Moses' opponents doubted or denied his commission or power, the greater and more surprising were the proofs he gave them. But Jesus did the very reverse: "For he did not many mighty works there, because of their unbelief." (Mat. xiv, 58.) Had he acted like Moses, he ought to have performed other great wonders; for the greater their unbelief, the greater ought his miracles to have been, and the greater would the honor have been of their conviction. Moses was greatly honored and esteemed by his brethren and countrymen; but Jesus was quite the contrary, he declares himself that no prophet is accepted in his own country. (Luke iv, 24.) Moses delivered the Israelites from the Egyptian bondage; did Jesus deliver the Jews from the power and yoke of the Romans? He indeed promised to "gather them as a hen did her brood," (Luke xiv, 34,) but this he never performed, though he knew this to be the chief part of the Messiah's character, and the desire and hope of the nation; yet he pretends to excuse himself by saying "they would not," when the contrary is really true.

Moses was forty days and forty nights with God on the mount; but of Jesus it is declared that he was in the wilderness as many days and nights with very different company, detained contrary to his will, famished, tossed and led about by the devil who must have been very superior in power to him, or he could not have used him so disrespectfully. Moses governed the Israelites forty years; did Jesus do the like or had he any command, post, or dignity?

Moses solemnly prepared the people, and appointed a time for the whole body of the nation to gather themselves in one place, to the end that they all might receive the law; did Jesus do the like? Moses delivered to the Israelites a system of laws, moral and political, by which they were to be governed; did Jesus do any thing like this?

I know it is pretended that he introduced a new dispensation; but this is very far from being clear, and I should be glad to be informed which of his laws (I mean those that are practicable) are new and not commanded or known before; there is not one to be found in the Evangelists, as I shall very clearly prove to you. Now if this be the case, how can he be made to answer the description "of his giving laws like Moses in the name of God Himself."

Moses published his laws in the most authentic manner; they were attested by God Himself; were those of Jesus published or attested in like manner? Moses took the people's express consent, who bound themselves and posterity, to observe and obey; did Jesus do any thing like it? In short, Moses proved himself to the satisfaction of all that he was a person sent by God; Jesus did not. From these, and many other instances, I think that it is very evident and clear that a more opposite character to that of Moses can not be produced either in their lives or deaths. If even, therefore, we suppose what is pretended that a person was promised who should be like Moses, and like him give laws; yet Jesus could never have been that person; for this passage can never be consistently applied to him. On the other hand the succeeding verses show evidently and plainly that Moses promised a succession of prophets.

Deut. xviii, 18-22: "I will raise them up a prophet from among their brethren, like unto thee, and will put my words in his mouth; and he shall speak unto them all that I shall command him. And it shall come to pass that whosoever will not hearken unto my words which he speak in my name, I will require it of him. But the prophet which shall presume to speak a word in my name which I have not commanded him to speak, or that shall speak in the name of other gods, even that prophet shall die. And if thou say in thine heart, How shall we know the word which the Lord has not spoken? When a prophet speaketh in the name of the Lord, if the thing follow not, nor come to pass, that is the thing which the Lord has not spoken, but the prophet has spoken it presumptuously: thou shalt not be afraid of him." The passage explains its own meaning. Joshua was the first of these prophets, as appears from the promise of God: "As I was with Moses, so will I be with thee; I will not fail thee, nor forsake thee," (Josh. i, 5,) and other passages in the book of Joshua (iii, 7; iv, 14, &c.); from which you will see that Joshua succeeded Moses as a prophet, director and governor; that God revealed and spoke to him in like manner as he did to Moses, in whose place he was appointed, that he was obeyed and feared in like manner as Moses was, all the days of his life; and to think otherwise, or to imagine that Jesus is meant here, is in every respect inconsistent and absurd, he being the most unlike the person promised, as is evident from all the circumstances of his life.

LETTER X.

Not being able to establish the inspiration of the Gospel, and the Messiahship of Jesus from the primary sense and plain literal meaning of Holy Writ, Paul and the Christian writers since his time obviate all difficulties at one stroke by pretending that none of the prophecies ought to be taken in their plain literal meaning; in other words, they will not allow the prophecies and perfectly plain passages to have any meaning at all, in order to impose on all such prophecies, and even on many historical passages of Scripture, what they call a spiritual, or figurative and typical sense and meaning of their own, such as best suits their purposes, accommodating by this means, as I have already shown, passages to events with which they have not the least connection, and even contrary to the express meaning of the verses cited. Besides this way of forcibly tearing their citations from all connection with the context in the books whence they are taken, adulteration of the passages is frequently employed by Paul, as anybody can see if he will be at the trouble of comparing his quotations with the original passages. But their principal engine is allegory and the typical scheme. Calmet explains allegory very properly when he says, "Allegory is a figure in discourse which we are then said to use, when we make the terms which are peculiar to one thing to signify another." This being the case, can allegory or type prove anything? And what may not be proved when terms and words peculiar to one thing are made to signify another? Can we suppose that the Almighty God of truth and eternity should, in an affair of the utmost importance, (an affair that concerns both learned and ignorant,) deliver Himself in such terms or words as must introduce into our minds ideas the most opposite and contrary to what His goodness intended to reveal and describe? Are we acting rationally and piously to think that the good and merciful God, condescending to instruct and enlighten, would give to His creatures instructions, commands, advice, and promises, which were puzzling, obscure, and uncertain, when the eternal happiness of their spirits was depending upon their conceiving and applying them aright. Can anything more unjust be imputed to God than to pretend He reveals one thing and means another? Yet this is precisely what they try to prove! Learning, art, cunning, industry, power, and every human invention is made use of for this purpose, to reject and set aside the words which, as coming from God, are infallible, and to pass off their own explanation in their place, as if they themselves were neither fallible nor interested, or were not liable to error, deception and imposition.

One invention, very much in favor with them, and used whenever it suits them, is to take and usurp the names by which the Jews are always meant,* and they boldly apply the name of Judah and Israel to themselves, as the following passage from "Divine Authority," vol. 1, page 162, very plainly admits:

"Whereas the Messiah's kingdom seems sometimes to be described with a particular regard to the Jews, and it is foretold that he should reign over them as their prince and shepherd, and that in his days Israel and Judah shall dwell safely, and in a happy state; there are two things which will entirely take off the advantage; the one is that the terms Israel and Judah and the house of Israel are not to be understood in the prophets, as precisely of the seed of Jacob, literally so called, or of the Jewish people and nation, but are sometimes designed for the church in general."

Here, then, by a dash of the pen, you have the Jews stripped of their name and the advantages of the promises made to them; and both the one and the other transferred to the church in general. Whenever they stand in need of it for their purpose, why, then they make use of it; but their turn being served, they very willingly part with it, and generally restore it to the right owner; for whenever the prophet reproves the people for their misdeeds, or whenever there is any calamity foretold, or punishment threatened to Judah or Israel, then the Jews are thereby meant; and upon such an occasion they are the literal seed of Jacob, and they will most certainly find it fulfilled and accomplished. But whenever they find any promises of good things, or happy days, then the Jews, or the literal seed of Jacob, have nothing to do with it; for the advantage of their name must be taken from them, and such things only belong to the Christian church, that is, to the mysterious seed of Jacob. Thus absurdly do they reason and make Scripture a too-edged sword to cut which ever way they please. Should not a reason be given why the literal sense should be applied at one time, and a different one at another? Particularly as by this rule they pretend "that the prophets intimated clear enough that a new dispensation was to be introduced, and a new covenant, different from that which God made with their fathers." (Div. Auth. 1, p. 101.) To prove this they refer to the following passage of Jeremiah (xxxi, 31 to the end): "Behold, the days come saith the Lord that I will make a new covenant with the house of Israel, and with the house of Judah: Not according to the covenant that I made with their fathers, in the day that I took them by the hand to bring them out of the land of Egypt, which my covenant (*b'rith*) they brake, although I was a husband unto them, saith the Lord. But this shall be the covenant that I will make with the house of Israel. After those days, saith the Lord, I will put my law (*Torah*†) in their inward parts, and write it in their hearts, and will be their God, and they shall be my people. And they shall teach no more every man his neighbor, and every man his brother, saying: Know the LORD; for they shall all know me from the least of them unto the greatest of them, saith the LORD; for I will forgive their iniquity, and I will remember their sin no more. Thus saith the LORD, which giveth the sun for a light by day, and the ordinances of the moon and of the stars for a light by night, which divideth the sea when the waves

*They even place these claims as headings into the Bible translations, contrary to the original text which has no headings to the chapters.

†*B'rith* is covenant, agreement; *Torah* is law, doctrine, religious knowledge.

thereof roar, the LORD of Hosts is His name: If those ordinances depart from me, saith the LORD, then the seed of Israel also shall cease from being a nation before me forever. Thus saith the LORD, If heaven above can be measured, and the foundations of the earth searched out beneath, I will also cast off all the seed of Israel for all that they have done, saith the LORD. Behold the days come, saith the LORD, that the city shall be built to the LORD from the tower of Hananeel unto the gate of the corner. And the measuring line shall yet go forth over against it, upon the hill Gareb, and shall compass about to Goath. And the whole valley of the dead bodies, and of the ashes and all the fields unto the brook Kidron, unto the corner of the horse-gate toward the East, shall be holy unto the Lord; it shall not be plucked up, nor thrown down any more for ever."

Now from this prophecy it plainly appears that God was to make a new covenant or agreement with the houses of Israel and Judah, or the Jewish nation, which covenant should not be broken like that made with their fathers to whom free choice had been left to live up to it, or not. But this covenant of agreement should be that the people should know and do the Lord's will and law as if by instinct (signified by His writing it on their hearts, &c.): and God, on His part, was to forgive and forget their iniquity and sin, was to restore and preserve them, and cause their city to be rebuilt, never more to be destroyed. This, in a few words, are the contents of the promised covenant, according to the clear sense and obvious meaning of the prophet, conformable and agreeable to the repeated promise made to the nation by all the prophets. The plain meaning of this prophecy, and the peculiar terms in which it is delivered, ought, one would think, to deter people from practicing their arts and imposing meanings, so different from, and so entirely contradictory to that of the prophet. He has entered into a particular description of the people who were to be parties or partakers of the new covenant; and he has also particularized and declared, not only its contents, but likewise in what it was to differ from the former one. Thus it plainly appears that God would enter into a new covenant with the Jews; but that a new law, or a new dispensation, was to be introduced, has no manner of foundation. That the new covenant was to be different from that which their fathers entered into is likewise plain and evident. But what has that to do with a new dispensation which as pretended was to be introduced? Does not the prophet declare in what the difference was to consist? The former covenant was conditional; by it the nation's happiness and welfare were made to depend entirely on the observance of that which they stipulated; and as they frequently failed and broke the conditions, they, in consequence, often received punishment. But the new covenant was to be formed upon an entirely new plan; by it the nation's happiness was to be permanent, lasting, unconditional; for they were to have such knowledge of God and His will, from the least to the greatest, as to insure duty and fidelity ever after, and this in such a manner that though all nations failed, yet the Jews should never be cast off, or cease to be a nation, for the same Almighty Power that had created and ruled the universe and gave laws to nature, would preserve and protect them.

The reasoning of Paul on this passage is most remarkable, and ought not to be passed in silence. He will have Jesus to be the mediator of it and reasons "that if the first covenant had been faultless, there had been no place for a second." (Heb. viii.) To these two assertions I shall only say, first, that the prophet neither points out Jesus, nor intimates anything concerning a mediator; and, secondly, had any other than Paul declared that what God did was faulty, so many arguments would be urged against him by Christian divines and such a defence be made of God's goodness and conduct that the impossibility of his committing any fault would be made so evident as should silence all such opinions. And there appears so little connection between the new covenant promised by the prophet, and the transaction related to have happened in the time of Jesus, that I can not see the least resemblance of the prophecy to the pretended completion. The comparison of a few points may help to set this in a clear light.

It is pretended that Jesus was the mediator of the new covenant; but how was this performed? Did he enter into any agreement or covenant with the house of Israel? No, the Jews know none, and history is entirely silent as to this circumstance, and not the least footstep of any such contract is to be traced. Besides no contract can be made without the consent of the parties; and if they did not give either their expressed, or tacit consent, the covenant, or contract, can never be either valid or binding. But was it at that time that God entered into a special relation with the houses of Israel and Judah, of being their God, and taking them for their chosen people?

Was it then that they were full of the knowledge of God, even from the least to the greatest?

Was it at that time that God forgave their sins and iniquity?

Were they at that time restored, never more to be cast off, or cease to be a nation?

Was then the time in which their city was rebuilt, never after to be thrown down?

Those particulars, it is well known, never came to pass, neither then, nor since. How then could the promised covenant take place? Should not every particular circumstance of the prophet's description be fulfilled and accomplished before they lay their claims? And are not things represented in the very opposite, or contrary extreme? For, instead of having God's law fixed in their heart, they are represented as being wicked and blind to the truth.

Instead of having their city rebuilt, never more to be destroyed, it is waste and in the hands of a barbarous and foreign nation.

Instead of having their sins forgiven, they are represented as committing at that very time the most atrocious crime of refusing the Messiah.

How then is this prophecy fulfilled? Has the application the least shadow of agreement with the promise?

But here they take shelter in their evasions, and fly for refuge to their arts and inventions, the strength of which let us examine.

They say that by the names of Israel and Judah not the Jews, but the Gentiles, are thereby intended and meant. It is the Christian church, under those denominations, that was to enjoy the peculiar privileges and advantages of the new covenant. Were they able to make out their claim, it would be but reasonable to grant their pretensions; but it happens that the prophet is so minutely circumstantial in his description that it effectually excludes any people or nation from being thereby intended, excepting the literal house of Israel, or natural seed of Jacob. Nothing even under the utmost violence done to the text, and a most unnatural meaning imposed on it, can give it a contrary sense. But certainly the liberty of imposing a sense and meaning on words different from that which they import according to their first and known acceptation and signification is such a violation as ought never to be admitted.

For, if words are made use of as signs to denote our ideas, what a confusion and subversion of language must ensue if a meaning contrary to that, whereof the words stand as a known sign, be arbitrarily imposed on them at pleasure? What is there, according to this scheme, that a person may not be made to say? But as this is the greatest and grossest abuse of language, the bare mentioning of it is sufficient to expose its absurdity. However, I should be glad to learn whence the authority of imposing an opposite, contrary, and different sense on Scripture is derived. I am sure no such liberty would be allowed to any person, even in the most common affairs of life. Ought not the pretenders to this privilege in this prophecy at least to have referred to some other passage wherein the houses of Judah and Israel are mentioned, and showing the inconsistency and absurdity of applying these terms to the literal seed of Israel, or Judah, or the Jewish nation, and then show their pertinency and exact agreement as applied to the Christian church? Was it for want of words in the Hebrew language that the Gentiles are called by that very name by which the Jews are always meant and intended? Can it be supposed that God would do that which must appear highly absurd in man? By no means; the very passage is plain and explicit against any such pretensions, and puts it out of all doubt that none but the literal houses of Judah and Israel were intended. For the new covenant was to be made with those whose fathers the Lord brought up from Egypt; with whose fathers He had made a former covenant; with those whose fathers had broken that covenant, notwithstanding He had behaved like a husband unto them. Now pray, whom does this description fit, the Jews or the Gentiles? If the Jews, then it was with them that God was to make the new covenant: and as it is they to whom, literally, the preceding particulars are alone applicable, so it is with them literally that the new agreement was to be made. But since the Gentile divines are so fond of being thought to be meant by the name of Israel, why do they not undertake to prove that it was not the ancestors of the Jews (literally) but theirs who entered into a former covenant—that it was not the fathers of the Jews (literally) who broke the covenant, and were punished but theirs? And then, after they have properly made all this out, it will be time to put in for that name, and claim the privilege of the new covenant. But, as it is natural to think that they will never even try to make out all this, they may perhaps make use of another invention, and pretend that the new covenant was to be spiritual. To this I answer that God made no such distinction, and as the former covenant was worldly and material, so does the new one describe and particularize things entirely of material nature, in particular that the house of Israel should never be cast off.

It may likewise be pretended that this covenant was to take place in heaven, and you may be referred to Paradise for its accomplishment; it is but putting heaven for Jerusalem, another invention often made use of. But, as if the prophet had foreseen such pretensions, he carefully and minutely describes the earthly Jerusalem, with the tower of Hananeel, the gates, the hills Gareb and Goath, the valleys, the fields, the brook Kidron, and the Horsegate, all of which puts it beyond dispute that he meant Jerusalem literally, and not Paradise nor heaven. Besides the words, "shall not be plucked up nor thrown down any more for ever," imply that a material place had been destroyed, which never could be said of a heavenly one.

When such substitutions fail of the desired effects then the allegorical artillery is brought into position, and applied to even the historical passages when the sense is most clear, as is plain and evident from every chapter of the writings that go under Paul's name. Thus, for example, he makes the patriarch's two sons, Isaac and Ishmael, into two covenants; (Galat. iv) Abraham's concubine he transforms into Mount Sinai. This same Mount Sinai he typifies into Jerusalem in bondage, although this same Jerusalem is typified by him into heaven. By the same art he pretends that God preached the Gospel to Abraham (Gal. iii, 8), and declares the baptism of the Israelites by their passing the Red Sea (I Cor. x, 1, 2). The water which the Israelites drank from the rock Moses struck he calls spiritual drink; and he not only makes that rock follow camp, but will have the rock itself to be the Messiah (I Cor. x, 4). In short, the Passover, the Tabernacle, and every thing in it, the Israelites' wanderings in the wilderness, the whole Jewish economy and history he turns into types. But if this method proves anything it proves that the same passages and events might prove any other things, and such proof would be fully as conclusive as Paul's and his followers. Please notice for instance that they make the serpent stand for the devil in Genesis (iii) and Rev. (xii, 9), John (iii, 14) declares "as Moses lifted up the serpent in the wilderness, even so must the son of man be lifted up," thus making the serpent testify Jesus as well as the devil. But we may prove by the same means, only carrying it to a later period in history, that this serpent (and its anti-type Jesus) caused the people to err by the worship which was paid to it, until King Hezekiah destroyed it. (II Kings xviii, 4.)

LETTER XI.

Founded on such whimsical fancies which surely nobody would admit as proof the well known fact that Christianity, or the doctrine of a human sacrifice, did not find any favor with, and but very few adherents among the Jews, even until this day, will not be wondered at; especially as we find that all the moral excellencies, claimed for Christianity exclusively, are but borrowed and purloined from the Sacred Writings of the Jews. Jesus, and after him, Paul, did not teach anything new in that respect.

The love of God is proclaimed, first, in the Pentateuch, (Deut. vi, 4, &c.,) and made the principal duty of man by all the other writers. The attributes of God,* as proclaimed by Moses are expressed with such simplicity that even the childish and untutored mind can understand them; and unsurpassed in sublimity, they are in full accordance with the every day witnessed law of nature, and therefore with reason.

The love of mankind, benevolence and justice in the intercourse with our fellow-beings, is by the preacher-prophets required as of all things the most needful and acceptable in the sight of the Eternal, while the formal observance of ceremonies of sacrifices, fasting, &c., is deprecated, and almost forbidden. "To what purpose is the multitude of your sacrifices unto me? saith the Lord: I am full of the burnt offerings of rams, and the fat of fed beasts; and I delight not in the blood of bullocks, or of lambs, or of he-goats. When ye come to appear before me, who hath required this at your hand, to tread my courts? Bring no more vain oblations: incense is an abomination unto me; the new moons and the Sabbaths, the calling of assemblies, I can not away with; it is iniquity, even the solemn meeting. . . . Wash ye, make you clean: put away the evil of your doings from before mine eyes; cease to do evil; learn to do well; seek judgment, relieve the oppressed, judge the fatherless, plead for the widow," &c. (Isaiah i, 11-18.) "Thus saith the Lord of hosts, the God of Israel: Put your burnt-offerings to your sacrifices, and eat flesh. For I spake not unto your fathers, nor commanded them in the day that I brought them out of Egypt, concerning burnt-offerings and sacrifices; but this thing commanded I them, saying: Obey my voice, and I will be your God, and ye shall be my people; and walk ye in all the ways that I have commanded you." (Jer. vii, 21-23.) "Wherewith shall I come before the Lord, and bow myself before the high God? Shall I come before Him with burnt-offerings, with calves of a year old? Will the Lord be pleased with thousands of rams, or with ten thousands of rivers of oil? shall I give my first-born for my transgression, the fruit of my body for the sin of my soul? He hath showed thee, O man, what is good; and what doth the Lord require of thee, but to do justly, and to love mercy, and to walk humbly with thy God?" (Micah vi, 6-8.)

The doctrine of a resurrection of the body, which some claim as the exclusive patentright of Jesus, had also become universal with the Pharisees, and is plainly expressed in Isaiah (xxvi, 19, "Awake and sing, ye that dwell in the dust: for thy dew is as the dew of herbs, and the earth shall cast out the dead.") Daniel (xii, 2, "And many of them that sleep in the dust of the earth shall awake, some to everlasting life, and some to everlasting shame and contempt,") and the second book of Maccabees. It is not my intention to go into the *pros* and *cons* of such a belief, nor into a history of the origin and development of Christianity. If you wish some very interesting information about these things, Geiger's Judaism and its history, and Dr. Wise's "Origin of Christianity," will give you all the points. I merely wish to explain the fact that to the Jew the idea of religion guiding the individual in all his actions and particularly in the intercourse with his fellow-beings had been preached long before the rise of the Gospel writings; but to the Greek and Roman world that had outgrown its mythological belief all these doctrines added the charm of novelty to their intrinsic value. The converts from these nations were entirely ignorant of the true import and meaning of Scripture citations, and took even adulterated passages just the same as genuine ones. For instance when Paul endeavors to prove the call of the Gentiles, he says in Romans (ix, 24-26): "Even us whom he hath called not of the Jews only, but also of the Gentiles, as he saith also in Osee, I will call them my people, which are not my people, and her beloved, which was not beloved. And it shall come to pass that in the place where it was said unto them, Ye are not my people; there they shall be called the children of the living God." Here he jumbles together two very different texts, and applies them as spoken of the Gentiles, which plainly only concern the Jews, as is evident from Hosea (i), to which please to turn.

* The authorized Bible Version is wanting in general, but its deficiency in giving the proper meaning is particularly apparent in the rendering of the attributes of God (Exod. xxxiv, 6, 7): "Self-existent, Eternal, Almighty, All-merciful and gracious; Long-suffering and abundant in beneficence and truth; keeping kindness unto the thousandth (generation), removing iniquity and transgression and sin, thus making innocent (again the soul); He doeth not restore pure (the body) for He Visiteth the iniquity of parents upon the children, and upon the children's children, unto the third and fourth generations."

In Hebrews (ii, 6-8) he tries to prove subjection to Christ by quoting Psalm (viii) which only speaks of man's dominion over the brute creation. In the same letter he quotes (ix, 20): "This is the blood of the testament which God hath enjoined unto you," from Exodus (xxiv, 8), instead of "the blood of the covenant."

In speaking of Melchizedek (Heb. vii, 2), he adds, "without father, without mother, without descent, having neither beginning of days, nor end of life; but made like unto the Son of God, abideth a priest continually," like if it was a description quoted from the Scriptures, while it is but a fancy of his own. Neither has the statement that Abraham gave him tithes any foundation on facts, as you may see in Genesis (xiv, 20) that he gave tithes (probably the provisions there mentioned) to Abraham. I will here observe that Melchizedek† or Adonizedek was the title of the kings of Jerusalem (Gen. xiv, 18, Josh. x, 1,) and means about as much as "His most just majesty," and after the conquest of Jerusalem (II Sam. v, 6-9, I Chron. xi, 4-9), David took his title, which fact, together with the bravery of the volunteers, the one hundreth and tenth Psalm commemorates.‡

It would require too much space to collate and compare all of Paul's quotations with the original passages. The above shown instances are, I think, sufficient to expose his sophistry, and you can multiply these *ad infinitum*, as every chapter and nearly every line of his writings will afford you an opportunity. I shall, therefore, not trouble with repetitions, but sum up the result by the observation that if the Evangelists and Apostles had been inspired (as is pretended), they must or should have known from the assistance or rather guidance of the spirit, the prophecies and passages which contained proof of what they advanced and asserted, and their bringing in verses that have not the least connection with the subject, is sufficient evidence of their want of inspiration.

To complete our inquiry (that nothing, though but seemingly material, may escape our examination,) it is necessary to attend to such other arguments and proofs as are made use of by theologians, as an addition to the proofs and evidence contained in the New Testament.

Foremost among these is Isaiah ix, 6, "Unto us a child is born; unto us a son is given; and the government shall be upon his shoulders, and his name shall be called Wonderful, Counsellor, the Mighty God, the Everlasting Father, the Prince of Peace;" all of which titles and epithets are ascribed to Jesus, as being God and man, urging that they are of such a nature as not capable of being applied to mere humanity; pretending, in consequence, that this description is one of a divine child, who was *wonderfully conceived, wonderfully born, wonderfully manifested.* (Univ. Hist. x, p. 459.) The wonderful conception and birth I have already considered in Letter V. As to his wonderful manifestation these historians make it to consist in "that the babe was wrapped up in swaddling clothes and laid in a manger."

As I have already observed chapters vii, viii, ix, x, and xi, 1-9, of the book of Isaiah form a continuous poem describing some events of the reign of Ahaz, his unbelief and its threatened punishment through the Assyrians, the birth and reign of Hezekiah, and the destruction of the Assyrian hosts. In the Hebrew original there is no division into chapters (which together with the partition into verses is a modern invention to facilitate reference) and consequently no headings to the chapters which greatly mislead in many instances, and only interrupt the flow of the narrative. The above quoted passage plainly concerns He-

---

†מלך *melek*, king, ruler, and ארון *adon*, Lord, are synonyms.

‡The Psalms are not all David's composition, but a collection of poems of different authors, from the time of Moses (Psalm ii, &c.) to the time of Nehemiah and even later.

Ps. cx.—To David—a Psalm.
The ETERNAL's message to my lord:
"Stay at my right hand,
"That I make thine enemies
"The stool unto thy feet."

Thy power's rod th' ETERNAL sends forth from Zion;
Rule in the vitals of thine enemies.
Thy people, so brave, is on thy muster day in sacred array;
From the womb, from the morn of life is thine the dew of thy youthful host.

Sworn has the ETERNAL, and he ne'er repents:
"Thou art a ruler forever;
"Upon my word, be Malchizedek."

The word signifies, "most just king," and was, as we have shown from Joshua, the title of the kings of Jerusalem, just as the Spanish Monarchs style themselves, "Most Catholic or most Christian Majesty."

zekiah for whose extraordinary character and reign I refer you to II Kings xviii, xxi, and II Chron. xxix to xxxiv. This poem is also called the "Dial of Ahaz," because Isaiah set, as it were, the time for Ahaz and his family; (Is. vii, 17-25) And on this dial the shadow returned or went back ten degrees by putting the conquest of the country off until after Hezekiah's death. But to return to our subject. The word אל (El) translated God, ought to be rendered in this place as in Moses' song (Ex. xv, 15,) where אלי מואב (Ele Moab) is properly translated "the mighty men of Moab." אבי אר (Abi Ad) rendered "everlasting father" is rightly translated *Pater Seculi*, Father of the Age by Arius Montanus, all of which expressions are literally true of Hezekiah as he had the courage to resist the King of Assyria, was the father of his age by purifying and restoring the national customs and worship, and administered the government better than his predecessor. The word אלהים (Elohim), on the plural form of which some wish to support the argument of a Trinity and by this the divinity of Jesus, is applied to Moses in Exodus (vii, 1,) "And the Lord said to Moses, see I have made thee a God (Elohim) to Pharaoh." From this passage certainly no one would wish to prove that Moses was a *triune* person. Besides, *Eloha*, *Elohim*, *El*, with the first signification of mighty, powerful, is applied to God when it ought to be rendered Almighty to men, when it may signify superior, hero, or judge; the context assists us in rendering it properly. Now when used of persons it would be perfectly absurd to claim a Trinity for them, how much more so when applied to God? Besides, if Elohim implies more than one, why not more than three?

Equally weak is the pretense that because the Scripture says, "Let us make man," that there was a consultation with the other persons of the Trinity; for any one acquainted with languages knows that the "plural of majesty" is used of one individual, without carrying the idea of a plurality with it. Thus the Scripture continues in the singular number, "So God created man in His own image, in the image of God created He him."

Protestants very justly reject the doctrine of transubstantiation, because it is manifestly contradictory to reason and sense; for as the eye can not forbear seeing that the object continues the same, notwithstanding any form of words, so the understanding can not forbear either assenting or dissenting, according to the agreement or disagreement of ideas—we having as sure a guide in the conduct of our understanding as we can possibly have in that of our senses. If any person was to assure me that one is three, and that three are but one, or that one simple unit was three simple units, and three simple units were but one simple unit, I should take such a person to be either crazy, or of having intentions to impose on me in the grossest manner. And were such a person to tell me that he had positive command from God to teach me any such propositions, I should certainly call his integrity into question; for my understanding would immediately give him the lie; for as God has not given me faculties to comprehend the proposition, how could He expect my assent? And in justice He could not command me to believe that which He had not enabled me to comprehend. But, on the contrary, God has laid down such propositions as are both in full accordance with our faculties and diametrically opposite to the doctrine of the Trinity. To instance a few: "Hear, O Israel, the ETERNAL our God is One;" (Deut. vi, 4.) "That the ETERNAL, (*Jehovah*,) He is God (*Elohim*, Almighty) in heaven above, and upon the earth beneath; there is none else." (Deut. iv, 39.) "Unto thee it was shown that thou mightest know that the ETERNAL, He is God, there is none beside Him." (Deut. iv, 35.) "See now that I, even I, am He: and there is no God with me; I kill and I make alive, I wound and I heal; neither is any that can deliver out of my hand." (Deut. xxxii, 39.) Let the Trinitarians reconcile the Trinity, or deified persons, to these texts, or to the following passages: "And thou shalt know no other God but me, for there is no Savior besides me." (Hosea xii, 4.) "Have not I told thee from that time, and have declared it? ye are even my witness. Is there a God besides me? Yea, there is no God; I know not any." (Isaiah xliv, 8.) "I am the LORD, and there is none else, there is no God besides me." (Isaiah xlv, 5.) "Look unto me and be ye saved, all the ends of the earth; for I am God, and there is none else." (Ibid. xlv, 22.) "To whom will ye liken me, and make me equal, and compare me, that we may be alike?" (Isaiah xlvi, 5.) "Remember the former things of old; for I am God, and there is none else; I am God, and there is none like me." (Ibid. 9.) In short, if there is no other "God but He;" "if there is none with Him," (or, if you please, in His essence); if there is "none besides Him;" if there is "none like Him;" if "He has no equal, nor any God able to save beside Him," and if God declares that "He knows not any God:" how vain, how impious is it to worship any other, or to pretend to put any such meaning on any part of Scripture!

In the New Testament there are many passages which directly contradict the divinity of Jesus. To instance a few: we are told that "Jesus increased in wisdom and stature, and in favor with God and man," (Luke ii, 52,) which is declaring him merely human; for what greater absurdity than to say that God increases in wisdom, or that He was grown in favor with Himself? Jesus declares, "my doctrine is not mine, but his that sent me," (John vii, 16); by which he claims himself to be only an agent, to do the will of his superior, and consequently could not be the same as he that had the power of sending; as he that sends, or commands another to go, can not be the same as he who goes and is commanded by a superior; for to command and to obey are different acts, inconsistent in the same person, unless a person can be said, not only to command himself, but also to obey himself, which is absurd. Again, Jesus declares of himself, "I go unto the Father; for my Father is greater than I." (John xiv, 28.) Consequently, he that has a superior can not be God. In another place John (xvii, 5) has the passage: "And now, O Father, glorify thou me with thine own self, with the glory which I had with thee before the world was." Here the writer lets him invoke his superior for that which he not only had not, but could not obtain of himself. For either he had that glory, or he had it not; if he had it, it was absurd to pray for what he had; and if he had it not, then could he not be God; for he that had the power to grant it, and to whom he prayed, must have been his superior. Besides he prays for a thing which he had "before the world was," of which (to make the passage sense) he must have been divested; but how absurd is it to suppose that the Deity divests himself, or is divested by another of his glory or of any of his attributes! Another passage (Mat. xiii, 32) declaring: "Of that day and that hour knoweth no man, no not the angels which are in heaven, neither the son, but the Father," excludes him of having knowledge which the Father only possesses. Now how can he be God, or of the same essence with the Father, and yet be ignorant of what the Father knew?

These passages are sufficient and unanswerable, and clearly prove that Jesus (in his life time) pretended not to any divinity; and so far was he from taking any of the divine attributes to himself that he rebukes one for only calling him "Good Master," and tells him, "Why callest thou me good? there is none good but one, that is God." (Mat. xix, 17.) I think a more determined and plain declaration can not be had.

LETTER XII.

There are some expressions of frequent occurrence in the New Testament that, though of no extraordinary or divine significance, may have been misconstrued by Greek converts through ignorance, and were afterward undoubtedly used by those who propagated the doctrine of the Trinity. Even the English reader is misled by these words, which are: son of man, son of God, and son of David. The Hebrew word בן (*ben*) besides the first and original meaning of "son" signifies also grandson, descendant, follower, disciple, and is greatly used in the formation of compound words when it very nearly corresponds to the English "like." Thus we translate בן מלחמה (*ben milchamah,*) literally son of war, by warrior, or warlike; בן נביא (*ben nabi*) pl. בני הנביאים, lit. sons of the prophets, by followers or disciples of the prophets; בן בליל (*ben b'lial,*) lit. son of Belial, by unruly man; בן שמנה יומים lit. son of eight days, by eight days old, &c. In some of these idiomatic expressions a literal translation would convey a wrong idea, just as the English idiomatic "man-of-war" translated literally into a foreign language, (for instance *Kriegsmann*, or *homme de guerre*) would give an entirely false meaning. "Son of man" is merely an elegant and poetic expression for man, and is like בן אלוהים (lit. son of God) "follower of God" frequently used in the plural number; בן רויר (lit. son of David) means "like David," and ought to be thus rendered, as the Jewish nation, in their distress and periods of subjugation by the Syrians and Romans, hoped to find or produce a second David, a successful warrior, that would conquer their enemies like the first David. This hope in the re-appearance of a ruler whose reign had been glorious was not confined to the ancient Jews; the Germans have their legend of Frederic I, Barbarossa, who only sleeps in the Kiffhauser mountain, ready to strike for a renovated German empire; during the defense against William (of Orange) the Irish hoped for a supernatural or miraculous deliverance by Baldearg O'Donnell. (Macaulay's Hist. of Eng. vol. ii and iii.)

But to return to our subject, such expressions as the above-mentioned, literally rendered into the Greek and Latin languages, conveying an ambiguous and wrong idea, assisted Jesus' deification, the germ of which was contained in the preaching of his first followers. Add to this the literal rendering of רוח הקורש (holy spirit, or better: inspiration) by "holy Ghost," and the Trinity is finished, ready for use.

This doctrine of the Trinity being once introduced, and made a fundamental doctrine of Christianity, all persons want to support their different opinions concerning it in some way, and try to force texts to their assistance. Yet they nearly all appeal to the witnesses of the Gospels to prove that which they themselves declare to be incomprehensible and unintelligible.

The very terms contradicting one another, and showing the folly of pretending to explain that which none can either understand or comprehend, soon occasioned such divisions among Christians, as are without parallel in history; each party damning, excommunicating, banishing, imprisoning, fining, and even murdering the other, in such a manner that I have often wondered that people who are so ready to apply God's judgment on other occasions, should not bethink themselves that these troubles came on the church as a judgment for their manifold absurdities and impieties.

The creed which establishes this doctrine is so full of contradictions and inconsistencies that one feels tempted to challenge any person to compose, within the same compass of words, any thing equal to it, or more repugnant to reason and common sense. For the truth of this I shall refer you to the Athanasian Creed, which is crammed down the throats of believers "as necessary to salvation," inflicting on unbelievers the most cruel punishments, even that of "perishing everlasting," concluding by saying: "This is the Catholic faith which except a man believe he can not be saved." But as it is impossible for any intelligent, reasonable man to believe the doctrine of the Trinity, those who pretend to it assert such things as are almost incredible. Bishop Beveridge, for instance, has the following passage in his "Thoughts on Religion" (Art. 3) on the Trinity: "This, I confess, is a mystery which I can not possibly conceive; yet it is a truth which I can easily believe; yea, therefore, it is so true that I can easily believe it; because it is so high that I can not possibly conceive it; for it is impossible anything should be true of the Infinite Creator, which can be easily expressed to the capacities of a finite creature; and for this reason I ever did, and ever shall look upon those apprehensions of God to be the truest, whereby we apprehend Him to be the most incomprehensible, and that to be the most true of God which seems the most impossible unto us." Who after this can believe the Trinity since it gives us notions of God so contradictory in themselves, and so inconsistent to His attributes? But this is not all; for the bishop continues, "Upon this ground, therefore, it is that the mysteries of the Gospel, which I am less able to conceive, I think myself the more obliged to believe, especially this mystery of mysteries, the Trinity in Unity, and Unity in Trinity, which I am so far from being able to comprehend, or indeed to apprehend that I can not seriously set myself to think of it, or to sum up my thoughts a little concerning it, but I immediately lose myself in a trance or ecstasy. That God the Father should be one perfect God of himself, God the son, one perfect God of himself, and God the Holy Ghost one perfect God of himself, and yet these three should be but one perfect God of himself; so that one should be perfectly three, and three perfectly one; that the Father, Son, and Holy Ghost, should be three, and yet but one—but one, and yet three! O heart-amazing thought, devouring, inconceivable mystery! Who can not believe it to be true of the glorious Deity? Certainly none but such as are able to apprehend it, which I am sure I can not, and I believe no other creature can, and because no creature can possibly conceive how it should be so, therefore I believe it to be so." I am tired of transcribing this nonsense, which is really what Christians must believe--a faith, or cause of faith, however, that I shall never be able to attain, neither do I believe the bishop himself ever did, if he was a rational, reasonable creature. Thus you see to what absurdities, inconsistencies, and incredibilities, those are led to believe who, contrary to Scripture, to reason, and to common sense, set up the Trinity.

There are but two passages in the whole New Testament which can be brought to the support of this doctrine, and they are John's "three in heaven," which we have already considered, and Matthew's (xxviii, 19): "Go ye, therefore, and teach all nations, baptizing them in the name of the Father, and of the Son, and of the Holy Ghost;" which bears every mark of being inserted long after Matthew's time when the doctrine of the Trinity had been started, and baptism instituted as a sacrament, in order to authorize both. There is, however, one method made use of to baffle all inquiries concerning this and other articles of the Christian faith, which is, to make them mysteries; every thing contrary to reason and common sense (as every thing peculiar to Christianity is) is a mystery. As they write to people of the same persuasion and way of thinking, it is very rare that their claims and reasoning meet any opposition; but every thing they say, though ever so absurd, is received with applause and approbation, as if they had demonstratively proved their point, or convinced their opponents. They triumph and exclaim against the Jews for willfully shutting their eyes and hardening their hearts against the (pretended) plain arguments and dictates of truth, concluding them to be under a national blindness, an infatuation. They will, indeed, invite people to make their objections; but woe to the poor creatures who undertake the task; for they are to expect no quarter: heresy, infidelity, and apostacy, will be proved against them; and defamation and ill-language will certainly ensue; for these challenging divines are generally very eloquent and expert at these weapons, in proportion as their cause is weak, and proof deficient.

I shall conclude this article with the opinion of two of the greatest minds the Anglo-Saxon race has produced. Mr. Wollaston says: "He who exists himself depends in no regard upon another, and (as being a Supreme Cause) in the foundation of existence to other beings, must exist in the uppermost and best means of existing; and not only so, but (since He is infinite and unlimited) He must exist in the best manner, illimitedly and infinitely; now to exist thus is infinite goodness of existence; and to exist in a manner infinitely good is to be perfect. There can be but one such being, that is, as it appears by Prop. 3rd that there must be at least one independent being, such as is mentioned in Prop. 1st, so now that in reality there is but one, because his manner of existence being perfect and unlimited. That manner of being (if I may speak so) is exhausted by Him, or belongs solely to Him; if any other could partake with Him in it, He must want what that other had, be deficient and limited; infinite and unlimited inclose all. If there could be two beings, each by himself absolutely perfect, they must be either of the same, or different natures; of the same it can not be; because thus both being infinite their existence would be coincident; that is, they would be but the same one. Nor can they be of different natures; because if their natures were opposite, or contrary, one to the other, being equal (infinite both and every where meeting the one with the other,) the one would destroy, or be the negation of the other."

The following is a translation of part of Mr. Locke's letter to Mr. Limborch, dated 2d of April, 1698. (See his works.) "The question you propose is reduced to this, "How the unity of God may be proved," or in other terms, "How can it be proved that there is but one God?" To resolve this question, it is necessary to know, before we come to prove the unity of God, what we understand by the word God.

The ordinary idea, and, I believe, the true idea we have of God, and of such who know His existence, is, that He is an infinite Being, eternal, incorporeal, and all perfect. Then, from this known idea, it seems to me easy to deduce the unity of God. In effect, a Being all-perfect, or otherwise wholly perfect, can not be but one only, because a Being all-perfect can not want any of its attributes, perfections, or degrees of perfection; for otherwise he would lack as much as would make him entirely perfect. For example: to have power is a much greater perfection than to have none; to have still greater power is a greater perfection than to have less; and to have all power, which is to be almighty, is a greater perfection than to want any part of it. This proved, two beings, almighty, are incompatible, because we should be obliged to suppose that one would necessarily will that which the other would, and, in that case, of the two the one in which the will is, must necessarily determine the will of the other, who could not be free, and would consequently want that perfection we have treated of. For it is better to be free than to be submitted to the determination and the will of another. And if they are not reduced to the necessity of willing always one and the same thing; in such case, the one might act or do that which the other would not, and then the will of the one would prevail over the will of the other, and of the two he whose power could not second his will can not be almighty; for he can not do as much as the other. Of course, then, there are not two almighty beings, consequently there can not be two gods. By the same idea of perfection we attain to the knowledge of God being omniscient, so that the supposition of two distinct beings each of which has power and distinct will is an imperfection that one can not screen his thoughts from the other, but if one can sever his thoughts from the other, then can not the other be omniscient, for not only does he not know that which may be known; but likewise does not know what the other knows. The same may be said of God's omnipresence. It is better to be in the vast extent of infinite space than to be excluded from the smallest part of space; for if one be excluded from any part of space, he can not operate nor know what is done in that space, and consequently can neither be almighty nor omniscient. If against this reasoning, it should be said that the two gods which they suppose, (or the thousands, for by the reasoning that there may be two, there may be two million, for there is no method of limiting the number,) I say if they suppose that several gods have one perfect almighty, that is, exactly the same power; and have also the same knowledge, the same will, and that they equally exist in the same place; it is only multiplying the same being. But, in the end, they do but reduce one supposed plurality to one true unity. For to suppose two intelligent beings, who know, will, and do incessantly the same thing, and have not a separate existence, is nothing more than to suppose, in words, one plurality, and to admit, effectually, one simple unity. For the being inseparably united by the will, by the understanding, by the action, and by the place, is as great a union as one intelligent being can possibly be united to himself; and consequently the supposing that where there is such a union there can be two beings is to suppose a division where there can be none, or a thing divided with itself." No addition is required to the plain, clear, and convincing reasoning of these scholars. I shall only apply to the subject of this letter the words of the excellent Archbishop Tillotson, when he tells us, "That if all the great mathematicians of all ages, Archimedes, and Euclid, and Appolonius, and Diophantus, &c., could be supposed to meet in a general council, and should there declare in a most solemn manner, and give it under their hands and seals that twice two did not make four, but five, that this would not in the least move him to be of their mind;" and of this opinion must all reasonable people be, by what names or epithets they may be called.

LETTER XIII.

Jacob's blessing to Judah (Genesis xl, lx) is famous both among Jewish and Christian commentators; the latter claim it to be a plain prophecy of Jesus, and consequently take great pains to show its literal accomplishment in him. But to be convinced that it is neither plainly nor literally fulfilled in Jesus, one need but observe not only the variety, but the contrariety of opinions which their commentators have run into. The terms which the Patriarch has made use of are such as increase the difficulty and divisions, every one explaining and deriving the sense and meaning of the words *shebet*, *mekhokek*, *ad* and *Shiloh*, and fixing their signification as best suits their different purpose. This you will find to be the real state of the case on consulting a few out of the many different authors who have commented on, or explained this famous passage, which is rendered in the commonly used Bible version: "The scepter shall not depart from Judah, nor a lawgiver from between his feet until Shiloh come; and unto him shall the gathering of the people be." (Gen. xlix, 10.) I do not suppose you expect I should enter into a critical examination, much less a confutation of the many different and contradictory opinions. This would be needless, since there is not one interpretation and application that was ever made, but what has been objected to and confuted by some other Christian author, so that you will find this task amply and fully done to your hands.

There is, however, of late a new interpretation and application started by the authors of the Universal History, who, I suppose, dissatisfied with interpretations hitherto made, have opened a new and different plan from all other (Christian) commentators. They pretend "that the Jews did not lose their scepter, Sanhedrin, or highest court of judicature, and supreme legislative power, till the heathens became converts to Christianity, of whom Cornelius was the first; that event denoting the gathering of the people, as foretold by the Patriarch," (vol. x, p. 317.)

To support this opinion, they (contrary to all other commentators) insist on the Sanhedrin's retaining the supreme legislative power (which they say the word scepter in the prophecy means) and represent Jesus' trial before Pilate in a light suitable to this view: "In order (they say) to set those right who, from the notion of the whole power of life and death being taken away before this time, have inferred that the scepter spoken of by Jacob was departed from Judah," (vol. x, p. 594.) The time of the scepter's departure from Judah is a point in which their commentators greatly differ, while the only thing they agree on is in placing the scepter's departure in the Sanhedrin's loss of power, and deem this circumstance necessary to the accomplishment of the prophecy. A few quotations will set this in a clear light: Basnage (Hist. of the Jews, iv, 21) declares: "That the Sanhedrin had lost the power of life and death; and when they were crucifying the Messiah, they acknowledged that the scepter was departed from Judah, since the Jews said to Pilate, 'It is not lawful for us to put any man to death.' This is the first period of the accomplishment of the oracle." Calmet (on the word Jesus) asserts: "That the Romans, who were masters of the country, had taken from them the power of life and death; they might pronounce a man guilty, but not condemn him in form, nor order his execution." Echard (Eccles. His. Intro. p. 16) speaking of Herod, says: "This was the first foreigner to whom the Jews became immediately subject, so that the ancient prophecy of the scepter's departing from Judah, is by the best critics supposed to begin to take place at this time." Prideaux (Connections, vol, iv, p. 932) declares that "Cyrenius having reduced Judea into the form of a Roman province, and, instead of their former governor of their own nation, placed a Roman Procurator over them, then began the fulfillment of this prophecy. For then, that is, at the time of this reduction of Judea to a Roman province, the scepter and the lawgiver from between their feet began to be taken away." These different opinions prove only that the literal application of this prophecy and its accomplishment in Jesus is very far from being as clear and evident as they pretend; for if it be a plain prophecy of Jesus and fully accomplished in him, why such contradictions and variety of opinions?

But the principal flaws in all these pretensions appear on examination of Jewish history. For it is a well known fact that the supreme legislative power (in which the scepter and lawgiver promised to Judah is made to consist in all their comments and applications) was never held by anybody, be he judge, king, prophet, or member of the Sanhedrin; for all the laws (חוק *khok*, from which *mekhokek* in the text is derived) moral, political, and ceremonial, were immediately enacted by the ETERNAL Himself in sight of all the people, as on Sinai at the giving of the law (ten commandments), or mediately by the hands of Moses' as the greater part of the law; and it would have been an affront to the Divine Legislator, as well as the highest presumption in any prince or judge of the Jews, to assume the power of giving or making laws, without special directions from the same Almighty Author of the laws of Israel, and even after such special direction it would only be the promulgation of a divine law, and not a legislative power in the prince, such power being utterly inconsistent with the theocratic Mosaic constitution. The holders of the sovereign power in Israel and Judah were but the executors of the law, not the makers of it.

Then, secondly, when the kingdom of Judah was destroyed by Nebuchadnezzar, the scepter, or independent government, ceased in Judah; nor did in Palestine any body out of the tribes of Judah ever govern after this event, as the Maccabees who restored the independence of Judea, and were elected kings by a grateful people in acknowledgment of their valuable services, were of the priestly tribe of Levi. Zerubabel and his few successors possessed but the shadow of authority under Persian supremacy as the interruption of the building of the temple amply witnesses.

The Sanhedrin (Greek *synedrion* assembly) were established and gained judicial authority only by the Maccabee Hyrcanus: but their power was reduced to a mere shadow, and made dependent on the Roman officers, ever since the first occupation of Palestine under Pompey. This is easily shown from those very historians, though they assert and pretend to make out the very reverse, to serve a turn. They tell us themselves that from a change which Gabinus made in the government (long before the birth of Jesus) the Jews "fell under the subjection of a set of domineering lords," and consequently lost their power by the change, (Univ. Hist. x, p. 376); and, though Hyrcanus II had afterward a grant of the government, as prince and highpriest, with privilege of judging all causes, it is evident that whatever power he left the Sanhedrin, it must have been very precarious, far short of the supreme legislative power. This appears from their suffering Herod to appear before them, "though summoned as a criminal, in such a guise as gave them to understand that he came not as a private person to be judged by them." And how could they possess the supreme power, without either the freedom of judging, or enforcing their sentence? That they had not privilege is very plain from the letters which Sextus Cæsar wrote to the Sanhedrin in their judicial capacity to intimidate them. (Univ. Hist. x, 385.) Can it be said they were the supreme legislators, and yet have their jurisdiction disclaimed by Herod who cruelly put to death all the members but two, for their proceeding in that very council? How insignificant must their power have been if they could not hinder the abolition of their ceremonies, and the introduction of foreign customs contrary to law; neither could they hinder a law of Herod from being imposed on them not only contrary to the law of Moses, but also contrary to the inclination of the whole nation.

Having thus proved that the scepter (independence) had departed from Judah long before the birth of Jesus, and that the supreme legislative power never was vested in Judah, it is self-evident that the blessing of Jacob can not be applied to Jesus at all, nor his Messiahship be proved therefrom.

I will now proceed to give you a construction put upon this passage by the learned and well known Rev. Dr. Wise; and for a better insight, I will begin with a vocabulary of the principal terms of the passage.

שבט (*shebet*) 1. Rod, staff. 2. Scepter, hence, independence, pre-eminence. 3. Tribe.

מחקק (*mekhokek*) from חק (khok) law, is of rare occurrence and used for lawgiver in Deuter. xxxiii, 21, as applied to Moses; in Judges v, 9, 14, it is rendered rulers and might be translated faithful. I take it to be the participle of a verb חקק to execute the law, hence faithful to the law, which sense it necessarily has in Prov. xxxi, 5.

שילה *Shiloh* is not translated in the English version. The same word recurs in Joshua and other later books, but is there, the name of a town. I derive it from שלל (shalal) to take or divide booty (like בזה from בז) and hence to signify victory or triumph; for at Shiloh (place of dividing the spoils, victory) the Israelites divided the land of Palestine among their tribes, (Josh. xviii, 1.) Most commentators translate it as if written שלו (sh'lo), he to whom belongs the empire, hence king.

יקהת (*yikhath*) occurs only once more in the Scriptures, viz: in Prov. xxx, 17, where it is necessarily rendered "obedience," (to *obey* his mother,) which makes it probable that it has the same meaning here. עד (*ad*) ever, forever; כי (*ki*) for.

Dr. Wise giving *shebet* the third meaning, translates: "No tribe shall depart from Judah, nor a lawgiver from among his posterity, until he come to Shiloh; and him the nations (of Canaan) will obey;" contending that this was an instruction of Jacob to his descendants, the tribes of Israel, to follow the leadership of Judah during the exodus from Egypt, and would terminate at Shiloh when they divided the land. Judah had, indeed, the front on the march Numb. x, 4), and was foremost in the encampment. (Numb. ii, 3.)

A German scholar (D. Arnheim, I think) translates: "Until he come from Shiloh, and him will the tribes obey," giving this part a prophetic turn and referring to Ahijah of Shiloh, who prophesied the rebellion and secession of the ten tribes from the kingdom under Rehoboam.

If you wish another prophetic application, allow me to give you one of my own. I translate: "The pre-eminence shall not depart from Judah, nor the faithful to the law from among his posterity forever, for his victory will come, and him will the nations obey," which translates all the words, leaves the parallel expression (common in the Hebrew) in the first part of the verse, and conforms both to the facts, and to the whole tenor of the Scriptures. For the pre-eminence of the mind, and the faithfulness to the mission of upholding religion, liberty, and the unity of the ETERNAL, have been and are still with Judah, even after the dereliction and dispersion of the ten tribes, and the progress of civilization, together with Scripture, promise the victory to these principles as the time when "the ETERNAL alone shall rule over all the earth, and His sole existence will be acknowledged." (Zach. xiii.)

LETTER XIV.

Extraordinary are the pains which have been taken, and the stress laid by Christian commentators on the famous prophecy of Daniel's* seventy weeks, as if Christianity could not subsist without it; or, as if the very being of religion depended on the application of this prophecy to Jesus, whom they make to be the Messiah, or Anointed, there mentioned. The passage (Dan. ix, 23, &c.,) is thus translated in the English Bible:

"At the beginning of thy supplications," (says the angel to Daniel,) "the commandment came forth, and I am come to show thee; for thou art greatly beloved: therefore understand the matter, and consider the vision. Seventy weeks are determined upon thy people, and upon thy holy city, to finish the transgression, and to make an end of sins, and to make reconciliation for iniquity, and to bring in everlasting righteousness, and to seal up the vision and prophecy, and to anoint the Most Holy. Know therefore and understand, that from the going forth of the commandment to restore and to build Jerusalem unto the Messiah the Prince shall be seven weeks, and three score and two weeks: the street shall be built again, and the wall, even in troublous times. And after three score and two weeks shall Messiah be cut off, but not for himself: and the people of the prince that shall come shall destroy the city and the sanctuary; and the end thereof shall be with a flood, and unto the end of the war desolations are determined. And he shall confirm the covenant with many for one week: and in the midst of the week he shall cause the sacrifice and oblation to cease, and for the overspreading of abominations he shall make it desolate, even until the consummation, and that determined shall be poured upon the desolate."†

The computations which are made of these seventy weeks, by the most learned, are so different and contradictory to each other, and the calculations do so vary from one another's hypothesis, as ought, one

*There is every probability amounting almost to a certainty, that the book of Daniel is not Daniel's production, but that its author lived under the Selucidan dominions. (Geiger's *Urtext*, and others.)

†This version is forced and mixed up; I will give one closer to the original below.

would think, to convince them of the impracticability of making the application of it to Jesus, and consequently, of the impossibilities of making it answer their purpose of proving Messiahship. Its obscurity is confessed by all, and you will hardly find two intelligent persons who will agree in their computations; difficulties surround them whichever way they take: how to make or bring out Jesus for the Messiah or Anointed who was to be cut off, is the result they aim at; but where to begin the computation of the weeks, how to continue them, and at what time to end them—so that every event mentioned may have the proper period of time in correspondence to the prophecy—are matters of the greatest difficulties and differences among the expositors. To make the prophecy answer the event they want to apply it to, they shorten or lengthen the chronology of those times, (which of itself is dark and perplexed,) extending or diminishing the duration of the reigns of Persian monarchs to what may best square with their different hypotheses which, after all the troubles and pains they take, are still under the most potent objections and insurmountable difficulties. There is appended to a family edition of the English Bible a ridiculous attempt at chronology which cuts the Gordian Knot in the following manner. The writer says: "In Daniel (ix,) it is mentioned, that there should be seventy weeks of years from the commandment of Cyrus to rebuild Jerusalem unto the death of Christ; it is therefore four hundred and ninety years from the restoration of the Jews to the crucifixion of Jesus," which is about as correct, and as close to the actual periods of history, as if one were to declare, that, since the captivity of the Jews was to last seventy years according to Jeremiah, therefore from the settlement of the English in Virginia to the Declaration of the Inde- ndence of the United States it is seventy years.

The authors of the Universal History, after mentioning in very contemptuous terms, (as it is their custom,) the differences which exist among the Jewish authors, and asserting their ignorance as chronological calculators, proceed to give the following account:

The Christians (they say,) are not exactly agreed, either in the placing of the beginning or end of these weeks, or in the calculations of those lunar or Jewish years; both differences, however, are inconsiderable, if duly attended to; the former is entirely owing to our imperfect knowledge of the chronology of those times; had we a sure guide in it, the points would not be long unsettled, but, whilst in this nnoertainty, one author will place the beginning at the decree of Cyrus, another at that of Darius, a third at that of Artaxerxes Longimanus, and each of them endeavors to stretch or shorten the chronology of each interval, as best suits his hypothesis, it is no wonder there is so little agreement among them, and so little certainty to be gathered from the whole dispute." (Un. Hist. x, p. 446.)

If these things are thus, can the Jews be blamed in rejecting their application of this prophecy, computed as is acknowledged "both without any perfect knowledge of the chronology of those times, or any sure guide in it?" Upon what grounds, then, can Christians pretend either to fix or urge this prophecy? And does it not betray pitiful shifts (or something worse,) in thus shortening and stretching each interval as best suits their different views, and is it not using unfair and unwarrantable means?

"Waiving (what these authors call) some minute differences," they proceed to give the system most universally received, and they tell us (Vol. x, 448,) that "the difference of time is trifling at most, but nine or ten years between those who make it longest and those who make it shortest; and who can wonder at it or urge it as an objection against this prophecy," &c. Against the prophecy nobody will, but against its application to Jesus a difference "of nine or ten years" is the strongest objection, for where there is a determined portion of time fixed, the accomplishment must be exact; otherwise, instead of seventy weeks (which commentators calculate at seven years each,) the angel ought to have said, seventy-one weeks and a half; ten years is therefore a very material difference, for it makes the time extend farther than the determined bounds set by the angel.

Their hypothesis is to begin the seventy weeks from the decree granted to Nehemiah by Artaxerxes, in the twentieth year of his reign (Neh. ii, 1), and end them at the death of Jesus; but to this computation there are unanswerable objections; it exceeds the four hundred and ninety years (70x7) by ten years, as their own historians acknowledge, or rather thirteen, as Dean Prideaux (Connect. ii, p. 403) makes it appear. He says, "And therefore, if the four hundred and ninety years of the seventy weeks be computed from thence, they will overshoot the death of Christ thirteen years, which being the grand event to be brought to pass at the conclusion of these weeks, it is certain they there can never have their beginning from whence they never can be brought to this ending." To remedy this evil, some have invented (though without the least foundation in history,) that Artaxerxes reigned ten years with his father, and pretended it to be the tenth year of his reigning alone; thus making up by invention what is wanting in exactness. Besides, according to this hypothesis, they make one continued series of time without making any epochs to the division, as made by the angel, and notwithstanding the angel speaks of the commandment already gone forth, yet they contradict him, and make that commandment to be one, given nearly ninety years after. I suppose with Prideaux (Connect. Vol. ii, p. 382, 386,) that the commandment mentioned by the angel to be that of Cyrus which he very learnedly proves to be the decree literally meant by the angel, declaring that it "can be applicable to no other restoring and rebuilding of Jerusalem, than that which was decreed and commanded by Cyrus at the return from the captivity; and therefore, if these words of the prophecy to restore and rebuild Jerusalem are to be understood in a literal sense, they can be understood of no other restoring and building of that city than that which was accomplished by virtue of that decree; and the computation of the seventy weeks must begin from the granting and going forth thereof." According to this opinion, the literal accomplishment of this prophecy must have its completion from the going forth of that decree; and whoever begins the same from any other, can not pretend to make it a literal prophecy. But there are other difficulties which arise from this hypothesis in common with others, such as the confirmation of the covenant with many for one week, (to which they are entirely silent,) the time of the Messiah's being cut off, the overspreading of abominations, which shall be taken notice of in my observations on the next hypothesis, that of the learned Prideaux, which these historians recommend, thereby conclusively showing that they are not satisfied with their own explanations.

Dr. Prideaux very judiciously objects to the calculations and hypotheses which terminate in Jesus in a different manner from his; he shows their absurdity, and the impossibility of terminating them in that event, and therefore begins his own computation of the seventy weeks, from the seventh year of Artaxerxes, when Ezra began to execute his commission. (Con. Vol. ii, p. 377.) For on calculating the time backward, he finds, from the death of Jesus to the execution of Ezra's commission, just four hundred and ninety years (Ibid. 381): he therefore takes the commandment mentioned in the prophecy, of the seventy weeks, or four hundred and ninety years, not literally, but in a figurative sense, (Ibid. 382) and this he does for a very obvious reason; for having proved, as I have before observed, that the commandment for restoring and building Jerusalem could be none other but Cyrus' decree, "If (he says p. 386,) the computation be begun so high, the four hundred and ninety years of the said seventy weeks can not come low enough to reach any of the events predicted by the prophecy, (he means of course the events to which Christians would apply the prophecy;) for from the first of Cyrus to the death of Christ were five hundred and sixty-eight years; and therefore, if the said four hundred and ninety years be computed from thence, they will be expired a great many years either before the cutting off, or the coming of the Messiah." As he begins his computation from a supposed figurative prediction of the angel, so he continues the events in the same sense, making the streets and city to mean figuratively, Church and State (Ibid. 415.) And the ditch, he makes a figurative expression, for good constitutions and establishment (Ibid. 416). Neither is he silent (as the authors of the Universal History are,) concerning the confirming of the covenant with many for one week;

he says (p. 416) this "was done by Jesus confirming for one week, that is, for the space of seven years, the covenant of the gospel with many of the Jews." But how he does this, when Christians as well as he himself (p. 380) declare and assert that his gospel "was not a temporal law, as was that of Moses; but to last forever, and to be a guide unto all righteousness as long as the world should last," and thus reduce it to only a seven years covenant, seems very strange and contradictory. Not less difficult is for him, how to make out that part of the prophecy, which declares that the sacrifice and oblations should cease in the middle of the last week; as they continued for a long time after the death of Jesus, with which event he closes the count of the period of seventy weeks. They have recourse in this difficulty, as they can not falsify the well known historical facts of their continuance until the destruction of the city, about forty years after, to the groundless pretense that "the sacrifices lost their efficacy, and became useless and insignificant, after the grand sacrifice of the savior of the world;" (Un. Hist. x, p. 449,) but for this you must take their word, for want of better proof. Most remarkable is the fulfilling of this part of the prophecy, as made out by Prideaux; for he has not the patience to wait till the death of Jesus, but anticipates it by half a week; for he tells us (Con. ii, p. 416): "that he should in the half past week, that is, in the latter part of it, cause the sacrifice and oblations in the temple to cease, and in the conclusion of the whole, that is, in the precise ending of the seventy weeks, be cut off and die, and accordingly (this he asserts with great assurance,) all this was exactly fulfilled and was brought to pass;" so that according to him, they must have lost their efficacy before the death of Jesus: and if this be so, what becomes of all the types of Christ's sacrifice, which they are made to prefigure? They pretend, by what rule of language I know not, that the overspreading of abominations "sufficiently prefigures the Roman eagles set up in the temple;" (Un. Hist. x, 449,) which is false in fact, none being set up there, as the building was in flames before it was taken, (Ibid. 663,) neither did the Romans there set up any idolatry at all. They are all so greatly perplexed how to make out and apply that part of the prophecy which mentions "the people of the prince that shall come," some applying the passage to the Romans under Titus, others to Jesus himself. But the first it can not be, because if the seventy weeks are applied to Jesus, all the events mentioned must of course have happened before his death; consequently, Titus with the Romans, who laid siege to Jerusalem many years after, can not be the person intended; neither can it be Jesus, who had no worldly power, nor command of any people to destroy the city. The prophecy declares positively, that the Messiah or Anointed was to be cut off after the sixty-second week; whereas the authors of the Universal History stretch it to the sixty-ninth week, and Prideaux to the seventieth, which is a contradiction of the prophecy; for, if the Messiah was not to be cut off till the sixty-ninth or the seventieth week, that period would undoubtedly have been fixed by the angel, and not the sixty-second. In short, considering their assertions made without the least foundation, and contrary not only to the prophecy, but also to facts, you will have less cause to be surprised at what is generally asserted by them concerning the finishing of transgression, making an end of sins, reconciliation for iniquities, and the bringing in everlasting righteousness, on all of which, and the sealing up the vision and prophecy, and the anointing the Most Holy, they run out and declaim most profusely; an instance of this you have in Prideaux, who makes all the above expressions accomplished, "in the great work of our salvation, undertaken by Jesus, fully completed by his death, passion, and resurrection. Being born without original sin, and living without actual sin, he was the most holy of all—he was anointed with the Holy Ghost, and with power to be king, priest, and prophet, which offered himself a sacrifice upon the cross, making thereby an end of sin, in so doing he did work reconciliation for us with our God." It is a pity that the learned author had not proved every one of these particular points; for it is impossible that any one can consider all these events thus put together, and think that they came to pass, or were brought about by Jesus. A transition of our thoughts, and a little reflection on the wickedness of the times in which he lived, the perpetual divisions, and continual crimes or unrighteousness of the church from the beginning down to this time, must surely make it not only impossible, but ridiculous to pretend any such fulfillments; the contradictions must appear so glaring to any person acquainted with the history of the church and its proceedings, as must occasion, nay, force, a conclusion entirely opposite; for it must naturally lead him to think, that nothing like that which is pretended ever happened, and that consequently the prophecy could never terminate in Jesus.

LETTER XV.

We are told by Father Calmet that there are many different hypotheses concerning Daniel's seventy weeks, even among Christian writers—some begin them from the first year of Darius, the Meade which is the epoch of Daniel's prophecy, and make them end at the profanation of the Temple by Antiochus Epiphanes. Others begin them from the first year of Cyrus at Babylon, and place the end of them at the destruction of the Temple by the Romans. Others fix the beginning at the first year of Darius, the Meade, and put the end at the birth of Jesus; Julius Africanus begins the seventy weeks at the second year of Artaxerxes, and makes them terminate at the death of Christ. (Cal. dict. see art. Weeks.) This Julius Africanus lived in the third century, and, I think, applied the seventy weeks to Jesus, which none of the Gospel writers or any other had yet done, though they lived late enough, every one having written according to their pretended accomplishment in the death of Jesus. Thus you see nothing is left unattempted to make out the accomplishment of this prophecy. "But," says the author of 'Grounds and Reasons,' (p. 250.) "let them understand by week, weeks of years, or what other portion of time they may see fit; let them understand by a year the Jewish or Chaldean, a lunar or solar year; let them begin the weeks in the year of Cyrus, or Darius, or Xerxes, or in the seventh or twentieth of Artaxerxes Longimanus, or when Daniel had his vision; let them fix the time of Jesus' birth, or beginning to preach, or death, when they please; and let them assign the time of the expiration of the seventy weeks, which is variously fixed, when they please; yet can not this prophecy be made to square the event they would refer it to, and will be after all subject to great difficulties." "Many other writers," (says Mr. Woolston, Dissert. on Dan. Weeks, p. 4,) "besides the Bishop of Litchfield, such as Dr. Clark, Dr. Marshall, Mr. Whiston, and Mr. Lykes, have most powerfully urged this prophecy against the author of the Grounds: and indeed it was unavoidable, and not to be passed over in silence by them since this author, by his insinuations, had objected to the obscurity of this prophecy, the difficulty of its application, and the difference amongst expositors in the computation of the time mentioned in it, and therefore the said writers against the Grounds were in the right on it, almost every one to contend for the truth of this prophecy, and to illustrate it; and if they had all jumped in their numerical and chronological notions with the least show of exactness, they had done something to the purpose. But alas! they are as unhappily divided amongst themselves as any before them, in their way of arithmetic and chronology, and good Mr. Whiston is so offended with the Bishop of Litchfield and Dr. Clark for their computation of Daniel's weeks, that he could not forbear writing against them."

These differences are enough to justify the opinion, that where there is so little agreement, little certainty can be expected; and you will less wonder at finding some of the most eminent Christian chronologists and commentators give up the application and its accomplishment in Jesus, and endeavor at a different computation and application by ending the seventy weeks, and the events mentioned in the prophecy, in the times of Antiochus Epiphanes; this is also the time assigned to this prophecy by some of the best Jewish authors.

I was once of opinion that no person could ever be able to know and ascertain the true meaning and import of this prophecy; it always appeared to me to be a particular revelation made to Daniel, who was favored with the foreknowledge of many future events, particularly with some remarkable transactions which would within a limited space of time befall his people; and as it was not necessary that any other person should have the like knowledge, a good many passages of his book are written in such terms as make inquiry very difficult. (Dan. viii, 26.) The divisions among commentators, who hardly agree in any one circumstance, helped to confirm me in this opinion, and their attempts to apply and extend the prophecy to a favorite event, or a particular hypothesis, rather than sincerely try to get at its true meaning, greatly increases the difficulties. I have shown the impossibility of extending it to one event to which it has, with great labor, been tried to make it answer. It now remains that I make it square with a very different event, to which I think it corresponds better. Probability is, in my opinion, the highest degree we can arrive at. By the angel, Daniel was made to know and understand its meaning and application; but as no other person was ever favored with the like privilege, it would appear presumptuous to attempt it. As this prophecy is largely and fully handled by many Jewish and Christian commentators who apply it to the same event, with little variation in their hypothesis, I shall refer you to them, and therefore shall be very short.

It appears from v. 2 of the ninth chapter that Daniel's prayer, and this subsequent revelation took place, on account of the construction which certain books, of that time, had put upon Jeremiah's prophecy of the captivity of Judah. After confessing the iniquity of his time, Daniel appeals to God's mercy for forgiveness of their sins, and for the introduction of those glorious, righteous, peaceable times on the globe, which are so often described by the prophets, and which period in mankind's existence the Pharisees called "the heavenly kingdom." They meant by this term universal peace and happiness on earth, and not the world of spirits where the Eternal Jehovah presided even before this globe's beginning. To his prayer the angel answers (the whole is in a vision): "Seventy weeks are accorded to thy people, and to the city of thy sanctuary, [either] to complete the wickedness and fill [the measure of] sins, or to atone for iniquity by introducing righteousness into the world, and thus seal vision and prophecy, and anoint the sanctum sanctorum," (that is, fulfill the prophecies by the righteous life which is the proper service of the Most Holy.) "Yet you may know and understand: since the prophecy (*dabar*) has gone forth to again build Jerusalem until the anointed prince [were] seven weeks." Or from the word of Jeremiah (xxv) in the first year of Nebuchadnezzar's reign until Cyrus who is by God through Isaiah* (xlv. 1) called "the anointed," there were seven weeks of forty-nine years. "And sixty and two weeks shall again be built wall, space, and ditch, even in troublous times. After the (*hashabuim*) sixty and two weeks an anointed will be destroyed and shall not have [help]" (*v'en lo*). The sixty-two weeks from the same time or four hundred and thirty-four years bring us to Judas Maccabeus, during which time the city was rebuilt in very troublous times, as is evident from the history of the Jews. After this epoch another Messiah, that is the legal, *anointed* Highpriest Onias, an upright, virtuous priest, an exception among the priests of the second temple, was cruelly put to death just after the sixty-second week. (2 Macc. iv.) We thus have two persons, two anointed ones, and a literal accomplishment by them of the prophecy, the words of which require two persons. Nothing can be more contradictory to the text than the forced translation, "unto the Messiah the Prince shall be seven weeks, and three score and two weeks;" for if the angel meant sixty-nine weeks, it would have been absurd to divide the time and announce two periods when he meant but one. My translation is perfectly conformable to the text, and agrees with the chronology of those times. Besides, Cyrus and Onias are properly termed Messiahs; but Jesus' right to that appellation is not so evident, as it can not be admitted as an adequate proof that they assert "he was anointed with the Holy Ghost," which phrase, rightly considered, is but an empty sound without any meaning at all.

But to proceed. "And the people of the prince, that will come, will corrupt (yash'chith) the city and the sanctuary, and its end [comes on as] by a flood, and until the end war and desolation are determined," which is a description of the doings of Antiochus Epiphanes and his army. (1 Macc. i, 20—24; 30—39; 2 Macc.

*According to the nearly unanimous opinion of Hebrew scholars the book of Isaiah, from Chap. xl to the end, is the production of a later prophet in the time of Cyrus.

vii, 16; 24—26.) "And he shall make a firm covenant with many for one week," is the covenant made by Antiochus with many who left the Jewish law to follow the customs of the Greeks. (1 Macc. i, 11—15.) "And in the midst of the week, he shall stop sacrifice and oblation, and [put] upon the battlements the abominations of the desolators," which happened accordingly; for he forbade in the middle of the week all service in the temple according to Jewish law, caused impure, Greek sacrifices to be offered, and idol altars to be built all over Palestine. (Ibid. 45, 54.) "Until the waste, which is firmly determined upon, shall be put upon the desolator," which also happened; for the Jews under the Maccabeean heroes overthrew the Greek-Syrian forces and regained their liberty.

Thus, sir, I have explained this famous prophecy, and you will judge for yourself whose explanation comes nearest to its meaning. Yet let me add that the righteous times for which Daniel prayed, and the future existence of which the whole tenor of Holy Writ implies, have no certain time fixed, but depends altogether upon mankind rendering themselves worthy of it. Still, whatever your opinion may be of my explanation of the prophecy, I may venture to assert that it can not be successfully applied to Jesus in a literal explanation; and if figurative comments are wanted, I doubt not such a one may be made out as would be much disliked by Christians; and why it should not be admitted, or be on the same footing, as those which they invent will be hard for them to show a sufficient cause.

LETTER XVI.

The fifty-third chapter of Isaiah is famous among Christian expounders: the whole is applied to and explained of Jesus. They tell us that he is therein described and represented as a person despised and rejected, as a man of sorrow and acquainted with grief; as one on whom the sins of the whole world were to be laid; as one who should offer himself to a ignominious death, and be chastised for our transgressions and iniquities—thereby redeeming lost mankind and working their reconciliation with an infinite and offended God—atoning with his life and suffering for original and actual sin; the whole human race (as they pretend) being slaves of the devil, and under God's wrath and damnation, as partakers of Adam's sin; God requiring infinite satisfaction, which not being in the power of any finite creature to make, could only be done by Jesus, as being God and man. It is really surprising to what lengths they stretch these doctrines; asserting that no person can be saved by his own merits, making salvation attainable only by the merits of Jesus, (that is, declaring we are only to be saved by proxy;) and they will have all good or beneficent works to be sinful without faith in Jesus, holding all accursed who believe in happiness hereafter by following the dictates of God, of mercy, justice and humanity. Thus one absurdity giving rise to another, they banish that charity which on many occasions they pretend to be the distinguishing characteristic of their religion; their own creeds proving this boast to have but little foundation. These doctrines and inventions are the foundation of the present system of Christianity, and are the consequences of, and have their foundation on the idea of original sin, from whence they draw a pretense for Jesus' sufferings and ignominious death, and the necessity of infinite satisfaction, that is, the necessity of one God dying to satisfy another, or the same God. It will be necessary to sift this matter and show its absurdity, and prove that there is no manner of foundation either in reason or Scripture for such invention; for as is judiciously observed, (Wharburton, Div. Leg. i, 83,) one of God's revelations can not contradict another, because He gave us the first to judge all others by; and it will be, therefore, vain to pretend that these doctrines are above reason, if they contradict reason and common sense, which faculties He endowed us with for the very purpose of discovering truth from error.

The ETERNAL's first revelation tells us in plain and unvarnished language—so plain as to be not possibly misunderstood—that Adam, and the other agents concerned in the first (or as they call it, original,) sin, had sentence pronounced on them by God Himself, which sentence was inflicted on the offenders; we have it (Gen. iii, 6—14) in the following words: "And the LORD God said unto the serpent, Because thou hast done this, thou art cursed above all cattle, and above every beast of the field; upon thy belly shalt thou go, and dust thou shalt eat all the days of thy life; and I will put enmity between thee and the woman, and between thy seed and her seed, it shall bruise thy head and thou shalt bruise his heel. Unto the woman He said, I will greatly multiply thy sorrow and thy conception, in sorrow shalt thou bring forth children, and thy desire shall be to thy husband, and he shall rule over thee. And unto Adam He said, Because thou hast hearkened unto the voice of thy wife, and hast eaten of the tree which I commanded thee, saying, Thou shalt not eat of it, cursed is the ground for thy sake, in sorrow thou shalt eat of it all the days of thy life," &c. This was God's own definitive sentence, which being executed on the different (or several) offenders, will any one say, that God required either a greater or a different satisfaction than that which He Himself imposed? Can any one say, that He was not satisfied with His own judgment?

Go wiser thou, and in thy scale of sense
Weigh thy opinions against Providence.—POPE.

Can there be a greater absurdity and contradiction, than to pretend that God Himself must suffer that He may pardon? How inconsistent (not to say impious,) are such doctrines! How unacquainted must those who propagate and inculcate such notions be with God and His attributes! Is it to be imagined that the sin of our first parents, after judgment and sentence were executed, should again be revived after some thousands of years? What tribunal or court of justice would allow this? Or who could be the appellants? Was it Adam that appealed against his Maker, or did the Almighty appeal against Himself, or His sentence? Is not such a proceeding, in fact, inflicting punishment on the Deity, as if He were the aggressor for giving a merciful sentence against Adam?

Snatch from His hand the balance and the rod,
Rejudge His justice, be the God of God.—POPE.

Can any thing be more ridiculous? and shall we believe people, nay, learned people, are serious, when they pretend to impose such absurdities for doctrines?

It is pretended that God being infinitely offended, required infinite satisfaction; but can God require of His creatures that which He never put in their power to give? Can we consistently with the natural notion we have of God, think He can act thus with His creatures, or that He in His infinite goodness can ever require more than is in our power to give? or, can finite creatures give infinite offense? But for argument's sake, let us suppose that such a satisfaction was necessary; and then let them tell us how it was possible that it should be made at all; for if God the Son (as is pretended,) be of the same essence with God the Father, how can one suffer and not the other? Besides, original sin must have equally offended the Father, Son, and Holy Ghost, since they are all but one, or of one and the same essence—for which reason all three must have required the like satisfaction; for as they all can have but one will, none could pardon without it; and why might not the Father or Holy Ghost be mediators as well as the Son, and if one could pardon or did not require infinite satisfaction, why not the other? And if we are told that nothing suffered by this satisfaction made on the cross but only the human nature, then they can not make out the satisfaction which they pretend was necessary; for if human sufferings were sufficient, there was no necessity for any satisfaction to be made by Jesus, as God and man. Adam, or any of his descendants, would have done as well. But let us inquire farther. Did Jesus make full satisfaction, or did he do it in part? If the first, pray what was it that was pardoned? Why, nothing; for the debt being fully paid, or satisfaction given, there was then, of course, no pardon; for supposing you owe me a sum of money, can it be said that I pardon you any thing on receiving payment, or satisfaction to the full amount? Would it not be ridiculous for me to say, I pardon you, having received the whole? Is it not equally absurd to say, pardon was obtained, when full satisfaction was made and given? But we may be told, that though full satisfaction could not be made, yet, that God accepted it and took it for such; if so, then they must allow, that God can pardon without full satisfaction, and if He can do thus, how absurd must it be to say, He required infinite satisfaction; and why He might not pardon Adam, on the punishment He inflicted, will be impossible for them to show. In short, they are reduced to this dilemma: If Jesus made full satisfaction, then there was no pardon; and if he did not make full satisfaction, then was there no necessity for either his sufferings or death. The Messiah, they say, was to die for the sins of the world; grant he did so; the natural consequence must then be, that mankind was restored; but nothing like this is pretended, for inquire in what the restoration consisted, and it vanishes to a mere nothing. Was the human race restored to any of its forfeited dignities? No. Was there any alteration in their affairs? No. Did the Jews receive any benefit or advantage by his coming? No; on the contrary, it is pretended that their doing that which was necessary to be done brought on their ruin. Can there be any thing more inconsistent or contradictory, than to pretend that the salvation of the whole world could only be brought about by the ignominious death of a person, and that the very act that introduced this salvation excluded those very people, through whose means it was obtained, from the benefit of it? How the Jews are upbraided for this very act, let all Christian writers witness: one and all agree, that for this sin not only the Jews' city and temple were destroyed, but that they brought thereby damnation on themselves and posterity. There is something very unaccountable in this affair; for Jesus must die that the world might be saved, and the Jews must be damned for the same reason. That Jesus was to suffer an ignominious death was pre-ordained, a thing settled by agreement; to this end and purpose, it is pretended, "he came into the world, the kings of the earth stood up, and the rulers were gathered together against the Lord, and against his Christ; for of a truth against the holy child Jesus, whom thou hast anointed, both Herod and Pontius Pilate, with the Gentiles and the people of Israel, were gathered together, for to do whatever thy hand and thy council determined before to be done." (Acts iv, 26.) That this was so, is evident from what John (xix, 11,) makes Jesus himself tell Pilate: "Thou couldst have no power at all against me, except it were given thee from above." Who can forbear lamenting this contrivance; who can forbear crying, O fatal necessity! Is it thus that the Almighty, the good and merciful God, deals His blessings to mankind, thus to deceive and doom to destruction the unhappy instruments which He was pleased to make use of in saving the world? Who could have suspected or believed that the Deity, who fills all things, should so contract His existence as to be contained in the womb of a woman, that He should take a human shape, and appear among us in disguise, doing all He could to hide from those to whom He was sent not only His divinity, but also the character of Messiah? (Matth. xvi, 20.) Was it to be imagined that the Messiah would in his discourses make use of nothing but dark saying and parables, that he might not be known? or as he is made to express himself, "that seeing, they may see, and not perceive, and hearing, they may hear, and not understand, lest at any time they should be converted and their sins should be forgiven them?" (Matth. iv, 12.) Is this conduct worthy of God? Is this the Messiah promised the Jews as their greatest good? Behold him using all the art he can from manifesting himself, "lest at any time they should see with their eyes, and should understand with their heart, and should be converted, and I should heal them." (Matth. xiii, 15.) Could it be imagined, that the Messiah would hinder the Jews in obtaining the means of being healed and forgiven? "And he said, Unto you it is given to know the mysteries of the kingdom of God: but to others in parables; that seeing they might not see, and hearing they might not understand." (Luke viii, 10.) The Jews did all in their power to be rightly informed, only desired a sign. But lest they should be convinced, they are refused; and a resolution is taken to give them no sign but the sign of Jonas (Matth. xvi, 4), which in fact was no sign, as it was never made good to them; for they were excluded from being present or seeing any of those transactions related of his resurrection; and I can not help thinking, that if his death brought on the desolation of Jerusalem, and the damnation of the Jews, it was none of their fault; since the grand secret was never disclosed to those who ought to have had the information; of this Jesus himself seems to have been sensible, "Father, forgive them, for they know not what they do," are said to have been his last and dying words, and St. Peter declares the Jews guiltless, "And now, brethren, I know, that through ignorance ye did it, and so did your rulers." (Acts iii, 17.)

It is, therefore, a great absurdity to pretend, that the destruction of the city and temple and the dispersion of the Jews were occasioned by putting Jesus to death. Was the destruction of the kingdom of Israel (which happened *seven hundred* years before Jesus,) owing to his death? Was the destruction of the city and temple by the Babylonians owing to his death? Were the many and frequent calamities which befell the Jews during the long periods of time of which the Bible gives us the history owing to his death? Was the entire demolition of Carthage and the entire distinction of her people owing to his death? Was the destruction of Polish or Irish nationalities owing to his death? No; we will be told that all such calamities were brought on by various political causes, and if so, why is not the last destruction of the Jewish city and temple imputed to the same political causes? Were not the Jews subject to the Romans long before the coming of Jesus? Were they not barbarously oppressed and ill treated by their extortionate governors, both before, in his time, and afterward? Was not this, together with a desire of recovering their liberties, and the being misled by some crafty and fanatical leaders, that which occasioned their revolt? They might as well pretend that all the misfortunes, which befell the Jews before the coming of Jesus were owing to his death, as to pretend that what afterward befell them was owing to this event, when it evidently appears that this was brought about by so many concurrent causes.

LETTER XVII.

The doctrine of original sin (for the purpose of frightening mankind into Christianity) and the necessity of Jesus' sufferings and death in satisfaction of it, appear very plainly to have been invented by his followers: the whole conduct of Jesus in our fragmentary and *ex parte* Gospels contradict it. We are told that, "as Jesus sat at meat in the house, behold many publicans and sinners came and sat with him and his disciples. And when the Pharisees saw it they said unto his disciples, Why eateth your master with publicans and sinners? But when Jesus heard that, he said unto them, *They that be whole need not a physician, but they that are sick.* But go ye and learn what that meaneth, *I will have mercy, and not sacrifice:* for I am not come to call *the righteous* (says he,) *but sinners to repentance.*" (Matth. ix, 10—13.) Nothing can be plainer and more to the point than this declaration of his; but how contradictory to the present system of Christianity let any one judge. Jesus, in explanation of his visits to bad and wicked individuals, declares that they that be whole need not a physician, but only those that are sick; but Christians insist that unless both the whole and the sick have one, they must be damned. Jesus declares that he came not to call the righteous, but sinners to repentance; but Christians insist that without *faith* they must be damned, repentance not being deemed by them sufficient. Jesus, a Galilean Jew, declares from Holy Writ (Hosea vi, 10), "that God requires mercy, and not sacrifice," but dogmatic Christians contradict him, and strenuously insist, that God could have no mercy *without* sacrifice. Is it possible that Jesus should have made such a declaration, if he knew that he himself was to be made a sacrifice, nay, a *necessary* sacrifice, to which he had, as Christians pretend, devoted and offered himself *willingly* and *freely?* But it is very plain that all pretensions of this sort have no manner of foundation; since it was with the utmost reluctance that he suffered. "My soul is exceedingly sorrowful, unto death," says he (Matth. xxvi, 38); he prayed very fervently: O, my Father! if it be possible let this cup pass from me," (Matth. xxvi, 29; Luke xxii, 42.) Here is what he earnestly desired, and what he besought in the utmost agonies—such as even made the sweat that came from him "as it were great drops of blood falling to the ground." (Matth. xxvi, 44.) The whole of this transaction evidently shows that he had not made any such agreement. For either he knew his death to be necessary, or he was ignorant of it: if the first, then was his praying to be exempted from that which was necessary, from that to which he devoted himself, and from that which he came to perform, absurd and ridiculous—and would have been thought so, had any common person acted in the like manner; for how could he so earnestly pray to be exempted from that which he knew was necessary for him to undergo, having freely offered himself? Was the desire of saving the world a matter of such indifference to him? Was his love to mankind abated? But if he knew not that his sufferings were necessary, or that, by his means, the world was to be saved: then could he not be that divine person which Christians make him; and consequently, if infinite satisfaction was necessary, or the death of God required, he could not be the person that could make it; that he could not be God is plain, not only from his whole conduct, but also from the circumstance of the angel's descent from heaven to strengthen him. (Luke xxii, 43.) Now, for God to be either in such agonies, or to stand in need of another's assistance, appears to be such an absurdity, as surely ought not to be mentioned; for of what service or use would the divine nature be, if it could not prevent human frailties and fears from getting the better of it, nor prevent its triumphing over it? On the whole, I think there redounds no honor to Jesus from the representations of this whole affair, since he prayed to be excused from it, and besought it with bloody sweats, it being done contrary to his inclination. "Not as I will," says he, "but as thou wilt," (Matth. xxvi, 39,) or, "Not my will, but thine be done" (Luke xxii, 42); so that, if he was a divine person, he must have had an opposite will to that of the Father, which, if so, will be difficult to be shown consistent; and either the Jews contracted no guilt, since there could be no salvation obtained without his sufferings; or salvation must be made the consequence of an obnoxious wicked act! To these sad dilemmas are they reduced.

We are told "that the whole economy of man's redemption is everywhere represented to us as an unsearchable mystery of divine wisdom and goodness, and as the object of our belief, and not of our comprehension; (Univ. Hist. x, 591) but, as this is the foundation on which the whole superstructure is built, I think that if the same be proved to be false, every thing that is built thereon must fall; for can that be made a matter of belief, which we not only do not comprehend, but which is contradictory in itself? Neither can it be made to answer any end or purpose at all; for as to original sin, they do not pretend that it is atoned for; it being an article of faith that all that are born are enemies to God, and slaves of the devil, and even children are doomed by the Romish Church to perdition if they die before baptism; and this they say is for original sin of which the children are most innocent; so that Jesus' death was of no service. And as to actual sin, we are as subject to be carried away by the flesh as our forefathers were, the same proneness to vice predominates in our weak natures, and experience will teach us that there is not the least alteration; so that his sufferings wrought us no cure. And as to any spiritual benefit, it is plain that by this scheme the world is in a worse condition than it was before; for the Jews by the law of Moses, and the Gentiles by that of nature, obtained salvation; but now the elect only are to be saved, and this saving doctrine is contracted to such narrow limits that it extends no farther than a particular sect; for the Roman Catholics send the reformed of all sects to the devil, and these in their turn do the like not only by them, but by all of different sects; for salvation is engrossed, and made the sole privilege of those within their own pale; and to the rest of mankind they show no mercy, as appears by their creeds. What was it, then, that his death redeemed the world from? Was it the cause of introducing true religion? His death for that purpose was needless, and it might have been done without his suffering. But where, or among what sect or party is this true religion to be found? Is it in the Romish Church? This the others contradict. Is it to be found in any particular sect? This will be denied by all the others. Of what benefit, then, were Jesus' sufferings and death? Could they in fact show the benefits arising from it, then indeed might they boast, and have some reason to apply the prophecy to him; but to pretend to impute it to him without proving the effects, is very extraordinary. How inconsistent are Christians in their doctrines! They tell us that Jesus atoned and made satisfaction for original sin, and yet declare that children are born with it. But again they pretend that it is done away by baptism, his death benefitting those only who received it—all others continuing under its penalty, the same as if he had not suffered; so that to be free from original sin (for which no one ever thought himself in any wise accountable) his death is not sufficient; the atonement being made to consist in baptism. And after all this they place the efficacy of the cure in the imagination; for they will tell you that Jesus did his part, and by his death freed every one from his sin; but it is necessary that you think so, for otherwise you can receive no benefit from it. You must therefore first think yourself under God's curse and indignation, and then imagine Jesus has freed you from it, that is, you must imagine yourself sick, and then imagine Jesus has cured you, and then you are sound and well; but if you have not strength of imagination sufficient to make you think yourself sick, and consequently, that you stand in no need of medicine, why then Adam's eating the forbidden fruit will rise in judgment against you, and you must be eternally damned. Is not mankind by this redemption scheme in a much worse condition than it was before? Was this the inestimable blessing which the world received by his death? Perhaps one in a thousand will be saved, and all the rest are to be damned. Now, how he carried our sorrows and our griefs, or how he bore our iniquities and our transgressions, or how he made atonement for our sins, and in what manner he justified us, are things which, I confess, I am not able to comprehend.

The Bible (Gen. ii, 7; Eccles. xii, 7,) and natural science tell us that man is composed of the material, animal body, and the divine immortal spirit, which is an emanation from God and the immaculate gift from Him to each individual. Only the body we receive from our parents, and it only is affected by their transgression as reason aided by experience teaches us. This the Bible also confirms: Visiting the iniquity of parents to the third and fourth generations. (See note to Letter XI.) The immediate descendant of Adam, Cain, is told (Gen. iv, 6, 7,) that his salvation, or eternal happiness depends on his own behavior, that he can rule over sin; that is, he can conquer his bad inclinations. And this is in accordance with reason; for can we suppose the God of truth, of purity, would inhale us an impure spirit, stained by somebody else's sin? Only our own sins affect us, and the all-kind Creator has declared that on our repenting and turning to Him with a reformed life, He would accept us and pardon us (See Isaiah lv, 7, and Ezech. xxxiii, 11), such acceptance on our repentance and amendment, being also agreeable to reason, and to God's mercy and goodness. Thus it must always have been, had Jesus suffered or not. Besides, if Jesus made satisfaction for the sins of the world, the past, present, and future sins, then can it be of no importance whether we be good or bad; for if that be so, our reward, or happiness, must be secured thereby, without good words or virtuous actions on our part. But it may be pretended that our reward depends partly on our own merits, and partly on the satisfaction which Jesus made,—imputing part of his own righteousness to make up our own deficiency. To this I answer: By this scheme Jesus was only a savior in part, and the redemption must be as incomplete as it is absurd; besides it takes from him the merit of having saved the world. For if our personal righteousness be necessary, or our repentance and amendment, then can not his death be any advantage to us, because upon these terms, as I have before observed, we always had assurance of being accepted. Nothing can be more contradictory than to pretend that a person (and a just one at that) was to suffer, that the wicked might receive a reward; for if that would be the case, men would be rewarded without regard to their merits; for personal merits must necessarily belong to the agent, and are connected with the very individual, inherent in himself, and no transfer can be made of them from one agent to another; consequently to claim another's merits is the most absurd and incoherent scheme that was ever invented. Is it reasonable that a person plead another's merits, and pretend to justify himself by faith? Will such a plea of justification avail a villain? and shall one who practices all the moral duties of life be damned, because he lacks that faith? Can it be made consistent with Holy Writ or reason, that the wicked be rewarded through faith, and to impute it to them for righteousness, while they deny to the good, who have led a life of goodness and virtue, the reward due to their merits? If God accepts faith, let them trust to it, and let there be no distinction between moral good and evil; but if good works be deemed necessary, why shall not he that practices them be benefitted thereby, let him belong to what sect or society, either choice or circumstances may have placed him in?* Shall the merits of one person benefit all others that will plead them, and shall not personal acts and righteousness avail those who practise them? Can any thing be more inconsistent with God's justice and mercy?

Thus you see, to what absurdities the scheme of Jesus' sufferings and death leads them, and those that through policy first published and spread this fiction could not foresee the consequences of reasoning from it. For, let us suppose that the Jews had received Jesus as their Messiah; that they had believed him to be God, and that they had paid him during life (terminated by old age as it would have been in the course of nature) the adoration paid to him by Christians since his death: what must have been the consequence? Must not the world have been damned, as a necessary consequence, because no atonement, no justification, no imputed righteousness, no faith could then have been pleaded, and in their absence all must have perished everlastingly? Are they, therefore, not under obligations to the Jews for performing the act, though wicked, as represented, since it has brought them salvation? How ungrateful they are for this benefit! Jesus underwent a momentary pain, and for that they reverence and adore him; the Jews were involved in the same act; they were appointed and elected to the work, but they are apportioned destruction and damnation for themselves and their posterity, for doing their part,—and are yet despised, ill-treated, and rejected by these very persons who pretend to reap the benefit. These are the absurdities attending this incomprehensible scheme; they are in the right, therefore, in calling it, "an usearchable mystery," and as such let those, who can, believe it!

*Of this opinion is Paul, writing to the Romans, (ii, 6 -10,) "God, who will render to every man according to his deeds: to them who by patient continuance in well-doing, seek for glory and honor, and immortality; eternal life: but unto them that are contentious, and do not obey the truth, but obey unrighteousness; indignation and wrath, tribulation and anguish upon every soul of man that doeth evil; of the Jew first, and also of the Gentile; but glory, honor, and peace, to every man that worketh good; to the Jew first, and also to the Gentile."

LETTER XVIII.

The absurdity and inconsistency of the doctrines treated of in my two last letters prove the impossibility of applying the prophecy, or making it answer the purposes intended thereby, as some pretend, that a two-fold death was implied in the sentence. They infer that Adam and his posterity were condemned both to a death of the body and a death of the spirit, from which they could only be released by the sufferings and passion of one, who was both God and man, in direct contradiction of God's plain words to Cain, the son of Adam. They produce a fictitious story of an agreement made between God the Father and God the Son, according to the terms of which the latter offered himself to be made a sacrifice on the cross, to appease the wrath of God the Father, and to atone by this ignominious death for Adam's sin; restoring the human race thereby to God's grace and favor, freeing them from the power of the devil, and from the penalties under which they must have continued, as no other satisfaction could have been accepted or deemed sufficient. We shall now, therefore, inquire into the foundation of this two-fold death. "In the day that thou eatest thereof *thou shalt surely die*," (Gen. ii, 17,)* is expressed in Hebrew by the words מות תמות (*moth tamuth*) (literally "to die thou shalt die,") or as the marginal note of the English Bible has it, "Dying thou shalt die." This is but the usual Hebrew form of expressing certainty and emphasis of a command, by placing the infinitive mood before the future tense or imperative mood. When Solomon passed sentence on Shimei, the very same phrase is made use of, "On the day thou goest forth, and passest over the brook Kidron, thou shalt know for certain thou shalt surely die." (Hebrew *moth tamuth*,) I Kings ii, 37.

*According to many Hebrew Scholars, the entire history of Paradise, the fall, Cain, and Abel, from Gen. ii, 4, to v, that is the ii, iii, and iv chapters, are the insertion of a much later writer, at the publication of a new digest of the Pentateuch Chapter v follows very naturally on ii, 3, continues the idea of man's creation in separate sexes and gives Seth as the first born son, without mentioning Cain or Abel,

The prophet Elisha uses the same phrase to Hazael in speaking of the certain death of Benhadad, king of Syria: The *Lord* hath shown me that he shall surely die. (Hebr. *moth tamuth.*) II Kings viii, 10.

When Saul doomed his son Jonathan to death he uses the same expression: "Thou shalt surely die, Jonathan." (Hebrew *moth tamuth.*) I Sam. xiv, 44. He also uses the same words when he sentenced the priest: "Thou shalt surely die, Abimelech." (Hebrew *moth tamuth.*) Ibid. xxii, 16.

From these and all other passages in the Scriptures where the same phrase is used, it is plain that this expression only denotes death of the body. Thus you see the foundation on which this grand superstructure is built. The sentence only signifies that on the day Adam ate the forbidden fruit he should commence to be mortal, or be liable to death. This is also in full agreement with reason and human experience. What we eat or take as nourishment into our body is prepared by the stomach and intestines for introduction into the blood, and modifies the functions of the bodily organs, and through these even the body itself. Death being the punishment by the operation of the law of nature, Adam was removed from his first happy abode, that he might be exposed to want and calamities, stimulating and developing his own powers, yet gradually causing decay and weakening the bond between body and spirit. The punishment being thus inflicted upon the transgressor, would it be just, in addition to the defects of body inherited from their progenitor by the law of nature that like begets like, to doom his race to eternal damnation of the spirit? Is such conduct reconcilable to the goodness and mercy of the *Eternal?* Supposing a legislator instituted a law, and enacted a certain punishment to be inflicted on those who transgressed that law: would not the infliction of another and greater punishment on the transgressor be unjust? And if unjust in human laws and tribunals, how much more so in the All-merciful God? In what a woful and miserable state must the whole human family be, if, notwithstanding they in all respects obeyed the will of God, they should ever continue under His wrath and heavy displeasure, both here and hereafter? To what purpose did He give laws, if those who practiced the duties enjoined by them were not benefited thereby? Can this be made consistent? No, this original sin—double-death opinion is invented to give a coloring to what is not, on any grounds *whatever*, to be maintained or supported.

Another trick to uphold this doctrine is that the history of the fall ought not to be taken literally. I can not better answer this evasion than in the words made use of by the authors of the Universal History. They say, (Vol. I, 135,) "It can not be denied, that some of the ancient philosophers affected such an allegorical way of writing to conceal their notions from the vulgar, and keep their learning within the bounds of their own school; yet it is apparent that Moses had no such design; and as he pretends only to relate matters of fact just as they happened, the well known passage: 'Not what goes into the mouth defiles the body,' is in itself sufficient proof of the fallibility and want of inspiration of the Gospel; for such a saying, indirect contradiction of God's well known physical laws can not have been spoken by inspiration. It is no doubt a production of the antijudaizing (or Paulinian) wing of early Christians, without art or disguise, it can not be supposed that the history of the fall is to be taken in a literal sense as well as the rest of his writings." Notwithstanding this plain and sensible deduction, these authors declare themselves of opinion that it was the Devil who made use of the serpent's body. That this beast stands for, and means the Devil, is also the opinion of almost every Christian commentator, (Dr. Clark tries to make it a monkey,) and it is particularly asserted by Dr. Sherlock, who has taken great pains to establish this point. But conscious that the passage as it stands could not bear that meaning, he adds, (Intent and Use of Prophecy, page 59,) "You will say, what an unreasonable liberty of interpretation this is; tell us by what rules of language the seed of the woman is made to denote one particular person (that is Jesus,) and by what art you discover the mystery of Christ's miraculous conception and birth in this common expression? Tell us likewise, how bruising the serpent's head becomes to signify destroying the power of sin and the redemption of mankind by Christ? As the prophecy stands there, (he ought to have said the *history*,) nothing appears to point out this particular meaning, much less to confine the prophecy (history) to it?" And I think that many good reasons ought to be given to his own objections, and a proper authority produced for giving this history any other sense; since, as he himself owns and readily allows that the expressions do not imply this sense. "We allow (he says, pp. 70,71,) that there is no appearance that our first parents understood them in this sense, or that God intended they should so understand them." Yet notwithstanding this he has, on doctrines of which our first parents knew nothing, on doctrines which "God never intended they should so understand," placed and established all the hopes and comforts of religion.

But whatever may be pretended, Adam by his fall forfeited that, whatever it it was, which he for a short time possessed, and was reduced to a state of labor, and subject to sorrow: yet it nowhere appears that they (he and Eve) were bereft "of a rational foundation for their future endeavors to reconcile themselves to God by a better obedience," (Intent and Use of Prophecy, page 61,) the best foundation, and indeed the only one, on which they could place their hope, (which I choose to give you in the Bishop's words;) and whenever this foundation was neglected, and dependence on a Mediator was introduced, you may then be sure that false religion and false worship took place; and it would be easy to prove that it was such schemes and inventions which gave the first rise to idolatry, and defaced true religion.

But whatever hopes this learned person makes our first parents to have different from a better obedience; or whatever foundation he is pleased to make necessary for the preservation of religion, by the hopes "that their posterity should one day be restored:" this much is certain, that any such dependence must have been ill-grounded; for if Adam's posterity was to be restored by the satisfaction made by Jesus on the cross, nothing like it was effected; for the serpent still labors under the curse; women still bear children in pain, and continue in subjugation to their husbands, (which some of them think the worst part of the curse;) the men still labor and endure sorrow; and death makes the same havoc as it did before. Let them represent things in what light they please, they still continue as they were.

To establish these doctrines they will have the serpent stand for, and be the Devil. But can anything be plainer than that every part of the sentence is only applicable to a literal serpent, a beast of the field, the being more accursed than any other beast, or above all cattle? Rank him with the brute creation; the Devil, I think, has nothing to do with this part of the curse. The serpent was to creep on his belly; in this punishment the Devil is also excluded. The serpent was also to eat dust all the days of his life; very improper food, hardly intended for the Devil, who they will scarcely admit mortal, as "the days of his life" imply. The serpent and his seed, and the woman and her seed were to be in continual enmity; the woman and her descendants were to bruise the serpent's head, whilst the serpent and his offspring, being by nature or by the curse made reptiles, should bite the others' heels, that being the part which they could most conveniently come at. This being a conflict between the woman and the serpent, and their offsprings, has the Devil any concern in this strife? Can words be made use of to denote plainer, that the whole concerns the serpent and his seed, and not the Devil, and that the woman and her seed are Eve and her descendants, and not Jesus in particular, as is pretended? That in this enmity and strife each should hurt the other as they had it in their power? Could the Devil hurt or bite Jesus in the heel, or has he any seed or posterity? It is plain, therefore, that the curse concerns the serpent only; he is represented at the first mention as an animal: "Now, the serpent was more subtle than any beast of the field which the LORD God had made;" (Gen iii, 2,) and for making a bad use of his subtlety he was punished. Now, had the serpent been actuated by the Devil, he could deserve no punishment. In short there is nothing in the whole sentence which concerns the Devil, neither can I find in this whole history any promise of a Messiah, nor any agreement between God the Father and God the Son. Indeed, such an agreement must be inconsistent, and would prove different wills in the Divinity; that is, there must have been one willing to make satisfaction and another willing to receive it.

while a third remained passive or neuter; acts as contrary to each other as any distinct beings are capable of, and inconsistent in the same God.

Thus you see the impossibility of proving what they pretend to, from the first eight verses of this chapter, and how contradictory to their claims it is in every respect. The remainder will appear not less so. Verse 9. "And he made his grave with the wicked and with the rich in his death," is the very reverse of what happened to Jesus; for in his death (it is related) he was with the wicked, being crucified between two thieves, while the tomb in which he was buried was that of Joseph of Arimathea, represented, as an honorable, just man.

V. 10. "He shall see his seed, he shall prolong his days, and the pleasure of the Lord shall prosper in his hand." Here are three blessings, of which none can be applicable to Jesus. As to the first, that he should see his seed, or have the pleasure of viewing his descendants, we do not hear that he had any children; the second promise of length of days, or long life, he did not enjoy as he is reported to have been executed at the early age of thirty-three years; and in regard to the third blessing of prosperity, their accounts of his poverty and sufferings contradicts it. To make out these blessings, they have recourse to the mystical application, though they pretend this whole chapter to be literal of him; they say that *seed* here does not mean *children* or descendants, but that the phrase denotes the *church*, or his followers, spiritually so called. But this has not the least foundation, as the Hebrew word זרע (*zerang*) is always used to denote descendants or posterity, and there is no such thing in all Holy Writ as spiritual seed or spiritual descendants. In the same manner they explain the Hebrew idiom, prolong his days, which always denotes long life, and pretend it means immortality. But this is but trifling, since immortality is not given as a privilege, but is general and common to every soul, the quality of even the wicked and the damned; so that length of days in the sense of immortality belongs to every departed spirit, and can only therefore be taken in its literal meaning as an earthly blessing. As to "the pleasure of the LORD prospering in his hands"—or prosperity—as they can not make it out *here*, they send us to his heavenly kingdom; but as they know nothing of it from any personal experience, you must take their words for it, at what such guesses may be worth.

V. 11. "By his knowledge shall my righteous servant justify many." This I have very plainly shown, he never did; therefore I will say nothing more on this head.

V. 12. "Therefore will I divide him a portion with the great, and he shall divide the spoil with the strong." This part of the verse is in no way applicable to Jesus; for, far from dividing a portion with the great, or having any spoil allotted to him, he never possessed any thing of his own, as he himself is said to have remarked. "Because he poured out his soul unto death" can not be said in truth of him, since his death was contrary to his will, and forced on him. How "he bore the sin of many" or "made intercession for transgressors," I have already considered.

Thus, sir, from the above objections and considerations it is evident that this chapter can not be truthfully applied to Jesus, neither can Christians prove therefrom the benefit which they pretend must be the necessary benefit of their doctrine.

LETTER XIX.

I remarked in a former letter upon the well-known fact the division of the Bible text, in chapters and verses, being comparatively a modern invention (dating back about 400 years) to facilitate references. The beginning of Isaiah's sermon, of which the fifty-third chapter forms but a part, is found in chapter 50, verses 4 to 11, which contain the introduction, stating his commission from the Almighty, and also the difficulty of the preacher's calling. In chapter 51, the prophet expresses the kindness of God to His people, promising them mercy, assistance, and liberation from their many oppressors, whose human weakness, wickedness and punishment, is eloquently described. In the 52d chapter these subjects are continued,—but I will let the words of the Seer speak for themselves, (lii, 7.): "How pleasant upon the mountains are the steps of him that carries the news of peace, the news of good things: announcing the message of help, and speaking to Zion: "Thy God reigneth!" [Hark,] the voice of thy watchmen! They lift up their voice; they shout joyfully all together, for with their own eyes they see, how the *Eternal* turneth [the fate of] Zion.

Begin the joyful song of praise, altogether, ye ruins of Jerusalem! For the *Eternal* has comforted His people, has liberated Jerusalem. Openly shown has the *Eternal* His holy power, before the eyes of all the nations; and all the ends of the earth see the help of our God.

Away! Away! Come out from there! Touch nothing unclean! Come away from out of their midst; be pure, ye armorbearers (*noze kheli*) of the *Eternal!* For not in haste shall ye come forth, nor hurry like fugitives; but before you goeth the *Eternal*, and your rear guard is the God of Israel.

[God saith:] "Behold, my servant shall be happy; he will be praised and exalted, and esteemed very high." Just as many were disturbed on his account, (so changed was he; had barely the looks of man, or the shape of human kind,) so will he astonish many nations, even rulers will shut up their mouths before him; for of what there was never told them, that they see; and what they never heard of, that they perceive. [They will exclaim in astonishment:]

"Who would have believed our report? Over whom has the *Eternal's* power been openly shown, for he grew up like a reed, like a sprout out of barren ground; he had neither beauty of form, nor comeliness, that we should have regarded him, no good looks that we should have liked him. Despised he was, and avoided by men; a man of sorrows, well acquainted with faintness; even as one, before whom one hideth his face, he was despised, and we thought nothing of him.

"Yet our own diseases he bore, and our own pains he carried, while we thought him to be punished, stricken by God, and oppressed. Yet was he made faint on account of our own wickedness, struck on account of our own sins; he was corrected for our perfection, and through his stripes health has come to us.

"We all erred like sheep, we are all turned, each one to his own way; but the *Eternal* visited on him the guilt that has been ours: crowded and tortured, he never opened his mouth; like a lamb led to the shambles, like a sheep mute before his shearers, he never opened his mouth. From assembly, even from courts of law, he was kept removed; and among his generation who would have thought, he was forbid from the land of the living for the sake of the wickedness of my people, for the disease that was on them. They placed his grave with [that of] malefactors, and [put him] with the rich [suicides,] even after he was dead; though he had committed no crime, nor had carried deception in his mouth."

Isaiah [xl, 1, 2, and xlix, 3,] calls the whole body of the Jews: "Jacob, my servant," and he states here that the Jew should be restored, though he had been so long despised, at which change the nations would be greatly astonished, and might exclaim that nobody would have believed, if they had foretold such a thing. For the Jew was hated, he even made a precarious living, under difficulties, without any particular attractions that would have shown him God's servant. The description of the scorn and contumely heaped upon him will be easily recognized by any one.

He had to bear every oppression, and was frequently killed with impunity, under the absurd pretense that he was rejected by God for killing God (Christ.)

Yet the wickedness was on the people's side, and the sufferings of the Jew gradually ushered in better times and more liberal views.

Under all these cruel oppressions the Jew never left his faith, never complained.

Though excluded from society; without just legal redress; through the wickedness of his cotemporaries, crowded into a "ghetto;" persecuted even after death by burial in the disgraced corner of the cemeteries amidst the graves of executed criminals and suicides, [literally true!] the Jew yet was guilty of no crime, and was nearer to biblical and historical truth than his persecutors.

All this is but part of God's government. We see but one side. Still, while Israel has thus, as it were, been offered as an atonement, he will succeed in carrying out the mission of God to spread truth and righteousness.

This end, which is ever present with the Jew, upholds and satisfies him; the knowledge of truth in his possession will turn many to righteousness, and at last the Jew will receive the just reward belonging to his service, and work as a martyr of religion and liberty.

The prophet then continues (chapter 54) with a joyful appeal to Judah to rejoice over this divine help and assistance, promising that like the waters of Noah would, according to God's word, never again cover the earth, so should also their prosperity never again be disturbed by affliction, for the Eternal and Almighty Creator would protect them.

Thus, I have given an exact translation, accepted by all Jewish commentators, and endorsed even by such high Christian authority as Bunsen. That this is the correct and proper meaning seems to appear from the complete connection which is thus established with the chapters that precede and follow the fifty-third.

The second psalm, which is sometimes urged as a prophecy pointing to Jesus as the son of God, appears to me but a Jewish or Israelitish war song. Moses is ordered [Ex. iv, 22,] to speak to Pharaoh: "Thus saith the *Eternal:* Israel is my first born (beloved) son." This idea is therefore frequently alluded to by prophets and poets, and it is not the least to be wondered at that a Jewish *Tyrtaeus* should embody it in song. The language of this song or Psalm points to a very ancient author; though if we translate *bar*, in the last verse by "*son*," we would have to assign it a place among the productions of the restoration, after the return from Babylon; as the word *bar*, with this meaning of *son*, does not occur in the earlier writings. *Bar*, in the signification of *son*, is Chaldean, and is only found in the Bible, in Prov. xxxi, 2. The best Hebrew scholars translate (Ps. ii, 12:) "Obey in purity," instead of "Kiss ye the son." Jerome (342—420 A.C.) renders it *adorate pure*. (Gesen., Art. בַּר.)

I think I have shown you that the Jews have good and satisfactory reasons for not accepting Christianity, and that their hopes for happiness and immortality are sufficiently well founded. May I hope that your spirit of inquiry is sufficiently awakened, to read hereafter critically, and form your own opinions uninfluenced by preconceived ideas.

APPENDIX.

ECCE HOMO!

SKETCH OF THE LIFE OF JESUS.

If we want to see men, as they have actually lived and acted, we must track them on the page of time, as the hunter tracks his game; we must notice every sign, every mark; we must carefully sift the real and actual, from the ideal and imaginary; we must scrape off the coloring and white-washing which the popular imagination, without regard to facts or actual occurrences, heaps upon its heroes.

"We are apt," says Guizot (Hist. Civ. Eur. Vol. I, p. 140,) "to fall into the great and common error, in looking at the past through centuries of distance, of forgetting moral chronology; we are apt to forget that history is essentially successive. Take the Life of any man — of Oliver Cromwell, of Cardinal Richelieu, of Gustavus Adolphus. He enters upon his career; he pushes forward in life, and rises; great circumstances act upon him; he acts upon great circumstances. He arrives at the end of all things—and then it is we know him. But it is in his whole character; it is as a complete, a finished piece; such in a manner as he is turned out, after long labor, from the workshop of Providence. Now, at his outset he was not what he thus became; he was not completed — not finished at any single moment of his life; he was formed successively. Men are formed morally in the same way as they are physically. They change every day. Their existence is constantly undergoing some modification. The Cromwell of 1650 was not the Cromwell of 1640. It is true there is always a large stock of individuality; the same man still holds on; but how many ideas, how many sentiments, how many inclinations have changed in him! What a number of things has he lost, and acquired! Thus, at whatever moment of his life we may look at a man, he is never such as we see him when his course is finished."

Take our own Washington. In 1755, under the ill-fated Braddock he fought as a British subject, an Englishman in feeling, for the very flag which he, twenty years later, so successfully opposed.

As an undoubted, reliable, and historical fact, we only have the remark of Tacitus, that Jesus suffered the *supplicium*, that is, crucifixion as the extreme penalty for treason, by sentence of Pontius Pilate, governor of Judea, under the reign of Tiberius. Here we are in full sight of the man, on natural ground; and by examining the country, population, and political aspect of the times, in which we find him, it is possible to trace the most prominent features and acts of his life, back to his first appearance before the public.

Jesus lived a Jew among the Jews in Gallilee, partook of their hopes and aspirations. The Jews, from Abraham down to the present, believed that their mission as a people was to spread true and correct ideas of God, to carry the blessings of a religion of love to all races and to all nations. Jesus is imbued with the same idea. The fragmentary Gospel narrative reports him saying to his countrymen: "Ye are the salt of the earth. . Ye are the light of the world. A City that is set on a hill can not be hid. Neither do men light a candle and put it under a bushel, but on a candlestick, and it giveth light unto all that are in the house. Let your light so shine before men (aliens and foreigners,) that they may see your good work, and glorify your Father who is in heaven."

But those times were not favorable to quiet development and growth. Great struggles were taking place within and without the Jewish commonwealth. Without, the iron hand of Rome was gathering heavy tribute, impoverishing the people. and creating by oppression a national republican party in opposition to foreign dominion, and Herodian royalists. To these republicans the mere name of a Roman was an eyesore, and they objected to counting time, and dating documents by the reign or consulship of a foreigner. By them Jesus is asked about the lawfulness of the tribute to Rome, but he is still on strictly moderate ground, and counsels submission to irresistible power: "Give to Cesar what is Cesar's."

But also within the commonwealth there were civil and religious divisions. The house of Zadok, (II Chron. xxxi, 10; Ezek. xl, 46,) the Sadducees, a hereditary priest-nobility, living by tithes and sacrifices, oppressed the people; yet, although their demands and exactions met opposition by the Essenes and the Pharisees, priesthood and sacrificial worship were so closely interwoven with the civil and religious law of the Jews at that time, that it seemed impossible to get rid of this incubus.

In such times, when the present is disagreeable and gloomy, people will turn their thoughts to the future. The Jews of that time, unable to cope with Rome, dissatisfied with the priest-ridden present, waited and expected a miraculous delivery from their oppressors. The belief in a sudden catastrophe, in the end of the world, in the appearance of a second David, afforded them relief and strength. Many passages in the older prophets were forcibly interpreted in support of this comforting belief.

Jesus, at first, had no idea to announce himself as the Messiah, the second David who should put every thing to rights again. When Peter says that he thinks him to be that person, Jesus expresses the utmost astonishment. In plain English his answer would sound: "This is no human idea; it is perfect inspiration, direct from God. You are a jewel, Simon! This is just what I want; it will rouse the people, and you shall be my lieutenant," &c. But knowing the watchful jealousy of the Roman goveruors and the Herodian family, he requests his followers to keep the matter a secret. About this time, Herod Antipas, tetrarch of Gallilee, had slain "John that was called the Baptist, who was a good man, and commanded the Jews to exercise virtue, both as to righteousness toward one another, and piety toward God, and so to come to baptism; for that baptism would be acceptable to Him, if they made use of it not in order to remove uncleanness, but for the purification (sanctification) of the body; supposing still that the soul was thoroughly purified beforehand by righteousness. Now, where others came in crowds about him, for they were greatly moved by hearing his words, Herod, who feared lest the great influence John had over the people might put it into his power and inclination to raise a rebellion, (for they seemed ready to do any thing he should advise) thought it best, by putting him to death, to prevent any mischief he might cause, and not bring himself into difficulties, by sparing a man who might make him repent of it when it should be too late. Accordingly, he was sent a prisoner, out of Herod's suspicious temper, to Macherus, and was there put to death." (Joseph. Ant. book XVIII, 5, 2.)

The papers from which the Gospel according to Luke was compiled, must have contained those political agitations. (Luke xiii, 31—35.)

As the situation was then in Palestine, the excitement spread rapidly. Great multitudes follow Jesus; their enthusiasm turns his head, and deludes him into confidence that he is God's instrument of liberation to his people. Strange rumors reach Jerusalem. The Pharisees, with national hopes and aspirations. hotheaded believers in miracles, and naturally superstitious, ask him to give them a sign in proof of his divine mission, as Moses and other prophets had done. The Sadducees, more rational, less given to excitement and religious enthusiasm, say that he will lead the nation into a disastrous insurrection. (John xi, 47—50.)

Jesus, having now gained firm faith in his Messianic mission, enters Jerusalem, goes to the temple, and carries every thing his own way. He tells his audience that.

in accordance with their hopes and ancient prophecies, the end of the world is nigh, the old world dies; and only the good and the true will survive the bursting of the old mother earth. (Matth. 24, 25; Mark 13.) But the expected miraculous assistance fails or delays; the Roman governor, in spite of intimidating tales and rumors of supernatural power, orders the arrest of Jesus, who tries to escape his fate by concealing himself with a few trusty followers. Here, in his hiding place, he thinks of resistance. The Gospel according to Luke reports his call for arms, (xxii, 36-38, that puts the learned Adam Clarke to a peck of trouble, in his Commentaries.) Too late! One of his followers treacherously guides to his hiding place a Roman detachment which brings him before the governor. Jesus does not deny his claims to royal office, but gives his firm conviction of his mission: "My kingdom is not of this world; this present world is in its last convulsions, is dying; my kingdom is of the new world that may arise at any moment out of the ashes of the present globe which is doomed to destruction."

To set at nought these pretentions of miracles, and to remove the cause of the popular commotion, Pilate has him scourged, and exposes him to the expectant multitude, with the words: "*Ecce homo!* Behold but a man! No worker of miracles! No God! Nothing supernatural!" delivers him to be executed as a political offender, according to the Roman law. It was one of the many executions ordered by the different Roman governors, which did not affect the people at large; hence the silence of Josephus on the subject.

The above appears to me the natural outline of the life of Jesus. His resurrection, and that of the other saints who are said to have accompanied him and showed themselves at Jerusalem, together with the miracles, are but the legendary embellishment of later times; currently believed in after-centuries, they found their way into the religious books.

ERRATA.

4th page, 1st column, 18th line from top, *Jew* should read Jews.

4th page, 2d column, 28th line from top, insert *next* after evidence.

5th page, 2d column, 17th line from top, *Perger* should read Peregr.

6th page, 2d column, 25th line from top, *Polycarpurs* should read Polycarpus.

7th page, 1st column, 19th line from bottom, insert *as* after acceptance.

7th page, 2d column, 19th line from bottom, *evidence* should read witness.

15th page, 2d column, 20th line from top, insert *no* after for.

15th page, 2d column, 14th line from bottom, insert *seen* after have.

16th page, 1st column, 18th line from bottom, insert *fulfilled* after be.

17th page, 1st column, 18th line from bottom, *xvii* should read vi.

17th page, 1st column, 13th line from bottom, *further* should read another.

18th page, 1st column, 29th line from bottom, *Seunacherib* should read Sennacherib.

20th page, 1st column, 20th line from top, *capitol* should read capital.

21st page, 2d column, 17th line from bottom, *vari* should read viri.

21st page, 2d column, 13th line from bottom, *deira* should read de ira.

21st page, 2d column, 3d line from bottom, *psunicularia* should read *pannicularia.*

22d page, 1st column, 4th line from top, *pmnit* should read punit.

27th page, 1st column, 14th line from bottom, *has* should read had.

30th page, 2d column, 18th line from top, *too-edged* should read two-edged.

31st page, 1st column, 29th line from top, *of* should read or.

36th page, 1st column, 22d line from bottom, insert ; after Almighty.

37th page, 2d column, 9th line from bottom, בליל should read בליעל.

40th page, 2d column, 6th line frm bottom, *xl, lx* should read xlix.

43d page, 2d column, [in note,] *Selucidan dominions* should read Seleucidan dominion.

47th page, 1st column, 35th & 27th lines from bottom, *Meude* should read Mede.

47th page, 1st column, 21st line from bottom, insert *first* after think.

47th page, 1st column, 17th line from bottom, *according to* should read after.

49th page, 1st column, 9th line from top, *desolators* should read desolator.

49th page, 1st column, 4th line from bottom, *a* should read an.

52d page, 1st column, 20th line from top, *distinction* should read extinction.

56th page, 1st column, 27th line from top, insert after *itself*, nine lines from 2d column, page 56, beginning at *the well known*, to *early Christians*, which lines are to be stricken from 2d column.

66th page, 2d column, 24th line from top, *indirect* should read in direct [in the lines to be transferred to 1st. column.]

(4

תולדת יצחק

M. B. Levy

Traunungsreden,

Postille

für jüdische Familien

von

Ig. W. Bak

Rabbi in Cztin, (Böhmen). vormals B. Gyula (Ungarn).

1. Heft.

Prag 1866.

Druck von Senders & Brandeis Rittergasse Nro. 408—I.

Verlag des Verfassers.

Vorwort.

Ich versuche hiermit dem ges. jüdischen Lesepublicum eine Reihe von Reden vorzulegen, die dazu angethan sein dürften, dieses Genre von Schriftthum nicht ganz nutzlos zu bereichern.

Daß ich mit Casual und mit Trauungsreden überhaupt und zuerst beginne, geschieht theils deßhalb, weil grade kein Zweig der Homiletik so sehr en **bagatelle** behandelt wurde — als, eben dieser — und zwar ist die Ursache dessen, einerseits das allzulocale Gepräge, welches dieser Gattung von Reden aufgedrückt wird und nicht selten aufgedrückt werden muß . . . so daß sie für ein größeres Publicum interesselos scheinen . . . anderseits aber gleichen diese Gattung Ansprachen zumeist so sehr einander an Stoff, Form und Behandlung, daß man sie gleichsam stereotyp nennen kann, und also abermals wenig oder kein Interesse für die Lesewelt haben — zu dem halten die meisten Redner diesen mächtig bewegten Augenblick nicht für geeignet um zu belehren*) . . . und wie sollten solche Reden dann der Oeffentlichkeit übergeben werden? Bedenkt man jedoch, daß die Menschen und ihre Verhältnisse sich mehr, oder minder überall gleichen, zieht man ferner in Betracht, daß ein jüdisches Auditorium immer aufmerksam und neugierig lauscht, berücksichtigt man schließlich, daß der Sitten- und Moralprediger jede Gelegenheit ergreifen soll und muß, um das Gotteswort eindringlichst zu lehren, so dürfte ein solches Vorgehen nichts weniger als zu rechtfertigen sein . . . Ja, wenn unsere Alten, selbst in Leichenreden erbauliche Betrachtungen einwebten, trotzdem doch der Tod schon an und für sich der überzeugendste Gelegenheitsredner ist

*) So kenne ich selbst einen klassischen und geistreichen Redner, der gewöhnlich die Trauungsreden dem Brautpaare so leise ins Ohr flüstert, daß es kaum etwas zu hören bekömmt.

warum nicht dann, wenn die Herzen aller Anwesenden der Freude erschlossen?

Da ich also diesen Zweig der Beredsamkeit, so wie Leichen- Trauer- und andere Gelegenheitsreden nicht minder ernst, wie Sabbat- und Festpredigten behandelte, so wage ich es hiemit solche, der Reihe nach, zu veröffentlichen. Und wenn ich auch von dem Dünkel, sie als Muster hinzustellen, weit entfernt, und selbst überzeugt bin, daß alles das, was ich an Sprache und Wahrheit aufbringe, von Andern viel schöner, besser und ausführlicher gesprochen sein mochte . . . so wird mir doch das Verdienst der Anregung, das jedem bessern Streben zu Theil wird, schwerlich abgesprochen werden.

Ich beginne aber theils auch deßhalb mit diesen, weil es nur allzubekannt ist, wie wenig Aufmunterung und Unterstützung leider dem jüdischen Autor a priori, sowohl von Seite der jüdischen Buchhändler, als auch von Seite des lesenden Publicums zu Theil wird — als daß er im Vorhinein es wagen könnte, sich an Größeres zu versuchen.

Und so mögen denn diese Blätter der gef. Lesewelt aufs Wärmste empfohlen sein, und so viel Anklang finden, daß es mir möglich werde, auch alles Sonstige, was ich durch neun Jahre meiner Amtsthätigkeit im Sinne Gottes und seiner Lehre, zur Ehre Israels und seiner heiligen Religion gesprochen und gelehrt, zum allgemeinen Nutz und Frommen zu veröffentlichen.

Daß diese, so wie meine sonstigen Reden kurz gehalten und der Kürze, so zu sagen, sich befleißigen, darf wohl nicht erst entschuldigt werden . . . Lehrte ja schon ein alter, bewährter Kanzelredner: Wenn ihr predigt, seid kurz und thuet das Maul auf!

Auf baldiges freundliches Wiedersehen.

Der Verfasser.

1.

Trauungsrede.

In Demuth stehen wir o Gott, vor Dir! um Deine Huld und Benedikzion gehen wir Dich, Vater im Himmel, herzinnigst an! auf daß dieses Bündniß, welches diese Deine Kinder nun im Sinne Deiner heiligen Lehre schließen wollen, ein gesegnetes und dauerndes sei. Amen.

וארשתיך לי לעולם — וארשתיך לי בצדק ובמשפט ובחסד וברחמים
— וארשתיך לי באמונה וידעת את ד'

„Und ich traue Dich mir an für immer, und ich traue Dich mir an in Recht und Billigkeit, in Huld und Zärtlichkeit, und ich traue Dich mir an in Treue und erkenne und liebe den Herrn!“

וארשתיך לי לעולם. Dieß, geliebte Beide, muß und soll das Schlag- und Losungswort jedes Brautpaares sein, wenn es sich unter dem Trauungsbaldachin zur ehelichen Verbindung eingefunden hat. Aus dem Herzen muß es dringen und von den Lippen muß es klingen, ich will Dich mir für immer antrauen, soll der Trauungsbaldachin anders zum Himmel einer neuen Welt und einer schönen Zukunft, und nicht das Leichentuch sein, in welchem die Vergangenheit der schönen Jugendzeit, die Blüthen süßer Hoffnungsträume begraben werden. „וארשתיך לי לעולם“ dieß muß so zu sagen Ihre Devise und die Parole ihres Lebens sein, wenn Ihnen dieser Himmel, der ihren Aufblick so sehr beschränkt und begränzt und einen so geringen Gesichtskreis biethet, ein Paradies unter seinen Zukunftsschleier bergen soll und nicht eine Hölle, an deren Pforte die Worte stehen: Lasset für immer euere Hoffnungen und euer Lebensglück zurück! Denn wahrlich nicht blos ein Freundschaftsbündniß ists, daß Sie gegenwärtig schließen, dabei jeder sich eine Hinterthüre so zu sagen offen läßt, um zu gelegener Zeit wieder seinen eigenen Weg gehen zu können, sondern aber einen Bund ewiger Liebe, Treue und Zärtlichkeit, der sich forterben soll von Zeit auf Zeit, auf Kind und Kindeskind; ein Bündniß, in welchem kein Vor und kein Zurück, kein Abseits und kein Allein gibt; ein Bündniß, in dem die Gedanken, das Wollen und Streben des Einen in den Gedanken und in dem Wollen und Streben des Andern verschmelzend aufgehen! Mit einem Worte, ein Bündniß, gewollt durch die Huld des Herrn; geweiht durch den Mund seines Priesters; gewünscht und beglückwünscht durch liebende Angehörige und Freunde! וארשתיך לי לעולם meine Lieben, mögen sie sich nun in traulicher und herzlicher Innigkeit zurufen, so der Segen Gottes auf diesem Ihren ehelichen Bündniß ruhen soll. Sowie aber das וארשתיך לי לעולם Ihr beiderseitiger Vorsatz sein muß, so liebe Glaubensbrüder müssen Sie des zweiten Satzes des angeführten heiligen Wortes וארשתיך לי בצדק ובמשפט ich will Dich mir antrauen in Recht und Gerechtigkeit, stets eingedenk sein, nach Recht und Gerechtigkeit, d. h. nach hergebrachter, guter, altjüdischer Sitte, nach welcher der Gatte nicht schon seine Pflicht hiermit erfüllt, so er seiner Gattin als treuer redlicher Ernährer und Versorger vorsteht, sondern aber erst dann, wenn er ihr in Treue und Liebe anhängt; sie schätzt, achtet, hoch in Ehren hält, und würdigt, würdigt nach Recht und Billigkeit als seines Lebens innere, bessere Hälfte; als die Begründerin einer beglückenden und segenbringenden Häuslichkeit; als Erzieherin eines werdenden Geschlechtes, durch welches man in Ehren fortleben und fortwirken will! וארשתיך לי בצדק ובמשפט muß der gute jüdische Gatte sich stets vergegenwärtigen, damit er niemals seiner Mißstimmung, seiner bösen Laune, seinem Zorne nachgebe! Immer müssen Recht und Billigkeit die Nachsicht zur Folge haben; immer soll und muß der Mann im Bewußtsein seiner Ueberlegenheit, seiner Kraft und Stärke in liebevoller Gewissenhaftigkeit ihr als Stütze zur Seite, niemals aber gegenüber, trotzig gegenüber stehen. Ihre heilige und unverletzliche Pflicht hingegen ist es liebe Glaubensschwester sich Ihrem Gatten stets בחסד וברחמים = in Liebe und in Zärtlichkeit, in Huld und inniger Anhänglichkeit hinzugeben und entgegen zu kommen. Ja, Huld und Zärtlichkeit heißen und sind die Blumenketten, die Gott dem Weibe anvertraut, um den Mann dauernd zu fesseln; das Weib im Bewußtsein seiner Schwäche soll es stets fühlen, daß es sich aufranken müsse an eine starke Stütze, welche für alle Zeiten ihr Gatte ist — damit die rohen Stürme des Lebens es nicht beugen und brechen — und wodurch sonst ist dieß wohl anders möglich als durch zärtliche Anhänglichkeit, durch liebevolle Innigkeit und trauliche Zuvorkommenheit?! Oh, des Weibes Aufgabe ist eine schöne, eine hohe aber auch eine schwere, denn sie darf nicht nur eine gute Gattin, sie muß auch eine tüchtige Hausfrau und nicht bloß Hausfrau, sondern auch eine umsichtige Erzieherin eines kommenden Geschlechtes werden! Die Quelle aber, woraus es alle diese Kenntnisse; der Born des Heils woraus auch der Gatte die Kenntniß seiner Pflichten, die Kenntniß von dem was Recht und Billigkeit ist, schöpfe, das sind die Worte וארשתיך לי באמונה וידעת את ד'. Im Glauben, in der Furcht, ja in der Erkenntniß des Herrn liegen all diese Geheimnisse; sie sind der Schlüßel zur Himmelspforte der Seligkeit wie zum dauernden Glücke des Erden und des häuslichen Lebens überhaupt. — Mit dem angestammten Glauben im Herzen, mit der Furcht Gottes vor Augen und mit der Erkenntniß Gottes im Sinne allein kann und wird dieser heilige Bund fortdauern — durch diese allein werden Sie lieber Glaubensbruder Ihren Pflichten als Mann und Gatte zu genügen, so wie sie liebe Glaubensschwester Ihre dreifache Aufgabe zu erfüllen im Stande sein! . . וארשתיך לי באמונה rufe ich Ihnen nochmals zu — dieß sei Ihr Gedenkspruch in allen Zeiten und unter allen Umständen des Lebens. Kann Ihnen dieß ja um so weniger schwer fallen, als Sie ja Beide von frühester Kindheit an bis auf den heutigen Tag solche im lebendigen Beispiele gesehen Und so segne ich denn dieses Bündniß ehelicher Einigung im Namen Gottes und seiner heiligen Lehre, die Euch zuruft: Liebet euch, vertraget euch und vergebet euch, wenn solches noth thut; traget miteinander die guten und die bösen Stunden und möge die Liebe nur erst mit dem Tode von Euch scheiden, also sei es. Amen.

קידושין.

2.

Deinen Beifall Herr! und Deinen Segen wollen wir uns erbeten für den heiligen Bund, den diese Deine Kinder, nun im Sinne Deiner Lehre für all die Zeit ihres Lebens schließen wollen — erhöre uns jetzt und allemal. Amen.

ויאמר ה׳ לא טוב היות האדם לבדו אעשה לו עזר כנגדו „Und Gott sprach, es ist nicht gut, daß der Mensch allein sei, ich will ihm eine Gehilfin schaffen, die ihm gegenüber sei."

Mit diesen Worten m. L. rechtfertigte der Herr, so zu sagen, die Mühen, die Beschwerden und die Lasten des Ehestandes — denn glauben Sie ja nicht, daß das eheliche Leben blos Rosen und nicht auch Dornen, blos Freuden und nicht auch Leiden, blos Genüsse und nicht auch Schmerzen bringt und biethet — und dennoch ist es nicht gut, daß der Mensch allein sei, und dennoch behaupten auch unsere Weisen, daß ein weiberloser Mann nur ein halber Körper, weil in der Ehe nur die Ganzheit und die Vollkommenheit des Mannes liege; wer ohne Weib ist hat keine Schutzmauer gegen die Sünde und gegen die Begierde, kennt die gemüthliche, häusliche Freude nicht und kennt das wahrhafte Glück, welches ausschließlich im Familienleben ruht, nicht — und sie haben gewiß recht, wie sie immer recht haben, da es nur von uns und ausschließlich von uns abhängt das eheliche Leben zur Quelle des fortdauernden Glückes und der Freude zu machen. „Ich will ihm eine Gehilfin schaffen, die ihm gegenüber — gegenüber, nicht aber zur Seite, wie ein Spiegel, stehe! Weil die Gattin den Glanz und das Glück des Gatten wiederstrahle, in ihr spiegle sich die Zufriedenheit des Mannes, die Ordnung des Hauses und die Flamme der Liebe ab!

Damit aber der Spiegel vollständig und klar zeige, dazu ist es vor Allem nöthig, daß er ungetrübt und blank sei, deßhalb soll und muß die Gattin dem Manne immer und immer ein freudenfrohes und heiteres Gesicht zeigen und darf niemals mürrisch, düster und zornig sein — denn wie sorgen- und kummervoll das Leben sich auch gestalten mag, das Haus muß sein frohes und heiteres Aussehn bewahren. Das Haus muß den Hafen der Ruhe bilden, in welchem alle Stürme machtlos, in dem aller Kummer schweige, alle Sorge schwinde und alle Düsterheit und Traurigkeit keinen Platz und keinen Raum finden. Wie jener unserer Weisen, der bei seiner Ankunft ein Klaggeschrei hörte, mit Zuversicht sagen konnte: „Es kömmt dieß nicht aus meinem Hause;" so muß dieß von jeder gutgeordneten Häuslichkeit gelten, so die Majestät des häuslichen Glückes nicht verdrängt und verscheucht werden soll*)! Der Spiegel soll ferner auch fein und nett eingerahmt sein, je netter und schöner der Rahmen, desto mehr spricht auch der Spiegel selber an — so soll auch die Gattin sich der Reinheit und der Reinlichkeit befleißigen — die Gattin stellt wohl das Haus, das Haus aber muß auch die Gattin darstellen! Der Spiegel soll und muß nothwendiger Weise auch eine angemessene Stelle einnehmen, so er gehörig das hineinschauende Bild wiedergebe, so soll und muß auch das Weib die richtige Stellung ihrem Manne gegenüber einnehmen, es darf sich weder zu hoch über ihn, noch zu tief unter ihm stellen, sie soll ihm, wie die Schrift sich so präzis ausdrückt, grade nur gegenüber stehn!

Dieß liebe Braut sind in wenigen Worten Ihre Pflichten als Gattin, Ihre Pflichten aber lieber Bräutigam als Gatte zeigt ebenfalls das angeführte Spiegelbild. Denn soll der Spiegel ein ganzes, ein grades, ein heiteres und helles Bild zurückwerfen, so muß eben ein Solches hinein schauen, darum heißt es auch so herrlich schön und wahr bei unsern Alten: זכה, עזר, לא זכה כנגדו! — weil eben das Weib, nur das Bild des Mannes reflektirt! Soll der Spiegel rein und blank sein, so darf ihn der Ma'n eben nicht anhauchen und beschmutzen mit dem Athem der Rohheit und mit der Sorge und dem Schweiße des Marktlebens — soll der Rahmen rein und nett und sauber sein, so muß der Gatte auch stets durch Fleiß und redliche Thätigkeit dafür besorgt sein, daß es dem Hause nie und niemals an dem Nöthigen und Nothwendigen fehle und mangle — so wie es ferner seine Sorge sei, daß sie den gehörigen Platz als Herrin des Hauses einnchme!

---

*) אין השכינה שורה לא מתוך עצבות וכו'.

Wer sein Weib nährt nach Umständen, kleidet nach Verhält-
niß und nicht weniger als sich selber ehrt, sagen unsere Weisen, von dem steht geschrieben: Friede ist in Deiner Wohne! Also sei es. Amen.

3.

An Deine Vaterhuld, Allmächtiger! wenden wir uns alle Zeit, und Du erhörest uns! Zu Dir kommen wir, so Leid uns befällt, aber auch wenn die Freude unser Herz erweitert und unsern Sinn erheitert und so stehen wir auch gegenwärtig freudig bewegten Gemüthes vor Dir — um Deines Himmels reichsten Segen herab zu beten auf das eheliche Bündniß, das diese Deine Kinder für ihre Lebenszeit, im Sinn Deiner geoffenbarten Lehre schließen wollen. Also geschehe es. Amen.

Der Schritt, den Sie nun meine Geliebten machen, ist nicht nur ein lebenswichtiger, sondern auch ein unberechenbar schwerer — denn wenn es heute zu Tage, da die Bedürfnisse so zahlreich, die Ansprüche so viel und selbst der einfachste Lebensunterhalt mit harter Mühe nur zu erschwingen ist — selbst wenn man so zu sagen sich nur allein durchzuschlagen und durchzukämpfen hat — um wie viel härter muß der Kampf des Lebens nicht erst sein, wenn es eine ganze Häuslichkeit zu versorgen und zu ernähren gilt — und doch! Sollten wir uns hiedurch abhalten oder gar zurückschrecken lassen, dem sittlich-göttlichen Gesetz, dem das Menschengeschlecht überhaupt und wir ins Besondere von je bis auf den heutigen Tag gefolgt, auch ferner zu folgen? O, davor wolle Gott uns bewahren! War es ja nur das jüdische Familienleben fast ausschließlich, das uns bis auf den heutigen Tag trotz all der, zahllosen Vernichtungsversuche, die gegen uns angewandt wurden unzerstörbar und stark machte und trotz unserer Unansehnlichkeit noch Würde und Ansehen verlieh —! Was uns aber heute mehr als sonst noth thut, das ist, daß wir uns dieses wichtigen Schrittes, den wir mit dem ehelichen Bündnisse thuen, genau bewußt seien und an heiliger Stätte uns mit guten Vorsätzen für das eheliche

Leben stählen und rüsten — und dazu ermahne ich Sie in diesem ernsten Momente durch folgendes Gotteswort: אשת חן תתמך כבוד ועריצים יתמכו עשר — Ein liebevolles Weib erhält die Ehre und Fleißige erhalten den Reichthum, und so liebe Glaubensbrüder ist es in der That; des Hauses und des Mannes Ehre muß des Weibes Hauptsorge sein, weil sie ausschließlich dem Weibe in die Hand gegeben ist, denn wodurch anders wird wohl des Mannes und des Hauses Ehre erhalten, als durch die Herzens- und Sittenreinheit des Weibes durch die Nettigkeit und Reinlichkeit; durch regelmäßige Ordnung, durch Sparsamkeit und Wirthlichkeit, und gehören diese Tugenden nicht alle dem Weibe zu? Vergeblich wahrlich müht sich der Gatte im Schweiße seines Angesichtes, dem Leben das Nöthige abzuringen, so das Weib leichtfertigen Sinnes das Gewonnene nicht zu würdigen weiß und alsbald zerrinnen läßt. — Nur bei zerrüttetem Hauswesen kann wirkliche Armuth Platz finden, nur bei vernachläßigter Wirthschaft kann des Mannes und des Hauses Ehre untergehn —; in geordneter Haushaltung kann bei der tiefsten Armuth, noch ein gewisser Ueberfluß herrschen. — Ueberhaupt ist man nicht arm, so lange man in Ehren lebt, denn die Ehre ist ein Kapital, dessen Zinsen und Zinseszinsen oft Kind und Kindeskind noch genießt. Ein liebevolles Weib sucht nicht in eitlem Putz und nichtigem Glanz des Mannes und des Hauses Ehre, im Gegentheil! spiegelt sich allzuoft das künftige Elend, der künftige Ruin, sowie die künftige Schmach und Schande des Mannes und des Hauses in solchem Glanze ab! Ein liebevolles Weib erhält aber des Mannes und des Hauses Ehre — durch ein würdevolles, schickliches, anständiges und bescheidenes Benehmen, durch ein einfaches und anspruchloses Tragen und Betragen im Hause und in der Gesellschaft; schließlich durch gute Zucht und fromme Vätersitte! Des Mannes und der Ehre des Hauses willen, muß die liebevolle Gattin so manches Ungemach und Leid sanft und still erdulden und ertragen . . denn des Mannes und des Hauses Ehre ist die Krone des häuslichen Staates, fällt sie einmal in den Staub, so ist auch die Zerrüttung eingetreten, die nur mit der völligen Auflösung endet. Mögen Sie daher liebe Glaubensschwester niemals es vergessen und immer sich an diesen Ausspruch halten! Ihnen aber lieber Glaubensbruder rufe ich die andere Hälfte des weisen Spruches zu: die Fleißigen erhalten den Reichthum! Fleiß! darin liegt das große alchemische Geheimniß aus Staub Gold zu machen. — Der Fleiß meine Freunde ist zwar ein so sehr bekannter Begriff, daß man kaum etwas über ihn zu sagen braucht und doch wird derselbe im Leben allzuoft mißverstanden und mißbraucht, denn nennt man nicht gar zu oft das rastlose, unermüdete Jagen und Mühen, ohne Ruhe und Halt, selbst an Sabbath und Festtagen — Fleiß! oh, ein solcher Fleiß erniedrigt uns, nimmt uns die Menschenwürde und wendet uns, wie die tägliche Erfahrung lehrt, von Gott und seinen Wegen ab! der echte Fleiß ist das ernstliche Streben und Wollen auf ehrliche, redliche und fromme Weise sich das tägliche Brod zu erwerben und das Erworbene, wie spärlich und karg es auch durch den Rathschluß Gottes ausgefallen sein mag, mit Umsicht verwalten und genießen הון מהבל ימעט וקובץ על יד ירבה. — Was durch Trug und Nichtigkeit errungen wird, das wird allzubald auch schwinden, was aber durch der Hände Mühen gesammelt und gespart wird, wird endlich zur Hülle und Fülle. Der wahrhafte Fleiß bedarf der Ruhe; ruht ja triebmäßig selbst die Ameise — das Muster des Fleißes und der Emsigkeit! Wohl soll die Ruhe nicht in Müssiggang und Faullenzerei ausarten und darum bestimmt unsere heilige Religion die Zeit der physisch n Ruhe zur Zeit geistiger Kopf- und Herzbildender Thätigkeit — weil nur Thätigkeit uns straff und munter erhält und immer zu neuer und doppelter Thätigkeit anspornt, welche zur Aufrechterhaltung unsrer Ehre und Würde unbedingt nö.hig ist — aber Ruhe in solchem Sinne ist unentbehrlich, weil erst durch sie der Fleiß geadelt, der Fleiß zur Tugend wird!

Ja sowie die Gattin stets bestrebt sein muß, des Mannes und des Hauses Ehre zu schützen und zu wahren, also beeifre auch der Gatte sich durch redliche Emsigkeit der Gattin liebevolles Walten anzuspornen und nach Gebühr zu würdigen! Wetteifernd müssen die Gatten sich stets zur Seite stehen, sonst tritt Muthlosigkeit, Mißmuth, Nachlässigkeit und alles Unglück in deren Gefolge ein! Die Fleißigen erhalten die Wohlhabenheit; wohlhabend aber sind wir alle Zeit, wenn wir uns in unserm Streben nichts vorzuwerfen haben und das Gewonnene dankbaren und zufriedenen Herzens hinnehmen. Und so schließen wir denn mit dem aufrichtigen Wunsche, es möge dieß Wort Ihnen fürs ganze Leben eingeprägt bleiben, um darnach zu thun, damit so Ihre nächsten Angehörigen את אשר ישנו פה עמנו היום, als noch Ihre spätesten Nachkommen diesen Tag und diese Stunde segnen und glücklich preisen. Amen.

4.

In Deinem Namen Herr! kommen wir freudig bewegten Gemüthes zu Dir! In Deinem Namen Herr! stehen wir betend vor Dir — betend um Deines Himmels besten und reichsten Segen für all die, die da gekommen sind, um sich vor Dir zu freuen —; betend vorzüglich für diese Deine Kinder hier, die pochenden Herzens Deinen Beistand und Deine väterliche Huld und Gunst für die Vereinigung ihrer Lebenspfade erwarten! und so mögest denn Du uns nahe sein in Deiner Gnade, um unser Beten und Wollen zu erhören und zu gewähren jetzt und immer. Amen.

ד׳ עמכם = Gott mit Euch! diesen kurzen, aber inhaltsreichen, markigen Abschiedsgruß unserer Altvordern, meine Theuern rufe ich Ihnen heute, in diesem wichtigen Lebensmomente zu, da auch Sie einen Abschied feiern, einen Abschied von den kindlich jugendlichen Tagen, an welche wir uns noch so gerne in den spätesten Tagen unseres Lebens erinnern; Abschied von den kindlichen Freuden und Spielen, die so reiz- und wonnevoll, Abschied letztlich von dem lieben Elternhause, wo so viel Güte, Sorgsamkeit und Annehmlichkeiten, so viel Huld und Zärtlichkeit uns umgeben und bewachen!

Sie Beide meine Lieben stehen nun am Scheidewege והימים הראשונים יפלו! In diesem Momente schließt sich Ihnen die gemüthlichste und frohsinnigste Epoche im menschlichen Dasein — und eine neue, unbekannte tritt an ihre Stelle, ein neues Leben erschließt sich Ihnen nun; ein neuer, wichtiger und selbst schwieriger Wirkungskreis nimmt von nun an Ihre Umsicht und Thätigkeit in Anspruch! und wie könnte ich Ihnen wohl als treuer

Lehrer und Freund eine bessere Zauberformel für diesen Ihnen noch unbekannten Lebensabschnitt, als Geleitwort, als sogenanntes צידה לדרך mitgeben, als eben die angeführten, inhaltsschweren Worte „Gott mit Euch!“ welche nicht blos einen Segenswunsch, sondern auch den goldenen Schlüßel zur Pforte des Glückes und der Seligkeit enthalten.

„Gott mit Euch,“ nicht nur im Heiligthume und so oft er angerufen werden muß, sondern aber alle Zeit, unter allen Umständen und allen Verhältnissen; bei all Ihrem Thun und Lassen, bei all Ihrem Sinnen und Beginnen! Stets müssen wir Gott im Herzen tragen, dann geht er mit uns und läßt uns niemals allein — stets müssen wir ihn vor Augen haben, dann sieht er und bewacht er uns fortwährend; — nie dürfen wir ihn außer Acht lassen, dann beleuchtet er unsere Pfade und schützt uns vor strauchelnden Netzen, wie es schon im Psalter heißt: שויתי ד' לנגדי תמיד כי מימיני בל אמוט = den Herrn hab ich stets vor meinem Angesicht — ist er zur Seite mir — so wank und schwank ich nicht! בכל דרכיך דעהו והוא יישר ארחותיך = Erkenn ihn an auf allen Deinen Wegen — dann ebnet er sie Dir zum Heil und Segen.

אין איש בלא אשה, ואין איש ואשה בלא שכינה

Nichts ist der Mann allein,
Ohne treuer Gattin Segen
Nichts zählt selbst Mann und Weib,
Ohne gottgefäll'ges Hegen.

behaupten schon unsere Alten.

ד' עמכם Nicht nur im Herzen, im Sinne und auf den Lippen, sondern aber in Werken und in Thaten. An den Pforten Eueres Hauses leuchte es schon dem Eintretenden entgegen, daß Alles und Jedes das Gepräge eines gottlieben Schaltens und Waltens, eines frommen jüdischen Für- und Vorgehens an sich trägt.

אשרי כל ירא ה' ההלך בדרכיו — יגיע כפיך כי תאכל — אשריך וטוב לך — אשתך כגפן פריה בירכתי ביתך — בניך כשתילי זיתים סביב לשלחנך — הנה כי כן יברך גבר ירא ה'. —

Heil dem, der fürchtet Gott den Herrn,
Und stets in seinen Wegen geht —

Den eigner Hände Mühen nährt!
Den Segen nur und Heil umweht —
Des-Gattin fruchtet gleich der Reb,
In seines Hauses stillem Kreis —
Wie Oehlbaum-Pflanzen, Kinder einst
Umgeben ihn — zum Ruhm und Preis!
Dieß, ja dieß ist Gottes Segen,
Für die, die folgen seinen Wegen!

'ד עמכם. Nicht nur in des Hauses stillem Walten, in dem gemüthlichen Kreise der Häuslichkeit, sondern aber aller Orten; im Handel und im Wandel, im Gotteshause, wie auf dem Markte des öffentlichen Lebens; in stiller Einsamkeit, wie ihm Gewühle der Freudeberauschten:

אשרי איש ירא את ה׳ — במצותיו חפץ מאד — גבור בארץ יהי׳ זרעו —
דור ישרים יברך — הון ועשר בביתו — וצדקתו עמדת לעד

„Wohl dem, den Gottesfurcht erfüllt
Dem Gotteswort das Herz mit Sehnsucht schwillt
Deß Folgenschaft wird fortbestehen auf Erden
Als biederes Geschlecht gepriesen werden,
Und während Ueberfluß sein Haus umquillt
Sein Ruhm die Nachwelt noch erfüllt.

'ד עמכם heiße es also von Ihrem Herzen, von Ihrem Hause und von Ihrer Thätigkeit in der neuen Phase Ihres Daseins, so Sie beide Ihren Wirkungskreis ausfüllen und das Glück an Ihre Fersen fesseln wollen!

Ich sollte zwar in diesem Momente von den ehelichen Pflichten, von Liebe und Treue und wie all die Tugenden sonst heißen, die das eheliche Leben unbedingt zu seiner glücklichen Fortdauer fordert, sprechen; schließen jedoch die angeführten zwei inhaltsschweren Worte nicht Alles was Pflicht und Tugend ist in sich? Können wir je fehlen, so wir Gott stets vor Augen und im Herzen haben?!

Mögen Ihnen daher diese Worte tief eingeprägt bleiben, damit dieses Gott geweihte Bündniß ein gesegnetes werde für alle Zeiten Amen.

5.

Deiner sittlichen Weltordnung gehorchend, stehen wir Herr vor Dir, um den Bund zweier liebenden Herzen zu heiligen und einzusegnen für alle Zeiten — und so beten wir denn zu Dir, Urquell des Heils und des Segens; Du wollest das Füllhorn Deiner Huld und Güte ausschütten über das Herzensbündniß, welches diese Deine Kinder hier, im Sinne Deiner heiligen Lehre und nach frommer Vätersitte schließen wollen, damit es ein heil- und segenvolles werde bis in die spätesten Zeiten, also geschehe es.

כאור השמש בבקר לא עבות — כבודת בת חן במושב ביתה — כנר במנורת הקדש — יפת תואר על טובת טעם — כאדני זהב על עמודי כסף — רגלי אשת חן צופיות הליכות ביתה.

Wie Sonnenglanz am wolkenlosen Morgen,
So glänzt das holde Weib im Haus verborgen —
Wie des heil'gen Leuchters hellleuchtendes Licht
Steht des Gemüthes Adel schönem Angesicht,
Wie goldne Säulen zu silbernen Füßen gestaltet
Ist holdes Weib, das sorglich wohl das Haus verwaltet.

In diesen wenigen Worten des weisen Ben Sira geliebte Beide! liegt das Glück und die Seligkeit des ehelichen und häuslichen Lebens! Nicht in dem Schimmer und in dem Glanze des Aufwandes, nicht in der Schönheit und in der bezaubernden Anmuth des Umganges und des Benehmens, und auch nicht im Reichthum und im Stolze vornehmer Abkunft besteht des Weibes Stolz und Ehre, sondern in der stillen Bescheidenheit; im Adel des Gemüthes und in guter Haushaltung und Verwaltung. Nicht damals, wenn die Sonne, ob unserm Scheitel brennt ist sie schön und erquickend — dann aber wenn sie halb verborgen aus dem Dunkel hervortritt und mit ihren Rosenfingern die Ausdehnung berührt. Nicht die flackernde Flamme, die ihre Zunge gen Himmel redet, thut dem Auge wohl; sondern aber die helle Kerze, die am heiligen Leuchter einen sanften Schimmer verbreitet; nicht an jedem Orte und an jedem Gegenstande ist des Goldes Anblick erquicklich schön, aber erst dann wenn es an seinem Platze ist!

Bescheidenheit ist des Weibes erste Zierde, denn ein unbescheidenes, schwatzhaftes und ein sich überall vordrängendes Weib gleichet einer Glocke, die; fortwährend läutend, zuletzt lästig und unausstehlich wird — das bescheidene hingegen gleichet dem Veilchen, das im Stillen duftet und erquickt — Das unbescheidene Weib gleicht dem schrillen Wecker an der Uhr des Hauses, während das bescheidene in ewig gleichem Takt des Hauses Räderwerk bewegt und pünktlich und genau die Zeit vertheilt nach Maß und Nutzen . . . Des Weibes zweite Tugend sei der Adel des Gemüthes, die feine Herzensbildung; ein Weib ohne Gemüthlichkeit ist eine Statue ohne Seele, eine Schlange in Gestalt einer Menschenhülle, ein gemüthloses Weib, das kein Gefühl für die Armuth und für die Leiden Anderer, kein Gefühl fü r alles Große und Erhabene besitzt, ein solches kennt auch die wahre hehre Mutterliebe nicht; ein solches Weib hängt nur insolange ihrem Gatten an, als das Glück ihn begünstigt, kennt die Mutterliebe nur, wie die Natur sie lehrt und gebietet . . . Ueberhaupt muß und soll das Weib, gefühl- und herzvoll sein, weil es für die Innerlichkeit geschaffen ist, zur Innerlichkeit aber gehört vorzüglich Gemüth und Herz! Ein herzloser Mann kann immer noch ein geistreicher Mensch und der Gesellschaft ein nützliches Mitglied sein, ein herzloses Weib aber ist eine Puppe, die höchstens einen Augenblick ergötzt, niemals aber dauernd fesselt. Die dritte Tugend, die das eheliche Glück vom Weibe fordert, das ist des Hauses nützliche Verwaltung, das ist die Vor- und Fürsorge der Gattin. Wie das Gottesauge muß das Weib des Hauses Licht und Leuchte sein und überall und stets Alles übersehen, so nur wird der Gatte am häuslichen Herde gefesselt, so nur wird das Haus zum Paradiese, das der Mensch in seinem Uebermuthe auf der Erde einst verloren. Nur wo der Gattin Sorge ist das Haus, dort gilt auch des Gatten Streben nur dem Hause, dieser vereinten Sorgsamkeit aber allein entspringt des Hauses Glück und Wohlfahrt. Wie Recht hat daher der Weise, wenn er ruft: Wie Sonnenglanz am wolkenlosen Morgen, so glänzt das holde Weib im Haus verborgen. Wie des heiligen Leuchters, hell glänzendes Licht, — so steht der Herzensadel schönem Angesicht. Wie goldene

Säulen zu silbernen Füßen gestaltet, — ist holdes Weib, das sorglich wohl das Haus verwaltet!

Und wie glänzend bewähren sich die goldenen Worte nicht an Ihrem Leben selbst, liebe Glaubensschwester! Nur allzufrühe haben Sie auf Gottes weisen Rathschluß den guten und liebenden Führer, den sorgsamen und guten Vater, den Sie sicherlich in diesem Momente allzuschmerzlich vermissen, verloren — und dennoch sind Sie herangeblüht und wohlgediehen zur Freude Ihrer Lieben und zur Wonne Ihres seligen Vaters, der Sie gewiß in diesem Augenblicke segnend umschwebt — wem aber haben Sie dieses, außer dem Herrn, der wohl ein allerbarmender Vater der Wittwen und Waisen ist, anders zu verdanken als der Bescheidenheit und dem treuen, sorgsamen und liebevollen Walten Ihrer zärtlichen Mutter?

Ihnen aber lieber Glaubensbruder rufe ich für die neue Lebensperiode folgende Worte desselben Weisen zur Beachtung zu:

„מתנה טובה בחיק ירא אלהים תנתן אשה ט״ב“

„Ein gutes Weib ist eine gute Habe
Dem Frommen nur wird sie von Gott zur Gabe.“ —

Ja, meine Lieben dem Frommen nur wird ein gutes Weib gegeben — und das lehrt außer dem Weisen, die tägliche Erfahrung — dort, wo der Gatte alles geistige und hehre Leben vernachlässigt und sich ausschließlich dem Materialismus und dem Lebensgenusse in die Arme wirft, dort folgt auch das Weib allzugerne dem Beispiele, denn das Weib trachtet vor Allem dem Manne zu gefallen, sei es durch Frömmigkeit, oder durch Gottlosigkeit — wohin aber die Gottlosigkeit im Hause und in der Familie führt — braucht wohl nicht erst gesagt zu werden.

Ach, wer predigte wohl unsern Eltern und Voreltern die gegenseitigen ehelichen Pflichten und Tugenden, und wie waren dennoch ihr Ehen — und Familienleben mit geringen Ausnahmen, so ehren- und musterhaft! wie kannten und erfüllten sie sie doch so gewissenhaft! Sie hatten aber einen Lehrer und Führer, der sie leitete und niemals im Stich ließ, und das war das untrügliche Gotteswort!

Ich erinnere Sie daher ernst und aufrichtig, so Sie Ihr häusliches und eheliches Glück dauernd begründen wollen, so geloben Sie es sich in diesem feierlichen Momente, nie von Gottes Wort und Gottes Wegen zu lassen; denn nicht die Liebe und nicht das Gold machen das Menschenherz für die Dauer glücklich und zufrieden. Dieß sind allzuoft Mittel zu unserem Wehe und Verderben, die Frömmigkeit allein adelt erst den Reichthum wie die Liebe, und bewährt sich stets sowohl im Ueberfluß wie auch im Mangel.

„Ein gutes Weib ist eine gute Habe
Dem Frommen nur wird sie von Gott zur Gabe."

Ach, wer wollte und sollte nicht schon um diesen Preis gottesfürchtig sein! wo gibt es denn wohl ein größeres Glück, eine hehre Wonne, als ein gutes Weib mit dem man die Freuden doppelt und das Leid nur halb fühlt!

Und so mögen denn diese Worte Früchte tragen und Sie beglücken in Ewigkeit. Amen.

6.

Zu Dir Herr! kommen wir in unsern freuderfüllten Momenten, damit Du sie heiligest durch Deine Nähe und segnest durch Deinen Beifall — auf daß sie nicht ohne segenreichen Einfluß auf unser ganzes Dasein, vorübereilendem Schatten gleich, verfliegen.

Und so stehen wir auch gegenwärtig vor Dir, Vater im Himmel, demütigen Herzens und Sinnes, um den Thau Deines himmlischen Segens herab zu beten auf die zarte Pflanze der Ehe, welche diese Deine Kinder nur in den Schoß der dunkeln Zukunft pflanzen wollen! auf daß sie gedeihe, Glück und Segen bringend für alle Zeiten. Amen.

Dunkel und wunderbar sind die Wege des Geschickes, dunkel und wunderbar die Wege, die e3 uns führt, damit wir am Ende um so heller und lichter die göttliche Vaterhand sehen, die uns dem Ziele zugeführt und um so sicherer und zuversichtsvoller ausrufen können: מאת ה׳ היתה זאת היא נפלאת בעינינו — זה היום עשה ה׳ נגילה ונשמחה בו. Von Gott dem Herrn ging dieß aus, was so wunderbar uns scheint — ja diesen Tag hat Gott bestimmt, damit wir dessen uns freuen, und frohlocken mit ihm."

Ja, meine Lieben. Sie müssen und sollen es in diesem Ihres Lebens wichtigsten Momente erkennen, daß Gott Sie für einander geschaffen, für einander bestimmt hat, und zwar schon daran, daß Sie auf so sonderliche Weise sich begegnet, kennen, achten und lieben gelernt, trotz der verschiedenartigsten Verhältnisse, in denen Sie beide bisher gelebt.

Diese Erkenntniß soll aber zugleich Ihr Lebensglück und Ihre dauernde Freude ausmachen, denn was gibt es wohl Erfreuenderes als das Bewußtsein, daß wir und Alles, was uns Frohes begegnet, Gott allein und ausschließlich zuzuschreiben und zu verdanken haben?!

Oh! Daß Ihnen der Herr dieses sichtbare Zeichen seiner unverkennbaren Huld so offen kund that, darin sollen Sie Beide, den allerbarmenden Vater der Waisen erkennen!

Keinen Vater und keine Mutter sehe ich hier freude- und wehmuthsvoll an Ihrer Seite stehen meine Lieben, Traurigkeit erfüllt Ihr Beider Herz! Das Bewußtsein der Verlassenheit und des Alleinstehens, oh, das ist eine so bewältigende Macht, daß allzuoft nur ein zu großer Muth dazu gehört, um sie zu bekämpfen, und mit Gleichmuth zu ertragen! Und so sehen Sie denn, wie tröstend Gott der Herr Ihnen zur Seite steht! Beide, Kinder einer und derselben Heimath, mußten Sie sich in der Fremde begegnen um sich für die Dauer zu vereinigen, um sich durch gegenseitige Liebe und Treue, die theuern Eltern die im Grabe ruhen zu ersetzen: מאת ה' היתה זאת sollen und können Sie froh mit dem Psalmisten rufen, wie der Psalmist aber sollen auch Sie niemals Gott vergessen, vielmehr aber in kindlicher Dankbarkeit stets beflissen sein sich Gottes Huld und Liebe zu erwerben und dauernd zu erhalten — denn ist überhaupt kein anhaltendes häusliches Glück ohne Gottesfurcht, Gottvertrauen und Gottesliebe denkbar, selbst dort, wo so zu sagen das Glück mit in die Wirthschaft gebracht wird, um wie viel weniger dort, wo Solches erst erworben wird!

Was die ehelichen Pflichten betrifft meine Lieben, hierüber will ich mich kurz fassen. Unsern frommen Altvordern ward wohl niemals über eheliche Liebe und Treue, über zärtliche Theilnahme und steter Zufriedenheit gepredigt, und doch wie glücklich und unerschüttert; wie ruhig und überselig flossen nicht ihre ehelichen Tage dahin! während bei uns allzuoft trotz der schönsten und herrlichsten Reden der Ehestand blos zum Wehestand, und das häusliche Leben blos ein ewig Widerstreben wird. . . Also nicht die schönen Worte sind's, die alsbald verklingen, aber die alte Gottesfurcht דא ביה כולא ביה! Wo diese herrscht, da wohnt das Glück; wo diese thront, da steht die Zufriedenheit als guter Engel wachend an der Pforte; wo diese ihren Sitz aufgeschlagen, da hat keine wie immer zerstörende Macht mehr Gewalt.

Sie Beide meine Lieben haben in frühester Jugend schon gehorchen gelernt ohne einen andern Lohn als den im Schweiße Ihres Angesichtes schwer Erworbenen — gehorchen Sie nun Gott dem Herrn, je williger und freudiger, und Sie werden noch in den spätesten Zeiten im trauten Familienkreise mit dem Psalmisten von diesem Tage rufen זה היום עשה ה' u. s. w. Amen.

7.

Um Deine Gunst o Herr! um Dein Wort mein Hort, und um Deinen Segen und Beistand Urquell des Segens flehe ich itzt und alle Zeit innigst zu Dir, erhöre mich und alle die da gekommen bewegten Herzens voll sehnlichster Wünsche. Amen.

Schön ist der Anblick, wenn die Erde die unheimliche Hülle des Winters ab — und das herrliche Grün des Frühlings anlegt, herrlich zu sehn ist es, wenn aus der trüben, sturmvollen Nacht die Sonne verjüngt aus dem Schoße der Finsterniß sich erhebt; beseligend ist es, wenn der Frevler aus der Tiefe des Sündenpfuhles zu einem neuen, gottreinen Wandel sich aufschwingt — schöner, herrlicher und entzückender aber ist es aus der Alleinheit heraus zu treten, um sich für die Lebenszeit in Freundschaft, Liebe und Treue zu verbinden und zu einen, denn wenn auch der Mensch selbst in seiner Alleinheit seinen Werth und seine Würde gleich dem Diamanten, der selbst ungeschliffen und ungefasst, schon seinen

Werth in sich trägt, so tritt doch der Mensch wie der Edelstein dann erst in seinem ganzen Glanze hervor, wenn ihm die letzte Glätte, die endnöthige Politur gegeben wird. — Das aber, was dem Kleinod die endnöthige Glätte, das ist dem Erdensohn die Weihe der ehelichen Verbindung! Und so wie das Gebet seinen Stützpunkt in dem ungeheuchelten Bedürfniß sich mit dem himmlischen Allvater in Verbindung setzen zu wollen, finden muß, also soll auch die Sorge ums Weltliche ihren Weihe- und Ausgangspunkt in etwas Besserm, Höhern, ja Göttlichen haben! Wann aber ist das Ringen ums Weltliche, die Sorge ums Irdische gerechtfertigter, geweiheter und heiliger, als eben wenn sie der Familie, Weib und Kind gilt?! Wo gibt es einen schönern, einen erhabenern Standpunkt für sie als diesen Horeb des irdischen Glückes?

Und darum geliebte Beide, ist das eheliche Leben so alt als das erste Menschenpaar, noch ehe es eine menschliche Gesellschaft, noch ehe es sonstige göttliche und menschliche Einrichtungen gab, da hatte schon das eheliche, das Familienleben Wurzel geschlagen für die ganze Zeitdauer des Menschengeschlechtes auf Erden. Und wohin wir auch unsere Blicke schweifen lassen, sei es nach dem entferntesten Norden, oder nach dem tiefsten Süden, zu den gesitteten und gebildeten Völkern, wie zu den rohen und wilden diesseits und jenseits des Erdgürtels — überall gewahren wir Mann und Weib, Ehe und Familie! Aber nicht ohne gewaltige und mächtige Unterschiede, denn während bei dem einen Volke das Weib nichts anderes als ein Eigenthum gleich jedem Andern, ist — bei Anderen wieder nur als Sklavin beachtet und geachtet wird — ist es das Judenthum, das der Würde des Weibes Eingang und Geltung bei allen zivilisirten Völkern der Erde verschaffte — das Judenthum behandelt das Weib nicht als Eigenthum, aber als Eigenthümerin mit Rechten und Pflichten, als Herrin des Hauses, nicht als leibeigen, sondern als Gehilfin, Freundin, als des Mannes zartere, edlere Hälfte! die gleiches Recht und gleichen Antheil an des Glückes Gaben haben soll! מצא אשה מצא טוב. Wem es ein Weib zu finden ist gelungen, der hat ein seltnes Glück errungen! Wie, aber? ist jedermann schon glücklich, der ein Weib gefunden? hat jedermann schon die Spitze des Glückes erklommen, er das Band der Ehe geknüpft und geschlossen? Ach! wie oft ist icht grade die Ehe, der Schoß der Zwietracht, des Haders, des Unheils und des Elends? hierauf aber meine Lieben läßt sich nur folgendes sagen: Allwo die Ehe im Sinne unserer heiligen Religion geschlossen und geachtet wird, allwo das Weib des Mannes Zierde, des Hauses Priesterin!

Allwo das Weib mit Treue waltet,
Und mustervoll im Hause schaltet —
Allwo das Weib, fromm, sanft und zart,
Und sorglich für die Zukunft spart —
Allwo das Weib den Gatten ehrt,
Als Krone — wie's die Liebe lehrt —
Allwo das Weib den Gatten liebt,
Stets ungeschwächt und ungetrübt —
Allwo das Weib stets Antheil nimmt,
An Freud und Leid von Gott bestimmt
Allwo das Weib nur das begehrt,
Was auch den Gatten ziert und ehrt —
Allwo das Weib besitzt ein Herz,
Das stets nur schlaget Gattenwärts!
Allwo der Mann auf Gott vertraut,
Und stets auf seinen Fleiß nur baut —
Allwo der Mann getreulich hängt,
Am Weibe, das ihm Gott geschenkt —
Allwo der Mann vertraut und baut,
Auf's Weib, das er sich angetraut —
Allwo der Mann bei Noth und Viel,
Der Gattin stetes Wohl nur will,
Allwo der Gatte stets bereit,
Zur Arbeit und zur Thätigkeit!
Allwo stets Mann und Weib zufrieden
Mit jenem Los, das Gott beschieden!

Alldort ist auch des Glückes Wonne, die Stätte der Eintracht die Fülle des Segens, der Horeb der Seligkeit! allwo hingegen das Mißtrauen sich ins eheliche Leben schleicht, da nagt die Verzweiflung an den innersten Kern der Glückseligkeit; allwo die Ansprüche, die Prunksucht und die Laune sich breit machen, da ist

Unfriede, Unheil und Trostlosigkeit! allwo Gottlosigkeit und Na
lässigkeit herrschen, da kehrt die Herzensruhe, der Frohsinn und
Behaglichkeit nie ein!

Und darum geliebte Beide! mahne ich Sie in diesem erns
Momente, stets eingedenk zu sein, daß nur Gottesfurcht und
genseitiges Vertrauen, Liebe und Treue, Frohsinn und Thätigke
Zufriedenheit und gegenseitige Achtung das eheliche Bündniß
einem gottgesegneten und glücklichen machen, darum fordere
Sie lieber Glaubensbruder nachdrücklich auf: daß Sie dieser Ihr
selbstgewählten Lebensgefährtin nicht nur ein redlicher Ernähr
und Versorger seien, sondern auch ein besorgter Führer über d
Dornen und Klippen am Wege des Lebens, sowie Sie liebe Gla
bensschwester, es sich zur Aufgabe und zur Pflicht machen möge
Ihrem selbstgewählten Gatten fort und fort eine glühende Lieb
zu beweisen, sich ihm hinzugeben mit einer Zuversicht, die kein
Schranken, mit einer Zärtlichkeit, die keine Gränzen und mit eine
Ehrerbiethung, die nichts Höheres auf Erden kennt! Mögen Si
es sich zur Aufgabe machen, diesem Ihrem Manne das Leben zu
verschönen und angenehm zu machen, seine Freuden und seine
Kummer gern, und bereitwillig mit zu fühlen, und mit zu empfin
den, mögen Sie es ferner als heilige Pflicht erachten das Hau
in guter jüdischer Sitte und Frömmigkeit zu leiten und zu regie
ren — denn wenn das gotterfüllte Weib eine wahrhafte Zierde
ein Schmuck des Mannes und eine Krone des Hauses ist, so is
das gottlose Weib ein Unding, eine Abart von Blume und Sta
chel, und wenn das gottgeweihete Haus ein Tempel — so ist da
gottleere Haus, wenn auch nicht immer die Stätte des Elendes
so doch auch niemals, die Stätte der Seligkeit. Mögen Sie beid
ferner es sich zum Vorsatze machen im Glücke bescheiden, im Un
glücke zuversichtig — bei Freuden tugendhaft im Leiden vertrauungs
voll, beim Reichthum sparsam, in Zeiten der Bedrängniß noch milde
im Ueberflusse genügsam, beim Mangel aber noch immer nicht gei
zig sein zu wollen!

Diese Fülle von Tugenden liebe Beide, die ich Ihnen al
aufrichtiger Seelsorger lehren zu müssen glaubte, mögen Sie sic
tief eingeprägt haben in den Tafeln Ihres Herzens, und sie pünkt-

lich und genau befolgen zum Glücke und zum Heile Ihres Lebens, für und für, also geschehe es.

8.

ויאמר ה׳ אלהים לא טוב היות האדם לבדו אעשה לו עזר כנגדו.

„Und Gott der Herr sprach, es ist nicht gut, daß der Mensch allein sei, ich will ihm eine Gehilfin machen, die um ihn sei." — Also lautete der Spruch des Herrn, als er in seiner Allweisheit den Entschluß faßte dem ersten Menschen das erste Weib zu geben!

Müssen wir aber nicht erstaunt fragen: welches Glück und welches Gut kann wohl in der Anhäufung und Vermehrung unserer Sorgen liegen? welches Glück und Gut in der Verzweifachung unserer Bedürfnisse? wie schwer fällt es dem Menschen nicht allzuoft sich allein das Nöthige in seiner ganzen Bequemlichkeit zu erstreben und zu erraffen und nun soll es noch des Menschen Lust und Glück vermehren, wenn er nicht nur für sich, sondern noch für ein anderes ihm gleich bedürfnißreiches Wesen zu sorgen und des Lebens Last zu tragen hat! „Ich will ihm eine Gehilfin schaffen die um ihn sei." Wie? das schwache, zarte Wesen Weib! Die zarte Blume im Erdeneden, die uns höchstens mit ihrem Dufte erfreut, mit ihrem Anblick erquickt und mit ihrer Liebe entzückt — sie, die schwanke Rose, die jeder Luftzug reizt und bewegt, sie soll eine Gehilfin sein dem starken, kampfgeübten Manne, der den rasenden Stürmen des Lebens trotzt, und auf geschwellter Woge des Windgepeitschten Ozeans das Schiff des Seins unerschrocken lenkt und leitet!? Sie die zarte Schlingpflanze, die ohne Stab und Stütze nur allzubald verwittert, sie soll dem Manne, der in seinen Plänen die Welt umfasset eine Gehilfin sein??

Also aber, meine Lieben! ist es dennoch, denn des Herrn Wort besteht fort und fort! und was auch nicht leicht der Verstand des Verständigen sieht, das empfindet gar oft ein frommes Gemüth! Wie? lieber Glaubensbruder, hast du nicht gar oft, wenn Deine wohlgeordneten Pläne draußen an den rauhen harten Klippen der Wirklichkeit gescheitert, wenn mannigfaches Leid auf Dich einstürmt — und die brandende Welle, Deinen Lebensnachen zu zerschlagen drohete und Du dich endlich nach Ruhe sehnend, in Deine stille Wohnung begabst, hast Du da nicht wehmüthig das Bedürfniß empfunden Dich mitzutheilen? Vergebens aber suchte Dein Auge den Gegenstand, der Dich verstanden, Dich getröstet, gestärkt und neuen Muth eingeflößt hätte! Und wenn hinwieder die Freude Dein übervolles Herz wie ein Alp drückte und Du beseligt aufjauchztest, fühltest Du da nicht ein namenloses Bangen, ein unaussprechliches Sehnen die Last Deiner Freuden zu theilen — vergebens jedoch suchtest Du das Wesen, das Dich begriffe, jeden Deiner Herzensschläge erwiedere und jeden Stral Deines freudetrunkenen Auges tausendfärbig wiedergebe. — Und wenn schließlich gar die quälende Sorge um die entfernte Zukunft — da die Tage kommen, an welche wir keine Lust finden, Tage an denen unsere Thatkraft bereits gebrochen, unsere Willensmacht geschwunden und unsere Lebenslust nur noch zur Lebenslast geworden — Dich beschlich, überkam Dich da nicht jener fromme Wunsch im Kreise einer treuen, liebenden Familie Dich zu sehn. — Ach! wie arm, wie freudenlos; ja wie elend erscheint uns nicht das ganze Leben, und schwelgten wir auch fort und fort in dem Genuß von Freuden — gedenken wir der letzten Stunde, wenn wir ohne Theilnahme, unbeweint und unbetrauert aus diesem Leben sollen! Oh wie gerne gäben wir in solchen Augenblicken das größte Glück, die unnennbarste Seligkeit, wenn ich so sagen darf, wie gerne trügen wir dann des Lebens schwerste Sorgen — für jenes zarte Wesen — Weib! das Gott der Herr in seiner höchsten Gnade zur Gehilfin uns gegeben!

Nun aber kannst Du, lieber Glaubensbruder! mit dem heiligen Dichter rufen מצאתי את שאהבה נפשי — ich fand was meine Seele sehnlichst wünschte! so ist es denn auch Deine Pflicht Deiner Lebensgefährtin ein mittheilsames Herz, einen dankerfüllten Sinn entgegen zu bringen, mit einem Worte ihr ein guter Gatte in des Wortes breitester und edelster Bedeutung zu sein!

An Ihnen aber theure Jungfrau ist es, Ihrem Gatten eine Gehilfin zu sein, indem Sie seine Lust und Last in Liebe und herzlicher Innigkeit tief mitfühlen und mitempfinden, an Ihnen als Gehilfin ist es, das redlich Erworbene zu sparen und zu bewahren, an Ihnen ist es als Gehilfin ihm durch eine wohlgeordnete Häuslich-

das Leben des Hauses zur höchsten Freude zu gestalten. Eben das Weib nicht für die rauhe Außenwelt geschaffen, weil eben Weib mit des Lebens Kämpfen und Stürmen nichts zu thun und haben soll, eben deßhalb muß es sich ganz der Häuslich- und den bessern Gefühlen hingeben — das Weib gleicht ge- n Schalthierchen, deren Stärke nur in ihrer Schale besteht — äßt es diese, so hat es seinen Schutz aufgegeben und wird als- n jeder harten Berührung und der Vernichtung ausgesetzt! Ich ihm eine Gehilfin machen, die um ihn sei — gibt aber das ib seinen eigenen Launen nach, seinen eigenen Wünschen und gehren, ist es dann um ihn und nicht vielmehr von ihm — er ihn?! Was die zarte und biegsame Feder in dem Werk der r, was die unsichtbare Seele in des Leibes Hülle, das ist, das das Weib dem Hause und dem Manne! In diesem Sinne ist es des Mannes Gehilfin, in diesem Sinne ist es um ihn, e Worte wollen Sie Beide bedenken, wenn Sie ihren Aufgaben sprechen und Ihr eheliches Bündniß zu einem glücklichen gestal- wollen für alle Zeiten. Also sei es. Amen.

Und nun ist dieß Ihr Herzensbündniß geschlossen nach der itte Moses und Israels, mögen Sie sich denn auch des Segens rdient machen, den ich Ihnen nun im Namen Gottes als Diener s Herrn ertheile:

יברכך ה׳ וישמרך

Gott segne Dich theures Paar mit den Glücksgütern dieser rde — und behüte Dich vor Stolz und Uebermuth und allen ebeln, die im Gefolge der Hülle und Fülle einzutreten pflegen.

יאר ה׳ פניו אליך ויחנך

Gott lasse sein Angesicht dir leuchten in Gnade, und gebe Gunst in allen Menschenaugen.

ישא ה׳ פניו אליך
וישם לך שלום

Gott wende dir Macht und Ansehen zu und schenke dir Voll- mmenheit, Glück und allseitigen Frieden für alle Zeit deines Le- ns. Also sei und geschehe es.

9.

עד הנה עזרנו ה׳,

Bisher hat Gott geholfen.

Also lieber Bruder in Gott, können Sie getrost mit
gottbegeisterten Seher rufen, wenn Sie den zurückgelegten Le
weg überschauen! Nicht ohne Mühe und nicht ohne große
schwerden sind Ihre Tage dahin geflossen, im Schweiße Ihres
gesichtes mußten Sie sich das, was Sie sind und haben, erri
— aber Gott der Herr hat geholfen, eben deswegen geh
Schön und ehrenvoll ist die Bahn der Arbeit, der Kunst und
Kunstfleißes — achtens- und schätzenswerth die Laufbahn des
beiters, aber auch nutz- und segenbringend: כפיך כי תאכל אשריך
וטוב לך So du genießest deiner Händemühen — so wird
Heil und Segen dir erblühen! Angelangt sind Sie zu dem sch
Ziele, das der gottergühte Dichter, Sänger und Seher dem
ßigen Arbeiter verkündet. Dein Weib gleicht fruchtbarem Weinf
im Innern deines Hauses! Wollten Sie aber nicht immer
Glückes sich erfreuen auf die zurückgelegte Lebensstrecke mit innig
Wohlbehagen sehn und rufen zu können: Bis hierher hat G
geholfen?! Oder glauben Sie etwa, daß die Arbeit, die Anstr
gung und der Fleiß allein, schon genügen und ausreichen um
für immer glücklich zu machen? und wenn wir endlich alt
schwach werden — und wenn es denn, wie die tägliche Erfahr
lehrt, trotz aller Anstrengung doch nicht immer nach unserem W
sche geht? Nein! lieber Glaubensbruder zu unserer Thätigkeit
hört auch und vorzüglich der Segen des Herrn, das Wohlwo
Gottes; die Liebe des himmlischen Allvaters, und um diese
gewinnen, dazu ist die Furcht vor dem Herrn, das Vertra
auf den Herrn und die Liebe zu dem Herrn unbedingt nöthig — so
der Psalmist dieß gerechter Weise voraussetzt, indem er sagt: רי כל
ירא ה׳ ההלך בדרכיו — „Heil dem Manne, der gottesfürchtig
und seine Wege nach den Seinen mißt“ und dann erst כפיך כי תאכל נ
Ja lieber Glaubensbruder Gottesfurcht, Gottvertrauen und Got
liebe, diese drei nur bilden das unzerreißbare Band, welches
Glück an unser Leben knüpft, diese drei bilden die feste Schli
um das eheliche Leben, daß es in Friede und in Freude fortbeste

Das Bündniß aber, das Sie nunmehr schließen, verlangt aber noch andere Pflichten von Ihrer Seite und zwar erstens, dau- Treue gegen diese Ihre selbstgewählte Lebensgefährtin, deren hick nun sichtbarlich in Ihre Hand gelegt wird, zweitens aber Zuversicht in ihre Anhänglichkeit und Liebe, denn wo sich das trauen ins eheliche Leben schleicht, da kömmt gleichzeitig das lück mit — drittens aber eine stets wohlwollende Behandlung, sie Ihnen auch weder Schätze, noch sonstige irdische Güter in lle zuführt! denn wahrlich nicht dasjenige Weib ist oft das Beste, mit vollen Händen kömmt, aber jenes ists, das uns ein Herz l Liebe, einen Sinn voll zarter Hingebung, ein Gemüth voll rmer Empfindungen mitbringt! und so frage ich Sie denn; b sie wohl gewillt dieses heilige Bündniß ein für allemal im inne unserer heiligen Religion und zur Erfüllung aller ehelichen lichten zu schließen, so geloben Sie dieß durch ein unverbrüch- hes „Ja" —

Und nun wende ich mich, liebe Glaubensschwester! an Sie; ch Sie können getrost in den Ruf einstimmen „Bis hieher hat ott geholfen" auch Sie sehen auf eine mit vielen Mühen, zurückge- gte Lebensstrecke zurück; auch Sie sind endlich ans Ziel Ihrer Wünsche gelangt — und also ist es denn auch Ihnen zu wissen öthig, was Sie auch für dieses neue Verhältniß zu thun haben, uf daß Sie auch in der entferntesten Zukunft noch, wie heute rufen können „Bis hierher hat Gott geholfen — denn liebe Glaubens- schwester gar wechsel- und veränderungsvoll ist das Leben des Menschen auf Erden — und was uns heute beglückt, kann morgen schon die Quelle unseres Elends sein! und wir sollten uns also unberathen in ein Bündniß für die ganze Lebenszeit einlassen, ohne uns früher um einen sichern Führer, um einen festen Stab zu bekümmern, der uns sicher durchs Leben geleite?! Dieser Führer aber und diese Stütze sind keine menschlichen und irdischen, sondern aber das Wort Gottes, das ich Ihnen nun in treuer Seelsorgerpflicht lehre.

Vor Allem ist es die Erfüllung der religiösen Pflichten, die Gott vorzüglich dem Weibe vorschrieb, denn ein frommes Weib ist zumeist auch ein gutes, ein pflichttreues und ein tugendhaftes Weib, sodann aber ist ehrerbietige Ergebenheit, diesem Ihrem selbstgewähl- ten Gatten Ihre unabweisliche Schuldigkeit, so wie es in der Schrift heißt והוא ימשל בך — denn wenn die Gattin auch des Ma Hälfte, seine Freundin und Lebensgefährtin sei, die gleiches und Antheil an des Glückes Gaben haben soll, so soll sie doch eingedenk sein, daß es der Mann ist, der da kämpft und ring arbeitet — und darum ist es ferner Ihre Pflicht, das Erarb treu zu sparen und zu bewahren, sorgsam zu erhalten und h hälterisch zu verwalten. — Es ist dieß beim Arbeiter um so n ger und nothwendiger, als es nur allzuoft Zeiten gibt da die H ruhen müssen, ruhen sollen! Ihre Pflicht ist es ferner, Ih Gatten beizustehn, so oft er Ihres Beistandes bedarf, sein Gew zu schätzen und in Ehren zu halten — ihn selbst aber stets zu ben, warm und innig, treu und wahr. — Ihre Pflicht ist es spruchlos und zufrieden zu sein; denn wenn auch das Handw wie das Sprichwort sagt, einen goldenen Boden hat, so gehört Mühe und Schweiß dazu um diesem hartem Boden das Nötl abzugewinnen!! Ihre Pflicht ist es, wenn es Noth thut, diesen ren Lebensgefährten zu stärken und zu trösten, wenn die Kraft schlafft und schwere Schweißtropfen den Unmuth auf die Sti locken, durch zarte Pflege und sinnige Zuvorkommenheit — so es ferner Ihre Pflicht ist, geduldig, sanft und nachsichtsvoll Launen des Ungemachs wenn solche eintreten, zu ertragen!

Ich frage Sie daher, sind Sie bereit Ihr eheliches Bün niß in diesem Sinne zu schließen, so geloben Sie dieß in diese ernsten Momente durch ein frommes, aufrichtiges Ja!"

Somit, o Gott! möge Dir denn dieser Bund der Treue u der Liebe empfohlen sein, auf daß Du ihn segnest, damit die Deine Kinder hier, noch in den spätesten Zeiten rufen könne עד הנה עזרנו ה' Amen.

10.

Um Deines Himmels besten Segen
Komm flehend ich, o Herr! zu Dir!
Um Deines Himmels besten Segen,
Für diese Deine Kinder hier!

Um ihnen Herr! Dein Wort zu lehren,
Das allbeglückend für und für,
Als Zehre für die Fahrt des Lebens,
Für diese Deine Kinder hier!

Um Deinen Segen, Deine Lehre,
Komm flehend ich, o Herr! zu Dir —
Auf daß durchs Leben sie geleiten
Herr! Diese Deine Kinder hier!
Amen.

Liebe Beide! Es gibt wohl unter allen religiösen und bürgerlichen Festen keines, das mit solcher Innigkeit, mit solcher Liebe Freude und Wonne gefeiert würde, als das Fest der Vereinigung zweier liebenden Herzen, als die Vereinigungsfeier zweier für einander geschaffenen Seelen! Und wenn es im Erdenleben wohl Momente gibt, in denen wir uns der Erde entrückt und dem Himmel, den Seligen näher fühlen, so zählt der Moment, in welchem Sie, meine Lieben sich gegenwärtig befinden gewiß zu denselben; denn gibt es wohl ein erhebenderes Bewußtsein als das, ein Haus zu gründen, eine Familie zu bilden, gibt es wohl eine schönere Empfindung als die, ein nützlicher Ring in der Kette der menschlichen Gesellschaft zu werden; gibt es schließlich wohl ein beseligenderes Gefühl, als das, daß jede unserer Empfindungen einen treuen Wiederhall findet!?

Sollen wir aber diesen ernstwichtigen Moment, da unser Herz geöffnet, unser Sinn erschlossen und unser Gemüth für alle bessere Eindrücke empfänglich ist — ja, sollen wir diesen Augenblick, in welchem sich so zu sagen, die Vergangenheit mit der Zukunft — wie zum Abschiede küßt — vorüber ziehen lassen ohne uns bewußt zu werden, wie so wir diese Freude der Vereinigung auch fortdauernd fest halten sollen? Gewiß nicht! und zwar um so weniger als wir ja nur allzugut wissen, wie schnell und flüchtig solche Momente im Leben dahinschwinden! Oder glauben Sie etwa, daß die sinnliche Liebe, das zarte Roth der Wangen; die liebliche Anmuth, und die entzückende Schönheit allein, schon ausreichen das eheliche Leben zu einem glücklichen und beglückenden zu machen? Ach, wie bald schwindet nicht das Alles! שקר החן והבל היופי. Die

Anmuth lügt, die Schönheit trügt, ruft schon der weise König! Wollen Sie aber sich stets dieser Verbindung freuen können, dann ist es nöthig, daß Sie die gegenseitigen Pflichten, die Sie mit gegenwärtigem feierlichen Akt, in dieser weihevollen Stunde sich so gerne aufbürden, die gegenseitigen Pflichten, die Ihnen unsere heilige Religion auflegt, genau kennen lernen und treu und willig befolgen! dann ist es Ihnen lieber Glaubensbruder zu wissen nöthig, daß Sie dieser ihrer nunmehrigen Lebensgenossin, die nun den treubesorgten Vater, die zärtlichliebende Mutter, das schützende Elternhaus verläßt und ihr Glück und ihr Geschick ausschließlich in Ihre Hände legt, stets eine wahrhaft standhafte Treue und Liebe bezeugen, und zwar nicht eine Liebe im gewöhnlichen, irdischen Sinne, aber eine solche, die in wahrer Achtung, in aufrichtiger Werthschätzung wurzelt; denn eine solche Liebe nur ist von ewiger Fortdauer, von unauflöslichen Banden umschlungen! Sie haben ferner dieser, ihrer Lebensgefährtin stets ein treuer und redlicher Ernährer und Versorger zu sein, ihr stets und immer schützend und schirmend zur Seite zu stehn — denn der Gatte ist der Regent des Hauses, die Pflicht des Regenten aber ist nicht nur zu herrschen, sondern auch ein schützender und versorgender Vater zu sein! Ihre Pflicht ist es schließlich Ihrer Lebensgenossin das Buch Ihres Herzens und Ihrer Gedanken stets offen zu halten, damit sie zu jeder Zeit darin lesen könne, oder mit andern Worten ihr vertrauungsvoll Freud und Leid stets liebevoll mitzutheilen, — Dieß sind die Pflichten, lieber Glaubensbruder, welche Sie Ihrer Lebensgenossin gegenüber zu erfüllen haben, sind Sie hiezu bereit so bestätigen Sie dieß durch ein ehrliches unverletzliches „Ja."

Und nun, liebe Glaubensschwester! wende ich mich an Sie, wenn es die Pflicht Ihres Gatten ist Sie aus Achtung zu lieben, so ist es hingegen wieder ihre Schuldigkeit dessen Liebe und Achtung zu verdienen, und zwar indem Sie ihm in glühender Zärtlichkeit anhangen, ihn lieben mit der ganzen Wärme eines kindlichfrommen Herzens; mit dem Zartsinn eines liebererfüllten Sinnes; mit der ganzen Hingebung eines gottdurchhauchten Gemüthes! Die Achtung und Werthschätzung des Mannes verlangt auch Achtung von Seite des Weibes. Er sei Ihr Schmuck und Zierde; der Stolz Ihres

Herzens, die Krone Ihres Hauptes und bilde den Glanz Ihres Hauses, Ihr Gatte sei Ihr redlicher Ernährer und Versorger, Ihr Stab und Ihre Stütze — nun so wissen denn auch Sie das Erworbene zu schätzen und mit Umsicht zu verwalten, so wissen denn auch Sie sich seines Schutzes zu erfreuen und dessen durch ein bescheidenes, frommes Benehmen stets würdig zu sein! Ihr Lebensgenosse soll stets mittheilsam gegen Sie sein, so seien Sie denn auch wahrhaft theilnehmend und mitempfindend, da nichts so sehr zur Liebe anregt als aufrichtige, herzinnige Theilnahme! Ich frage Sie nun, sind Sie ein für allemal entschlossen diese Ihre ehelichen Pflichten stets zu erfüllen, so sprechen Sie dieß aus durch ein aufrichtiges „Ja!"

Und nun, möge denn Gott der Herr ihre frommen Vorsätze vernommen haben und Ihnen seinen Beistand und seine Hilfe verleihen, daß Sie sie auch ausführen können, denn אם ה' לא יבנה בית שוא עמלו בוניו בו. „So Gott nicht baut das Haus des Lebens — so mühen die Meister sich vergebens! doch behaupten schon unsere frommen Alten הבא לטהר מסייעין לו der aufrichtig dem Guten nachstrebt, dem verhilft auch Gott dazu! also sei es. Amen.

11.

Unser erster Gedanke gilt Dir Allmächtiger, der Du des Segens Quell und Ursprung bist, und so richten wir denn unser erstes Wort an Dich, an Dich Vater im Himmel! das inbrünstige Gebeth — Du wollest uns nahe sein in dieser Stunde, da so viele im Stillen zu Dir bethen! zu Dir flehen wir innigen Herzens; Du wollest die Ehe, welche wir nun im Sinne Deiner heiligen Lehre einsegnen wollen, zu einer friedlichen, glücklichen und kummerlosen gestalten, für alle Zeiten. Amen.

Liebe Beide!. Wenn ich Sie blos an das Muster einer zufriedenen und glücklichen Ehe verweisen wollte, so hätte ich Ihnen nichts anderes zu sagen, als „Gehet hin und ahmet Euern Eltern nach."

Denn wie viele schwere und trübe Zeiten, wie viele kummervolle und trübselige Stunden; wie viele sorgenvolle Tage und Nächte sie auch durchleben mußten, so blieb ihr eheliches und häusliches Leben doch stets ein zufriedenes und unerschüttertes ein mustergiltiges und nachahmungswerthes!

Doch nicht bloß zeigen will ich Ihnen das helle Bild einer guten Ehe, ich will Sie aber zugleich lehren, wie ein gutes eheliches und häusliches Leben zu gründen ist, den Grundpfeiler zu einer dauernd glücklichen Ehe will ich Sie aufrichten lehren, und dazu zitire ich das ewig reiche und unerschöpfliche Gotteswort, welches lautet: על כן יעזב איש את אביו ואת אמו, ודבק באשתו והיו לבשר אחד „Es verlasse darum der Mann seinen Vater und seine Mutter und hange seinem Weibe an, so daß sie ein Wesen ausmachen!"

Daß das eheliche Leben der gegenseitigen Liebe bedarf, wie die Pflanze Thau und Wärme, braucht wohl nicht erst gesagt zu werden, da eine liebelose Ehe einem deckelosen Hause gleicht, das eine Zeitlang wohl feststehn mag, doch nur allzubald durch die Zeitstürme zerfällt und zu Grunde geht! Wohl läßt sich die Liebe nicht erkämpfen und nicht erkaufen אם יתן איש את כל הון ביתו באהבה בוז יבוזו לו = Und gäbe man auch alle Schätze für die Liebe hin, so wäre doch Verachtung nur der Gewinn! die Liebe aber muß ja auf gegenseitige Achtung beruhen, und diese läßt sich wohl erringen und gewinnen — und ehret und achtet die Gattin im Manne die Stärke, die Kraft und das Streben, so würdige und ehre der Gatte im Weibe, die zärtliche und aufrichtige Anhänglichkeit, das fromme und treue Walten im Hause und endlich die Schwäche und die Verlassenheit desselben.

Hier, an der Schwelle des ehelichen Tempels muß der Gatte all die Vorzüge, die er etwa seiner Gattin zuvor hat zu den Füßen derselben, resignirend niederlegen, sowie die Gattin wieder auf die etwaigen ihrigen verzichten muß!

Gleich müssen beide Ehehälften sich dünken, gleich an Vorzügen und Ansprüchen, gleich an Rechten und Pflichten, so nur bewährt und bewahrheitet sich das ! והיו לבשר אחד

Und so wie das Weib kein anderes Bild, als das ihres Mannes im Herzen trage — wie es heißt: . . . והוא ימשל בך Nur Er herrsche in dir, also lebe auch der Gatte nur in ihr, mit ihr; durch und für sie — nicht nur im Hause und dem Scheine nach, sondern überall und immer — und müssen selbst Vater und Mutter, wie die Schrift will, in den Hintergrund treten, damit die Gattin ganz des Mannes Herz ausfülle.

Sie liebe Glaubensschwester, werden ferner in dem zärtlichen Elternhause verbleiben und gewiß stets beflissen sein Ihren Eltern eine gute und dankbare Tochter zu sein, doch dürfen sie niemals vergessen daß Sie nicht blos Tochter, sondern auch Gattin, nicht blos Kind, sondern auch Weib und im beschränktern Sinne auch Hausfrau sind.

So treten auch Sie mein Freund, nicht nur als Mann und Gatte ein neues Verhältniß an, sondern auch als Kind und Sohn! und Sie werden hoffentlich nicht nur ein guter, treuer und liebender Gatte s in, sondern auch ein dankbarer Sohn — wie Sie es bisher den Urhebern ihrer Lebenstage, so auch den Begründern Ihrer Selbstständigkeit und Ihres ehelichen und häuslichen Lebens sein! Denn so nur meine Lieben wenn gleiche Gefühle und Empfindungen sie beseelen — wenn Sie liebe Glaubensschwester trotz des Elternhauses eine musterhafte Gattin — und Sie mein Freund trotz Ihrer Selbstständigkeit als Mann und Gatte, doch schmieg- und biegsam als Sohn und Hausgenosse sein werden, dann erst wird ihre Ehe eine segensreiche und musterhafte, eine heilvolle und beneidenswerthe sein, und bleiben, Amen.

12.

Zu Dir Herr! erheben wir betend unsere Herzen und unsere Blicke, auf daß Du uns nahe seiest mit Deinem Segen, denn den Du segnest, der ist gesegnet! um Deine himmlische Vaterhuld beten wir für diese Deine Kinder beide — die nun nach Deinem heiligen Rathschlusse das heilige Band der Ehe für ihr lebelang um ihr Dasein schlingen wollen! möge es ein heiliges und ein segensreiches sein für alle Zeiten. Amen.

Friede, Eintracht und innige Uebereinstimmung bilden das große Geheimniß der Natur in ihrem Bestande und in ihrem segensreichen Wirken! Friede, Eintracht und allseitige Harmonie sind die Säulen, auf welchen der Tempel des menschlichen Glückes und des menschlichen Heils ruht — und Friede, Eintracht und fortwährender Einklang sind es auch, die das Haus und die Familie fest und für die Dauer erhalten. Darum heißt es auch so wahr und treffend bei unsern Alten: אם אין שלום אין כלום = Wo kein Friede herrscht, da zählt auch alles Andere nichts!

Was jedoch Friede, Eintracht und Uebereinstimmung sind, das will ich Ihnen in diesem ersten Momente pflichtgetreu zur Darnachachtung ans Herz legen.

Wenn Sie liebe Beide wähnen, daß dort schon wahrhafter Friede herrscht, allwo es weder Zank noch Streit und Hader gibt, und daß dort schon dem ehelichen Frieden Genüge geleistet ist, allwo keine Gelegenheit zum Unfrieden gesucht und gebothen wird — so irren Sie — einen solchen negativen Frieden nennt man mit Recht Ruhe! und die herrscht ja allzuoft selbst unter Feinden — das eheliche Leben aber verlangt mehr, verlangt einen Frieden, der sich äußert in gegenseitiger Liebe, Achtung und Zuvorkommenheit! die eheliche, häusliche Eintracht wünscht mehr; sie verlangt ein fortwährend vereintes Streben mit allen zu Geboth stehenden Mitteln zu dem einen Ziele, welches das Glück und die Seligkeit des Ehelebens ist! Die eheliche Uebereinstimmung wünscht und begehrt ein gegenseitiges Eingehn in den Willen und in die Empfindungen des Einen und des Andern! und dieß ist wahrlich beileibe nicht so leicht als Sie liebe Beide denken und glauben mögen — zu solcher Harmonie gehört Geistes- und Herzensbildung — Gotteserkenntniß und vorzüglich wahrhafte Gottesfurcht! wo diese herrscht, da wohnt auch die Liebe, die Sanftmuth; die Geduld und die Ausdauer — da thront die Arbeitsamkeit, welche das Leben versüßt, die Sparsamkeit, die das Haus füllt und endlich die Wirthlichkeit, welche es angenehm macht!

Die eheliche Verbindung meine Lieben gibt zu so vielen erbaulichen Betrachtungen Anlaß, daß ich Ihnen wohl recht viel sagen hätte, doch ziehe ich es vor, Ihnen vorzüglich die Eintracht warm ans Herz legen, weil דא ביה כולא ביה — und so wie unsere Aeltern mit Recht behaupten אם אין שלום אין כלום, also wagen wir den Satz umkehrend, zu behaupten, daß dort, wo allseitige Übereinstimmung und Eintracht herrschen, dort auch Alles und zwar allen Gute ist!

Der wahrhafte Friede erzeugt Genügsamkeit, wo aber gäbe es Glück, ohne Genügsamkeit — oder wo hat je das Mißgeschick Platz gegriffen neben der Zufriedenheit?

Das Leben meine Lieben ist reich und mannigfach an Wechselfällen — nicht immer geht es nach unserem Wunsche, sondern allzuoft gegen denselben — ein Mißmuth bemächtigt sich unser, sollen wir denselben etwa ins Haus bringen und da zur Geltung kommen lassen? Nein, liebe Glaubensgenossen, das Haus sei eine Andachtsstätte, in dem die Liebe ihren Altar habe — und so wie wir beim Eintritt in die Gottesstätte den Staub des Alltagslebens und der gemeinen Sorge von uns schütteln sollen, also sollen wir beim Eintritt in den liebgeweihten Kreis der Häuslichkeit, jede Sorge und jeden Kummer an der Schwelle desselben lassen, um ausschließlich der Liebe und der Zärtlichkeit zu leben! Der Liebe und der Zärtlichkeit, die sie liebe Glaubensgenossen im Herzen tragen sollen, deren Stamm Sie stets zu hegen und zu pflegen haben, Ihre Sorge sei es Ihrem angetrauten Gatten das Marktleben mit seinen Sorgen und mannigfachen Beschwerden zu erleichtern ja vergessen zu machen; vergessen zu machen durch zarte Zuvorkommenheit, durch innige Anhänglichkeit und freundliche, liebevolle Theilnahme.

Nicht immer, meine Lieben geschieht von jeder Seite das Nechte und Rechte, gar oft werden bald von der Einen, bald vor der andern Seite Fehler begangen — doch wo wahrhafter Friede ist, ist es auch mit wenigen, sanften und belehrenden Worten abgethan, wie schon der Weise lehrt — ועל כל פשעים תכסה אהבה. Wehe aber, allwo eine Rechthaberei sich geltend macht, dort ist alsbald der goldene Friede gewichen, das häusliche Glück zerstört und auf den Ruinen desselben sitzt alsdann das Unheil als kreischende Eule, die all die guten Engel, die im Hause weilen und walten sollen, verscheucht.

Doch Sie, lieber Glaubensbruder, sind ja ein Namensbruder und Nachkomme jenes großen Ahnen von dem geschrieben ist, daß er ein אוהב שלום ורודף שלום war, so wie Sie liebe Glaubensgenossin eine verlassene Waise sind, welcher der Gatte nunmehr Alles sein soll und wird — und so liegt schon in diesen Zufälligkeiten eine gewisse Bürgschaft Ihres friedlichen und harmonischen Zusammenlebens und Wirkens. Möge es also geschehen. Amen.

13.

Liebe Beide! Es ist ein schwerer, ein wichtiger; ja ein lebenswichtiger Schritt, den sie nun vor Gott dem Herrn und den Menschen thuen und darum wollen wir uns die Hilfe und den Segen Gottes erflehen für jetzt und für alle Zeiten, möge er uns in Gnade erhören. Amen.

כי אל אשר תלכי אלך ובאשר תליני אלין עמך עמי ואלהיך אלהי =
denn wo du hingehst will auch ich hingehn, und wo du weilst, will auch ich weilen — ist ja Dein Volk auch mein Volk und Dein Gott auch mein Gott!" Also liebe Glaubensschwester sprach einst die fromme, anhängliche Ruth zu ihrer Schwiegermutter, und das liebe Glaubensschwester sei stets auch Ihr frommer Vorsatz diesem Ihren künftigen Lebensgenossen gegenüber. Wo du hingehst, will auch ich hingehn" Wie? soll etwa die Gattin, deren Wirkungskreis der häusliche Herd, deren Streben das Frohmachen des Gatten deren Ringen die Ordnung des Hauses sein soll und muß — dem Manne, dessen Beruf es ist zu säen und zu erndten; zu erstreben und einzuheimsen, auf jeden Tritt und Schritt folgen? Verträgt sich dieß mit der Würde des Weibes, von dem es heißt כל כבודה בת מלך פנימה, daß die Herrlichkeit und die Zierde des Weibes die Gemüthlichkeit und die Innerlichkeit?

Indessen gibt es nicht auch ein frommes Geleiten im Geiste, ein wirkliches Mitgehn im Herzen und im Sinne? Wenn der Mann hinauszieht in's Gewühl des alltäglichen Lebens um das tägliche Brod zu erwerben und die treue Gattin ihm ihre heißen Segenswünsche nachsendet, und für ihn und seine redlichen Bestrebungen zum Spender alles Guten aufrichtig betet, geht sie da nicht mit ihm? Und wenn der Gatte draußen kämpft und erwirbt und die treue Genossin zu Hause sich nur kärglich einrichtet, weil sie seine Arbeit, seine Mühe und seinen Schweiß würdigt und mitempfindet, ist sie da nicht mit ihm? und wenn die Gattin stets sehnsuchtsvoll dem abwesenden Gatten entgegenharrt, um ihn durch ihre Liebe, durch ihre Zuvorkommenheit, wie durch ihre Fröhlich- und Freundlichkeit für die Sorgen und Mühen des Alltagslebens zu entschädigen — ist sie dann nicht abermals mit ihm? und wenn schließlich der Gatte den einen Ort, allwo das Glück und das Geschick ihm nicht wohlwollen, weil eben dort seine Bestimmung nicht ist, verläßt, um ein besseres Los hier oder dort zu finden, und die Gattin ihm vertrauungsvoll, ohne zu zögern und zu murren, ja selbst aufmunternd, folgt! geht sie da im eigentlichen Sinne nicht mit ihm? כי אל אשר תלך אלך. Nur wohin du gehst, gehe und folge auch ich im Geiste, nur an Deiner Seite will ich mein Glück; nur in Deiner Nähe meine Seligkeit finden — und zwar weil ja Dein Volk auch mein Volk, und dein Gott auch der Meine ist! weil ja Dein Thun und Deine Gesinnung der Meinigen gleicht — weil auch Du ja als Jude denkst, strebst und fühlst und nur mit Gott aus- und eingehst!

So aber wie es der aufrichtige Wille dieser Ihrer Lebensgefährtin ist, und sein muß, ihnen auf dem Rosen — und Dornenpfad des Daseins ungetheilten und willigen Herzens zu folgen, so sei auch Ihr Vorsatz lieber Bräutigam ובאשר תליני אלין. Wo du weilst, will auch ich weilen, mit andern Worten, wo Du bist dahin ist auch mein Sinnen und Trachten, mein Streben und Wollen gerichtet, jeder meiner Gedanken gilt Dir — und wo ich auch bin, überall schwebt Dein Bild mir vor, tröstend und ermuthigend, erfrischend und stärkend! Kein Genuß und keine Freude, kein Vergnügen und keine Lust spricht mich an, so du nicht Theil an dieselben nimmst, und zwar weil ja Dein Volk mein Volk und dein Gott auch der Meine ist! weil Deine Pflichten ja auch Meine sind — weil wir beide ja nicht nur uns selbst angehören, sondern auch unserem Stamme und unserem Gotte — ihnen aber können wir nur durch ein vereintes, frommes Streben und Zusammenwirken dienen!

Mögen denn also diese frommen Vorsätze Sie nie verlassen und Sie können getrosten Herzens und frohen Sinnes der Zukunft, die in Gottes Vaterhand ruht, entgegensehn und entgegengehn.

Zu Dir aber, o Gott, ist unser Herz und unser Sinn erhoben. — Laß dieses Bündniß, welches diese Deine Kinder nunmehr schließen, ein unzertrennliches, ein glückliches; ein frohes und ein heiliges sein. Amen.

14.

„Es gibt im Menschenleben Augenblicke, in denen wir dem Weltgeist näher sind als sonst“ und zu jenen gehört unstreitig dieser, in welchem sich zwei liebende Herzen mit einander für die Lebensdauer verbinden. Dieser, in welchem Wehmuth und Wonne, Freude und Bangigkeit, Nacht und Morgen so zu sagen sich begegnen. Denn, während wir in solchem Momente die frohe und sorglose Jugendzeit, die fröhlichen Jugendspiele und die jugendliche Leichtfertigkeit, das zärtliche Elternhaus mit seiner Gemüthlichkeit zurücklassen — treten wir urplötzlich in die dunkle, dichtverschleierte Zukunft und unwillkürlich fragen wir uns: Wird auch der Ernst des Lebens fröhlich und heiter an uns vorbeiziehen? Werden die Wolken, die den schönsten Frühlingshimmel selbst, zuweilen verdüstern — uns blos einen Moment belästigen, oder werden sie das Schiff unseres Daseins an den Klippen des Lebensmeeres scheitern und zerschellen lassen?

Sie beide, meine Lieben, stehen in diesem Momente an dem Scheidewege, wo die frohe Vergangenheit von der düstern Zukunft sich scheidet, und so ziemt es sich denn auch, daß diese Fragen an Sie herantreten und eine Lösung beanspruchen! Aber gibt es denn auch eine Lösung? Welches Menschenauge wäre scharf und weitsehend genug um den dichten Schleier, den Gott der Herr in seinem Erbarmen dem „Wird“ vorgezogen, zu durchdringen? Gewiß keines! aber eines vermögen wir doch! und das ist: unsere Zukunft selber, glücklich und beglückend zu gestalten — weil wahrlich diejenigen welche Glück und Wohlfahrt nur von Außen und von äußern Umständen und Zufälligkeiten erwarten, können dem wanken und schwanken Nachen gleich, hin und her auf den Wässern des Daseins geschleudert werden und endlich untergehn — diejenigen aber welche wissen, daß Glück und Unglück tief in unserem Innern geboren und großgezogen werden, —, die werden auch einsehen, daß es blos und ausschließlich von uns abhängt, ob wir glücklich oder unglücklich sein wollen! Denn wahrlich nicht in den Schätzen dieser Erde, nicht im Ruhm und im Ansehn und auch wahrlich nicht im Wissen und im Erkennen — liegt das Glück, grade diese sind gar oft die Hebel zu unserem Verderben, das lehrt die Vernunft, das Gotteswort und die tägliche Erfahrung — was uns aber unstreitig beglückt und beseeligt und was vorzüglich geeignet ist, das eheliche und häusliche Leben dauernd glücklich zu erhalten, das sind: Gottesfurcht, Gottvertrauen und gegenseitige anhaltende Liebe! ירא את ה׳ בני ומלך „Fürchte Gott, mein Sohn! und Du bist ein für allemal, ein von allen Umständen und Verhältnissen unabhängiger König! ועם שונים אל תתערב — so daß Du nie mit den Veränderlichkeiten und Wechselfällen des Lebens ins Gemenge kömmst — ברוך הגבר אשר יבטח בה׳ והיה ה׳ מבטחו heißt es ferner, Heil dem Manne, der in Gott sein Vertrauen setzt; denn dessen Vertrauen wird auch durch Gott gerechtfertigt sein und nie zu Schanden werden! Schließlich aber rufe ich Ihnen zu: ראה חיים עם האשה אשר אהבת — betrachte das Leben als ein Gemeinschaftliches mit der Dir von Gott zugetheilten Lebensgenossin — indem Du sie liebest — Gottesfurcht, Gottvertrauen und Liebe kann und darf aber auch nie und niemals von Seite des Weibes vermißt werden und darum mögen die angeführten Gottessprüche Ihnen stets gegenwärtig sein, auf daß Sie sie befolgen, damit Ihr ganzes Leben, ein vorzügliches, aber Ihr eheliches ein glückliches und beglücktes sei, was Gott gebe. Amen.

15.

Eine Quelle,
Silberhelle,
Schuf Gott der Herr —
Huld und Segen,
Mild wie Regen,
Stralt um sie her!

Himmelswonnen,
Reicht der Bronnen,
Im Goldpokal —
Allen Lippen,
Die da nippen,
Am Silberstral.

Heilig Beben,
Licht und Leben,
Stralt von ihm aus —
Er nur schmücket,
Und beglücket,
Feld, Flur und Haus!

Diesen Bronnen
Hehrer Sonnen,
Nennt Liebe man —
Sie belebet,
Sie nur hebet,
Zu Gott hinan!

Liebe, ja Liebe, daß ist der Zauberstab, mittelst dessen Gott die Welt ins Dasein rief, sie leuchtet in den Myriaden Sonnen am Himmelszelt; sie lockt die Blumen aus der Erdentiefe ans Tageslicht; sie schimmert und glänzt und duftet in deren Farben und Würzen! Liebe ist der Athem der Natur, sie allein erfüllet alle Räume und alle Wesen — und sowie die Luft alles durchdringt und nöthiger Weise Alles im All und das All selbst durchdringen muß, so ist die Liebe, der moralische Kitt, die moralische Anziehungskraft der Wesen all im Weltall!

Wenn dieß aber schon von der Liebe im Allgemeinen, im Großen und Ganzen gilt, um wie viel mehr erst bei dem ehelichen Bündniß, da ist sie das Leben selbst! Auf Liebe nur kann der Tempel des ehelichen Glückes aufgeführt und dauernd erhalten werden, in der Ehe muß es heißen . . . אני לדודי ודודי לי „Ich gehöre meinem Freunde an, und mein Freund mir!"

„Ich gehöre meinem Freunde an," müssen Sie sich liebe Glaubensschwester stets sagen, wie auch das Leben sich gestalten mag — nicht nur dem Namen und dem Scheine nach, sondern mit ganzem Herzen und ganzer Seele, mit all meinem Trachten und Thun; mit all meinem Sinnen und Beginnen; mit all meinen Anlagen und Streben! Ich gehöre meinem Freunde an, in thätiger sich äußernder Liebe, denn wenn die zärtlich liebende Gattin das Erworbene, haushälterischer Weise auch zu erhatten bestrebt ist — ist das nicht ein Beweis inniger Anhänglichkeit? und wenn im Hause die höchste Reinheit und Reinlichkeit herrscht, und Alles und Jedes das unverkennbare Gepräge der tiefsten Sorgsamkeit an sich trägt, heißt das nicht abermals אני לדודי? und wenn ferner das Weib unter allen Umständen und Verhältnissen stets ein anständiges, nettes und bescheidenes Aeußere, niemals aber einen übertriebenen Glanz und Prunk zur Schau trägt, spricht das nicht wieder „ich gehöre meinem Freunde an?" —

Ich gehöre meinem Freunde an, indem seine Freude auch die meine, sein Schmerz auch der meinige; sein Stolz und seine Zierde auch mein Schmuck und meine Ehre ausmachen!

Oder, sollte die Gattin etwa nur insofern ihrem Gatten angehören, als er ihr Ernährer und Versorger, ihr Stab und ihre Stütze im Leben und durch das Leben ist; insofern als er ihre Bedürfnisse und Wünsche erfüllt, gehört sie dann ihm und nicht vielmehr sich, ja ausschließlich sich selber an!

אני לדודי rufe die Gattin stolz, denn im Hause ist er mein Abgott und auf dem Lebensmarkt ist er mein Gebet und meine Sorge!

So aber, wie Sie, lieber Glaubensbruder, zu fordern und zu wünschen berechtigt sind, daß diese ihre Lebensgefährtin das אני לדודי zum Ziele ihres Strebens mache, so ist es auch anderseits Ihre Aufgabe, daß Sie auch die andere Hälfte des angeführten Spruches stolz rufen könne, dann soll und muß der Gatte auch nur für sein Weib und in seiner Gattin leben — dann muß auch sein Dasein nur dem ehelichen und dem häuslichen Glücke geweiht und gewidmet sein. — Mein Freund gehöret mir, ausschließlich mir — im Hause und auf dem Markte bin ich sein Gedanke, mir allein ist sein Streben und Ringen geheiligt; die Liebe zu mir beseelt ihn zu fortdauernder Thätigkeit, verleiht ihm stets aufs Neue Muth und Beharrlichkeit; meinethalben unterzieht er sich gerne den Sorgen und Mühseligkeiten des Alltagslebens, erträgt er freudig Frost Hitze und wie all die Beschwernisse des Lebenskampfes sonst heißen ודודי לי soll das Weib in stolzem Bewußtsein stets rufen können: mein Ich allein lebt in seinem Herzen, ich allein bin sein Trost im Ungemach, so wie ich allein das Ziel seiner Lust und Freude bin! deßhalb ruft die Schrift: Mann und Weib mache nur ein Wesen aus, Eins im Wünschen und Wollen, Eins in Freud und Leid; Eins im Denken und Fühlen!

Wo solche Liebe thront, da wohnet auch das Glück, wo solche Liebe wacht, da ist des Hauses Wohl geborgen, wo solche Liebe waltet, da schaltet niemals Unfriede und Unzufriedenheit. — Solch Liebe jedoch beruht auf gegenseitige Achtung, sonst ist die innigste heißeste Liebe nur ein bald zu verflüchtigender Rausch — Achtung aber verdient ja die Gattin schon wie unsere Alten behaupten, weil sie uns von Sünden abhält, weil sie die Erzieherin eines kommenden Geschlechtes ist; Achtung schon deßhalb, weil sie dem Gatten ihr Vertrauen schenkt, und ihr Glück und ihr Geschick ausschließlich in seine Hände legt. Achtung verdient aber vorzüglich diese Ihnen von Gott bestimmte Lebensgenossin, weil sie einem guten Stamme entsprossen, und eine sorgfältige Erziehung genossen — Achtung und Werthschätzung verdient aber auch der Gatte seines ernsten Wollen und Strebens halber, seiner Vor- und Fürsorge wegen; der Manneskraft und Manneswürde willen — Achtung als Regent des Hauses, als der vom Herrn zum Beherrschen eingesetzter Leiter und Führer des Weibes!

Mögen Sie sich denn an diese Lehren halten zu Ihrem Heile und zu Ihrem Wohle für alle Zeiten. Amen.

16. *)

Zu Dir mein Gott! kommen wir in allen ernsten und wichtigen Momenten unseres Lebens, und so stehen wir denn auch in diesem ernsten lust- und wonneerregten und bewegten Momente vor Dir, um im Namen all der hier in diesem feierlichen Augenblicke mit theilnehmenden Herzen Anwesenden, Deinen Segen und Deinen Beifall zu erflehen für den Bund der Treue, für das eheliche Bündniß, das diese Deine Kinder hier, im Sinne Deiner heiligen Lehre ein für allemal zu schließen gewillt sind. Mögest Du es o Gott, ein dauerndes und segenreiches werden lassen. Amen.

זאת הפעם עצם מעצמי ובשר מבש״ו !

„Diesmal ist es Wesen von meiner Wesentlichkeit und Leib von meinem Leibe“, so sprach der Vater und erste der Menschen, als Gott der Herr ihm das Wesen zugeführt, welches seinem Dasein erst die rechte Weihe verlieh, seinem Leben und Lieben erst die Krone aufsetzte und seinem Streben erst die ächte und rechte die ernste und wichtige Richtung gab — und das ist das Familienleben in seiner erhabensten und edelsten Bedeutung; denn in

*) Gehalten in Ofen im Jahre 1864.

ihm erkannte er nicht nur das Meisterstück der göttlichen Schöpfung, das ihm an Gestalt und Form nach Außen gleich kam, sondern, worüber er sich vorzüglich, und mit Recht zuerst freuete, es war der göttliche Funke des Geistes, der ihm von der Stirne und aus den Augen jenes Wesens entgegen leuchtete. Ja, er fühlte es, daß er es hier nicht mit einem Geschöpfe, das ihm fremd an Gefühl und Neigung, fremd an Wollen und Können, fremd an Streben, Dichten und Trachten, sondern mit einem verwandten, verwandt an Leib und Seele, verwandt an Fühlen und Empfinden, verwandt an Herz und Gemüth, verwandt an Sinnen und Wollen, verwandt an Fähigkeiten und Thätigkeiten, zu thun habe! und deßhalb rief er begeistert, dem Herrn dankend זאת הפעם עצם מעצמי ובשר מבשרי — deßhalb aber können auch Sie *) lieber Glaubensbruder in diesem lebenswichtigen Momente, der Zukunft froh und heiter entgegensehend ausrufen זאת הפעם u. s. w. Beide ein und demselben guten und edeln Stamme entsprossen, Beide ein und dieselbe frommjüdische Erziehung genossen; Beide voraussetzlich von denselben Gefühlen und Empfindungen durchtränkt — wie sollte da die nöthige Eintracht und Harmonie, welche die Seele des ehelichen Lebens, den Grundton des glücklichen Familienlebens bildet, nicht vorauszusetzen sein?? Ja, wie sollte einem Jünglinge, der nicht wie so viele seines Gleichen in unserer Zeit, die ihre schönsten Tage in Saus und Braus, so zu sagen, hinbringen, und dann wenn der Ernst des Lebens an sie, mit all seinen unabweichlichen Forderungen hinantritt, nur Blasirtheit und gebrochene Manneskraft, unfähig zu jeder nützlichen Thätigkeit, vorfindet, sondern seit seiner frühesten Jugend sich dem würdevollsten Ernste hingegeben; einem Jünglinge, der stets voll kindlicher Liebe dem Wohle seiner Eltern gelebt, mit einem Eifer und mit einer Liebe, die Ihnen noch in den spätesten Tagen die süßeste Erinnerung sein wird — wie sollte einem Solchen nicht die glücklichste Ehe voraus zu sehen sein? Welch eifriges Streben und Wollen, wird nicht erst Sie beseelen, wenn es dem eigenen Heerde, wenn es Ihrem doppelten „Ich“ gelten wird!

*) Der Bräutigam war der Oheim seiner Braut.

Und dennoch gehört zum Glücke, ja zur Glückseligkeit des ehelichen Lebens mehr als blos Ernst und unausgesetzte Thätigkeit; es verlangt auch Frohsinn und Heiterkeit, denn das Haus im engsten Sinne sei ein Gotteshaus, ein Asyl, wohin alle unsere bessern Gefühle und Bestrebungen sich richten müssen, weil es der höchste Zweck derselben sein muß! So aber wie wir an der Schwelle des Gotteshauses den Staub des Alltagslebens und der gewöhnlichen Sorgen von uns rütteln und schütteln müssen, ebenso muß der Gatte an der Schwelle seiner Behausung alle Sorgen und Kümmernisse des Markt- und Geschäftslebens von sich werfen, um ausschließlich der Familie im engsten Kreise zu leben, um die höhern und edlern häuslichen Genüsse zu genießen, mit einem Worte, um das Leben auch von seiner idealen Seite mit Bewußtsein zu hegen und pflegen. Nur von einem solchen gemüths und seelenvollen Haus- und Familienleben, wie es unsere Altvordern gelebt, gelten die schönen und herrlichen Worte der Schrift: מה טבו אוהליך יעקב משכנותיך ישראל כנחלים נטיו כגנות עלי נהר כאהלים נטע ד׳ כארזים עלי מים „Wie schön sind Deine Zelte Jacob, Deine Wohnungen Israel! wie Bäche langgedehnt, unaufgeregt von den gewaltigsten Stürmen, wie Gärten am bewässernden Strom, über die wol die entfeßelten Winde hinrasen, niemals aber sie ihrer Fruchtbarkeit, ihres Blumenschmuckes und Duftes berauben können, wie Aloen, die Gott gepflanzt, unter deren reichem, kühlenden Schatten es sich so bequem und angenehm von der ermattenden Arbeit und der quälenden Tageshitze ausruhen läßt — wie Zedern am Wasser, durch deren Blätter wohl ein gewaltiges Rauschen, wie mächtiges Gottesflüstern, brausen mag, ohne sie zu verrücken oder gar zu entwurzeln!

Ja, außer dem Ernst und der Thätigkeit, außer der Heiterkeit und dem Frohsinn gehört von Seite des Gatten auch ein sogenannter feiner Takt und überaus zarter Sinn zur Vervollständigung des ehelichen Glückes. Und grade dort, wo wir uns so Manches vergeben zu können, glauben, ist ein achtungs-, würdevolles Benehmen um so nöthiger, und auch um so klüger und nützlicher!

Doch auch für Sie, liebe Glaubensschwester, liegen in den Pflichten des Mannes Ihre zu erfüllende Obliegenheiten — da jede Pflicht, die Mutter anderer Gegenpflichten ist. Wenn also der Ernst und die Thätigkeit die erste Pflicht des Mannes, so soll auch die Gattin, dieß im vollesten Werthe zu würdigen wissen, durch Sparsamkeit und häuslichen Fleiß; durch Wirthlichkeit und kluge Haushaltung, und wenn der Gatte stets freundlich, froh und heiter sich zeigen soll, so muß auch die Gattin immer durch Frohsinn, Gemüthlichkeit nnd Ruhe, durch liebevolle Zuvorkommenheit und Zärtlichkeit fort und fort bemühet sein des Mannes gute und frohe Laune zu erzielen und zu erhalten und etwaige Sorgen und trübe Wolken, die sich allzuoft wider unser Willen und Wollen auf unsere Stirne drängen, durch liebevolle Theilnahme zu verscheuchen trachten, und wenn schließlich das Glück und die Glückseligkeit der Ehe vom Gatten Takt und Zartsinn fordern, so ist gewiß das Weib, dessen ganzes Wesen Zartheit bildet, bilden soll, nicht minder, ja vielmehr hiezu verpflichtet und Laune und Zorn, jene bösen Feinde des Ehebundes, die das Weib entstellen, wie schon ein großer Meister sang. Ein aufgereiztes Weib gleicht einem schwarzgetrübten Quell, aus dem der Durstigste nicht trinken möchte, niemals in sich aufkommen lassen!

Ja, Sanftmuth und Nachsicht bedarf das Weib von Seite des Gatten, Sanftmuth und Zartheit müssen aber auch die steten Begleiter der Gattin ihrem Manne gegenüber sein.

Da jedoch nicht selten alle menschlichen Voraussetzungen trügen, da ferner das wechselvolle Leben nicht selten solchen Formen und Gestaltungen und Wandlungen unterworfen, wie kein Menschenauge sie vorauszusehen vermag und kein Gemüth ahnen kann, so will ich Ihnen mit den Worten des Predigers eine Regel fürs Leben mitgeben, die in allen Verhältnissen des Lebens beglückt und beseligt, so wir sie gewissenhaft befolgen und die heißt: את אלהים ירא ואת מצותיו שמור כי זה כל האדם denn wo Gotteswort geliebt und geübt wird, da bleibt das Leben ungetrübt, da ist Gottes Segen aller Wegen. Amen.

17.

Geliebte Beide! So oft es mir von Gott gegönnt ist, ein liebendes Paar nach göttlichen und menschlichen Gesetzen zu verbinden, so oft bin ich auch von einem Frohsinn, aber auch von einer gewissen Wemuth ergriffen — denn freuet es mich einerseits, daß der Sinn fürs eheliche, fürs Familienleben, diesen Glanzpunkt Israels seit urdenklichen Zeiten noch nicht aus unserer Mitte geschwunden, noch nicht bei uns erloschen, so ergreift mich doch anderseits der wehmühtige Gedanke, „wird diese Ehe auch eine glückliche und beglückende, eine beseligende und fortdauernde sein? wird sie das hehre Ziel, das in der Ehe liegt auch erreichen? wird der eine und der andere Theil auch die Rechte, welche ihm das Bündniß einräumt vernünftiger Weise, mit Billigkeit und Mäßigung genießen, und anderseits auch die Pflichten, welche dasselbe dem Einen und dem Andern auferlegt, in Treue und Gewissenhaftigkeit erfüllen? Doch welches sind die Rechte und Pflichten dürften Sie mit Recht fragen?

Wolan denn, ich will sie Ihnen in wenigen Worten lehren, mögen Sie ihnen Ihre Herzen erschließen, und sie tief in die Tafeln Ihrer Herzen einprägen, damit dieß Bündniß, das Sie, nun vor Gott und den Menschen für die Lebensdauer schließen ein fortdauernd glückliches und beglückendes sei.

Amen.

אני לדודי ודודי לי!

„Ich gehöre meinem Freunde und
mein Freund mir.“

Also sprach einst das treue Israel von Gott seinem himmlischen Verlobten, und sollen auch Sie, liebe Glaubensschwester das stets Ihrem Gatten gegenüber fühlen und empfinden. Ich gehöre meinem Freunde an! ach wo gäbe es wohl eine Menschen- oder Engelszunge, die in so wenigen Worten soviel, ja derart Alles sagen könnte, als es diese wenigen Worte in diesem Verhältnisse thuen! Ich gehöre meinem Freunde an, was will es anders sagen, als: all mein Thun und Lassen, all mein Denken und Trachten, all mein Fühlen und Wollen sei nur ihm geweiht, gilt nur ihm und ausschließlich ihm! Was will es anders sagen, als: Mein Leben und Weben, mein Wünschen und Begehren sei ihm, und nur ihm zu gefallen! Ja, was will es anders sagen, als: sein Wille sei auch der meine, seine Freude ist auch die meinige, aber auch seinen Schmerz, seinen Kummer und sein Leid will ich wie er selber tragen, wie er selber fühlen und empfinden! Ich gehöre meinem Freunde an, weil ich mich willig ihm hingegeben in Liebe und Treue, in unvergänglicher Anhänglichkeit und aufopfernder Zärtlichkeit!

Oder soll und will die Gattin ihrem Manne nur insofern angehören, als er sie in Treue ernährt und versorgt, ihre Wünsche erfüllt und ihren Ansprüchen willfährt — oh, dann gehört sie ja nicht ihm, vielmehr aber er ihr, oder sich selber eigentlich und ihren Leidenschaften an! dann gleicht sie ja nicht der Braut Israel, die ihrem himmlischen Verlobten alles zu opfern bereit, vielmehr aber einer entarteten Tochter, die ihren Eltern stets die schwersten Opfer auferlegt — die Elternliebe stets mißbrauchend. — Nebst diesen Pflichten aber, die Ihnen liebe Glaubensschwester, durch das eheliche Verhältniß, in das Sie jetzt treten auferlegt, ist aber Ihr Gatte von Ihnen als Gehilfin, auch thätige Mithilfe, vermöge seines schweren aber ehrbaren Gewerbes — Ihre Anspruchslosigkeit, Reinlichkeit und Wirthlichkeit zu beanspruchen berechtigt! — denn wie oft müssen und sollen die Hände nicht ruhen, und wie oft kann nur das Ersparte retten, was die Zeit versagt und abkargt.

Sind Sie also gewillt aus ganzem Herzen Ihrem Gatten zuzurufen אני לדודי, so bekräftigen Sie dieß durch ein frommes williges „Ja".

Und nun lieber Glaubensbruder, wenn es die heilige Pflicht Ihrer Gattin ist, Ihnen ganz anzugehören mit ihrem Leben und Weben, Thun und Lassen, Denken und Fühlen, so ist es auch, Ihre unverbrüchliche Schuldigkeit, ihr ein mittheilendes Herz entgegen zu bringen, denn Liebe nur, kann Gegenliebe fordern, Treue nur, kann Gegentreue wünschen und verlangen! Ihre selbstgewählte Lebensgefährtin soll nicht nur אני לדודי, sondern mit vollem Rechte auch rufen können ודודי לי, auch mein Freund gehört ganz und gar nur mir, auch er lebt nur mit mir und für mich! Sie werden Ihrer Gattin ein ehrlicher und redlicher Versorger sein, dafür bürgt Ihr ehrenhafter Stand — seien Sie ihr aber auch ein zärtlicher Freund, ein derart liebender Gatte, wie er geeignet das zärtliche Elternhaus zu ersetzen. Denn wenn auch die Schrift, dem Manne die Herrschaft über seine Gattin einräumt, so ist es nicht die eines Herrschers über seinen Untergebenen, sondern die des liebenden Vaters über sein geliebtes Kind, die des starken Beschützers über seinen Schützling; die des himmlischen Herrn über sein ihm verbundenes Israel!

Was der Mann draußen im gewerbthätigen Leben, das ist die Gattin im häuslichen Kreise, und darum soll und muß sie sich der Achtung des Mannes erfreuen, sowie der Mann die Ehrerbiethung des Weibes genießen muß.

Sind sie also entschlossen, dieser Ihrer Lebensgefährtin zuzurufen. „Ich gehöre Dir an" in Treue und Liebe, mit Dir und für Dich allein will ich leben und wirken, so bekräftigen Sie dieß durch ein männliches „Ja".

Wie nun dieß Ihre beiderseitigen Rechte und Pflichten — wie Sie nun Beide sie feierlichst zu schätzen und zu erfüllen gelobt, so wolle Gott sie gehört und Ihre stillen Wünsche erhört haben für alle Zeiten. Amen.

18.

Dir, Unsichtbarer und doch Allgegenwärtiger! klopfen unsere freudig gestimmten Herzen entgegen! Um Deinen weihenden und segenreichen Beifall beten wir innigst zu Dir in diesem wonnetrunkenen Momente, um Deinen fruchtbringenden Segen flehen wir aus ganzer Seele zu Dir Vater der Menschen כי את אשר תברך מבורך „Denn wen Du segnest, der ist gesegnet — und darum rufen wir "השקיפה ממעון קדשך מן השמים וברך" Schaue doch herab von Deinen Himmelshöhen und segne den Bund, den diese Deine Kinder hier für alle Zeit ihres Lebens einzugehen gewillt sind mit Frieden und Zufriedenheit, mit Liebe und unversieglicher Wonne. Amen.

Wenn schon jedes halbwichtige Bündniß, das wir im Leben schließen wollen, einer reifen Ueberlegung, eines wohldurchdachten Entschlusses, gegenseitiger Bedingnisse, und einer gewissen Sicherstellung nöthig hat, selbst wenn es nur für einen beschränkten Zeitraum von Halt und Dauer sein soll, um wie viel mehr soll und muß dieß nicht da der Fall sein, wo zwei Wesen von verschiedener

Stellung und geistiger Gestaltung sich für die Lebensdauer aufs Engste und Innigste mit einander verbinden wollen! Und wenn schon jede sonstige Verbindung im Leben, so oft wider unsere Vorausberechnung, und trotz mannigfacher Garantien an tausend und tausend unvorhergesehenen Klippen scheitert und zerschellt, um wie viel mehr muß die Furcht uns, bei dem Bündniß, das für's ganze Leben eingegangen wird, überkommen, ob es denn auch von glücklicher Dauer sein werde! Und dennoch verlangt die sittliche Weltordnung grade diese Verbindung zumeist und am lautesten, und dennoch haben die Menschen von je bis auf den heutigen Tag diesem Rufe zumeist gefolgt und sich zumeist auch wohl und glücklich dabei befunden. Wahrlich es ist ein gar starker Beweis für den Ausspruch unserer Weisen, daß הקב"ה יושב ומזוג זיוגים daß es der Herr selber ist, der diese Art Bündnisse bestimmt; daß es die Stimme des Herrn ist, die da rief: „Der Mann verlasse Vater und Mutter und hänge in Liebe seiner Gattin an.“ —

Ist dem aber also, werden Sie denken, wozu der reifen Ueberlegung, wozu der guten Vorsätze u. s. w. Da die Bürgschaft schon in dem Willen Gottes liegt! Und doch was geschähe denn im Leben sonst, es hätte der es nicht im Voraus bestimmt! Wenn das Glück unsern Fersen folgt, oder Leid und Kummer uns begegnen, hat der Herr es nicht im Voraus gefügt — und müssen wir deßhalb nicht streben das Eine zu erreichen und zu erhalten, und dem Andern zu entgehen und auszuweichen?

Allerdings kann die Wahl der Gatten nur durch des Herrn besondere Gnade eine glückliche und beglückende sein! Müssen und sollen wir aber grade hier die Hände müßig in den Schoß legen und nicht vielmehr durch unser Thun und Streben die Wahl des Herrn nachträglich zu rechtfertigen trachten?!

Doch womit und wodurch — dürften Sie fragen, können und sollen wir in den Rathschluß Gottes zu unserem Glücke und fortdauernden Heile eingreifen? Oh, nichts ist leichter! Ich spreche nicht von der nothwendigen gegenseitigen Liebe und Werthschätzung, welche dieses Ihr Bündniß ins Leben rief — ich rede auch nicht von der Versorgung des Gatten einer — und der treuen Besorgung der Gattin anderseits, da Sie Beide ja bereits das Leben mit seinen Mühen und Sorgen kennen und zu würdigen wissen. Ist aber in dem Einen und dem Andern schon die Sicherheit einer glücklichen Fortdauer dieser Verbindung? Gewiß nicht! Denn kann das was die Zeit geboren, nicht auch mit der Zeit verloren gehn? Wie oft wechseln nicht die menschlichen Gefühle! Wie oft brechen nicht das menschliche Streben, Thun — und Wollen durch mannigfache Verhältnisse gleich einem schwanken Rohr zusammen! Darum meine Theuern müssen wir die Garantie in etwas Höherem, Besserm; ja, Göttlichem suchen! Was aber ist göttlicher denn innige Gottesfurcht? בכל דרכיך דעהו והוא יישר ארחותך Erkenne Ihn auf allen Deinen Wegen — so ebnet er sie Dir zum Heil und Segen! Die Gottesfurcht ist es, die uns hält und sicher stellt in allen Verhältnissen, sie erst gibt der aufrichtigen Liebe die rechte Weihe; sie verleiht dauernden Muth nnd stete Thatkraft; sie setzt dem Familienleben die Krone des Glückes auf und umgibt es mit dem Strahlenkranze unvergänglicher Zufriedenheit! Wo die Gottesfurcht das Scepter führt, da herrscht Treue und Arbeitsamkeit, Mitgefühl und Ordnung; redliches Streben und zärtliches Besorgen! Fehlt diese aber, da mangelt der eigentliche Kitt — und über Kurz oder Lang wie fällt da Alles aus einander; die Liebe altert, die Treue wankt; die Thatkraft schwindet, die Zufriedenheit weicht das Glück ist zerstört und das Eheleben wird ein Weheleben, wofür der Himmel Sie bewahre! Amen.

19

*) Te hozzád, nagy hatalmas isten! fohászkodnak sziveink ezen örömtelt perczben, Te hozzád, ki az aldás szt. kútforrása vagy, forrón imádkozunk, hogy e házaságot, melyet gyermekeid szt. akaratod és parancsolatod szerint kötni akarják boldog 's boldogitó legyen. amen.

Kedvesim!

E perc önökre nézve oly fontos, az egész életökre oly nagy befolyással, hogy mint hü lelkészük lehetetlen elhallgatnom annak fontosságát és a házaság nehezitő körülményeit, önnök hasznára ki ne fejeznem. A házaság t. J. nem baráti véd-és dac-szövetség, a mely csak önérdekből kötettik, és ha az érdek épen annak feloldását követeli, megint feloldatik, a házaság sem nem csupa rokonszenvből eredett összekötetés, mert érzeményeink változásánal fogva mily könnyen változhatik rokonszenvünk ellenszenvvé!

De a boldog és boldogitó házaság sokkal többet kiván, sokkal többet követel—ő azt akarja, hogy a kettőből csak legyen egy a lélekben egy a gondolásban; egy az érzésben, egy az akaratban, egy szóval, a mint a szt. irás azt kifejezi והיו לבשר אחד hogy egy lénnyé legyenek. Itt, a házaság szt. Küszöbén meg kell szünni az egyik mint á másik önérdeke, mert csak azért alkotá a teremtő a nőt az ember oldalbordájából, hogy mutasson miképen hiányos az ember vagy a férfi a nő nélkül és miképen a nő csak a hiány potolásápa szolgáljon — azért már bölcseink is kimondták, hogy a nőnélküli ferfi isak פלג גופא az az félember, vagy más szavakkal . . . כל השרוי בלא אשה שרוי בלא חומה בלא שמחה וכו׳ a. a. a nőnélküli ember védőfal és minden öröm nélküli sat. és mi a férjnélküli nő — azt csak mindenki úgy is tudja! a hol a házaság nem a legszorosabb egység, ott az sohse megfelelend szt. feladatának, sohse a jó isten boldogitó és szerencséltető akaratának. A házasági szövetség az emberi társaságnak alaposzlopa, az alaposzlopban pedig az egyik kőnek a másikhoz oly erősen kell ragaszkodnia, hogy csak erőszakos kéz által feldúlható.

En annál inkább önnőket az egyességre figyelmeztetnem kell, minthogy ön t. mennyasszony, mint szeretett egyetlen egy gyermeke édes szüleinek, talán oly gyenge szokásokat vett tel, melyek az új állopotjával nem egyezhetők 's igy a mitől az isten önnőket megóvja, e házaság temploma, romba dülne! és ámbár hogy az ön tapasztalaságában t. vőlegény nagyon is bizni lehet, a feladat mégis némelykor oly nehéz, hogy

*) Auf Verlangen der Betreffenden ward diese Ansprache in ungarischer Zunge gehalten.

gyakran nem egy, sem kettő inkább a türelmet elvesztette, inkább e viszony édes jármát nyakáról levettette, mintsem igyekezték volna az egyességet hosszú tűrelem által alapitani, mintsem feladták voloa szokásaik leggyengébb egyikét!

Igyekezzék tehát mindig az egyetértést és az összehangzatot létre hozni és allandóan fenntartani azon meggyűződés által, hogy az isten önnöket egymás iránt teremtette, és biztos vagyok hogy önök még a legkésőbb időkben is, ezen óra boldogságáról örömmel emlékezni fognak.

En önt t. M. nagyon miveltnek, úgy mint önt t. V. nagyon tapasztaltnak tartom, mintsem szükségesnek tartsam önnöket e visszony több kötelességeire figyelmeztetni — és igy tehát csak azt mondom: szeressé-ek egymást és boldogok lesztek. Amen.

תולדת יצחק.

Trauungsreden

von

Ig. W. Bak,

Rabbiner in Amschelberg.

II. Heft.

Prag, 1869.

Druck von Senders und Brandeis. Rittergasse Nr. 408—1.

Verlag des Verfassers.

Seinem alten, ehrwürdigen Vater, dem belesenen Talmudisten, dem geistreichen und rühmlichst bekannten **Agadisten,**
Herrn

Josef L. Bak,

ד׳ יהדש כנשר נעוריו

Rabbinatsassessor in Szegedin,

widmet in kindlicher Liebe, Ehrfurcht und Dankbarkeit
diese Blätter.

der Verfasser.

[illegible]

[illegible]

Herrn

Josef F. Klink,

[illegible]

[illegible]

[illegible]

[illegible]

Der Verfasser.

Eine Antwort als Vorrede.

Geschätzter Freund!

Ihre werthen, sehr freundlichen Zeilen, habe mit Bedacht, ja mit Andacht, wie Sie eben wünschten, zwei und mehrmal gelesen.

Mit Recht, fragen, und sagen Sie: Haben Sie denn auch nur die nackten Köften, welche Ihnen die Veröffentlichung des 1. Heftes Ihrer Traureden verursacht, schon eingebracht? ואתה בא להוסיף עליהן Wissen und kennen Sie denn noch immer nicht die Munifizenz des jüdischen Lesepublikums für „jüdische Sachen?" oder wollen Sie durchaus die par Gulden, welche diese Reden Ihnen בשעתן eingetragen haben mögen, wieder los werden? Oder kitzelt Sie etwa gar die Sucht zu schriftstellern, diese leidige Epidemie, die bereits unter den Kindern grassirt?! So schreiben Sie denn in Gottes Namen, Novellen, reißen Sie Witze; „machen Sie in Journale," legen Sie sich aufs Kritteln und Kritisiren, arbeiten Sie an Eisenbahn- und sonstige Actien-Projekte; kurz, schreiben Sie judenfreundliche Brochüren unter kristlichem Namen oder pseudonyme Pamphlete, oder was sonst für Gattung Zeug, nur nicht hebräisch, oder Jüdisch-religiöses — wenn Sie Leser finden und Geld verdienen wollen.

Ja, ich könnte noch Jüdisches im Allgemeinen hingehen lassen, aber Predigten, Casualreden, und noch dazu Trauungsreden, die doch, und mögen sie noch so geistvoll angelegt sein, immer nur ein und dasselbe bezwecken, ein und denselben Stoff behandeln; ein und denselben Ein- und Ausgang haben, Solche zu veröffentlichen, würde ich — bleiben lassen. Nicht etwa, weil dieser Zweig der Literatur schon überhaupt, und dieses Genre insbesondere, schon so reich und gut vertreten ist, als es eben wünschenswerth. Im Gegentheile! wenn man Salomon, Mannheimer, Jellinek und noch andere, geringe Ausnahmen abstrahirt, ist die gesammte Predigt-Literatur nichts als Maculatur, kaum des Durchblätterns werth. Aber diese Uiberfluthung eben von ganz mittelmäßigen oder gar schlechten Predigten verleidet einerseits dem Publico das Lesen derselben überhaupt und verschlechtert anderseits den Geschmack dessen derart, daß es in der That zwischen Gut und Schlecht gar nicht mehr unterscheidet, gar nicht mehr unterscheiden kann.

Und was dieses Uibel noch verschlimmert — wenn es überhaupt noch der Verschlimmerung fähig ist — das ist bald die gewöhnliche Lobhudelei, bald die vornehme Abfertigung, wenn nicht gar totale Ignorirung, von Seite der jüdischen Blätter, derartiger Produkte!

Während die Triller irgend eines Kehlkünstlers, der graziöse Pas irgend einer Tänzerin u. s. f. ganze Zeitungsspalten füllen, natürlich Alles im Interesse der Kunst und des guten Geschmackes . . . ja, während jüdische Blätter gewöhnlich die Backen voll nehmen, wenn irgend ein obscures Federvieh in irgend einem Winkelblättchen Gift und Galle speit gegen Juden, und Judenthum, die doch Amalek, Bileam und Haman überlebten, und lange fulminante

Gegenartikel schreiben, oder aber lange und breite Auszüge bringen, wenn irgend ein christlicher Schriftsteller sich bewogen fühlte, der Judenheit, oder dem Judenthume Gerechtigkeit wiederfahren zu lassen, haben Selbe im Interesse der Wohlredenheit überhaupt, die doch in unserer Zeit ein so mächtiger Factor des öffentlichen, politischen und sozialen Lebens, und im Interesse jüdischer Kanzel-Beredsamkeit und des jüdischen Publikums, das die Synagoge resp. die Predigt — man mag denken und sagen, was man will — doch ausschließlich zu bilden und zu veredeln hat — — keine Worte erfrischender und ermunternder Belobung und auch keine strengen, aber auch gerechten Tadel's.

Und nun, geehrter Freund, sehen Sie, indem ich Ihre Ansichten an die Spitze eben dieser Casualreden stelle, daß ich Ihren klugen und wohlgemeinten Rath — nicht befolgte, wie sehr ich denselben auch vom Gesichtspunkte der Vernunft aus, würdige und zu würdigen verstehe!

Ich mag und will es durchaus nicht versuchen, Ihren triftigen Gründen vernünftige Gegengründe entgegen zu setzen, wiewol Sie allerdings die Dinge zu schwarz sehen und keineswegs zu bedenken scheinen, daß die Zeit endlich denn doch das ihre thut, um das Korn vom Spreu zu sondern, ferner nicht zu bedenken scheinen, daß das pure Interesse denn doch eine zu große Kleinlichkeit im Leben solcher Menschen ist, die einer bessern und idealern Weltanschauung leben! Soviel jedoch will ich Ihnen bemerken, daß das schwache Menschenherz auch seine kostenreiche Bedürfnisse hat, vorzüglich wenn es den verzeihlichen Wahn hegt, ein Schärflein zum Bessern beitragen zu können — der Beifall aber, den diese Reden als lebendige Worte verdienter, oder auch unverdienter Weise gefunden, ist eben der Vater dieser Einbildung, es könnten dieselben auch jetzt noch, als blos geschriebene Figuren, noch einiges Interesse haben — und wer möchte mit den Waffen der Vernunft das minder stark gerüstete Herz bekämpfen! —

Zum Schlusse noch die Bitte: Lesen Sie diese Reden, wenn es Ihnen Ihre Zeit und die Stimmung eben gestatten, und lassen Sie mich dann ohne Weiters Ihr gründliches Urtheil über Selbe, mag es loben, oder tadeln, hören — und seien Sie versichert, daß ich Ihnen für aufrichtiges Lob und ehrlichen Tadel gleich verpflichtet bleibe, wie ich stets war und bin Ihr aufrichtiger Freund

Amschelberg.

20.

Einleitung.

פ׳ תולדת

ד׳ מנת חלקי וכוסי — אתה תומיך גורלי — חבלים נפלו לי בנעימים — אף נחלת שפרה עלי — אברך את ד׳ אשר יעצני — אף לילות יסרוני כליותי — שויתי ד׳ לנגדי תמיד — כי מימיני בל אמוט — לכן שמח לבי — ויגל כבודי!

Du Herr! mein Kelch, mein Freudenmal!
Du warfst mein Los mir allzumal!
So lieblich fiel mein Los mir zu,
Und auch mein Gut begünstigst Du!
Ich danke Gott, der mich berathen hat,
In Nächten schwerer Sorgen, kummersatt. —
Stets dacht' ich Gott vor meinem Angesicht,
Ist er zur Rechten mir, so wank ich nicht!
Drum freuet sich, drum jauchzet meine Brust —
Und meine Ehre auch, erfreut sich drum in Lust!

So betete, so dankte und lobte der fromme Sänger und König, wahrscheinlich bei einer Angelegenheit, die ihm lebenswichtig, bei einer Angelegenheit, von der sein Lebensglück abhing.

Wie schwer und sorgenvoll fließen da nicht die stillen Nächte dahin, wie schwer wiegt da nicht, das „Soll ich, soll ich nicht" in der Wagschale unserer stets wankenden und schwankenden Vernunft! denn wer kann den Schleier der Zukunft auch vom nächsten Morgen nur lüften, um wie viel weniger erst den, der langgedehnten und gestreckten Zukunft!

Und als er sich denn doch entschlossen und Gott es ihm wohl ausfallen ließ, da rief er begeistert, Gott dankend: „Ich danke Gott.“ u. s. w.

Und warum ließ denn aber auch Gott seinen gefaßten Entschluß, derart gedeihen und gelingen? Nun denn, Sie haben es gehört, geeh. B. weil er sein Lebensglück und seine Zukunft, zuvor Gott anheim gestellt hat „Gott hab' ich stets“ u. s. w. rief er, und deßhalb vermochte er auch zuletzt aufzujubeln: לכן שמח לבי.

Nun aber stehen auch Sie, gel. B. einen lebenswichtigen Entschluß auszuführen, da. Wie oft mögen auch Sie bedacht haben: Gott, mein Gott! wird dieses Bündniß auch ein Dauerndes ein Glückliches, ein Segensreiches sein?! Und wer könnte und möchte Ihnen dieß verargen? Wie so mancher Jüngling ist wegen dieser wohlbegründeten Besorgnisse gar nicht, wie so manche Jungfrau nur erst spät der natürlichen und göttlichen Bestimmung gefolgt!

Und gleichwohl ist der Entschluß gar leicht und bald gefaßt, denkt man nur mit dem Psalter ד' מנת חלקי u. s. w. hält und hat man mit dem frommen König, nur Gott vor Augen stets — dieß gel. B. wollen Sie bedenken und Sie werden allzeit mit demselben rufen אברך u.s.w. allezeit mit ihm frohlocken לכן שמח rc. Das bethen wir und Gott erhöre und gewähre uns — Amen.

Liebe Beide!

Der Wochenabschnitt erzählt uns von der eingegangenen Ehe zwischen Jizchak und Rebecka ויהי יצחק בן ארבעים שנה בקחתו את רבקה בת בתואל... לו לאשה — ויעתר יצחק לד' לנוכח אשתו...

Wenn man diese Herzensverbindung, die unser Erzvater Jizchak eingegangen, vom Standpunkte menschlicher Einsicht und menschlicher Vernunft im Voraus hätte beurtheilen sollen und wollen, wer hätte derselben das Glück und den Segen, dessen sie sich sodann erfreuete, voraus gesagt, ja auch nur zu ahnen gewagt? Jizchak ein wohlgereifter, in des Mannes schönster Blüthe stehender Mann, der sich selber schon im Leben eine Stellung hat errungen und Rebecka, ein verzärteltes, junges Elternkind, dem noch die Amme an die Seite gegeben werden mußte! Jizchak ein Jüngling der herangereift ist in der Schule der Erfahrung und sich der vollen Würde eines Mannes bewußt war und Rebecka, die unsere Weisen, parabolisch als dreijähriges Kind bezeichnen, unerfahren, nicht einmal noch ihrer Ehre als zartes, weibliches Wesen eingedenk; Jizchak der Sohn Abrahams an der Seite einer Sarah erzogen und Rebecka, ein spielendes und tändelndes Mädchen, das sorglos aus Lust und Laune mit den andern Ortsmädchen zum Brunnen lief... Welche Verbindung!

Diese kindliche, ja wir möchten sagen, kindische, jugendliche Rebecca, die vorweg nichts, als ein Bischen Herz hatte, sollte urplötzlich eine würdige Gattin, eine tüchtige Hausfrau; eine fromme Abrahamstochter werden, mit einem Worte, die gute Mutter, in deren Zelt er sie gebracht, vollkommen ersetzen? Wie mußte da der böse Leumund, der so gerne Schlimmes voraussieht und profezeiht, sich schadenfroh aussprechen. Welche klägliche Reibungen mußte da der klügelnde Menschenverstand voraussehen und befürchten! Und rechtfertigten sich etwa diese Voraussetzungen! Ward dieses Herzensbündniß nicht ein Glückliches, ja ein Musterhaftes und Neideswerthes? Nun so hören wir! Schon die Schrift gibt ihm das Zeugniß mit den Worten: Als Jizchak sie gebracht in die Hütte seiner Mutter Sara, da ward er getröstet über den Verlust seiner seel. Mutter. Unsere Alten jedoch, die so klar zwischen den Zeilen zu lesen verstanden, geben hiezu folgende weitere Erklärung: Solange die fromme Sara lebte, war das Haus die Stätte sabbathlicher Zurückgezogenheit, die Stätte strenger Sittlich- und Sittsamkeit.. solange die fromme Sara lebte, war das Haus der Gastfreundlichkeit, der Milde und der Armuth offen.. eine Stätte der Sparsamkeit und der Wirthlichkeit, wo das redlich Erworbene durch Fleiß, Thätigkeit und nützliche Verwendung sich verdoppelte, und wie es von der Heldenfrau im Liede heißt: בלילה לא יכבה נרה. Alles das wäre mit dem Tode Derselben, naturgemäß gewichen — denn wo die Frau dem Hause fehlt, da fehlt naturgemäß dem Haus die Gottheit, — mit Rebecka jedoch, da kam die alte Sitte, der frische Fleiß; der alte Segen wieder!*)

So glücklich fiel dieses Herzensbündniß aus!

Und welche Mittel wandte denn wohl dieser erfahrene Jizchak an, daß dieß ihm so wohl gelang, daß er mit dem Psalter

*) Midrasch zur Stelle.

rufen konnte הבלים נפלו u. s. w. Wandte er vielleicht Strenge statt des Zartsinns, barsche Unfreundlichkeit, statt der Liebe an! Nichts von all dem, sondern Jizchak bethete zu Gott seiner Frau gegenüber, berichtet das Gotteswort, Gott stellte er sein Glück und sein Geschick anheim, שויתי ד' ꝛc. rief und bethätigte er und darum ließ auch Gott seine Wabl gelingen, Jizchak bethete לנוכח אשתו u. z. כי עקרה היא, weil sie vermöge ihrer Jugendlichkeit eben noch unfruchtbar an solchen Tugenden war ...

In diesem herrlichen Vorbilde, will ich Ihnen denn, lieber B. Alles gesagt, alles gelehrt und gezeigt haben, was nöthig und nothwendig ist, damit dieses Ihr Herzens- und Seelenbündniß ein Segensreiches und Heilvolles werde; denn es ist dieß Musterbild ein so Passendes und Gelungenes, daß jemehr Sie es anschauen und betrachten, desto mehr werden Sie sich daran erbauen, daran erheben, um es ihm nach zu thun?

Ihnen, liebe Braut, aber, soll ebenfalls die junge und doch tüchtige Rebecka der Schrift, als Muster zur Nachahmung dienen, denn die Aufgabe, die Ihnen mit diesem Augenblicke auferlegt wird, ist keine Kleine und keine Geringe, so wie es auch die jener Rebecka nicht war; denn Sie sollen diesem Ihren Gatten nicht blos eine gute, treue, ja zärtliche Gattin, nicht blos eine würdige, musterhafte Hausfrau; und nicht blos eine bescheidene, sittsame Abrahamstochter werden... sondern, indem Sie in das Zelt seiner braven Mutter — das sie vor Kurzem erst verließ, um in das ewige Reich einzukehren ... in Tngend vollkommen ersetzen .. damit es auch da wie dort heißen könne (*ויביאה יצחק u. s. w.

Dieß aber wird Ihnen nur dann vollkommen gelingen, wenn auch Sie den Blick zu Gott erheben und aufrichtig seinen Beistand sich erbeten werden, wie unsere Weisen der Rebecka nachrühmen . . wenn auch Sie einstimmen und bethätigen den Ausruf .שויתי ד'

So nur werden Sie allezeit auch in den Ruf des frommen Psalters einstimmen אברך ד' אשר יעצני ꝛc. Das gebe Gott. Amen.

---

*) Der Zufall wollte, daß der Name des Bräutigams in der Thal יצחק war.

21.

פ׳ ויצא.

So oft es mir auch schon, unter den mannigfachsten und verschiedensten Umständen und Verhältnissen, gegönnt war, Ehen, die im Himmel geschlossen werden, hier, auf Erden einzusegnen, war ich doch noch niemals so sehr ums Wort verlegen, ich gestehe es aufrichtig, als eben in diesem Augenblicke, da ich mit innigster Theilnahme eines aufrichtigen Freundes, das Gotteswort über die Bedeutung und hohe Wichtigkeit des ehelichen Lebens an Sie, geschätzte Braut, richten soll — denn ich kenne nur allzusehr Ihren gebildeten Sinn, Ihr fein- und zart-fühlendes Herz, ich weiß nur allzugut wie sehr Sie sich bereits als tüchtige Hauswirthin, als musterhafte Freundin dieses Ihres künftigen Lebensgefährten; als treue und zärtliche Vorsehung des Kindes, das Gott nunmehr Ihrer weitern Hege und Pflege anvertraut, bewährt, was also könnte und sollte ich Ihnen in irgend welcher Beziehung dieses neuen Verhältnisses, in das Sie nun treten, sagen? Auch Sie, werther Freund, haben sich bereits als treuer und aufrichtiger Gatte, als redlicher Ernährer und Versorger, als Mann und Mensch, in dieser Worte edlerer Bedeutung vollkommen erwiesen, woran also hätte ich Sie in diesem Augenblicke noch zu mahnen? Ihre Herzen haben sich überhaupt schon längst gefunden, wenn Ihre Lippen es auch noch nicht ausgesprochen, Sie kennen und haben einander achten gelernt; Sie vertraueten einander in gegenseitiger, wahrhaft geschwisterlicher Zuneigung und rechtfertigten dieses Vertrauen auch vollkommen und in würdigster Weise! Ja, Gott hat Ihre Herzen derart für einander geschaffen, daß selbst die sogenannte Volksstimme — Sie für einander bezeichnete . . Was also brauch und kann ich Ihnen ans Herz legen, damit dieses Ihr eheliches Bündniß ein Beglückendes werde?!

Und trotz alldem, meine Lieben, ist all das allein nicht angethan das eheliche Leben für die Dauer und ununterbrochen, unter allen Umständen und Verhältnissen, jenen sanften Schmelz, der dem Auge wohlthut, jenes gewisse Etwas, das das Leben würzt; und jenen steten Reiz der Neuheit, der dem Leben und Lieben so unbedingt nöthig ist, zu geben, wenn die Tugend im Allgemeinen, die Tugend im Großen und Ganzen (— im Gegensatz zu einzelnen und vereinzelten Tugenden —) und die Gottesfurcht ins Besondere, nicht im Hause walten! Um so mehr als die menschlichen Gefühle nur allzuwandelbar, und was uns heute beglückt kann morgen schon, wie es nur allzuoft geschieht, die Quelle unserer Leiden sein, und was unsere Fantasie so oft Schönes sich gebildet, nimmt in Wirklichkeit nicht selten ganz andere Gestalten an . . Daher ist es die Tugend einer — und die Gottesfurcht anderseits, die all unser Thun und Lassen durchdringen und verherrlichen müssen, wenn das Leben überhaupt, und das eheliche und häusliche Leben ins Besondere, sich stets, wenn auch nicht immer so glücklich und wolkenlos, wie wir es wünschten, doch stets gleich freundlich und erträglich sein soll!

Jacob, erzählt uns das Gotteswort, diente sieben Jahre um Rachel, und trotzdem strichen dieselben ihm wie einzelne Tage dahin . . Wären es Schönheit und Anmuth, wären es sonst weibliche, äußere Vorzüge; ja wären es bloß einzelne Tugenden gewesen; die auf den ernsten Jüngling einen solchen Eindruck hervorbrachten, wie würden sich da, schon die Minuten zu Jahren gedehnt haben, wenn wunderbarer Weise die äußern Reize und Vorzüge Rachels, durch diese lange Zeit nicht hart gelitten, und die einzelnen Tugenden noch immer neu und ihren vollsten Zauber behalten haben sollten! Aber nein! die Schrift setzt wohl weislich hinzu באהבתו אתה. indem er sie liebte . . . d. h. nicht sich selbst, nicht sein leibliches Ich und das Interesse seines Hauses liebte er in ihr, sondern ihr eigentliches Wesen, den Adel ihres Herzens, die Frömmigkeit ihrer Gesinnung; ihren schönen und herrlichen Lebenswandel, der an der Sonne seiner Liebe, wie die junge Knospe, immer mehr und mehr seine würzigen Düfte und seine Farbenpracht entfaltete . . . und deßhalb war diese Liebe ewig jung und glühend wie am ersten Tage, und dauerte über das Grab hinaus und pflanzte sich auf Kind und Kindeskind noch fort . .*) denn Tugend und Frömmigkeit altern nicht, sind fruchtbar stets an

*) Ich bemerke hier in Wehmuth, daß Diejenige, an welche ich diese Worte richtete, bereits im Grabe modert, zum unsäglichen Schmerze ihres Gatten und Aller, die sie näher kannten.

Neuem und biethen immer Anziehungspunkte, die den bessern Mann dauernd fesseln. . .

Tugend und Frömmigkeit zieren wohl auch den Mann und machen ihn zum Menschen in des Wortes edlerm Sinne, dem Weibe aber fehlt ohne dieselben die eigentliche Weiblichkeit, jener zarte Farbenschmelz, jener würzige Blumen-Duft, die sein eigentliches Wesen ausmachen.

Tugend und Frömmigkeit geben dem Hause jenen unentbehrlichen Nimbus, den keine heilige Stätte, wo inniger Herzensfriede und Freude herrschen sollen, entbehren kann und darf.

Können es ja auch nur Tugend und Frömmigkeit gewesen sein, die Ihre Schritte bis zu dieser ersehnten, schönen Stunde geleitet haben — da die beiden sonstigen Schutzengel, die wir Vater und Mutter nennen, Sie, gel. B. ja nur allzufrüh verließen . . . können es ja nur Tugend und Frömmigkeit sein, denen auch Sie — geehrter Freund, es zu verdanken haben, daß Gott Ihnen zum zweiten Male eine Lebensgefährtin zuführt, deren höchstes Streben Sie zu beglücken ist!

Bannen Sie daher diese beiden Schutzengel nie und nimmer aus Ihren Herzen und aus Ihrem Hause, denn sie setzen dem Glücke die Krone dauernder Seelenfreude auf, während sie dem Unheile den vernichtenden Stachel rauben . . Tugend und Frömmigkeit lehren uns das Leben, wie es sich eben gibt, mit stetem Gleichmuth hinnehmen . . und dieß allein ist schon geeignet uns glücklich zu machen. Und so segne Sie denn Gott. Amen.

22.

Einleitung.

פ׳ וישלח.

שמש ומגן ד׳ אלהים — חן וכבוד יתן ד׳ — לא ימנע טוב — להולכים בתמים — ד׳ צבאות! אשרי אדם בוטח בך!

Sonn' und Schild ist Gott der Herr!
Huld' und Ehr' verleihet er!
Das Heil entzieht er nimmermehr
Den, die da wandeln fromm einher,

Drum Heil dem Menschen, Gott, mein Herr!
Der dir vertraut und Niemand mehr.

So fühlte, so dachte, so sprach in kluger Erfahrung der fromme Fürst, der des Lebens Sollen und Wollen, des Menschen Thun und Denken, aber auch Gottes Macht und Güte gar genau kannte. Er wußte und sprach es aus, daß Gott der Herr das Weltall erleuchtet und erwärmt in und mit seiner Liebe, daß Gott der Herr ein mächtig Schild dem Schwachen, eine feste Stütze den Wankenden und eine starke Schutzwehr dem Beengten und Bedrängten; er wußte und sprach es aus, daß Gott es ist, der nicht nur Freuden und Leiden, sondern selbst Gunst und Ehre, welche Güter die Menschen doch in ihrem Eigendünkel gewöhnlich ihren eigenen Verdiensten zuschreiben, mit eigener Hand vertheilt, er wußte nnd sprach es aus, daß Gott es ist, der in seiner Gerechtigkeit, das Gute niemals unbelohnt und die Guten nie des Guten entbehren läßt — und darum rief er denn voll Zuversicht Heil dem Menschen, Gott mein Herr! — der Dir vertraut, u. s. w.

Gar oft geliebte Beide, gibt es Augenblicke im Menschenleben, da wir schwankend und unentschlossen, zagend und zögernd stehn bleiben und die Frage an das Geschick richten möchten; Welches wohl der rechte Weg sei, der uns dem erwünschten Ziele, dem erhofften Glücke, dem wir Alle zustreben und entgegen gehen möchten, zuführe? Doch vergebens schauen wir uns da um die sicher führende Hand um, vergebens ziehen wir unsere Vernunft unser Wissen und Können zu Rathe, kein Urim und Tumim gibt Kunde von dem, was die Zukunft wohlweise unsern Blicken entzieht, keine Stimme als das hohle Echo unserer bangen Zweifel antwortet.

Doch nein! es gibt eine sichere Hand, die uns über die Klippen des Lebens hinüber setzt, es gibt eine Stimme, die da ruft und antwortet — זה הדרך לכו בו und der fromme Psalter ist es, der sie kennt und nennt mit den Worten: Sonn' und Schild ist Gott der Herr, — Huld und Gunst verherrlicht Er — Er läßt das Gute angedeihen, denen, die sich fromm ihm weihen — Heil wird denen, die ihm trauen — und stets auf seine Liebe bauen.—Und dieser sichern Hand wollen wir Herr! auch das Geschick dieser Deiner Kinder hier, am Scheidewege dieses ihres wichtigsten Lebensabschnittes, anvertrauen und diesem Rufe wollen sie folgen, damit sie glücklich und beglückt, gemeinsam und vereint des Lebens Wege gehen für alle Zeiten. Amen.

Geehrte Freundin! geschätzter Freund!

Als unser Altvater Jacob, wie der Wochenabschnitt uns erzählt, den siegreichen Kampf mit den feindlichen Mächten, die sich ihm auf seiner Wanderung durchs Leben hindernd und hemmend in den Weg stellten beendet hatte, da rief ihm Gottes Stimme zu לא יעקב יאמר עוד שמך כי אם ישראל כי שרית עם אלהים ואנשים ותוכל Nicht Jacob soll ferner dein Name genannt werden, sondern Israel, weil du gekämpft mit Menschen und Mächten und siegtest.

Man hat die Welt schon oft mit einem Tummel- und Kampfplatz und das Leben mit einem steten Kampfe verglichen! Und mit Recht! denn der Greis, der an des Grabes Rand und der strebende Mann, der in der Jahre schönster Mitte, sowie der Jüngling und die Jungfrau, die das Dasein nur von seiner rosigen Seite und des Lebens schwere Lasten und Sorgen noch nicht kennen, kämpfen sie nicht Alle mehr und minder, willig oder unwillkührlich, bald mit den Schranken und Gränzen, die die Vorsehung unserem Streben im Allgemeinen gesteckt, bald mit den Hemmnissen, die das Leben und so zu sagen, seine Vertreter uns biethen und bald wieder gegen Neigungen und Abneigungen? Und wie Wenige doch können nach Beendigung dieser schweren Kämpfe mit Befriedigung zurückschauen, wie Wenige die sich den würdigen Namen Israelit, Israelitin erkämpft und ersiegt! Ja wie Viele gehen nicht im Gegentheile dieses edeln Namens und Rufes im Lebenskampfe verlustig; wie Viele treten nicht vom Schauplatze des Daseins, mit dem weniger ehrenvollen Namen Jacob ab, ohne den Namen Israel auch nur je erworben zu haben!

Und gleichwohl liegt in dem Streben und Ringen nach dem Rufe und wohlverdienten Namen Israel, Israelitin, allein und ausschließlich, des Lebens Glück, und gleichwohl macht dieß allein das Leben dieser Kämpfe werth; und gleichwohl macht auch dieß das Glück und das Heil des häuslichen, des ehelichen und des Familienlebens aus! denn dort wo das Ringen und der Kampf sich wie der Name Jacob besagt, um die Ferse, um des Lebens letzte Güter, um Vortheil und vergänglichen Gewinn handelt, da wird das Haus höchstens eine Vorrathskammer, ein Speicher, wo wir unsere wichtigen Errungenschaften aufspeichern, da sinkt das Haus zur Esse herab, wo wir unsere Pläne für den Lebensmarkt schmieden... und wenn es hoch kömmt, zur Ruhestätte, wo wir blos von den Mühen des Tages und der Sorgen ausruhen! Das Haus soll aber weder dieß noch jenes allein sein, sondern eine Stätte beseligender Gemüthlichkeit, ein Ort geistiger Erholung und Erhebung ein Eden wo neben dem Baume des Genusses und des sogenannten Lebens auch der Baum des höheren Strebens und Webens blühen und gedeihen soll! Wie aber wäre dieß möglich, ohne aufrichtiges Wollen und Ringen nach dem wohlverdienten Namen Israel!

Sie werden es daher gel. B. wohl begreiflich finden, wenn ich Ihnen in diesem Augenblicke, wo das Leben mit seinem ganzen Ernst an Sie herantritt, in diesem Momente, wo Sie von der sorg- und kummerlosen Vergangenheit Abschied nehmen und mit dem frommen Altvater rufen אעשה גם אנכי לביתי Auch wir wollen ein Haus bilden, auch wir wollen für unsere Gemüths- und Herzens-Bedürfnisse sorgen, mit dem Gottesworte zurufe לא יעקב u. s. w.

Ich finde diesen Zuruf und diese Ansprache um so angezeigter und gebothener, als ich eben nicht erst nöthig habe, Sie auf die sonstigen Pflichten des Ehestandes, auf die sonstigen Tugenden des häuslichen- und Familienlebens, die zum Glücke desselben erforderlich, aufmerksam zu machen, denn welche Tugend überhaupt und welche Lichtseiten eines musterhaften Ehe- und Hausstandes hätten Sie, geliebte Beide! nicht von frühester Kindheit an, schon im Hause Ihrer Eltern nicht gesehn! Haben sich ja außerdem Ihre Herzen in Liebe gefunden und was ist wohl geeigneter zu beglücken als die Liebe, diese edelste Triebfeder alles Segenbringenden auf Erden!

Ich finde diese Mahnung und diesen Zuruf um so gebothener, als. trotz des guten Beispiels und .der frommen Lehren im Elternhause nichts leichter von der Jugend unserer Zeit genommen wird, als eben mit dem Streben nach dem dauernden und segenreichen Namen und Ruf eines wahren Israeliten, einer aufrichtigen Israelitin und gleichwohl ist dieß hehrer Mitzweck der jüdischen Ehe und Häuslichkeit! denn die Tugend überhaupt und die ehelichen, häuslichen Tugenden und die Liebe insbesondere, machen uns wohl zu Menschen und sind wohl angethan uns zu beglücken den Ehrennamen Israel aber für die Mit- und Nachwelt gibt uns erst das häusliche Leben im Sinne Gottes und Israels!

Und was wars und ists denn noch, daß den Ruf und den Namen Ihres gottseligen Vaters, den Sie, theuere Freundin, gewiß jetzt recht schmerzlich an Ihrer Seite vermißen — zu einem so segenreichen in unserer Mitte erhielt und erhält? Wahrhaftig nicht seine Geistes- und Herzensbildung allein, nicht sein menschenfreundlicher Beruf,*) dem er sein Leben weihete, ausschließlich — sondern vorzüglich weil er sich neben Diesem und Jenem den ehrenvollen Namen Israel erkämpft und ersiegt!

Ich wende mich gel. Freundin, mit dieser Mahnung auch, ja vorzüglich an Sie, weil wie sehr auch das Welt- und Geschäftsleben den Mann draußen und allzuoft zum Schaden seiner Religion, beeinflußen mag, wenn die Gattin nur als עקרת הבית das Haus im Sinne Gottes und Israels lenkt und leitet, so wird und muß sich stets auch an den Mann der Name Israel bewähren!

Und so mögen denn diese Worte die Richtschnur Ihrer Gesinnungen und Handlungen werden und dieses Ihr Herzensbündniß und Ihr eheliches und häusliches Leben, dem sonst alle Bedingnisse, die dasselbe zu einem Glücklichen gestalten müssen, nicht mangeln, wird gewiß ein Solches sein, daß Sie noch in den spätesten Zeiten mit dem Psalt. froh und freudig aus Uiberzeugung rufen werden שמש ומגן ד׳ u. s. w. das wünschen, das bethen; das hoffen wir und mit uns Alle, die sich Ihres Glückes freuen in Ewigkeit

Amen.

---

*) Derselbe war ein rühmlichst bekannter Arzt.

23.

Einleitung.

פ׳ וישב.

רם ד׳ — ושפל יראה — וגבוה ממרחק ידע!

Erhaben hoch ist Gott der Herr —
Und auch das Nied're siehet er . .
Er kennt das Hohe von der Ferne,
Er kennt das Gras und auch die Sterne!

Ja, Er sieht und kennt, Er weiß und liebt Alles, jedem und Allen ist er ein Vater, ein liebender Vater — und das sind und bedeuten die Worte des frommen Königs, die wir anführten.

Und wer erkennt dieß nicht zu jeder Zeit, an allen Umständen, und an seinem eigenen Leben, wie hoch oder nieder die göttliche Vorsehung uns auch im Leben gestellt haben mag. Keiner und Keines ist von Ihm vergessen, Alles und Jedes ruht an seinem Vaterherzen; Jedem gibt er Freud und Leid, Genuß und Wehe; Wonne und Trübsal — Und dieß erkennen wohl auch Sie Beide in diesem ungetrübten Augenblicke verständigen Sinnes und dankbaren Herzens an.

Und so weil Gott alles sieht und kennt, wollen wir denn bethen: Er wolle dieß Ihr eheliches Bündniß mit seines Himmels bestem und reichsten Segen beschenken für alle Zeiten. Amen.

Das Gotteswort erzählt uns mit den Worten ויחלם יוסף etc. Wie der Jüngling Josef in seiner Ländlichkeit als Hirtenknabe, so schöne Träume geträumt, von Glück und Ansehn, von Größe und Hoheit, von Macht und Würde. Träume, wie sie wohl alle Jugend, schlafend und wachend träumt — denn, wer wollte in seiner Jugend vorzüglich, sich die dunkle Zukunft nicht so rosig und duftig als eben die Fantasie reicht, ausmalen und gestalten!

Aber erfüllten sich denn auch die Träume dieses fantasiereichen Josef? Ja wohl! aber welche dornen-, sorgen- und kummervolle Wege mußte er erst durchwandeln, in welche mannigfache Verhältnisse erst eintreten und sich heimisch machen . . .

Doch wie? verlor er da etwa den Muth, die Hoffnung; die erforderliche Ausdauer? Keineswegs! im Gegentheile aber, in jedes neue Verhältniß sich schickend und fügend ging er immer voll frischen Muthes, voll würdigster Zuversicht und Gottvertrauens in und an Dieselbe und hielt sich mit zähester Ausdauer stets aufrecht in Denselben . . Und auf solchen Muth, auf solche Unablässigkeit und Gottzuversicht will ich Sie l. Glbnschw. in diesem ernsten Augenblicke für das schwierige Verhältniß, in das Sie treten, verweisen, damit auch Sie muthig und mit Ausdauer sich Demselben widmen und niemals verzagen.

Ich nenne das Verhältniß schwierig, weil Sie nicht nur ein gutes, treues und wirthliches Weib, nicht nur eine mitthätige, sparsame Frau einer Behausung sein sollen; sondern auch heilige Pflichten als erziehende, und sorgsame Mutter, gleichzeitig übernehmen müssen . . . Und gleichwohl ist schon jede Einzelne dieser Pflichten geeignet das ganze Dasein eines Weibes in Anspruch zu nehmen und auszufüllen. Wie leicht tritt in solchem Falle nicht Entmuthigung und Verzagtheit ein, wie leicht tritt nicht wenigstens Eines auf Kösten des Andern in den Vordergrund, so daß das Weib die Hausfrau, oder die Wirthin die Mutter verdrängt . . Dem aber sollen und werden Sie ausweichen, wenn Sie stets das leuchtende Beispiel, das ich Ihnen in Josef gezeigt, vor Augen haben werden —

Ihnen aber l. Glbrdr. dem ich mit Recht Reife und Erfahrung zumuthe . . . rufe ich in Rücksicht eben dieser schweren Pflichten, die Ihrer Gattin auferlegt sind . . zu ihr ein guter, liebevoller und strebsamer Gatte zu sein, und die guten Hoffnungen, die sie in Sie setzt nach Möglichkeit zu rechtfertigen! denn wo ein solches Streben herrscht, da bleibt der Erfolg, wie uns die Geschichte unseres Helden Josef lehrt, nicht aus, da schon das Streben selber ein halber Erfolg!

Und so sei denn diese Ihre Ehe eine glückliche כי רם ד׳ ושפל יראה וגבוה ממרחק ידע Amen.

24.

פ׳ הנ״ל

Einleitung.

שבענו בבקר חסדך — ונרננה ונשמחה בכל ימינו.

Früh Morgens sättige uns in deiner Gütigkeit,
Auf daß wir jauchzen freudig froh durch die Lebenszeit!

So bethete inbrünstig der Gottesmann, und wir und Sie, l. Beide, in diesem frohen, schönen Augenblicke, bethen es ihm gerne nach — denn nur, solange des Lebens Blüthen und Blumen, solange des Lebens Früh- und Frühlingszeit; solange des Lebens junger Morgen und jugendliche Kraft uns duftet und glänzt und innewohnt, solange nur beglückt uns die Freude, erfreut uns das Glück; schmerzt uns das Leid empfindlich, ist aber einmal die Jugendkraft gebrochen, des Lebens Lenz dahin; der Morgen unseres Daseins trübe und wolkig, dann, dann sind wir wohl für die Leiden und Kümmernisse wohl weniger empfänglich und empfindlich, aber auch für die Freuden und Wonnen weniger zugänglich, auch diese lassen uns kalt und nüchtern . . . Und darum bethet der Gottesmann und Wir und Sie mit ihm „Am Frühmorgen unseres neuen Daseins Herr! laß uns glücklich sein, damit wir uns durch's ganze Leben freien!" Und dieß Ihr inniges Gebeth wolle Gott erhören an der Schwelle und am Frühmorgen dieses Ihres neuen Verhältnisses. Amen.

Es ist allerdings ein gar nicht zu verargender Wunsch, all sein Lebelang glücklich sein zu wollen — und wer trüge ihn nicht im Herzen und auf den Lippen!! Wie aber? ist ein solches Begehren auszuführen auch in unserer Macht? Oder hätten wir bloß die Hände müssig in den Schoß zu legen und es dem lieben Gott anheim zu stellen, daß er uns beglücke? das Gotteswort gibt uns Antwort darauf und zeigt uns gleichzeitig das einzige Mittel, welches hiefür ganz allein zweckdienlich ist, und so lautet das Gotteswort ויהי ד' את יוסף ויהי איש מצליח. . . .

Und Gott war mit Jos. und er war beglückend und glücklich — Und wie kam es denn, daß Gott mit ihm war? Welche Verdienste hatte er sich denn schon erworben, daß Gott mit ihm sein sollte? Aber die Schrift sagt es eben in den angeführten Worten; es kam daher, daß auch Jos. stets mit Gott war, daß er ihn stets im Herzen und vor Augen hatte; daß er bei all seinem Thun und Lassen an Gott dachte; all sein Wissen und Können, Gott zuschrieb, in Freud und Leid, in Noth und Liebe, kurz allüberall Gottes Nähe und Gottes Vaterhand fühlte und empfand — und so war er ein treuer Sohn, ein redlicher Diener; ein großherziger Herr, ein guter Gatte und ein liebender

Vater — und so war auch Gott mit ihm und er war beglückend und selber glücklich!

Auch Ihr Streben lieber Bräutigam ist und muß es sein, diese Ihnen von Gott bestimmte, und von ihren Eltern Ihnen zugeführte Lebensgefährtin glücklich zu machen, wohlan so seien auch Sie wie Josef stets mit Gott, und Gott wird alle Zeit auch mit Ihnen sein, damit auch Sie werden ein איש מצליח — beglückend und glücklich.

Freilich muß das Glück nicht nur in äußerlicher Hülle und Fülle gesucht werden, denn Solche bleibt oft bei der wahrhaftesten und aufrichtigsten Frömmigkeit aus, aber wo Gott ist, da herrscht jedenfalls jene Herzensruhe und jene häusliche Innigkeit, die allzuoft neidenswerther als Reichthümer sind. . Ist Gott mit uns so gibt er uns Kraft zu nützlicher Thätigkeit, die jede Noth bannt und Kummer und Sorgen leicht erträglich macht.

Aber auch Sie liebe Braut haben nicht bloß das Recht, durch diesen Ihren Gatten beglückt zu werden, sondern auch die heilige Pflicht ihn zu beglücken, zu beglücken durch all die weiblichen und häuslichen Tugenden, wie Sie sie im Elternhause üben gesehn, vorzüglich durch Einfachheit, Bescheidenheit und Anspruchslosigkeit! . .

Gott, sagen unsere Alten, ist die Vorsehung des Mannes, der Mann, die des Weibes und des Hauses — deßhalb muß der Mann mit Gott sein, Weib und Haus ausschließlich dem Manne leben. Beide müssen ihn stets anmuthen, beide ihm Friede und Freude, Ruhe und Beruhigung gewähren — So wird das Gebeth שבענו בבקר auch Erhörung und Gewährung finden. Das wolle Gott bis in der Zeiten Späteste. Amen.

. 25.

Einleitung.

פ׳ יתרו.

ואני-קרבת אלהים לי טוב-שתי בד׳ אלהים מחסי-לספר כל מלאכותיך!

Und ich!
Die Nähe Gottes ist ein Glück für mich!
In Gott setz mein Vertrauen ich —
Sein Thun zu künden feierlich!

So spricht sich der fromme Sänger aus, während eines jener zallosen Momente im Menschenleben, da Gottes Macht und Güte sich seinem Geistesauge klarer und deutlicher als sonst offenbart hatte.

Und welches Menschenleben hätte nicht solche Augenblicke, welches Menschenleben wäre so arm an Freuden und Wonnen, daß es nicht von Zeit zu Zeit mit dem frommen Sänger Gottes Macht und Güte preisen, der fühlbaren Gottes Nähe und des gerechtfertigten Hoffens auf Ihn, sich so recht freuen wollte!

Ja, alles freuet sich und hoffet, der Wurm, dessen ganze Welt, die kleinste Erdscholle, wie der freie Vogel im weiten Gebiete der Luft, die Lilie und der Schmetterling; der Fürst und der Bettler und die Wittwe und die Waise . . Allen gibt Gott Lust und Freude, alle erfreuen sich seiner Macht und Güte . . der Mensch allein jedoch hat das Bewußtsein dessen, der Mensch allein kann dieß sein Bewußtsein Gott gegenüber dankend aussprechen . . .

Und daher l. B., die Sie des Lebens Bitternisse schon gekostet, Sie fühlen jetzt gewiß um so stärker mit dem dankbaren Psalt. wie die Nähe Gottes beglückt, wie das Gottvertrauen beseligt, und wie wohl und noth es thut, Gottes Macht und Güte zu preisen und anzuerkennen, denn der freudigste Augenblick im Menschenleben' da sich das Herz zum Herzen findet, ward auch Ihnen von Gottes Liebe gegönnt — Seien Sie daher dessen stets eingedenk und Sie werden die beseeligende Gottesnähe allezeit empfinden, allezeit Ihm gerne vertrauen; seine Macht und Güte gerne anerkennen und dankend erzählen, anknüpfend an diese segens- und freudenreiche Stunde — das wolle Gott. Amen.

זכור את יום השבת לא תעשה כל מלאכה . . —

So lautet bekanntlich das vierte Geboth, das Gott unsern Vätern vor Jahrtausenden geoffenbart hat, und wie allgemein dasselbe, als Solches, auch gehalten ist, so entspricht es doch auch passender Weise unserem Zwecke bei dieser Gelegenheit — abgesehn davon, daß Sie l. B. dem ehrenhaften Arbeiterstande angehören —um Ihnen Beiden einige nützliche Winke für das Herzens- und Seelenbündniß, welches Sie nun fürs Leben schließen — mit zu geben.

Sechs Tage weist uns der gütige Schöpfer zur Arbeit in jeder Woche an und nur einen Tag zur Ruhe. So schwer ist das Leben, so hart der Erwerb; so mannigfach die Arbeit, so zahlreich die menschlichen Bedürfniße; so gering die menschliche Kraft, daß erst nach sechstägiger Arbeit, nach sechstägigem Mühen uns Ruhe, Friede und Freude gegönnt ist . .

Ist das nicht ein gar herrliches Sinnbild des ganzen Menschenlebens!

Sabbatruhe, Sabbatglück; Sabbatfreude und Sabbatseligkeit, wie selten kehren sie zu uns ein, wie selten kommen sie in unser Herz, in unsere Hütten! Die Mühen und die Leiden, der Kummer und die schwarzen Sorgen hingegen, diese stellen sich gar zahlreich und nur allzuoft ein! und wohl uns, wenn dieselben nur sechsfach die sabbatlichen Glücks- und Freuden-Zeiten überragen!

Sollen wir darob verzagen? Nimmermehr. Im Gegentheile; das Bewußtsein gerade, daß Gott der Herr in seiner Macht und Güte das Leben so geschaffen und gestaltet hat, muß unser Vertrauen auf Gott allein, stärken, muß die Nähe Gottes, wo sie eintritt, um so fühlbarer machen und unser Herz und unsern Mund mit Dank und Lob gegen Ihn erfüllen.

Aber auch das eheliche Leben, m. L. ist mehr ein gemeinsames Tragen, denn ein gemeinsames Behagen, mehr ein gemeinsames Thun, denn eine gemeinsames Ruhn und hat mehr Werktags- denn sabbatliche Momente, darum nennt auch das Gotteswort so wahr und weise das Weib, die Gehilfin des Mannes, weil das Weib die nützliche Thätigkeit des Gatten anspornen und erleichtern soll, durch häusliche Mitthätigkeit und sonstige weibliche Tugenden — denn ist der Mann seinem Weibe gleichsam Vater und Mutter zugleich, indem er sie redlich nährt, schützt und währt, indem er sie liebt und niemals betrübt, soll und muß der Mann bedacht und bestrebt sein, die Freuden und Wonnen, die das Leben allerdings auch reichlich bietet, zu erhaschen, zu genießen und mitgenießen zu lassen, nicht im rauschenden, schwellenden Leben draußen, sondern gottfreudig am häuslichen Herd, im häuslichen Kreis; en famille so zu sagen אתה ובנך etc. . . . soll der Mann, wie gesagt, auch inmitten der Tagesmühen eingedenk sein der sabbat- und feiertäglichen Momente, wie die Schrift es ausdrükt mit den Worten זכיר u. s w. so muß auch das Weib diese Freuden und Wonnezeiten mit herbei führen helfen, durch Wirtlichkeit, Frohsinn und Heiterkeit, mit vorbereiten, dieselben im Sinne Gottes zu feiern, denn ויום השביעי שבת u. s. w. Oh', Gott sendet sie, seine Ruhe- und Festzeiten, seine Freuden- und Friedenstage — an uns nur ist es sie zu nützen.

So und nicht anders wird das Leben im Großen und Ganzen erträglich, so gedeiht das eheliche und häusliche Leben; so ist die Mühe und Arbeit keine Last und kein Fluch, sondern eine Lust, denn die Hoffnung auf Ruhe und Rast auf Friede und Freude, die nicht trügt, würzt die Mühe verschönt die Arbeit, lohnt den Fleiß und krönt das Streben mit glücklichen Erfolg. Amen.

26.

Einleitung.

פ׳ תרומה.

אנא ד׳ הושיעה נא — אנא ד׳ הצליחה נא!

Oh, Ewiger hilf! und steh mir bei, o, Gott, laß es gelingen doch!

Es muß ein gar wichtiger Augenblick, ein gar wichtiges Vorhaben und Unternehmen gewesen sein, daß der fromme, gottgeliebte, liebliche Sänger Israels also inbrünstig zu seinem Gotte bethete!

Und wie natürlich ist nicht ein solch Gebeth, zu einer solchen Zeit! hängt ja alles Gelingen und alles Glück nur von Ihm allein ab, wie derselbe es voller Bewußtsein schon früher aussprach ימין ה׳ עושה חיל. Nur Gottes Rechte, schafft alles Große.

Und welches Menschenherz könnte sich enthalten in solch bedeutungsvollen Augenblicken ein Stoßgebeth solcher Art auszusprechen? Nun aber gibt es gewiß im ganzen Menschenleben keinen hehrern Augenblick, kein wichtigeres Vorhaben, von welchem unseres Daseins ganzes Wohl oder Wehe der Art abhienge, als, wo zwar zwei gleichartige Wesen, jedoch verschieden an An- und Einsichten, verschieden an Gewohnheiten und Neigungen; verschieden vielleicht selbst an Gefühlen und Empfindungen, einander für die Lebensdauer, Liebe und Treue, Gegenseitigkeit und Uebereinstimmung geloben . . . Wer möchte und sollte da nicht mit dem frommen Sänger bethen אנא ד׳ u. s. w.

In der Ueberzeugung daher, daß auch Sie, liebe Beide dieses innige Gebeth, gegenwärtig, dem Psalt. inbrünstig nachfühlen, sprechen auch wir es aus und bethen: Gott wolle diesen Ihren frommen Wunsch erhören und gewähren, und dieß Ihr Herzensbündniß gelingen lassen. Amen. . .

ועשו לי מקדש ושכנתי בתוכם.

Und sie sollen mir machen ein Heiligthum, daß ich unter ihnen wohne! dieser Ruf, der einst an ganz Israel erging, als Dasselbe einen ewigen Bund mit Gott einging, damit Er stets mit Ihm sei, ergehet heute auch an Sie, geehrte. Denn auch Sie wollen und wünschen, daß Gott in Ihrem Hause, auch Sie wollen und wünschen, daß Gott Sie schütze und beglücke; auch Sie wollen und wünschen, daß Gott Ihnen stets nahe sei mit seiner Hilfe im Leid und mit seinem Segen im Glücke! Nun denn so gilt es auch da ועשו לי מקדש So ists denn an Sie aus Ihrem Hause ein Heiligthum zu machen, ein Heiligthum durch Frömmigkeit und Liebe; ein Heiligthum durch Gemüthsruhe und Genügsamkeit, ein Heiligthum durch Gottvertrauen und jüdische Zucht und Sitte!

ועשו לי u. s. w. Mögen sie mir nur ein Heiligthum bereiten, so will ich ohne Weiter's unter ihnen wohnen, ruft Gott — dieß sollten alle Menschen einsehn — — doch die Meisten, die Ihn dann erst herbei wünschen, wenn sie ihn am Nöthigsten haben, dürfen sich kaum beklagen, wenn er ihnen auch dann fern bleibt!

Oh . . . . welches Verhältniß bedarf mehr des göttlichen Schutzes, des göttlichen Beifalls und des göttlichen Segens, als eben das Eheliche und Häusliche, von welchem, wie gesagt, unser ganzes Lebensglück, oder Wehe abhängt!

Armuth und Reichthum, Hoheit und Niedrigkeit; Leben und Tod, was sind sie im Vergleiche zu einem seelenvollen, glücklichen Familienleben, im Vergleiche zu dem steten Elend einer mißlungenen Häuslichkeit! Wer aber sein Haus zum Heiligthume gestaltet, wo der Gatte seine Kraft dem Weibe, und die Gattin ihr ganzes Sein dem Manne opfert, zum Heiligthume, wo der Mann die Gattin sozusagen anbethet, und die Frau den Mann verehrt, zum Heiligthume, wo Mann und Weib nur einen Willen, den des himmlischen Hausherrn nämlich, haben, da wohnt und thront Gott und mit Ihm, was göttlich und beglückend ist für alle Zeiten, weil Gott und Gut unzertrennliche Begriffe sind.

Mann und Weib, sagen unsere Alten, geben in ihrer Ganzheit eine Anschauung Gottes — Wolan so müssen denn Mann und Weib auch Gott im Herzen, Gott im Hause haben ועשו לי u. s. w. so ihr Haus ein Heiligthum sein soll, so muß auch ihr Herz und ihr ganzes Innere, ihr Fühlen und Denken mir geweihet sein. . .

Ich verweise Sie um so ernster auf dieß Heiligthum des Herzens und des Hauses, als die materielle Richtung der Zeit, den Gott des Weltalls, sozusagen immer mehr aus dem Weltgetriebe drängt und allein auf das Asyl des Hauses und des Herzens beschränkt und beengt!

Und somit glaube ich Ihnen denn das Nöthigste und Wichtigste für die gemeinsame Lebensreise und Lebensweise, die Sie nun antreten und beginnen, mitgetheilt zu haben, beachten Sie es wohl für alle Zeiten. Amen.

27.

Einleitung.

פ׳ כי תשא.

אלהים למדתני מנעורי-ועד הגה-אגיד נפלאותיך-וגם עד זקנה ושיבה
אל תעזבני-עד אגיד זרועך לדור-לכל יבוא גבורתך !

Von Jugend an bisher, hast du mich Gott! beraten,
Und darum will ich künden deine Wunderthaten!
Und auch in des Alter's hohen Tagen,
Wolle deine Huld mir nicht versagen!
Bis ich verkündet deine Macht dem Zeitgeschlechte,
All den Kommenden, die Stärke deiner Rechte!

Und diese, oder ähnliche Gefühle mögen es wohl sein, die auch Ihren Geist in dieser freudenreichsten Stunde Ihres Lebens, beschäftigen, da auch Sie mit dem frommen, dankbaren Säuger, in des Wortes eigentlichster Bedeutung rufen können: Von Jugend an bis her, hast du, o Gott, mich geleitet und gelehrt . . . denn, hervorgegangen aus dem Schoße der Entbehrung, frühe verwaist und führerlos, sind Sie nicht hinabgesunken zu jener Hefe der Alltäglichkeit; zu jenem Pöbelhaufen, der stets am Karren der sogenannten Existenz sorgenvoll einherkeucht, um endlich jene, schwindlige Höhe so vieler Menschen von Gestern, zu erreichen und zu erklimmen, sondern wie geleitet von Gottes Vaterhand, wie unterrichtet und belehrt von Gottes Weisheit, haben Sie sich einem edlen und heiligen Berufe gewidmet, der noch immer leider nicht genug gewürdigt ist, und daher des Mannes beste Kraft und Stärke bis ins hohe Alter ungeschwächt fordert und erheischt.

So rechtfertigt sich auch in diesem Augenblicke das Gebeth וגם עד זקנה u. s. w. doppelt, damit ich deine Macht und Güte künde dem kommenden Geschlechte denn was ist wohl beglückender als der Rückblick auf ein ehrenhaft zurückgelegtes Dasein was beseligender, als die Erinnerung an die überstandenen Mühen eines mit Erfolg gekrönten, bessern Strebens!!

Aber auch Sie l. Glsch. müßen jetzt mit dem gekrönten Ps. tief empfinden, wie Gott Sie, von frühester Kindheit bis zu dieser schönen Stunde geleitet und gelehrt, geleitet an und durch die Hand eines einsichtsvollen Freundes, der Ihren Geist, Ihr Herz und Ihr Gemüth für das Nützliche, Güte und Schöne herangebildet, geleitet an und durch die Hand eines lieben und liebenden Freundes, der Ihnen diese schöne Stunde bereitet hat in edelster Großherzigkeit; geleitet bis zu dieser schönen Stunde, da Sie ein warmfühlendes Herz und einen starken, sichern Arm gefunden, der Sie schützend, ehrend und nährend, kummer- und sorgenlos durch das Leben zu führen gewillt ist — auch Sie fühlen sich gewiß gedrängt Gottes Huld und Liebe in diesem Augenblicke dankbar anzuerkennen; auch Sie bethen jetzt gewiß dem frommen König nach, das Er Ihnen seine Gunst und Liebe niemals entziehen und versagen wolle, auf daß auch Sie einst, in trautem Familienkreise, nach der Jahre reichsten und segenvollsten Fülle erzählen können seine Macht und Güte. Amen.

מלאו ידכם היום לד׳, ולתת עליכם היום ברכה.

Weihet euere Macht, euer Thun und Können, heute, Gott dem Herrn, damit ihr gebet heute auf euch Gottes Segen.

So rief der Gottesmann einst seinem Volke, bei einer andern Gelegenheit wohl, und in einem andern Sinne zu, aber passender Waise, rufe auch ich, als Lehrer des göttlichen Wortes, Ihnen L. B. diese weihevollen Worte in diesem Augenblicke zu: denn auch Sie wollen ja Gottes Beifall und Gottes Segen für diese Ihre Herzens- und Seeleneinigung, auch Sie wollen ja diesen Freudentag als Quelle fortdauerden Glückes, als Born des Segens und des Heils; auch Sie wollen ja diesen Tag mit goldenen Buchstaben in die Tafeln Ihres Herzens zum ewigen Gedenken verzeichnen und so gilt denn hier wie dort der Ruf מלאו ידכם היום u. s. w.

Wohl brauch ich Sie, gel. Fr. wie ich Sie genau kenne, nicht erst auf die Wichtig- und Heiligkeit dieses Herzens- und Seelenbündnisses aufmerksam zu machen, denn Sie sind geistes- und herzensgebildet genug, als daß Sie dieß nicht von selber genau wissen sollten, ich brauche Sie ebensowenig auf all die heiligen und schönen Pflichten, welche aus dieser dauernden Verbindung schon für jeden Gatten überhaupt, und für den Berufsmenschen, dessen Aufgabe es ist, gott- und menschengefällige Menschen zu erziehen und heranzubilden, und daher vorzüglich als Muster der Häuslichkeit dastehen soll und muß, . . ins besondere hervorgehen, aufmerksam zu machen . . denn ich kenne Sie als vorzüglich dankbeflissenen Sohn, als wahrhaft opferwilligen Bruder; als einen Menschen milden Herzens überhaupt — wie sollten Sie also nicht auch ein fürsorgender, treuer, ja zärtlicher Gatte sein! Oh, ich brauche Ihnen nicht einmal das מלאו ידכם zu zurufen, da ja Ihr ganzes Leben einem heiligen gott- und menschengefälligen Berufe gewidmet ist, wenn ich Ihnen also trotzdem diese Worte ins Gedächtniß rufe, so geschieht dieß nur des Nachsatzes wegen ולתת עליכם היום ברכה um Ihnen meine innige Theilnahme, meines Herzens beste Wünsche kund zu geben, um Gottes reinsten Segen auf diesen Ihren Herzensbund herab zu bethen!

Ihnen aber, th. Glb. gelten diese Worte in ihrem ganzen Umfange, in ihrer weitesten Bedeutung, denn wenn schon das ganze weibliche Dasein, blos ein Herzens- und Gemüthsleben, schon die ganze weibliche Wesenheit gewissermaßen etwas Höheres und Besseres sei, so gilt dieß um so mehr dort, wo das Weib nicht mit-thätig in das profane Weltgetriebe und Geschäftsleben hinaus treten muß, wo das Weib, wie es bei Salomo heißt, als Königstochter ihre Ehre und Würde ungeschmälert wahren kann, vor jedem rohen Anhauch der Außenwelt! . . Es muß das Leben der Gattin dort ein so innigeres, seelenvolleres und gemüthlicheres sein als der Beruf des Gatten, wie hier, ein so schwieriger, so ernster und strenger ist, hier muß das Leben und Streben des Weibes vorzüglich der Heiterkeit des Hauses und des Mannes gelten; hier muß das Haus vorzüglich eine Stätte der Freude und der Wonne sein durch all die weiblichen Tugenden und Annehmlichkeiten, die des Mannes Herz erfreuen, weil nur ein frohes, fröhliches Gemüth, nur die Hoffnung auf des Hauses Freude und Glück die Berufsmühen überhaupt, und die Mühen dieses Berufes ins besondere, leidlich und erträglich, ja überhaupt, möglich machen . . . Und sagen wir es nur grad heraus, soll der Lehrer in seinem heiligen Beruf wirken, mit Erfolg wirken, so muß er dem frohen kindlichen Gemüthe auch ein heiteres frohes Herz entgegen bringen, ein Solches aber gibt und schafft nur die Gattin, das Haus!

Wollen Sie also diesen Tag zur Quelle des fortdauernden Segens machen, so liegt dieß eben nur an Ihnen, wie schon unsere Weisen lehren: des Mannes Segen, hängt nur von des Weibes Streben ab!

Es wird Ihnen dieß hoffentlich diesem Ihrem Gatten gegenüber um so eher gelingen, als derselbe, wie gesagt, ein warmfühlendes und dankbares Herz besitzt, und ein solch edles Streben vollkommen anzuerkennen und zu würdigen weiß.

Seien Sie also dieser Worte stets eingedenk, um ihnen nachzuhandeln und nachzuwandeln und Sie werden alle Zeit mit dem frommen Pf. rufen können: Von Jugend an bis her, hast du uns Gott geleitet und gelehrt — und deine Wunderthaten stets an uns bewährt — denn, noch in des Alter's hohen Tagen — wird er Ihnen Seine Liebe nicht versagen — auf daß Sie erzählen spätem Zeitgeschlechte — die Macht und Güte seiner Rechte. Amen.

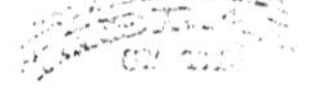

28.

פ פקודי.

ויכס הענן את אהל מועד וכבוד ד' מלא את המשכן Und ein Gewölk bedeckte die Stiftshütte, und die Herrlichkeit Gottes füllte die Wohnung. So lesen wir in dem Gottesworte. Und ein Zelt der Bestimmung für Jedermann, der der sittlichen Weltordnung folgt, und ein Haus und eine Familie gründet, muß das eheliche und Familienleben allezeit und unter allen Umständen bilden, wenn die Herrlichkeit Gottes es füllen, wenn Gott darin wohnen; wenn Friede, Freude und dauerndes Wohl drin stetig bleiben sollen.

Das אה' מ' war eine Stätte des Friedens, in welchem alles weltliche Geräusch keinen Platz hatte und eine Stätte der behoglichsten Ruhe soll und muß auch das Haus sein wenn es seiner Bestimmung entsprechen soll — Das Stiftszelt war eine Stätte strengster Ordnung, wo Jedes und Alles am rechten Platze war, jedes und alles nach Vorschrift und Norm ging . . auch das Haus, will es seiner Bestimmung entsprechen, muß eine so wohl geordnete Stätte sein, wo nicht nur dieß und jenes, sondern auch Mann und Weib ihre richtige Stellung einnehmen . . . . auch das Haus muß nach Vorschrift und Gesetzen geleitet werden! Das Heiligthum war die Wohne der Ehrfurcht vor Gott und der Achtung und Liebe gegen Mitmenschen, die sich in demselben als Kinder eines Vater's betrachteten, eine Stätte gegenseitiger Achtung, Liebe und Ehrfurcht soll auch das häusliche אהל מועד sein allwo der Mann das Weib achte und würdige als treue Lebensgefährtin, als ordne nd Vor- und Fürsehung seines Hauses und Hauswesens; als gute Mutter seiner Kinder . . . als schwaches, hilfloses Wesen, das nur von seiner Obsorge abhängt, als Erwählte und Erwünschte seines Herzens, allwo aber auch das Weib den Mann achte, ja ehrfürchte, als redlichen Ernährer und Versorger, der im Schweiße seines Angesichtes das tägliche Brod erwirbt . . . Ja so wie die Stiftshütte mit einem dichten Gewölk be- und verdeckt war, weil dieselbe mit der Herrlichkeit Gottes gefüllt und erfüllt war, also soll und muß auch das Heiligthum des Hauses vor der geräuschvollen und lärmenden Außenwelt durch einen dichten Wolkenschleier sabbatlicher Stille, Ruhe und Friedfertigkeit, gesondert und abgeschnitten sein, kein neugieriges fremdes Auge darf sich hinein drängen wollen, keine Zunge daran ihren Stachel wetzen können, wenn anders die Herz- und Gemüthlichkeit darin wohnen, Glück und Zufriedenheit drin walten sollen! Die Gotteswohnung war schließlich dazu bestimmt, ein Ort traulichen Zusammenseins mit Gott, dem Allvater im Himmel, zu sein, der nicht durch Gemeinheit der Gesinnung und niedriger Handlungsweise entweihet werden durfte, ein Heiligthum des traulichsten Zusammenlebens von Mann und Weib, muß auch die Stätte des ehelichen und Familienlebens sein.

Dieß m. L. gilt von jeder Häuslichkeit . . . Jedes Haus muß einem א'ה'מ gleichen, wenn die Herrlichkeit Gottes dauernd drin wohnen soll, wenn wir uns wohl und behaglich drin finden sollen . . . Ihnen aber legen wir dieß um so mehr ans Herz, weil einerseits Ihr Glück, als Waise, uns um so mehr am Herzen liegt und weil anderseits - und dieß gilt Ihnen m. Fr. das Vertrauen, daß diese Verlassene in Sie setzt, auch gerechtfertigt zu werden verdient, denn merken Sie wohl! jede Beleidigung und jede Kränkung, die ihr widerführe würde auch das Herz ihrer alten Mutter, würde jeden Einzelnen in dieser Gottesgemeinde verletzen . . . .

Und so bethen wir denn, es möge sich an Ihre Behausung bewähren ויכס u. s. w. Amen

---

29.

Einleitung.

פ' פקודי.

ראה אל עבדיך פעלך — והדרך על בניהם — ויהי נועם ד' אלהינו עלינו — ומעשה ידינו כוננה עלינו — ומעשה ידינו כוננהו.

Laß Deinen Dienern sehen, Herr! Dein Wunderthun,
Und Deine Herrlichkeit auf ihren Kindern ruhn!
Zeig Deinen Beifall uns, o Gott! Dein lieblich Walten,
Und unser Thun, das laß zum Heile sich gestalten!

Laß, was wir schaffen nun, zum Segen fortbestehn,
Und festige, was wir thun zum Nimmeruntergehn!

Und dieses fromme Gebeth und diesen heißen Herzenswunsch des heiligen Sängers, spreche auch ich theilnehmenden Herzens in diesem Augenblicke, sowohl für die Eltern dieser Deiner Kinder, Gott mein Herr! als auch für diese selber, aus; denn was mag wohl das Herz der Eltern in diesem Augenblicke mehr erfüllen, das Gemüth derselben mehr bewegen und erregen als der fromme Wunsch und das inbrünstige Gebeth: Es möge und wolle Gottes Herrlichkeit, Gottes Huld und Güte sich an ihren Kindern offenbaren und kund thun! Und was ist wohl von Ihrer Seite geschätztes Brautp. gerechtfertigter, als der fromme Wunsch: Es wolle und möge Gottes Beifall und Gottes Segenfülle, dieses Ihr inniges Herzens- und Seelenbündniß, diese Ihre gemeinsame Lebensreise und Weise, die Sie nun antreten, geleiten und mit bestem Erfolg krönen!

Ist doch das Bündniß so wichtig, ist doch diese Gemeinsamkeit so schwer wiegend im und für's Leben! Denn nur nallzuwahr ist und bleibt des Sängers Wort „Darum prüfe, wer sich ewig bindet, ob sich das Herz zum Herzen findet; denn ach, das Menschenherz hat wie der Ozean seine Klippen und seine Tiefen und das Schifflein des ehelichen und häuslichen Lebens — und damit unser Lebensglück — kann eben so gut daran scheitern und untergehen, wie auch auf der glatten Spiegelfläche desselben ruhig dahin gleiten . . je nachdem es dem Lenker und Leiter in der Höhe gefällt! Wie sehr ist es daher bei diesem so wichtigen Lebensentschlusse zu bethen nothwendig ויהי נועם u. s. w.!

Und so wolle uns denn erhören und gewähren, o Gott und diese Herzensverbindung zu einer Glücklichen und Beglückenden gestalten, daß sich bewähre והדרך על בניהם — — ומעשה ידינו כוננהו. — Amen.

ויכס הענן את אהל מועד וכבוד י״י מלא את המשכן!

Und fürwahr, soll und will die Wohnung erfüllt sein von Gottes Herrlichkeit, soll und will die Wohnung voll sein göttlicher Majestät — und welche Behausung und welche Stätte wollte dieß nicht! und welches Haus und welche Wohnung wollte nicht geschützt und gestützt, beglückt und segenerfüllt sein von der Gegenwart und Nähe Gottes! so ist es hier wie dort nöthig, daß das Haus eine Stiftshütte, ein Gotteshaus, daß das Haus bedeckt und verhüllt sei von einem dichten Gewölk!

Doch, fragen Sie geehrtes Brautp. wie dieß zu machen sei? so antworte ich mit dem Gottesworte: וידעת כי שלום אהלך ופקדת נוך ולא תחטא. = Liebst Du es, daß Deine Behausung eine Stätte des Friedens, eine Stätte der Zufriedenheit; eine Stätte der Eintracht und der Gemeinsamkeit sei, dann gedenke und bedenke, daß diese Deine Wohne laster- sünden- und fehler-frei bleibe! denn das Gotteshaus, meine Lieben, ist nicht deßhalb ein Haus Gottes genannt, weil die Menschen daselbst ihre Säufzer und Gebethe zu Gott empor senden, sondern vorzüglich weil es unbefleckt von menschlichen Schwächen und Gebrechen ist; vorzüglich, weil es die Stätte des Friedens und der Eintracht zwischen den Menschen ist; vorzüglich weil es reinigende Kraft besitzt und den Menschen, der im Außenleben so viel an Reinheit verliert, wieder würdig seines Schöpfers macht. So aber und grade so soll und muß das Haus sein, eine Stätte gegenseitiger Verehrung und Hochachtung des Mannes gegen die Gattin und des Weibes gegen den Gatten, eine Stätte, frei von jeglicher Sünde; eine Stätte inniger Eintracht und Uebereinstimmung, eine Stätte reinigender Kraft gegen die Rostflecken des Verkehrs und des Geschäftslebens, die nur allzuoft des Gatten Sinn für's Bessere, des Gatten Herz für's Edlere abstumpfen, durch häusliche Herz- und Gemüthlichkeit!

Sind dieß aber die Bedingungen, wodurch das Haus zum אהמ wird, so muß, wenn die Majestät Gottes mit ihrer beglückenden Nähe, und ihrem segenspendenden Füllhorn drin wohnen soll, auch ein Gewölk die Wohne bedecken und umhüllen, denn ה׳ אמר לשכון בערפל; nur dort, wo die stille Bescheidenheit, die nützliche geräuschlose Thätigkeit; die andachtsvolle Frömmigkeit herrschen, dort wohnt, dort waltet Gottes Huld und Güte.

Soll daher in der Stiftshütte, die Sie nun geehrtes Brautpaar jetzt errichten, die Majestät Gottes residiren, so darf weder der aufgeblasene Hoch- und Uebermuth im Glücke, noch der Stolz und die rauschende Prunksucht sich breit machen im Hause— denn אני את דכא ושפל רוח אשכון lautet das Gotteswort, nur neben der Demuth und Bescheidenheit wohne und weile ich. Ja, nur dann, wenn in Mitte des geräuschvollen und lärmenden Außenlebens selbst, das Haus von einer sittlich bescheidenen Gotteshausstille umrahmt und eingefasst ist וכבוד ד' מלא את המשכן dann füllt die Herrlichkeit Gottes ohne Weiters, dauernd, die Wohnung.

Ich unterlasse es all den Tugenden, die das Eheleben, sowohl von Seite des Gatten, als auch von Seite der Gattin erfordert, das Wort zu reden, da ich weiß, daß Sie lieber Bräutigam trotz Ihrer Jugend, trotz langer Abwesenheit vom väterlichen Hause und trotz stetem Weilen und Leben in Mitte einer Großstadt, die so viel Verlockendes und Verderbendes hat, denn Sitten und Tugenden Ihres frommen väterlichen Hauses treu geblieben, da ich weiß, wie Sie durch Thätigkeit, männlichen Ernst und reele Strebsamkeit sich so frühe eine Stellung und einen weiten Kreis von Freunden verschafft, so gebe ich mich einerseits, und hoffentlich mit Recht, der Hoffnung hin, daß Gott Ihnen auch eine dermaßen würdige Gattin schenkt, und anderseits der gerechten Erwartung, daß Sie, geehrte Braut, gewillt sind diesen Ihren Gatten zu beglücken, da er Ihnen dieß in Liebe zutraut und selber Sie beglücken will, dazu gebe Gott Ihnen seinen Beistand. Amen.

30.

Einleitung.

פ׳ שלחלך

שבענו בבקר חסדך ונרננו ונשמחה בכל ימינו.

Am Frühroth unseres Daseins sättige uns mit Deiner Huld, auf daß wir jubeln und uns freuen durch alle unsere Tage!

So bethete Mose inbrünstig zu Gott und wer hätte wohl Besseres zu wünschen, und wer möchte wohl Besseres sich erbethen? Am Frühroth, am Morgen unseres Lebens; in unseren

Jugendtagen, am Beginne unserer Laufbahn, wenn wir noch voll Kraft, und Saft, blühend und glühend im Lebensfelde stehen; wenn unser Herz noch empfänglich, unsere Sinne noch frisch unser Muth noch ungebeugt und ungebrochen, dann, o Herr! sättige uns mit Deiner Huld und Güte, noch ehe da kommen die Tage des Alters, die Tage der Lebenssätte, von denen wir sagen: Es sei keine Lust in ihnen!

Und diese Bitte und dieses Gebeth richten wir an Dich in dieser Stunde im Namen dieser Deiner Kinder, die am Beginn ihrer gemeinsamen Wanderung durchs Leben zu Dir kommen, um den hoffnungsreichen Bund der Ehe zu schließen! sich freuen Sättige sie mit der Fülle Deiner Huld, damit sie frohlocken und durch alle Tage ihres Lebens, Amen.

Als Gott unsere Vorältern in das verheissene und heißersehnte Land Canaan führen wollte, da sprach er, wie das Gotteswort uns erzählt, zu Mose, er solle Männer mit dem Auftrage sich genau umzusehn und zu prüfen, ob es gut oder schlimm, welche Licht- und Schattenseiten welche Vorzüge und Fehler es habe . . dahin absenden, und da ruft er ihnen auch zu: והתחזקתם ולקחתם מפרי הארץ — והימים ימי בכורי ענבים Und seid muthig, daß ihr holet von den Früchten des Landes — und die Zeit war die Zeit der Traubenreife!

Und in ein unbekanntes Land m. L. in das gelobte und geliebte Verhältniß ehelicher Gemeinsamkeit wollen auch Sie ziehen— sollten daher nicht auch Sie erst die Freuden und Leiden, die starken und schwachen Seiten, die Rosen und Dornen des Ehestandes kennen lernen und prüfen! oder glauben Sie etwa, daß dieß Verhältniß nur Wohl und nicht auch Wehe hat? daß dieser Stand nur Genüsse und nicht auch Schmerzen biethet?" daß dieser Garten nur Blumen und nicht auch Disteln trägt? Ruft ja schon der deutsche Sänger „Wer sich von dem goldenen Ringe u. s. w.'

Wohl ist es ein gar wunderschönes, gar prachtvolles Land das Land der Ehe, Blüthen und Blumen voll Süße und Duft, Früchte voll köstlichen Labsals, Bäume voll schattiger Blätter; Quellen voll perlenden Nasses gibt es da in Hülle und Fülle, man nennt sie gegenseitige Liebe, Treue, innige Theilnahme u. s. w. wo aber auch giftige Schlangen, und häßliche Kröten, schädliche Giftpflanzen und unheimliches Gefieder gibt es daselbst, es sind das all die bösen Leiden, die unausweichlich jeder größern und ausgedehnteren Thätigkeit und Obsorge auf dem Fuße folgen . . . Wo es überhaupt Freuden gibt, da fehlen auch die Leiden nicht, wo es Früchte gibt, da fehlt es auch nicht an nagenden Würmern und wo es kühlenden Schatten und Ruhe athmet, o, da gibt es auch glühend brennende Sonnenstrahlen und gar mächtige Stürme!

Und wohl uns, wenn Gluth und Kühlung, wenn Aufregung und Ruhe; wenn Lust und Last nur gleichmäßig vertheilt und einander die Wage halten!

והתחזקתם ולקחתם u. s. w. Muth und Ausdauer muß der Gatte im Kampf des Lebens bewähren, so er genießen will die Früchte des Lebens überhaupt und die Früchte des häuslichen Edens insbesondere, Muth und Ausdauer in ihrem Berufe als Gattin und Hausfrau muß auch das Weib bewähren, wenn es die Freuden des Ehestandes, trotz so mancher Bitternisse, die das Leben biethet, nicht entbehren will!

Soll der Mann in seinem Streben, in seinem Fleiße und in seiner nützlichen Thätigkeit nicht ermüden und ermatten, so muß die Gattin ihn durch Liebe, Theilnahme und rege Mitthätigkeit — und bestünde diese auch nur in ermunternden Worten — ihn stets von Neuem muthvoll anspornen, und soll die Gattin auch ihrerseits in ihrer weiblichen Wirksamkeit nicht erschlaffen und stets froh und fröhlich den Obsorgen für des Hauses Wohl und Ordnung und für des Mannes Lust und freundliches Behagen bedacht und thätig sein, so darfs auch von des Mannes Seite an Ermunterung und Aufmunterung nicht fehlen והתחזקתם Beide müßet Ihr mit Muth, Ausdauer und Standhaftigkeit an die dauernde Eroberung des heiligen Landes und Standes der Ehe gehen, denn das Haus bedarf der beiden Säulen und Stützen — und ist der Gatte der Repräsentant der Kraft und Stärke בֹּעַז, so ist das Weib die Bereitende und Ordnende! יָכִין . .

והתחזקתם Seid nur immer voll guten Muthes, ולקחתם, also werdet Ihr auch die Früchte genießen, denn kein andauerndes

Streben bleibt über kurz oder lang unbelohnt, — um so mehr als — והימים ימי בכורי ענבים — Ihr steht ja Beide noch in der Jugend schönster Blüthe, in den Tagen, wo der Muth sich erst erprobet, in den Tagen wo nützliche Thätigkeit noch ein Bedürfniß, in den Tagen, wo des Lebens Lust noch doppelt angenehm und des Lebens Last noch seine drückende Schwere nicht hat. — Und so möge denn Ihr Gebet, שבענו בבקר u. s. w. kein fruchtloses sein, Amen.

31.

Einleitung.

פ׳ חקת.

אלהים יחננו ויברכנו — יאר פניו אתנו סלה

Gewär, o Gott! uns deine Gunst und deinen Segen,
Erleucht mit deinem Angesicht uns, aller Wegen!

Dieß Gebeth m. L. dürfe Ihnen in diesem Augenblick ganz aus der Seele gesprochen sein, denn, wann und wozu bedürfen wir wohl mehr der göttlichen Huld und Liebe, des göttlichen Mitwollens und Segens, als eben wenn wir in ein neues, uns unbekanntes Verhältniß treten, als eben wenn wir einen so kühnen Griff in die Urne des Geschickes; einen so wichtigen Schritt in die Zukunft vorwärts thuen! Wann und wo haben wir des Lichts und der Erleuchtung nöthiger, als eben auf dem Pfad des ehelichen Lebens, der wohl der Rosen, aber auch der Dornen hat, so wir die Einen nicht zertreten und durch die Andern nicht verletzt werden sollen!

Und darum kommen und bethen wir denn auch zu Dir, Urquelle der Liebe und des Lichtes gewähre deine Gunst dieser im Sinne deines heiligen Willen's zu schließenden Vereinigung zweier für einander geschaffenen Herzen, und laß ihnen Dein leuchtendes und erleuchtendes Angesicht voranstrahlen, auf dem Wege ihrer gemeinsamen Wanderung durch's Leben. Amen.

דרך המלך נלך לא נטה ימין ושמאל die grade, breite Königstraße wollen wir gehn, wollen weder Rechts noch Links abneigen.

Mit diesem Vorsatze im Herzen, mit diesem Grundsatze auf den Lippen zogen einst unsere Väter' wie uns das Gotteswort erzählt, dem Lande Edom entgegen, mit diesem Vor- und Grundsatze zogen sie durch die Wüste des Lebens; durch aller Herren Länder dem ersehnten Lande der Freiheit . . des Heiles . . . zu, in Freuden und bei Leiden!

Und auch Sie, m. L. sollen mit diesen Worten, mit diesem gediegenen Vor- und Grundsatz, die neue Bahn, die Sie heute antreten, beginnen und fortsetzen! denn diese Königstraße allein ist der rechte Weg, sie allein führt zum guten Ziele; sie allein wahrt und wehrt uns, daß wir nicht abbiegen weder Rechts noch Links!

Und Ihr kennt gar gut den herrlichen breiten Königsweg, denn es ist eben der Weg, den jener große Weltenkönig, der den Sternen ihre Bahnen, dem Thierkreis seinen Lauf und den Menschenkindern überhaupt und uns Israeliten ins Besondere, vorgeschrieben und vorgezeichnet hat!

Gar viele Wege m. L. führen zum und ins Verderben, ein einziger nur, der דרך המלך allein, führt zum Wohl und Heile, der Weg der Gottesfurcht und des Gottvertrauens — überall und allezeit! und nicht minder im gemeinsamen Leben der Ehe und der Familie!

Gottvertrauen muß der Mann besitzen, wenn er hinaustritt in das Leben um fürs Leben das Nöthige zu erstreben כי הוא הנותן, לך.כח לעשות חיל weil Gott es ist, der dir Kraft verleihet zu erwerben. Er allein verleihet Muth, allen Hindernissen, die sich uns entgegen stellen die Stirne zu biethen; Er allein gibt Kraft und Ausdauer die allzuoft verlorenen Mühen, wieder aufs Neue zu bezinnen! גול אל ד' מעשיך וכו' dem Ewigen stelle dein Thun anheim, und dein Sinnen und Beginnen wird auch festen, starken Boden hab:n; Gott überlasse dein Thun, dann werden deine Gesinnungen auch grade und gottgefällig sein und sicher auch gelingen.

Wer auf Gott vertraut, dem vertrauen auch die Menschen, weil er eben ihr Vertrauen nicht zu suchen braucht, wer auf Gott vertraut ist im Glücke doppelt glücklich und wird in Noth und Leid nicht verzagt und hoffnungslos, wie es heißt: תריב גדולת

mag mein Glück sich mehren — ותסוב = oder mir den Rücken kehren — תנחמני = Du wirst mir immer Trost gewähren!

Thut also dem Manne und dem Gatten Gottvertrauen Noth, so ist das Weib es, welches allein durch Gottesfurcht seinen Pflichten, als Gattin, Hausfrau und Mutter eines künftigen Geschlechtes zu genügen im Stande ist—denn das Haus ist das Reich des Weibes, welches Reich aber könnte bestehen ohne wahre, aufrichtige Gottesfurcht, welche allein die Richtschnur für alles Gute und Edle ist! .

Die Gottesfurcht verleihet dem Weibe Anmuth und Reitz, die den Gatten dauernd fesseln, macht es zur guten Mutter und besten Erzieherin ihrer Kinder, deren erste und beste Lehrerin sie ist und sein soll . . . שקר החן u. s. w. sagt daher mit Recht der weise König —

Gottesfurcht und Gottvertrauen lehren bethen und Arbeiten, und das ist der דרך המלך den Gott der Herr Sie führen wird. wie es heißt ואזניך תשמענה דבר מאחריך לאמר זה הדרך לכו בו כי תאמינו וכי תשמאלו so Ihr abbiegen wollet nach Rechts oder Links!

Und so segne Sie, denn Gott und behüte Sie, erleuchte Sie und schenke Ihnen seine Gunst; kehre Ihnen zu sein stralend Angesicht und gebe Ihnen Glück. Amen.

32.

Einleitung!

פ׳ בלק.

זאת מנוחתי עדי עד־פה אשב כי אויתיה

Dieß sei mein Ruhort für immerdar,

Da will ich weilen, weil ichs gewünscht fürwahr!

In diesem Wunsch des Ps. der dem Gotteshause galt auf Zion, stimmt stillschweigend, sowohl der Jüngling als auch die Jungfrau ein, wenn sie dem Rufe ihres Herzens, der Stimme der sittlichen Weltordnung, ja der segenbringenden Einrichtung Gottes folgen und sich in Liebe vereinen, um ein Haus und eine Familie zu gründen!

זאת מנוחתי Hier, in meiner Häuslichkeit will ich ausruhen von des Lebens Lasten, Mühen und Sorgen, dieß sei der Ruhepunkt, dem ich im Lebensdrange und Lebenszwange stets zusteuern will; dahin sei mein Wähnen und Sehnen immer und überall gerichtet, rufe und ruft der Jüngling, der aus seiner Alleinheit, so zu sagen, heraustritt, um sich eine Lebensgefährtin anzugeloben, anzuleben und anzulieben. פה אשב, hier sei für die Lebensdauer mein Sitz und meine Ruhestätte, weil ich es selbst gewünscht, rufe und ruft die Jungfrau ihrer Behausung zu, die, nach dem Willen Gottes und der Bestimmung ihrer besorgten Lieben und Liebsten, sich einem Manne im Vertrauen hingibt, um eine gute Gattin und eine tüchtige Hausfrau zu werden.

Und in diesem Rufe und in dem ganzen tiefen Ernst dieses Willens und Wollens liegt auch die Bürgschaft des ehelichen Glücks und der glücklichen Fortdauer desselben.

Möge daher dieser Vorsatz Ihr ernster Gedanke und Ihre feste Uiberzeugung in diesem Augenblicke hehrerer Weihe sein, damit diese Ihre Ehe eine glückliche und beglückende werde. Amen.

מה טוב אהליך יעקב משכנותיך ישראל —

Wie schön sind doch deine Zelte Jacob! deine Wohnungen Israel! So rief in göttlicher Begeisterung der heidnische Seher, als er Israel's Lager- und Hüttenleben mit seinem scharfblickenden Auge übersah — Und dieser Lobesruf und dieser Ausdruck der Ver- und Bewunderung erscholl er nicht von je bis auf den heutigen Tag über das Lager- und Hüttenleben Israels, aus dem Munde Aller, die es kannten?! Und mit Recht! denn wer, der ein Auge für die Wahrheit hat, und wer, der ein Herz für Gemüthlichkeit besitzt, und wer, dem Sinn für den Ernst des Lebens innewohnt, könnte es uns abstreiten, daß die jüdische Ehe, das jüdische Haus- und Familienleben einen seltnen Reitz besaß, der wie ein ewiger Frühling mit all seinen Blüthen und Düften anmuthete!

Welche Keuschheit und Sittsamkeit bei weltlicher Verlockung, welche Wirthlich- und Sparsamkeit im Uiberflusse; welchen Genügsamkeit und Zufriedenheit beim Mangel, welch' würdiger Ernst im Frohsinn; welche Trostseligkeit im Schmerze, welcher Friede im Unmuthe und welche Uibereinstimmung in jeglichem Willen und

Wollen herschte nicht im Palaste wie in der ärmlichsten Hütte Israels!

Was Wunder wenn es allgemein hieß מה טובו u. s. w.!

Was aber war es denn eigentlich, daß dem also war? War es etwa die sogenante, oder gar sinnliche Liebe? o die schwindet ja naturgemäß, mit jedem Tage mehr aus der menschlichen Brust — o, die fühlen und pflegen ja auch andere Völker — weit mehr! oder war es etwa der leidige Druck und die Ab- und Zurückstoßung von Außen, die unsere Väter zwang, sich wie eine Schnecke in ihre Häuslichkeit zurückzuziehen und auf sie zu beschränken!? Nun wie kam es denn, daß diese Regel keine Ausnahme hatte, weder in den Zeiten des Unglücks noch in den Tagen des Glückes? wie kam es, daß der Druck, der sonst nur zerstörend, vernichtend und demoralisirend wirkt, da grade so Herrliches und Großes schuf? —

Doch nein, m. L. weder dieß noch jenes, noch irgend etwas Weltliches und Vergängliches war es, die das bewirkten, die einzige Triebfeder dessen war das jüdisch — religiöse Leben, die jüdische Religion war es, welche das Weib weihete und zum unverletzlichen Heiligthume machte, wie schon die Trauungsformel „Du sollst mir geheiligt sein" besagt, sie war es, die den Gatten zum weihenden und geweiheten Priester machte; sie, die sich als beglückend und beseligend bewährte, sie schaffte Segen, Trost, Friede und Genügsamkeit ins Haus; sie schließlich machte das Haus zur Stätte der Ruhe und die Wohnung zum Paradies der Traulichkeit und des fortdauernden Glückes!

Und wollten nicht auch Sie, daß es von Ihrer Behausung ebenfalls stets heiße מה טובו u. s. w.? Gewiß! nun denn, so beherzigen Sie diese Mahnung — leben Sie nach guter, alter, frommer jüdischer Sitte, denn die Religion lehrt, die Vernunft predigt und die alte lebendige Erfahrung bestätigt ihren Werth!

זאת מנוחתי . . Diese Uiberzeugung lebe in Ihnen als Gedenkwort fort, und Ihre Ehe wird eine segenvolle und gepriesene sein für alle Zeiten. Amen.

33.

פ׳ בלק.

Einleitung.

Dir Unsichtbarer, und doch Allgegenwärtiger! schlagen unsere Herzen entgegen, um Deinen Beifall und um Deinen fruchtbringenden Segen beten wir aus tiefster Seele zu Dir, Vater im Himmel! כי את אשר תברך מבורך denn, wen Du segnest, der ist gesegnet; zu Dir beten wir Gott! השקיפה ממעון קדשך מן השמים וברך schaue wohlwollend herab aus Deinen Himmelshöhen auf den Freuden- und Friedensbund, den diese Deine Kinder für die Lebensdauer einzugehen gewillt sind und segne ihn mit der Fülle alles Wohles. Amen.

מה טובו אהליך יעקב משכנתיך ישראל! Also rief einst, wie das Gotteswort uns erzählt, ein berühmter judenfeindlicher heidnischer Seher, der aber Geist und Herz besaß . . als er in das schöne sittlich und fromme Haus- und Familienleben Israels schauete — und mit diesen Worten th. Verlobte! will auch ich in diesem ernsten weihevollen Augenblicke ihre Aufmerksamkeit auf meine wohlgemeinten Rathschläge zum Heile dieses Ihres Herzensbündnisses lenken, damit es ein Glückliches und Beglückendes sei — Und nichts ist hiezu passender als eben die angeführten Worte . . denn das eheliche Leben gleichet einem Bau, um aber ein gelungenes wohnliches Gebäude aufzuführen, dazu bedarf es eines weisen Planes, guter Materiale als Baustoffe; dann aber tüchtiger, rüstiger und fleißiger Hände — und so wenig als derjenige ein schönes und wohnliches Haus aufführen wird, der plan- und zwecklos nur Stein an Stein reihet, und sowenig als derjenige eine sichere Stätte zu Wege bringt, der unbedacht, des Hauses Grund auf Sand setzt, das jeder Wind erschüttert, der gar umstößt; und sowenig je ein Haus vollendet und vollkommen wird, wo die Hände schwach und faul . . so wenig wird auch das Haus und die Familie, d. h. die Ehe eine vollständige, eine solide und zweckendsprechende, allwo der Plan; das eigentliche Bewußtsein, allwo die sogenannten Baustoffe und der nöthige Fleiß, das emsige Bestreben fehlen!

Nun ist wohl der erste Zweck der ehlichen Wohne, die Vereinigung und Beglückung zweier mit und für einander leben wollender Wesen — doch soll das Haus etwa deßhalb die Stätte der Selbstsucht und des Eigennutzes sein, abgeschlossen von und vor der Außenwelt? durchaus nicht! denn so wenig als der einzelne Körpertheil von Bedeutung ist, wenn er nicht verbunden mit dem Ganzen, den ganzen Körper ausmachen hilft — so wenig entspricht der einzelne Mensch, das einzelne Haus seiner höhern Bestimmung, wenn sie sich nicht nach Außenhin den immer sich erweiterden Familien- und Menschenstamme anschließen und den großen Gesammtzweck der Menschheit fördern helfen!

וירא את ישראל שוכן לשבטיו = erst als Bileam sah, wie die Einzelnen sich zu Familien und zu Stämmen zusammen thaten, wie sie da, Einer gestützt auf den Andern, Einer geschützt durch den Andern; wie Keiner und Keines vereinzelt und vereinsamt da stand— — da erst überkam ihn der Gottesgeist ותהי עליו רוח ד' und er rief מה טובו אוהליך יעקב u. s. w.

Welches wohl die guten Baustoffe sind, die zur Aufführung des ehelichen Hauses nöthig? das braucht wohl kaum gesagt zu werden, sie heißen gegenseitige Liebe und Werthschätzung, gegenseitiges Zu- und Vertrauen; gegenseitige Hilfe und Theilnahme u. s. w. u. s. w. Sind sie aber auch ausreichend? Allerdings! wenn nur der Kitt nicht fehlt und der ist hier die Religion, die Frömmigkeit und die jüdische Sitte! Wenn die Liebe und die Treue und die Achtung und das Vertrauen angewehet sind vom Odem Gottes, wenn über all die Tugenden der Glanz der Religion sich ergießt; wenn die gute alte Sitte aus all und jedem hervorleuchtet, dann ja dann ist auch um bei dem Bilde zu bleiben—der Bau solid und für die Dauer!

Ja, erst als der scharfblickende Bileam sah, wie Israels Familien- und Stammweise neben einander lagerte ותהי עליו רוח ד' d. h. wie ein Geist, der Geist Gottes über das Ganze sich ergoß, wie ein Geist, der Geist Gottes es durchzog und belebte, da erst that er seinen Spruch מה טובו אהליך יעקב u. s. w.

Und soll ich nun noch von der nützlichen Thätigkeit und von dem nöthigen Fleiß sprechen, die das Haus zur Vollendung seiner inneren und äußeren Verschönerung hat ... Nun Sie wissen und haben es ja Beide erfahren, wie Sie nur dem Fleiße und der Thätigkeit diese schönste Lebensstunde zu verdanken haben — ohne Fleiß und Thätigkeit geht das solideste Haus seinem Untergange und dem Ruin entgegen, wie es so wahr heißt בעצלתים ימך המקרה ובשפלות ידים ידלף הבית! = Durch Faulheit senkt sich das Gebälk, durch müssige Hände träuft das Haus!

Sie Beide stehen noch in des Lebens Blüthe, an Rüstigkeit und Kraft gebricht es Ihnen nicht; eine lange Zukunft harrt Ihrer, so nützen Sie sie denn zu Ihrem Wohle, zur Freude der Ihrigen; zur Ehre Gottes und zum Nutzen der Menschheit, mit einem Worte, zum nachahmungswürdigen Muster, daß es stets von Ihrem wie vom ganzen Familienleben Israels heiße מה טובו u. s. w.

Amen.

34.

Einleitung.

פ' ויקב.

בידך עתותי! = In deiner Hand o Gott! liegt mein Geschick!

Mit diesen zwei inhaltsschweren Wörtchen sprach der fromme König seine ganze Zuversicht, sein ganzes Gottvertrauen; sein ganzes Fühlen und Denken über alle Begegnisse seines reichen wechselvollen Lebens aus!

Und in diesen wenigen, aber schwerwiegenden Worten liegt in der That der erhabendste und erhebendste Trost, das erhabendste und erhebendste Bewußtsein in den manigfachsten leidigen und freudigen Verhältnissen und Ereignissen des Daseins.

Mit diesem Gefühle im Herzen, mit diesem Ausspruch auf den Lippen und mit dieser Ueberzeugung in all unserem Thun und Lassen, können wir uns stets getrost und in bester Zuversicht der dichtverschleierten Zukunft überlassen, denn es ist ja Gott, der liebreiche Vater, der unser Geschick in seiner Hand hält, und welches Kind könnte und wollte zweifeln an das Wohlwollen und die Güte eines so barmherzigen, allweisen und allgütigen Vaters, wie es Gott all seinen Geschöpfen ist!

Dieser festen Zuversicht und dieses festen Vertrauens aber bedürfen auch Sie, m. L. jetzt, da Sie sich entschließen den schweren, lebenswichtigen Schritt zu thun, nämlich sich für die Lebensdauer in Liebe zu vereinigen — Ich sage diesen lebenswichtigen Schritt, weil es in der That nichts Geringes ist, für den Jüngling, der bis zur Stunde nur für sein eigen „Ich" zu sorgen hatte, nunmehr auch für das Wohl und die Zufriedenheit eines zweiten Wesens zu streben — kein Leichtes und Geringes ist, für die Jungfrau, die des Lebens Mühen und Streben nur so zu sagen, vom Hörensagen, und das Haus-, Ehe- und Familienleben, aus Mangel an Gelegenheit, nur vom flüchtigen Anschauen und nur von der rosigsten Seite kennt, plötzlich, ja urplötzlich eine gute Gattin, eine treue mitthätige Gefährtin und eine umsichtige Hausfrau, in des Wortes ganzer Bedeutung zu werden — und doch müssen all diese Tugenden gleich mit, in das eheliche Verhältniß gebracht werden, weil sie sich sonst weder anlehren noch anpredigen lassen.

Mit der Ueberzeugung aber בידך עתותי, daß Gott unser Geschick väterlich leitet, gelingt Alles, ist all unser Thun und Lassen; all unser Streben und Hoffen gerechtfertigt und wohl geborgen und so fühle ich es denn, wie Sie dies dem frommen Ps. nachdenken und nachfühlen, damit diese Ihre Ehe eine gelungene werde. Amen.

Damit Gott unser Geschick leite und zu unserem Besten leite, müssen wir uns und unser Geschick auch ihm anvertrauen d. h. in seinem Sinne handeln und wandeln: והיה עקב תשמעון .. ושמר ה' אלהים לך את הברית ואת החסד .. ואהבך וברכך! Und so ihr gehorsamen werdet den Anordnungen Gottes, so wird Gott dein Herr dir in Liebe wahren das Bündniß, die Huld und die Angelobung .. und dich lieben und segnen.

Und dieses an ganz Israel ergangene Versprechen, ergehet heute auch an Sie l. Verlobte, es ist dieß eine Bedingung, ohne welche nicht, eine Bedingung, ohne welche schon das Dasein überhaupt wenig Trost und Sicherheit bietet, das eheliche Glück insbesondere aber kaum denkbar ist!

Und wer sollte und wollte um solchen Preis nicht gerne den weisen Vorschriften gehorchen! Was opfern die Menschen nicht Alles an Gut und Blut und allzuoft selbst an Ehre und Seligkeit, nur um dem trügerischen Schattenbilde des sogenannten Glückes nachzujagen — während das Wahre doch nur von dieser Bedingung abhängt!

Ist denn dieß aber auch wahr? werden Sie vielleicht im Gedanken fragen . . und wie kömmt es doch, daß so viele, die in Gottes Wegen nicht gehen und nach keiner Vorschrift nicht thuen, dennoch in Hülle und Fülle leben und genießen, und so mancher der in Frömmigkeit so fest an Gottes Lehre hält, kummer- und sorgenvoll, wie ein Fremdling, durch's Leben schleicht? diese Frage, m. L., die sich uns so oft im Leben aufdrängt, ist freilich auch hier am Platze, aber ebenso deren Beantwortung . . . wer das Glück nur im Glanz und im Schimmer; in der Hülle und Fülle der Lebensgüter, mit einem Worte nur im Aeußeren sucht, der freilich mag sich immer glücklich fühlen, wenn solches Blendwerk ihn umgibt, ob auch sonst das Herz vor Furcht und Unersättlichkeit von Innen blutet, der mag und wird sich stets unglücklich fühlen, wenn der goldene Regen und Segen ihm nicht stets sattsam in den Schoß fällt . . Nun aber offenbart sich Gottes Huld und Liebe an seine Lieben und Treuen, gar oft, nicht blos durch Reichthum und Ueberfluß, sondern durch ein Gedeihen von Innen nach Innen, das von der Außenwelt fast unbemerkt, uns aber desto glücklicher und glückseliger macht? Gesunde Hände und gesunder Sinn, Lebensfrische und Lebensmuth; Friede und Herzensruhe, Eintracht und Genügsamkeit, das sind Güter ganz anderer Art, und die gibt Gott ganz bestimmt, denen, die Ihm gehorchen und diese beglücken auch weit mehr als jene, denn diese können uns nicht geraubt werden, und können nicht verloren gehen; sie sind andauernd, hatten fest und steigern mit jedem Tage unser Wohl und unser Wohlbehagen!

Und Sie m. L. haben ja am Wenigsten Ursache an Gottes Vaterhuld zu zweifeln, im Gegentheile! denn so wie der Profet unsern Vorvätern zuruft עיניכם הראות את כל מעשה ד׳ הגדול אשר עשה so kann ich Ihnen, heute mit vollen Fug und Recht zurufen, Sie mögen es bedenken l. Br., wie nur Gott, trotz der Ihnen mangelnden beiden Stützen von Vater und Mutter, an Sr. Vaterhand geleitet und geführt und Ihnen diese Freudenreichen geschenkt, Ihnen eine Lebensgefährtin zuführend, die Ihre Liebe und Werthschätzung im vollsten Maße verdient . . . zurufen: Sie mögen es eingedenk bleiben l. Braut! wie Gott Sie so liebenden Herzen und Händen anvertraut hat, die in wahrhaft aufopfernder und elterlicher Liebe für Sie, bis zu dieser schönen Stunde gesorgt und Sie einem Ziele zuführen, dem Sie so glücklich entgegen gereift!

Seien Sie daher überzeugt, daß unser Geschick stets in Gotteshand ruht, damit Sie stets in seinen Wegen wandeln, auf daß sich an Sie bewähre . . ושמר ד' u. s. w. Das gebe Gott!

Ihnen aber, edle Wohlthäter, die Sie hier in uneigennützigster Weise Vater- und Mutterstelle so liebreich vertreten, möge das Bewußtsein dieser Hochherzigkeit ein weiterer Sporn für sich und Andere sein, solche Großthaten noch recht Viele zu fördern, und es wird sich an Sie bewahrheiten ,ונתתי לכם בביתי ובחומתי יד בנים ושם טוב מבנים ומבנות, שם עולם אשר לא יכרת. = Und ich werde euch verschaffen in meinem Hause und in meinen Mauern ein Denkmal und einen Namen, der besser als Söhne und Töchter, einen Namen für die Ewigkeit, der nie schwinden soll. Amen.

34.

Einleitung.

פ׳ ואתחנן.

שומע תפלה עדיך כל בשר יבוא! = Der Du Gebete erhörst, zu Dir kommt jegliches Wesen.

Es ist dies eine Wahrheit m. L., die keines weiteren Beleges und Beweises bedarf. Denn von der Pflanze angefangen, die zu ihrem Gedeihen Sonnenschein und Regen braucht, bis zum Herrn der Erde, dem Gott Alles zu Füßen gelegt, dessen Herz aber bald Schmerz bald Freude fühlt, Alles blicket auf zu Gott, bald betend, bald dankend, ja betend und dankend zugleich! Und so falten denn auch wir dankend die Hände zu Dir, Allmächtiger! der du diese Freudenstunden diesen deinen Kindern gegönnt, sich in Liebe und in Treue für das ganze Leben zu vereinen, betend, Du wollst diese Vereinigung eine dauernde und segensreiche werden lassen. Amen.

שמע ישׂ־אל ד' אלה־נו ד' אחד. Merke wohl Israel, der Ewige unser Gott ist ein einig einziger Gott! Diese Einheit und Einigkeit Gottes, welche das oberste Prinzip unserer heiligen Lehre bildet, dieser Grundsatz der Einigkeit und der Einheit macht auch im gesellschaftlichen und im Haus- und Familienleben den Grundzug, ja die Seele unseres ganzen Daseins und Strebens aus. Immer und überall zieht sich dieser erhebende Gedanke wie ein rother Faden durch das Gewebe unserer Pflichten תמים תה־ה עם ד' אל־היך Eins und einig sollst du dich mit deinem Gotte fühlen — als ein Strahl der Gottessonne hast du dich zu betrachten, nicht als etwas gesondertes, außerhalb Desselben Stehendes, sondern in und mit Ihm fühlen und mit Ihm denken, in und mit Ihm handeln und wandeln — ואהבת לרעך כמ־ך heißt es vom geselligen Umgange; wie dein eigen „Ich“ sollst du deinen Neben- und Mitmenschen betrachten, du wie er bist nur ein Tropfen von dem großen Menschen-Ozean, den alle einzelnen Menschen zusammen ausmachen ומי כעמך גוי אחד wird uns, Israel speziell bezeugt .. Hier gilt nicht mehr das Bild vom Meere, welche die einzelnen Tropfen, noch das der Sandwüste, die aus den einzelnen Sandkörnern gebildet ist. — Die Einheit und Einigkeit Israels entspreche und entsprach auch stets den einzelnen Gliedern eines einzelnen Körpers, wo das Wehe und Wohl des Einzelnen den ganzen Organismus wohl oder schmerzlich affizirte, und so und nicht anders verhält es sich auch mit dem Ehe-, Haus- und Familienleben והי־ לבשר אחד ruft die Schrift, Mann und Weib sind nicht blos Glieder eines und desselben Körpers, sondern sollen und müssen wie Leib und Seele einander derart durchdringen und ergänzen, daß Eines ohne das Andere nicht denkbar sei! So muß die Kraft, die Strenge; der Fleiß und der Ungestim des Mannes durch die Ruhe, Milde, Heiterkeit und Sanftmuth des Weibes gelindert und gemildert . . die Schwächen, die schönen Hoffnungen die lieblichen Träume und sonstigen Zartheiten der Gattin durch; die Tugenden des Gatten gerechtfertigt und vor Ueberschreitungen gewahrt werden.

Denn ebensowenig fürwahr als der schon eins und einig mit seinem Gotte ist, der so nebenher mit Ihm geht, sich ins Unvermeidliche fügt u. s. w. und ebensowenig als der eins und einig mit der menschlichen Gesellschaft, der nur das thut was er muß und nur unterläßt was er soll . . und ebensowenig als schon derjenige eins in und mit seinem Volke ist, weil zufällig ein und dasselbe Land sie geboren ein und dieselbe Religion sie zu ihren Bekennern zählt, ebensowenig ist es genug wenn der Gatte sich in die Laune des Weibes fügt und das Weib sich in den Willen des Mannes schickt . . dieß ist allerdings Lebensklugheit, diese aber schwindet ja allzuoft, wenn die Leidenschaften und die Erregtheit uns aufstacheln — die Einheit aber, welche die Ehe bewähren soll, muß eben aus der innigsten Verwebung, aus dem innigsten Ein-Leben beider hervorgehn!

Ein solches Ein-Leben hat keine Pflichten (insofern als Solche gegen unser eigen „Ich“ nicht von der Natur uns auferlegt . . .) und bedarf keiner Rechte . . . macht aber die Ehe zu einer glücklichen und das Haus zu einer dauernden Stätte der Seligkeit, und so rufe ich Ihnen denn zu והיו הדברים האלה אשר אנכי מצוך היום על לבבך Amen.

36.

Einleitung

פ׳ עקב.

שמחו בד׳ Freuet euch in Gott!

Diese Worte ruft der fromme, hocherfahrene König oft und wiederholt seinen Brüdern zu. Und mit Recht! weil nur eine solche Freude ohne Täuschung, nur eine solche Freude schmerzlos, nur eine solche Freude von steter Dauer und ewigem Halte ist.

Gar oft m. L. freuet sich das Menschenherz ohne Gott, ja gegen und wider Gott, ohne zu bedenken, daß Gott es ist, der sie ertheilt, ohne zu bedenken, daß es erst von seinem Beifalle oder Mißfallen abhängt, ob wir uns mit Recht gefreut, oder wie es allzuoft geschieht, grade die Freude nicht die Quelle unserer Leiden werde!

Die trüben, wie die heitern Loſe liegen in Gottes Vaterhand und eben darum rathet der fromme Pſalmiſt uns allen und jedem, der ſich freuen witt, ſich in Gott zu freuen, d. h. ſich Gottes Uibereinſtimmung, Gottes Beifall und Gottes Wohlwollen und Segen zu erflehen. Wann und wozu aber iſt dieß nöthiger als eben zu der Zeit und zu dem Bunde, wo zwei Weſen einander Liebe geloben, und zu lebensdauernder Gegenſeitigkeit verbinden.

Und ſo bethen wir denn zu Dir: Wolle o Gott die Ehe welche von dieſen Deinen Kindern nun in der angenehmen Hoffnung, es werde dieſelbe ihr Leben verſüßen und verſchönen, geſchloſſen wird, anch atſo ſich bewähren und die ungetrübte Freude, die jetzt ihr Herz erfüllt, gerechtfertigt ſein durch ihr ganzes Daſein Amen.

כל המבוה אשר אנכי מצוך היום תשמרון לעשות למען תהחיון ולרבותם = Alle Gebote, die ich dir gegenwärtig aufrage, ſollt ihr merken auszuführen, damit ihr lebet und groß werdet.

Und wahrhaftig dieſe Worte haben heute wie zur Zeit als ſie geſprochen wurden noch ihren vollen Werth, noch ihre ganze Bedeutung es gitt eben nur der Probe, es witl nur den ernſten Entſchluß — Und nichts iſt in der That leichter, aber auch nichts ſcheint ſchwerer; denn was kann für denjenigen, der in der Uiberzeugung lebt, daß Gutes wie Schlimmes ausſchließlich von Gott kömmt u. z. Jenes in Folge unſeres Gehorſames gegen Gott und ſeiner beglückenden Anordnungen, und dieſes in Folge unſeres Mißachtens ſeiner weiſen Vorſchriften leichter ſein als in Gottes Wegen gehen, ſeine Vorſchriften achten, ſie lieben und ausüben.

למען תהיון ורביתם ſagt das Gotteswort, hierunter wollen die Menſchen freilich Reichthum, Reichthum und nichts als Reichthum verſtehen! Gibt denn aber auch der Reichthum Leben überhaupt und tebt etwa nur der Reiche? macht etwa nur der Reichthum groß? das Gotteswort ſagt Anders! יגיע כפיך כי תאכל אשרך וטוב לך So du dich redlich durch deiner Hände Mühen nährſt, dann Heit und wohl dir, der Weiſe und Erfahrene hat andere Uiberzeugung — שן קה שנת העובד והשבע לעשיר אינו מניח לו ל׳י מתו ruft er der Schlaf des Arbeiters, und mag er viel oder Wenig genießen, iſt gar ſüß, während der Uiberfluß allzuoft dem Reichen den Schlaf raubt! der Reichthum verſchönt, verſüßt das Leben, aber das eigentliche Leben mit Allem, was drum und dran hängt, ehe es der Verschönerung bedarf, hängt von der Befolgung der göttlichen Anordnungen ab — Ja ist nur das Leben würdig und der Verzierung werth, so folgt schon dieselbe und bleibet sicher nicht aus.

Nichts scheint aber auch schwerer, sagt' ich, und das lehrt die tägliche Erfahrung, die geringe Anzahl der wahrhaft Glücklichen unter den Menschen.

Das sogenannte Leben ist freilich einerseits zu schwer anderseits zu verlockend, als daß er stets und überall mit dem Gottesworte Hand in Hand gehen könnte, dafür aber soll und muß das Haus um so mehr die Hege- und Pflege-Stätte desselben sein — da nur das fromme Weib überhaupt eine gute, bescheidene und anspruchslose Gattin, eine tüchtige Hausfrau; eine zärtliche sorgsame Mutter, nur der frome Mann ein treuer liebender Gatte, ein redlicher Freund seines Hauses und Herdes, ein strebsamer Versorger der Seinen und ein guter Vater und Erzieher seiner Kinder werden und sein kann!

Alle Pflichten, sagt das Gotteswort, müssen erfüllt werden, so wir leben, mehr und groß werden wollen — Merken und üben Sie sie stets und aller Orten Amen.

37.

Einleitung.

פ׳ עקב.

יהי חסדך ד׳ עלינו כאשר יהלנו לך.

So komme Deine Huld, Herr! über uns, wie wir auf Dich hoffen.

Und nur in dem Maße, wie wir auf Gott vertrauen, zu Gott hoffen und harren, in dem Maße läßt Gott auch Seine Huld, Seine Milde und Seine Liebe über uns walten.

Wann aber bedürfen wir mehr des Vertrauens und der Zuversicht auf Gott, als eben wenn wir in das wichtigste Verhältniß des Daseins, in das des ehelichen und häuslichen Lebens, eintreten, da unser Leben einen doppelten Werth, unser Streben ein zweifaches Ziel; mit einem Worte, unser ganzes Sein und Wirken eine doppelte Gestalt annimmt.

Mit welch hohem Ernst tritt da das Außenleben einer und das Leben nach Innen anderseits an uns heran! und wir sollten da nicht ernst unser Vertrauen auf Gott allein setzen, der es nur allein auch rechtfertigen kann!

Und gewiß denken und fühlen Sie gegenwärtig dem frommen Ps. nach יהי חסדך u. s. w. so wie auch wir die frohe Hoffnung hegen und aussprechen; es werde Gott dieses Ihr eheliches Bündniß ein gelungenes sein lassen durch alle Zeit Ihres Lebens

Amen.

לא על הלחם לבדו יחי׳ האדם כי על כל מוצא פי ד׳ יחיה האדם׳

Nicht durch und für das Brod allein lebe und strebe der Mensch, sondern durch und für Alles, was der Mund Gottes hervorgebracht lebe der Mensch.

Und dieser Mahnung und dieser Aufforderung und Aufmunterung folgt Jeder, der den Namen Mensch, in des Wortes besserer Bedeutung, tragen will, und folgt bewußt oder unbewußt Jeder, wenn er aus der Vereinzelung, aus dem ausschließlichen Leben für sein eigen „Ich“ hinaustritt um seine Sorgfalt sein Mühen und Streben, sein Leben und Lieben zu theilen, zu theilen mit einem ihm verwandten Wesen; um ein Haus und eine Familie zu gründen!

Wie schal und fahl ist nicht das Leben, solange es sich allein und ausschließlich nur um die Achse unseres „Ichs“ bewegt, und mag die Sanduhr unseres Daseins noch so glücklich abrinnen, es fehlt ihm doch jener Farbenton, der das Auge ergötzt, jener Reiz des wohlthuenden Wechsels; jene Ebbe und Fluth der mannigfachsten Freuden und Leiden, die das eheliche, häusliche, Familienleben in so reichem Maße biethet; es fehlt ihm doch jenes bessere Ideal, jenes hehere Gemüths- und Seelenleben; jene Frische und Herzlichkeit, die das Leben erst des Lebens werth macht!

Darum und daher ist das Haus, die Ehe und die Familie so alt wie das Menschengeschlecht, daher rührt die innige

Theilnahme der Menschen überall und immer, an diesem weihevollen feierlichen Act; daher der feierliche Ernst, die tiefe Bewegtheit und Erregtheit unseres Selbst in diesem wichtigen Augenblicke.

Bewußt oder auch unbewußt fühlen wir die ganze Schwere und Bedeutung dieses Verhältnisses, bewußt oder auch unbewußt, wie gesagt, lallen unsere Lippen, schlagen unsere Herzen die Worte יהי חסדך u. s. w. dem frommen Bether nach!

Und mit Recht!

Hoffen und Vertrauen Sie daher nur und Allemal auf Gott und Gott wird Ihr Vertrauen stets rechtfertigen, bedenken Sie, daß der Mensch nicht allein fürs Brod, für die nichtigen und flüchtigen Güter dieser Erde allein streben soll, sondern auch fürs Höhere, für den Geist, für Herz und Gemüth, und Sie werden es fühlen und einsehn, wie nur das Haus und die Familie die besten, ja die alleinigen Förderer dessen sind. Das gebe Gott.

38.

Einleitung.

פ׳ עקב.

גדלו לד׳ אתי ונרוממה שמו יחדיו!

Verherrlicht den Herrn mit mir, zusammen wollen wir Seinen Namen lobpreisen.

An Euch, Ihr Väter und Mütter, in diesem froherregten Kreise, an Euch Ihr Brüder und Schwestern in dieser lustgestimmten Versammlung; an Sie l. B. die da gekommen um sich vor Gott im Sinne seiner sittlichen Weltordnung und seiner heiligen Lehre für die Lebenszeit zu vereinen in gegenseitiger Liebe und Treue, an Sie Alle ergeht der Aufruf des gottbegeisterten Sängers, weil Ihnen ein seltnes Glück wiederfährt, weil Ihren Herzen eine zwiefache Freude gewährt, weil Gott es Ihnen gegönnt in dem engsten Rahmen einer Spanne Zeit eine solche Summe Glück's an sich und den Ihrigen zu genießen und zu empfinden.

Und so lasset uns denn Atle, die zunächst den innigsten Antheil an dieser Freude haben, Gott loben und Dank sagen, gleichzeitig aber auch bethen, innigst bethen: Er wolle dieser zwiefachen Freude anch seine zweifach segensreiche Dauer, ein ungeschmälert und ungetrübtes Glück verleihen, damit Sie sich durch alle Zeit dieser Doppelfreude zwiefach freuen. Amen.

כי ד׳ אלהיך מביאך אל ארץ טובה = Denn der Ewige Dein Gott bringt und führt Dich in ein gutes Land!

So und mit diesen Worten ermuntert Moses sein Volk zur Dankbarkeit und zum steten Gehorsam gegen Gott, und mit eben diesen Worten witt auch ich Sie bei dieser feierlichen Gelegenheit, passender Weise, für diese Gefühle, ein für allemal aufmerksam machen. Denn auch Sie treten wohl in ein neues Verhältniß, aber der Herr hat es Ihnen in Seiner Güte, gar sehr erleichtert, so daß Sie froher und leichtern Herzens dasselbe, wie jeder Andere sonst, antreten können — da Ihre Herzen einander seit frühester Jugend kennen, da Sie mit einander durch die zartesten Bande der Blutverwandtschaft verbunden und atso nicht erst nöthig haben einander zu nähern, einander erst kennen zu lernen; Und so, indem Sie einer und derselben Wurzel entstammt, einem und demselben Stamme entsprossen, werden hoffentlich anch Ihre Gefühle und Neigungen sich in Allem und zu jeder Zeit aufs Freundlichste und Uebereinstimmendste begegnen — Was aber ist mehr geeignet und dazu angethan das Glück und den Segen des ehelichen Lebens zu fördern und dauernd zu erhalten, als eben die gegenseitige Uebereinstimmung in Allem und Jedem.

Ist denn aber die Harmonie in Allem und Jedem auch atte Zeit heilsam? Will denn auch das Menschenherz immer und überall nur das Gute und Beste? Weiß denn anch der Erdensohn immer und überall was wahrhaft gut und heilsam?

Darum aber ruft ja die Schrift zuerst ושמרת את מצות ד׳ אלהיך וללכת בדרכיו וליראה אתו Willst Du in dem neuen guten Verhältniß anch stets gut berathen sein, so mußt du dieses Gotteswort hatten, willst Du auf dem Lebenspfade niemals straucheln, so mußt Du S e i n e Wege gehn; willst Du nie und nichts fürchten, so fürchte Ihn!

גדלו לד׳ אתי Preiset den Namen Gottes mit mir, denket und handelt stets so, daß der Name Gottes durch Euch gepriesen und verherrlicht werde, ונרממה שמו יחדיו dann wird es uns wohl gegönnt sein in den spätesten Zeiten noch, Seinen Namen in Liebe und Dankbarkeit zu erheben. Das wolle Gott!

39.

Einleitung.

פ׳ נצבים.

ואני תמיד עמך — אחזת ביד ימיני — בעצתך תנחני — ואחר כבוד תקחני.

Und stets bin ich, mein Gott! bei Dir,
Drum führst Du selbst, die Rechte mir —
So leit' mich stets nach Deinem Rath,
Den rechten Weg, der Ehre Pfad!

Und dieses Gebeth wollen auch wir in gegenwärtigem Moment der Lust und Freude anstimmen, בעצתך תנחני wollen wir bethen, damit Sie einst, d. h. noch in späten Zeiten rufen können אחזת ביד ימיני.

Wohl müssen wir bei jedem Vorhaben, bei jedem Unternehmen dieß Gebeth im Herzen und auf den Lippen haben, weil von Gott allein jedes Gelingen, von Gott allein jede Ausführung abhängt, aber nie und niemals muß es ernster um's Herz, nie und niemals heißer auf den Lippen brennen, als in dem Augenblicke, da zwei Herzen einander stete Liebe, fortdauernde Treue und inniges Eins-sein-wollen geloben! Wer hiezu Gottes Hilfe und Beistand, hiezu Gottes Führung und Leitung nicht zu bedürfen glaubt, o, der darf sich nicht wundern, wenn er, nicht an Gottes Hand, irre und wirre geht, der darf sich auch nicht beklagen, wenn ihn nicht Gott den rechten Weg, den Pfad der Ehre, den neidenswerthen Pfad des Glückes führt!

Aber Sie, l. Bräut. haben ja durch Ihre bereits zurückgelegte Lebensstrecke, als treuer und muthiger Diener unseres geliebten

Landesvaters bewiesen, daß Sie eingedenk Ihres Gottes, an seiner Hand, durch seinen Rath den Pfad der Ehre gewandelt, und so geben wir uns denn der gegründeten Hoffnung hin, daß Sie auch in diesem lebenswichtigen Schritte, von Gott geleitet, an seiner Hand geführt, glücklich und beglückend durch das Leben gehen werden, an der Seite dieser Ihrer Gattin, die Ihnen Gott der Herr bestimmt, geben uns der guten Hoffnung hin, daß auch Sie l. B. Ihr Herz zu Gott erheben mit der innigen Bitte „Leite mich o Gott in deinem Rath“ damit auch Sie den Pfad der Pflicht, den beglückenden Weg des Guten wandeln — und so erhöre Gott Sie Beiden. Amen.

„Denn das Geboth, daß ich dir heute auftrage, es ist dir nicht wunderbar, und nicht entfernt — Es ist nicht im Himmel, daß du sagest, wer steigt wohl in den Himmel und hott und lehret es uns, daß wir's thuen, und es ist nicht Jenseits des Meeres daß du sagest wer geht wohl über's Meee und hott und lehrt es uns daß wir's vollführen, denn die Sache liegt dir sehr nahe, im Munde und im Herzen, daß du es ausführest.“

Gilt dieß m. L. von atten Pflichten gegen Gott und Menschen, weit es uns gewißermaßen, als vernünftigen und geselligen Wesen, angeboren und angemessen ist, Gott und die Menschen zu lieben, mit Gott und den Menschen in Uibereinstimmung zu leben — — wie soll es dem Einzelnen schwer fatten, in Liebe und Eintracht, sich einem in Liebe und Treue ihm anfügendes und anschmiegendes Wesen, an zu teben und an zu tieben? Wenn es nur, wie das Gotteswort lehrt, attein von unserem Witten und Wollen abhängt, uns als gott- und menschengefällig zu bewähren — und es hängt nur von unserem Willen ab — wiewohl es trotzdem so manches schwere Opfer kostet, warum sollte es uns schwer fatten unserem eignen Ich in einem uns zweiten Selbst, sozusagen, in Liebe zu leben? „Die Sache ist ja sehr nahe,“ denn sie liegt ja nur in dem stets ruhigen, sanften, milden und belehrenden Worten einer und im theilnehmenden, weichen und milden Herzen anderseits!

O, das Glück und die Seligkeit des Ehe und Hausstandes ist nicht in jener himmelshohen Region des sogenannten Glückes zu suchen, daß Du dächtest, wer kann wohl so hoch steigen und sie hoten לא בשמים היא, — grade in jenen hohen Regionen ist sie gar oft eine gar seltne Pflanze sie ist aber auch nicht außer deinem Gesichtskreise, jenseits der Fläche des bewegten Lebens — Meeres, daß Du dächtest, das geräuschvolle Alltagsleben sei nicht angethan, ein so lieb-und seelenvoles Leben zu führen לא מעבר לים היא'. . im Gegentheile aber, dein unmittelbares Ich allein, trägt dieß Glück, dein unmittelbares Ich allein kann Dich beglücken, denn es ist Dir ja im Munde, wenn Du es nämlich ausspricht, das ואני תמיד עמך, ist Dir ja im Herzen, nämlich, Dich vom Rathe Gottes leiten zu lassen!

O, das Geboth, das ich Dir heute l. Bp. auftrage, es ist nicht wider — es ist nicht übernatürlich, und liegt auch nicht außer Deiner Begriffs— und Herzens-Sfäre, im Gegentheil, der Verstand predigt, das Herz lehrt es; Liebe, Gegenseitigkeit; Mithilfe und wie all die ehelichen Tugenden heißen, sie wurzeln in uns, sie wollen ausgesprochen und bethätigt sein — es hängt nur von unserem Willen und Wollen ab. Seien Sie Beide, deß eingedenk, und Sie werden es fühlen und einsehn, daß Gott Sie an seiner Vaterhand den Weg der Ehre und den Pfad des Glückes führen wird. Also geschehe es.

Rede

bei Eröffnung der isr. Volksschule in B. Gy. im Jahre 1861.*)

Wenn ich sie, m. L. geladen, der Einweihung dieses Institutes, das uns nach tangem, unausgesetzten mühevollen Streben, ins Leben zu rufen, gelungen, anzuwohnen, so mögen sie nicht glauben, daß eine Schule überhaupt erst der Weihe und der Heiligmachung, wenn ich's so nennen darf, nöthig habe . . . O nein! eine Schule ist vielmehr ein ohne Weiters Allzugroßes, ein an und für sich Allzuheiliges, als daß es erst einer Weihe von Außen, einer Weihe durch schwache Menschenworte und strömten Solche, von den Lippen eines Hohepriesters selbst — bedürfte! Und schon unsere Alten erkannten und zeichneten die hohe Wichtigkeit der Schule aus, indem sie behaupten: יאהב ד' את שערי ציון מכל משכנות יעקב — שערים המצוינים בהלכה מכל בתי כנסיות שבישראל d. h. Gott liebt mehr die Pforten, die gezeichnet und bezeichnet sind durch den fördernden Fortschritt, denn atte Gotteshäuser Israels!

Und mit Recht! denn in diesen manifestirt sich blos der blinde Gtaube, in jenen aber das lebendige Wissen, da bekundet sich der starre Stillstand, dort der Fortschritt des menschlichen Geistes hier wird blos das Gefühl, dort aber der Sinn und Geist geweckt und gebildet — die atlein den Menschen Gottähnlichkeit geben . . hier sotten wir Juden, dort aber gleich mit nützliche Mitglieder der Gesellschaft, Bürger des Vaterlandes; mit einem Worte, vorzügliche Menschen in jeder Bedeutung, erziehen und heranbilden! בה"כ מותר לעשותו כה"מ. Aus einem Gotteshause darf ohne Weiters ein Lehrhaus gemacht werden, heißt es ferner bei ihnen, während eine Schule niemals zum Gotteshause erniedrigt werden darf! לא נחרבה ירושלים אלא על שבטלו בה הבל תנוקות של בית רבן — Auch Jerusalem verlor erst dann atten Hatt und atle Stütze, als die Schulen vernachlässigt, und der eigentliche Lebensodem aus dem siechen Staatskörper schwand! rufen sie so sinnig als wahr! denn in der geistigen Fortbildung der Jugend liegt die Fortdauer und die Stärke eines Volkes, nicht in der Höhe und Fütte der Generation selber . . .

*) Aus andern Gelegenheitsreden, die mit Nächstem erscheinen werden, so ein geschäztes jüd. Lesepublikum dem Verfasser nur einigermassen seine Gunst nicht versagt.

Also, nicht um diese Anstalt erst einzuweihen, sind wir hier versammelt, denn hier, wie nirgend's gelten die Worte der Schrift: כי המקום. אשר אתה עומד עליו אדמת קדש הוא ja, jede Schule ist eine erquickende Oase in der Wüste des Lebens — und um das Bild zu vervollständigen, setze ich hinzu, sie ist und gleichet auch dem biblischen Dornbusche, weil sie ach, gar so viele Stacheln, den bewährtesten und strebsamsten Kräften . . . biethet, sie ist und gleichet dem Dornbusche, weil auch da wie dort die Glorie und Majestät Gottes aus derselben hervorstralt! ! aber um uns den Begriff und die Bedeutung der Volksschule klar und deutlich zu machen, wollen wir uns Einiges zu Gemüthe führen — Es ist dieß um so nöthiger, als sonst kein Institut soviel Anfechtungen und Kämpfe zu erdulden hat, als eben die jüd. Volksschule . . . und dieß eben liegt nur, theils im Mißverstande, theils in der Mißdeutung des Begriff's und des Wesens der Volksschule — denn während der Eine dieselbe für eine Bildungs — ja, für eine Ausbildungsanstalt hält, aus welcher das Kind berufsvollkommen fürs practtische Leben kommen soll, glaubt ein Anderer, sie sei blos ein nothwendiges Uibel, dem das Kind, sobald als möglich entwachsen sein müsse . . und während ein Dritter sie für eine Erziehungs-Anstalt ansieht,, in welcher nebst der Theorie des Wissens, auch die Praxis des sogenannten Bonton's beigebracht werde, meint ein Vierter, sie sei ganz und gar — von Uibel, und diene höchstens als Versorgungsanstalt für einige Individuen, die wir Lehrer nennen, denn die Schule soll — nun was soll die Schule? den Gemeinde-Säckel füllen helfen, nicht aber leeren und ausbeuten! . . u. s. w. u. s. w.

Gehen dann solche Illusionen, solche chimäre Voraussetzungen, wie es nicht anders zu erwarten, in die Brüche, dann heißt es, wir sind betrogen, die Schule hat nichts geleistet; die Lehrer nichts ausgerichtet u. s. w. Die Volksschule ist aber weder dieß noch jenes, sondern einfach und nichts anderes, als die Pflanzstätte, wo die jungen Zweiglein in den Boden gesetzt werden, damit sie keimen und Wurzel schlagen sollen, um dann erst in die höhere Schule des Lebens versetzt zu werden — die Volksschule hat blos die im Kinde schlummerden Fähigkeiten und Anlagen für Wissen und Kennen, für Frömmigkeit und gute Sitte; für Zucht und Anstand zu wecken, nicht aber auszubilden und heranzureifen; die Volksschule ist erst der Boden, allwo das Kind biegsam, bildsam und empfänglich gemacht werden soll für die Schule und fürs Leben, sie selbst ist weder das Eine, im eigentlichen Sinne, noch das Andere; mit einem Worte, sie ist erst und allein die Vorbereitung — hier erst geht der sogenannte Gährungsprozeß zwischen dem vorhandenen Rohstoff und dem zu weckenden Geiste vor — — daß er aber regel- und vernunft-gerecht vor sich gehe, das ist die schwere Aufgabe der Lehrer!!

Ja, dieser schweren Aufgabe, nämlich, das anvertraute Kind durch und durch zu kennen, durch genaue und scharfe Beobachtung, damit nie und niemals der rechte Moment versäumt und verpaßt werde, muß der Lehrer gewachsen sein, so er seinem Gewissen und seinen Pflichten entsprechen will.. Und wie der pflichtbeflissene Lehrer, weder stets strenge noch immer milde sein darf, weil sonst die zarte Kindespflanze durch allzuviel Sturm verwittern und durch allzuviel Sonne verdorren und hinwelken würde, ebenso darf er auch weder zu pedantisch an der starren Vorschrift, noch zu rationelle an dem freien Geiste, hangen, denn das Eine tödtet, das Andere verwirrt zu sehr das schwache Kindervermögen . . der Lehrer aber soll und muß mit und neben dem Kinde nur das erwachsene, vernünftigere Kind sein, d. h. spielen!

Unsere Zeit, m. H. Lehrer! verlangt, und nicht mit Unrecht, daß der Unterricht schnell, gründlich und leicht d. h. angenehm sei . . . wie aber wäre dieß möglich, wenn der Lehrer nicht wie ein guter und besorgter Gärtner stets bedacht wäre, den zarten Kindespflanzen, zur rechten Zeit, Licht und Wärme, Kühle und Schatten zuzuwenden? wie wäre dieß möglich, wenn der Lehrer nicht ausschließlich und mit Liebe seinem heiligen und schweren Berufe obläge? wie wäre dieß denkbar, ohne daß sich der Lehrer mit zum Kinde, unter den ihm anvertrauten Kindern, mache?

Soll aber der Lehrer seinem heiligen Berufe derart entsprechen können, so ist es vor Allem nöthig, daß demselben das Leben und Streben nicht anderweitig, durch die Sucht zum Tadeln und sonstigen Uibeln, die leider in unserer Mitte so Gang und Gäbe nicht verleidet und verbittert werde . . . der Lehrer muß seinen Kindern mit frohem, heitern Gemüthe, und mit freundlich strahlendem Antlitze entgegen treten können, wie Moses, der erste und größte Lehrer, dessen Gesicht freudestralte, wenn er sein Volk belehrle — wie es so schön heißt: וראו בני ישראל את פני משה כי קרן עור פני משה = So oft die Kinder Israels das Gesicht Moses sahen, so erglänzte und, erstrahlte es von dem erglühenden Bewußtsein seines großen und erhabenen Berufes, erst ! ויכל מדבר אתם ויתן על פניו מסוה erst als er aufhörte mit und zu ihnen zu reden, da überzog seine Stirne wieder der tiefe Ernst des Denkers, das Gewölk himmelan ragender Gedanken —

Wie aber wäre dieß vom Lehrer in des Wortes gewöhnlichem Sinne zu verlangen, wenn ihm statt Achtung Mißachtung, statt Anerkennung Tadel und statt Aufmunterung, Entmuthigung zu Theil wird?

Soll der Lehrer seinem Berufe entsprechen können, so muß ihm das Elternhaus an die Hand gehn, am Wenigsten aber darf es der Schule entgegen wirken; Weckt die Schute zur Frömmigkeit, so darf das Elternhaus keine Irreligiösität, am Wenigsten dem Kinde gegenüber zeigen, muntert der Lehrer zum Selbstfleiße auf, so müssen die Eltern ihn leiten und bewachen; eifert die Schule zur Zucht und Sitte an, so muß das Elternhaus strenge darüber wachen, daß das Kind von jedem bösen Beispiele, von jeder unzüchtigen Rede, von jedem unkeuschen Worte fern bleibe, da nichts so schädlichen Einfluß auf das weiche Kindesgemüth übt, als eben das böse Beispiel in Thaten und in Worten!

Dieß gilt von jeder Volksschule, von atten Lehrern — was diese unsere Schute betrifft, wotten wir vorerst bedenken, wie viet Unebenheiten wir noch zu ebnen, wie verschieden geartet unsere Jugend, wie mangelhaft unsere Lehrmittel, wie geringe nnsere Kraft — mit einem Worte, daß sie eben erst im Werden ist!

Trotz dieser Mängel jedoch, sotten Sie überzeugt werden, daß unser Streben und Wollen, ich rede auch in Ihrem Namen, meine Herrn Lehrer, dieses Institut nach Möglichkeit und unserer schwachen Kräfte gemäß zu fördern und auf die Höhe der Zeit zu bringen, ein Ernstes und Redliches sein soll — Damit es uns aber auch gelinge, bethen wir, o Gott, und Herr, zu Dir:

אשר מפי עוללים ויונקים יסדת עוז!

Schütte deinen besten Vatersegen über dieses Heiligthum aus, und lasse die darin zu erziehende und heranzubildende Jugend gesund an Körper und Geist, gesund an Herz und Sinn heranblühen und gedeihen zur Freude ihrer Eltern, zum Ruhme ihrer Lehrer; zum Stolze ihres Volkes, zum Heil und Segen des th. Vaterlandes und der menschl. Gesellschaft. Schenke Stärke und Ausdauer o Gott, den Lehrern, damit sie muthig das Tageswerk, das sie beginnen auch ruhmvoll ausführen — mögen sie stets eingedenk sein, wie flüchtig die Zeit, wie groß und schwer das Tagewerk; wie viel der zu besiegenden Hindernisse, wie groß aber der Lohn; das erhabene und erhebende Bewußtsein, die Anerkennung der bessern Mit- und Nachwelt; der Lohn, dessen wir keiner entrathen können, der Lohn des Vaters im Himmel droben, und schließlich wie der Hausherr drängt, der Hausherr im fisischen Sinne des Wortes, es ist die Gemeinde die sich den besten Erwartungen hingibt mit den Worten כלו מעשיכם! es ist aber auch der Hausherr im heheren Sinne, und auch Der ruft לא עליך המלאכה לגמור u. s. w. . . . .

Deinen Segen flehen wir ferner an, Herr! für all diejenigen in unserer Mitte, die bereits ihr Schärflein zur Unterstützung dieser Anstalt beigetragen und für Alle die zu ihrem fernern Gedeihen beitragen wollen!

Und so rufe ich denn! והיה ראשיתך מצער ואחריתך ישנא מאד

Amen.

Lightning Source UK Ltd.
Milton Keynes UK
UKOW06f1050270217
295416UK00002B/873/P

9 781330 016695